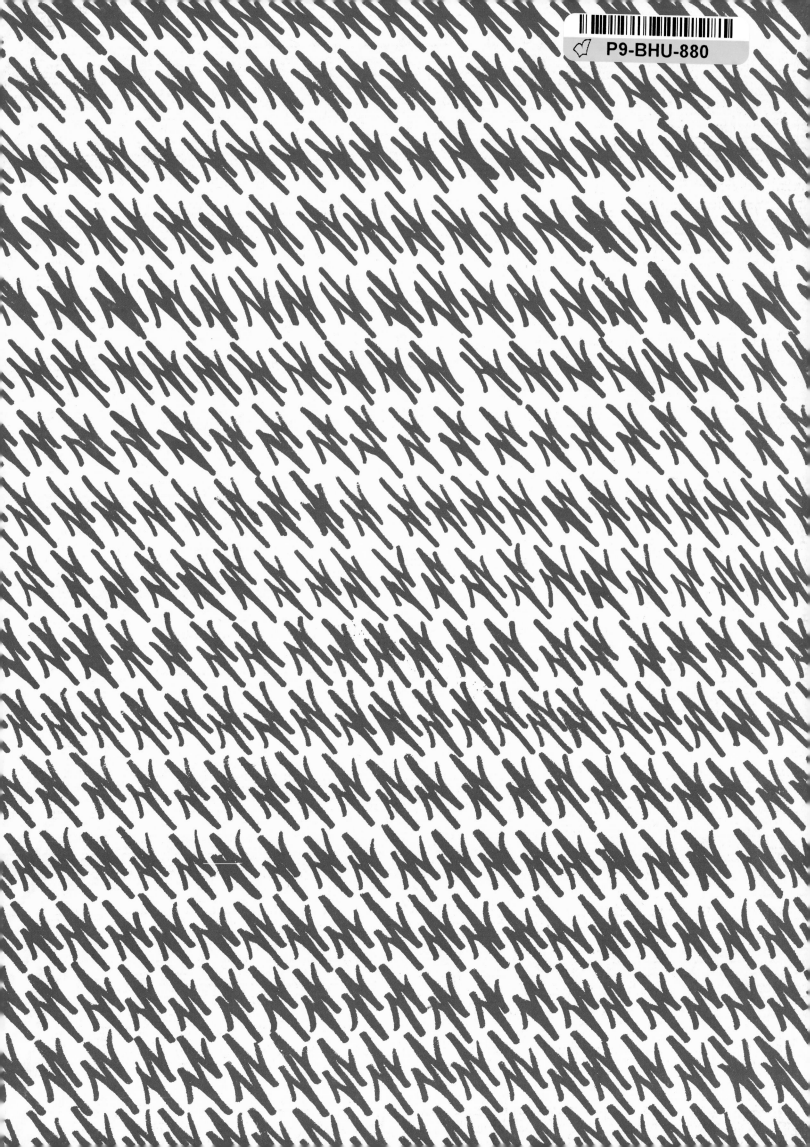

THE HOHOKAM

HAURY, Emil Walter. The Hohokam, desert farmers & craftsmen: excavations at Snaketown, 1964–1965. Arizona, 1976. 412p ill bibl index 74-31610. 19.50. ISBN 0-8165-0445-8

CHOICE   *NOV. '76*

History, Geography &
Travel
   Ancient (Incl.
   Archaeology)

tall
E 78
A 7
H 37

The Hohokam is one of the more important archaeological works published in recent years. The intention of the author is to put to rest the controversy about the Hohokam that has arisen over the 30 years between his first work at Snaketown and his return in 1964. It appears unlikely that this new work will lay to rest that controversy. The title gives the reader a clue to the assumptions the author makes: typifying all Hohokam culture by what was found at Snaketown. Although a most impressive site and book, it is unlikely that either characterize Hohokam cultural variability any more than New York City is typical of all American culture. The book is exceptionally well done, profusely illustrated, and obviously the result of a major archaeological project. With index, appendices, and an extensive bibliography, the book will become a classic archeological reference work, although many archaeologists will disagree with details and conclusions drawn by the author. It is aimed at the professional and graduate student in prehistory, although a more general audience may find the book stimulating and interesting. The profusion of illustrations will also broaden its appeal.

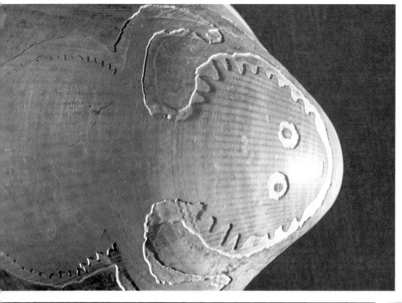

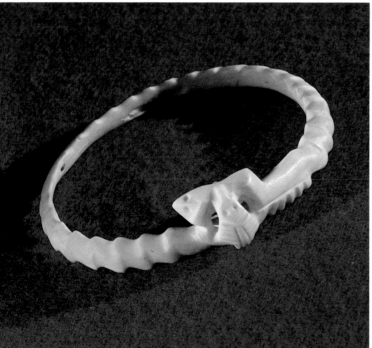

SELECT EXAMPLES
OF HOHOKAM ART

Clockwise from upper left:
  Etched shell, Sedentary Period, A.D. 900–1100
  Pottery plate, Colonial Period, A.D. 700–900
    and Pottery effigy jar, Sedentary Period, A.D. 900–1100
  Stone sculptures, Colonial Period, A.D. 700–900
  Bone hairpin, Sedentary Period, A.D. 900–1100
  Shell bracelet, Sedentary Period, A.D. 900–1100

THE HOHOKAM

DESERT FARMERS & CRAFTSMEN

Excavations at Snaketown, 1964-1965

Emil W. Haury

Published by
THE UNIVERSITY OF ARIZONA PRESS
Tucson, Arizona

In Collaboration With
SOUTHWEST PARKS AND MONUMENTS ASSOCIATION

About the Author ...

Emil W. Haury, a past President of the Society for American Archaeology and of the American Anthropological Association, has received the Viking Fund Medal in Anthropology and appointment as the Fred A. Riecker Distinguished Professor in Anthropology at the University of Arizona. A member of the National Academy of Sciences, the American Academy of Arts and Sciences, and the American Philosophical Society, he received his early training in archaeology from Byron Cummings at the University of Arizona.

Among Haury's notable archaeological activities are his excavations at Mogollon Village and the Harris Site, multidisciplinary research at Ventana Cave, and work at the Naco and Lehner sites. In 1930 he began active field research with Gila Pueblo. His excavations at Roosevelt 9:6, and Snaketown, and his analysis of Cushing's early work at Los Muertos, made him a key figure in defining the culture of the Hohokam. Included among his book publications are *The Stratigraphy and Archaeology of Ventana Cave, Arizona* (with other authors) and *Excavations at Snaketown, Material Culture* (with other authors), as well as a multitude of professional articles.

In 1937, at the University of Arizona, Haury became head of the department whose name subsequently was changed from Archaeology to Anthropology. A year later he became Director of the State Museum at the University of Arizona. He held both positions until 1964. During this time, under Haury's direction, field schools at Forestdale and Point of Pines converted countless students into professional archaeologists.

THE UNIVERSITY OF ARIZONA PRESS

Contents

Illustrations

Tables

Author's Note

In the early 1920s Byron Cummings, head of the Department of Archaeology, University of Arizona, was busily engaged in uncovering the famous ruin of Cuicuilco a short distance south of Mexico City. In 1925, he invited me to join him. His willingness to accept an eager novice "sight unseen" gave me the unprecedented and awesome opportunity to assist in unlocking Cuicuilco, a monumental truncated cone, from the grip of the Pedregal lava flow which engulfed it several thousand years ago. What an introduction to archaeology that was!

By a quirk of history, the work at Snaketown would later expose a miniature Cuicuilco in Mound 16. It duplicated Cuicuilco's flat top, many-layered sides, and even had a palisade reminiscent of the cromlech that circled the base of the Mexican structure. Although we did not know it in 1925, Cuicuilco was built close to the time of Snaketown's founding, and we were then a number of decades away from fully realizing how close the ties really were between the ancient people of southern Arizona and those of Mesoamerica. My early exposure to Mexican archaeology and the opportunity to investigate a derived society must stand as the most rewarding experiences of my career.

In 1964, the Honorable Stewart Udall, Secretary of the Department of Interior, declared Snaketown to be eligible as a Registered National Historic Landmark. The Gila River Indian Community, composed of Pima and Maricopa Indians, accepted this opportunity with enthusiasm. A bronze plaque noting "This site possesses exceptional value in commemorating and illustrating the history of the United States" was presented to Lloyde Allison, then governor of the Gila River Indian Community, on April 3, 1965. The ceremony took place in the amphitheater formed by Snaketown's old ball court. About five hundred Indians, rising to the spirit of the occasion, made it both momentous and joyous.

Recognizing that Snaketown preserves traces of the oldest irrigation system in the United States and that it is the foremost example of the history of irrigation north of Mexico, the Gila River Indian Community Council passed Resolution GR-106-65 on August 18, 1965, reiterating the same thoughts in Resolution GR-447 of March 6, 1968, petitioning authorities to preserve these historic values by bringing Snaketown into the National Park System. The signing of Public Law 92525 by President Richard M. Nixon on October 27, 1972, saw the fulfillment of that dream. Snaketown thus became a link in a chain of resources, including Casa Grande National Monument and the surviving Indian communities along the Gila River, which dramatically illustrate more than 2,000 years of desert living by the River People.

Three long-planned developments which materialized in quick succession made it possible in 1964–65 to pursue the restudy of Snaketown. These events were my relinquishment in September 1964 of all administrative duties related to the Arizona State Museum and the Department of Anthropology of the University of Arizona; the granting of a sabbatical leave from the University of Arizona for fiscal year 1964–65; and the award from the National Science Foundation of a grant (No. GS-450) in support of the field investigations. Certain personnel salaries and other costs were borne by the University of Arizona. I am indirectly indebted to Harold S. Gladwin for an important fraction of the support through residual dollars derived from the transfer of the Gila Pueblo Archaeological Foundation to the University of Arizona in 1951. Without these various kinds of assistance the work could not have been carried out at the planned level. To Sherwood Carr, then Assistant Comptroller in the University's Business Office, I owe much for having made easier our compliance with complicated state fiscal policies.

The privilege of working on the Gila River Indian Reservation was freely given us by the Gila River Indian Community Council over which Lloyde A. Allison presided as governor at the time. His assistance and the interest in and enthusiasm for our work expressed by all members of the Tribal Council was a continual source of encouragement. Bureau of Indian Affairs officials, notably the late Superintendent Minton Nolan and his successor Kendall Cummings, deserve special recognition for assistance rendered on many occasions.

To the Pima Indians and the several Maricopa Indians who made up the field force, thirty men on the average, and the two ladies in the laboratory, goes a large share of the credit for our success in the endeavor. They are people of good humor, gentle, dependable, and a joy to work with. The fact that they readily identified themselves with the people whose remains they were uncovering was of no small help. I would like to note each one by name; but singling out a few must stand as a symbolic recognition of all: the late Fred Marrietta who logged more than 1,000 hours as the skillful operator of the backhoe; Ruppert Hall, speaker of the Piman language, English, and a passable German, who, as cartographer Gell's chief assistant, quickly became proficient in the art of mapping; Joe Thomas, to whom fell the lonely task of keeping the site under surveillance nights and weekends, in fact at all times when we were not working; Amenda Lewis and Evelyn Jones, who, between them, probably washed and marked more old Indian pottery than have any other modern Indians; men like Raymond Cawker, David Moore, and Leonard Stone, who, in their respective ways, were helpful by offering guidance at the right times; and finally, an old and good friend of Gila Pueblo days of the 1930s, Jones Williams, who worked with me at Roosevelt 9:6 and then again at Snaketown. Our rapport with all of these people and their families came to a climax on April 17, 1965, when they invited all of us non-Indians to a well-planned

The Snaketown field crew, 1964–65. *Top Row:* (left to right) Roger Pedro; Leroy James; Fred Marietta, Jr., Larry Porter; Iver Sunna; Fred Marietta, Sr.; Leonard Manuel; Joseph P. Marietta; Joseph O. Marietta. *Middle Row:* Clinton Lewis; Everett "Moon" Howard; Eldridge Cross; David Moore; Jones Williams; Delbert Lewis; Job Hayes; George Kyyitan; Raymond Cawker. *Bottom Row:* Eddy Harrison; Rupert Hall; Leonard Stone; Dennis Williams; Justin Miller; Larry Lewis. *Inset:* Lab crew members Amenda Lewis and Evelyn Jones.

social occasion as an expression of their thanks for our efforts and our presence in their midst. The Snaketown staff will long remember the sincerity and the substance of the thoughts voiced on that day.

It may seem trite to say that the professional success of the 1964–65 restudy of Snaketown resulted from the dedication and the expertise of the staff. The fact remains that this is true. It is therefore my privilege and pleasant obligation to express my deep debt to each one of them: the late William Wasley, as second in command, for wide-ranging assistance in solving both professional and logistical problems, and especially for his help in the area of irrigation canal testing; to two of the three archaeologists on the force, Al Lancaster and James Sciscenti, whose experience in Hohokam site digging was new, both having worked extensively in different parts of Anasazi territory. Alfred Johnson, on the other hand, had good familiarity with Hohokam dirt archaeology. These varied backgrounds proved to be a decided asset, for each man, in his own way, applied special skills and insights to his respective assignment. The variability in approaches never ceased to amaze me, and after initial misgivings, I became convinced that the end product would come off the better for it.

As cartographer, Jonathan Gell was faced with one of the toughest jobs imaginable, initially to reestablish the 1934–35 grid system and then to maintain map control over fast-moving and widely dispersed labor crews, not to mention the work of the machine. Yet the job was superbly done by dint of long and arduous hours. The maps of Snaketown and its features reflect this because they are professional, accurate, and complete. The master map of the site, done by his own hand, Figure 1.6, brings together the efforts of 1934–35 and 1964–65.

Helga Teiwes-French, a German-trained photographer, brought to the task of photo-recording a talent rarely found in archaeological endeavors. Despite the fact that this was her first field assignment, she quickly mastered the light, angle, subject matter, and physical problems to provide consistently excellent results. The high quality of studio-made plates in this report attest to her expertise in this area as well. Her contribution to this work has immeasurably reduced the need for lengthy word descriptions.

To Mary Anne Stein fell the responsibility of managing the laboratory at the Santan Day School where we lived, ably assisted by Susan T. Adams, both graduate students in anthropology. Keeping the daily accumulation of specimens in order, washing, mending, and cataloguing them as required, and readying the mountains of broken pottery for analysis, was a never-ending and demanding task, ably discharged. Theodore C. Contes, a newcomer to archaeology but nevertheless intrigued by it, was employed as business manager. His presence and versatile handiness enormously eased my own concerns about fiscal management and maintenance.

Much of the overseeing of the living arrangements of the staff fell upon the shoulders of my wife, Hulda, who has the knack of resolving awkward problems quietly. To all of the foregoing members of the on-site staff I shall always be grateful, for they were there to help solve problems, not to create them.

Mr. and Mrs. Manice deForest Lockwood, then of New York, joined the force as volunteers, electing a winter in the sun over a business assignment in foggy London. A former student at Point of Pines, "Chip," helped where needed in the field, from profile mapping to guiding visitors, and his wife "Aggie" did yeoman service in systematizing the record keeping in the laboratory. Their presence and generous help was deeply appreciated.

Julian D. Hayden, while not a resident member of the staff, paid weekly visits to Snaketown from Tucson to oversee the health and care of the indispensable machine, the backhoe. Besides contributing his knowledge of mechanical equipment and ground conditions, he stood by and gave sage counsel on a variety of archaeological matters, drawing on his deep experience as a participant in the excavations of the Grewe site by the Los Angeles-van Bergen Expedition in 1928, in the first Snaketown operation, extensive work in Pueblo Grande ruins near Phoenix, in the University Indian Ruin, Tucson, and in Ventana Cave. His contributions to the present endeavor are not to be underestimated.

Colleagues on the campus of the University of Arizona were liberal in giving time and aid in many related areas. They are: E. B. Sayles, Curator Emeritus of the Arizona State Museum and member of the first Snaketown expedition; Paul E. Damon, Chief Scientist, Laboratory of Geochronometry, for approving gratis service in making a number of the radiocarbon assays of Snaketown samples; C. Vance Haynes, then of the University of Arizona, who supervised the early radiocarbon laboratory work and who contributed his evaluation of the results, as well as supplying helpful information about Gila valley terrace geomorphology; Austin Long, for his work on organic samples when he was in charge of the Smithsonian Institution's Radiation Biology Laboratory, and the later determinations he made for us when he returned to oversee the University of Arizona's radiocarbon laboratory; Robert L. DuBois, then Director of the University of Arizona's Archaeomagnetic Laboratory and later pursuing similar studies at the University of Oklahoma, for his important help in clarifying chronological problems through the recovery of archaeomagnetic data from fired clay samples; Vorsila Bohrer, Department of Botany, University of Arizona, who worked diligently on pollen extraction from Snaketown soils with disappointing results, but who found rewards in the carbonized plant residues screened from trash and other sources; Kenneth Bennett and Walter H. Birkby for reports on the meager human skeletal remains, unburned and cremated, respectively; Ralph W. G. Wyckoff, for x-ray spectrometry analysis of various materials; Robert T. O'Haire, Arizona Bureau of Mines, for assistance in identifying minerals; Robert W. Hoshaw, Department of Botany, for guiding Carlos Caraveo in efforts to grow algae from spores presumed to be present, but were not, in the calcareous lining of canals; Anne Colberg-Sigleo, Laboratory of Isotope Geochemistry, for trace-element studies of turquoise; Raymond N. Rogers, then graduate student in geochronology and long-time staff member of the Los Alamos Scientific Laboratory, New Mexico, for x-ray diffraction and x-ray fluorescence spectrometry analyses of canal lining and potsherds, respectively; Bryant Bannister and William J. Robinson, Laboratory of Tree-Ring Research, for tree-ring determinations of carbonized architectural wood; Richard Sense, for mineralogical observations of pottery; Laurence A. Carruth, Department of Entomology, for identification of mud dauber nests from Hohokam houses; Joseph C. Bequaert, for freshwater and land shell identifications; Allan D. Halderman, Agricultural Engineering, who assisted me in understanding certain problems in irrigation hydraulics; and William F. McCaughey and E. T. Sheehan, Agricultural Biochemistry, for analysis of the resist which was used in the acid etching of shell.

Assistance from the following persons is also gratefully acknowledged: Thomas W. Mathews, Jerry L. Greene and Charmion R. McKusick, of the Southwestern Archaeological Center, National Park Service, Globe, for the identification of mammalian and avian remains; W. L. Minckley, Arizona State University, and Stanley J. Olsen, University of Arizona, for additional studies of zoological materials; Hugh C. Cutler and Leonard W. Blake, Missouri Botanical Garden, St. Louis, for study of burnt corn; L. G. Hertlein, California Academy of Sciences, San Francisco, for the identification of marine shells; John S. Sigstad, University of Missouri, for examination of red mudstone samples; Richard B. Woodbury, University of Massachusetts, for making available to me his field data resulting from investigations of the Snaketown canal; Clement C. Meighan and Leonard J. Foote, University of California, Los Angeles, for obsidian hydration dating tests, and to Don Crabtree of Kimberly, Idaho, for illuminating discussions about Hohokam lithic technology. Other professional colleagues helped in innumerable ways when called on. To name them all would be tedious to all but them, but they should know that their efforts have not been forgotten.

Artifact restorations were ably done by Jerry Beard through the Work-Study program of the University of Arizona. Assisting me in the laboratory on certain phases of the work was Dudley Meade who also, with Geoffrey A. Clark, Wesley Jernigan, Karen Young, Jon Czaplicki, and Deborah Hondorf, provided the art work for this book. Their efforts are identified as follows:

Meade: Figures 5.3, 5.4, 6.3, 6.4, 6.9, 9.4, 9.8, 9.11, 9.16, 9.17, 9.19, 12.2, 12.5, 16.8, 16.9, 17.2, and 17.3; Clark: Figures 11.17, 13.14, 13.15, 13.20, 15.17–15.23, and 15.25; Young: Figures 11.28, 11.29, 12.14, 13.1, 13.29, 13.30, and 15.28; Hondorf: Figures 5.13, 6.7, 6.8, 6.11, 6.13, 6.16, 6.18, 8.27, 8.37, 8.40, 11.14, 11.31, 12.93, 12.110, 13.2, 13.27, 14.5, 15.10, 15.11, 16.4, 16.5, 16.7, 16.10–16.12, 17.1, A2.1, A3.1–A3.3, A4.1, A5.1–A5.9, A6.1, A9.1–A9.2; Czaplicki: Figure 12.106; Jernigan: Figure 8.3.

Jonathan Gell assembled Figure 1.6. Charles R. McGimsey III supplied Figure 16.13. All other drawings are my own.

Funds for maintaining laboratory activities after the close of the excavations were provided by the Wenner-Gren Foundation for Anthropological Research (Grant No. 1930), New York, the Office of the Coordinator of Research, the Graduate College, the Department of Anthropology of the University of Arizona, and an anonymous donor. My indebtedness to all persons involved is hereby expressed.

Many courtesies were extended to me by people who were interested in the work. One of these was from the late Donald H. Bacon of Chelsea, Michigan, who made a gift of a Paradome, a compact collapsible structure which served us well as a field storehouse. To all others who aided the operation but who have gone unnamed, I extend deserved thanks.

An important product of the photographic endeavor was some 6,000 feet of motion picture film, taken and edited by Helga Teiwes-French to make a 40-minute documentary account of the excavations. The University of Arizona Foundation generously supported the venture in its final stages of development to bring it to completion.

Involved at the administrative level from the beginning of the field work to the completion of this report was Raymond H. Thompson, Director of the Arizona State Museum, the immediate sponsoring unit of the University of Arizona. His understanding of our problems and his willingness at all times to abet the effort were essential to its success. I hope he finds some satisfaction in the knowledge that the Museum for which he is responsible houses the most comprehensive artifactual and documentary collection in existence which has been derived from a single village of the Hohokam people.

Appreciative recognition also is due the University of Arizona Press for effecting publication of this book with which achievement the Southwestern Parks and Monuments Association has collaborated. I extend special thanks to Elaine Nantkes for her expert editorial assistance and to Ida Edwards for invaluable help during proof-reading and indexing stages.

To the late Frances T. Slutes, my secretary for more than two decades, I must pay tribute for unfailing encouragement and help during the planning stages of the Snaketown work. My personal sadness is deepened because she did not live to see the fruits of her efforts.

Finally, in reflecting on all of those persons who helped shape the restudy of Snaketown, it would be thoughtless of me not to mention the role played by my sternest critic and former director, Harold S. Gladwin. His many doubts about earlier interpretations, eloquently argued in 1942 and again in 1948, demanded answers. These, I felt, could not be given on the basis of reworking the data available to us, but only on new findings. It was he, therefore, who sent me back to Snaketown.

Those persons who are familiar with the activities of archaeologists in the American Southwest since the end of the nineteenth century know that their aims and goals have been in a continuing state of metamorphosis. The 1960s, when Snaketown was being restudied, was a decade of searching for values, a quest for the "relevancy" of what archaeologists do to the complex social problems of the times.

While I eagerly welcome the direct and practical benefits of archaeology to the modern scene, those do not seem as impelling as another value which has strongly motivated my own involvement in the discipline. Barnaby C. Keeney, Chairman of the National Endowment for the Humanities from 1966 to 1970, prompted by the Endowment's partial funding of the recovery of a Greek merchant vessel carrying a cargo of amphorae, grinding stones and almonds, and which came to grief more than 2,200 years ago off the coast of Kyrenia, Cyprus, had the following to say:

The kind of fascination and excitement inherent in such a discovery is hard to define. But it is real, because the continuity of human concerns is real. It is quite possible to be too much the prisoner of one's own time, unable to appreciate that the ways of men and of institutions can vary and can change. The humanities can be the antidote to that without diverting one from present problems. There is a cultural environment as well as a physical one to be protected and preserved and made enjoyable, and it is in that sense that even the "wreck of the Kyrenia" can contribute to the quality of life available to us.

(From the Fourth Annual Report, National Endowment for the Humanities, 1970)

With this thought in mind, let us turn to the desert village of Snaketown.

E. W. H.

PART ONE

INTRODUCTION

1. Background

In January 1888, Frank Hamilton Cushing probed the knolls in the Salt River valley of southern Arizona that marked the site of La Ciudad de los Muertos, the City of the Dead. As leader of the Mary Hemenway Southwestern Archaeological Expedition, he was the first to initiate a sustained and purposeful effort to learn something about the Indians whose architectural mounds dotted the floors of the desert valleys. The wonder at the time was how a presumed primitive group of people could carve out an existence and develop a society that left behind monumental structures in a harsh and forbidding environment.

It was in that same month—January 1888—that Sylvester Baxter, correspondent for the Boston Herald, joined the expedition and wrote a piece titled "The Old New World" (*Boston Herald,* April 15, 1888), in which he called attention for the first time through a national news medium to the remains of an agricultural Indian tribe that exploited the desert by irrigating their parched lands. This prosaic bit of information is lost today, in the 1970s, in our modern emphasis on and achievements in water technology and concern about an impending water crisis. But seen in its rightful perspective, what the native Americans accomplished more than two millennia ago established the model that we, as European immigrants, were to emulate and build upon.

In retrospect, Cushing's work must be acknowledged as the first well-organized, expertly staffed, and abundantly financed effort to understand the prehistory of the then little-known southwestern United States. After those pioneering efforts, however, the pendulum of attention swung to the north, to the land of the Cliff Dwellers; Southern Arizona was largely forgotten.

The archaeological investigations that were made later in the desert have been ably reviewed by Gladwin (1937: 12-18) and need not be detailed again here. Since 1937, the principal efforts have either been born of the depression, as the studies at Pueblo Grande near Phoenix (Hayden 1936–1940, unpublished notes; Schroeder 1940) and the University Indian Ruin near Tucson (Hayden 1957), or the result of salvage efforts associated with reservoir construction, as those near Gila Bend (Wasley 1960; Wasley and Johnson 1965), and highway building, as south of San Xavier Mission (Greenleaf, Ariz. BB:13:49 and 13:50, 1975), near Snaketown (Johnson 1964), and in Phoenix at Las Colinas (Hammack 1969).

There were, of course, some notable exceptions to emergency-born excavations, such as Kelly's work in the Hodges site (1938), the Amerind Foundation's studies in the Babocomari, Santa Cruz, and San Pedro valleys (Di Peso 1951, 1956, 1958; Tuthill, 1947), and the Arizona State Museum's work in Papaguería (Scantling 1940; Withers 1973; Haury and others 1950). Useful information came from all of these, particularly on the nature of the Hohokam in areas marginal to the presumed heartland in the Gila-Salt River valleys. On a broad front, the archaeological story was unfolding slowly.

The initial excavations at Snaketown in 1934–35 did as much to expand our knowledge of this culture as had all of the cumulative efforts before. A long developmental period was recognized as preceding the horizons then known; the cultural inventory was markedly expanded and definite notions about a chronology as related to the Christian calendar were voiced. These findings were reported in 1937 (Gladwin, Haury, Sayles, and Gladwin). Furthermore, influences from the centers of high culture in Mesoamerica were recognized as a vital force in shaping the Southwestern society. Some of the basic implications of Hohokam beginnings were difficult to accept: the relatively earlier age for the achievement of certain ceramic and other cultural attributes than was the case among the Anasazi, as an example, and a conviction that in the most arid part of the Southwest the advance from food gathering to food production through irrigated agriculture did indeed lead the field of similar endeavors by others.

While Gladwin's position and his ideas about the Hohokam seemed firm in 1937, a few years later he began to have second thoughts. Reevaluation of the Snaketown data was first aired by him in 1942 and again in 1948, and others tried their respective hands at making new arrangements of the chronological information available.

In a sense, all the juggling of the data had its good effects because it sharpened the interest in the Hohokam. An unhappy side effect was the lost motion and energy, but most lamentable was a dormant period of about twenty years when our knowledge was not advanced.

This chaotic state of affairs convinced me that the only way to solve the dilemma was by launching new studies, that the only reasonable way to argue the points under contention was with the shovel. I fully expect that the information presented in this report will be submitted to the same critical scrutiny given the findings of 1934–35, and this is as it should be.

Because the site of Snaketown was "revisited," however, my own position becomes doubly vulnerable. A valued friend was overheard to say, "He's returning to the scene of the crime!" But, since my convictions about the accuracy of the reporting of the 1934–35 work were unwavering, whether or not a "crime" was committed became a moot point. During the debates that followed the issuance of the 1937 report on Snaketown, my voice was not raised. Now, armed with fresh data I will present objectively what was learned, with no thought of self-fulfillment. To do otherwise would challenge the integrity of the archaeologists on the project—Wasley, Lancaster, Johnson, Sciscenti, Gell and Hayden—as well as my own. Each of these men was given maximum freedom in conducting his respective assignment, and each exercised appropriate skepticism about the meaning of his findings. They were not intellectually bound to me. They may not, nor do I expect them to, subscribe to everything set down on these pages, but they know that the records of their work form the backbone of my presentation and that those documents are not privileged. The incisiveness each of my colleagues displayed during the excavations, and the enthusiasm they showed when specific time relationships in the cultural remains became clear, lead me to believe that they saw the main outlines of Snaketown's history as I do.

Fig. 1.1. Hohokam country. *(Top)* The Gila River valley, looking west from Gila Butte toward Snaketown, 5 km (3 mi) distant. Estrella Mountains are in the background. *(Bottom)* View east from Gila Butte toward the Santan Mountains. Dominant tree is the exotic tamarisk from Africa. Dust pall generated by vehicular traffic on unpaved roads indicates quiet air of early morning. Irrigated fields lie below the cholla- and saguaro-studded slopes of the butte.

MEANING OF HOHOKAM

Probably the earliest known use of the word "Hohokam" appears in Benjamin Hayes' *Scrapbooks of California Indians*, which are now in the Bancroft Library. They were written by a John D. Walker of unknown connections. Bancroft acquired the scrapbooks in 1874 or 1875, and how much older the Walker document is is not known. In describing his visit among the Pima Indians, Walker noted, "They have many traditions among them. Some of them concerning the migration of a people whom they call 'Hohokam,' ancients or extinct people" (Quoted by permission of the Director, the Bancroft Library, University of California). Russell was probably the first investigator to use the word in professional literature (1908: 24), and his interpretation of the meaning was "That Which Has Perished."

Generally, the label is said to mean "those who have gone," with the word "vanished" often substituted for "gone." But some of our workmen went to considerable pains to explain to us that the common interpretation was not exactly what the Pima word meant. Literally *hokam* means something that is "all used up," essentially the same as Russell's explanation. A characteristic of Piman languages is the manner of pluralizing the word by duplication of the first syllable. Thus *hokam* is one thing all used up, and *hohokam* means more than one. It was pointed out to us that if a tire on one's automobile blows out it is *hokam;* if two go, *hohokam*. So, as the Pimas pass by the ancient Indian villages that dot their reservation, they think of them as "used up." This interpretation may not be as romantic as the one in general use, but it comes close to saying what the Pimas are thinking. Either way it serves the purposes of the archaeologist well. And the name has caught on outside professional circles, for there are motels, subdivisions, and packaged ice cubes that carry the label.

THE PHYSICAL SETTING

If a traveler speeding along on Interstate 10 between Tucson and Phoenix is aware of the moment he crosses the Gila River at Gila Butte, his eyes take in a scene of desolation. He is then only 5 km (3 mi) east of Snaketown, and the dry windblown riverbed would provoke questions as to how anyone could ever make a living in this inhospitable environment. It must be pointed out, however, that what we witness today is vastly different from the landscape the Hohokam first saw when they penetrated this land. It comes as a surprise to learn that before the white man tampered with the Gila River, its valley was the "best practical route from the Rocky Mountains to California across the southern desert region" (Bryan 1925: 119). This was due to the permanent flow of water, a resource that made the difference between success and failure, whether for travelers or for the agricultural people who wanted to exploit the land.

The most useful sources for information of a technical nature on the country the Hohokam favored are to be found in the Water Supply Papers of the United States Geological Survey (Bryan 1923 *a* and *b*; Ross 1923; Bryan 1925; Hoover 1929). El-Zur's probing into the field of environmental anthropology (1965) also contains wide-ranging and detailed data of the Hohokam habitat, but his work is available in dissertation and microfilm forms only. It is not my intention to dwell at length on the river, but enough must be said to acquaint one with the particular facets of the physical setting that the Hohokam faced and to which they needed to adapt if they were to survive in it.

Rising in New Mexico, the Gila River flows westward through alternating canyons and flat valleys until it reaches the Colorado River north of Yuma. In the final 325 km (about 200 mi) of its search for the sea, the stream passes over the broad flat plains that separate the low but rugged north-south trending mountain chains that dominate the Basin and Range Province of the western United States. Some of the basins are filled with deep alluvium trapped by the forces of nature as the neighboring mountains were reduced in mass by erosion. The upper and younger layers of this alluvium have been rearranged many times by the action of sheet flooding and by the more persistent work of the perennial streams, as the Gila and the Salt, that flow over them. Through geologic time this action has tended to flatten the landscape and to reduce the vertical distance between the bed of the river and the rich lands nearby. In this way nature set the stage for a particular kind of land utilization by man involving directed transport of water (Fig. 1.1).

Snaketown is located on the north bank of the Gila River at 111° 55' 3″ west longitude and 33° 11' 2″ north latitude. To place it with respect to more familiar landmarks, it lies about 20 km (12 mi) west-northwest of Sacaton and about the same distance southwest of Chandler, Arizona (Fig. 1.2).

The elevation above sea level at Snaketown is 358.15 m (1,175 ft) and the east-to-west slope of the land is a gentle 2 m or less per km (6-8 ft per mi). The low relief of the landscape, excluding the mountains, is emphasized by examining the transverse section of the valley as given in Figure 1.3. The higher ground, the upper terrace, is well drained and beyond the reach of river floodwaters. Snaketown occupies this surface. The edge of the upper terrace drops off about 3 m to merge with the surface of the lower terrace. The lower terrace is tillable land composed of humic sand and silt loam. The historic Pima fields and canals are still in evidence (Fig. 8.4), and these have effectively erased any obvious traces of Hohokam use of the terrace for farming. The 50-year or 100-year flood probably inundated this surface, adding to the richness of the land and offsetting any damage to it by over-cultivation. Mesquite is struggling to reestablish itself on the abandoned fields but against great odds because it is regularly harvested by the local Indians for fuel.

The margin of the lower terrace falls off about 1 m to join the floodplain. The floodplain is scarred by small, braided water channels caused by flood discharges from tributary streams below Coolidge Dam. Sparse scrub growth dots the floodplain, becoming heavy along the banks of the river channel. The river's trench, now typically dry and floored with heavy sand (Fig. 1.4), is about 2 m deep and 15 to 20 m wide, though these dimensions vary locally.

The distance from Snaketown to the river is about 1 km. Although signs of shifts in the channel in antiquity are to be seen, the sequence of changes has not been determined and we do not know where the channel stood when the village was inhabited. In all probability, however, the changes in the position of the channel have been minimal in the last two thousand years. Old photographs and other information show that the main difference between now and older days has been a deepening of the river's trench, which spelled disaster for the Pimas who were irrigating the fields on the floodplain below Snaketown, for they could no longer divert river water into their ditches. This happened at the beginning of the twentieth century.

The riverine environment that the Hohokam knew probably was a greater asset to them than we realize in the 1970s. There are enough accounts from the nineteenth century (Bryan 1923*b*: 64-67) to indicate that the riparian growth at the river's banks and marshy areas along the drainage was dense and provided a haven for game and water birds. The river itself supported fish life, comprising perhaps as many as a dozen species (Russell 1908: 83), as well as some shellfish. Most of these resources were harvested, as evidenced by remains in the village. The water was said to be clear when not in flood and up to 2 m in depth. Incredible as it seems, an amphibious craft, a 16-foot boat with wheels carrying three men and the family of one of them, made the journey from the Pima country to the Colorado River in October, 1849 (Bancroft 1889: 487). While a limited kind of navigability of the Gila, if uncertain, was thus demonstrated, I am not citing it here in support of the contention occasionally heard that the Hohokam migration into their desert habitat was waterborne.

Successful and sustained use of the Gila River's waters for

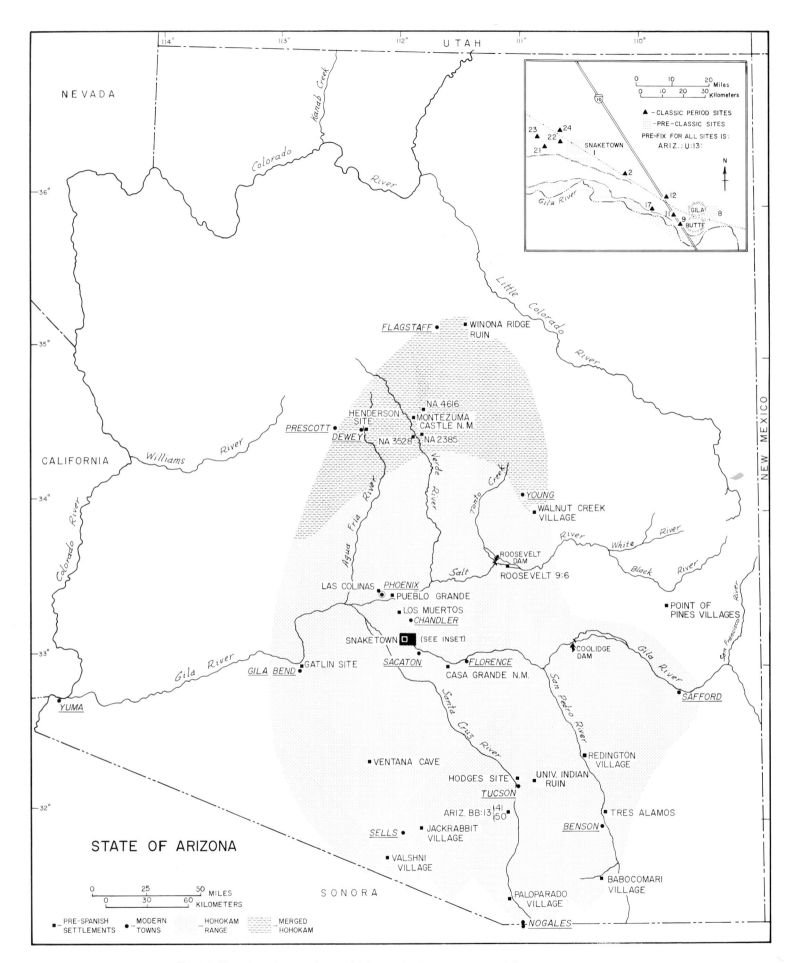

Fig. 1.2. Map of southern and central Arizona showing the location of Snaketown with respect to other ruins in the Hohokam territory and the former range known to them. The maximum territorial spread was experienced during the Sedentary Period, about A.D. 1000.

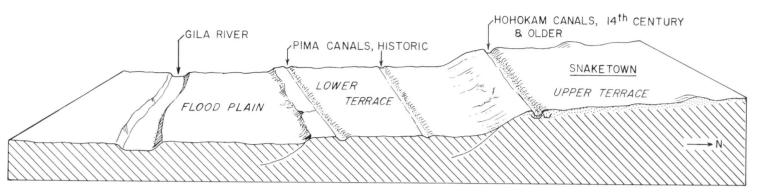

Fig. 1.3. Schematic transverse section of the Gila valley from Snaketown south to the river. No scale.

Fig. 1.4. The Gila River at Snaketown in its typically dry state (left) and after a winter rain (right). Most of the native riparian vegetation has been crowded out by tamarisk.

irrigation depended on the quantity available and the reliability of the flow. The Pimas experienced crop failures for want of water either because of drought every fifth year (Russell 1908: 66) or because the white settlers upstream used it all. The latter problem would not have plagued the Hohokam, except as their own kinsmen upstream may have cut into the supply. But there must have been times of hardship, because when the river ran dry, native foodstuffs, notably mesquite beans and the fruit of the saguaro, had to be relied on. All of these difficulties were overcome, as shown by Snaketown's long occupancy.

The river water used by the Pimas historically is said to have been highly saline, enough so that in time fields were rendered sterile, a problem solved by repeated flooding with irrigation water to dissolve and wash away the salts (Russell 1908: 87). This practice, carried out along many miles of the stream and over centuries of time, might well have had a marked effect on water quality. The calcareous lining in the fourteenth century canal and the absence of a similar crust in earlier ditches suggest a possible increase aboriginally in the mineral content of river water.

Although the key element in the Hohokam habitat was the river, it would have done little to promote the kind of economy the inhabitants wanted without the rich lands adjacent to the stream. Furthermore, these lands had to be reachable by canals. A choice had to be made between desirable and less desirable plots for tilling because the quality of soil varied, depending on the alkalinity, permeability and richness in plant nutrients, factors determined by genesis of the soils, and subsequent treatment by man or nature. Perhaps trial and error, but more importantly, experience, led to qualitative judgments of soils.

Climatic measurements at Sacaton, the nearest weather station to Snaketown, show an extreme annual temperature range of 108°, from 9° to 117° F (U.S. Weather Bureau reports; Arizona Experimental Station Bulletin 130), and a diurnal range that may exceed 50° in the 1970s. The mean annual temperature is about 70° F. The growing season between killing frosts is close to 260 days, long enough to permit double cropping of selected domesticates, a practice followed by the Pimas. The average annual rainfall is about 0.25 m (10 in). Since Sacaton is 30.5 m (100 ft) higher than Snaketown, any differences that exist between the two places would be in the direction of slightly higher temperatures and less rainfall at Snaketown. Precipitation is heaviest in July and August and again in December and January in two patterns: torrential downpours often highly localized, and the large and more gentle storms of winter. The rarity of snow was dramatically brought home to us, when on March 10, 1935, a sharp winter squall dropped several inches of sleet and snow on our camp. One of our Pima workmen was celebrating his twenty-fifth birthday that day, and this was the first snow he had seen on the reservation. Ironically, the storm's limits matched the boundaries of Snaketown. Half jokingly, the coincidence was explained as our punishment for meddling in the site.

The natural resources of water and land, added to the climatic ingredients of high temperatures and related high evaporation, low rainfall with attendant low humidity and a maximum number of sunny days leading to a long growing season, set the stage for the development of irrigated agriculture. The Hohokam were motivated to pursue this pattern of subsistence, and an account of their successes will become an important part of this report.

Beyond the dry statistics of the physical setting, the Hohokam habitat had an ethos peculiar unto itself, a quality best experienced to understand it. Perhaps it is the combination of many things that establishes in a resident the feeling of peace and tranquility and an honest appreciation of the contrasts between the searing heat of the day and the bone-rattling chill of the night; the powder-dry land one minute, a quagmire the next; the unbelievable mirages in the morning and the crystal-clear night sky; the dust devils, the dimensionless vistas ending in a ragged mountain backdrop that reminds one of pasteboard cutouts, and the smell of the desert

after a rain. Together, these add to the quality of life sought in the twentieth century. It is easy to convince oneself that these environmental influences were felt by the Hohokam in the tenth century as well. While difficult to quantify and to support with hard information, the enduring character of Hohokam society was, in large measure, a product of their nearly perfect adaptation to a desert homeland. Until the balance of native Pima culture was upset by white settlers in the nineteenth century, when their water rights were ignored, the Pimans reflected a mode of living that stretched back in time more than 2,000 years.

PLANT AND ANIMAL LIFE

The indigenous plant and animal resources available to the Hohokam are still seen in the biota of today, but there have been marked changes. Bohrer's review of the plant communities (1970) should be consulted by those with particular interest in plant ecology. The main modification in plant distribution along the Gila River itself was caused by the retention of the waters behind Coolidge Dam, beginning about 1930, although the effects were felt considerably earlier when the river's flow was heavily drawn on upstream for land tillage. At this time there was a reduction in the dominant element of the riparian vegetation—namely, cottonwood, willow, ash and mesquite. The replacement vegetation is the exotic *phreatophyte*, tamarisk, from Africa. Extensive land reclamation for agriculture in the area must also be considered as having had an effect on the local ecology. Native noncultivated food plants were well represented in the plant communities, saguaro, mesquite and cholla being the main ones; the archaeological record shows that they were drawn upon in early times (Bohrer 1970) as well as historically by the Pimas.

The discussion of animal remains found at Snaketown (Appendices 5-8) provides a partial list of the creatures that might have been identified a century ago. But animals, as plants, have experienced drastic population changes. Again, the principal cause has been that the loss of river water has denied the numerous waterfowl and marshbirds the kind of habitat they need. The fish are gone, as are the mollusks, the muskrat, and the beaver. Agricultural developments and the gun have driven the deer to the fastnesses of the nearby mountains, and the antelope and the mountain sheep have retreated to even remoter refuges. The only creatures that abound in the way the Hohokam may have known them are the several kinds of rabbits, the smaller rodents, the fox, coyote, and reptiles. Broadly speaking, the Hohokam-Pima ecosystem, which served the Indians well for more than two millennia and which doubtless underwent subtle changes due to their exploitation, fell tragically and irreversibly the victim to twentieth century pressures and is today a poor reminder of what once was there.

THE HOHOKAM RANGE

While the foregoing description of Hohokam habitat applies to the Gila River valley and by extension to the Salt River valley, we know that all Hohokam people were not restricted to a riverine habitat. This fact came out when the survey efforts of the Gila Pueblo Archaeological Foundation were summed up in a series of reports focusing on the range of the "Red-on-buff Culture" (Gladwin and Gladwin 1929a, 1929b; 1930a, 1930b; 1935). Attention has also been called to the Desert Branch of the culture specifically (Haury and others 1950: 2-21) because adjustments to a nonriverine environment in Papaguería had to be made in order to survive. Hohokam adaptability has also been demonstrated by the existence of their sites in the foothills of the desert mountain ranges and up to elevations of about 1,500 m (5,000 ft) above sea level, east of Prescott in the Henderson site (Weed and Ward 1970). Furthermore, it is becoming increasingly apparent that, along with geographic adaptability, they also merged readily with other people, as seen not only in the aforementioned site but in the Verde Valley (Breternitz 1960) at Winona (McGregor 1941: 278) east of Flagstaff, and again south of Young, Arizona, on Walnut Creek (Morris 1969a; 1970). But although they exploited any environment in which they found themselves, they seem to have felt most at home and comfortable in a riverscape setting. This same affinity is still reflected in the name the Pimas use when speaking of themselves as *Äkima O'otam*, River People.

In Figure 1.2 the distribution of Hohokam sites is shown in a generalized way, recognizing an outer northern band where cultural blending seems to have taken place. The questions that this phenomenon evoke are deserving of further attention, particularly the nature of the merging and the temporal correlation of the Hohokam with their neighbors. The southern boundary is left indefinite, because where this is eventually placed depends on how the people in extreme southern Arizona and northern Sonora are defined, a problem marginal to the present task. Snaketown's location is nearly central in the range, and because it yielded abundant early material, had such a long life, and grew to be as large or larger than any other Hohokam site known, I tend to look upon it as a likely candidate for the original and parent Hohokam village.

THE OLD VILLAGE OF SNAKETOWN

Well-known as the name Snaketown is, the derivation of the word is not generally understood. Its coinage springs from a logical, though not mutually beneficial, relationship between rodents and reptiles. The heaps of garbage collected by the Hohokam became desirable nesting places for rodents because they provided slightly higher, and therefore better drained, ground than the adjacent flat terrain, and the matrix of the mounds was a soft earthy mass making burrow-digging easier than in the harder surrounding desert. The result was a rising rodent population, which in turn attracted reptiles which thrive on them—rattlesnakes, including sidewinders and other serpents. When, in the late 1870s, a dozen or so Pima Indian families established a new site on the old one because of the availability of tillable land on the lower terrace, they observed the higher reptile population here than elsewhere and called their new home "Skoaquick," the Place of the Snakes, or, "Skâ' kâik," Many Rattlesnakes, as given by Russell (1908: 23).

Ordinarily, this would have been considered a place to avoid, but the total number of snakes we encountered during some fifteen months of excavation did not exceed a dozen, including those disturbed by our digging. They posed no threat to our work; if anything they sharpened our powers of observation.

While the Pimas had a reason for christening the place Skoaquick, there was another justification for the name, of which they were not aware. This was the heavy reliance the Hohokam placed upon the snake in their art, whether painted on pottery or carved in shell and stone. Snaketown was well named and deserves to be recognized as an aboriginal village of distinction in the annals of the arid Southwest.

The choice of the site of Snaketown is difficult to assess. The land on which it resides, about 1 km² in area, looks like any other comparable area of desert for a long distance up and down the valley. Why should this precise spot have been selected? The answer to this question probably lies in a set of circumstances which subtly distinguished the place from others that appeared similar and which reflect an uncanny ability on the part of Snaketown's founders to read the resources of the environment.

As one becomes familiar with the environment, three characteristics stand out as having had probable significance in selecting the site. Two of these deal with water and one with land. First, Queen Creek, which rises under the Pinal Mountains some 97 km (60 mi) to the east, flows generally in a westerly direction; after it leaves the confines of its rock-walled canyon at Superior, it

debouches onto the flatlands, spreading out dendritically to find the Gila River. Snaketown is in the path of this discharge. While there are a few defined channels that carry flood water in wet times, there is also much sheet flooding which effectively returns water to the underground aquifer. One arm of this reservoir passed under Snaketown, providing the opportunity to gain domestic water by digging a well no more than 3 m deep. Surface evidence of this condition is to be seen in the distribution of mesquite trees whose roots must tap a good water supply. This fact obviously did not escape the Hohokam.

The second attraction was the nearness of the village site to arable land on the lower terrace and to good land on the upper terrace as well. Third, and perhaps most important of all, was the feasibility of diverting Gila River water from several miles upstream through a canal to the tillable lands nearby. Only people with water management skills would have recognized this possibility. In short, the conditions for sustaining life on the desert were at hand: water to drink, land to cultivate, and water to nurture the crops, and these resources occurred in ideal combination. The selection of the site seems disarmingly simple.

At the time of settlement, the maximum difference in elevation between high and low ground was not much over 2 m. Topographic changes from occupation resulted in the filling-in of some lowspots, creating others by quarrying underlying materials, the growth of trash mounds up to 4 m deep and the building of other mounds for specific purposes, and, finally, a slight elevation of the edge of the upper terrace representing canal cleanings and the spoil dirt from numerous canal remodelings.

The flatlands location of Snaketown and the eventual dispersal of residence units over nearly a square kilometer of landscape, together with the absence of closeby natural refuges, suggest that the choice of location was not influenced in the slightest by fear of a hostile people. Except for the aridity of the environment, the natural setting imposed no barriers to free and easy communication from the outside world with the people of Snaketown.

The mounds of Snaketown and the long slightly-crescentic sides of the large ball court provide the only conspicuous relief on the flat surface of the upper terrace. Although the elevations are easily recognized (Fig. 1.5), only the trained eye identifies them as unnatural features in a landscape that occasionally shows the weak duning of blow sand. The sixty mounds appear to be randomly deployed (Figs. 1.6 and 1.8; see also Gladwin and others 1937, Fig. 2), the sizes depending in part upon the length of time they were in use or the number of people who contributed to their mass. Most of the mounds owe their origin to the villagers' desire to keep the residential premises clean and unlittered, a trait we usually do not associate with early people. The Hohokam must be given credit for a tidiness of mind and behavior that caused them to dispose of waste products either in pits or on selected spots where the mounds developed. Sheet trash is locally present but, with few exceptions, the deposits are thin. In spite of the apparent orderliness of waste disposal, the decomposing organic matter on the dumps and the use of them as latrines must have given Snaketown a special quality which escapes the archaeologist of today. Happily this is true, because the investigator must spend much time studying refuse to learn the habits of the people who produced it.

The exact limits of Snaketown are not easily drawn. The grid system as originally laid out encompassed approximately one square kilometer. It included all but one of the sixty mounds and only about half of the fourteenth century canal that bordered the village along its southern margin. Several Classic Period sites to the west were also excluded. The label Snaketown, therefore, applies arbitrarily to the pre-A.D. 1100 part of the settlement. References to the abandonment of Snaketown do not imply that the region was emptied of people, because there are numerous nearby enclaves that carry the record of occupation to 1400 or a little later.

Fig. 1.5. Examples of refuse mounds that, to the trained eye, announce the presence of an old village.

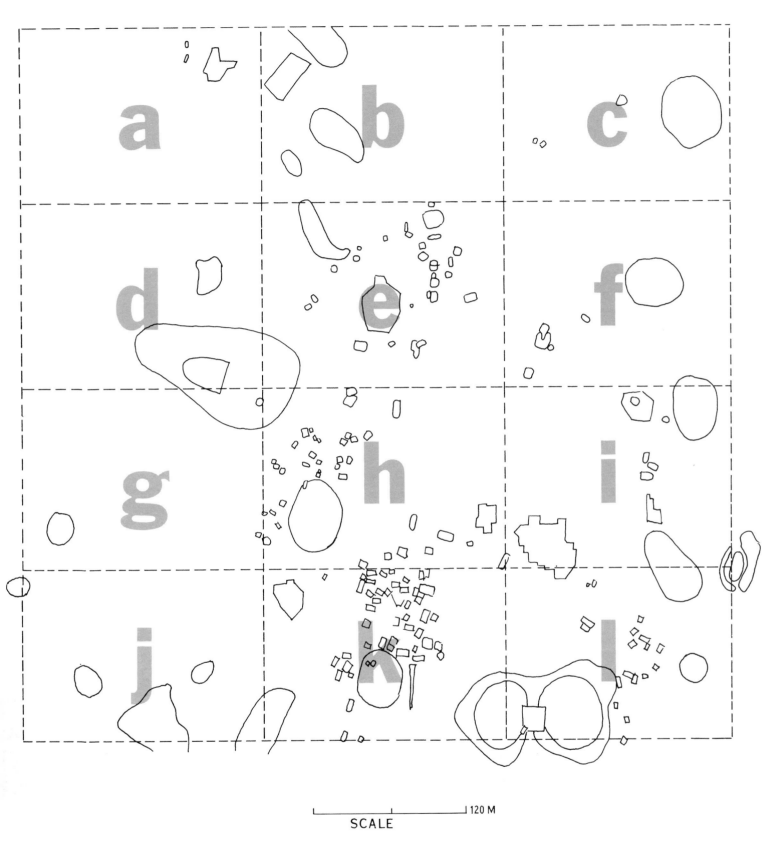

|⊢————|————|————————⊣ 120 M
SCALE

Fig. 1.6 Sectionalized general map of Snaketown. Lettered blocks correspond to facing pages that follow. Only the obvious surface features and the excavated structures of 1934–35 and 1964–65 seasons are shown. The full deployment of mounds may be seen in Fig. 1.8. Vacant areas in the map do not necessarily mean an absence of features since all parts of the village were not equally tested. Exploratory trenches and tests have been omitted. Outlying coordinate blocks with few or no features are not shown. Collated and drafted by Jonathan Gell.

KEY TO SYMBOLS

$+_{7F}$ — GRID BLOCK CORNER

$_4$ — HOUSE NUMBER, 1964-5 EXCAVATIONS

④ — HOUSE NUMBER, 1934-5 EXCAVATIONS

16/27 — HOUSE 16 SUPERPOSED OVER HOUSE 27

○ ◦ — HEARTH, UNDERLYING HEARTH

• · — POST HOLE, UNDERLYING POST HOLE

◎ — ROASTING PIT

◡ — ADOBE PLASTER OR CONSTRUCTION

▲ — BALL COURT MARKER STONE

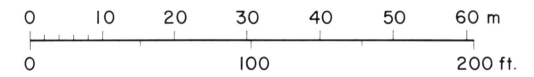

CONTOUR INTERVAL 0.5 METER

$+$ 3 D

$+$ 3E

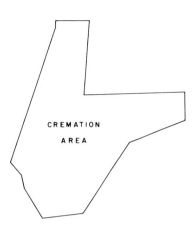

CREMATION
AREA

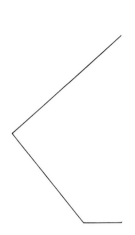

$+$ 4 D

$+$ 4E

a

$+$ 5 D

$+$ 5E

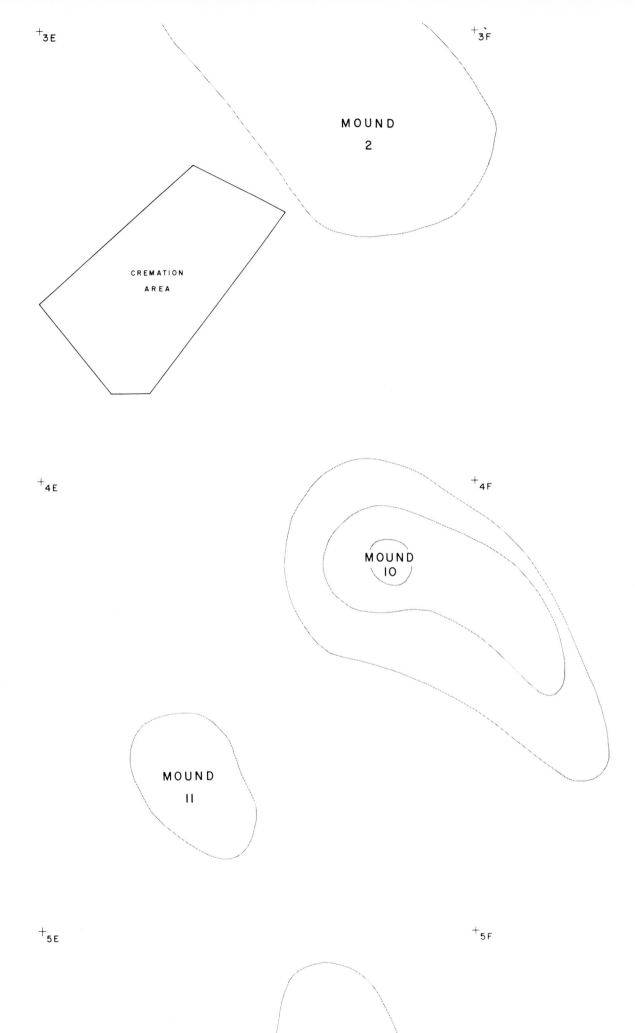

+3E

+3F

MOUND
2

CREMATION
AREA

+4E

+4F

MOUND
10

MOUND
11

+5E

+5F

MOUND

+ 3G   + 3H

KEY TO SYMBOLS

+ 7F — GRID BLOCK CORNER

4 — HOUSE NUMBER, 1964-5 EXCAVATIONS

④ — HOUSE NUMBER, 1934-5 EXCAVATIONS

16/27 — HOUSE 16 SUPERPOSED OVER HOUSE 27

o ◌ — HEARTH, UNDERLYING HEARTH

• ˙ — POST HOLE, UNDERLYING POST HOLE

◎ — ROASTING PIT

⌣ — ADOBE PLASTER OR CONSTRUCTION

▲ — BALL COURT MARKER STONE

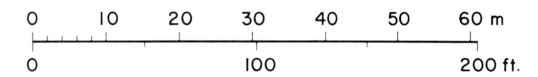

CONTOUR INTERVAL 0.5 METER

+ 4G   + 4H

b

+ 5G   + 5H

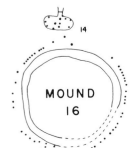

$+_{3H}$ $+_{3I}$

KEY TO SYMBOLS

$+_{7F}$ — GRID BLOCK CORNER

₄ — HOUSE NUMBER, 1964-5 EXCAVATIONS

④ — HOUSE NUMBER, 1934-5 EXCAVATIONS

16/27 — HOUSE 16 SUPERPOSED OVER HOUSE 27

○ ◌ — HEARTH, UNDERLYING HEARTH

• · — POST HOLE, UNDERLYING POST HOLE

◎ — ROASTING PIT

⌐ — ADOBE PLASTER OR CONSTRUCTION

▲ — BALL COURT MARKER STONE

0	10	20	30	40	50	60 m

0			100			200 ft.

CONTOUR INTERVAL 0.5 METER

$+_{4H}$ $+_{4I}$

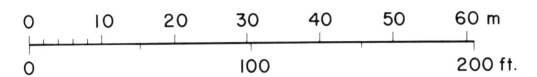

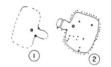

$+_{5H}$ $+_{5I}$

+ 3 J

+ 3 K

REMATION
AREA

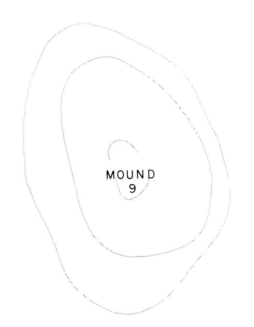

+ 4 J

MOUND
9

+ 4 K

C

+ 5 J

+ 5 K

+ 6 B   + 6 C

KEY TO SYMBOLS

$+_{7F}$ — GRID BLOCK CORNER

4 — HOUSE NUMBER, 1964-5 EXCAVATIONS

④ — HOUSE NUMBER, 1934-5 EXCAVATIONS

16/27 — HOUSE 16 SUPERPOSED OVER HOUSE 27

○ ○ — HEARTH, UNDERLYING HEARTH

• · — POST HOLE, UNDERLYING POST HOLE

◎ — ROASTING PIT

⌒ — ADOBE PLASTER OR CONSTRUCTION

▲ — BALL COURT MARKER STONE

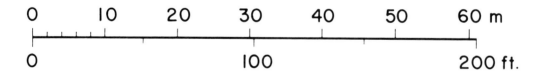

0   10   20   30   40   50   60 m

0   100   200 ft.

CONTOUR INTERVAL 0.5 METER

+ 7 B   + 7 C

d

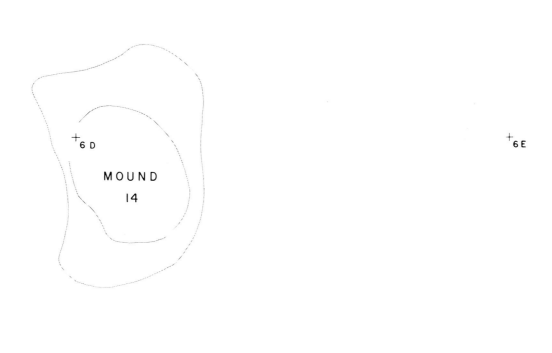

MOUND
14

$+$ 6 D

$+$ 6 E

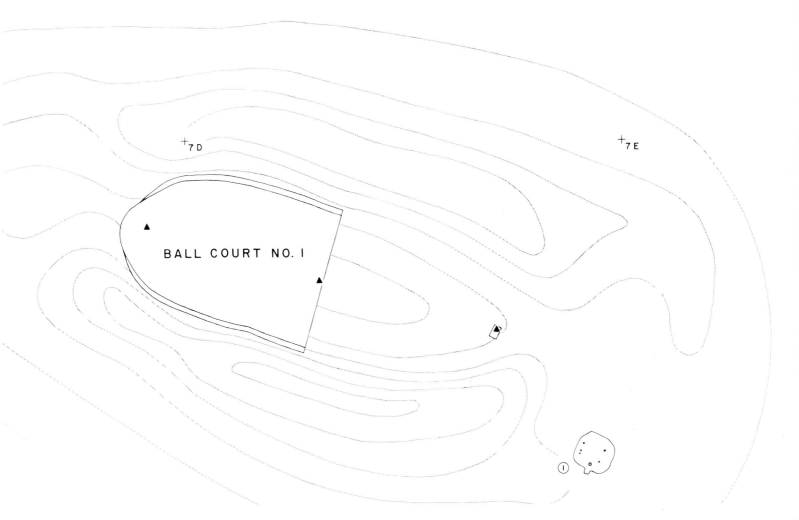

$+$ 7 D

$+$ 7 E

BALL COURT NO. 1

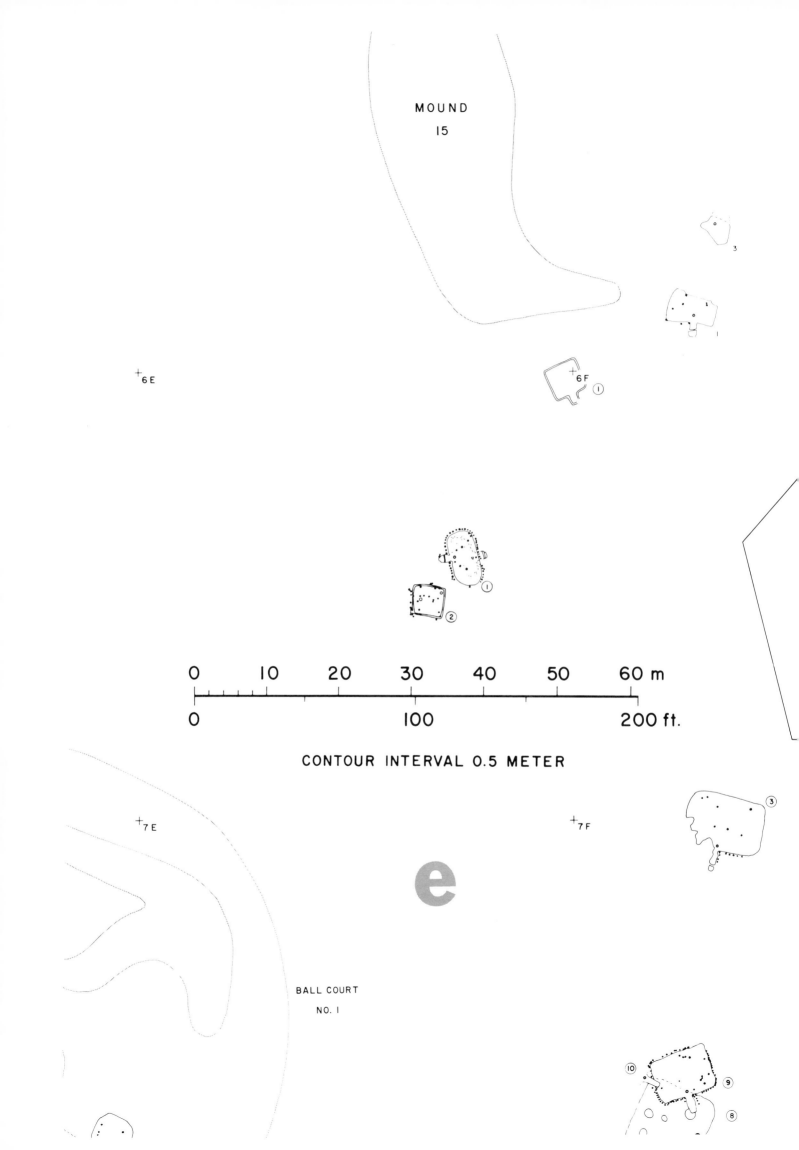

MOUND

15

3

1

+ 6 E

+ 6 F ①

①

②

| 0 | 10 | 20 | 30 | 40 | 50 | 60 m |

| 0 | 100 | 200 ft. |

CONTOUR INTERVAL 0.5 METER

3

+ 7 E

+ 7 F

e

BALL COURT

NO. I

⑩

⑨

⑧

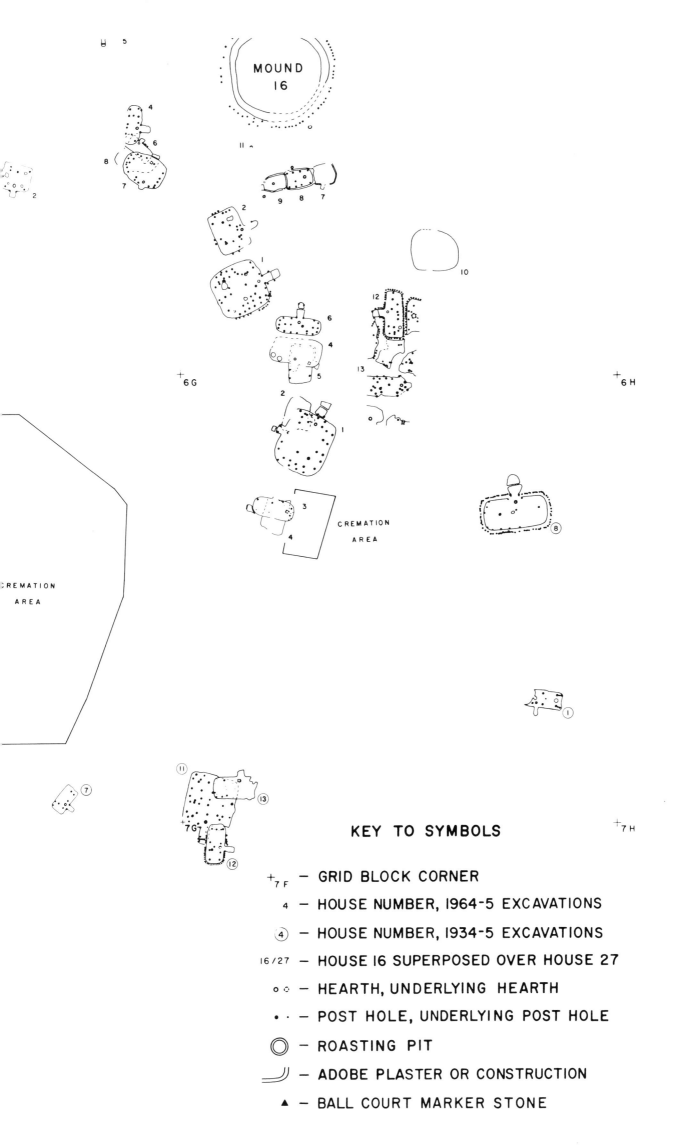

MOUND 16

CREMATION AREA

CREMATION AREA

+ 6G   + 6H

+ 7G   + 7H

+ 7F

KEY TO SYMBOLS

+ 7F — GRID BLOCK CORNER

4 — HOUSE NUMBER, 1964-5 EXCAVATIONS

④ — HOUSE NUMBER, 1934-5 EXCAVATIONS

16/27 — HOUSE 16 SUPERPOSED OVER HOUSE 27

○ ○ — HEARTH, UNDERLYING HEARTH

• • — POST HOLE, UNDERLYING POST HOLE

◎ — ROASTING PIT

╯ — ADOBE PLASTER OR CONSTRUCTION

▲ — BALL COURT MARKER STONE

+ 6 H

+ 6 I

2

1

2

1

+ 7 H

+ 7 I

f

I

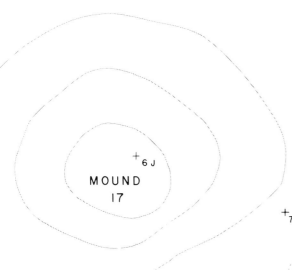

$+_{6J}$

MOUND
17

③

$+_{6K}$

KEY TO SYMBOLS

$+_{7F}$ — GRID BLOCK CORNER

4 — HOUSE NUMBER, 1964-5 EXCAVATIONS

④ — HOUSE NUMBER, 1934-5 EXCAVATIONS

16/27 — HOUSE 16 SUPERPOSED OVER HOUSE 27

○ ◌ — HEARTH, UNDERLYING HEARTH

• · — POST HOLE, UNDERLYING POST HOLE

◎ — ROASTING PIT

⤸ — ADOBE PLASTER OR CONSTRUCTION

▲ — BALL COURT MARKER STONE

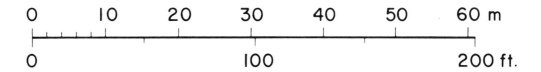

CONTOUR INTERVAL 0.5 METER

$+_{7J}$

$+_{7K}$

②

MOUND
25

$+$ 8 B

$+$ 8 C

$+$ 9 B

$+$ 9 C

MOUND
28

+ _{8 D}

+ _{8 E}

KEY TO SYMBOLS

+ _{7 F} — GRID BLOCK CORNER

4 — HOUSE NUMBER, 1964-5 EXCAVATIONS

④ — HOUSE NUMBER, 1934-5 EXCAVATIONS

16/27 — HOUSE 16 SUPERPOSED OVER HOUSE 27

○ ⊙ — HEARTH, UNDERLYING HEARTH

• · — POST HOLE, UNDERLYING POST HOLE

◎ — ROASTING PIT

⌣ — ADOBE PLASTER OR CONSTRUCTION

▲ — BALL COURT MARKER STONE

0	10	20	30	40	50	60 m

0	100	200 ft.

CONTOUR INTERVAL 0.5 METER

+ _{9 D}

+ _{9 E}

g

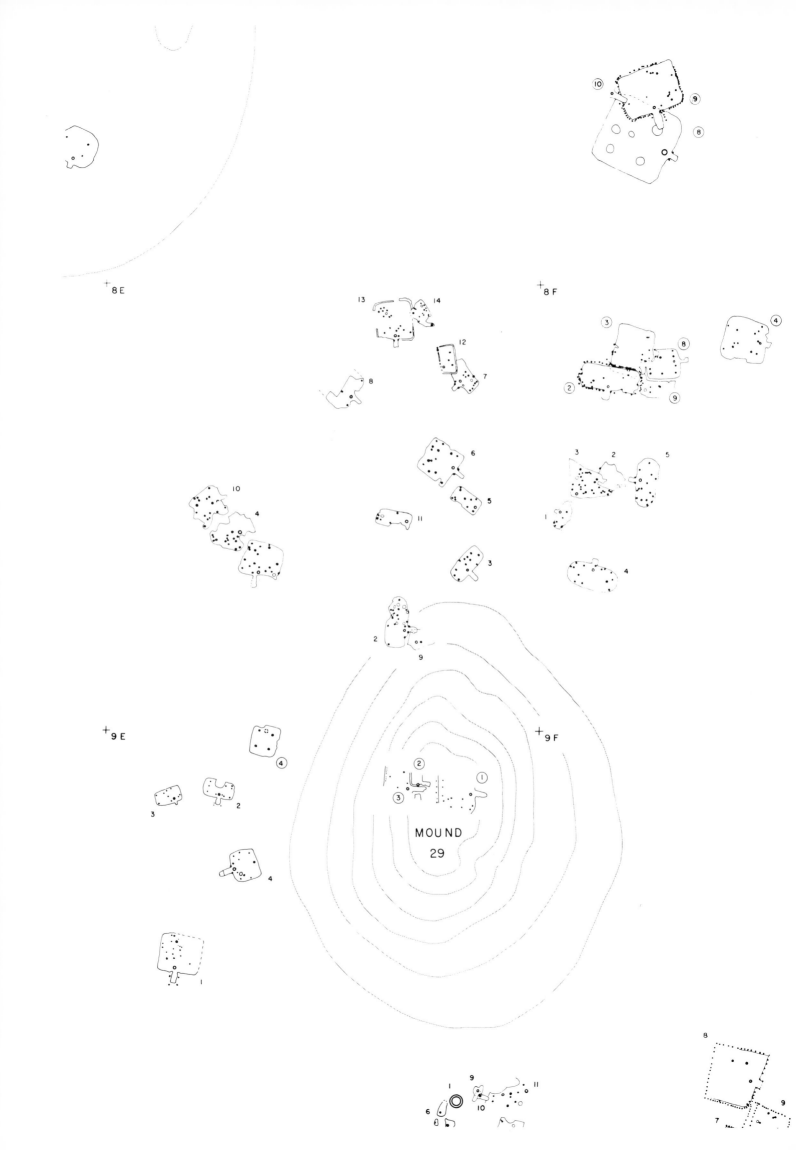

CREMATION
AREA

$+_{8G}$　　　　　　　　　　　　**KEY TO SYMBOLS**　　　　　　　　$+_{8H}$

$+_{7F}$ — GRID BLOCK CORNER

4 — HOUSE NUMBER, 1964-5 EXCAVATIONS

④ — HOUSE NUMBER, 1934-5 EXCAVATIONS

16/27 — HOUSE 16 SUPERPOSED OVER HOUSE 27

○ ◌ — HEARTH, UNDERLYING HEARTH

• · — POST HOLE, UNDERLYING POST HOLE

◎ — ROASTING PIT

⌣ — ADOBE PLASTER OR CONSTRUCTION

▲ — BALL COURT MARKER STONE

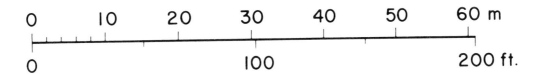

0　　10　　20　　30　　40　　50　　60 m

0　　　　　　　100　　　　　　　200 ft.

CONTOUR INTERVAL 0.5 METER

$+_{9G}$　　　　　　　　　　　　　　　　　　　　　$+_{9H}$

CREMATION
AREA

⑥

3

IMA
ROUND
HOUSE

⑧

5

1

5

4/10　　　　5

2

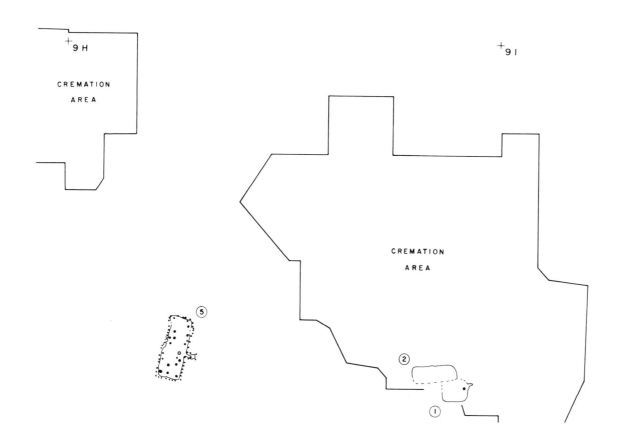

KEY TO SYMBOLS

+$_{7F}$ — GRID BLOCK CORNER

4 — HOUSE NUMBER, 1964-5 EXCAVATIONS

④ — HOUSE NUMBER, 1934-5 EXCAVATIONS

16/27 — HOUSE 16 SUPERPOSED OVER HOUSE 27

o ∘ — HEARTH, UNDERLYING HEARTH

• · — POST HOLE, UNDERLYING POST HOLE

◎ — ROASTING PIT

⌣ — ADOBE PLASTER OR CONSTRUCTION

▲ — BALL COURT MARKER STONE

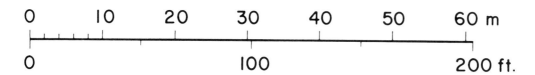

CONTOUR INTERVAL 0.5 METER

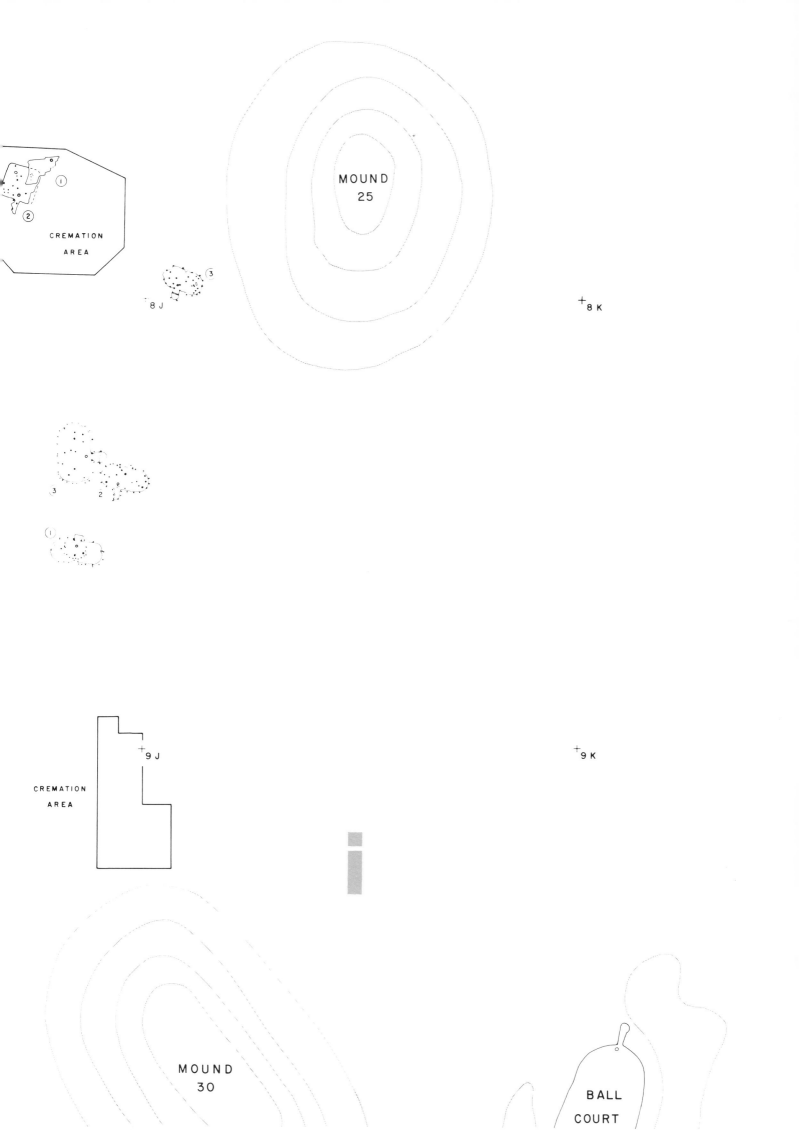

CREMATION
AREA

① ②

MOUND
25

③

⁺8 J

⁺8 K

③ 2

①

⁺9 J

⁺9 K

CREMATION
AREA

MOUND
30

BALL

COURT

$+$ 10 B

MOUND
27

$+$ 10 C

KEY TO SYMBOLS

$+$ 7 F — GRID BLOCK CORNER

4 — HOUSE NUMBER, 1964-5 EXCAVATIONS

④ — HOUSE NUMBER, 1934-5 EXCAVATIONS

16 / 27 — HOUSE 16 SUPERPOSED OVER HOUSE 27

o ◌ — HEARTH, UNDERLYING HEARTH

• · — POST HOLE, UNDERLYING POST HOLE

◎ — ROASTING PIT

⌣ — ADOBE PLASTER OR CONSTRUCTION

▲ — BALL COURT MARKER STONE

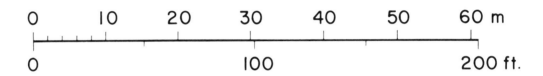

CONTOUR INTERVAL 0.5 METER

$+$ 11 B

$+$ 11 C

MOUND
26

12 B

12 C

3

4

+ 10 D

+ 10 E

2

+ 11 D

+ 11 E

MOUND
41

MOUND
42

MOU
43

j

+ 12 D

+ 12 E

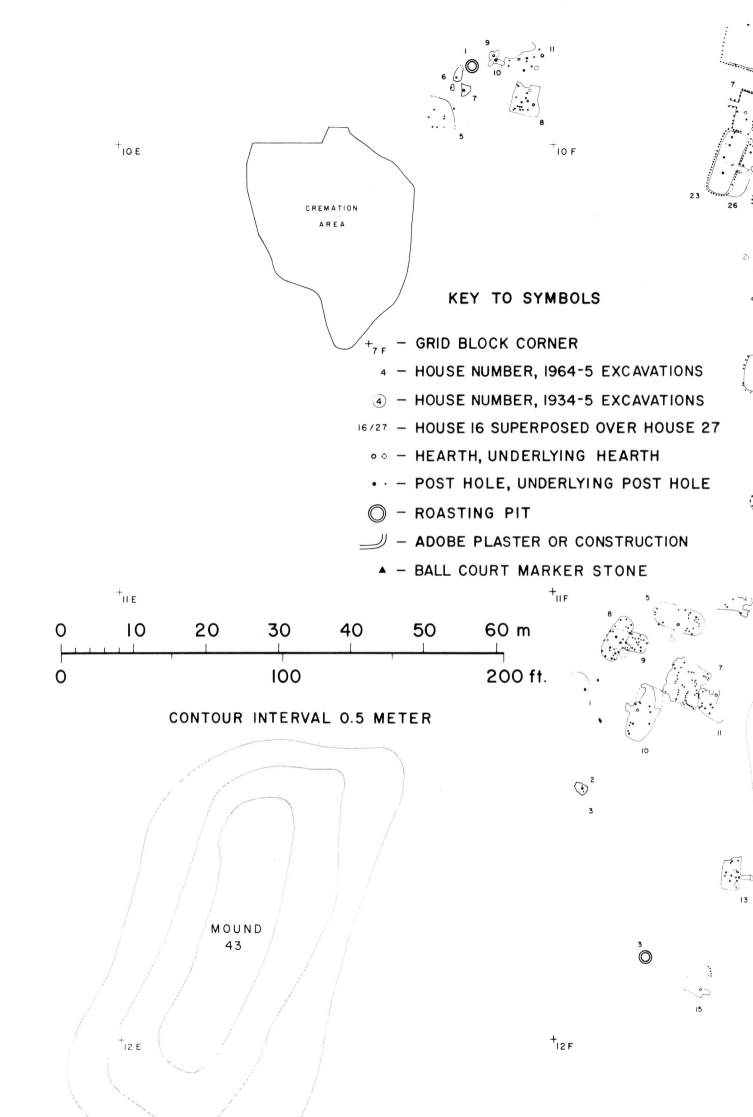

CREMATION
AREA

KEY TO SYMBOLS

$+_{7F}$ — GRID BLOCK CORNER

4 — HOUSE NUMBER, 1964-5 EXCAVATIONS

④ — HOUSE NUMBER, 1934-5 EXCAVATIONS

16/27 — HOUSE 16 SUPERPOSED OVER HOUSE 27

○ ○ — HEARTH, UNDERLYING HEARTH

• • — POST HOLE, UNDERLYING POST HOLE

◎ — ROASTING PIT

⌐ — ADOBE PLASTER OR CONSTRUCTION

▲ — BALL COURT MARKER STONE

0   10   20   30   40   50   60 m

0   100   200 ft.

CONTOUR INTERVAL 0.5 METER

MOUND
43

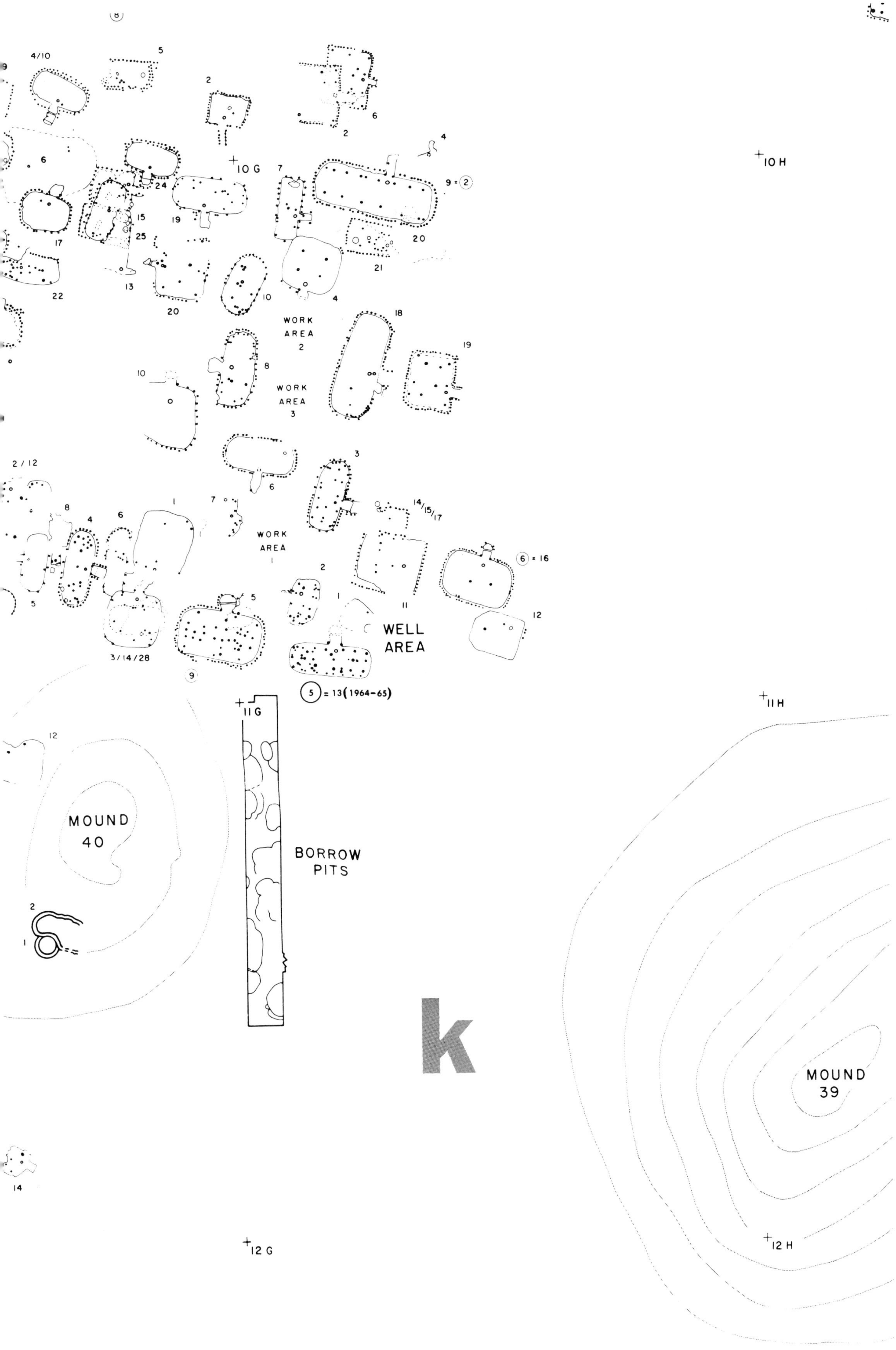

(8)

4/10

5

2

9

6

6

2

2

4

+10 G

7

9 = (2)

+10 H

6

24

15

19

20

20

17

25

21

13

10

4

WORK
AREA
2

18

22

20

8

19

10

WORK
AREA
3

2/12

3

8

1

7

14/15/17

8

4

6

WORK
AREA
1

6 = 16

5

2

1

5

11

12

5

WELL
AREA

3/14/28

9

(5) = 13(1964-65)

12

+11 G

+11 H

MOUND
40

BORROW
PITS

2

1

k

MOUND
39

+12 G

14

+12 H

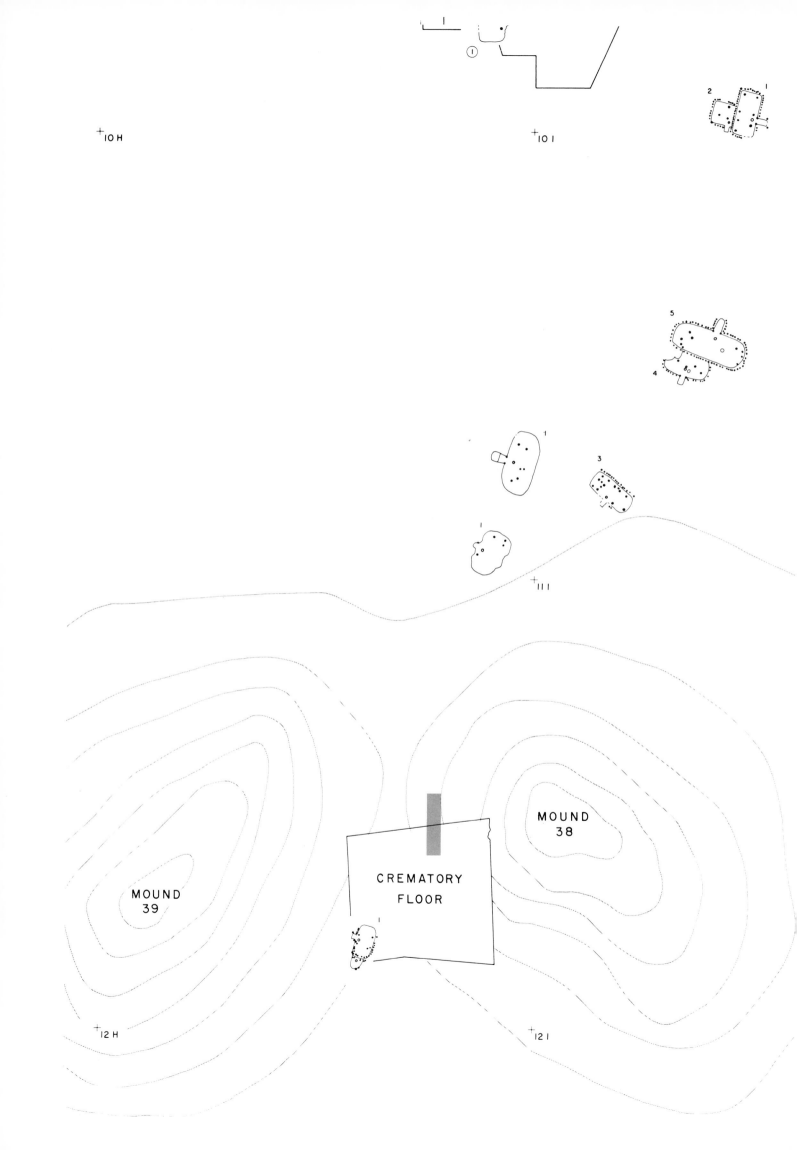

MOUND
38

MOUND
39

CREMATORY
FLOOR

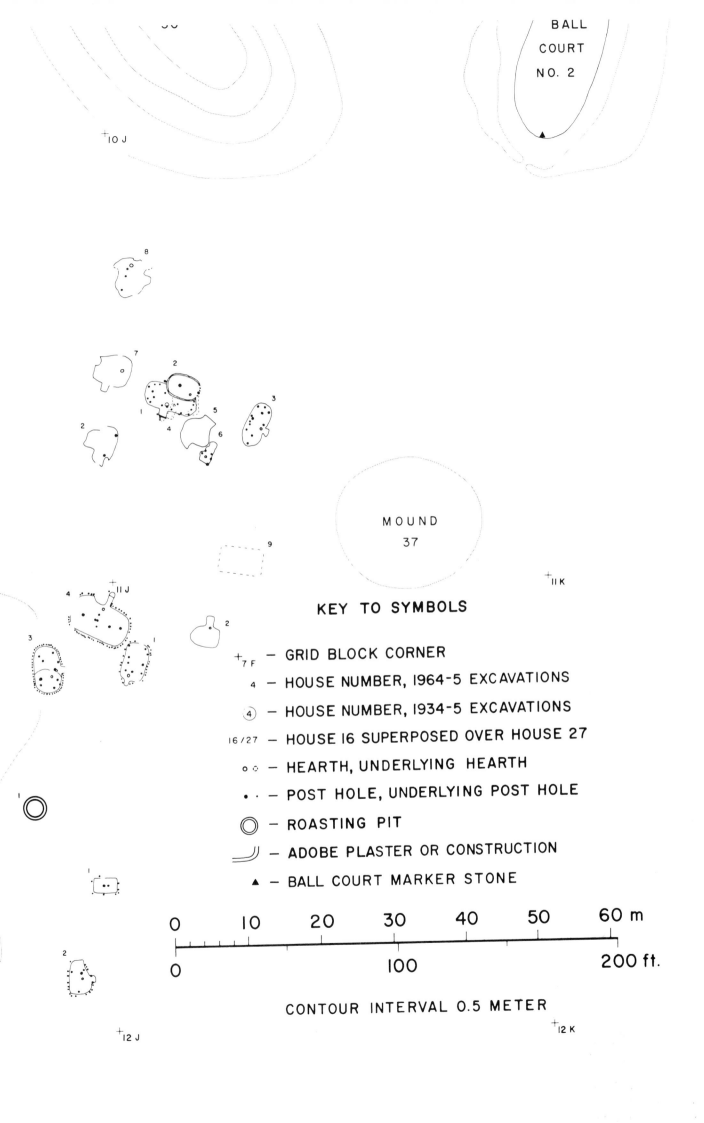

BALL
COURT
NO. 2

MOUND
37

KEY TO SYMBOLS

$+_{7F}$ — GRID BLOCK CORNER

4 — HOUSE NUMBER, 1964-5 EXCAVATIONS

④ — HOUSE NUMBER, 1934-5 EXCAVATIONS

16/27 — HOUSE 16 SUPERPOSED OVER HOUSE 27

○ ◌ — HEARTH, UNDERLYING HEARTH

● ∙ — POST HOLE, UNDERLYING POST HOLE

◎ — ROASTING PIT

⌣ — ADOBE PLASTER OR CONSTRUCTION

▲ — BALL COURT MARKER STONE

0	10	20	30	40	50	60 m

0		100		200 ft.

CONTOUR INTERVAL 0.5 METER

THE MODERN VILLAGE OF SNAKETOWN

Modern Snaketown (Gladwin and others 1937: 1-4) was one of a number of new villages established after peace was declared between the Pimas and Apaches toward the end of the nineteenth century. The same resources that were attractive to the Hohokam also appealed to the Pimas: the availability of shallow domestic water, good land on the lower terrace, and the feasibility of building a canal system to serve those lands. Southworth (1919: 127) states that in about 1868 Indians from Sratuka (Wet Camp), on the south side of the Gila, crossed the river and founded Snaketown, or Skukaika. They irrigated the lower terrace but experienced increasingly difficult times at the end of the century because of water shortage due to drought and to heavy upstream use. When the rains finally came in 1904–05, a disastrous flood washed out the canal heading along with about 500 acres of arable land of the nearly 1,800 acres that once were under cultivation (Southworth 1919: 127). Numerous efforts were made to realign the canal intake, the remains of which are still traceable in the early 1970s. But the deepening of the Gila River channel had gone so far that soon after 1910 agriculture at Snaketown was all but dead. The residents stayed on, finding wage work whenever possible to eke out a slim existence.

A walk over Snaketown in the 1970s reveals few traces of the widely dispersed houses of Pima Indians living on the site in the mid-1930s (Fig. 1.7). Destruction of the buildings has been hastened by the salvaging of reusable materials, but even so it is surprising that so little remains. The present surface remnants consist of low mounds of rubble marking the sites of a few houses. The most prominent housemounds are situated on the slightly higher ground on the southern margin of the upper terrace, the elevation having been caused by the maintenance and other activities related to the prehistoric irrigation canal. One architectural mound here is still partially capped by a concrete slab, the pulpit area of the village's church. It was also reported to us that a store once stood in this area. The low earthen rings marking the locations of the old-time round house, called *ki*, are difficult to see, but seven of them were noted and one was excavated (Gladwin and others 1937: Pl. XVI). Evidently the Pimas at Snaketown were conservatives, for Russell makes special mention of the fact (1908: 153) that the residents were retaining the old house form in the face of government efforts to encourage the construction of adobe houses.

Other surface traces of the Pima occupation are concentrations of refuse near the houses, consisting of broken glass, metal, porcelain, and fragments of native pottery, mixed with ashes from kitchen hearths. Partially filled wells and occasional lengths of barbed wire, survivals from fenced plots, may also be seen.

Fortunately, J. C. Fisher Motz, Gila Pueblo's cartographer in 1934–35, mapped the Pima features that have been incorporated in Figure 1.8. Without his work, after only thirty years, we would be hard pressed to come up with a reasonably accurate idea about the extent of the Pima reoccupation of Snaketown. Fisher Motz indicated the ruins of seven round houses; sixteen flat-roofed houses of wattle and daub, in use or abandoned at the time of mapping; three similar structures in an advanced state of disrepair; nine out-buildings of various kinds; four wells, one of which, located south of Ball Court 1, was still functioning in 1934–35, and a dozen fenced areas of different sizes.

The dispersed residency pattern was normal for Pima villages, and in no way was it incongruous with the manner in which space was used by the ancient villagers. House clusters reflect the extended family social grouping, and they occurred either inside or outside of fenced enclosures. Placement in several cases was close to the old trash mounds, but never on them. Fenced areas, on the other hand, were established with no regard for mounds.

It is difficult to estimate the size of the population of modern Snaketown when it was at its peak. Possibly no more than a dozen families lived there at any one moment, which could mean 50 to 60 people. One can guess that it would require 15 to 20 able-bodied men to keep the ditches in order and to till the fields. All of these, however, may not have come from Snaketown, since people on the south side of the river crossed it to farm the land below Snaketown (Southworth 1919: 127). In 1934 when the first archaeological studies of the site were undertaken, modern Snaketown consisted of three families living on the edge of the upper terrace, one family at the edge of Mound 15, an elderly couple along the east side of Mound 40, an old gentleman south of the large ball court, and a couple to the southeast barely beyond the limits of the old site, a total of about 17 souls. Those who wished work were employed by Gila Pueblo, and three men were put on the work force. While this was a momentary boost to the local economy, it could not last, and by 1940 modern Snaketown was dead. In a sense it was a replay of what had happened to the ancient village, though the forces that brought on the demise in each case were not the same.

During our work in 1964–65, a number of visiting Pimas told

Fig. 1.7. Modern Pima house and related structures in 1935. Gila Pueblo's tent camp is visible extreme upper right; test trenching is in progress (beyond house).

E. B. Sayles photo

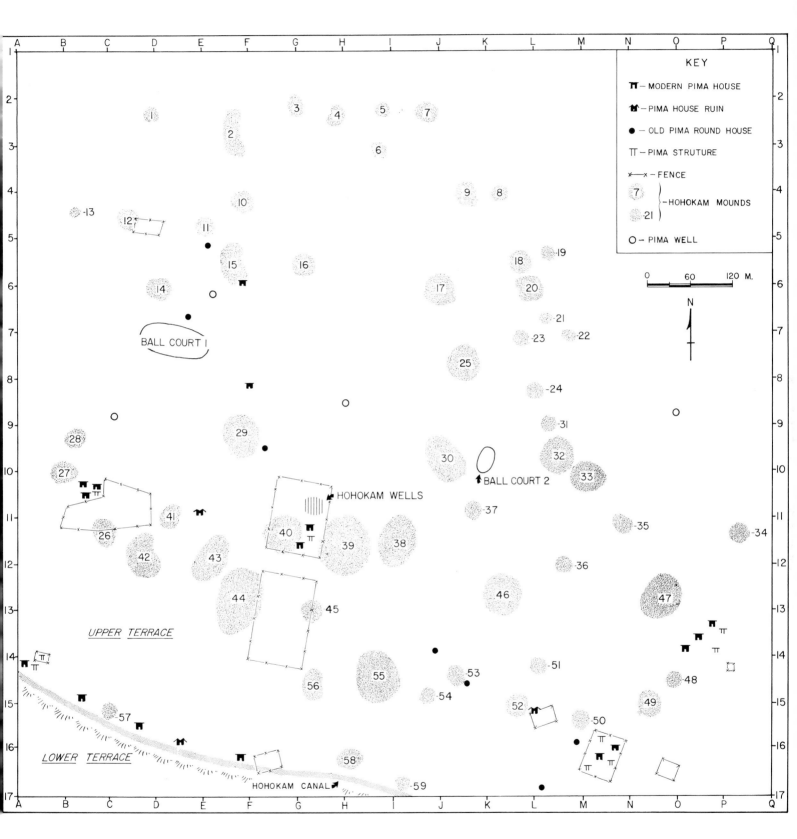

Fig. 1.8. Map of Snaketown showing the widely dispersed structures, abandoned and in use, of modern Snaketown in 1934-35. (Cartography after J. C. Fisher Motz)

us that they were either born at Snaketown or lived there during childhood. Standing at the edge of our excavation, the uniform reaction was, ''We didn't realize that all this was under our feet!'' Although they were aware that people had lived on the spot in the distant past, the nature of the evidence was not understood.

Modern Snaketown provides the archaeologist with a clear and documented case of the reoccupation of an old site after a long period of abandonment. This is a concept often used to explain the presence of diverse cultural materials, particularly when certain vestiges appear to be out of chronological context with the main evidence a site produces. In this case the distinction between the two uses is easily made because of the presence of glass, metal, porcelain, and other non-native goods. But suppose the reoccupation would have taken place before the introduction of European hardware to the Pimas of 1700 or 1750. The Pima *ki*, the round house, could not have been drastically dissimilar from the Hohokam structures, and the red-on-buff Pima pottery could have been fitted into the older ceramic tradition. The judgment might be made that, while there was a hiatus in the occupation, the late residents were probably related to the older ones. On the other hand, the archaeologist of the distant future, and for the sake of the argument, unfortunate enough not to have access to documentary sources, might see the European types of goods as reuse of the site by a totally different kind of people. Perhaps this is useless speculation, but to me modern Snaketown holds an important lesson for the archaeologist when it comes to interpreting the observations he has made. The stone axe with an iron shovel in a modern cache, and the cache of Pima pots, an enamel coffee pot, iron trivet and other objects on the floor of an ancient house, reviewed later, are only the more obvious cases of association that could lead to mistakes in interpretation. We are saved this embarrassment by having a record of the founding of modern Snaketown and the sharply contrasting non-native cultural goods, the beginnings of which must be traced to another continent.

2. Goals, Logistics, and Notes on Methods

In 1964 when the National Science Foundation was approached for funds to support the Snaketown work, the principal goals were stated as follows: (1) to reexamine the basis for the Hohokam chronology by employing improved stratigraphic and cross-dating techniques, and by using new dating tools, radiocarbon and archaeomagnetic analyses among them, which had not yet been devised in the 1930s; (2) to develop a clearer picture than now available of Hohokam origins by expanding knowledge of the initial cultural phases and to attempt to link these to the San Pedro Stage, the terminal manifestations of the Cochise complex; (3) on the basis of the anticipated new data, to evaluate the kind, extent, and time of Mesoamerican influences known to have been exerted on the Hohokam; and (4) to concentrate on the history of irrigated agriculture.

High aspirations declared at the time of seeking funds for a project are seldom fully realized. The difference between intent and accomplishment could be disastrous in the eyes of a grant-making institution, were it not for the fact that the phenomenon is well understood and that unattained goals may be offset by unanticipated discoveries. This is the case in part with the present endeavor.

The first goal, establishing the age of Snaketown, was reasonably well met, although the explicit and unequivocal data hoped for were not obtained. The information gained in support of the second goal led me to reverse my position with respect to Hohokam origins. Instead of an indigenous people, influenced by cultural factors flowing out of the south, I now see them as migrants from Mexico, possessing a well-developed water technology, a hypothesis developed elsewhere. Little new ground was gained on the third goal, but the concept of strong Mesoamerican ties was not weakened either. Perhaps the most significant gains were in the area of the economic base of Hohokam society, and our new knowledge of irrigated agriculture from the moment of Snaketown's founding has far-reaching implications. Furthermore, our overall understanding of these desert people has been strengthened through clarification of the architectural story, the introduction of the concept of artificial platform mounds, new information on food practices, and a host of minor subjects.

I consider this work, together with prior efforts, to be little more than a beginning toward achieving an understanding of the broad outlines of Hohokam society. We know something about the elements in the environment upon which they depended and the technologies they possessed to make the most of them. Some trends in cultural development can also be detected. But until the chronology is well established and progress has been made in blocking out the artifactual inventory, particularly in a spectrum of remains that spans nearly 1,500 years, little can be done to investigate questions of social interaction, of processes that induced change or promoted stability, or even the long-term impact organized agriculture had on the practitioners. My historico-cultural approach will therefore be a disappointment to those who

are searching for articulation of hypotheses of a processual nature with appropriate tests. These will come in due time. Meanwhile, I make no apology for reporting what was found and what I think the derived information means. Of no small importance to me is the desire to reach the nonprofessional as well as the professional. Hopefully the dust-dry portions of this report will be offset by others which the reader can relate to and appreciate more easily the people under investigation.

The original report on Snaketown, Medallion Paper No. XXV (Gladwin, Haury, Sayles, and Gladwin 1937), has been relied on heavily in preparing this supplement. Much duplication has been avoided in so doing, though it places an added burden on the reader who wishes to piece the results of the two investigations together. Happily, the original volume, long out of print, is available once again through the University of Arizona Press and the help of friends.

The chronological scheme and the names for periods and phases used in the following pages are the same as established in 1937. Only the Santan Phase, the last substage of the Sedentary Period (Gladwin and others 1937: 170), has been deleted for lack of verification. While a phase appears to be needed here to smooth out an abrupt transition between the Sedentary and Classic periods, Snaketown did not provide the information to fill the void. A forthcoming report (Hammack, Weed, and Huckell; in press) on excavations in Las Colinas, Phoenix, promises to end the uncertainty about the existence of a Santan Phase. The outline of periods and phases given in Table 2.1 will serve as a guide to the discussions that follow.

The substance of this report is intended to clarify the criteria that are recognized as phase hallmarks, the temporal order of the same, and the correlation of the sequence with the year values in the Christian calendar.

In 1934–35, Gila Pueblo's staff was housed in a tent camp on the site of Snaketown. Hand-pumped water from an old Pima well

TABLE 2.1

An Outline of Periods and Phases

Period	Phase	Approximate Time
Classic	Civano	Ending about A.D. 1450
	Soho	
Sedentary	Sacaton	Ending about A.D. 1100
Colonial	Santa Cruz	Ending about A.D. 900
	Gila Butte	
Pioneer	Snaketown	Ending about A.D. 550
	Sweetwater	
	Estrella	
	Vahki	Beginning about 300 B.C.

provided the first requisite of life. With improvement of roads, the ancient village has become much more accessible, and the logistics in 1964–65 dictated that off-site living would be the best solution to the residence problem. A reorganization of the elementary school system on the reservation had led to the abandonment of the Santan Day School, located a few miles northwest of Sacaton, and arrangements were concluded with Bureau of Indian Affairs officials to lease the property for the duration of the Snaketown work.

The cluster of buildings was ideally suited to our needs. A duplex housing unit sheltered the staff, and the school's kitchen and dining room were easily converted into a laboratory and darkroom. Three classrooms provided further space for drafting and for storage. The ten-mile daily commuting trip to the site was more than offset by the advantages the school offered for living and working with all customary utilities and facilities available.

This arrangement, however, left Snaketown vulnerable during non-working hours. Two house trailers were moved onto the site, one occupied by the guard, Joe Thomas, the other serving as a field office. A fuel tank, small machine shed, Paradome supply shelter, a lunch table shaded by the largest tree on Snaketown—a tamarisk from Africa!—and sanitation facilities were the only onsite developments.

The grid system employed in 1934–35 was reestablished with the thought that this would be less confusing than to adopt a new plan of horizontal control (See Appendix 1 for Cartographer's statement). Coordinate intersections were marked by 5 x 5 cm wooden stakes, the interval being 60 m. East-west lines were numbered, and north-south ordinates were lettered, the beginning point being in the northwest corner with stake 1A. The northwest corner marker in each grid block was the designator stake for that block. Features such as houses, cremations and pits were then serially numbered within each block, House 2:9E being an example. Subsidiary triangulation points could easily be established within a 60-m square area if conditions called for it. Vertical control was maintained by establishing an arbitrary "Snaketown datum." The relief in the large area the village covers is so negligible that this dimension had little use.

About 85% of the area of Snaketown is flat terrain, lying between mounds and the embankments of the ball courts. There are no surface clues of buried features. To find these requires probing by hand, mechanical, or instrumented means. We learned in 1934–35 that hand digging, whether by continuous trenching or spaced test pits, was a slow and costly process and that in the small area exposed in a pit extant features could not always be recognized. While some hand testing was still done in 1964–65, heavy reliance was placed on the backhoe. In the soft soil of Snaketown this machine could explore a large area in an hour, pinpointing enough promising spots to keep a crew of twenty men busy for a week or more working out the details. Use of the backhoe in canal testing hastened the work by at least a factor of ten over hand labor, and it opened the door to a much wider geographic investigation of the system than would have been possible otherwise.

The careful study of trench profiles provided useful guides in planning the lateral excavations, labeled "profile-plan digging" in the field. This means simply that a single feature, as for example, a crematorium, could be cleared with little expansion of the trench. A series of superimposed house floors or irrigation canals, however, presented another problem. With two dimensions visible, the third could be estimated better, and both the digging technique and the backdirt placement could be approached more sensibly.

We noted that trench profiles, etched naturally by drying out, by wind, and perhaps by temperature changes, often brought out subtle differences in the matrix that could not be recognized by scraping the trench faces immediately after digging. On a long-term excavation, leaving the trenches open and studying them periodically has its rewards.

Stratigraphic testing was adjusted more or less to the nature of the deposit. The methods used are reviewed in reference to specific tests. Snaketown lends itself especially well to controlled sampling because of the soft soil and lack of hard and massive architectural remains. Disturbances by man and animal did, at times, however, erase the latent chronological values of a deposit.

A by-product of the conventional stratigraphic test was the application of a micro-sampling method in which the residue from mechanical screening was further hand-sifted through a window-size screen. This separated everything larger than the screen size but smaller than the ¼ or ½ inch mesh size of the previous screen. Nearly a hundred samples varying from 5 to 10 kg in weight were taken from trash of all phases. In the laboratory, the screenings were slowly poured into water to float off the carbon. This fraction consisted of finely divided pieces of charcoal, carbonized plant parts, and seeds, which were separately boxed and prepared for submission to an ethnobotanist. The inorganic concentrate was painstakingly searched for micro-minerals, wastage from shell or stone work, artifacts such as beads, and small faunal remains. The amount of labor invested in this step was great, but the results obtained warranted the effort.

The organic fraction led to the detection of the presence of certain domestic plants at an early date, as for example, cotton. Variations in the relative abundance of carbonized native food versus domestic food plants have suggested cyclical periods of plenty and want (Bohrer 1970).

The micro-mineral fragments for the most part were derived from working with minerals, and the presence of a few not represented by other kinds of samples was detected in this way. The evidence for making mosaic units of turquoise in the oldest horizons at Snaketown was determined by this sampling technique.

Perhaps most meaningful of all are the data drawn from the faunal remains, the tiny bones, whole or finely fragmented, that are usually lost in coarser screening operations. These provide new insights into the dietary habits of the Hohokam.

Laboratory procedures included cleaning, repairing, and the cataloguing on the spot of the prime materials in the Arizona State Museum system, followed by packing and periodic shipping to the Museum. The vast amount of pottery accruing from the excavations, whether from random probes or stratigraphic sampling, was washed and analyzed within a few days of recovery. This provided quick knowledge of the nature and age of the deposits being dug, information which in many cases allowed more intelligent planning of further work. The typological analysis provided the basis for quantitative evaluations, by count or by weight, and permitted an almost immediate reduction of mass by simple selection. Some samples, for reasons of purity, richness of associated details, or other reasons, were held intact. Other lots were reduced to representative samples as, for example, pit contents, and still others were severely culled where stratigraphic placement or other conditions held little value. Of the total pottery yield of about 1.5 million sherds, approximately 30% was retained.

All of the materials accruing from the 1934–35 and the 1964–65 Snaketown excavations, cartographic, photographic, field records of directing personnel and laboratory analyses, are permanently housed in the archives of the Arizona State Museum. The two collections of artifacts have been merged into one.

While no substitute has yet been devised for pick-and-shovel probing in the ground as a means of locating subsurface features in an archaeological site, advances are being made in the development and application of detection devices. Froelich Rainey, Director of the University Museum, University of Pennsylvania, and also Director of the Museum's Applied Science Center for

Archaeology, together with Hugh Bergh, then of Princeton University, spent nearly a week at Snaketown in January 1965 testing the reaction of several pieces of equipment to desert soils. More is said about this work in Appendix 3 by Bergh. Suffice it to note here that the experiments proved the capability of the proton magnetometer to locate hearths and burned areas with ease. Most of the anomalies detected in resistivity were excavated immediately for verification purposes.

Since this type of prospecting has been little used in Southwestern archaeology, further observations are worthwhile. The most easily identified feature was Roasting Pit 1 in Block 11 I (Fig. 9.9c), the heavily burned sides of which, and the thermally-fractured rock filling, markedly influenced the magnetometer (Fig. A3.1). Although this feature would have been found had it been in the path of a test trench, the quickness and relative ease with which a large area could be examined for anomalies made a deep impression on us. No surface clues indicated its presence.

Another station, detected in Block 10 I, produced weak readings on the instrument, but the level of resistance was enough to make testing seem worthwhile. The anomaly developed into an irregularly shaped borrow pit filled with trash and lenses of ashes. The refuse contained much shell wastage, the leavings of a shell craftsman's work, and a large Sacaton Red-on-buff cauldron (Fig. 2.1). This vessel, the ash beds, and the slight evidence of burning in the pit were the elements to which the magnetometer responded.

A number of instrument transits across the irrigation canals made by Rainey and Bergh and independently by Wasley were instructive only up to a point in providing data on canal sections. Hopes of being able to plot the course of canals by this method or even of identifying canals where no surface evidence exists were not fulfilled. Resistivity readings were not consistent enough to permit the construction of canal profiles.

The hint in Bergh's account (Appendix 3) that the results of a total magnetometer survey of Snaketown, coupled with certain other kinds of information, might permit the identification of subsurface features of a desired age *before* excavation, would be a boon of the first order and an advantage little short of magic. His idea should be pursued.

While the proton magnetometer is a useful search tool in that "hot spots" can be quickly identified with it, places where it fails to respond may still yield valuable archaeological information. The technique does not relieve the excavator from testing the neutral areas.

Finally, the code designation for Snaketown in the archaeological survey made by Gila Pueblo about 1930 was Gila Butte 1:1. In the Arizona State Museum inventory the site is listed as Arizona U:13:1. The concordance for the Classic Period sites follows:

Gila Pueblo	*Arizona State Museum*
Gila Butte 1:2	Arizona U:13:21
Gila Butte 1:3	Arizona U:13:22
Not listed	Arizona U:13:23
Gila Butte 1:4	Arizona U:13:24

These villages were assigned to the Soho Phase (Gladwin and others 1937: 83) of the Classic Period on the basis of limited digging. Our more extensive work indicated that they were later and should be related to the Civano Phase. No testing was done in Arizona U:13:23, but, in all probability, it was no different than the others nearby. For locations of these sites, see Figure 1.2.

Fig. 2.1. Large Sacaton Red-on-buff cauldron in an area of ashes and lightly burned soil, detected by a proton magnetometer.

PART TWO

ARCHITECTURE

3. Houses

Unlike residences with limitations placed on them by the living rock walls of a cave, the contours of a mesa, or the slope of the land, the houses built in Snaketown were essentially unhampered by geography. Good sense dictated the avoidance of the lower terrace for fear of flooding, but on the upper terrace almost any spot was as desirable a homesite as any other. The freedom from environmentally imposed restrictions undoubtedly has something to do with the openness of the village, with its wide sprawl occupying roughly a km² (about 0.4 mi²), as did also the need for more space demanded by a rising population. Yet, while the scattering may have been a response to a permissive nature, there must also have been an influence from within the society, a belief that close spacing of houses was not the key to quality living. If there were rules of residence, they were imposed by the society, not by nature.

Seen broadly, the open character of Snaketown lasted from its inception to the introduction of above-surface, multi-storied, adobe structures near the beginning of the fourteenth century—as, for example, Casa Grande. This represented a sharp switch in residence philosophy. But the new pattern lasted only a short while, for by the time Father Kino arrived in the Gila valley in 1694, the Pima Indians were living in villages that mirrored the pattern of old. Bartlett's description (1854: Vol. 2, 233 ff) is a significant early account of a Pima village, and a recently discovered painting by Seth Eastman (Fig. 3.1) is perhaps the earliest visual portrayal. Had he painted a thousand years earlier, the result would have been about the same.

The lack of architectural compactness and the nature of the Hohokam house introduce a number of practical recovery problems for the archaeologist. The typical house had side walls and roof of reeds internally supported by a framework of posts and other structural elements variously put together and externally veneered with dirt. A covered extension from one long side afforded some protection for the entry, which normally included a step down to the floor, sometimes barely below the then extant desert level or as much as one meter below it. Unless the house burned, nothing remained of the superstructure; the principal evidence of the structure is the floor, generally of specially prepared material that made following it relatively easy. When a structure collapsed, the resulting pit, or in rare cases a slight mound, was soon erased by acts of man and nature. At Snaketown not a single house of Sedentary Period age or earlier was recognized by surface evidences. They were all discovered by test trenches or other excavations. Recalling now the dimensions of Snaketown, larger than a square kilometer (250 acres), the task of locating dwellings becomes clear. The advantages of machine trenching can best be illustrated by noting that the hand digging of the 1934–35 operation led to the uncovering of 40 houses, while the 1964–65 venture netted 166 excavated structures, not counting the Classic Period sites. Finding and tracing the houses depended on extensive and sensitive probing.

Figure 1.6 is a map of Snaketown bringing together most of the architectural remains uncovered in both efforts. Fewer than the 206 houses found are shown because some of the floors noted in the field sheets were too patchy to determine house form. Also, some architectural remains lay outside the area included in the map, an omission dictated by scale problems. The Classic Period sites, Arizona U:13:21, 22, 23 and 24 lie on the western fringes of the larger occupied area (Fig. 1.2, inset).

To clarify further the nature of the sample, Figure 3.2 provides information about the number of houses uncovered assignable to various phases, and their distribution by block in the Snaketown grid system. The recorded distribution of houses, in part, is a function of our more or less arbitrary selection of places to dig and the limiting of stripping operations to only a few areas. The time-frequency figures, on the other hand, underscore two circumstances of interest: the highest number of houses and the greatest geographical spread in the site (in 24 of 34 grid blocks tested) occurred during the Sacaton Phase. This is a clear reflection of the fact that the maximum population in Snaketown's long history was reached at that time.

Beyond that, the large number of Sacaton Phase houses also tells us that man's destructive activity was missing from the scene thereafter. Snaketown proper was abandoned by the end of the Sacaton Phase, and no one was there to intrude upon the latest structures by overbuilding. In general, the older the house the more susceptible it was to mutilation by later house construction or by other disturbances of the ground (Fig. 3.3). This condition, together with a reducing population as one recedes in time, is responsible for the fewer units uncovered in the early phases. Although more Pioneer Period houses might be wished for in the sample, the evidence available is indicative of what happened to the Hohokam architectural idiom in the village as time passed.

The house deployment as shown in Figure 1.6 indicates one major area of architectural concentration, encompassing Blocks 10F and 10G and spreading beyond them. Seen from the air (Fig. 3.4) the situation seems complex indeed, and it was. Although almost the entire house-building history of Snaketown is compressed into this locale, at no time, excepting the Sacaton Phase, were there more than a few houses standing simultaneously. The apparent reason for the desirability of this locality for residences was its nearness to a shallow underground water source, tapped by wells that were exposed in the large test pit (upper left corner of Fig. 3.4).

Blank areas on the master map (Fig. 1.6) do not necessarily mean that these were unoccupied spaces, for much of Snaketown's acreage was inadequately tested. This fact, perhaps more than any other, has a direct bearing on the evaluation of the settlement pattern and the inability, at this point in the investigations, to detect with confidence house arrangements that might have been dictated by social or other forces.

Fig. 3.1. Nineteenth century village of the Pima Indians on the Gila River. Watercolor by Seth Eastman, early 1850s. Bartlett Drawing No. 192. On deposit in the John Carter Brown Library from the Museum of Art of the Rhode Island School of Design. Reproduction arranged through Thomas R. Adams, Librarian, The John Carter Brown Library, Brown University. First published by Robert V. Hine in *Bartlett's West,* 1968, illustration 36.

PERIOD	PHASE	GRID BLOCK																																		AZ.U:13.21	AZ.U:13.22	SUB-TOTAL	GRAND TOTAL
		3C	4H	5F	5G	6E	6F	6G	6H	6I	7D	7F	7H	7I	7J	8B	8E	8F	8I	9E	9F	9G	9H	9I	10D	10F	10G	10H	10I	10J	11F	11H	11I	11J	15E				
SED. CLASSIC	CIVANO																																			6	10	16	16
SED. CLASSIC	SOHO																																						
SED. CLASSIC	SACATON	_2_	_2_	5	11	_2_	_1_	_1_ / 2							_1_	1	2	2	_2_		3	1			2	_1_ / 24	_2_ / 10	1	4	7	6		3	2				_14_ / 86	100
COLONIAL	SANTA CRUZ				1	_1_		2 / 1									2	2		_1_ / 1	_1_ / 1	_1_	_1_			1	1	4					1					_7_ / 16	23
COLONIAL	GILA BUTTE			2	1			1									1	1		2	1				2				1		2							14	14
COLONIAL	COLONIAL																2			1	2						1											6	6
PIONEER	SNAKETOWN						_1_	_1_	_1_		_1_			_1_				_1_	_1_ / 1		2					1	1				1			1				_7_ / 7	14
PIONEER	SWEETWATER							_1_										_1_ / 3									1				1		1					_2_ / 6	8
PIONEER	ESTRELLA							_1_										1			1																	_1_ / 2	3
PIONEER	VAHKI											_1_	_1_ / 1								1																	_2_ / 2	4
PIONEER	PIONEER		1														5			1	1	1					2				2							13	13
	UNPLACED										_1_	_1_	_1_				2	_3_	_1_ / 1		1				1	2	2				1		3					_7_ / 13	20
	SUB-TOTAL	_2_ / 2	_2_ / 2	8	13	_2_ / 2	_2_ / 2	_5_ / 4	2	1	1	3	2	1	1	1	14	5	4	3	4	11	10	6	2	4	28	21	1	5	9	14	1	4	2	1	6	10	_40_ / 181	221
	GRAND TOTAL	2	2	8	13	2	2	9	2	1	1	3	3	1	1	1	14	9	3	15	10	7	1	2	4	29	23	1	5	9	14	1	4	2	1	6	10	221	

_2_ = 1934-'35 — 2 = 1964-'65

Fig. 3.2. Distribution of houses in Snaketown by grid block and phase, and by phase only in the Classic Period sites. The 1934-35 frequencies are from Gladwin and others 1937, Fig. 19.

Fig. 3.3. Houses 10 (foreground), 4, and 1, and an unnumbered fragment (lower right) illustrate the mutilation of old houses by later occupants of Snaketown. All floors pictured were assignable to the Pioneer Period but not to phase (Block 8E).

Fig. 3.4. This mosaic of more than sixty house floors represents a cross-section of Snaketown's architectural history. The round-appearing floor (left center) and the large square structure (bottom) are the youngest and oldest buildings, respectively, in the group shown.

ANALYSIS

It is both impractical and unnecessary to give the detailed plan for every one of the 181 houses cleared. Examples of "normal" structures, as well as aberrant ones, will be examined with some care. Out of this approach should come some appreciation of the architectural modes and changes therein through time. For those who will be dissatisfied with this treatment, the records of all structures are on permanent file in the archives of the Arizona State Museum where they may be consulted.

The detection of a house floor was followed by tracing it carefully with a trowel. Some floors, made directly on the natural matrix, were especially difficult to develop. Compactness, a slight color variation caused by trampling and the grinding of charcoal into the soil by feet, and, most importantly, a hearth and other features, were the guidelines followed. Where floor material differed from the matrix in color and texture, having been laid down specially, the uncovering process was relatively simple.

The arrangement of holes in the floor and around its edge was the chief clue to the nature of the superstructure, aided on rare occasions in burned structures by the survival of charred structural elements. Floor holes in some houses made no sense at all, and only in a few structures was the arrangement "clean," that is, unencumbered with holes that had no apparent meaning in the overall design. Irregularities must be explained by the fact that all roof support posts need not have been set in holes (Woodward 1933), and all floor holes did not hold posts that were connected with the roof. Modern Indian houses in northwestern Mexico and in Papaguería often show water jars or metates supported a meter or so above the floor by a forked tree stem; or racks and shelves for the storage of goods. There is no sure way to separate roof and non-roof related elements by an inspection of the surviving holes in the floor. Therefore, when roof support patterns are identified as typical of one or another horizon, the plans generally represent a synthesis of the evidence from a number of structures.

Upon the completion of any one house, further probings were always made to test for multiple floors in single houses, and to detect deeper floors which might be indicative of overlapping structures. It was this type of investigation that led to the disclosure of the massed and superimposed houses in what appears to have been the heart of the village (Fig. 3.4).

The time-ordering of house units was based on the following criteria:

1. The stratigraphic relationship to other floors or features when present, establishing no more than the order of succession.
2. The contents of the house pit, separated as to fill and floor contact specimens. Most of the material recovered was random broken pottery. Such material is helpful but not absolutely indicative. Its utility depends upon a variety of human activities and natural circumstances responsible for the filling of the house depression. The best dating clues were whole or crushed vessels on the house floor, meaning that they were in use when the house was destroyed. A notable exception to this "rule" is discussed on page 68.
3. By radiocarbon and archaeomagnetic dating techniques, both of limited value because so few houses produced carbon and archaeomagnetic samples were taken only from structures exemplary of the presumed architectural sequence.
4. The shape of the house, if all other controls failed. This criterion, however, could be applied only if enough of the house floor was preserved to establish the form, and if the reservoir of information about houses in general became large enough to reveal the evolutionary pattern of the architectural idiom.

While precise dating, as has been achieved in the Anasazi region by tree-ring studies, was not possible, I have faith in the correctness of the general developmental picture of Snaketown's architecture. It should always be borne in mind that in another village the story may not be exactly the same, for individual or social group requirements both may have been different, or there may have been subtle environmental effects that are not obvious to us now. What this means is that hard and fast architectural period criteria cannot be set up. Broad trends, however, may be identified.

As an aid to talking about house forms, a simple typology will be used. Since changes are identifiable to period rather than to phase, the code system adopted is based on a letter or letters from the period name, together with a number. For example: C1-1 means Classic Period, Type 1 structure; S-2 means Sedentary Period, Type 2 structure; C is Colonial Period; and P is Pioneer Period. Frequency figures related to types include the 1934–35 excavations as listed by Sayles (Gladwin and others 1937: Fig. 19). Appendix 2 identifies and quantifies the architectural recoveries by phase, block, house number, and type.

The following synopsis of Snaketown architecture proceeds from the recent to the early remains.

Classic Period

For reasons not known in the early 1970s, the heart of Snaketown was abandoned by A.D. 1100 or soon after. Life continued, however, both east and west in a number of definable settlements. Most or all of these are of Classic Period age with little or no surface evidence of older beginnings. Three of these villages, closest to Snaketown on the west (Fig. 1.2, inset), were given varying attention: house remains in Ariz. U:13:21 and 22 were partially cleared in order to establish the architectural mode and other cultural traits, and Ariz. U:13:24 was tested only sufficiently to be certain of its position in the time scale. While these villages may have been established in the Soho, or the initial phase in the Classic Period, the weight of the evidence we were able to gather indicates that they were chiefly assignable to the Civano Phase, roughly A.D. 1300 to 1425. This revises Sayles' identifications of the sites as dating from the Soho Phase (Gladwin and others 1937:83). Since there are no recognizable evidences of settlements younger than A.D. 1425 but still pre-Spanish, these villages are considered to mark the end of the prehistoric record of human use of the Gila valley in the immediate environs of Snaketown.

They are situated well back on the terrace, the farthest one being nearly 1 km distant from the edge. This is no different than the "suburban" limits of Snaketown in the Sacaton Phase. What is different, however, is the sharply contrasting nature of the architecture, the clumping of rooms built on the ground surface in late times versus the scattered sunken houses of earlier days. The two patterns of residency represent a sharp contrast in the ideas of what the mode of housing should be. Although no clear traces of canals survive, it may be assumed that domestic water was brought to these settlements by small ditches from the main waterway at the edge of the terrace.

ARIZONA U:13:21

Only six houses and fragments of several others were cleared in this village (Fig. 3.5). Judging from the presence of three sizable trash mounds, there probably were ten times as many houses as we exposed. Yet, the sample is large enough to permit several inferences.

Houses 1 to 4, Types Cl-1, were independent units in the village (Fig. 3.6a-c), duplicating the system followed at Snaketown. Houses 5 and 6, Types Cl-2, however, begin to show an arrangement that brought rooms together into a contiguous or connected relationship (Fig. 3.6d). On the basis of looseness or compactness of organization of rooms, the latter condition being the more advanced in a typological sense, Ariz. U:13:21 should be older than Ariz. U:13:22 (Fig. 3.8). Ceramic and other cultural evidences are not helpful, however, in supporting this idea.

ARIZ. U:13:21

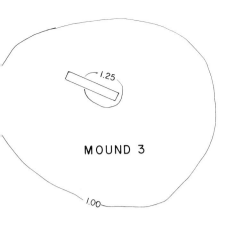

MOUND 3

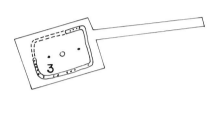

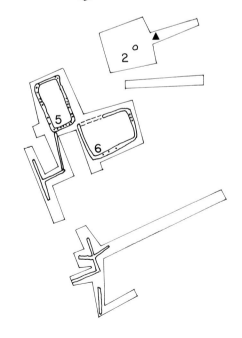

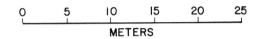

⊂⊃ = ADOBE WALLS

⊂∙∙∙∙∙⊃ = ADOBE WALLS, POST REENFORCED

○ = HEARTH

∙∙ = FLOOR POST HOLES

▲ = BURIAL

▭ = AREAS TESTED

CONTOUR INTERVAL .25 M.

N

| 0 | 5 | 10 | 15 | 20 | 25 |

METERS

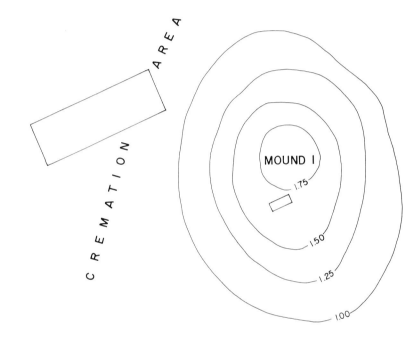

CREMATION AREA

MOUND 1

1.75

1.50

1.25

1.00

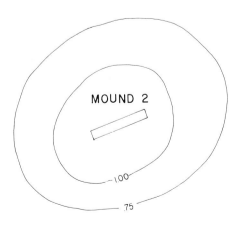

MOUND 2

1.00

.75

Fig. 3.5. Plan of Ariz. U:13:21

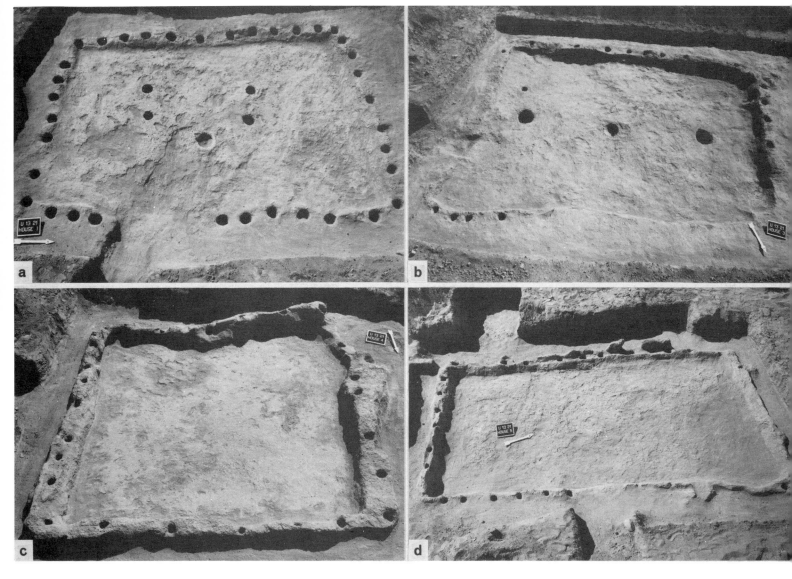

Fig. 3.6. Houses in Ariz. U:13:21, Civano Phase. (a) House 1—only bare remnants of adobe walls survive, but post reinforcing of wall is well shown (Cl-1). (b) House 3—position of roof support posts suggests single main beam (Cl-1). (c) House 4—vertical stone slab in south wall probably marks entrance (Cl-1). (d) House 5—note wall stub, upper left corner (Cl-2). Arrow length is 0.5 m.

The architectural mode of the phase may be generalized as follows: house floors of prepared clay were built on the existing desert surface or lowered slightly below it to eliminate soft desert soil; floor plan dominantly rectangular, corners squared and floor area averaging 15 m²; side walls were vertical of puddled adobe, average thickness 25 cm, reinforced internally with more or less regularly spaced posts 10 to 15 cm in diameter; highest preserved wall, 20 cm; internal roof support post plan variable, not always present or not detected; rooms were side entered without benefit of passage, no evident consistency in orientation; hearths circular, more or less central in floor, clay lined.

Houses that stood alone have been designated Cl-1 in the typology, and those that were contiguous to others are Cl-2. This division may seem unwarranted, but it recognizes my thinking that separateness or contiguity of houses represents a basic shift in residence philosophy and needs, therefore, to be recognized.

ARIZONA U:13:22

This village, the nearest of all Classic Period sites to Snaketown proper, best illustrates the arrangement of the living units of the times. Figure 3.7 shows how the symmetry of the overall structure unfolded by trenching when viewed from the air. The ten rooms cleared of fill were deployed within a compound

wall (Fig. 3.8), and it may be presumed that other rooms still exist in the areas not tested. Also we cannot be sure that outside of the compound wall, single house units may not be present as well. Material for the adobe structures was apparently obtained from the depression located west of the compound. It may also have served as a pond for storing domestic water, either surface derived or canal fed, although no evidence of the latter device exists.

Once again, generalizing, the room configuration is rectangular; rooms may be contiguous, attached to the compound wall or separate from it; floors were of prepared clay, the level roughly coinciding with the desert surface at the time of construction; floor area 10 to 15 m²; walls rise from below floor level in a prepared trench, of post reinforced adobe, or puddled adobe blocks as indicated by drying cracks; internal roof support posts absent; rooms were side entered, generally in midsection of long axis; hearth position variable but most often midway between entrance and room center. In the architectural typology, all rooms in this site are classified as Cl-2, even Room 4 which probably was linked to the compound wall originally.

A number of special features need further attention. The custom of digging trenches for wall foundations below floor line was not detected in Ariz. U:13:21 (Fig. 3.9). Post reinforced walls were made by setting poles an average of 25 cm apart (Fig.

Fig. 3.7. Tracing the walls of Ariz. U:13:22.

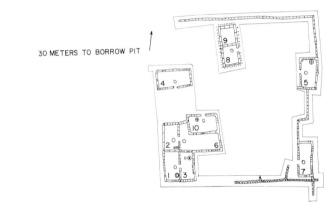

30 METERS TO BORROW PIT

Fig. 3.8. Map of Ariz. U:13:22.

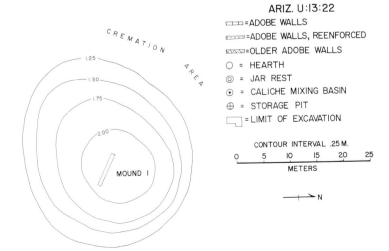

CREMATION AREA

1.25
1.50
1.75
2.00

MOUND I

ARIZ. U:I3:22

⊏⊐ = ADOBE WALLS
⊏∵∵⊐ = ADOBE WALLS, REENFORCED
▨▨ = OLDER ADOBE WALLS
○ = HEARTH
◎ = JAR REST
⊙ = CALICHE MIXING BASIN
⊕ = STORAGE PIT
⊐ = LIMIT OF EXCAVATION

CONTOUR INTERVAL .25 M.

0   5   10   15   20   25
METERS

N

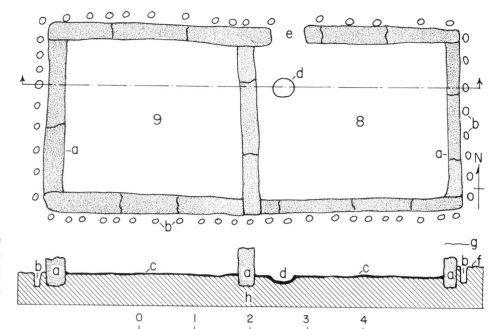

Fig. 3.9. Ariz. U:13:22. Plan and section of Rooms 8 and 9 (CI-2): (a) adobe walls laid up in blocks and courses and set in a trench; (b) outside posts; (c) floor; (d) hearth; (e) door; (f) old surface; (g) present surface; (h) native soil.

METERS

3.10b,c), stuffing adobe with a high caliche content between them, and finishing both faces with a 5 cm thick layer of adobe plaster. Both room and compound walls were given this treatment. A second method of wall construction consisted of laying up adobe in blocks and courses and sometimes setting poles outside the walls. Rooms 8 and 9 are examples of this (Figs. 3.9, 3.10a). Wall height for either type of construction was not determinable. There is no apparent time difference between these two methods of wall-building, for both occur in the same room (Rooms 2 and 3). The variations appear to have been a matter of

personal choice (See Hayden 1957: 7ff for further discussion of these and related wall types).

A number of the rooms had two floors (Fig. 3.11), testifying to their renovation or reoccupation, judged to be a short-term difference on the basis of associated pottery. Entries were at or near floor level, but Rooms 6 and 9 evidenced no side entrances. In the former the atypical location of the hearth suggests a roof entrance. None of the rooms cleared had doors opening through the compound wall.

Clay-lined hearths, several shallow pits presumed to be for

Fig. 3.10. Ariz. U:13:22, CI-2. (a) Rooms 8 and 9, adobe walls made in segments laterally and courses vertically. Reinforcing posts ring the walls exteriorly. (b) Room 5, with post reinforced adobe wall. (c) Room 7, central platform is part of upper floor with hearths. (d) Salt eroded surface of compound wall. The sloping surface (outside to left) indicates wall had suffered complete attrition.

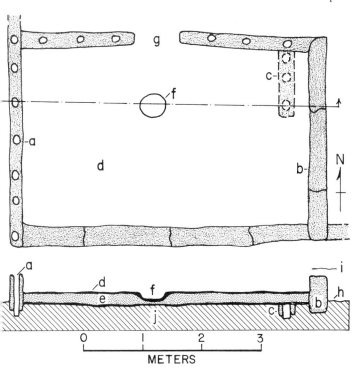

Fig. 3.11. Ariz. U:13:22. Plan and section of Room 2 (Cl-2): (a) post reinforced adobe wall; (b) adobe wall, laid up in blocks and courses; (c) pre-room adobe wall; (d) second floor; (e) first floor with relatively clean fill above; (f) hearth; (g) door; (h) old surface; (i) present surface level; (j) native soil.

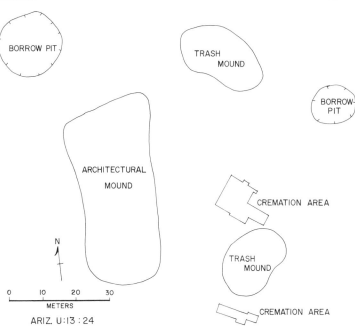

Fig. 3.12. Plan of Ariz. U:13:24, Civano Phase.

storage, a possible jar-rest pit, and a caliche mixing basin were the only floor features noted. Artifactual materials were sparse, and no metates were found in place. The evidence indicates that abandonment was peaceful and all useful goods were removed.

Walls of the kind used in this village were highly susceptible to salt erosion, a good example of which was observed in the older segment of the compound wall at the northeast corner (Fig. 3.10d). Hayden (1957: 105-111) has analyzed this phenomenon in detail. Considering the fact that the normal wall thickness of this style of adobe architecture was only 25 cm, and that basal weakening by salt erosion would not take long, the pole reinforcing of the walls makes good sense. The posts prevented structural collapse when the adobe could no longer effectively support a roof by itself, as long as imbedded post ends did not rot. I am inclined to believe that the internally pole-strengthened adobe wall and salt erosion have a cause and effect relationship, perhaps endemic to the Gila-Salt river region by reason of a long ancestral tradition of pole and mud wall construction. The essential construction differences were vertical walls in contrast to the older slanting ones, and using more adobe than wood instead of vice versa in earlier times.

ARIZONA U:13:24

The third and last Classic Period site tested lies a few hundred meters north of Ariz. U:13:22 (Fig. 1.2). Its plan follows the by-now-familiar pattern of a house unit, adjacent trash mounds, cremation areas and depression, either for water storage or the relic of the source of building materials (Fig. 3.12). The results of random testing and the recovery of 16 cremations clearly establish this site as coeval with the preceding two discussed. The architectural unit, judged to be compact on the basis of surface evidence, undoubtedly resembles Ariz. U:13:22.

* * *

Although Casa Grande National Monument is the type example of architecture for the Civano Phase, we know that there were many other villages in both the Gila and Salt river valleys in the fourteenth century, and that bigness and multi-storied buildings were among their characteristics. The Civano Phase communities, on the other hand, that were a part of greater Snaketown, were small geographically independent settlements. The points to be borne in mind about these houses that contrast so sharply with the earlier ones in Snaketown are: they were clusters of single-story, contiguous structures, within a compound wall, rectangular in form, erected on or near the desert surface, limited by vertical adobe walls which were either internally post-reinforced or of solid adobe laid up in blocks and courses, and side entered without passages. The developmental links were from types S-1 to Cl-1 to Cl-2.

This massive adobe architectural mode represents an intrusion into the Hohokam territory, often attributed to the Salado people. The answer, however, may not be as simple as that. Identifying the origin and tracing the development of Classic Period architecture will be left for others to investigate, since it was terminal in the long Snaketown sequence.

Sedentary Period

About fifty percent of all houses cleared of debris were datable to the Sacaton Phase. Houses of this time establish the maximum geographical limits of Snaketown, and they also exhibit more variability than do the domiciles of any other phase.

HOUSE TYPE S-1 (FIGS. 3.13, 3.14)

A total of 66 houses of this type were uncovered; a number of them were fragmentary.

Floor. Depth below desert surface at time of construction variable, 0.15 to 0.60 m, average 0.25 m; elongate, typically round-ended but always round-cornered, plan sometimes elliptical; material is mixture of clay and caliche, giving floor a light-buff color and distinct, therefore, from the reddish-brown color of Pioneer Period floors and the natural desert matrix; thickness 0.05 to 0.15 m (Fig. 3.15a); refurbishing of floors not uncommon; floor edge may have groove and occasionally a clay lip or rim 0.5 to 0.8 cm high (Fig. 3.14d); area highly variable ranging from 13 to 40 m², average 20 to 25 m². (For typical plans see Gladwin and others 1937: Figs. 21 to 27.)

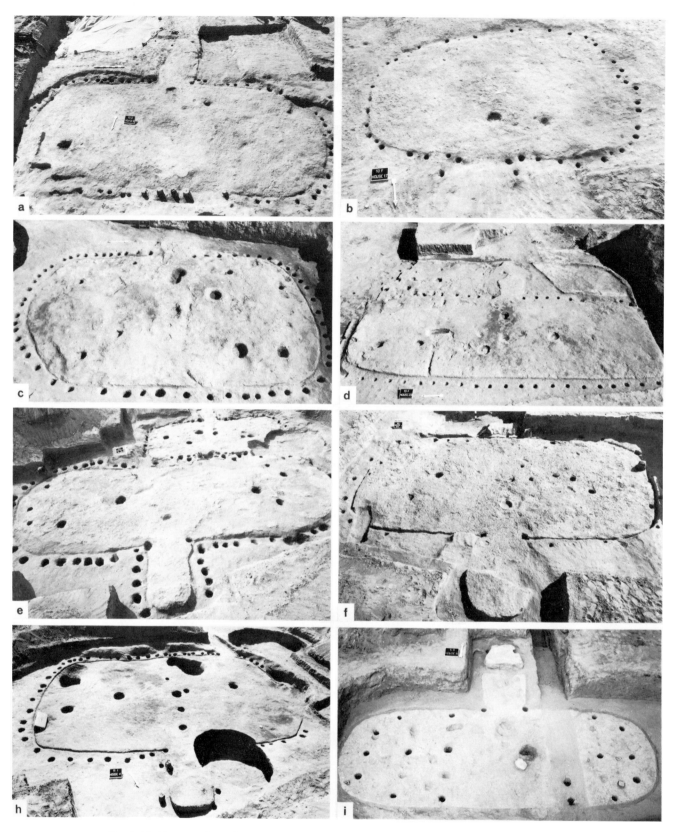

Fig. 3.13. Houses of the Sacaton Phase, S-1 Type. (a) House 6:10G, no evident interior roof supports; charred posts in foreground. (b) House 17:10F, shallow structure without evident interior roof supports; entrance passage not well defined. (c) House 3:11I, good example of outer wall post arrangement with a probable 4 or 5 interior roof supports. (d) House 23:10F, overlaps and mostly destroyed House 26:10F of the S-2 type (upper right). (e) House 5:10I, shows two main inner support posts and position of structure enclosing entry. House 4:10I, distance, is Gila Butte Phase. (f) House 1:10I, has two support post holes in central long axis; entry step partially destroyed. (g) House 4:11I, has center axis post arrangement; pits were later than house, filled with Sacaton Phase refuse; metate, left, had apparently been leaned against house wall. (h) House 6:5G, one of the best examples of roof support post arrangements with secondary posts ringing house's edges; entry stepped with transverse groove; vertical band is trench cut by testing machine.

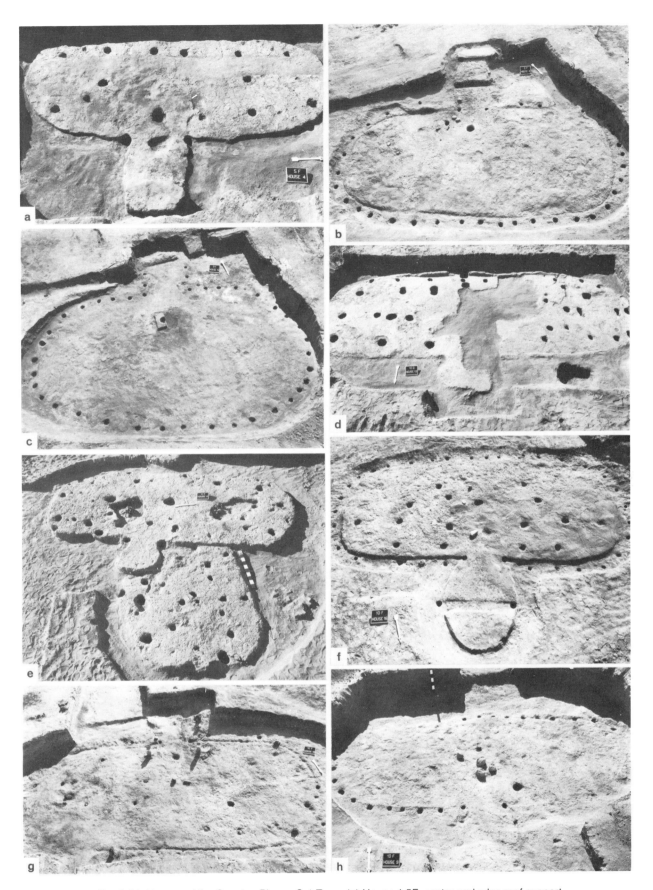

Fig. 3.14. Houses of the Sacaton Phase, S-1 Type. (a) House 4:5F, center and edge roof support posts well delineated; entry passage has possible water catchment pit. (b) House 4:9F, no evident interior roof supports; entry stepped, stone slab riser has been dislodged. (c) House 10:9F, directly below House 4 (b), side wall posts do not match, suggesting a major rebuilding on the old plan; groove lacking. (d) House 13:10G, shows floor edge lipping and extensive disturbance in central area. This house was cleared in 1934-35 and labeled House 5:10G. Its reexcavation in 1964-65 was not discovered until maps of the two seasons were coordinated, thereby unexpectedly validating the accuracy of the 1964-65 grid system. The pit, lower right, contained Cache 1:10G, narrowly missed in 1934-35. (e) House 8:11F, overlapping and partially destroying House 9. (f) House 16:10F, shows transverse groove at base of riser in egg-shaped entry. (g) House 19:10F, note especially the notched stones set up in triangular pattern around hearth. (h) House 9:10F, arrangement of clay trivets next to hearth.

[55]

Fig. 3.15. Architectural and other details related to Sacaton Phase houses. (a) House 9:10F, an example of floor renovation. (b) House 6:10J, entry with prepared caliche-clay riser ending in a sill. (c) House 3:10F, parallel roofing poles about 10 cm in diameter, of Douglas Fir. (d) House 4:10G, charred reeds at base of wall, inner face. (e) House 9:10F, clay trivets in relation to hearth, circled but not excavated. (f) House 4:10G, charred *petate* in floor; width of compound elements, about 3 cm. (g) House 2:10J, twilled mat impression on side wall.

Entrance. Generally in midsection of long side of house; orientation evidently optional; a sample of 33 houses gives following results: 11 north, 10 south, 7 east, 3 west, 1 northwest, 1 southeast; length equivalent to one-third to one-half of house width; shape may be parallel-sided (Fig. 3.13e) but typically slightly bulbous to egg-shaped (Fig. 3.13f,h); the presence of a step was evidently determined by the depth of the house; when present the riser was treated variously: a simple step of caliche-clay flooring without or with a molded sill on upper tread probably to control surface drainage (Fig. 3.15b), rarely faced with a thin slab of mica schist (Fig. 14.1a); risers of small horizontally laid logs were also used (Gladwin and others 1937: Fig. 21). The transverse groove sometimes seen in the entry apparently was designed to accommodate the bottom log when this device was used (Fig. 3.14b,f); a sizable pit in the entry of 5F:House 4 may have served as a water trap (Fig. 3.14a); entrances were covered by extensions of the roof and house side walls.

Roof. The deployment of postholes in the floor is the basis for inferring the nature of the roof. But the picture is confused by the fact that little uniformity is evident. Some floors yielded no evidence of internal supports (Fig. 3.13a,b) while in others the distribution was random. Post alignments parallel to the long axis in three rows, near floor edges and centrally placed, appear to be the mode (Fig. 3.13h). In most houses, the roof probably had a slight gable or central ridge. The lack of formality may indicate that the engineering of the roof was influenced by the nature of the structural elements. Mesquite timbers, the principal wood used, come in twisted and irregular lengths. Secondary timbers, brush and reeds, the latter probably *Phragmites communis,* and a light covering of clay, completed the roof proper.

[56]

Side Walls. Typically, the house floor was ringed with mesquite posts about 10 cm in diameter and spaced an average of 25 cm apart. These rose either vertically or at a slight slant to meet the roof plate. In some instances the side walls appear to have been sturdy enough to support the roof. Horizontal lashings between vertical members would have helped to hold in place the closing materials between them, as for example, reeds and brush. A final covering layer of clay completed the shell. The groove at the floor's edge and inside the ring of posts received the butt ends of reeds which lined the interior of the house at floor level (Fig. 3.15d).

Hearth. The standard location of the hearth in Hohokam houses was about midway between the geographic center of the room and the inner edge of the entry, suggesting that no smokehole was provided in the roof. The native Pima *ki* similarly was not equipped with a vent, although the Maricopa house did have one. Hearth diameters averaged 0.25 m, and they were almost always precisely fashioned of good quality clay by lining a pit excavated into the floor. The hard-baked hearth linings have been singularly useful in archaeomagnetic age determinations. Relining of hearths often accompanied the replastering of floors.

Trivets. Functionally related to the cooking process and thus to hearths are the prepared clay lumps specially made and used in trios to support pots over beds of coals. The objects themselves are discussed elsewhere (Fig. 13.28). While many houses produced no evidence of trivets, they probably were in regular use. In four instances trivets stood near hearths (Figs. 3.14h; 3.15e) but they were also used at some distance from the fireplace, as indicated by the associated ashes. Supplementary cooking areas were apparently dictated by convenience. House 1:10J was equipped with two sets of trivets.

Other. Built-in features, such as notched stones, have been discussed elsewhere. In the floors of a few houses were caliche mixing basins. There is no evidence that they were contemporaneous with the houses in which they were found; most likely they post-dated the collapse of the structure. This kind of disturbance also applied to a number of pits in the floors, which may or may not have been house connected. Some of these, particularly when near hearths, probably were jar rests. Still another factor that may confuse one's ideas of the arrangement of roof support posts are holes in the floor in which posts were imbedded to support platforms or even a log with triple forking to hold a water jar, a feature I have seen in Papago homes. It is clear that internal fixtures of this kind cannot be reconstructed except through the greatest accident of preservation.

Unfortunately, Sacaton Phase houses were generally barren of artifacts, even when the house was overtaken by fire. Identification of specific work-areas in houses has therefore not been possible, except the obvious activity that centered about the hearth.

Overbuilding of S-1 type houses was not uncommon, either by closely following the outlines of the older house (Fig. 3.14b,c) or without regard to the configuration of the previous house (Fig. 3.14e).

HOUSE TYPE   S-2 (FIGS. 3.16, 3.17, 3.19)

Eight houses of this type were uncovered. In spite of the relatively extensive excavations in 1934–35, houses of the type about to be described were not found, and have not been reported from other investigations in Hohokam sites. This should serve as a warning that data recovered in archaeological ventures are never finite, that new twists in the record may emerge with the next thrust of the shovel.

Floor. Distinct features are form and size: squarish with rounded corners and slightly convex sides; for eight complete houses, floor area ranges from 30 to 55 m², average 42m², or almost twice the area of house type S-1. Other floor details much as in S-1. Floor depths from 0.5 to 0.75 m except House 3:10F which was literally on the surface, needing excavation with no more than trowel and broom.

Entrance. Short and stubby in relation to size of house and dominantly parallel-sided; entry to House 1:6G was evidently originally directed north, subsequently changed to west (Fig. 3.17); no standard orientation is evident, but south openings are most numerous; steps present if floor depth required same for easy exit.

Roof. The norm appears to be a four-post plan, establishing a flat roof over the central area; secondary posts imbedded near floor edge supported horizontal beams against which side-wall poles were leaned. House 3:10F, destroyed by fire, provided an interesting roof detail: closely laid parallel logs about 10 cm in diameter bridged the space between primary horizontal roof members (Figs. 3.15c, 3.16b). These proved to be Douglas Fir, *Pseudotsuga menziesii* (*P. taxifolia*), identified by Robert C. Koeppen of the Forest Products Laboratory, Madison, Wisconsin (through the University of Arizona Laboratory of Tree-Ring Research and also by Bohrer 1970: 426). Diameter uniformity of five adjacent logs suggests careful selection of the building units. The nearest source at the present time for this species is in the Pinal Mountains south of Globe, about 120 km (75 mi) east of Snaketown.

Side Walls. As in S-1, although post molds were generally not found where floors were built on trash. House 4:10G gave abundant evidence of the inner reed lining (Fig. 3.16e), but whether the present horizontal position with respect to the floor edge was the original one could not be verified.

Hearth. Always near entry, otherwise no different than S-1 hearths.

Discussion. The north-south arrangement of S-2 houses, evident in Figure 1.6, I do not believe to have much meaning. Several structures are far enough off to the sides to suggest that the apparent axial alignment was the product of where we excavated. Even given this condition and the fact that the largest of the S-1 houses match the floor area of the smallest S-2 houses, the shape nevertheless remains as the distinctive feature. Whether S-2 houses served a different function than the others cannot now be determined. Goods on the floor appear to be strictly of a domestic nature, even to the presence of matting (*petate*) in the southwest quadrant of House 4:10G, a likely sleeping area (Figs. 3.15f, 3.16e).

It is plausible to believe that the ancestry of S-2 houses of the Sacaton Phase is traceable backward in time to the P-4 type of the Vahki Phase, with a link through P-3 (Fig. 3.28). The supposition that the architectural form had limited or a special use and remained essentially unchanged because of a stable social system cannot be discounted.

The stratigraphic record sheds no light on the earliness or latenesss of S-2 houses within the phase. Houses 1:6G and 26:10F were abandoned before Snaketown was; but the others may have survived until the village's end. Analogous structures in the Classic Period have not been reported.

HOUSE TYPE S-3 (FIGS. 3.18, 3.19)

Three houses of this type, House 3:9G and Houses 9 and 18:10G, were uncovered. They are like S-1 type structures except for one important character: size. Respectively, the floor areas were about 56, 58, and 52 m² as compared with the average of 20 to 25 m² for S-1 houses. This doubling of floor area, one might think, should have some meaning beyond the mere desire of the owner to have a large house. But the clues of use that remain are not particularly helpful.

With respect to architectural details, notable points are: House 3:9G shows three rows of roof supports, one along a central axis and two parallel rows between centerline and house edge; paired posts were used in a number of cases, not surprising in view of the size of the span. The roof of House 9:10G appears to have been of the same form, although the centerline posts were not detected (Fig. 3.19). Entrance orientations were north, east, and south; all

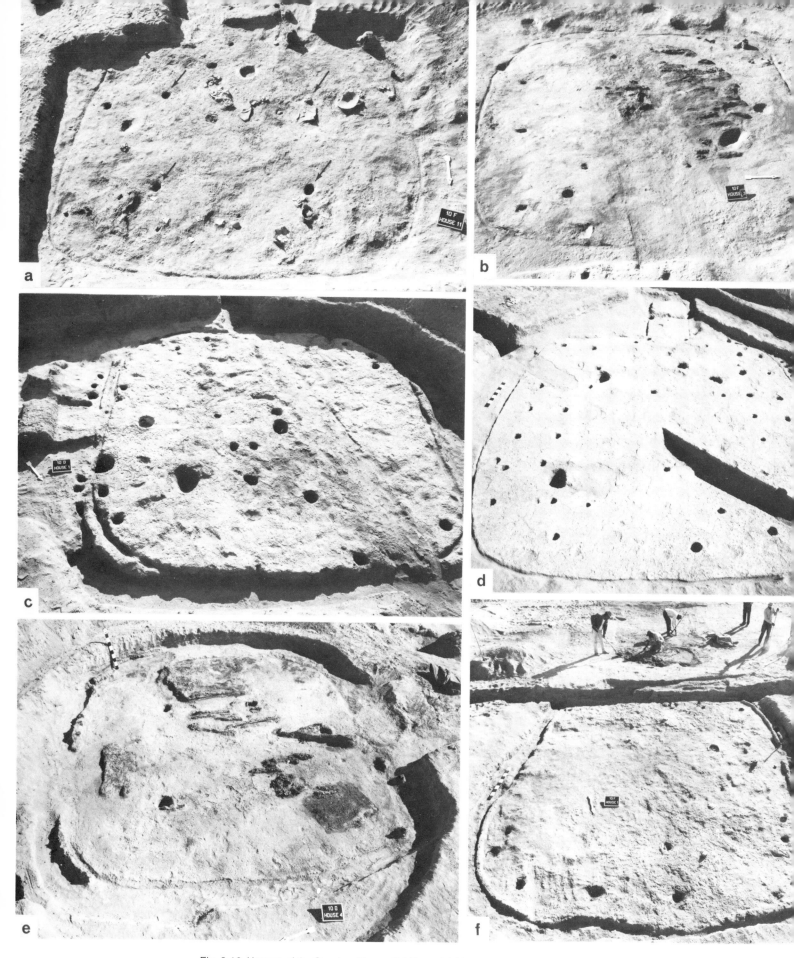

Fig. 3.16. Houses of the Sacaton Phase, S-2 Type. (a) House 11:10F, one of the smaller houses of the type; burned, with some artifacts in floor; arrows indicate 4 main roof supports. (b) House 3:10F; burned, Douglas Fir roof beams on floor. (c) House 1:10D, illustrates floor lip and groove inside outer wall posts. (d) House 1:5G, note double rows of auxiliary roof support postholes outside the 4 main supports, the 4th of the set was apparently removed by the trenching machine. (e) House 4:10G, burned, roof timbers and supports were mesquite; dark square area, lower right is charred remnant of floor mat. (f) House 1:10F, pronounced floor lip with groove outside of it.

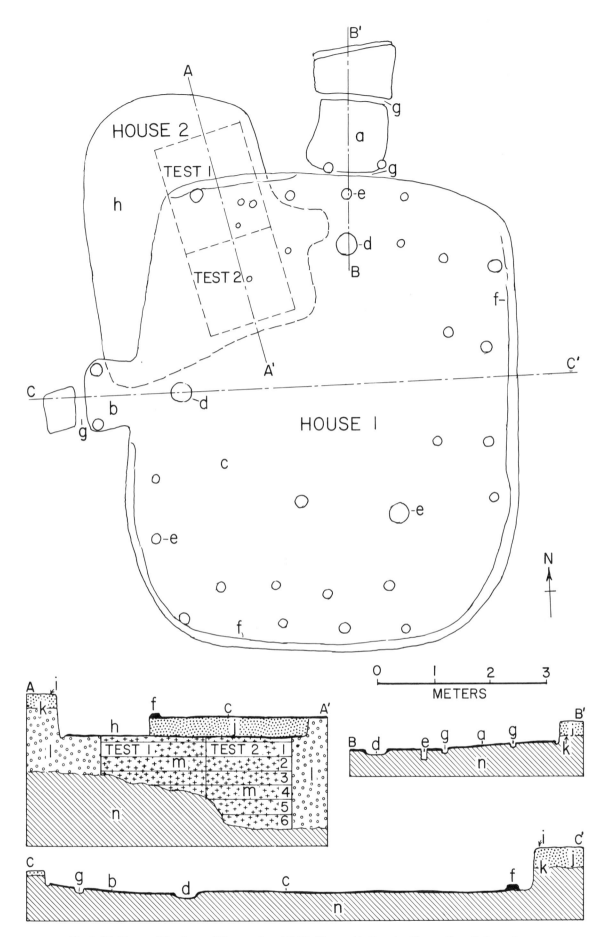

Fig. 3.17. Plan and Sections of Houses 1 and 2:6G. House 1 is Sacaton Phase. Type S-2 overlaps House 2, Santa Cruz Phase, Type C-1, which in turn was built over a Vahki Phase trash deposit. (a) original entrance, groove (g) suggests entry was closed when (b) west entry, was made; (c) floor of House 1; (d) hearths, no evidence that north hearth was abandoned when entryways were changed; (e) roof support holes; (f) adobe rim of floor; (g) grooves; (h) floor of House 2; (i) present surface; (j) cultural debris; (k) old surface; (l) untested refuse; (m) Vahki Phase trash as revealed in Tests 1 and 2, excavation levels are indicated; (n) native soil.

Fig. 3.18. Houses of the Sacaton Phase, S-3 Type: (a) House 3:9G; (b) House 9:10G.

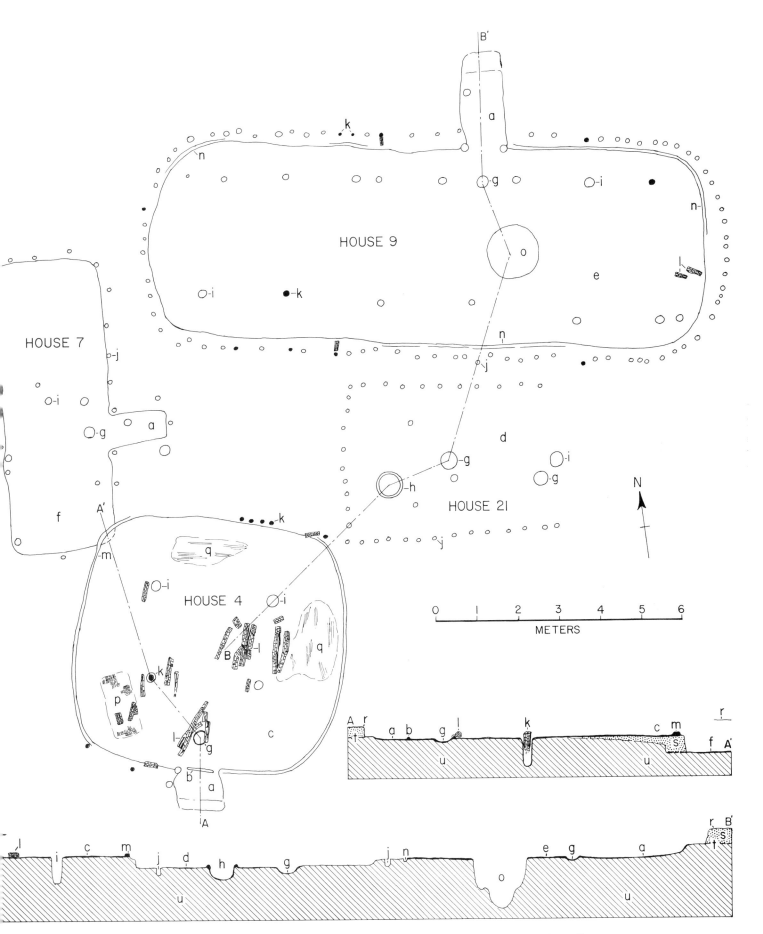

Fig. 3.19. Plan and sections of a group of houses in 10G: (a) entrance passages; (b) adobe sills;
(c) floor of House 4 (Type S-2, Sacaton Phase); (d) floor of House 21 (Type P-2, Pioneer Period);
(e) floor of House 9 (Type S-3, Sacaton Phase); (f) floor of House 7 (Type C-2, Santa Cruz Phase);
(g) hearth; (h) large clay-lined pit with rim, burned; (i) interior roof supports; (j) exterior side wall
pole holes; (k) charred timbers, *in situ*; (l) charred roof beams on floor; (m) adobe floor rim; (n)
groove; (o) pit, probably younger than house; (p) area covered by *petate* (?) sleeping mat; (q)
carbonized reeds; (r) present surface; (s) cultural deposit; (t) old surface; (u) native soil.

were parallel-sided, and House 3:9G had a stone riser effectively pinned into place by vertical tabular stones imbedded in the ground (Fig. 14.1a). House 18:10G had two hearths near each other, apparently both in use at the same time.

The three houses were destroyed by fire, but there was a notable lack of cultural material of a resistant nature in all of them when the conflagrations took place. A few items on the floor of House 9:10G warrant special mention. Mountain Sheep horns, all charred, were found along the south wall near the west end, in the center of the floor, and a third set was found in the east end of the house. Special significance was attached to the horns of Mountain Sheep by the Pima (Russell 1908: 82), a concept that may be an ancient one. Their presence in this instance lends some credence to the idea that the structure fulfilled a special need in Hohokam society, perhaps that of a council house, as was once used by the Pima (Russell 1908: 155), with a capacity up to 80 people. The house under discussion could easily have accommodated that many persons and more. The question arises, if this interpretation has merit, why there should be three such structures in close proximity. If the S-3 structures were functionally similar, it may be that they were built sequently, after the loss of one by fire in turn, but all within the time of the Sacaton Phase. Another possibility is that they were linked with tribal cults or associations, but the existence of these is purely conjectural.

One further and most curious aspect of House 9:10G needs mention. On the floor, in the eastern half, were found three fragmentary, though restorable, Snaketown Red-on-buff plates. Under normal circumstances these would be used as indicators of the age of the house; but in this case other lines of evidence show the improbability of the association.

In the first place, the house form is typically of the Sacaton Phase and has no counterparts among the limited number of Snaketown Phase houses cleared. Second, although not directly superimposed on Houses 7 and 21:10G (Fig. 3.19), the differences in floor levels and the nature of the related filling materials established House 9 as postdating the other two. One may only guess how it came about that pottery no younger than A.D. 500 should have found its way into a house 500 years later. In the construction of House 9, Pioneer Period refuse was disturbed (witness the pit below floor line and near the center of the structure, and House 21). The Snaketown vessels in question might have been encountered at this time and retained as omens of good luck. The mystical potency of ancient artifacts is not a strange idea among primitive people generally, and the case of a Pima medicine man having a Hohokam slate palette in his kit is relevant (Russell 1908: 112). In sum, this phenomenon and the presence of the Mountain Sheep horns suggest, but do not prove, that the super-houses of the Sacaton Phase served special purposes.

HOUSE TYPE S-4 (FIGS. 3.20 a, b; 3.21)

Two houses of this type were uncovered. The small curious structures of a kind heretofore unreported in Hohokam sites were jocularly labeled "bathtubs" in the field. The better preserved of the two, House 2:10J, is the basis for the description.

Floor. Elliptical, depressed at least 0.6 m below surface; of mixed caliche-clay, continuing without seam into side wall; area about 9 m² and somewhat less for House 9:5G. The latter was refloored.

Entrance. Lipping of wall in House 2:10J, evidently worn by feet, is present close to hearth, oriented to the southeast, 0.6 m above floor. This represents a high step, unmatched in any other structures. The entry of House 9:5G was oriented to the west-southwest, marked by a low step.

Roof. Three postholes in rough alignment, one near center of floor, and one at each end outside of wall, were the only hints of

roof type, probably a horizontal gable supporting slanting poles down to side wall.

Side Walls. Clay-caliche mixture, puddled, cast continuously from floor, 0.15 m thick, laid against excavated surface; sloping outwardly about 10° from the vertical, maximum height preserved 0.65 m. Patches of a thin coat of plaster remain.

Hearth. Precisely circular, clay lined, undercut. Location close to entrance but original hearth in House 9:5G was near center; when latter structure was refloored, hearth was moved to west end near entrance.

Other. The impression of a twilled mat was observed along the north margin of House 2:10J extending from the floor upwards on the wall face for about 0.2 m (Fig. 3.15g).

Both houses were barren of artifacts except for the ever-present broken pottery, among which were a few worked pieces and intrusive types, expectable accompaniments in trash.

The absence of any clues as to the purposes served by these two houses leaves only speculation in the search for an explanation. The presence of hearths indicates use over extended periods of time; smallness of floor limited the number of persons that could be accommodated, and no traces remain of associated domestic activities. The silhouettes of the structures must have been low and unobtrusive in the village, almost as though they were hideaways. As a guess, they may have been menstrual huts. If so, neither of them was far removed from domiciles, and they were far more formal than the temporary brush shades employed by the Pimas (Russell 1908: 155). Another possibility is the use of such a structure by the aged. Russell vividly describes the unhappy lot of an old Pima at Sacaton, living in a hut "8 feet square that contained a little straw and the single blanket that served to cover him" (1908: 192).

HOUSE TYPE S-5 (Fig. 3.20b,c)

Two houses of this type were uncovered. Although few in number, S-5 houses assume an important place in the architectural styling because they forecast the form and construction methods of some of the Classic Period houses. I will return to this thought again.

Floor. Rectangular with square corners or with rounded corners and slightly convex sides; depths not certainly ascertainable; material as in S-1 structures; area about 7 m².

Entrance. Not definable.

Roof. Internally supported as best recorded by House 8:5G (Fig. 3.20c).

Side Walls. Adobe walls 10 cm thick and preserved only to a height of 15 cm. They are not thick enough to have supported much weight, hence presumption is that they sloped up to meet horizontal stringers as in S-1 houses.

Hearth. Burned area only on floor in House 12:8E, southeast corner; formal hearth in House 8:5G, east half, was intentionally plugged (Fig. 3.20b).

Other. Stratigraphically both of these structures overlapped Colonial Period houses; in the case of House 8:5G, it post-dated the adjacent S-4 type structure.

The floor area of both of these units is small, within the range of S-4 structures and well below what appears to have been the minimum requirement for a residence. For this reason S-5 houses are believed to have been built to meet a specific need, perhaps no different than S-4 type buildings. But more than any other structures, they begin to reflect the architectural form that was to become an important theme in the Soho and Civano phases (Johnson 1964: 149-150; p. 50, U:13:21 herein). Evidently experimenting with a different architectural style began late in the Sedentary Period, presumably inspired from without because the models existed easterly.

Discussion. Seen broadly, the architecture of the Sedentary

Fig. 3.20. Houses of the Sacaton Phase, Type S-4 (a, b); Type S-5 (b, c). (a) House 2:10J, elliptical, partially destroying the stratigraphically older House 1 (Type S-1). (b) House 9:5G (S-4, foreground) east border destroyed by House 8 (S-5) which also overlaps House 7, Santa Cruz Phase (C-1). Mound 16 on the left. Plug in House 8 hearth has been removed. (c) House 12:8F (Type S-5) overlapping House 7, Colonial Period structure. Age of floor fragment at left not determined. (d) House 1:11J. A one-of-a-kind structure, with offset entry and long axis at right angles to normal pattern. Not typed.

Period exhibited a variability that has not been recognized before, brought out by the relatively greater number of units studied. It may be that structural diversity existed in earlier phases, but proof of this must await further excavations because the resources are few in number. A sequence in the building forms within the Sacaton Phase is not discernible except for the probability that the S-5 type houses are late and the stepping stone to new kinds of houses to come in the Classic Period. One senses that, although building standards did exist, there were departures from the norm, probably no more than a response to the owner's choice. Figure 3.20d is one of these variants, the only one of its kind.

Architecture specifically motivated by religious forces, except platform mounds, has not been identified. Nothing comparable to the kiva is known. But the giant-size S-3 type units, probably council houses, are logical additions to the building inventory. The differences between S-1 houses, the mode and in the main

line of Hohokam architectural development, and S-2 units are not readily explained, unless the latter are holdovers from what appears to have been the dominant early Pioneer Period form.

The frequent overlapping of Sacaton Phase houses over others of the same general age is reviewed elsewhere as one of several indications of a long duration of the phase. Only a small percentage of the S-1 type houses were destroyed by fire, and few had artifacts on the floors in numbers and kinds that might have suggested any cataclysmic withdrawal from the village. On the contrary, orderly abandonment appears to have been the case. Consistent burning, however, was noted for the three S-3 structures; but whether willfully set or not is not ascertainable.

Arbors, shades, and windbreak walls were probably known to the Hohokam as they were to the early Pimas; but the identification of informal constructions of this kind is not always simple or sure.

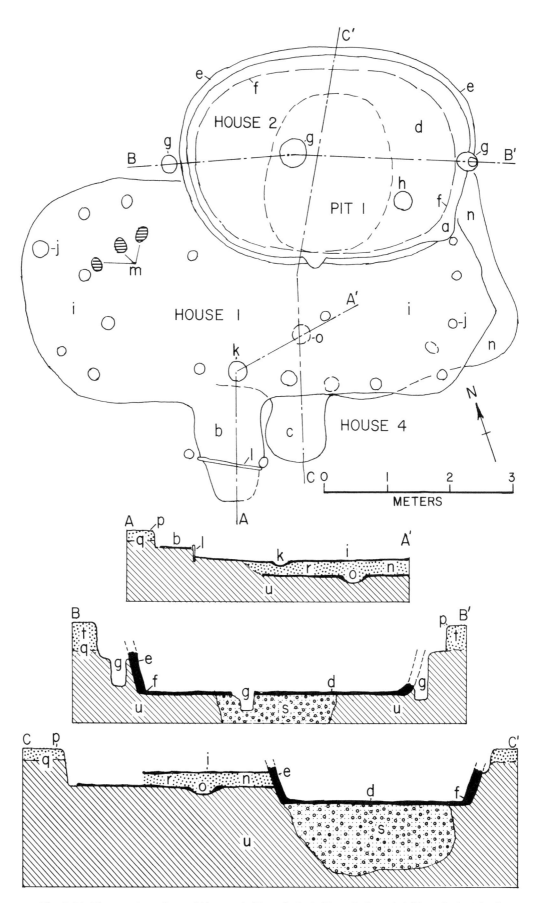

Fig. 3.21. Plans and sections of Houses 1 (Type S-1), 2 (Type S-4), and 4 (Type S-1) 10J; all Sacaton Phase: (a) entrance to House 2; (b) entrance to House 1; (c) entrance to House 4, (d) floor, House 2; (e) sloping adobe wall; (f)e at floor line; (g) roof support posts; (h) hearth; (i) floor, House 1; (j) roof support posts; (k) hearth; (l) stone slab riser; (m) clay trivets; (n) floor, House 4; (o) hearth; (p) present surface; (q) old surface; (r) cultural debris; (s) Sacaton Phase trash in Pit 1; (t) sheet debris on old surface; (u) native soil. The succession of events was as follows: (1) excavation of Pit 1 and filling with trash, (2) construction, use and abandonment of House 4, (3) construction, use and abandonment of House 1, (4) construction of House 2.

Colonial Period

Of the 43 Colonial Period structures, 11 were too fragmentary to use in establishing a typology. The remaining 32 were classified as follows:

HOUSE TYPE C-1 (Fig. 3.22a)

Santa Cruz Phase, 4 examples; Gila Butte Phase, 1; not assignable to phase, 1. (See also Gladwin and others 1937: Fig. 28 for another example.)

Essentially the same as S-1 houses in all details, although the entry is never elliptical. Due to smallness of sample, all the details of S-1 houses cannot be duplicated.

C-1 houses were about in the midpoint of a long tradition of a type used by the Hohokam, a tradition that started in the Pioneer Period with the P-1 structures (Fig. 3.23b,c), passing successively into C-1, S-1, and finally finding expression in a somewhat modified form of Cl-1 (Fig. 3.28).

HOUSE TYPE C-2 (Fig. 3.22b-e)

Santa Cruz Phase, 11 examples; Gila Butte Phase, 7; not assignable to phase, 2 (Gladwin and others 1937: Figs. 29, 30; Haury 1932: 8-47).

Floor. Plan rectangular, clay-caliche mixture having light buff color; edge may have groove but lip not observed. Floor area average is about 20 m² but House 3:9E is exceptionally small with a floor area of about 7 m² (Fig. 3.22e).

Entrance. Parallel-sided, usually placed near midpoint of long side; one instance of expanding entry noted (Fig. 3.22d); no consistency in orientation; may be stepped, depending on depth of floor below surface level; no examples of stone risers observed, but this practice is known elsewhere for the period (Haury 1932: Fig. 12).

Roof. Evidence for interior post arrangement not satisfactory to reveal if there was a consistent pattern; probability is that auxiliary lines of supports near and parallel to edges were the norm (Fig. 3.22c).

Side Walls. Basically as in S-1 structures.

Hearth. Usually well-made, in standard location near entry; but sometimes no more than an informal burned area on the floor in the usual hearth position.

Type C-2 houses were the mode for the Colonial Period.

HOUSE TYPE C-3 (Fig. 3.22f-h)

Santa Cruz Phase, 3 examples; Gila Butte Phase, 2; not assignable to phase, 1.

Floor. Rectangular, but less elongated than C-2; corners usually square; floor material prepared as in C-2 but may also be on native soil and therefore of reddish-brown color; edge groove observed in one instance, and there are two cases where circumambient posts are set in a wide shallow groove (Fig. 3.22g,h). Floor area ranges from 25 to 48 m², average 33 m².

Entrance. Parallel-sided, oriented either east or south, may be stepped.

Hearth. Usual position near entry; clay lined basins.

Roof. Information lacking.

In terms of shape and relatively greater size, C-3 houses represent a Colonial Period survival of the large Pioneer Period rectangular houses (Type P-2). Nothing about C-3 structures hints at any use other than domestic.

Seen broadly, Colonial Period houses are in the mainstream of Hohokam residential architecture. All types had antecedents in the Pioneer Period.

Pioneer Period

Only 17 of the 31 houses dated to the Pioneer Period could be assigned to phases with reasonable certainty, and only 18 could be used in the typological analysis because so many of the floors were too fragmentary to reveal the original form. An example is seen in Figure 3.23a, House 12:11F, under Mound 40. The stratigraphic relationships were often good, as in this case, but past human activity did much to destroy the integrity of the structure. Although small, the sample does give us an insight into the nature of the oldest houses in Snaketown which introduce interesting questions about their origins. Far from being simple, small, or primitive, some of the first buildings were as far along the developmental line as were the later ones, and they required as much or more engineering skill to erect as did any structures in the Gila-Salt river valleys except the multistoried houses of the Classic Period, like the famous Casa Grande. Furthermore, the typological range was large, as the following inventory brings out.

HOUSE TYPE P-1 (Fig. 3.23b,c)

Snaketown Phase, 4 examples; Sweetwater Phase, 1 example.

Stylistically House 2:9E is similar to the smaller S-1 type buildings except that the ends are somewhat less rounded and the entry is not bulbous. The pattern of internal roof supports and hearth position are not dissimilar. The floor area was about 11 m² and remodeling of the hearth was evident.

The structure under consideration was destroyed by fire during its occupancy, resulting in the recovery of 27 catalogued artifacts on floor contact, providing an uncommonly broad range, for Snaketown, of associated items. These included various utilized stones, choppers, axes, a proto-palette, mano, red ochre, charred corn and 10 pottery vessels, 8 of which were Sweetwater Red-on-gray (Figs. 12.50, 12.51). The cluster of artifacts clearly establishes the age of the house as Sweetwater Phase, and the proto-palette and the ridged axes are consistent with this assignment, as indicated by other data.

Long after the destruction of this house, a pit (Pit 6:9E) 1.30 m in least diameter was intruded through the floor in the midsection of the north edge. It was filled with refuse dominantly of the Gila Butte Phase as inferred from about 2,000 potsherds. While the stratigraphic sequence is consistent with other chronological evidence from Snaketown, radiocarbon samples collected in the pit and the dated corn from the floor of the house have given confused and contradictory results. In this case, as is explained elsewhere, priority in dating value is given to the physical evidence of associated cultural material and to stratigraphy. A probable age between A.D. 100 and 300 is put upon this house. From the architectural point of view, this means that the S-1 houses, the norm for the Sedentary Period, had antecedent forms that dipped well back into the Pioneer Period.

HOUSE TYPE P-2 (Fig. 3.23d-g)

Snaketown Phase, 1 example; Sweetwater Phase, 1; Estrella Phase, 1; not assignable to phase, 4.

Floor. Rectangular, corners square, on native soil, reddish-brown in color; floor edge groove not well developed, posts in groove when present. Floor area ranges from 15 to 35 m², average 28 m².

Entrance. Parallel-sided, short in relation to size of floor, no evident step in entry; orientation inconsistent.

Roof. Preferred distribution of roof supports appears to have been in rows set in about one meter from house edges, suggesting a flat central roof area; other posts positioned as needed.

Side Walls. Closely spaced poles, about 0.25 m apart in reasonably precise alignments, presumably leaning in to rest on horizontal stringers. No evidence of side wall construction details has survived. Groove to engage reed ends used as lining layers of side wall generally not present.

Hearth. In normal position, clay lined.

P-2 houses appear to have been well established in the Pioneer Period and were perhaps most commonly in use toward the end of the period. Persistence into later times is evidenced by the almost identical C-3 houses of the Colonial Period.

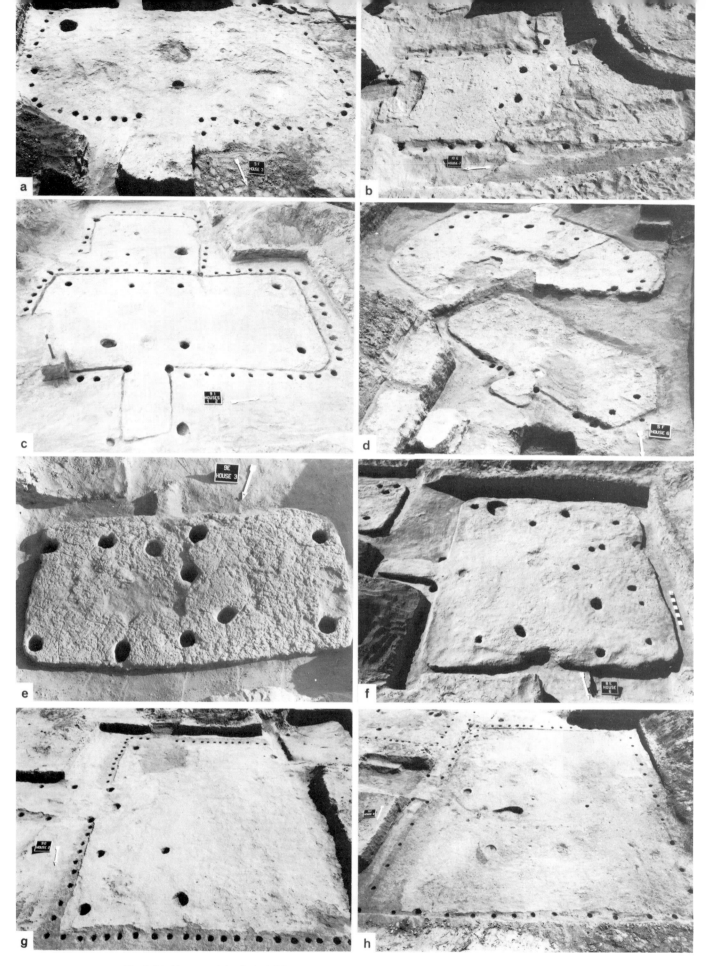

Fig. 3.22. Houses of the Colonial Period. (a) House 3:9F; no evident internal supports, closely set sidewall posts, no groove detected; Type C-1. (b) House 7:10G; Santa Cruz Phase; side posts in groove; corner of House 4:10G (Type S-2) overlaps corner (upper right). (c) Houses 1 (foreground) and 2:9I; both Gila Butte Phase, excellent example of inner and outer supports in relation to groove; Type C-2. (d) House 6:5F; Gila Butte Phase; flared entry; House 4, Sacaton Phase (above) partially destroyed in exposing House 6; Type C-2. (e) House 3:9E; Gila Butte Phase; an exceptionally small structure with inner supports; Type C-2. (f) House 6:8E; Santa Cruz Phase; Type C-3. (g) House 2:9G; Santa Cruz Phase; east outer wall post alignment destroyed by test trench; Type C-3. (h) House 8:9F; Gila Butte Phase; Type C-3.

[66]

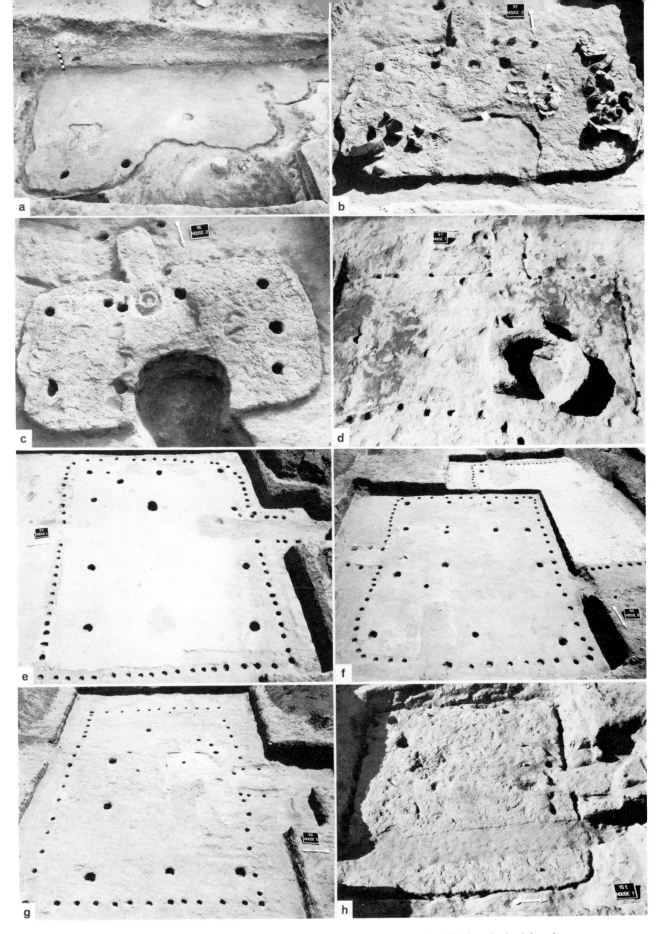

Fig. 3.23. Houses of the Pioneer Period. (a) House 12:11F, mutilated before its burial under Mound 40; white-topped pillar is cremation 5:11F; not typed. (b) House 2:9E (Type P-1) with many floor contact artifacts; Sweetwater Phase. (c) House 2:9E with artifacts removed and intrusive pit cleared of trash (Gila Butte Phase). (d) House 7:9F (Type P-2), phase undetermined; residual block with circular pit is locus of Cache 2:9F, Sacaton Phase; semicircle of postholes belong to House 3:9F, Colonial Period. (e-f) Houses 1 and 6:9G (Type P-2) classic examples of the type, Snaketown Phase. (g) House 5:9G; (Type P-2) Estrella Phase. (h) House 1:15E (Type P-3) side wall posts were set in pronounced groove; pit in extreme upper left corner was for mixing caliche-plaster; Snaketown Phase (see. Fig. 8.19 for plan).

[67]

HOUSE TYPE P-3 (Figs. 3.23h; 3.24a)

Snaketown Phase, 7 examples; Sweetwater Phase, 2. (See also Gladwin and others 1937: Figs. 32, 33, 34, 35.)

Type P-3 houses are separately listed because of their squarish shape in contrast with the previous ones which are dominantly rectangular. Construction particulars follow the pattern already established for P-2 buildings, with the notable exception that the roof was usually supported by four main posts set a short distance in from the corners. This roofing system was almost certainly a response to the geometry of the house, being the most efficient method of developing the superstructure. The floor areas range widely, from 15 to 35 m^2, though the average is about 22 m^2.

HOUSE TYPE P-4 (Figs. 3.24e; 3.25)

Estrella Phase, 2 examples; Vahki Phase, 4 examples.

Two exceptionally large structures uncovered in 1934-35, House 1:7H and House 8:7F (Gladwin and others 1937: Figs. 34, 35), both assigned to the Vahki Phase, were believed at the time to be domestic units. Gladwin (1948: 118), in reassessing the Snaketown data, preferred to look upon them as of likely ceremonial use. The addition of three more large houses of early Pioneer Period vintage to the inventory once again reintroduces the probability that the majority of the Vahki Phase structures were large and that they were in fact domestically used. It does not seem likely that our excavations in both major efforts should have been so selective as to uncover only ceremonial houses, four out of four houses, or four out of five houses, if Gladwin's addition of House 8:8F (1948: 118-119) as a Vahki Phase House, is accepted. More will be said about these later.

Since House 5:9E (Estrella Phase) and House 1:7H (Vahki Phase) were either highly fragmentary or not well preserved, the following description is based on House 1:9F, a well-preserved floor (Fig. 3.24e).

Floor. Depth below extant surface 0.5 m, roughly square with rounded corners; floor material mixed caliche and red clay about 3 cm thick; a narrow groove outlines the floor edge and extends along sides of entry passages; rim or lip not present in this house, but in House 1:7H clay applied to excavated face of pit rose 10 cm above floor level and outside the floor groove; floor area, not counting entryways, 52 m^2, average for the three houses, 51m^2.

Entry. Two, in the midsections of the south and north walls, slightly less than 1 m wide and nearly 2 m long; floors gently sloped and probably terminated in steps.

Roof. Four large main support posts with auxiliary interior posts as needed; smoke holes not likely, considering position of hearths in relation to house's entrances; main posts were probably mesquite but no evidence remains. The holes receiving them were exceptionally large and elongated at floor level, either to ease the task of bringing large timbers into vertical position or to simplify the task of clearing out the meter-deep pits. An offset in the bottom of each hole suggests the excavator worked in it rather than from floor level (Fig. 3.25d,e).

Side Walls. Formed by posts, probably leaning inwardly to meet horizontal stringers supported by four main vertical timbers; 10 to 15 cm in diameter, spaced from 20 to 50 cm apart; charred remnants of a few elements indicate that mesquite wood was used; inner reed lining of wall at floor level is inferred from presence of trough.

Hearth. Two, positioned near beginning of entry, circular, carefully clay-lined, the north hearth having a raised rim; south hearth was damaged in original testing.

Other Noteworthy Features. The impression of a twilled mat was discovered in the floor between the north hearth and the center of the dwelling. Under the mat, pressed into the clay floor, a number of shell beads and a fragment of abalone shell were recovered, hinting that the mat may have been a sleeping pad and that the inhabitants slept in a bejeweled state. Otherwise the floor was barren of artifacts excepting a cache of historic materials over the southwest major posthole (Fig. 3.25). This consisted of nine badly corroded tin cans, an enamelware coffee pot, two buckets, an iron three-legged cooking stand, a sawed beef bone, three plainware clay jars, and three red-decorated jars of historic Pima manufacture. A turquoise pendant, probably archaeological in origin but found by the Pimas, was also included in the cache.

Reconstructing the events that led to the bizarre placement of contemporary materials on a house floor with a probable age of more than 2,000 years, one begins with the fact that the Pima Indians reinhabited Snaketown near the end of the nineteenth century and that one of their customs was burying the possessions of a deceased person separately from the corpse. In this case, the excavator, striking the hard floor of the house, may have become discouraged and deposited the goods partly on the floor and partly over the fill of a posthole.

That the association is coincidental and the occupation of the house and the deposition of the goods were widely separated in time is verified by the historic nature of the material, by the fact that we have no knowledge the Pimas ever built houses of the kind involved, by the physical impossibility of simultaneous occupancy of the same space by the house post and the cultural items, and by the ceramic contents of the house pit and the postholes. The approximately 7 kg of potsherds, about 1,500 units, were 99.99% Vahki Plain and Vahki Red, the fortunate accident of almost no human activity involving building or ground moving in the area occupied by the house after its abandonment. Finally, the archaeomagnetic assay of the north hearth indicates the age to be about 300 B.C. The generally accepted tenet that floor artifacts date the room can be shown to have exceptions and this is a prime example.

The dual entry system of House 1:9F was not duplicated by any other large structures of the Vahki Phase, but it must be pointed out that two of the four houses studied were too fragmentary to ascertain whether or not they were endowed with these features. House 8:7F definitely did not have two entrances (Gladwin and others 1937: Fig. 35), and the fourth unit, House 1:7H, was not explored in the critical area because of a complex of superimposed floors of later houses (Gladwin and others 1937: Fig. 34). Nevertheless, this departure from the normal single entry in Hohokam houses of later times, along with the great size of the early houses, does raise the question of the relationship of social customs and architectural forms. Sayles speculated that the large Vahki Phase houses may have been community structures (Gladwin and others 1937: 82), and Gladwin saw them as fulfilling ceremonial functions (1948: 118).

It is pointless to argue vehemently for a position that differs from either of these on the basis of the scant evidence we have, but a guess in another direction can be made. I doubt that the large Vahki structures were ceremonial and the concept of community use I would replace by the idea that extended family residence under a single roof may be nearer the truth. Under this system multiple hearths and double entrances or single hearths and entrances might be options that the residents exercised.

HOUSE TYPE P-5 (Fig. 3.24b)

This single example is not assignable to a specific phase. The small, rectangular, well-floored structure with a hearth appears to have been end-entered but without a passageway. The floor area is only 8 m^2, which would appear to remove it from the usual family-house category. The presence of a hearth suggests occupancy, rather than storage, perhaps as a menstrual retreat.

HOUSE TYPE P-6 (Fig. 3.24c)

Sweetwater Phase, 1 example. Distinguished from Type P-5 by its side entrance and absence of hearth. Structure had pronounced floor groove to engage butt ends of inner reed lining and some traces of outside posts, indicating a sturdy construction; floor area 6.5 m^2, the smallest building recorded in the entire site. Probably a storehouse.

Fig. 3.24. Houses of the Pioneer Period. (a) House 4:9E (Type P-3) larger floor holes were apparently storage pits; Sweetwater Phase. (b) House 5:8E (Type P-5), probably entered through west end as determined by hearth position, not assigned to phase. (c) House 1:11I (Type P-6) Sweetwater Phase. Floor delineated by pronounced groove, side entrance. (d) House 13:8E (Type P-7) a true pit house, late Pioneer Period. (e) House 1:9F (Type P-4), Vahki Phase. Note especially double entry and hearth plan.

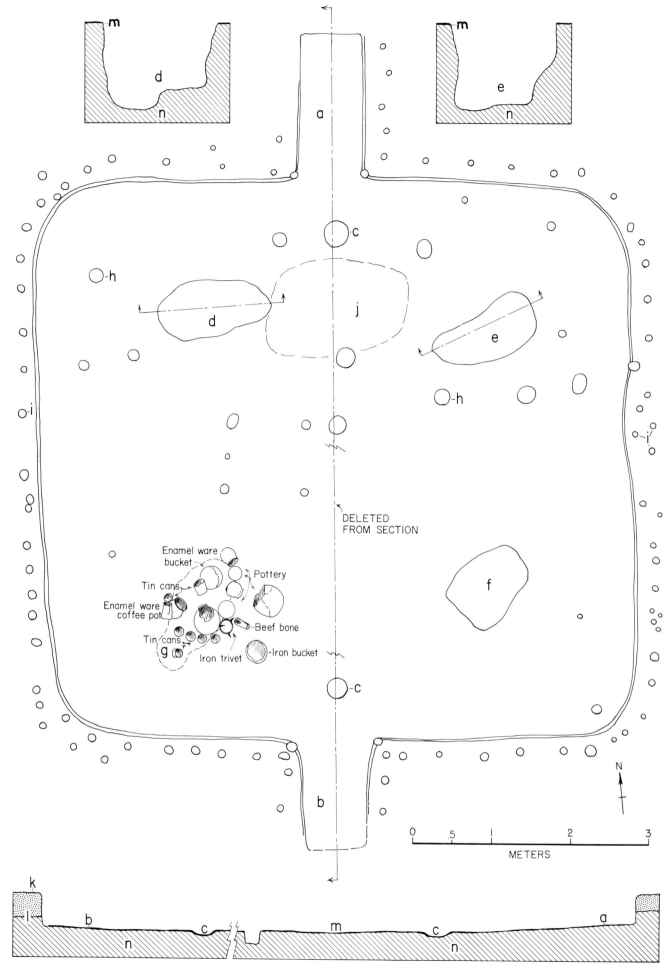

Fig. 3.25. Plan and sections of House 1:9F, Type P-4, Vahki Phase: (a) north entrance; (b) south entrance; (c) hearths; (d, e, f) primary postholes (note sections of d and e); (g) primary posthole covered by cache made by Pima Indians in recent historic times; (h) secondary internal roof supports; (i) holes for side wall posts; (j) area of floor showing mat impression; (k) present surface; (l) old surface with sheet trash above; (m) house floor; (n) native soil.

HOUSE TYPE P-7 (Figs. 3.24d; 3.26)

Pioneer Period, not assignable to phase, 1 example. The reason that House 13:8E has been given a special position in the house typology is because it deviates in a particular way from all other structures: the normal Hohokam residence has been described as a house in a pit, meaning that, although the floor was sunken, side walls rose to meet the roof from the floor level. Pit houses, on the other hand, make use of the ground as side walls, the height being determined by the depth of the floor, and structural side walls rose from the ground surface to meet the roof.

The house in question, although badly mutilated by later pit-digging and house overbuilding, nevertheless revealed enough of the perimeter and the entry to provide a good notion of its shape and characteristics.

Roughly square in outline with rounded corners, the made caliche-clay floor turned up to continue as plaster on the excavated pit sides, rising to a maximum height of 0.5 m and rounded toward the horizontal to what was probably the ground surface at the time. Roof supports rose from the floor, but no traces of outer wall poles were found. The structure was side-entered with no evidence of a step in the entry. Floor area about 25 m².

Early Pioneer Period trash was penetrated when House 13 was built (Fig. 3.26d) and the house, in turn, was partly destroyed by the digging of Pit 8:8E, which was filled with Snaketown Phase trash; still later its eastern edge was partially overbuilt by House 14. Due to extensive damage, it was not possible to date the latter, although it must have been of late Pioneer or early Colonial Period vintage. House 13 could not have been younger than the Snaketown Phase and may have been substantially earlier. This evidence, along with House 1:7H of the Vahki Phase (Gladwin and others 1937: Pl. XX a), signifies that the concept of the plaster-lined pit had early beginnings at Snaketown, but the architectural yield also makes it clear that the idea was never heavily exploited. The relative softness and instability of desert soils, particularly noticeable in the Snaketown area, may have helped determine the house-in-pit mode common to most Hohokam villages.

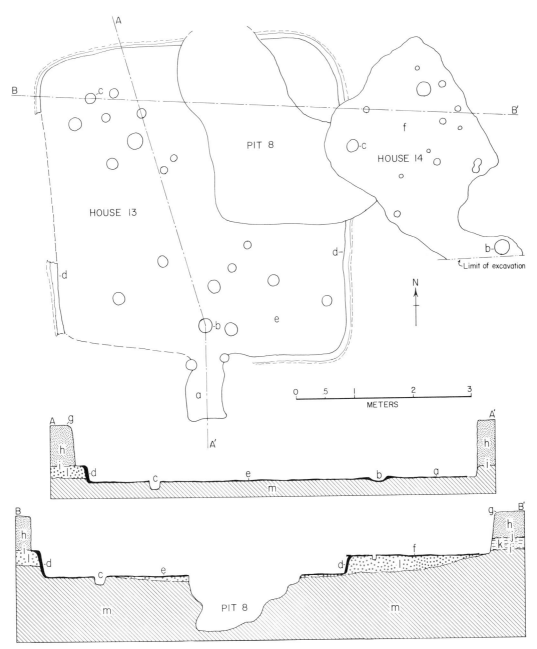

Fig. 3.26. Plan and sections of Houses 13 and 14:8E and Pit 8:8E. House 13 is Type P-7, late Pioneer Period. (a) entrance; (b) hearths; (c) floor holes, (d) caliche-clay side walls of House 13; (e) floor, House 13; (f) floor, House 14; (g) present surface; (h) cultural debris; (i) probable surface when House 13 was occupied; (j) probable surface when House 14 was occupied; (k) sheet refuse; (l) pre-House 13-age refuse; (m) native soil.

ARCHITECTURAL COMPARISONS

The architectural story of Snaketown shapes up substantially differently in the early 1970s than it did after the mid-1930s effort. The addition of 181 new architectural units to the original inventory of 40 is clearly the reason this is so. It can be argued that a doubling of the present number would show still other unexpected nuances and that the conclusions now drawn are as deficient as were the earlier ones. While this undoubtedly is true, emendations to the former generalizations must still be made on the basis of the new data.

First, let us examine trends, or the lack of them, with respect to construction details. There is no recognizable consistent difference in house-pit depth through time. Floor depression was apparently a matter of personal choice; some floors were near the surface or up to 0.5 m in depth in all phases except the Civano, when surface construction was the mode. Although the Hohokam architectural idiom was a unit structure built in a pit, the use of the excavated pit wall as part of the house wall was known in the Pioneer Period but only sparingly used. In general, a light-colored floor material, derived from heavy caliche admixture with clay, is a diagnostic for some Colonial and practically all Sedentary Period houses; a red-brown applied clay mixture, or similarly colored natural soil, was a good but not infallible clue of a Pioneer Period house. Entrance passages, usually centrally located in the long side of a house, revealed no preferred directional orientation at any time, and there are no evident temporal differences as to whether or not the entry was stepped, or in its length relative to the width of the house. The passage cover, or hood, appears to have remained the same structurally throughout time. Stone or adobe treads and the ellipsoid entry were criteria for Sacaton Phase structures.

The standard position of the hearth at all times was about midway between the point where the entrance passage left the house floor and the centerline drawn on the long axis of the dwelling. Almost invariably it was carefully made with wet adobe, sometimes with a slightly elevated lip. In general, Pioneer Period hearths were basin-shaped (Fig. 3.27a). While this shape persisted into later periods (Fig. 3.27d), vertical-sided or slightly undercut hearths were the mode (Fig. 3.27b,c,e-g). Consistent size or depth differences in time were not detected; multiple hearths in a single-entry house were rarely present, although remodeling of the usual lone firepit was commonly done (Fig. 3.27h, i). The smallness of the hearths and the limited extent of the burn area adjacent signify that large fires were not built in them, that embers must have been brought in from a larger outside fire. As indicated before, the position of the hearth in the floor probably means there was no smokehole in the roof and that the entry served as the outlet. The early historic Pima houses, undoubtedly the lineal descendents of the old Hohokam structures, also lacked smokeholes (Russell 1908: 155). Apart from the hearth's important role in supplying energy for cooking, heating, and to a lesser degree light, the baked clay has given the archaeologist a new and useful tool for age determinations through archaeomagnetic studies.

Roof construction basically followed two patterns, largely determined by the engineering requirements of the floor shape: a four-main-post plan was usual for square houses, and a two-main-post support for a ridge type roof, employing auxiliary supports near the edges was normal for long-axis houses. These two forms are not mutually exclusive temporally; however, the large squarish building was evidently dominant at the beginning, giving it a slight chronological edge. Structural materials were locally derived in the main, and mesquite was the primary wood wherever heavy supports were needed; juniper was also identified, and in one case, House 3:10F, selected poles of Douglas Fir were employed, possibly collected as driftwood in the Gila River. Brush from nearby desert growth, reeds from the river's edge and swampy spots, and adobe from underfoot filled the other material

needs for house building. Stone was sparingly used, an omission easily understood when one realizes that the nearest source was about 5 km (3 mi) away.

Side walls at all times rose in a gentle slope from the floor level to meet the horizontal beams of the roof above. The structural members, averaging four or five to the lineal meter, provided the framework for the external matting of brush and reeds, the reinforcing materials for the final veneer of adobe. The interior lining of reeds started in the floor groove, but no evidence exists that it ever was carried more than a reed length, about 1 m, above the floor. Interior plastering appears not to have been done.

One of Sayles' conclusions after reviewing the architectural remains uncovered in 1934–35 was that "The development from early to late is clearly seen, the trend being from the large square houses of the Vahki Phase, becoming progressively smaller, but still square, or rectangular, in the Estrella, Sweetwater and Snaketown phases; changing to rounded corners in the Santa Cruz Phase; and elliptical in the Sacaton Phase, an evolution which leads up to the prototype of the Pima round house" (Gladwin and others 1937: 79). Gladwin found this generalization unacceptable; in 1948 (112-123), after a careful reanalysis in which floor areas were computed, he concluded that "... there was no abrupt or progressive change in the size of houses which were used only as dwellings at Snaketown" (118). He did recognize that structures in the three periods of his modified chronology arranged themselves in two size categories: houses with floor areas of 35 m² or less he considered as dwellings; buildings with floor areas above that figure, ranging up to 110 m² (House 1:7H), he believed to have served a special function, namely ceremonial, and their large size led him to call them Great Houses.

In the light of present information, it appears that the ideas of both Sayles and Gladwin are in need of some modification, or at least consideration should be given to alternative ideas. Looking at the size factor first, it is demonstrable that rooms with large and small floor areas were present in all periods. Yet, overriding this fact, there should be some other basis than size to aid in the determination of function. Unfortunately at Snaketown little collateral help is available, as, for example, specialized architectural features and interior furnishings and equipment. So, the judgments must still largely be subjective in nature. The super-large structures of the Vahki Phase (Type P-4) revealed only evidence of domestic use and some hint, because of double entries and hearths, of possible multiple family occupancy. Spacious houses with 50 m² floors continued in use through time (Types S-2 and S-3), although the record for the Colonial Period is blank in this respect, probably a vagary of excavation. The only structures which possibly qualify as having been nondomestic in nature were the three of the S-3 type, one of which (House 3:9G; Fig. 3.18a) produced floor materials that were different from the norm as described earlier. Sayles' label of "community houses" (Gladwin and others 1937: 82) may be appropriate for these.

In Figure 3.28 an effort has been made to summarize visually what the present work has shown. Although charts of this kind tend to oversimplify the story, they do have some utility in bringing together scattered information into some kind of a design. The following points need particular emphasis because they are at variance with what we thought we knew about Hohokam architecture previously:

1. The greatest typological diversity was in the Pioneer Period, in which the prototypes for essentially all building forms of later times existed. The exception was the mode established by the rectangular, adobe-walled, contiguous surface rooms of the Civano Phase, a tradition introduced into the Hohokam area in later times and therefore new to it. The presence of the large houses at the beginning of the period, whose construction demanded a higher engineering skill than at any time, has a certain bearing on one's beliefs about the origins of Hohokam architecture. The oldest houses were not the efforts of a fumbling, experimenting group of people. They exhibited mastery over house

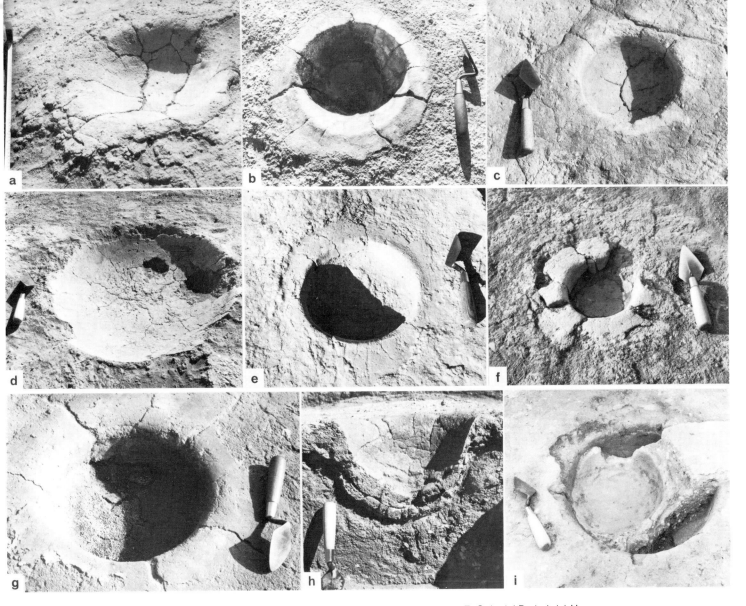

Fig. 3.27. Hearths. (a) House 10:8E, Pioneer Period. (b) House 11:8E, Colonial Period. (c) House 7:10G, Santa Cruz Phase. (d) House 12:5G, Sacaton Phase. (e) House 4:10F, Sacaton Phase. (f) House 7:10F, Sacaton Phase, the smallest hearth found. (g) House 14:11F, Sacaton Phase. (h) House 3:11I, Sacaton Phase, remodeled. (i) House 9:5G, Sacaton Phase, remodeled.

building, as they did over problems of irrigation and other aspects of their culture, from the beginning.

2. The Pioneer Period form diversity is most likely a reflection of functional differences: multiple and single family occupancy of houses probably coexisted from the start, a factor that undoubtedly determined size; and P-5 and P-6 types exhibit nonresidential qualities, introducing inferred storage and menstrual hut uses. On the question of size, Gladwin endeavored to show that the small square, or "normal" sized, house was contemporaneous with the large ones in the Vahki Phase (1948: 117-118) on the basis of the excavator's field determination. The structure in question is House 8:8F. Subsequent study by Sayles of all dating factors involved persuaded him to put this house in the "Unplaced" category. For this reason the type has not been included in Figure 3.28 in the Vahki Phase. I wish to note, however, that future work will undoubtedly reveal the existence of small square houses alongside the large ones from the beginning of Hohokam residency in the Gila valley.

3. The rectangular, square-cornered structure and the round-ended or ellipsoid house, whose beginnings were in the Pioneer Period, became the dominant themes in the Colonial and Sedentary periods, respectively; and the square or squarish house also had a long history, at least through the Sedentary Period.

4. The developmental sequence of Hohokam architecture is not as clear-cut as was originally believed. Building forms did not change uniformly with phase or period, and they cannot be used with the same precision as can pottery in identifying time periods. The substance of this generalization is that individual options in domicile construction probably overrode the dictates of social structure or the architectural canons of the times if they existed. It can be said that, in all probability, more large houses and more square houses were in use during Snaketown's early years than any other kinds, that rectangular houses dominated in the Colonial Period, that ellipsoid houses were the normal type in the Sedentary Period, and that the Classic Period was noted for its adobe-walled, supra-surface, contiguous buildings and the introduction of the compound idea.

The only form missing in all of the early periods is the round house. This house form does show up as the historic structure of the Pimas. Gladwin objected (1948: 115) to Sayles' derivation of the Pima house from the Sacaton Phase elliptical house on the grounds that it did not logically follow the rectangular contiguous room theme of the Classic Period; but this is not a difficult transition to make when we know that S-1 type houses and modifications thereof were still in use in the Classic Period (Hastings 1934; Ambler 1961) and recognize the fact that above-ground adobe-walled buildings and compounds were innovations associated with the Salado expansion into Hohokam territory. The Pima house, in my opinion, represents the retention of the old Hohokam architectural idiom, a not insignificant argument in favor of Hohokam-Pima continuity.

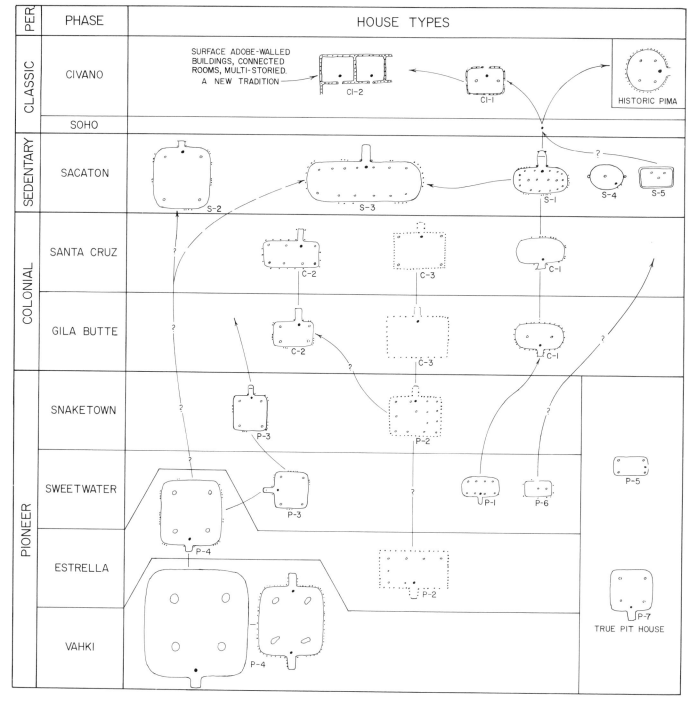

Fig. 3.28. Synoptic chart of Hohokam house types by phase and period with suggested lines of descent or influence. House sizes are relative.

MISCELLANEOUS CONSIDERATIONS

The idea enunciated by Gladwin that the large houses were ceremonial, particularly those of the Vahki Phase, has been reiterated by others (Wheat 1955: 195). For reasons already stated, I reject this idea, believing instead that the Vahki Phase houses filled the basic needs of sheltering family life, whether singly or in groups. Large houses in later times may have been places for community gatherings. The double use of houses for secular and sacred activities may well have taken place, but the fact remains that none of the Hohokam architectural forms give clear evidence that any buildings comparable in use to the great kivas, or even the small kivas, ever existed. This suggests a sharply different religious organization from that of the Anasazi and Mogollon among whom, even in the distant past, specialized buildings were known.

On the assumption that the Hohokam were equally religious, is it fair to ask what took the place in their society of structures earmarked for nonsecular functions among the other groups? The ball court, for one, may have filled some of these needs, although the extent of the rituals associated with the games can only be surmised. The platform mounds and the large crematory floor at the edge of Mound 38 strike me as more likely candidates. Rather than closed structures, which might be construed as an extension of the temple idea, the Hohokam may have favored the open air as the appropriate place to communicate with the elements of the unobservable universe. For this a flat surface may have sufficed.

Burning of Houses. In view of the high flammability of Hohokam houses—a spark from the hearth lodged in the super-dry elements of the roof above would quickly burst into flame—it is something of a surprise to find that only 10% of the houses excavated gave clear evidence of destruction by fire. Considering the incomplete nature of some of the houses and the fact that others were only partially cleared of debris, it may be that the incidence of burned buildings was actually somewhat higher than noted above. But at best it could not have been much higher. Since the ratios of burned houses to sample size in any one phase remain about the same, one cannot say that destruction by burning was more prevalent at one time than another, ruling out the possibility of a wholesale conflagration that might have resulted from hostile action or destruction of a village by choice of the occupants upon abandoning it.

The scarcity of material goods on house floors, and the minimal amount of what may be taken to be roofing material in the fill of the house pits, raise the question as to whether or not the Hohokam dismantled houses on occasion, thereby reducing the chance for relatively more burned structures. Although the Pimas in the early days did burn the domicile upon the death of the owner and destroy his personal property, they also followed the practice of covering the grave of a deceased person with the timbers of his shed or storehouses (Russell 1908: 193). One wonders whether the Hohokam who burned the dead, but evidently not the houses at death, dismantled the buildings when the owner died and used the timbers as fuel to consume his mortal remains. This could be a reasonable explanation of the low incidence of burned houses at Snaketown. Such a custom would have reduced the need to forage for wood to feed the funeral pyre.

In those houses where burning was evident, the amount of charred wood remaining was always nominal. Compared with the average pueblo room destroyed by fire the contrast in the amount of residual charred structural wood is extreme. Smothering of the fire by inorganic materials, as for example clay, when the roof collapsed, was undoubtedly the main factor in this kind of preservation. What the conditions suggest is a heavy layer of roofing clay up to 0.3 m thick, in pueblos, which snuffed out the flame, and a light earth covering in Hohokam houses which allowed the more complete combustion of structural materials before and even after roof collapse.

Whether the Hohokam had set areas within their houses where particular activities took place cannot be ascertained because the evidence, material goods essentially, was too sparse to establish patterns. The standard position of the hearth, near the entrance, did determine where inside cooking was done and the main place for the source of heat. But trivets (Fig. 3.15e) and occasional ash beds elsewhere on floors indicate a response to other needs. Too few metates were found to say that any given part of a house was preferred for milling work. Presumed sleeping mats in one case (Fig. 3.15f) were near the corner, a good spot for avoiding drafts; but in the second instance the mat was in line between the two entries of the house (Fig. 3.25j). Storage jars appear to have been out-of-the-way near the floor's edge in the back of the house. Until we have better information than Snaketown has provided, not much more can be said about the Hohokam use of space, except that the mildness of the climate favored relatively more activities outside the house during the year than was the case where the winters were colder and longer.

The presence of mud dauber nests, preserved by the fires that destroyed some dwellings, tells us that house pests existed then as now. The wasp responsible for these has been identified as a species prevalent today, *Sceliphron caementarium* (Drury), (by Howard E. Evans, Museum of Comparative Zoology, Harvard University, and through L. A. Carruth, Department of Entomology, University of Arizona). Mud dauber nests were recovered in association with Vahki, Snaketown, and Sacaton Phase features, thus spanning the life of the village. Their presence in houses burned during occupancy, indicated by artifacts on the floor, suggests that the wasps and man were co-residents. Reed impressions on the nests support the statement made earlier that house interiors were not plastered.

SETTLEMENT PATTERN

As a preface to this subject, reference should be made to a historic Pima house, and some consideration should be given to the number of houses that may have stood in Snaketown through-

out its long history. Dramatic evidence of what happens to a flimsy structure is seen in the fate of the last surviving Pima round house standing near Snaketown in 1934. Its architectural mode and the details of construction accurately reflect the older Hohokam buildings. This house was pictured in 1937 (Gladwin and others: Pl. XVb), and it is reproduced again here (Fig. 3.29a). The site of the structure was revisited in 1964, and what we saw, after some searching, is shown in Figure 3.29b. In the span of thirty years the house was transformed from an occupied building to an annular ridge of soil representing the melting down of the mineral covering of the reeds and whatever was left of the internal framework. A single upright protruding stump of a roof support post testifies to the destruction of the house by fire. It is a safe conclusion that in not too many years ahead even the existing surface traces will have vanished and that the only means of gaining knowledge about the structure would be the excavation of the hard-packed floor and the reconstruction of the roof by the presence of carbonized reeds, roofing elements, and the arrangement of the post molds in the floor.

Here, then, is a glimpse of archaeology in the making, of the human forces, assuming the house was intentionally set afire, and natural forces that reduced the building to only a few traces of its former self. The archaeologist can learn as much from it by excavation as he can learn from the houses uncovered in Snaketown, except for one dimension: the Pima house was still occupied when first seen. Its lone resident was an old-timer of about 70 years, a Mr. Bichemgottem, and he could be plied with questions: "Why did you build here? When? Who helped you? Why this kind of house (when the vogue on the reservation was already the rectangular flat-roofed house)?"

Being alone, and aged, he built the house about 1915 on that spot so as to be near his son and family, a distance of several hundred meters. The kind of house was what he knew from childhood, and besides, it was warmer than the newer houses then being built. This is the kind of information that is denied us when we talk of Snaketown's houses. I am led to wonder how the archaeologists of the future, having excavated Mr. Bichemgottem's round house and his son's rectangular house, contemporaneous absolutely, would explain the difference in type and location. Kinship, age of the occupants, unwillingness to break away from the old tradition and presumed better comfort, were factors. How do we recapture these values for houses 2,000 years old?

Our sample of 207 houses at Snaketown, 16 rooms cleared in the Classic Period site not included, represents probably less than 3% of the domestic structures that once stood in the village. This figure, frankly, is a gross estimate, based on a number of assumptions. The first assumption states that the average yearly population was 500 people during the life of the village from 300 B.C. to A.D. 1100, a span of 1,400 years. The population undoubtedly fluctuated from a possible minimum of 100 at the time of founding to as many as 2,000 during the Sedentary Period when the village attained its maximum extent. Considering family size as four souls, and using the idea that each family had its own house, then at any one moment, 125 houses may have stood in the village.

The next unknown value is the length of time any single house served its occupants. Termites, fire, and neglect would tend to shorten the life of a house, as would a social custom that dictated the house be set afire or dismantled when the owner or a member of the family died in it. Mr. Bichemgottem lived in his structure about 25 years, the value I shall use. In any century, therefore, using the figures of 125 units standing at any one moment, times a life span of 25 years, there would have been 500 structures. The estimated fourteen-century span of the village now added to the equation indicates that as many as 7,000 houses might have once made up Snaketown. But since all of the figures given are highly speculative, lengthening the life span of a house, increasing fam-

Fig. 3.29. Pima Round House (ki) in western outskirts of Snaketown: (a) as it was in 1934, occupied by Mr. Bichemgottem; (b) as it was in 1964.

ily size, or reducing the population would shrink this value. On the other hand, the opposites of the above factors would inflate the 7,000 figure. Whether one's attitude is conservative or liberal at this stage really makes no difference: the point is clear that Snaketown once had many, many houses, and that our understanding of Hohokam architecture is based on viewing only a tiny fraction of the potential whole.

The maximum number of houses, whatever the figure, that once graced the village can never be studied. The older the structure the more vulnerable it was to destruction by later house overbuilding or to other human activities; therefore, the increase in the number of houses assignable to the later phases (Fig. 3.2) is not only an expression of an expanding population but is also due to the survival factor, for no one was on hand to destroy the late houses once the village was abandoned.

Thus, preservation, the age of the house, and the vagaries of our testing determined the nature and place of the architectural evidences, a not too sound basis for determining patterns in house deployment. But let us look at what we have.

Efforts to plot house distribution by phase produced some general impressions but not much information of a specific nature. For example: An increase in the area occupied through time is evident. A reasonable basis for measuring this is the number of grid blocks in which houses of different ages were found. The tabulation follows, excluding the Classic Period because the residence pattern was different at that time:

Period	Phase	No. of Grid Blocks
Sedentary	Sacaton	24
Colonial	Santa Cruz	14
	Gila Butte	10
Pioneer	Snaketown	12
	Sweetwater	5
	Estrella	3
	Vahki	3

Taken at face value, the figures suggest that Snaketown was a growing village with spurts in the late Pioneer and again in the Sedentary Period. Another product of this effort is the impression that the heart of Snaketown was about in the same place throughout its life. The clustering was probably a response to the availability of domestic water in what has been termed the well area. But the discovery of an occasional house some distance from the core is basis enough for believing that strip excavation might alter the present idea. It has not been possible from the data at hand to detect any plan or rhythm in directional or aerial expansion.

Russell states (1908: 184), "When a youth married he brought his wife to the home of his parents if there was room for them; if not, a house was built nearby and the families ate together." This was the basis for the clustering of houses in early Pima villages. However, I cannot convince myself that the tight grouping of houses, as, for example, in grid blocks 10F and 10G (Fig. 1.6), was attributable to this social custom. Determining the house-to-house relationship is not simple because we cannot be sure of simultaneous occupancy and because the excavations were spotty. The clearest example of a likely, functionally related house grouping is discussed in the review of work areas as specific units of the village (Fig. 12.2). In short, no "grain" or even loosely organized plan in the overall arrangement of houses with respect to each other, or in relation to refuse mounds, is discernible. Unfortunately, plans of early Pima villages seem not to exist; but a few surviving pictures (Fig. 3.1) give the same impression of roominess that evidently was true of Snaketown.

The open spaces between nodes of house densities were probably due to a deep seated desire to spread out, to avoid close living with neighbors where sanguine ties did not exist. This is a sharply different outlook than typifies Anasazi and Pueblo living. In all probability, the open spaces were not "green" spaces. Instead, they were well trampled, taken up with work areas, trash mounds, and cremation plots. There is no hint in the data available to suggest that gardens existed within the village itself.

Seen broadly, it does appear that some rules governed the deployment of houses in relationship to Ball Court 1. Trash mounds and related houses lie to the north and east; to the south is a large, open flat area and no appreciable occupation extended to the west. In other words, the ball court in question was situated on the western edge of Snaketown bordered on the south by an apparent vacant space. Testing there revealed much sheet trash, up to 1 m in depth, and a few widely scattered houses at some distance from the court. I have the distinct feeling that this area was somehow functionally related to the ball court, a use that may have discouraged the building of residences. Since it has not been thoroughly explored, one can only speculate what that use may have been. The activities that took place in the court must have been important not only to Snaketown but to neighboring settlements as well.

The absence of courts of the same age in the villages within many miles suggests that Snaketown may have been something of a mecca for the region. Furthermore, one may imagine that activities extended over several days. Given these conditions, then, a congregating place for visitors, joined by local residents, would have been needed. Occasions of the kind envisioned would be times for the exchange of goods as well as a time for visiting. Not inconceivably, the area in question could have been the market place. Markets as an institution were well developed in Mexico for centuries past, but the idea has not been clearly established as having existed in the villages of the American Southwest. If the Snaketown clearing was a proto-plaza, an informal unbounded space, earmarked for gatherings and possibly commerce, it may be presumed to be of the same age as the construction of the ball court, some time between A.D. 500 and 700. Since the ball court was certainly Mesoamerican-inspired, the plaza would be a predictable and compatible related trait (Jennings et al., 1956: 97, 113). For the Sedentary Period, Wasley and Johnson (1965: 37-8) report what appears to be a formalized example of the plaza with well-made floor and adjacent houses in a site near Gila Bend. Future studies, whether at Snaketown or other large Hohokam villages, would do well to pay attention to this problem.

Finally, a word about the origin of Hohokam architecture. Two qualities stand out when one reviews Pioneer Period houses: (1) forms were more diversified at that time than during any of the subsequent periods, and (2) from the moment of Snaketown's founding, the largest buildings ever erected by the Hohokam were a part of their architectural inventory. These conditions suggest that, along with pottery-making, canal-building, shell-carving, and other attributes of the Vahki Phase, the mode of house-building was equally as much a part of the cultural complex. This view implies that the architectural idiom was well established elsewhere, some place to the south in Mexico which is yet to be identified.

Although pit houses were being built in southern Arizona before the appearance of the Hohokam (Sayles 1945: 1-4) a direct connection between the Cochise culture and Hohokam architectural traditions does not seem likely on typological and other grounds, minimizing the probability of any local influences. Furthermore, the unorganized character of the secular Hohokam village contrasts sharply with the planned sacred centers of Mesoamerica, ruling out the far south as a possible point of origin. For these reasons, the most promising place to search for the source of the Hohokam house is in the northern frontier of Mesoamerica and the time horizon should be as early as the middle of the first millennium B.C. or perhaps a little later.

If differences in details of form and construction are disregarded as having primary diagnostic value in architectural evolution, then the Hohokam house was amazingly stable throughout its long history. Whether or not this is a reflection of an equally stable social system remains to be demonstrated.

4. Ball Court

The identification of a large elongated depression with high crescentic sides as a ball court in the 1934-35 excavations (Gladwin and others 1937: 36-49) introduced a new element into the Hohokam way of life, a trait which further accentuated the presumed affinity of these desert people with those of Mexico. A feature of great size, with its end units nearly as long as a football field, the No. 1 ball court at Snaketown stood out as the only truly monumental construction in their architectural repertoire. The ensuing years saw much attention paid to similar structures in the Southwest, and these yielded helpful information about ball court distribution, typology, and age. Kelly's survey in 1963 showed that approximately 90 courts are known and that at the time of his study eight had been tested and 15 partially or wholly excavated (155, 109ff). By now those figures have been substantially increased with the consequence that probably more courts have been tested in the Southwest than in Mesoamerica whence the idea was derived. Although far more is known today than at the time of discovery, many tantalizing questions persist. Considering the nature of the remains and the difficulty of recovering reliable information about the activities that went on within the courts, it may be a long time before a clear understanding of the ball court's role will be gained.

As for the two Snaketown courts, nothing new can be added that alters the story as originally stated. No further digging was done, or could be done, in Court 2, the smaller of the two units related to the Sacaton Phase, as it was completely cleared before. We had no intention of conducting any comprehensive work in Court 1, believing that the untouched half should stay that way until proper provisions can be taken to protect the fragile surfaces from weathering. The west half, opened in 1934–35, has suffered serious erosion since then (Fig. 4.1). Its restoration should be a part of any future work that is done in it.

Probings that were made in Court 1 were as follows: (1) a limited test in the south bank, to verify the findings of 1934–35 (Gladwin and others 1937: 38-41), namely, that traceable surfaces of the embankment representing different stages of construction or repair, do indeed exist, and that in the core of the embankment no pottery later than the Gila Butte Phase occurred. In both instances the earlier results were repeated. The original estimate that Court 1 was built sometime during the Gila Butte Phase remains unchanged, though the use of the structure extended well into the Santa Cruz Phase if not to the end of the Colonial Period; (2) a north-south trench through the east end unit was made with the hope of detecting the surface extant at the time the court was in use. Clear proof of this was not obtained (see below), but I believe that the end units, now little understood, could be instructive if painstakingly excavated. Such work should reveal more specific details than we now have about form and the existence of structures as suggested by Ferdon (1967: 9-10); and (3) a controlled screened test (7D: Test 1) in the east annex, taken in 0.25 m levels, provided the following information as excerpted from the analysis of 13.385 kg of broken pottery (about 2,500 sherds). The base of the annex, or what may be presumed to have been the

floor at the time of use, was 0.75 m below the present surface. The pottery from the highest two levels was dominantly Santa Cruz Red-on-buff, grading to nearly "pure" Gila Butte Red-on-buff in Level 3. Below this level, the pottery was mainly of the Sweetwater Phase. The annex was evidently built upon Pioneer Period trash during the Gila Butte Phase, and its use evidently extended into the Santa Cruz Phase. The potsherds in the levels above the assumed floor were uncommonly small, perhaps broken by the trampling of human feet.

At the time of construction, the floor of the ball court was lowered only about 0.5 m below the existing desert floor. The earth thus removed would have been far short of the bulk required to build the sides to the heights we see them today. Earth from other sources was needed. Machine-dug trenches in the environs of the court located several borrow pits which may have been exploited for this purpose. It may be assumed that earth was not brought in from any great distance, rather that the closer the supply the better. Immediately to the southeast lies a large area where an average of 2.0 m of desert material was removed. Subsequently the hole was used for dumping trash. Except for a thin surface veneer of refuse of mixed ages, the underlying mass was clearly assignable to the Gila Butte Phase. A rough calculation of volume yields a figure of around 4,000 cubic meters that now lies below what appears to be the natural desert floor. This is not far from an estimate of the mass that existed in the court's embankments. If the assumption is correct that the earth did come from the borrow pit in question, then the Gila Butte Phase trash that fills it provides supporting evidence for the age of the initial construction. To account for the pottery content in the earth of the embankment it must be assumed further that some contemporary trash was gathered with the rest of the earth.

A large depressed area about 50 m northwest of the court may also have supplied bulk for the court. The nature of the buried caliche surface hinted that human activity had modified it. Mound 14 lies immediately to the east of the depression and during its formation in the Sacaton Phase much of the refuse spilled over into the pit. Gila Butte and Santa Cruz Phase pottery was present in minor quantities, but since controlled testing was not done here we cannot be certain that a true stratigraphic situation existed. It can be said with reasonable certainty that more bulk than appears to have been taken from the southeast pit was needed to build the sides and the end units of the court, and the pit in question was in a strategic position to supply some of it.

As noted before, south of Court 1 stretches a flat, open space, the largest of its kind in Snaketown. If the institution of the market could be proven as a part of Hohokam life, then this would have been the ideal place for it. People drawn from miles around for intervillage games in the court might also have taken advantage of the occasion for trading and fraternizing. Coincidentally or not, the bronze plaque designating Snaketown a Registered National Historic Landmark was awarded to Lloyde A. Allison, then Governor of the Gila River Indian Community, on April 3, 1965, in the ball court, and all of the food preparation for the

Figure 4.1. Ball Court 1, looking east towards Gila Butte. The west, or near, half shows erosion damage after excavation in 1934-35 (compare with Plate VIII, Gladwin and others 1937). Note related and other important features as labeled.

Court 2

Court 1

Borrow Pit Area

Mound 39

Mound 29

Area Without Houses

festive occasion and the dances took place in the open space to the south of it.

Ferdon (1967) has questioned the identification of the court as a place in which a ball game was played. He holds that a comparative study of Hohokam and Mesoamerican ball courts fails to show the existence of essential shared features. Alternatively he argues that the courts were dance plazas which have their modern surviving counterparts in the cleared floors and especially built impermanent structures used in the Vikita celebration of the Papago Indians. Ferdon argues eloquently but, from my point of view, not convincingly, for he fails to take into account the differences that distance may make in the modification of transmitted ideas and most importantly, the vastly different building resources the two environments provided. The Hohokam had to work with adobe, not stone, and this would affect the geometry and the final appearance of the structure. The fact is that the architectural analogies between Mesoamerican and Hohokam courts are far closer and more numerous than are the shared features of the Hohokam courts and the Vikita dance plaza. While I am inclined, therefore, to cling to the original identification, in a sense the argument is academic, for there is no reason why dances could not have taken place in the courts along with other activities.

It is worth noting that the Pimas referred to Court 1 at Snaketown as "Bat Man's Dancing Place" and that, according to them, the high side embankments were formed by two facing lines of dancers, alternatingly advancing and retreating toward or from each other, and each line, at the end of its retreat, kicked the dust underfoot backward. In time the high dirt ridges were formed! This mythical explanation of the feature as it exists probably extends as well to identifying it as a place for Bat Man to dance! I would further argue that if a prototype of the Vikita dance plaza is present in Snaketown, it is to be found in the empty area south of Court 1.

The significant aspect of courts among the Hohokam, whatever transpired in them, is that the genesis of the idea that produced them is inescapably southern, a conclusion supported not only by the obvious physical analogies and by the wide distribution of ball courts in Mesoamerica but also because it was only one of many elements in a constellation of attributes that so clearly helps in identifying the Hohokam as a northern outlier group from the southern high cultural nucleus.

At the same time it must be granted that an orderly pattern of distribution, in space or time, has not been established; but this applies to many other elements as well, and it may be concluded that the record is still too spotty to lead to the convincing results one wants or that diffusion was discontinuous. Beals notes that a ball game played with a rubber ball in a prepared court and with other associated elements extended north as far as the Sinaloa and Fuerte Rivers in Sinaloa (1932: 113), and Di Peso excavated a stone court at Casas Grandes in Chihuahua (1968). These occurrences bring the complex to within about 500 km (300 mi) of southern Arizona, not a great distance obstacle to overcome when one thinks of the transmission of cultural elements along well-established routes. It is interesting that in the state of Guanajuato, where some parallels with the Southwest seem to occur, ball courts are later than those to the north (Braniff 1965: unpublished ms), a situation that might be taken to favor littoral diffusion which Beals' studies suggest (1932: 113).

5. Mounds

Inevitably, societies with a fixed residential pattern accumulate wastes that must somehow be taken care of. The Hohokam did this either by dumping refuse into pits of their own making or by piling it up in selected spots, thereby, in time, contributing to the topographic relief of the village. Due to a few of the mounds that were built by design as platforms and several other trash mounds that were modified by surfacing them to achieve the same end, the whole mound complex is thought of as kind of an architectural expression. The mounds of "pure" refuse, long in forming, do express a point of view and a behavior pattern on the part of the Hohokam, and the platforms are the result of a desire to fulfill an apparent ritual need. Whichever way one views the mounds, as garbage piles to avoid, or as symbols of a way of life, they nevertheless are the features more productive of information than any others on the site.

Deployment of the sixty mounds appears to have been a matter of convenience and at the option of the house owners that used them. Comparisons of house and mound contents show some of them to have been contemporaneous, and when one examines house distribution it becomes clear that a number of them were located at the edges of mounds in use. At best, this closeness must have had its disagreeable side effects. There is some evidence, though it is not altogether convincing, that living on the downwind side of a mound, to the east or northeast, was avoided. Unfortunately, our work was not extensive enough to encompass all of the terrain around a single mound, which, if done, might provide an accurate base for judging house-mound arrangements and for determining how many households were using a trash pile at a given moment. A mound's growth rate and the waste-production rate might be reconstructed from this kind of data.

Snaketown's mound distribution was examined specifically with the idea that symmetry of arrangement, or planned groupings, might reflect a northern extension of the religious center concept of Mesoamerica. This possibility seemed particularly attractive with the identification of Mound 16 as a platform, whose construction was completely unrelated to refuse disposal. However, no convincing alignments came out of the examination. In general, the greatest concentration of mounds coincides with the densest assemblage of houses—a logical cause and effect relationship. Mention should be made, however, of the fact that Mound 39, with its three stages of capping, was immediately adjacent to the large crematory floor and that this floor was built over nonsecular looking hearth complexes. Furthermore, when the crematory floor fell into disuse, it was over-built by Mound 38 which, in its terminal stage, is believed to to have been capped. The close arrangement of architectural elements, with ritual uses that extended over several centuries, may be the most we can expect in Hohokam villages as expressions of their ideas of how secular and sacred features relate to each other. I see no evidence to support the thought that formalized ritual centers were ever a part of the Hohokam way of life.

Mound sizes varied considerably, dependent in part on intensity and length of use. The lowest ones rose barely a meter above the desert floor, while the highest, or deepest, reached 3 to 4 m. Actual trash depth exceeded this figure by as much as 2 m, where mounds grew over trash-filled pits. The greatest lateral extent of the largest mounds was in excess of 60 m. These ancient garbage heaps and the absence of mounds resulting from the collapse of houses provide a sharp contrast between early Hohokam sites and those of other Southwestern archaeological tribes and, more dramatically, from most other American sites, north or south as well. Usually piles of rock rubble or earthworks establish the presence of massive religious or domestic structures. But not until Classic Period times, when the erection of above-surface adobe-walled buildings was the vogue, does one see elevations in the Gila and Salt River valleys identifiable as house mounds. The heart of Snaketown had none of these, but a few did exist in the outskirts (see Ariz. U:13:21 etc).

Twenty-nine of the 60 mounds were tested, some perfunctorily and a few extensively. The essential information about these is given in Table 5.1. Mounds of all sizes were examined, and it is believed that the typology developed in the following pages is representative but not final. It is evident from the list that there were more active collecting spots of refuse in the Sacaton Phase than at any other time. A number of them do have successive phases represented as measured by the ceramics. It is also apparent, however, that the practice of mounding refuse does not run through the entire history of the site. The custom began sometime in the Pioneer Period and was well established by Snaketown Phase times. Morris (1969b:49-50) notes the mounding of Vahki Phase trash in the Salt River valley; but to my knowledge, this evidence has not been duplicated elsewhere. As a speculation, it appears at Snaketown that mounding may have been the consequence of an expanding population, that when refuse accumulation exceeded the volume of available borrow pits and other excavations earmarked for filling, one alternative was to go up. This is what was done.

MOUND TYPES

In 1934–35 only four mounds were tested, Nos. 11, 29, 40, and 58. On the basis of these efforts it was inferred that all of the mounds were composed of trash, though the thought lingered in the minds of some, that house mounds might also be represented (Gladwin and others 1937:7-9). Through the work of Wasley (1960) and our own recent explorations of Snaketown, we now know that the situation is more complicated than was originally believed.

The broad categories of mounds are distinguishable as follows: Type 1, those composed of "pure" trash, with heavy ash, pottery, and general refuse content, showing a physical structure, or "grain," which reflects the manner and direction of mound

TABLE 5.1

Inventory of Tested Snaketown Mounds

Mound Number	Type 1	2	3	Nature of Test	Ceramic Age*	Remarks
9	x	x		T-trench, backhoe	Sacaton	Trash structured south end, clean soil north end
10	x			N-S trench, backhoe, east end of mound	Sacaton	Trash loose, has some structure
11	x			Stratigraphic	Sacaton	Gladwin and others 1937: Fig. 10
12		x		N-S trench, backhoe	Sacaton	
14	x			E-W trench, backhoe	Sacaton (SC, GB)	Has flat top but no capping
15	x			N-S trench, backhoe	(Sac) Santa Cruz, Gila Butte	
16			x	Completely uncovered	Sacaton	Formal platform (see Chap. 5)
17	x			E-W trench, backhoe	Sacaton over Pion. Per. fill	
24	x			E-W trench, backhoe	Sacaton	
25	x			E-W trench, backhoe	Sacaton (SC, GB)	
26		x		N-S trench, backhoe	Sacaton (SC)	
29	x			Stratigraphic	All Phases	Gladwin and others 1937:25–31
30	x			Central pit, backhoe	Sacaton (SC, GB)	Trash exceptionally soft
32	x			NW-SE trench, backhoe	(Sac) Santa Cruz, Gila Butte, Snaketown	
33	x			NS & EW trenches, backhoe	Sacaton (SC, GB)	Grain of deposit weakens east half
38	x			Wide trench & stripping with machine	Sacaton on older premound fills	(See Chap. 5)
39	x	x		Stratigraphic & stripping	Sacaton & older	(See Chap. 5)
40	x	x		Stratigraphic	Gila Butte, Snaketown & older	(See Chap. 5)
41	x			NE-SW trench, backhoe	Sacaton (SC) Gila Butte, Snaketown	Growth N to S
42	x			N-S trench, backhoe	Sacaton	
43	x			2 E-W trenches, backhoe	N Tr. Sacaton S Tr. SC, GB	Growth S to N
44	x			L-trench, NS-EW backhoe	Sacaton	Growth N to S; over 3 burials
45		x		T-trench, EW-NS backhoe	Santa Cruz (GB, ST)	
46	x			NE-SW trench, backhoe	Sacaton	
47		x		E-W trench, backhoe, & stratigraphic	Sacaton-Santa Cruz transition	
55		x		E-W trench, backhoe	Sacaton (SC)	
57	x			Pit test, backhoe	Sacaton, Santa Cruz, Gila Butte	
58	x			Hand-dug trench	Sacaton	Gladwin and others 1937:55
59	x			E-W trench, backhoe	Sacaton (SC)	

*Dominant phase given as Sacaton or Santa Cruz; present but not dominant (Sac) or (SC).

growth. Type 2, mounds with some refuse content, but containing a predominance of desert soil, generally exhibiting no structure and no hard capping. Type 3, platform mounds, either (a) trash accumulations capped with a caliche-clay mixture, or (b) mounds especially built of desert soil according to a preconceived plan in fulfillment of presumed ritual requirements.

Type 1: Trash

These are the most numerous, 19 of the 29 tested having exhibited Type 1 characteristics. They required the most time in growing, by the gradual accretion of trash, and they most clearly reflect the Hohokam attitude toward garbage disposal. No consistent pattern of directional growth is discernible, and we have no meaningful data on the growth rate-time relationship. This undoubtedly varied from mound to mound, dependent upon the intensity of use. The dominance of Sacaton Phase refuse in terms of numbers of mounds and in volume as well, may be attributed to the apparent fact that the village's population maximum was reached at that time. No tests were developed which might have provided information on changes through time in the per capita amount of refuse produced. I do not believe that anyone has seriously looked at the question of whether or not increased agricultural efficiency stemming from improved water control devices influenced the waste output, a problem not completely unrelated to twentieth century living.

Looking at mound composition more closely, it is evident that refuse generally was dumped on a sloping surface, once the height of a meter or more was reached. Lateral growth was the result. What determined the height limit is not known. Some subtle cultural factor was at work, for the angle of repose of the refuse would have permitted it to be piled much higher, thereby taking up less space in the village. Onto the discard heap went just about everything for which no further use was foreseen. While no detailed volumetric studies were made of the contents, mostly because of the variability of the elements from one part of a mound to another, the relative order of components would read as follows: soil, wood ash and charcoal, broken pottery, stone residue, shell and bone. The high soil content of mounds probably was the consequence of tidying the premises around houses by sweeping and gathering the dirt with the scattered debris.

One must remember that organic refuse on the mounds, such as corn stalks, and other plant remains, probably bulked as large as did the inorganic fraction. Continuous layers of white ash, up to 5 m in extent, suggest that the combustible trash was set afire from time to time. This would have had some salutary hygenic effects, for the mounds may be presumed to have also been used as latrines. Fire, decomposition, and settling combined to reduce the mounds to their form today.

In addition to making stratigraphic tests in mounds using coarse mesh screens, fine siftings with window screen were made periodically to recover the more minute materials that are usually lost. Microminerals, representing the remnants of work done on minerals, were recovered in this way, as were many charred seeds which constituted the basis for interesting speculations about Hohokam subsistance (Bohrer 1970) and comminuted bone which tells us something about early dietary habits.

It is clear to me that Snaketown's trash mounds are capable of revealing far more information than we were able to extract from them. Their principal value in this study was as sources for data essential to chronology building. But a project focusing on the obscure as well as the obvious components and blending physical, chemical, botanical and cultural analytical methods would be most rewarding.

Type 2: Mixed Trash and Desert Soil

Nine of the mounds tested were composed predominantly of desert soil. The pottery content in them was low, and occasionally thin lenses of dumped refuse appeared in the side walls of the test trenches as the only evidence of "grain" in the otherwise homogeneous matrix. In size and shape these differ in no way from Type 1 mounds, but the surfaces do exhibit fewer potsherds and a relatively higher concentration of caliche pebbles. While those mounds of this type tested gave no evidence of having been hard-surfaced, the possibility that they were once capped and subsequently modified by erosion cannot be discounted. If they were surfaced, the reason for their existence becomes clear, for they would then match the characteristics of Type 3 mounds discussed next. If they were not surfaced, they might still have filled the need for elevated platforms. The essential step in the search of proof of it would be missing. An alternative explanation is that Type 2 mounds represent the accumulations of powdery soil cleared from the desert surface in areas where new houses were to be built. The low pottery content could be explained in this way, and pauses in mound building would have provided the opportunity to add an occasional basketload of trash. If this idea has merit, then cyclical house-building might be inferred.

Mound 9 was classifiable as Type 1 and Type 2 at the south and north ends, respectively, and the same sharing of characteristics was evident in Mound 38. This suggests that, in the minds of the people, a clear distinction between the categories devised here was not made. Although most of the Type 2 mounds are assigna-

ble to the Sacaton Phase, Mounds 15 and 45 provide evidence that the practice which prompted their construction extended well into the Colonial Period.

Type 3: Platform

Mounds of this type introduce a relatively new element into the inventory of Hohokam attributes, namely, the construction and use of artificial elevated platforms. Wasley's work in the Gatlin site (1960) near Gila Bend, Arizona, was the first to bring the existence of earth platforms into clear focus. The Gatlin mound convincingly illustrated that construction was staged, that enlargements of the core mound were made periodically, and the presence of ancillary structures. The total complex may be presumed, on comparative data from the south, to have been designed for ritual use. The original construction and all subsequent modifications were datable to the Sacaton Phase.

Guided by the Gila Bend evidence, we consciously searched for platform mounds at Snaketown as tests were made, convinced that this feature was known generally to the Hohokam and was not unique to the discovery locale. In this we were not disappointed because it is possible to amplify the known record by the following cases.

MOUND 40

Although Wasley believed that the Gatlin mound and all of its related parts were erected in no more than a century (1960:261), perhaps between A.D. 1000 and 1100, one suspects that the beginning of the idea of platforms was somewhat earlier. Probable ancestral forms came to light during the extensive testing of Mound 40. The evidence is here presented as the hypothetical first and simplest Hohokam efforts to strive for elevations with hard floors, conjecturally for ritual use. The prepared surfaces in question are seen in Figure 6.4 in which they are related stratigraphically to other features, and again in Figure 5.1. Layer 2, the lower of the two surfaces, was detected in trenches and test pits over an area of about 10 m in both directions. How much farther it extended we do not know. It was laid down over what was initially a low trash mound on a slight natural rise in the village. This indicates that the Hohokam were responding to a need for a floor that stood above the surrounding desert level. The age of the floor is clearly established by the fact that it rested upon refuse of the Snaketown Phase and trash of the same horizon was dumped on it when it fell into disuse. In terms of the Christian calendar, it appears that the idea of elevated surfaces was picked up by the Hohokam at least by A.D. 500.

The higher, and somewhat later, capping (Fig. 5.1-4) was thinner but more compact than the deeper surface, and we were not able to trace it over as large an area. It seems to have been subjected to considerable disturbance. Its age could be either Snaketown or Gila Butte Phase.

MOUND 39

As the largest artificial hillock in Snaketown, Mound 39 was selected for a series of stratigraphic tests with the hope that it would yield information about all or most of the village's life. Abundant sherds on the surface, ashy soil, and a low quantity of caliche nodules suggested the mound was composed of trash. It is elliptical in shape, the 70 m long axis trending southwest-northeast. The exploratory trench with its three control columns sliced through the mound's short axis, from northwest to southeast (Fig. 6.2). The outcome of this work showed the mound to have had an unpredictably complicated history. Although the stratigraphic, or chronological, results we sought were somewhat reduced in value because of the events affecting the mound, the unexpected features more than made up for the loss. It is these that now concern us.

Fig. 5.1. Profile in Mound 40: (1) Pit 2, filled with Snaketown Phase trash; (2) older capping layer of clean desert soil with a prepared surface; (3) Snaketown Phase trash; (4) younger capping layer; (5) predominantly Gila Butte Phase trash.

Figure 5.2a and b are composite photographs of the north and south faces of the trench respectively and both merit close scrutiny. Directing attention to a first, we see on the left two remnants of upward sloping well-packed layers of caliche-clay (2 and 4). The lower of the two layers (2) rests on stratified trash in which the lenses of ash more or less parallel the hard surface, except as one goes deeper where the slope of the strata is reversed. Layer 4 rests on a cushion of refuse about 0.5 thick (3) with faintly developed structure. The two hard layers in question, if projected, would extend out into space. The implication is that they have been truncated by the removal of the underlying material that extended to the west. This interpretation is supported by the structure of the refuse in the south face of the trench (Fig. 5.2b,1) where the relationship of the slope of the mound's surface to the "grain" of the refuse also indicates that truncation took place. It will be noted that in this profile the capping layer is thin to absent, but the equivalent surface is well delineated.

Unit 5, in both trench faces is a massive bed of refuse totally lacking in structure. It rests on the upper capping layer (4) or on the extension of the surface it occupies. We noticed that when refuse was disturbed by us, all depositional lines were destroyed and the resultant mass was homogeneous in texture exactly like the unit under discussion. It may be safely concluded that the old mound, or a sizable part of it, was physically moved eastward, thereby shifting its summit to a new location. At the same time some additional refuse was introduced as suggested by the analysis of the pottery content in the test labeled Column 3.

The results of the stratigraphic tests in Mound 39 are given in detail elsewhere. Suffice it now only to recapitulate the essential

times when events affecting the mound took place. The rubbish below the premound desert floor was mainly of the Pioneer Period. Mound-building started in the Gila Butte Phase carrying into the Santa Cruz Phase, when the first capping layer (2) was laid down. Still during the same phase more trash accumulated, and it, too, was capped (4). The relocated refuse (5) was mixed Santa Cruz-Sacaton phase material, as already noted, the latter increasing in frequency in the eastern flanks of the mound.

Finally, the translocated refuse was covered with successive layers of caliche-clay, intercalated locally with thin strata of charcoal (6). As much as 0.4 m thick in spots, this layer was traced over about 75 m² on top of the mound, and there were reasons to believe that the area was only a fraction of the surfacing that once was there. This unit has suffered extensively from erosion and from pitting by curio seekers in recent years. It is not known, because of this damage, whether the locally detected multiple surfaces were the result of repairs or vestiges of staged renovations. The only feature detectable on the uppermost floor was a hearth, a circular clay-lined basin, matching in kind the hearths in houses. A Sacaton Phase assignment for unit 6 is certain.

In summary, the sequence of events as exposed in the trench through Mound 39 is given schematically in Figure 5.3. The three essential facts that emerge are: (1) Hills of normally accumulated trash were sometimes surfaced with a material that could be compacted into a durable floor. (2) Increased elevations were achieved by the further addition of refuse which was capped. (3) The geographical center of an eminence could be shifted by translocating the mass of the original mound. Added to what we know about Mound 40, these actions can now be identified as having spanned a time period beginning in the Snaketown Phase of the Pioneer Period to the Sacaton Phase of the Sedentary Period.

MOUND 38

The density of caliche nodules and the scarcity of pottery on the western slope of Mound 38 suggested that it may have been capped at one time. Testing in the form of a wide trench from the western edge to the mound's center, and a right angle machine-dug trench to the north perimeter, did not produce definitive results in support of this idea. However, interesting and possibly meaningful features did result from the operation, and they should be noted.

The south profile of the main trench, as seen through the camera's eye, is reproduced in Figure 5.2c. The western flank of the mound, from the end of the trench to about one-third the way beyond the first shovel and toward the second one proceeding toward the left, overlapped a hard and heavily burned crematory floor (1). This feature is reviewed elsewhere. Farther to the left, or east, some stratification lines begin to appear at the base of the mound (2) representing a sheetlike accumulation or, at best, the beginning of a mound of refuse attributable to the Snaketown and Gila Butte phases. At the extreme left, obvious mounding of trash took place (3) in the Sacaton Phase which, out of the picture, rose to a height of over 2 m. Sequent to that event was the addition of up to a little more than 1 m of relatively clean desert soil (4), slightly mounded in the center of the profile. Some charcoal and ash bands are visible in this unit near the top. This part of the mound meets Type 2 criteria. The "valley" created between units 3 and 4 was then filled with refuse (5), as was also the area west of unit 4 which, because of its lack of depositional lines, indicates it was transported from some other place. Finally, an indistinct layer of clean material (6) covers the crest and western slope of the mound, the source of the caliche nodules observed earlier. This rather complicated history is schematically reviewed in Figure 5.4.

Even though the evidence for a capping layer in Mound 38 is not convincing, I believe it had one. Subsequent erosion and disturbances have destroyed its character. Perhaps most important

Fig. 5.2. Trench faces illustrating composition and succession of events in Mound 39 and Mound 38. *(Top)* North face of trench through Mound 39: (1) eastern edge of original mound, structured trash exposed, Santa Cruz Phase; (2) truncated caliche-clay capping remnant; (3) weakly structured trash, Santa Cruz Phase; (4) remnant of second caliche-clay capping; (5) unstructured trash, moved from another source, some probably from the original mound to the west, mixed Santa Cruz-Sacaton phases; (6) final capping of mound with caliche-clay, locally interspersed with layers of charcoal, Sacaton Phase. *(Center)* West portion of south face of trench through Mound 39: (1) truncated structured trash of original mound, upper layers Santa Cruz Phase, deeper layers with opposite grain, Gila Butte-Snaketown phases; (2) old mound surface, capping layer thin to absent; (3) structured Santa Cruz Phase trash; (4) mound surface showing thin remnants of capping, equivalent to *4* above; (5) structureless trash, moved, mixed Sacaton Phase and earlier trash; (6) caliche-clay capping layer with a thin veneer of Sacaton Phase refuse above it. Vertical scorings indicate places (toward camera) where stratigraphic test columns 1 (right) and 2 were made. *(Bottom)* South face of trench in Mound 38: (1) crematory floor extending under flank of mound and westerly; (2) layered refuse, mixed Snaketown-Gila Butte Phases; (3) structured Sacaton Phase trash considerably disturbed by rodents; (4) nearly clean soil, some intercalated charcoal and ash beds; (5) churned trash, probably moved from another locality, Sacaton Phase; (6) indistinct surface band, less trashy and containing more caliche pebbles, possibly capping remnant. Open burrow was old rodent tunnel, cleaned out by owl which took possession shortly after trench face was established.

is the fact that this investigation revealed another effort to construct a mound intentionally by incorporating preexisting refuse heaps. The "clean" zone, unit 4, helps to explain Type 2 mounds as probably having been platforms, and it reinforces the notion that the Hohokam made more use of artificially prepared mounds than the few obvious examples we have found would indicate.

The crematory floor was dated as early Sacaton Phase. The extension of the mound over the floor, an intentional act, must then be younger. However, why this was done and what prompted the abandonment of the crematory area cannot be answered.

MOUND 16

Mound 16 was a low, circular elevation in the site, barely a meter high and roughly 15 m in diameter. It lacked the usual heavy surface layer of broken pottery, the ashy matrix, and the extensive holes and mounds left by burrowing animals that characterize Type 1 trash mounds. However, these qualities, together with moderately dense scattering of caliche nodules, attracted us to this most unimpressive hill. There was nothing about its location, in the northern sector of the village, that called special attention to it. An east-west backhoe trench quickly established the fact that the mound was indeed made of clean desert soil and that artificial faces and surfaces existed within it. Little doubt

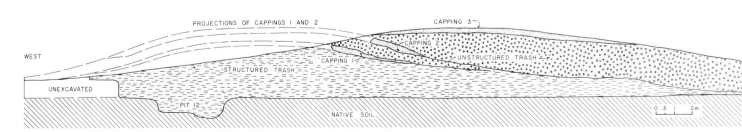

Fig. 5.3. Section through Mound 39 showing schematically how projections of capping layers 1 and 2 extended over the old, original mound, and how these related to the later rebuilt mound with its capping (3) on unstructured refuse.

Fig. 5.4. Schematic summary of events in history of Mound 38 as exposed in south face of test trench: (1) crematory floor over older cremations and hearths; (2) locally concentrated Snaketown or Gila Butte Phase trash; (3) Sacaton Phase trash, structured; (4) predominantly culture-free desert silt; (5) translocated refuse, predominantly Sacaton Phase; (6) probably remnant of capping layer.

remained at this stage that careful exploration would produce evidence for a type of structure previously unknown at Snaketown. Sciscenti and crew were assigned to the task, predictably, a difficult one. Tracing subtle soil changes, distinguishing between erosionally and artificially made features, detecting old surfaces produced by the trampling of feet or by the addition of thin veneers of clay, and developing the gross nature of the mound consumed about 2.5 months of digging time with a work force varying from two to six. Ultimately the effort was richly rewarded by the information gained (see front cover).

The following pictorial record will testify to the expertise with which the work was done. One fact emerges clearly from this experience—that in our search for information about Hohokam mound-building inclinations, we cannot afford to leave any mounds uninvestigated.

Premound Construction. The area occupied by the mound originally was subjected to what appears to have been normal village activity. Pockets of trash and sheet refuse, all of the Sacaton Phase, were exposed by the test trenches (Fig. 5.5). Some interspersing of blow sand in thin layers was also noted. Intently more interesting were fragments of a large floor that may have extended beneath the entire mound. Although seen only in patches (Figs. 5.5, 5.6, and 5.7), the floor was consistently made of a caliche-clay mixture, and the remnants occurred on the same horizontal plane. A hearth and adjacent pit may be seen in profile B-B′, and locally burned spots were also noted. A thin covering of sand, fine gravel, and white salt stains left by the evaporation of water trapped in pockets indicate that the floor at one time was exposed to the weather. These conditions suggest that the floor was associated with a special use area as, for example, a plaza serving a number of houses, as noted by Wasley and Johnson (1965: 37-38) in the Citrus site near Gila Bend. The location of Mound 16 may have been determined by the prior existence of the floor and the activities that took place on it.

The potsherds from the various floor and prefloor tests were dominantly of the Sacaton Phase. There was some admixture of older materials.

Mound Construction. The heart of the mound was the product of an intentional earth-moving operation (Fig. 5.5). Although we cannot be certain that the test trench sectioned the core at its greatest diameter, it appears that a deposit of clean reddish-brown silty clay with inclusions of caliche nodules, some coarse sand and fine gravel, was brought in and piled up to a depth of 1 m and a width of about 7 m. The mineral constituents of the core match those in the subsoil in the immediate area of the mound. A sufficiently deep excavation would have tapped the sand-gravel stratum that lies below the clay-silt-caliche layer. It may be assumed that the mound's central bulk was not transported far. The next step was widening the mound by adding relatively clean silty sand around the core to expand the diameter to about 14 m. Pottery in this material suggests that it was scraped from the desert's surface nearby. Structure lines were visible over short distances in this matrix, some apparently representing artificial depositional surfaces, others silting lines from rain.

The absolute sequence of subsequent events was difficult to establish due to the fragile and eroded nature of the mound material. It was not always possible to be certain whether modifications recognized in the uncovering process were planned additions or remodelings necessitated by erosion. The absence of, or our failure to detect what appeared to be, staged increments around the whole circumference of the mound, tends to reduce the force of the argument that the Hohokam purposefully masked the old facings by adding new ones.

The clearest evidence of additions to the mound was seen in the southeast quadrant in two cross-sections (Fig. 5.5). The western edge and the north face in the step area failed to produce any hints of similar additions in those parts. Traces either of the mound facings or the related floor areas would certainly have remained

even where erosion took place, had the remodelings extended all the way around. Removal of the facings by the Hohokam to alter the plan of the mound is possible, but such acts seem unlikely. The reason for limiting remodelings to the east and south sides of Mound 16 is not apparent.

The facings consist of a caliche-clay mixture, applied wet in a stiff plastic condition. The surfaces, where best preserved, showed smoothing, perhaps by hand, followed by implement polishing seen on a limited part of the second facing on the south side. The accretions were applied directly on each other, except where erosion had produced hollows that required bulk to fill them.

Eight surfaces were definable, each a thin veneer, somewhat variable in thickness and slope with respect to each other (Figs. 5.5, 5.6, and 5.7). Gradual filling around the mound slowly reduced its height. As a consequence, each succeeding facing had less vertical height than its predecessor. The last surface, No. 8, in fact, was not a facing at all but only a hard topping on fill material which reduced the hillock on the east side to a smoothly contoured mound (Fig. 5.8).

The walking surfaces associated with the various facings were traceable several meters away from the mound. Sections through them revealed that pads of silt and soil separated the floors, representing either intentional or natural accumulations between refurbishings (Fig. 5.9). How much time elapsed between floor constructions is not known. The physical conditions described demonstrate that there was a purpose behind these changes, and the lack of circuit uniformity of the floorings and facings must be explained in the same terms.

Associated with the last surface, 8, after Mound 16 had lost its truncated cone character, holes spaced about 0.5 m apart were dug circumferentially around the mound, located an average of 1 m out from the old mound faces (Fig. 5.5, 5.6, & 5.12). If posts were set in these, a plausible inference, the effect would have been that of a palisade. There were just enough interruptions in the ring of holes, the largest gap being on the north, to make impossible the identification of an opening that may have existed to provide entryway to the mound. A few miscellaneous holes in the area of the mound, probably postholes, were recorded, but not enough were located to suggest any plan, if one ever existed. The absence of postholes on the mound itself tends to rule out the possibility that the palisade was the side of a building that completely covered the mound. Note should be made of a large hearth that occurred on surface 8, outside of the palisade on the southeast side. Weathering and rodent activity have largely destroyed the nature of the mound's flat top. A small patch of hard floor, less than a square meter in extent, with flat-lying sherds on it, may represent the level of the original surface. This was capped with a thin (5 to 10 cm) layer of reddish adobe, a remnant of what probably was the last surface treatment given the mound. Slender lenses of wood ash were noted on the mound, but no formal hearths were encountered.

On the north side of Mound 16 a set-back in the middle part of the sloping face appears to have served as a step. It extended about 6 m along the face feathering out at the ends, where it was lost in the uniform slant of the mound's edge. The intentional nature of this feature is revealed by the section cut through it (Fig. 5.10) in which the manner of applying and shaping the adobe on the soft core material is clearly visible. Hints of a step on the west and southwest segments of the face were detected, but the feature could not be developed with certainty.

No effort at ornamentation by modeling the plastic adobe was seen. A trace of red pigment occurred on the floor associated with the second facing on the east northeast side of the mound, but it was so limited that the intentional painting of surfaces cannot be claimed.

Figures 5.11 (top) and 5.12 show Mound 16 after exploratory trenches through it were filled but before the facings on the east

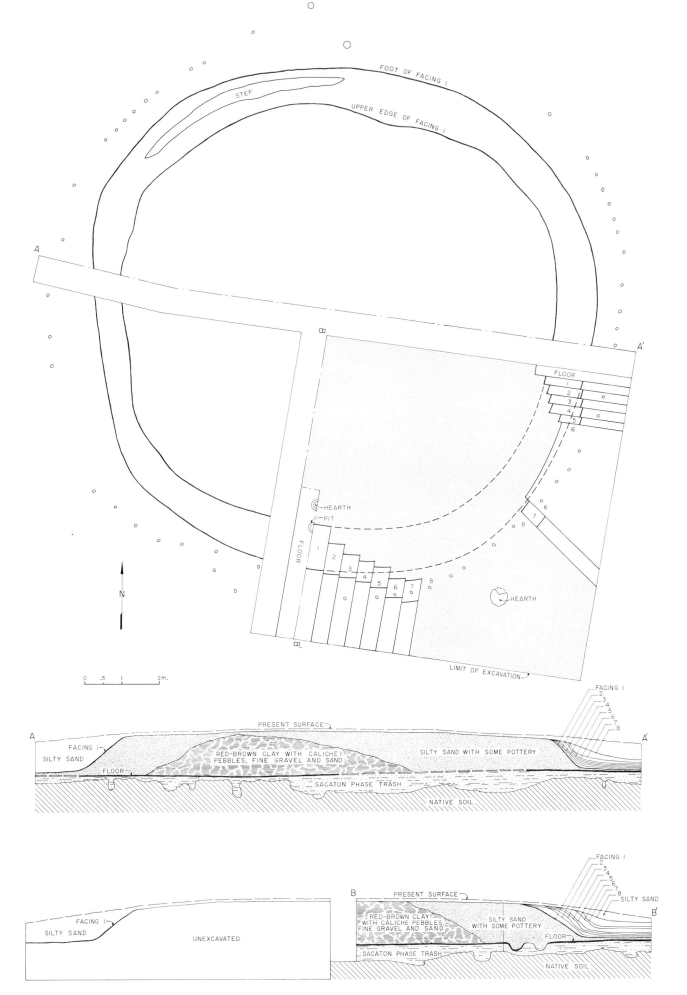

Fig. 5.5. Plan and sections of Mound 16, an artificial platform. Stippled south-east quadrant represents surface 8, the terminal stage of the mound, on which there was a hearth and the presumed palisade. Facings exposed on east side have been transposed to A-A' profile for reasons of clarity. Also see Figures 5.6 and 5.7.

Fig. 5.6. Mound 16: Sectional staggered view of increments 1 through 8, resting on the subfloor east side of mound. Arc of holes represents probable position of palisade associated with surface 8.

Fig. 5.7. Mound 16: Surfaces and related floors as exposed on the south side. Numbers match those in Figure 5.6.

Fig. 5.8. Mound 16: The mound as it must have appeared when last used. Surfaces 5 through 8 are visible, lying outside of the face of the mound. Note that holes for (?) posts appeared on surface 8.

side were traced. Ignoring the exposed sequential facings on the southern margin, the overall impression of the mound is probably close to what one might have seen in the later stages of its use.

At the conclusion of the work, the sloping faces, the walking surfaces, and the major part of the mound's top were covered with plastic sheeting and finally a layer of dirt up to 0.25 m thick. An effort was made to restore the contours of the mound as we found them and to provide the maximum protection for the fragile features below. Hopefully, the precaution of the plastic film will make the uncovering of the mound at some future time far easier than was our task. The smallness of Mound 16 makes it manageable as an exhibit under a roof.

House Relationships. Although some stripping up to 5 m away from the mound was done to detect possible related features, consistent distant testing was not done. The principal architectural features on the south, west, and north sides were probably exposed, but the east side was not explored. The houses closest to the mound were those to the south and north (Figs. 1.6 and 5.11 bottom), but some, as for example, Houses 7, 8, and 9:5G, were older than the mound. Houses 11 and 14:5G, on the south and north sides respectively, were apparently contemporary with the mound. The floor of the former was lowered through some of the laminated surfaces, related to the mound and it must, therefore, have been built toward the end of Mound 16's use. That a house should have been built so close to it, literally on its flanks, is surprising, and it may denote a fading of the mound's function.

House 14 was judged to be contemporary with the initial construction of the mound as the walking surface associated with the first facing lipped against the house edge. By form, placement in relation to Mound 16, pottery content, and nature of floor material, both houses were clearly datable to the Sacaton Phase.

I see no basis in the data at hand to think of the mound's use as being limited to special social or religious units within the community. It is worth noting that the nearest trash mounds were more than 60 m away from Mound 16. This detachment is interesting in the light of the dependence upon trash mounds earlier in Hohokam history to provide the elevations demanded by their doctrine.

Dating. The various ways for dating Mound 16 are: (1) evaluating age of premound events, (2) noting the contents of the mound, ceramics and otherwise, (3) the age of the litter on the various walking surfaces, and (4) the relationship of the mound to houses that have been assigned to phases. Where mixtures occur, or where pottery of different ages is directly associated, only the most recent material has any real dating value. In each of the above categories, Sacaton Phase ceramics are the latest present and, in fact, the only cultural remains with reliable time value. The conclusion is inescapable that Mound 16 dates from the terminal period of Snaketown's life, the Sacaton Phase, and that its construction, remodelings, and use were limited to this phase. The Gatlin mound near Gila Bend (Wasley 1960) was determined to be of the same age.

Fig. 5.9. Mound 16. Exposed section on east side of mound showing the floor under the mound and surfaces 1, 2, 3, and 5. The thickness and different character of the surfacings are readily seen in the vertical section. Surface 4 is indistinct here.

Fig. 5.10. Mound 16: The configuration of the step on the north side is here shown by the contrast between the applied adobe (coarse layer with white inclusions) and the more homogeneous and softer core of the mound.

Fig. 5.11. Mound 16: *(Top)* As seen from the southwest. The facing here was irregular, probably due to erosion and to little or no repair work. *(Bottom)* As seen from the south showing relationship with Houses 7, 8, and 9:5G, left to right.

Fig. 5.12. Mound 16: Aerial view from the north. The step is clearly visible as is the circular arrangement of presumed postholes. The east facings and related surfaces were not yet exposed when picture was taken.

DISCUSSION

On the basis of the various surfaced mounds at Snaketown and the Gatlin Site, we may conclude that the concept of artificial platforms, built purposefully and with design above the then extant ground level, did not become formalized among the Hohokam until the Sedentary Period. It was preceded, however, by a period of some centuries, beginning probably as early as A.D. 500, when the need for elevated platforms was met by covering existing trash mounds with a layer of adobe that would compact and provide a durable surface underfoot. Unsurfaced trash mounds, because of the ashy nature of the matrix, would have been quickly made useless as dance platforms by choking clouds of dust. That refuse mounds were surfaced to solve the dust problem is a logical assumption. Mound 16 represents a refinement of the platform concept because it did not incorporate a preexisting elevation of a radically different material.

An alternative explanation for the occurrence of caliche-clay surfaces on trash is that mounds of this material were occasionally covered with fresh dirt to seal in their foulness as a sanitation-control measure. However, most of the mounds tested, even though of dense trash, revealed no such layers. Furthermore, the shifting of the geographical center of the mound, as in Mound 39, and the nature of Mound 16 would not be explained by the suggested alternative. This idea may be abandoned.

Figure 5.13 illustrates in synoptic form the sequence of prepared surfaces and platforms as identified at Snaketown. Historically the progression was from the simple to the more developed, from a rudimentary state, Mound 40, to a finished structure, Mound 16. The former could not have been identified as a part of the chain without the intermediate and latest units. To state this in another way, Mound 16 leaves no doubt in the mind about its total artificiality. Although principally composed of trash, Mound 39 with its three stages of capping is also convincing proof of de-

signed behavior. The probable existence of a surface in Mound 38 would not have been detected at all without Mounds 39 and 16, and the prepared surface in Mound 40 would not have been acceptable as a prototype expression of the idea without Mounds 39 and 16 either. In short, all examples of the phenomenon begin to cohere in a way which makes for a logical explanation.

The platform idea at Snaketown seems to have spanned at least 600 years, from before A.D. 500 to 1100. If we think of this feature as a Mesoamerican inspired trait, and I see no persuasive alternative to this, there is nothing incongruous in so early an appearance of the feature among the Hohokam which, in fact, was late when compared with the first millennium B.C. spread of temple mounds into the Southeastern United States (Wicke 1965). Truncated pyramids and cones had already been long established among the high cultures of Mexico before the platform concept diffused northward. At a more specific level of comparison, the idea that an elevation was a proper place for ritual practices, phased construction, the use of a step or steps, and modification of the form of the mound by shifting the geographical center, possibly in respose to a concept related to calendrical cycles, are explicit reminders of southern ties.

Cuicuilco, a late Pre-Classic truncated cone of monumental proportions (Cummings 1933) and dated to the centuries immediately before the time of Christ (Jiménez Moreno 1959:1042), establishes an architectural baseline for round flat-topped structures. However, more than a thousand years separate it from Mound 16, to say nothing of size, material, and cultural differences. Flat-topped cones or squat cylindrical buildings are known in later sites, and Meighan informs me that some ruins in western Mexico have mounds that resemble Snaketown's Mound 16. Unfortunately, no detailed reports about them are available.

The two presently known totally artificial Hohokam mounds of the Sedentary Period, Mound 16 at Snaketown and the Gatlin Site structure, bear little resemblance to each other. The latter was nearly rectangular in plan and had several ancillary and connected structures, while the former was a truncated cone without satellite units. However, the two share earth construction with adobe facings, sloping sides, flat and largely featureless tops, and frequent remodelings. The palisade was not seen in the Gatlin mound. Functionally, there was probably little difference between the two.

The religious fervor that inspired the construction of these mounds evidently faded after the Sedentary Period, resulting in less frequent construction of them. Las Colinas was an apparent later surviving example (Hammack 1969). They may, however, have been transformed into something else, whose nature has not yet been clearly identified. The Classic Period is characterized architecturally by massive mounds with house remains on top of them. Pueblo Grande and Mesa Grande in the Salt River valley, Compound B at Casa Grande, and the Adamsville site in the Gila valley, and the University Indian Ruin in the Santa Cruz valley, testify to the widespread occurrence of the feature. House overbuilding apparently increased with time (Schroeder 1953:190), suggesting an expanding secularization of mounds if those under discussion were originally inspired by the older nonsecular platforms. A similar trend may be represented in Pottery Mound, New Mexico (Hibben 1966). More than 85 years after Cushing started his landmark excavations in Los Muertos we still suffer from a scarcity of extensive and systematic explorations in the villages of the Classic Period as a basis for testing continuities of some of the earlier Hohokam traits, platform mounds among them, into more recent times. Doyel's work (1974) in the Escalante Ruin is a step in this direction.

Russell notes (1908:205) that historically the Pima Indians held dances on low rounded natural mounds. Two such hills he mentioned, one near the railroad siding at Sacaton and the other near Gila (Double) Butte, 5 km (3 mi) east of Snaketown and adjacent to a Hohokam site excavated by Johnson (1964: Fig. 5). This

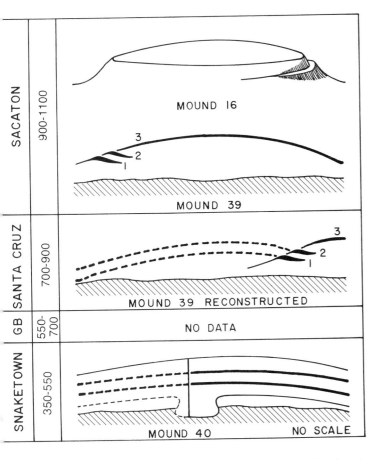

Fig. 5.13. Synoptic chart giving known changes in form of surfaced platform mounds.

recent Pima practice may be a faint reminder of earlier and better-established habits of mound building.

During its final stage, when the sloped facing which gave the mound definiteness was lost by overbuilding making a rounded hillock, Mound 16 was surrounded by what appears to have been a palisade of poles. With the loss of a clearly defined mound summit, the palisade may have represented a kind of containment for the area considered appropriate for ritual functions. While the comparisons with the present may have little meaning, nevertheless, it is worth noting that among the Pimas sacred places, some of which are said to be graves, were encircled with stones (Russell 1908: 255, Pl. XXXIX c). Johnson excavated one of these during the course of highway salvage operations near Gila Butte, but he failed to find the medicine man said to be buried there. The chances are that the places mentioned by Russell were no more than sacred spots or shrine areas. A closer parallel is the circle of ocotillo poles enclosing the children's shrine near the Papago village of Akchin (Chesky 1942:4-5). The idea of encirclement of sacred places may have old beginnings.

Finally, most mounds at Snaketown, and presumably those in other Hohokam sites as well, were the result of their tidy habits—the concentration and piling-up of refuse. A minority were inspired by ritual motives. None of the mounds tested were collapsed buildings, and it is doubtful if any of the mounds not tested were of this kind either. We must look to the Classic Period for the house, or architectural, mound.

The concentration of refuse in mounds started in about the middle part of the Pioneer Period. From the beginning of the period, however, and continuing throughout its span, the volume of trash in pits exceeded the amount of refuse collected in mounds, a generalization based upon observations rather than on quantified data. In the Colonial Period, the pendulum swung in the other direction. Mounded refuse far outstripped subsurface deposits by volume, a trend that became intensified in the Sedentary Period. Trash heaps attributable to the Sacaton Phase were the largest individually; there were more of them, and they were more widely spread than were the mounds of earlier phases. Snaketown reached its maximum territorial limits during the terminal phase of its life, just before the residence pattern changed from the ranchería type of settlement to the clustered houses of the Classic Period.

A question that can be raised but not answered at this time concerns the effect that the steady accumulation of wastes over so long a time had on the occupants of the village itself, particularly the influence of the great bulk of refuse present in the Sacaton Phase. Twenty-five of the 29 mounds tested showed significant fractions, or were wholly composed, of Sacaton Phase trash. If we extend this ratio to the 60 mounds recognized on the site, then close to 80% of the mounds were active refuse collecting spots in the final decades of the village's life. Certainly in our terms, and possibly also in those of the Hohokam, this situation would have posed a major threat to the environment and to community health. The apparent population increase, and a likely related increase in the per capita production of trash, could have resulted in an insidious and detrimental condition with which they could not cope. Instead of choking on it and being engulfed by their own wastes, they may have paid the price by moving away.

PART THREE

THE STRATIGRAPHIC RECORD

6. Methods, Tests, and Results

To this point in the presentation of the data from Snaketown, the existence of a chronology, of a phase sequence, has been taken for granted. The structure and the order of a changing culture used is the one published earlier (Gladwin and others 1937). Since the temporal placement of the artifactual and other remains discussed hereafter will continue to be dependent on the same system of classification, it seems imperative at this time to review the stratigraphic record as determined in 1964–65. Several troublesome problems related to analytical procedures are discussed elsewhere (pp. 197ff), and these should be understood before final judgment is passed on the findings that follow. As will be seen, the information gained in the new investigations calls for no major overhauling of the 1937 time system.

Many simple acts performed by the Hohokam, such as throwing out a basketful of refuse, digging for clay, or enshrining the bones of a deceased relative, left some record of the event in a way which often permits relating it in time to the traces of other events. Similarly, the larger activities shared by a number of people, for example, house building, canal excavation, and platform mound construction, also were performed in a time-relationship to other acts whose traces were already on hand. One of the main goals of the archaeologist is to arrange these events in a chronological system as the necessary prelude to most other kinds of studies.

There are several processes by which the time ordering of events may be achieved. These range in the degree of accuracy from gross relative arrangements, in which the time factor is unknown, to methods that not only order but provide a reasonably accurate basis for estimating the number of elapsed years between events and where these stand in relation to the Christian calendar. The dating methods based on year counts are reviewed in another section. For the present we will look only at the stratigraphic record.

Happily, Snaketown lends itself admirably to the application of the stratigraphic technique of excavation because of its long occupancy. Deep refuse deposits presuppose the passage of time, hopefully enough so that the fragmented contents of the various layers will reflect some changes in cultural modes and styles. Evidence for the realignment of canal systems, refurbishing of platform mounds, the building of house floors over older ones and over pre-existing pits, and the intrusions of pits and cremations into features already there, are present in abundance. The duplication of stratigraphic relationships provides the kind of verification that helps to rule out the strange and aberrant circumstance; instead they lead to the conviction that the implied order is indeed correct.

It is not necessary to dig much in the refuse or in houses of different ages to realize quickly that the shreds of evidence of the times differ. Since most of these tattered remnants are potsherds, the burden of the first ordering of a chronological scheme rests upon them. This means initially the establishment of types, made possible by the assumption that there was a slow and continuing stylistic change; second, the arrangement of types in a sequential order by applying the principle of stratigraphy mentioned above; and third, on the basis of other cultural attributes, such as houses, stone, bone, and shell artifacts associated with specific pottery types, to round-out our understanding of how the society is to be characterized at different times. These simple rules governed the initial work at Snaketown. They were spelled out in 1937 (Gladwin and others:19-22), and I see no reason to depart from them now.

The Hohokam pottery chronology stands, I believe, as one of the finest demonstrations of ceramic typology in all of the Southwest. The reasons for this lie in the simple facts that numerous readily identifiable attributes were responsive to change, that the changes came in an orderly fashion, and that the time factor was a long one, more than a millennium. Further, the mass of the material was also an asset because the typing process applied to smaller samples would have yielded less convincing results. Tens of thousands of potsherds from the same source speak more eloquently than do hundreds.

METHODS OF TESTING

Some 40 controlled stratigraphic tests in trash, mounded or in pits, were made. The aggregate potsherd yield was over 500,000 units. The tests varied in level thickness from 0.25 to 0.5 m, depending on such factors as depth of deposit, richness of ceramic content, and the nature of the suspected changes. The size of the area tested was also variable, determined by the diameter of the pit, if small, or by practical logistical reasons if the deposit was essentially limitless, as in a mound. Deep sheet trash was tested in blocks 2 x 0.5 x 0.5 m when a long continuous profile was desired (Fig. 6.1). Column testing, as in Mound 39, was on a 2 m square plan if conditions permitted. We did not believe that limiting the sampling procedures to comparable volumes of trash was necessary, considering the ends we had in mind.

The refuse in all controlled tests was passed through a mechanically driven screen with a mesh size of ½ inch. Basic sorting of pottery, shell, bone, and fractured stone was done on the spot as the cultural remnants rolled off the end of the screen. Periodically, microsampling was done as described elsewhere. The potsherd yield per cubic meter of trash varied from about 2,000 to 8,000 units. In most cases these were weighed by type rather than counted, thereby saving much time. The results of weighing and counting, in test cases, have proven to be essentially comparable (Johnson, personal communication), although arguments have been made that using both methods of quantifying yields more information than does either one by itself (Solheim 1960).

When features were not involved in the testing, as for example, house floors, arbitrary levels were used as a matter of expediency even though some grain was evident in the matrix. Mound 29

Fig. 6.1. Stratigraphic testing in deep sheet trash, using the continuous sectional method.

TESTS
Mound 39

Because of its size, Mound 39 held prospects for producing a long stratigraphic record. Also its nearness to the deep disturbances toward the northwest, resulting from digging for water, suggested that features below the mound might be anticipated. Accordingly, three test areas, each 2 m square, were laid out on an east-west line across the short dimension of the mound. The central test, Column 2, on the crest of the mound, was flanked to the west 6 m by Column 1 and to the east 6 m by Column 3 (Fig. 6.4). Expected depths up to 4 m demanded that a continuous trench be cut through the mound on the axis of the tests as a safety measure against cave-ins of the soft trash. Partial burial of a workman in the 1934–35 operation had taught us the need for this precaution. The trench was machine-dug, and its floor proceeded downward as the tests were deepened (Figs. 6.2a,b,c). By the time sterile soil was reached in the test areas and the trench was completed, we had an excellent opportunity to explore for sub-mound features (Fig. 6.2d) and to examine the mound faces in detail. This rewarded us with information about the mound's use as a platform. Also, being able to examine the structure of the mound in a continuous profile provided the basis for determining how the mound grew, and this, in turn, made clearer our understanding of the tests.

Approximately 40 m^3 of refuse were screened in the three tests. The pottery yield aggregated some 780 kg, of which about 33% (250 kg) was decorated. Expressed in another way, the sample amounted to roughly 100,000 sherds, of which about 33,000 were painted and therefore readily typable. This part of the sample constituted the prime means of establishing the history of the mound in relation to the span of the village's life. Pollen samples were taken from nearly all stratigraphic units, but the results were negative because the conditions within the mound were not favorable to pollen preservation. Fine-screen samples, taken from about half of the test levels, gave helpful data about plant and animal remains.

The results of the quantitative analysis of pottery from Mound 39 are given in Figure 6.3, *a* being the numerical tabulation and *b* the graphical presentation of the values. The main points to be noted are: (1) The order of pottery types is comparable in all tests. (2) There are no sharp-line transitions from one type to the antecedent ones, suggesting the mound grew by gradual accretion and that stylistic changes in pottery were smooth and orderly. (3) No single level produced only one type of pottery, but in most cases, dominances were sharply emphasized. (4) The mixture of types in any one level is partly the result of the arbitrary testing system and partly the product of other factors, such as the migration of sherds up or down. Worth noting is the fact that more early types were present in late trash than were late sherds in early contexts, a possible reflection of the upward movement of trash by rodents. (5) The inter-column comparison reveals that the oldest part of the mound was tapped by Column 1 on the west side, a fact supported by the physical structure of the mound as well.

This brings us now to a recapitulation of Mound 39's history; reference to Figures 5.2 a and b, 5.3, and 6.4 will be of assistance in understanding what happened. The area occupied by the mound was first covered with sheet trash of Pioneer Period age exhibiting a mixture of types of different phases, as revealed in the bottom level of all tests. Then the mound began to grow, the core being somewhere to the west of Column 1 as indicated by the inclination of the refuse strata. In succession, the events were: laying down capping layer 1; covering same with a layer of unstructured refuse; adding capping layer 2; destroying the mound except the eastern edge and shifting the center of the mound to the east; and, finally, adding capping layer 3.

amply demonstrated that changes in pottery types tended to take place over larger rather than smaller distances, whether horizontal or vertical (Gladwin and others 1937:25). To state this in another way, the volume of trash discarded by the Hohokam was so large that stylistic changes in the contained cultural materials were, in most cases, detectable by comparing specimens meters rather than centimeters apart. Where obvious features appeared, as superimposed house floors or the several levels of a platform mound, these phenomena were used, of course, as the basis for separating samples.

An inventory of all stratigraphic situations shows that about 100 instances were studied, ranging from simple cases of house floor on house floor, to long sequences representing the interrelationships of pits, houses, cremations, and refuse. It is clearly impractical to itemize all of these circumstances in detail. Key stations will, however, be examined closely, for it is upon these that the main burden of chronology-building must rest.

The selection of places to test was made in two ways. First, visually, guided either by such physical properties as the apparent depth of a trash mound, thereby forecasting a possibly long record, or, the concentration in an area of potsherds of a particular phase which needed further study. Also, subtle topographic changes not readily attributable to natural causes were selected for further investigation. Second, and most often, stratigraphic situations were revealed in the course of systematic testing which were not detectable by surface indications. Long backhoe trenches were particularly helpful in exposing profiles that required follow-up work. In a site like Snaketown, I consider this opportunistic approach to the selection of test sites to be more valid and productive than following the prescriptions of an artificial sampling technique.

Fig. 6.2. Stratigraphic testing of Mound 39. (a) Column 1, staked out, being prepared for strata removal by providing machine-dug access trench from side. (b) Beginning removal of top layer of Column 2. (c) Columns 1 and 3 have been completed. Basal levels of Column 2 protected with plastic sheeting during removal of adjacent refuse. (d) Hand-trenching below base of mound for premound features.

The main mass of the material in the new mound was unstructured, an indication of moved or intensively disturbed trash (Fig. 6.4). What we are concerned with now is where this material came from. Levels 1 to 5 in Columns 2 and 3 show Santa Cruz and Sacaton Red-on-buff mixtures, but deeper levels retain hints of a sequential relationship. If all of the bulk of the transferred mound came from the earlier one, we would expect a dominance of Santa Cruz Red-on-buff in the upper levels of Columns 2 and 3. But the presence of Sacaton Red-on-buff indicates the probability that trash of that phase was introduced from other mounds or as currently accumulated refuse and that a mixture resulted. The relatively "pure" Santa Cruz Phase trash in Column 2, Level 5, and Column 3, Level 4, suggests that the original mound extended well to the east. Using the youngest pottery in the unstructured trash as a guide, we can say that the rebuilding of Mound 39

took place during the Sacaton Phase, or between A.D. 900 and 1100. The painted pottery recovered from the thin veneer of refuse on top of capping layer 3 was 98% Sacaton Red-on-buff.

Although Vahki Phase remains were not detected in this series of tests, and the Estrella, Sweetwater, and Gila Butte Phase materials were less abundant than might have been desired, the results nevertheless come nearer than any other tests made in 1964–65 in demonstrating the full Snaketown sequence in one mound.

In Figure 6.3a, the pottery foreign to Snaketown, appearing as intruded elements in the trash of Mound 39, has also been tabulated. Hohokam phase equivalents of the trade pieces can quickly be established by reference to the level and phase identifications given in Figure 6.4. These samples have been incorporated in the over-all study of intrusive types reviewed later.

Columns	Levels	Painted Pottery by Period and Phase: Sedentary — Sacaton — Sacaton Red-on-buff		Colonial — Santa Cruz — Santa Cruz Red-on-buff		Colonial — Gila Butte — Gila Butte Red-on-buff		Pioneer — Snaketown — Snaketown Red-on-buff		Pioneer — Sweetwater — Sweetwater Red-on-grey		Pioneer — Estrella — Estrella Red-on-grey		Totals		Plainware Totals		Foreign Pottery: Kana-a Black-on-white	Deadman's Black-on-red	San Lorenzo Red-on-brown	Mimbres Bold Face Black-on-white	San Francisco Red	Reserve Smudged	Alma Plain	Rillito Red-on-brown	Rincon Red-on-brown	Unidentified Redware	Unidentified Black-on-red
		Kilograms	Percent	Kilograms	Percent	Kilograms	Percent	Kilograms	Percent	Kilograms	Percent	Kilograms	Percent	Kilograms	Percent	Kilograms	Percent											
1	1	.185	2.15	8.310	96.57	.055	.64	.045	.52	.010	.12			8.605	13.98	25.855	15.60	1			1						1	
	2			12.075	98.89	.100	.82	.030	.25	.005	.04			12.210	19.84	30.605	18.47											
	3			15.380	95.03	.680	4.20	.115	.71	.010	.06			16.185	26.29	42.680	25.75				1	1	2					
	4			3.930	40.29	5.460	55.97	.365	3.74					9.755	15.85	26.265	15.85	1				1					1	
	5			.010	.10	1.555	15.61	8.380	84.14	.015	.15			9.960	16.18	17.790	10.73											
	6							4.155	93.79	.245	5.53	.030	.68	4.430	7.20	16.615	10.03					3						
	7									.245	60.49	.160	39.51	.405	.66	5.910	3.57											
TOTALS		.185	.30	39.705	64.51	7.850	12.75	13.090	21.27	.530	.86	.190	.31	61.550	100.00	165.720	100.00	2			2	5	2				2	
2	1	6.405	75.22	1.955	22.96	.085	.99	.055	.65	.015	.18			8.515	8.48	18.160	8.69											
	2	11.815	84.15	2.155	15.35	.050	.36	.020	.14					14.040	13.97	20.625	9.87				2	1				1		1
	3	3.035	14.72	17.475	84.77	.065	.32	.015	.07	.025	.12			20.615	20.52	30.795	14.73											
	4	7.800	31.51	16.785	67.82	.165	.67							24.750	24.63	48.145	23.03		2			2	2				1	
	5	1.205	6.60	16.290	90.00	.805	4.40							18.300	18.22	31.270	14.96					2			1	1		
	6			.415	5.20	5.950	74.61	1.460	18.31	.110	1.38	.040	.50	7.975	7.94	25.995	12.43										1	
	7					.075	1.26	5.495	92.35	.380	6.39			5.950	5.92	31.535	15.08					1						
	8							.275	84.62	.030	9.23	.020	6.15	.325	.32	2.530	1.21					1						
TOTALS		30.265	30.12	55.070	54.81	7.195	7.16	7.320	7.29	.560	.56	.060	.06	100.470	100.00	209.055	100.00		2		2	7	2		1	2	2	1
3	1	9.820	99.55	.020	.20	.025	.25							9.865	11.22	19.140	12.32					5					1	
	2	22.310	99.07	.175	.78	.035	.15							22.520	25.61	24.015	15.46	2			1	1						
	3	10.740	62.05	6.485	37.46	.055	.32	.030	.17					17.310	19.69	29.020	18.68					2				1		
	4	1.090	7.60	13.070	91.15	.135	.94	.045	.31					14.340	16.31	21.595	13.90					3						
	5	.465	2.70	13.625	79.15	2.885	16.76	.215	1.25	.025	.14			17.215	19.58	33.440	21.53						1					
	6			.025	.41	.875	14.29	4.750	77.55	.445	7.26	.030	.49	6.125	6.97	25.200	16.22					2		1			1	
	7					.065	11.82	.445	80.91	.030	5.45	.010	1.82	.550	.62	2.925	1.89			1								
TOTALS		44.425	50.53	33.400	37.99	4.075	4.63	5.485	6.24	.500	.57	.040	.04	87.925	100.00	155.335	100.00	2		1	1	13	1	1		1	2	

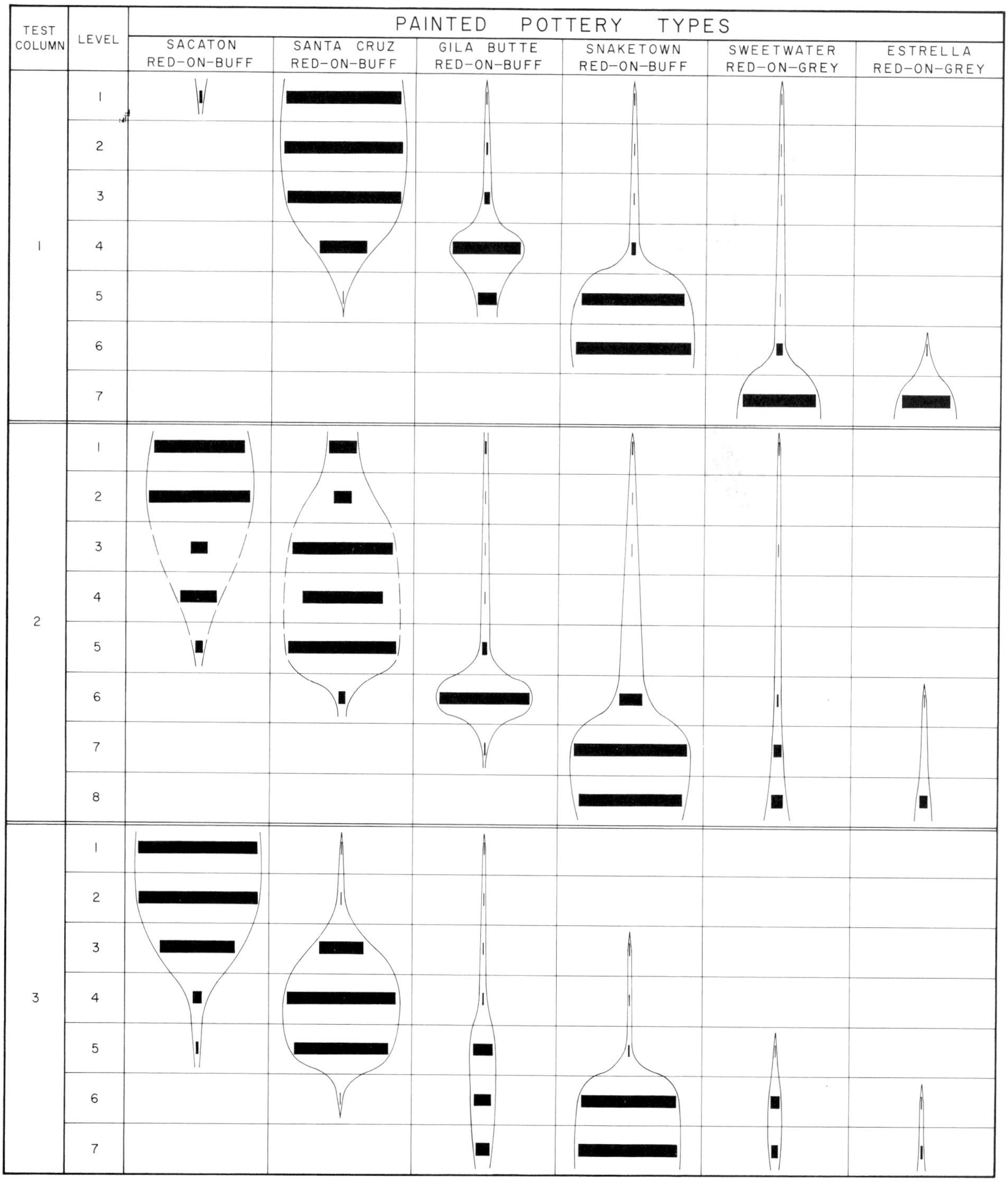

PERCENTAGE SCALE FOR GRAPH BARS 0 25 50 75 100

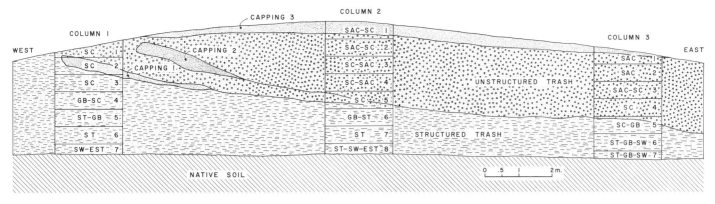

Fig. 6.4. Section through Mound 39 showing its basic structure, capping layers and the location of test columns. Abbreviations in levels stand for pottery type dominances in the order given.

Mound 40

A small test was put into Mound 40 (Block 11F) in 1934–35, which produced Colonial and Pioneer Period pottery types. Further probing was considered worthwhile because the volume of the mound promised to supply adequate pottery samples from consecutive layers to illustrate more sharply than we had seen up to then the nuances in the transition of styles separating Snaketown and Gila Butte Red-on-buffs. It was on this borderline that the taxonomic division between the Pioneer and the Colonial Periods was based. Further, it was believed that more extensive testing might reveal the reasons for mixtures of early Pioneer pottery types in some of the later samples. In this we were not disappointed, for early premound pits, a large roasting pit, and the initial examples of mound capping as a step in making platforms, came to light (Fig. 5.1).

A number of adjacent 2 x 2 m tiers of tests were made, exposing a considerable portion of the mound and pits below it. The area involved early in the effort is shown in Figure 6.5 with screening of the refuse in progress. Approximately 125 m³ of material were removed, half of it screened. The pottery sample resulting from the closely controlled tests amounted to 507 kg, or nearly 100,000 units.

We need to concern ourselves with only one of the tests made, Tier 9/26, because it best illustrates the time span of the mound. Test levels were made at 0.25 m intervals instead of the usual 0.5 m depth, a circumstance which led to a more refined analysis of the deep trash than was usual. This test came within the boundaries of Pit 41, thereby providing information on a premound feature and stratigraphic data drawn from a trash depth of 3.25 m. The location of the test with respect to the pit is given in Figure 6.6. The aggregate weight of the pottery recovered was over 75 kg, representing about 1,400 sherds. Type frequencies are tabulated in Figure 6.7.

Proceeding from the surface downward, the youngest trash in Level 1 was predominantly of Gila Butte Phase age; mixed Gila Butte-Snaketown Phase trash was represented in Levels 2 and 3; and Snaketown Phase pottery predominated in Levels 4 and 5. The sample from Level 6 was small because a part of the mass was the lower platform surfacing, but the pottery present was mainly Snaketown Red-on-buff; Levels 7 and 8 were dominantly Sweetwater Phase; Levels 9 to 13 revealed only a trace of painted

pottery, the most consistent type being Sweetwater Red-on-gray. The contrast in amounts of this type between Levels 7 and 8 and those below, suggests a probable downward drifting of Sweetwater Red-on-gray by rodent action (Fig. 12.9) to become mixed with what most likely was refuse of the Vahki Phase. Plainware was not differentiated in the analysis, but the difficult-to-establish transition from Vahki Plain to Gila Plain came at about the level of the first mound capping. Vahki Red, the only redware present occurred in minuscule amounts, mainly in the deeper levels, a fair reflection of its earliness and the minor role redware played in the ceramic tradition.

In Figure 6.6, the main events recognized in this part of Mound 40 are schematically summarized: I, the digging of Pit 41, probably during the Vahki Phase, and its filling with presumed Vahki Phase trash, topped later with refuse of the Sweetwater Phase, restoring the ground surface to near its original level; II, the digging of Pit 1, a large roasting pit which, after heavy use, became filled with Sweetwater refuse indicating that it dated from that phase or earlier; III, excavation of Pit 2, a large rambling hole, heavily burned, which became filled with trash of the Snaketown Phase. This fact and the physical relationship of Pit 2

Fig. 6.3. Analysis of pottery from stratigraphic tests in Mound 39. (top) Quantitative tabulation. Redwares were not included because the aggregate weight of Vahki Red and Sacaton Red was only 0.140 kg. (below) Bar diagrams of types by level, revealing both vertical transitions in dominances and type mixtures horizontally.

Fig. 6.5. Testing in the stratified trash of Mound 40.

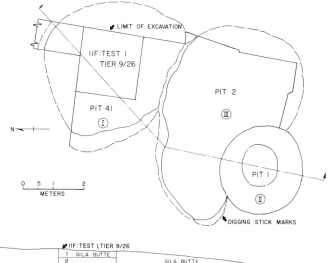

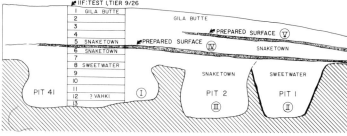

Fig. 6.6. Section through a part of Mound 40 showing the relationships between premound pits, capping layers, trash, and the location of Test 1:11F, Tier 9/26.

to Pit 1 place both the digging and the use of Pit 2 in the Snaketown Phase. Waste material of this time continued to accumulate to the north and east of Pit 2, representing the beginning of the formation of Mound 40. Event IV was the application of a caliche-clay mixture to provide a hard surface on the soft refuse of a low profile mound. This came at the juncture of Levels 5 and 6 in the stratigraphic test labeled Tier 9/26. Then came the accumulation of Snaketown Phase trash on top of the capping which was covered in turn by introduced surfacing material, shown as event V. Finally, further accretions of trash in the Gila Butte Phase terminated the mound's growth.

While only three certain phases, Gila Butte, Snaketown, and Sweetwater, and a probable fourth, the Vahki Phase, are represented in this sequence, the variety of phenomena involved adds substantially to the clarity of the succession of changes noted in the cultural remnants. The results of tests labeled Tiers 1, 2, 4 and 12, based on 430 kg of pottery, consistently confirmed the Gila Butte, Snaketown, Sweetwater sequence.

Although houses dating from the Santa Cruz and Sacaton Phases were situated near Mound 40, trash of those times was not dumped on the mound. This provides us with a hint that factors other than convenience determined where refuse was thrown. One wonders whether or not an ancient oral tradition that Mound 40 once was used ceremonially could have discouraged the discarding of garbage upon it. The people of the Snaketown and Gila Butte Phases, particularly the latter, felt no such restrictions, however, for they dumped nearly a meter of refuse on the upper prepared mound surface.

Houses 1 and 2:6G and Subfloor Trash

Neither of the two foregoing tests—Mound 39 and Mound 40—provided clear evidence of a Vahki Phase complex, identified in 1934–35 as a ceramic horizon free of painted pottery. One of several deposits that provided data for such a condition was a thick layer of rubbish resting under floors of Houses 1 and 2 in Block 6G (Fig. 3.17). Two controlled tests were made below

SOURCES	POTTERY TYPES						
LEVEL	GILA BUTTE RED-ON-BUFF	SNAKETOWN RED-ON-BUFF	SWEETWATER RED-ON-GRAY	ESTRELLA RED-ON-GRAY	VAHKI RED	PLAINWARE (NOT SEPARATED)	TOTAL
1	.785	.125				1.850	2.760
2	.940	.650				3.050	4.640
3	.575	1.310	.035			7.770	9.690
4	.275	2.040	.090		.005	7.525	9.935
5	.080	1.360	.165			7.115	8.720
----------LOWER PLATFORM SURFACE----------							
6	.115	.475			.010	4.750	5.350
7	.050	.075	.980	.020		9.315	10.440
8	.020	.040	.330	.015	.020	6.310	6.735
9			.090	.010	.035	2.610	2.745
10	.005	.005	.055		.060	2.810	2.935
11			.065		.075	3.950	4.090
12			.045	.005	.040	4.405	4.495
13			.045	.010	.020	3.160	3.235
TOTAL	2.845	6.080	1.900	.060	.265	64.620	75.770

Fig. 6.7. Pottery type frequencies in Mound 40, Test 1:11F, Tier 9/26 (in kilograms).

SOURCES	POTTERY TYPES									
LEVEL	SACATON RED-ON-BUFF	SANTA CRUZ RED-ON-BUFF	GILA BUTTE RED-ON-BUFF	SNAKETOWN RED-ON-BUFF	SWEETWATER RED-ON-GRAY	ESTRELLA RED-ON-GRAY	VAHKI RED	VAHKI PLAIN	GILA PLAIN	TOTAL
1	2.950	.005	.020	.005			.020		★	3.000
2	1.400	.040	.040	.020					★	1.500
--------------------HOUSE 1 FLOOR--------------------										
3	.100	1.800	.100						★	2.000
4	.050	6.900	.050						★	7.000
--------------------HOUSE 2 FLOOR--------------------										
1		.260			.005		.690	12.550		13.505
2		.055					.370	5.760		6.185
3		.025					.215	4.720		4.960
4		.010		.005			.315	4.545		4.875
5							.075	1.235		1.310
6		.005					.065	1.630		1.700
TOTAL	4.500	9.100	.210	.030	.005		1.750	30.440		46.035

★ = GILA PLAIN NOT SEPARATED

Fig. 6.8. Quantitative results of stratigraphic tests in fill of Houses 1 and 2:6G and in subfloor deposits. Upper levels 1 to 4 do not coincide geographically with Levels 1 to 6 in Tests 1 and 2; also the pottery sample was only roughly analyzed in upper levels, and values are estimates on painted types only. Figures in Levels 5 and 6 reflect presence of these levels in Test 2 only because of high native soil in Test 1. Values are in kilograms.

House 2, the overlying deposits not being included in the test area because the presence of the deeper trash was not known when the house floors were cleared. However, by stratigraphy, by house type and by pottery, the latter removed in 4 levels above the house floors, we may extend the record as given in Figure 6.8. On an adequate sample of about 4.5 kg of painted sherds (about 700) House 1 was of Sacaton Phase age; House 2, with a heavy concentration of Santa Cruz Red-on-buff in the fill and on the floor (9 kg, about 1,400 units) was Santa Cruz age or older. Then, picking up the test results, an abrupt change to dominantly plainware and redware was noted. Quantitatively Tests 1 and 2 were so comparable that the values have been combined, aggregating a sample total of 32.5 kg, or about 6,500 sherds. It is interesting to note here that Santa Cruz Red-on-buff which was heavily concentrated above the floor of House 2 contaminated the sample in reducing amounts in going down. Rodent tunnels were observed extending from above House 2 floor down to Level 6, and it may be presumed that the intrusions were attributable to this cause. Otherwise, except for single sherds of Sweetwater Red-on-gray and Snaketown Red-on-buff the sample was impressively unmixed, consisting of Vahki Plain and Vahki Red.

House 5:10F and Well No. 1

A deep deposit of trash under House 5:10F matches in most respects the circumstances described in the previous section. In clearing House 5 it was noted that soft refuse continued below the floor and that it extended beyond the floor limit in a westerly direction immediately south of the entry (Fig. 6.9). A trench probe along an east-west axis detected the rim of a pit about 2 m in diameter and 0.4 m below the floor line. As the workmen continued down, the pottery-rich deposit was separated into three gross levels as a way of determining whether or not closer controlled testing would be worthwhile. This was called Test 1. A quick analysis of nearly 16,000 sherds (57 kg) showed that we were dealing with a plainware-redware complex further characterized by pottery fragments of vessels with thin walls. The few painted sherds present were of Colonial and Sedentary Period vintages, considered to have drifted downward from the higher levels where these types were dominant.

Test 2, with five levels, was then made which yielded another 13,000 sherds (about 48 kg). Finally, to empty the pit, suspected by now of being a well (Fig. 6.10) because it penetrated deeply into a sand aquifer, Test 3 was made in three levels. This effort netted another 5,700 pottery fragments (22 kg), making a grand total of about 35,000 units from some 6 m³ of fill. The results of the analysis of the three samples are given in Figure 6.11.

The sherds coming from the fill and floor of House 5 were predominantly of Sacaton Phase age, and the architectural type places the structure in this phase as well. The subfloor accumulation of about 0.4 m in depth and resting on the native soil line was a layer of sheet trash of mixed Sacaton, Santa Cruz, and Gila Butte phases, though the values for painted pottery of all types were low. Once below the rim of the pit, that is, below Level 1 in all tests, the total number of painted sherds was further reduced, amounting to about 20 in a sample of more than 25,000 fragments of Vahki Red and Vahki Plain. These cannot be accepted as contemporary components of the redware-plainware complex, but instead, they must be considered to be downward intrusions from the later deposits above. The total absence of the earliest Pioneer Period painted and grooved pottery, hallmarks of the Estrella Phase, supports the idea that this accumulation dates from the initial, or close to the initial, stage of pottery production at Snaketown. According to the criteria developed in 1937 (Gladwin and others), the deposit is assignable to the Vahki Phase. Taken

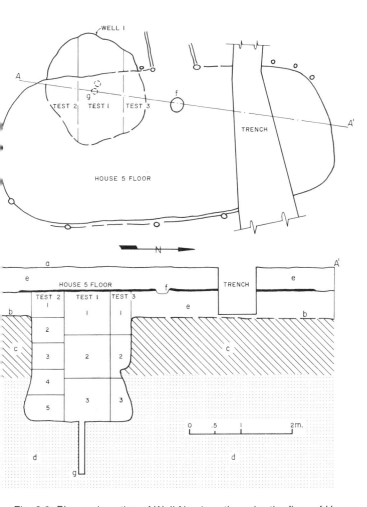

Fig. 6.9. Plan and section of Well No. 1 partly under the floor of House 5:10F, Sacaton Phase. Scheme of stratigraphic sampling is given in sectional view. (a) present surface; (b) surface from which well was dug; (c) silty-clay native soil; (d) sand and fine gravel; (e) mixed Santa Cruz-Sacaton Phase trash; (f) hearth in floor of House 5; (g) auger tests.

Fig. 6.10. Removing and screening the trash content of Well No. 1 under the floor of House 5:10F.

SOURCES		POTTERY TYPES								
TEST	LEVEL	SACATON RED-ON-BUFF	SANTA CRUZ RED-ON-BUFF	GILA BUTTE RED-ON-BUFF	SNAKETOWN RED-ON-BUFF	SWEETWATER RED-ON-GRAY	ESTRELLA RED-ON-GRAY	VAHKI RED	VAHKI PLAIN	TOTAL
1	1							1.700	28.940	30.640
	2							.685	8.260	8.945
	3							.325	17.050	17.375
2	1	.075	.175	.095	.010	.030		.600	3.860	4.845
	2		.050	.010		.015		.770	8.500	9.345
	3				.010		.005	.845	8.540	9.400
	4						.010	1.700	12.045	13.755
	5		.015					.510	9.960	10.485
3	1	.220	.025	.010				.170	4.500	4.925
	2		.015	.010				.220	6.460	6.705
	3							.190	10.100	10.290
TOTAL		.295	.280	.125	.020	.045	.015	7.715	118.215	126.710

Fig. 6.11. Pottery frequencies by weight (kg) from Tests 1, 2 and 3 in Well No. 1, under House 5:10F. Test 1 was not screened and late painted types were not analyzed but frequencies may be presumed to be proportional to results in Tests 2 and 3. Some Gila Plain was probably present in upper levels and counted as Vahki Plain.

with the subfloor samples under Houses 1 and 2 (6G), the evidence for this horizon is greatly strengthened. The typology is correct, as is the stratigraphic position, even though several phases are omitted.

An impressive detail shared by the samples derived from the two foregoing sources was the quantity of pottery that permeated the refuse. This high density, exceeding 5,000 fragments in a single cubic meter, was rarely equaled by pottery occurrences in refuse of other phases. While the circumstances of trash collection, within the confines of a pit or well, may have had some influence on pottery frequency, I think it to be more likely that this condition reflects a high level of pottery production in the initial stage of the village's life and that the history of the potter's art had progressed far down the road beyond the point of invention.

Well Area 10G

In the foregoing instances of superposition, we have seen examples of sequent pottery stages in a typologically smooth order, receding in time through the Sacaton, Santa Cruz, Gila Butte, Snaketown and Sweetwater phases. In Mound 39, indications of the Estrella Phase were noted, and in separate situations Vahki Phase residue was identified as occurring under much younger trash or houses. To strengthen the early relationships and particularly to establish the temporal position of material attributable to the Estrella Phase, we turn to a series of tests in the well area, Block 10G. How deep trash came to be in this locality is explained elsewhere. In all, 17 tests, most of them screened, were made as indicated in Figure 6.12. The recurrent excavations by the Hohokam to make walk-in wells inevitably led to some mixing of the accumulations, but useful data emerge nevertheless.

Five tests, Nos. 5, 6, 11, 15, and 17, have been selected as worthy of close inspection. The quantitative data are given in

Figure 6.13; profiles, where meaningful, are shown in Figures 9.2 and 9.3.

Tests 5 and 6 were adjacent to each other and can be regarded essentially as one. Test levels were arbitrary in part, but where marked physical differences were discernible, the natural strata were followed. It is evident that the matrix consisted of dumped refuse interspersed with silts and sands derived from well excavations and surface wash. Level 1 began 0.25 m below the natural surface because this layer had been stripped in recovering rodent dispersed pieces of the sculptured stone in Cache 1:10G and before the depth of the stratified deposit was determined. The mixture of pottery of all phases in Levels 1 and 2 probably existed in the stripped layer as well, and we may assume that little information was lost.

Test 5 cut into the northeast corner of House 13 (Fig. 6.14) of Sacaton Phase age, which means that Level 2 and those below were pre-Sacaton, a state borne out by the analysis. An interesting sidelight on this situation was the discovery that House 13 was originally dug in 1934–35 (House 5:10G). This became evident only when the structure was plotted on the base map of the site.

The value of Tests 5 and 6 is in the fact that Estrella Red-on-gray was the dominant painted pottery in Levels 3 to 6, resting below Sweetwater Red-on-gray. While some downward intrusion of late pottery is seen, these amount to tiny fractions of the total pottery yield, some 30,000 pieces (154 kg).

Tests 1, 2, 3, and 4, immediately to the east of Tests 5 and 6, parallel the results of the latter in an aggregate sample of about 62,000 potsherds (about 270 kg). This at least demonstrates some lateral as well as vertical uniformity so that the probability of a false stratigraphic situation is minimized. The sequence manifested in the physical nature of the deposits and the nuances in the art styles between Estrella and Sweetwater Red-on-gray convincingly support the existence of a lineal development between the two types.

Test 11, located about 3 m south of Test 5, is included because the upper levels show a somewhat higher incidence of later pottery types than did the others, albeit the samples are mixed. Level 1 produced a few pieces of glass derived from Pima refuse associated with a house that was still inhabited near the test area in 1935. The apparent inversion of Gila Butte over Snaketown Red-on-buffs in Level 4 and the proportionally high incidence of Sweetwater Red-on-gray can only be taken to mean that the deposit was subjected to considerable churning. The physical structure of the ashy deposits, Levels 1 to 5, however, did not reveal this. Below Level 4 the Sweetwater-Estrella Red-on-gray relationship matches that seen in other tests. These conditions are reflected in a sample of about 15,000 potsherds (65 kg).

Tests 15 and 17 were contiguous to each other and a few meters east of Test 11. With minor variations they duplicate the trends already seen; mixtures of later types in the upper levels and Sweetwater Red-on-gray giving way to Estrella Red-on-gray on going deeper. Taken jointly, this evidence is based on about 21,000 sherds (95 kg).

What these various tests reveal, discounting the surficially mixed materials, is an Estrella-Sweetwater Red-on-gray association in the mid-levels which raises the questions as to whether or not this is a true reflection of what took place or whether it is a function of disturbances. I think there is some truth in both conditions, namely, that there was a time when the Sweetwater style was rising from the Estrella base and both styles coexisted as probably was the case with most other pairs of sequent types; but the impression of an extensive overlap has been increased by mixing.

More important is the fact that on going down into the deeper levels the quantity of the Sweetwater type was sharply reduced, being present only as a few isolated, and doubtless intruded, units. Estrella Red-on-gray was clearly the dominant form. The inference may be drawn, supportable not only by the cir-

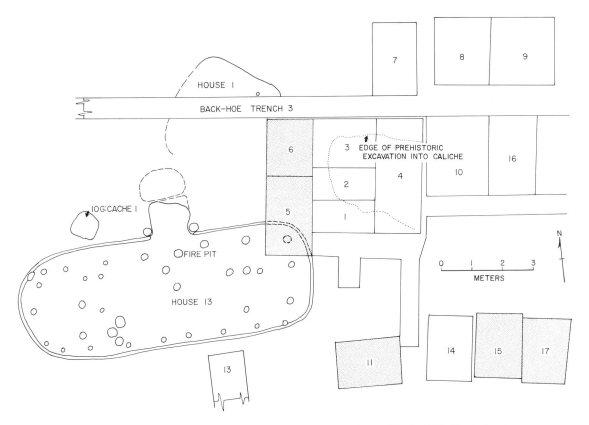

Fig. 6.12. Numbered stratigraphic tests in deep trash of well area (Block 10G). Shaded tests are reported on in text. Test 12 was off the map.

Fig. 6.13. Pottery frequencies by weight (kg) in selected tests in the well area, Block 10G.

WELL AREA TEST NO.	LEVEL	SACATON RED-ON-BUFF	SANTA CRUZ RED-ON-BUFF	GILA BUTTE RED-ON-BUFF	SNAKETOWN RED-ON-BUFF	SWEETWATER RED-ON-GRAY	ESTRELLA RED-ON-GRAY	VAHKI RED	PLAINWARE	TOTAL
5	1	.030	.055	.020	.035	.055	.020	.050	3.075	3.340
	2		.260	.020	.040	.895	.135	.475	19.830	21.655
	3		.015	.005	.010	.290	.320	.260	9.910	10.810
	4		.025	.015	.015	.380	1.520	1.320	50.195	53.470
	5					.005	.235	.405	9.125	9.770
	6						.065	.130	4.355	4.550
	7							.060	1.085	1.145
	8								.350	.350
TOTAL		.030	.355	.060	.100	1.625	2.295	2.700	97.925	105.090
6	1	.030	.035	.015	.010	.090	.040	.040	2.230	2.490
	2	.075	.115	.065		.225	.150	.050	5.055	5.735
	3		.120	.040		.060	.170	.080	9.300	9.770
	4		.005			.015	.315	.280	12.545	13.160
	5		.015			.015	.085	.220	8.815	9.150
	6		.015			.025	.105	.425	8.020	8.590
	7								.165	.165
	8			.020					.080	.100
TOTAL		.105	.305	.140	.010	.430	.865	1.095	46.210	49.160
11	1	.075	.080	.085	.060	.090	.005	.110	1.455	1.960
	2	.210	.035	.320	.200	.060	.010	.090	7.140	8.065
	3		.045	.275	.310	.085	.040	.075	10.110	10.940
	4		.030	.480	.230	.460	.035	.060	14.330	15.625
	5			.010	.005	.065	.075	.090	9.910	10.155
	6			.010	.020	.040	.190	.170	10.325	10.755
	7				.005	.010	.175	.225	5.065	5.480
	8						.080	.040	1.335	1.455
	9						.010	.020	.950	.980
TOTAL		.285	.190	1.180	.830	.810	.620	.880	60.620	65.415
15	1	.035	.085	.010	.090	.075	.030	.035	4.775	5.135
	2	.030	.135	.065	.360	.055	.040	.025	8.950	9.660
	3		.015	.045	.210	.510	.140	.245	11.085	12.250
	4			.010	.360	.295	.170	.110	10.775	11.720
	5			.005		.015	.150	.195	10.735	11.100
	6			.005	.010	.005	.090	.365	11.385	11.860
TOTAL		.065	.235	.140	1.030	.955	.620	.975	57.705	61.725
17	1	.210	.065	.020	.050	.020	.020	.005	3.785	4.175
	2	.055	.070	.060	.095	.075	.005	.015	5.800	6.175
	3		.015	.005		.125	.205	.175	9.050	9.575
	4			.015		.025	.060	.110	6.145	6.355
	5				.005	.015	.085	.295	4.715	5.115
	6						.040	.050	2.385	2.475
TOTAL		.265	.150	.100	.150	.260	.415	.650	31.880	33.870
GRAND TOTAL		.750	1.235	1.620	2.120	4.080	4.815	6.300	294.340	315.260

Fig. 6.14. House 13:10G and its relationship to the stratified deposits below the floor, visible in the profile behind the meter stick. Photo was taken before Tests 5 and 6 were made.

cumstances in this series of tests but from others as well, that there was a moment in the ceramic history when Estrella Red-on-gray was being made to the exclusion of any other painted forms and that this type marked the beginning of the painted tradition in the Hohokam sequence at Snaketown. By the same token, it can be demonstrated that there was a moment when Sweetwater Red-on-gray was the ruling type although the Estrella style may have lingered on.

In several of the well area tests, on reaching the bottom of the culture-producing layers, only plainware and redware were recovered. This might be indicative of a Vahki horizon as the beginning of the series, but the samples are small, and since Estrella Red-on-gray occurs in such minute percentages in relation to the total pottery yield, the inference is not a safe one to make.

Of the large sample of potsherds recovered, close to 130,000 (about 575 kg), in the well area tests enumerated and including Tests 1 to 4, less than 2% was Estrella Red-on-gray. This emphasizes the fact that when the painting of pottery became the vogue, not much of it was produced. The minuscule level of production complicates identification because, conceivably, a large sample of plain and red pottery might be studied without detecting the presence of painted pieces. Because of this situation, quantities have been stressed in the previous paragraphs as a condition necessary to the successful reading of the data.

A by-product of no small importance in making these stratigraphic tests is the recovery of associated materials. Our knowledge of when certain elements either appeared or were present in the cultural complex is largely dependent upon their associations in trash contexts. Although subject to the same displacements as sherds, duplication of the associations is a kind of test that leads to acceptance. Figurines, worked shell, stone artifact types, jewelry, and the nature of related animal bones and carbonized organic remains all become a part of the picture.

Tests 2:10D and 4:10F

The best evidence in support of a Sweetwater Phase, or of any for that matter, is the association of ceramic and other goods in cremations or on the floor of a house. House 2:9G stands out as particularly significant in this respect. That there were ample deposits of refuse of the time was also demonstrated by a number of tests, Column 1 of Mound 39 having been one of them. Two others are added as further evidence.

Test 2:10D was a relatively shallow pit with a depth of slightly over 2 m. The structure of the deposits (Fig. 6.15) showed the upper 4 layers to have been homogeneous and those below showing heavy trash interspersed with some water-laid silts and sand. The impression is that the pit filled rapidly, at least up to the midpoint, once the filling process began.

The pottery return of about 4,100 units (almost 21 kg), somewhat lighter than usual, shows a considerable mixture of materials in the upper 4 levels. An essentially pure sample of Sweetwater Phase rubbish came from Levels 5 to 8 (Fig. 6.16). The undercutting at the bottom of the pit suggests the excavation was initially made to recover the caliche-clay matrix commonly seen in house floors.

Test 4:10F offers a more complex situation, particularly in the upper half of the two-meter deep deposit. As is often the case, the

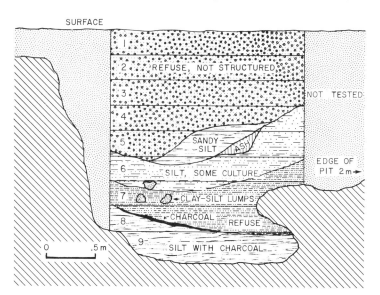

Fig. 6.15. Profile of Stratigraphic Test 2:10D.

TEST NO.	LEVEL	SACATON RED-ON-BUFF	SANTA CRUZ RED-ON-BUFF	GILA BUTTE RED-ON-BUFF	SNAKETOWN RED-ON-BUFF	SWEETWATER RED-ON-GRAY	ESTRELLA RED-ON-GRAY	VAHKI RED	PLAINWARE	TOTAL
10D: TEST 2	1	.030	.225	.070	.005	.015			1.535	1.880
	2		.055	.135	.020	.105	.005	.010	2.450	2.780
	3		.040	.035		.170		.020	3.675	3.940
	4			.010		.110		.010	1.760	1.890
	5	.005				.055		.010	3.375	3.445
	6					.055	.005	.010	2.225	2.295
	7					.130	.015	.005	1.980	2.130
	8					.075			1.055	1.130
	9					.025		.005	1.400	1.430
TOTAL		.035	.320	.250	.025	.740	.025	.070	19.455	20.920
10F: TEST 4	1		.090	.040	.095	.035	.015	.040	2.000	2.315
	2	.050	.140	.060		.080	.010	.030	1.925	2.295
	3	.945	.285	.145	.085	.110		.065	14.010	15.645
				FLOOR OF HOUSE 5:10F (SANTA CRUZ PHASE)						
	4		.340	.260	.040	.185	.010	.050	8.435	9.320
	5		.165	.195	.080	.750	.080	.210	15.710	17.190
	6		.120	.150		1.510	.045	.330	18.200	20.355
	7		.035			1.305	.040	.120	19.030	20.530
	8		.005	.020		1.660	.345	.110	27.705	29.845
TOTAL		.995	1.180	.870	.300	5.635	.545	.955	107.015	117.495

Fig. 6.16. Pottery frequencies by weight (kg) in two stratigraphic tests.

upper levels produced mixtures of early and later materials, emphasized by the presence of iron, beef bones, and a piece of rubber, attributable to nearby Pima occupation. Furthermore, the edges of two caliche house floors appeared on the north side of the test in Level 2; at the bottom of Level 3 the test encountered the floor of House 5:10F, a late and mutilated structure but not clearly assignable to phase. Although the deposit gave up moderate amounts of Gila Butte and Santa Cruz Red-on-buff in Levels 4 and 5 (Fig. 6.16), Sweetwater Red-on-gray increased sharply and continued to the bottom where Estrella began to pick up in predictable fashion.

These two tests do not exhaust all possibilities that might be cited to clarify the discreteness and temporal position of the Sweetwater Phase. The stratigraphic position is unequivocal, in my opinion, and the typological characteristics of Sweetwater Red-on-gray designs are the connecting links between the Estrella and Snaketown painting traditions.

COMPILATION OF CASES

The instances of superposition of pottery types reviewed in the preceding paragraphs are summarized graphically in Figure 6.17. The majority, though not all, of cases of stratification, representing a complex variety of features and situations, are also shown. The evidence for change ranges from the gradual transitions in pottery types from one to another, as in the unbroken continuum of a deep trash deposit, to the marked contrasts in pottery derived from features in close proximity to each other, such as houses, pits, cremations, and caches, whose relationships were not sequent.

The initial assumption that pottery differences reflect age differences is clearly correct because, if it were not, the repetitive nature of the stratigraphic record would not exist. What we see is a consistency of pottery type occurrences with respect to others which establishes the basis for making predictions. The 1964–65

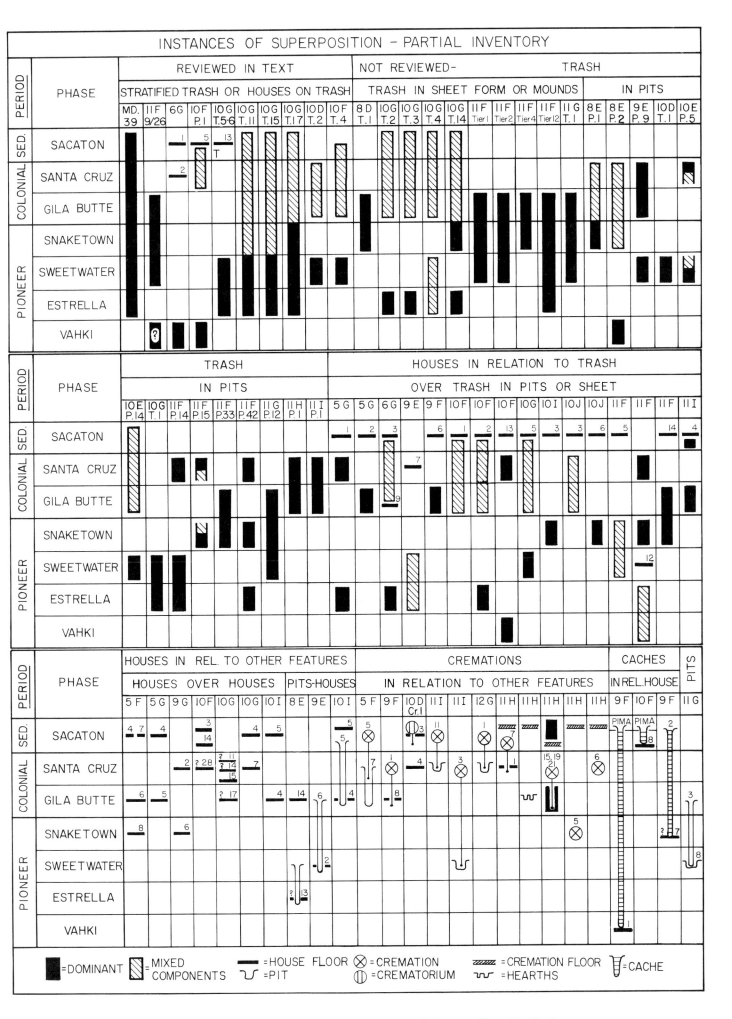

Fig. 6.17. Partial inventory of instances of stratified remains at Snaketown. Phase identifications are based on associated pottery.

STRATIFIED TRASH IN SHEET FORM OR MOUNDS

PROVENIENCE	GRID SQUARE	NO. OF LEVELS	REMARKS
TEST 1	8D	5	Gila Butte changing to Snaketown.
TEST 2	10G	7	Late mixed (1-4), Estrella (5-7).
TEST 3	10G	7	Late mixed (1-4), Estrella (5-7).
TEST 4	10G	8	Late mixed (1-3), Sweetwater-Estrella (4), Estrella (5-8).
TEST 14	10G	8	Late mixed (1), Snaketown (2-5), Estrella (6-8).
MOUND 40, TEST 1, TIER 1	11F	7	Gila Butte (1), Gila Butte-Snaketown (2), Snaketown (3-5), Snaketown-Sweetwater (6), Sweetwater (7).
MOUND 40, TEST 1, TIER 2	11F	8	Gila Butte-Snaketown (1-3), Snaketown (4), Snaketown-Sweetwater (5), Sweetwater (6-8).
MOUND 40, TEST 1, TIER 4	11F	3	Gila Butte-Snaketown (1-2), Snaketown (3 and below).
MOUND 40, TEST 1, TIER 12	11F	9	Gila Butte-Snaketown (1-2), Snaketown-Gila Butte (3), Snaketown (4), Sweetwater (5), Sweetwater-Estrella (6-9).
TEST 1	11G	5	Gila Butte (1), Snaketown-Sweetwater (2), Sweetwater (3-5).

STRATIFIED TRASH IN PITS

PROVENIENCE	GRID SQUARE	NO. OF LEVELS	REMARKS
PIT 1	8E	6	Gila Butte-Santa Cruz (1), Snaketown-Gila Butte (2), Snaketown (3-6).
PIT 2	8E	6	Santa Cruz-Snaketown, Gila Butte (1-3), Vahki (4-6).
PIT 9	9E	6	Santa Cruz (1), Santa Cruz-Gila Butte (2), Gila Butte-Sweetwater (3), Sweetwater (4-6).
TEST 1 (PIT UNNUMBERED)	10D	6	Mixed late sheet trash (1-2), Sweetwater (3-6).
PIT 5	10E	4	Santa Cruz (1), Santa Cruz-Sweetwater (2), Sweetwater (3-4).
PIT 14	10E	6	Late mixed sheet trash (1-2), Santa Cruz-Sweetwater (3), Sweetwater (4-6).
TEST 1 (PIT UNNUMBERED)	10G	3	Sweetwater (1), Estrella (2-3).
PIT 14	11F	6	Santa Cruz (1-2), Sweetwater (3-5), Estrella (6).
PIT 15	11F	5	Mixed Santa Cruz-Snaketown (1-4), Snaketown (5).
PIT 33	11F	6	Gila Butte (1-2), Gila Butte-Snaketown (3-6), stylistically a sample that bridges the classic forms of Gila Butte and Snaketown.
PIT 42	11F	9	Santa Cruz (1-2), Snaketown (3-4), Estrella (5-9).
PIT 12	11G	8	Gila Butte (1-4), Gila Butte-Snaketown (5-6), Sweetwater (7-8).
PIT 1	11H	4	Santa Cruz (1), Santa Cruz-Gila Butte (2), Gila Butte (3-4).
PIT 1	11I	4	Santa Cruz-Gila Butte (1), Gila Butte (2-4).

HOUSES OVER TRASH IN PITS OR IN SHEET FORM

PROVENIENCE	GRID SQUARE	NO. OF LEVELS	REMARKS
HOUSE 1 (SACATON), OVER TRASH	5G	4	Santa Cruz (1), Santa Cruz-Estrella (2), Estrella (3-4).
HOUSE 2 (SACATON), OVER TRASH	5G	4	Gila Butte (1-4).
HOUSE 3 (SACATON), OVER HOUSE 4 (GILA BUTTE), OVER TRASH	6G	4	Mixed Sacaton, Santa Cruz, Gila Butte, Vahki (1-3), Vahki (4).
HOUSE 7 (SANTA CRUZ), OVER PIT 13	9E	1	Sweetwater-Estrella.
HOUSE 6 (SACATON), OVER PIT (GILA BUTTE)	9F		
HOUSE 2 (SACATON), OVER PIT 1	10F	5	Sacaton-Santa Cruz-Gila Butte (1-2), Estrella (3-5).
HOUSE 1 (SACATON), OVER SHEET TRASH	10F		Mixed Sacaton-Santa Cruz-Gila Butte.
HOUSE 13 (SACATON), OVER PIT 3	10F	4	Santa Cruz (1-2), Vahki (3-4).
HOUSE 5 (? SACATON), OVER TRASH	10G	8	Sacaton-Santa Cruz-Gila Butte (1-4), Sweetwater (5-8).
HOUSE 3 (SACATON)	10I		Over small pit filled with Snaketown trash.
HOUSE 3 (SACATON), OVER SHEET TRASH	10J		Santa Cruz-Gila Butte.
HOUSE 6 (SACATON), OVER SHEET TRASH	10J		Snaketown.
HOUSE 5 (SACATON), OVER PIT 9	11F	2	Snaketown-Sweetwater (1), Sweetwater (2).
SURFACE TRASH (SANTA CRUZ OVER SNAKETOWN)	11F		Over House 12 (Sweetwater), over sheet trash (Estrella-Vahki).
HOUSE 14 (SACATON), OVER SHEET TRASH	11F		Gila Butte on Snaketown.
HOUSE 4 (SACATON)	11I		Over sheet trash (Sacaton-Gila Butte), over Pit 8 (Gila Butte).

HOUSES OVER HOUSES	
PROVENIENCE	GRID SQUARE
HOUSE 4 (SACATON), OVER HOUSE 5 (GILA BUTTE)	5G
HOUSE 4 (SACATON) AND HOUSE 7 (SACATON), OVER HOUSE 6 (GILA BUTTE), OVER HOUSE 8 (SNAKETOWN)	5F
HOUSE 2 (SANTA CRUZ), OVER HOUSE 6 (SNAKETOWN)	9G
HOUSE 3 (SACATON), OVER HOUSE 14 (SACATON), OVER HOUSE 28 (? SANTA CRUZ)	10F
HOUSE 11 (? SANTA CRUZ), OVER HOUSE 14 (? SANTA CRUZ), OVER HOUSE 15 (SANTA CRUZ), OVER HOUSE 17 (? GILA BUTTE).	10G
HOUSE 4 (SACATON), OVER HOUSE 7 (SANTA CRUZ)	10G
HOUSE 5 (SACATON), OVER HOUSE 4 (GILA BUTTE)	10I

PITS THROUGH HOUSES	
PROVENIENCE	GRID SQUARE
HOUSE 14 (EARLY GILA BUTTE), OVER UNNUMBERED PIT WITH SWEETWATER TRASH, CUT THROUGH HOUSE 13 (? ESTRELLA)	8E
PIT 6 CONTAINING GILA BUTTE TRASH, CUT THROUGH HOUSE 2 (SWEETWATER)	9E
HOUSE 5 (SACATON), OVER PIT 5 WITH SACATON TRASH, CUT THROUGH HOUSE 4 (GILA BUTTE)	10I

CREMATIONS IN RELATION TO PITS OR HOUSES	
PROVENIENCE	GRID SQUARE
CREMATION 5 (SACATON), INTRUDED IN PIT 7 (SANTA CRUZ GRADING TO GILA BUTTE)	5F
CREMATION 1 (SANTA CRUZ), INTRUDED IN HOUSE 8 (GILA BUTTE)	9F
CREMATORIUM 1 (SACATON), INTRUDED THROUGH HOUSE 3 (SACATON), OVER HOUSE 4 (SANTA CRUZ)	10D
CREMATION 11 (SACATON), INTRUDED IN PIT WITH SANTA CRUZ TRASH	11I
CREMATION 3 (SANTA CRUZ), INTRUDED IN ROASTING PIT 1 (? SWEETWATER)	11I
CREMATION 1 (SACATON), INTRUDED IN PIT WITH SANTA CRUZ TRASH	12G
CREMATION FLOOR (SACATON), OVER HOUSE 1 (SANTA CRUZ), WITH CREMATION 7 (SACATON), INTRUDED THROUGH IT	11H
CREMATION FLOOR (SACATON), OVER COOKING PITS (GILA BUTTE)	11H
MOUND 38 TRASH (SACATON), OVER CREMATION FLOOR (SACATON), OVER CREMATIONS 15, 19 AND 21 (SANTA CRUZ), INTRUDED IN GILA BUTTE TRASH	11H
CREMATION FLOOR (SACATON), OVER CREMATION 5 (SNAKETOWN)	11H
CREMATION FLOOR (SACATON), OVER CREMATION 6 (SANTA CRUZ)	11H

CACHES IN RELATION TO HOUSES	
PROVENIENCE	GRID SQUARE
HISTORIC PIMA CACHE ON FLOOR OF HOUSE 1 (VAHKI)	9F
HISTORIC PIMA CACHE ON FLOOR OF HOUSE 8 (SACATON)	10F
CACHE 2 (SACATON), ON FLOOR OF HOUSE 7 (PIONEER PERIOD)	9F

MISCELLANEOUS	
PROVENIENCE	GRID SQUARE
PIT 3 (GILA BUTTE), INTRUDED IN PIT 8 (SWEETWATER)	11G

Fig. 6.18 (left and above): Supplementary information on various types of cultural stratigraphy in Snaketown.

findings duplicate and therefore support the data presented in 1937 (Gladwin and others) outlining the Hohokam pottery chronology.

Given the present stage of Hohokam investigations, I see no real alternatives to the indicated pottery sequence. All investigators would not necessarily have drawn the lines separating types, hence phases, in the same way as used here; but different taxonomies probably would not alter the overall picture much. Another debatable point is the magnitude of time assignable to a type or to the sequence as a whole. This problem will be reviewed later.

Figure 6.18 lists instances of stratigraphic situations portrayed in Figure 6.17. The quantitative results are not included here for reasons of economy, but they are on file in the archives of the Arizona State Museum.

In this context, reference may be made again to the superposition of canals. While the canals are not as certainly dated as are the refuse deposits or houses, the overlappings observed cover the total span of the village's occupation and are so indicated in Figure 8.32.

The preceding partial inventory of stratigraphic cases requires summarization. Discounting Pima intrusions and canal overlaps, the evaluation in Table 6.1 is made on a two-category basis: (1) number of cases of direct superposition in which the most recent pottery type rests conformably on the immediate antecedent, and (2) number of cases where the younger types lie over older types, but not in direct succession.

The descending order of frequencies is not surprising, being a function of decreasing opportunities for superpositions as one approaches the founding of the village, and an increasing population coming up in time. The failure to note any clear cases of Estrella-on-Vahki trash may be construed as a weak link in the sequence, but three instances of this relationship were noted in the earlier work (Gladwin and others 1937:Fig. 9). At least a dozen instances of Estrella rubbish resting under later refuse, eight of these being in a directly sequent relationship before Sweetwater, leave little room for questioning its chronological position. A part

TABLE 6.1

Inventory of Stratigraphic Cases of Pottery Type Sequences

Phase*	Direct Sequence (No. cases)	Broken Sequence (No. cases)
Sacaton	17	37
Santa Cruz	10	24
Gila Butte	16	20
Snaketown	12	14
Sweetwater	10	11
Estrella	0	0
Vahki	—	6

*Beginning with most recent phase and ending with earliest in sequence.

of the problem may stem from the difficulty of identification, for if Estrella Phase refuse was laid down on Vahki Phase trash and any downward mixing of Estrella Red-on-gray sherds ensued, the whole deposit would have been called Estrella Phase.

Although the Snaketown ceramic sequence has been developed by a variety of internal stratigraphic controls as reviewed in the preceding pages, other evidence which tends to validate the ar-rangement is presented later. The repetitive nature of the data and the orderliness of the typology establish a base from which we may proceed to use the pottery types as indices in arranging other cultural remains in a relative time order, depending on the sound-ness of the association. Houses, stone tools, cremations, shell, and other artifacts may thus be assigned their rightful place in the sequence.

PART FOUR

SUBSISTENCE ACTIVITIES

7. Food Collecting

Most activities of the Hohokam, whether secular or sacred, related to the acquisition, production, and preparation of food. Intimate knowledge of the soil and what it supported was the key to survival, for the well-being of the society was insured only so long as man's relationship to this vital element in nature was not abused. Snaketown's long uninterrupted history, some 1,400 years, declares at once that the human attitude toward nature's bounty was indeed in balance and that the subsistence pattern the Hohokam developed was successful. The energies expended in canal construction and maintenance and the labors in the fields were the prime investments that bought them security and assured their longevity as a people. Yet, there are signs in the fragmentary record of what they relied upon for food that they did experience hard times. Abundance was not always a characteristic of their economy. It was during moments of dietary deficiencies that anything edible became acceptable, as we will see later.

There is no simple way of determining Snaketown's sustaining area. Produced foods would have been limited mainly by the extent of the related canal system, probably not exceeding more than a half-dozen miles in any direction at the time of peak population. But there is always the possibility that small garden plots were maintained much farther from home as adaptations to peculiar topographic conditions or as determined by special cropping needs.

Foraged foods, plant or animal, for the most part came from no greater distance than could be traveled round-trip in one day. Except for Bighorn Sheep, the taking of which would have required hunting expeditions to the Estrella and Superstition mountains as the nearest sources 25 to 65 km (15 to 40 mi) away, other edible products could have been gathered much closer to the village. For the importation of "exotic" foods there are no data. As an estimate, perhaps up to 95% of the food required by the residents of Snaketown came from an area no larger than 15 km (about 10 mi) from the village up and down the valley and no farther than a few kilometers north or south of the river. Beyond these limits, competition with other villagers would almost certainly have resulted.

In some ways, the information bearing on Hohokam exploitation of natural resources, both plant and animal, is better than the record of their achievements as farmers. Their collecting skills resulted from a long familiarity with the desert. It should be observed that the desert in which they lived was a succulent one, capable of supplying a variety of foodstuffs to an extent better than was true of most other Southwestern sub-environmental zones. The immediate question that arises is how the Hohokam balanced their food-collecting and food-producing activities to keep the larder maximally full. There is no way of knowing how much of their caloric intake came from agriculture or from collected natural foods. It was doubtless somewhat better in favor of produced foods than the roughly 50-50 ratio observed for the Pimas (Castetter and Bell 1942: 56-57).

PLANTS

Bohrer's excellent study (1970) of plant remains from Snaketown was based on a limited number of samples from burned rooms, ranging in quantity from a handful to 8.5 liters (2 gal). Her examination included a restudy of some of the specimens reported by Castetter and Bell (1942: 33) from the 1934–35 excavations. But the most rewarding information was provided by the charred plant parts recovered with a fine-mesh screen and water flotation from about 100 samplings of trash of different ages.

Bohrer has established a high degree of correspondence between the Pima and Hohokam in their dependence on native foods (1970: 420), and in both cases it is clear that fruits of the saguaro (*Carnegiea gigantea*) and mesquite (*Prosopis juliflora*) were staples. To these should also be added various chollas (*Opuntia*) that supplied young joints and buds, and the screwbean (*Prosopis pubescens*), a relative of the mesquite. The role of the stately giant cactus (Fig. 7.1) as a supplier of food for Indians in recent and ancient times has probably been underestimated. The abundance of the saguaro in desert areas favorable to its growth, dependable fruiting no matter how dry the preceding months have been, the relative ease with which the fruit may be harvested, the variety of ways in which the fruit may be processed for consumption and storage and its nutritive values, made it a prime resource. The Indians recognized this fact by starting the new calendar year at the time of the saguaro fruit harvest (Russell 1908: 35). Wine could be produced from the juice, and fermented wine produced acid to etch shells. Furthermore, the seeds had utility in tanning hides, at least historically, and the internal ribs of the cactus became structural elements in house-building. Without the saguaro the story of survival in the desert might be written differently.

Similarly, mesquite and mescrew, widely available in the desert, provided abundant and reliable food, building materials, and fuel. The probable integration of the saguaro and mesquite harvesting periods with double annual plantings by the Hohokam, as proposed by Bohrer (1970: 424), may have been unique in the Southwest as a regimen of food acquisition.

In addition to the foregoing, many other seed crops were exploited by the Hohokam, among which the *Amaranthus* and *Trianthema-Chenopodium* complex may have been the most significant (Bohrer 1970:417-419). We have no knowledge of Hohokam use of plant leaves and tubers as food sources. Broadly speaking, Papago and Pima dependence on native foods, so well described by Russell (1908) and Castetter and Bell (1942), accurately mirrors the ancient Hohokam practices.

The presence of charred seeds in refuse prompted Bohrer to ask two questions (1970: 414): Why were they there and what did the fluctuations in their distribution mean? Charring, as a by-product of parching, a common method for preparing seeds for eating or

Fig. 7.1. The giant cactus (*Carnegiea gigantea*) was an unfailing source of food.

storage, probably accounts for the seeds in the trash. Variations in the distribution, expressed as a seed concentration index, Bohrer attributes not to chance but to increased wild food gathering associated with low crop yields (1970: 420-423). This idea, further correlated with high water levels in the Gila River and the effect of local rains, is a most challenging approach to the study of Hohokam food problems. Bohrer is the first to admit, however, that available samples are not sufficient to establish the trends from good to bad in crop production in any one phase which stretched through several centuries. In other words, to say that crop failures characterized the Gila Butte or Sacaton phases on the basis of a few samples would be incorrect because the data reflect only upon a moment of time in either of those periods. The designing of a totally different sampling method is needed to test her hypothesis effectively.

In review, a case can be made for maize and beans as having had the highest priority as produced foods in the minds of the Hohokam and the saguaro-mesquite combination as holding the top spot among collected foods. This pattern appears not to have changed for more than two millennia. Stable environmental conditions favorable to the production of foodstuffs by man and nature appear to have prevailed although nominal fluctuations, whether man or nature induced, are suggested by the profile developed from pollen taken from refuse (Bohrer 1970: 426-428).

ANIMALS

Bones of animals collected for food or for other useful by-products constitute a surprisingly small fraction of Snaketown's trash. Relative to the volume of dirt moved, the derived animal bones, whether measured by weight, by pieces or by minimal

faunal count, were far below the customary level of retrieval in Southwestern sites, particularly those of the Anasazi. I do not believe that this represents an aversion to eating meat but rather that the animal population immediately available was in short supply or that vegetal products, whether grown or gathered, were favored by the Hohokam. A low hunting efficiency does not appear to be the answer and a minimal utilization of bone for tools is not responsible either. The conditions of preservation in the ground were favorable as evidenced by the soundness of the bones that were recovered. In short, the impoverished nature of animal utilization, on the basis of present information, is not readily explained. If a scant meat supply was available and if the yield of a vegetal protein was small, for which there is some indication, then the Hohokam diet may have suffered seriously from protein deficiency.

Mammals

A highly detailed report on the mammalian fauna by Greene and Mathews of the Southwestern Archeological Center, National Park Service, formerly in Globe, Arizona, is included as Appendix 5. The study is based on an examination of 1,688 bone units, representing about 33% of the total Snaketown sample. The authors believe that the conclusions reached would be unaffected by a review of the whole collection. Their analysis does not, however, take into account the tiny fragmented bones recovered by flotation. These are treated separately (Appendix 7). At the present time—the early 1970s—we do not have adequate comparative data to make full use of the information they have provided in Figures A5.2 to A5.9, but their efforts should stimulate others to make similar studies.

Nineteen animals, identified as to order, genus, or species, compose the list (Fig. A5.2). Except for cattle (*Bos taurus*), the mammals represent a typical arid lands fauna of rabbits, rodents, and hoofed animals. Considering the dependence the Hohokam placed on a riverine environment, it is surprising that water mammals are not included in the new list, although the muskrat was noted in the original work (Gladwin and others 1937: 156). In terms of numbers of animals taken, rabbits outnumbered all other mammals by a ratio of 3:2, and the Black-tailed Jackrabbit was dominant among the Llagomorpha by 2:1. Most usable meat per animal, however, came from the Artiodactyla, and the Mule Deer provided most of that. These values given in Figures A5.7 and A5.8 offer no real surprises except for the low frequency of the Bighorn Sheep. McKusick, in an unpublished study of fauna from a Classic Period site near Sacaton (Ariz. U:14:8), finds evidence of the increased dependence on the Bighorn Sheep in late prehistory, a trend already begun in the Sedentary Period as indicated by the data from Snaketown.

Historically the Pima and Papago were heavily dependent on the Bighorn Sheep, and early writers noted enormous deposits of skulls and horns of the animal encountered in their travels. The custom of having special depositories for certain animal bones in the distant past may account for the scarcity of the Bighorn in Snaketown. In addition, taking it meant making hunting trips to mountain ranges, the nearest being the Estrellas about 25 km (15 mi) distant. Related problems of transport may have affected the amount of bone residue of the animal available to us. A hint of the importance of the Bighorn to the Hohokam is seen in their art, for it was sculptured in stone, modeled in clay, carved in bone, and painted on pottery.

The absence of bison in the present list suggests that the six instances reported in the first study of Snaketown (Gladwin and others 1937: 157) were indeed anomalous and that parts of the animal were undoubtedly introduced into the village as bones. Clearly, the bison did not figure in the Hohokam food supply. The Pima reoccupation of Snaketown in the nineteenth century introduced the *Bos taurus*, or cattle bones, into the site.

The fifteen bone elements identified as dog, *Canis familiaris*, came from Vahki and Estrella phase contexts. Although absence of the animal in later phases may be due to the vagaries of sampling, another explanation has been suggested to me by a colleague, Theodore Downing. His field records for Zapotec and Nahuatl groups in Mexico show that dead dogs were disposed of by throwing them into nearby rivers. The fact that Snaketown yielded no dog burials might stem from such a custom.

The early occurrence of the dog in Snaketown is consistent with the data from Ventana Cave where the earliest association was with cultural material dating to 2500 B.C. or before (Haury 1950: 158).

An unusually high percentage of bones, whether of large or small animals, is burned. Coloration ranges from scorched black through deep brown to calcined white. Roasting parts of animals might produce charred bone-ends, but not the whole bone, and boiling would not yield the results observed. In short, food processing appears not to have been the main cause for this condition. However, the analysis of burned bones representing the principal meat producers (Figs. A5.7 & A5.8) reveals that almost half of the Artiodactyla bones were burned, while the effects of fire are seen on only about 20% of the rabbit bones. This difference is doubtless related to the methods used in preparing the meat. Periodic removal of the organic cover of trash mounds by fire may be held partly responsible, particularly in scorching the fine bones that were components in human waste. However, trash-filled pits exhibit no in situ burning, yet they produce heat-altered bones, indicating that the condition was acquired before disposal. In all probability the Hohokam threw bones in the hearth after the meat was cleaned off, thereby taking advantage of the grease in them as a little extra fuel. It should be noted that a few cremations had associated nonhuman bones, which were not artifacts, burned equally as hard as the human ashes. There is no easy explanation for these occurrences.

Estimates of the usable meat through time (Fig. A5.8) clearly reflect the Mule Deer to have been the principal producer. Although the rabbit was taken in large numbers, it yielded only a small fraction of the meat protein available to the Hohokam. The moderate phase difference in the dependence on these two animals is probably not significant, but the late increase in the use of Bighorn Sheep does appear to be a meaningful trend.

Reptiles

Lizards and snakes typical of the desert habitat today were identified among the micro-vertebrate remains (Appendix 7). Occurrences of the bones with the remains of other food animals suggest that these creatures, too, were eaten. Though the evidence is slim, it is noteworthy that poisonous species as, for example, the Gila Monster and the sidewinder are not represented. Their lethal nature may have been a deterrent, but it is more likely that they were avoided because of their association with the spirit world, hinted by frequent depictions in Hohokam art.

Fish

Before the waters of the Gila River were contained by modern reclamation practices, the Pima Indians viewed fish as a desirable source of food. Fish were caught by hand and impaled on a stick through the gills or the body. Set in the ground in front of a fire, they were roasted and eaten on the spot (Whittemore 1893: 56). It appears that fish-eating was a custom of long standing in the Gila valley, for bones were recovered from refuse of all ages in Snaketown. Vertebrae were the most common elements representing "pan-size" fish for the most part, but bones of much larger fish were also noted. Although about half of the test samples from fine screening produced evidence of aquatic life, the low yield from general refuse digging suggests further that fish did not constitute a large fraction of Hohokam animal diet. In this connection it is interesting to note that, while the Pimas ate fish, they did not distinguish species, having only one name for all kinds (Russell 1908: 83). The occasional drying up of the river during droughts may be responsible for the relatively low emphasis on fish as a source of food.

The fish remains studied by Olsen (Appendix 7) and Minckley (Appendix 8) represent different parts of the faunal sample separated by our collecting methods. If the results of only one of these examinations would be reported on, we would have a biased view of Hohokam fish use. The gross bones identified by Minckley came mostly from the coarse screening of trash. His fraction of the sample suggests that emphasis was on catching large fish, some weighing as much as 22.5 kg (50 lb). The assumption is that these came from the river rather than canals. The bones reviewed by Olsen were recovered in the fine screening of trash after removal of the larger residues. His data show that no fish over about 0.5 kg (1 lb) were taken and that most of them were of fingerling size. The difficulty of catching small fish in an open stream, except under ideal netting conditions and with good equipment, suggests to him that the canals were the prime source because the more restricted waters and fewer places for the fish to hide made their capture easier. We can be sure that the Hohokam took fish of all sizes and that several methods of preparation were known, principally roasting and drying. Like other small creatures, fingerlings were eaten whole and raw.

The fish species identified by Olsen and Minckley offer no surprises for they have all been present historically in the Gila and Salt rivers and related canals. Both agree with Miller (1955: 132-133) that the sturgeon (*Acipenser*), reported in 1937 (Gladwin and others: 157), was an incorrect identification, the bones having been those of the squawfish, *Ptychocheilus lucius*.

Minckley notes that marine fish bones are limited to otoliths, the earbones of croakers, prized for their ornamental value. There is no evidence that the sea was drawn upon for food by the Hohokam.

In a stern indictment of the white man, Miller observes (1961: 398-99) that six or seven species of fish have become extinct in the American Southwest and that "... at least 13 others have been either locally exterminated or so endangered that they too may soon vanish. These 19 or 20 species constitute almost 20 percent of the known aboriginal fishes of Western North America (north of Mexico)." He further notes that "... nowhere else in North America has the upset of natural conditions been more strikingly reflected by biotic change than in the arid Southwest, particularly in southern Arizona. Overwhelming evidence indicates that modern man, rather than climatic change, has been the chief agent in producing the observed changes." There is "... little evidence that the aborigines had much effect on the original fauna."

Birds

In spite of a conspicuously small sample of avian remains, Charmion R. McKusick of the Southwestern Archeological Center, formerly in Globe, Arizona, has been able to identify 68 individual birds representing 32 genera, species and subspecies (Appendix 6). This suggests that the Hohokam made extensive use of birds and that they had developed effective means of capturing them. Water birds were doubtless taken often, not surprising considering the nearness of the Gila River. Deep still water in the river is indicated by the presence of a diving and a stiff-tailed duck. The absence of water fowl in the Sacaton Phase I believe to be the result of inadequate sampling rather than a reflection of changing collecting habits of the Hohokam.

From the relatively high incidence of birds with yellow plumage and the presence in the collection of wing bones and pectoral girdle elements, it may be inferred that extensive use was made of feathers. Presumably the macaw and parrot, the only exotic species in the avian list, supplied brightly colored feathers as well.

It is difficult to determine which birds were eaten. McKusick observes that only mockingbirds, orioles, blackbirds, and sparrows were identified in what is presumed to represent fecal remains. These are the smaller birds which could have been eaten whole, accounting for the highly fragmented nature of the bones. If this thought is true, then certainly the larger birds would also have supplied food, but the manner of consumption would have been different and the bones would not have been crunched up. Although the turkey was listed as present in the avifauna derived during the first work at Snaketown (Gladwin and others 1937: 156), this bird was extremely scarce at best, and there is no basis for believing that the Hohokam domesticated or even kept it.

In general, the birds noted by McKusick are those that would have been expected along the Gila River and in the adjacent desert terrain before the river was dried by impounding its water behind Coolidge Dam. There are no species that might be used as indicators of significant environmental changes. The sage hen (Gladwin and others 1937: 156-157) is the only bird totally absent in the desert today.

Parrots and macaws, imported from Mexico for their bright plumage, are by no means rare in the Southwest. Hargrave's detailed study (1970) notes no fewer than 145 archaeological occurrences in 24 sites widely scattered through Arizona and New Mexico. He states (p. 53) that "Trade in macaws was established in the Southwest about 1100, or slightly before . . .,".

A certain respect for the birds, and a suggestion that they were regarded as prized items, is seen in the fact that they are frequently found as burials. The random presence in Snaketown of the Thick-billed Parrot and the Scarlet Macaw would not command a second look except that the age assignments add a new and unexpected dimension to the parrot-macaw problem. An unidentified species of macaw, the Scarlet Macaw and the Thick-billed Parrot were recovered in Sweetwater Phase contexts and possibly as early as the Estrella Phase in the case of the macaw not identified as to species. Other instances range from Snaketown-Gila Butte to Santa Cruz phases. By the calendrical reckoning used here, these colorful birds were introduced by A.D. 100, and their use may be presumed to have been continuous, as they became available, after that time.

Traffic in live birds evidently began much earlier than has been suspected and it would appear that the trade routes were kept open, indicating an active rather than a passive contact situation. Further, if birds were carried northward, we may believe that other goods were being passed along the trade channels as well. Why it should have taken nearly 1,000 years for parrots and macaws to reach the Anasazi from the Hohokam country is not readily explained, although I suspect it is due to the fact that far more attention has been given to villages and towns dating after A.D. 1000 than to those of earlier centuries, and the chances, therefore, for recovery of the evidence in late sites have been vastly increased.

McKusick believes she recognizes a trend in bird usage at Snaketown based on three groupings of species (Appendix 6). Going from early to late, there are: (1) waterfowl, quail, doves, and Sparrow Hawk; (2) a wider range of species than before, including the Common Raven, Marsh Hawk, parrot and macaw; and (3) emphasis on hawks and absence of waterfowl and macaws. Once again I suspect that this trend is more apparent than real and that it is the product of sampling. Failure to collect

waterfowl and to have the macaw during the late Colonial and Sedentary periods, a time of great cultural activity, does not seem reasonable. Of note, however, is the late emphasis on the taking of hawks, matching what happened among the Western Pueblos at about the same time.

McKusick is impressed by the fact that no eagles and owls appeared in the avifauna although they are listed as present among the bones recovered in 1934–35 (Gladwin and others 1937: 156). Unfortunately little attention was paid in those days to bone frequencies. One is led to wonder whether the apparent scarcity or absence of eagle, vulture, and owl remains could, in any way, be linked with the Pima belief that these birds are the causes of certain sicknesses (Russell 1908: 263). If the Hohokam had similar ideas, collecting these species might have been avoided. The Pima attribute the same dire effects to the hawks, but a number of species of hawks are represented in the Snaketown collection spanning the full life of the site.

As is documented elsewhere, birds of various kinds figured prominently as a motif in shell carving, stone sculpturing, and pottery painting. In the latter, water fowl and the quail were favored, a possible reflection of the importance of these species in the food chain.

Arthropods

The fill of a Sacaton Phase house (1:10 I) produced a 3.9 cm long fragment of the immovable pincer claw of a marine swimming crab. Henry B. Roberts, Senior Museum Specialist, Division of Crustacea, of the National Museum of History, Washington, D.C., kindly identified the specimen as representing the genus *Callinectes* (Family Portunidae), but because of the range of variation exhibited by the fingers of several species, identification to the species level cannot be made with certainty. Since most of the marine shells known to the Hohokam originated in the Gulf of California, the probability is that the crab-claw in question came from there as well. The most abundant crab in the gulf is *C. bellicosus* (Stimpson), the species probably represented here.

A plausible explanation for the presence of a marine crab in Snaketown is that the claw, and perhaps other parts of the exoskeleton, were brought back from the coast with shells as an item of curiosity, to show the "folks back home" examples of the strange life that occurs in the ocean. It suggests the possibility that Snaketown residents made the trek to the ocean, because it is not likely such items would normally pass from hand to hand as a trade item.

Mollusks

The fresh water clam *Anadonta dejecta* (Lewis) was used infrequently as a source of raw material for making ornaments. Relevant to this discussion is the fact that highly fragmented *A. dejecta* shells were present in most of the samples recovered with a fine screen. This suggests use of the fragile-shelled mollusk as a food source. It was prevalent in the Gila River and could have been collected readily. The excessive fracturing of the shell may have been due to the barbarous custom of eating the animals whole, shell and all, as is discussed later. This interpretation seems likely because the shell was present in trash samples of all phases, but it was not until the Santa Cruz Phase and later that we have evidence of the shell's use in ornament production.

8. Food Production

Advanced knowledge of methods to control water ranks the Hohokam high as a food-producing society. Their cultigens, however, we know from charred remains only, a state of affairs that tells us immediately of the woeful incompleteness of the record. There is no evidence that animals of any kind were kept and bred as a food source.

CROP FARMING
Maize

Expectably, the prime cultivated crop was maize (*Zea mays*). Cutler and Blake's examination of the samples recovered (Appendix 3), consisting of nine lots of shelled corn of varying amounts and about two dozen cobs, has provided several significant pieces of information. The most revealing of these is that small-grained and small-cobbed races were typical of the early phases and that these were augmented by larger-grained and larger-cobbed kinds of maize in the later phases. This trend was originally observed by Jones in the 1934–35 ethnobotanical collections from Snaketown reported and commented on by Castetter and Bell (1942: 30-34). While the present sample consists of popcorn and flour corn, it may be assumed that sweet corn was grown as well. Nearly all of the races of maize identified at Snaketown were cultivated until recently by the Pima and Papago Indians.

Cutler and Blake observe that most of the changes in maize followed the Gila Butte Phase, or after A.D. 700. They equate the Gila Butte Phase with the Georgetown Phase of the Mogollon Culture as seen in Tularosa Cave (Martin and others 1952) and note that this was a time of stress, marked by increased dependence upon natural plant foods. While maize samples from the southern Arizona desert are inadequate to match this line of evidence, Bohrer (1970: 422), on the basis of seed concentrations in refuse, has indicated the possibility of increasing crop failure after the Gila Butte Phase. This idea, reached by two independent routes, should be pursued in future studies of Hohokam agriculture.

If a period of stress did exist, it may have been countered by the importation of new races of maize which were better adapted to withstand the stress, if environmentally caused. Considering the fact that during the Santa Cruz Phase, artistic achievements in stone sculpture and other arts reached their peak of excellence, it does not seem likely that the suggested trend toward increasing crop failure was severe enough to adversely affect the vigor of the society.

Using the Pima ecosystem as a model, Bohrer believes (1970: 424-425) that the Hohokam may have planted two crops a year: one in the spring, the other in the fall. Crop failures or reduced yields at either time could be supplemented by the fruiting of the saguaro in July and the collecting of mesquite and mescrew beans in September, an ingenious blending of nature's bounty and of man's activity in his quest for food.

Bohrer's observations on this problem have far-reaching implications, and they deserve to be quoted in full (1970: 424-425):

If the early Hohokam farmers followed the proposed ecosystem, then they followed a planting calendar that selected maize seed for cold and drought resistance at an accelerated rate. The spring planting of maize subjects it to near freezing temperatures in the seedling stage. Late fall harvests encourage selection for a strain of maize resistant to cold temperatures. Protoplasmic endurance of high and low temperatures has been shown to be an inheritable characteristic. True drought resistance is associated with the same physiological conditions manifested by cold resistance (Ferry and Ward 1959: 58). The Hohokam accelerated the rate of selection for both cold and drought resistance by raising two generations per year. What better streamlining could maize receive before it spread to the higher elevations of the American Southwest? It is hardly surprising that the Pima grew maize so drought resistant that they could mature a crop on but one irrigation (Castetter and Bell 1942: 89). Modern breeders have not approached such a record.

It appears to me that what we want and need to know about Hohokam maize culture is still dependent on future studies. Present knowledge does, however, permit a few inferences. While one might suppose that races of maize occurring in early times in the mountains and in the desert would be different in their responses to grossly varying growing conditions, Cutler and Blake observed (Appendix 3) that the maizes of Tularosa Cave and Snaketown were closely related. This applies notably to Vahki Phase maize of roughly 100 to 300 B.C. in Snaketown and to the Pinelawn Phase and Pre-Pottery Phase maize of Tularosa Cave with an age span of before 150 B.C. to about A.D. 500. This situation inspires some thoughts with respect to the spread of the cultigen in early times but post-dating the considerably older diffusion of popcorn of the kind found in Bat Cave.

Since it is logical to believe that the Hohokam introduced varieties of maize as a part of their agricultural complex when they arrived in the Southwest, and their place of origin was most likely in the subarid northwestern Mesoamerican frontier, adaptations in maize to an arid environment may already have been made before it reached the Southwest. From this point on, applying Bohrer's hypothesis of double planting, resistance to freezing temperatures would have had to be achieved before the time of Christ if transmission of maize was from the Hohokam to the Mogollon area. This does not seem likely. A second option is that races of maize growable in the Hohokam and Mogollon domains, respectively, made the adaptations in Mexico and that they spread northward at about the same time, several centuries before Christ. This postulate holds that the northward expansion followed two routes, the Sierra Madre corridor over which cold resistant races passed and a lowland, coastal route favorable to drought resistant races.

How the Southwest did in fact receive maize is dependent upon far more archaeological data than are now available, improved dating methods for areas concerned and advanced ethnobotanical knowledge bearing on adaptive factors as related to the peculiarities of the regional environments. The fact that most of the races of maize grown by the Hohokam at Snaketown were also the kinds grown by the Pima and Papago suggests to me that drought-resistant strains had a long history and that the adaptation to aridity had indeed been made in Mexico. At the moment, therefore, I am inclined to favor the idea of a two-pronged dispersion of maize before 200 B.C.

Questions of crop yields per acre, storage of harvests and modes of maize preparation beyond whole kernel parching and reduction of kernels to flour by grinding, remain unanswered. The smallness of the amounts of shelled corn recovered may mean that these lots were held in reserve for seed. Storage in jars was probably the norm, but there is one lot from a Vahki Phase house (1:7H) which appears to have been contained in a small hamper made of closely spaced wooden rods 7 to 11 mm in diameter. How these were held together is not known.

Beans

The earliest occurrence of the common bean (*Phaseolus vulgaris*) at Snaketown was in the Estrella Phase (Bohrer 1970: 425). Since samples from later phases have been noted, it may be assumed that the bean was cultivated in the interim as well. Furthermore, it may be supposed that the bean was known from the time of founding of Snaketown as one of the original components of the agricultural complex. It appears in Mexico by the third millennium B.C. if not before (MacNeish 1964: 536).

Special interest is attached to the presence of the tepary bean (*Phaseolus acutifolius*). Only one occurrence was noted at Snaketown, the association being with a Sacaton Phase house (8:6G) (Jones, as reported in Castetter and Bell 1942: 32). Teparies came to the attention of the botanists early in the twentieth century when they were collected as a field crop among the Papago and Pima Indians. Grown experimentally, more than 70 distinct kinds were recognized (Freeman 1918: 3). It is reported that the Indians distinguished sharply between the common bean, as the *frijole*, and the tepary bean.

The heavy reliance placed upon this legume in recent times by the Papagos and Pimas belies the meagerness of the archaeological record. No evidence of the tepary was found in Ventana Cave (Haury and others 1950: 161), but teparies have been reported from a village located several miles south of Tucson and dating about A.D. 900 to 1200 (Bohrer, Cutler, and Sauer 1969: 4-5). An eighth century A.D. occurrence has been noted in a Basketmaker site of southwestern Colorado (Carlson 1963). There probably are numerous unreported cases of the tepary since, if found in small number and particularly if charred, they might be mistaken as small individuals of the kidney bean.

The importance historically of the tepary stems from its drought resistant quality and because, whether dry-farmed or irrigated, it outyielded the *frijole* by four times as determined in a series of experiments reported by Freeman (1918: 44-50). Although Freeman believed that the prehistoric Indians domesticated the tepary from wild ancestral plants growing in the canyons of the Southwest and northern Mexico (1918: 55), the origin may, in fact, be much farther to the south because it has been reported as a component of the Coxcatlan Phase, 5200 to 3400 B.C. in the Tehuacán Valley, 240 km (150 mi) south of Mexico City (MacNeish 1964; Kaplan 1967: 208-210).

Pumpkins

Because of the perishable nature of *Cucurbita*, parts of this food plant are less likely to survive charring than are hard-seeded plants like maize and beans. This condition does not fully explain, however, the essential absence of squashes in the botanical remains from Snaketown. Rind fragments were associated with Cache 2:9F, Sacaton Phase, probably *Lagenaria* sp. A *Cucurbita* pollen grain was identified from a Snaketown Phase context, but it is not known that this specimen signifies a cultivated species (Bohrer 1970: 425). Pumpkins were grown extensively by the Pimas at the turn of the century. Seeds were parched for eating, and meat was preserved by cutting into strips and drying (Russell 1908: 71). If pumpkins were an important food source to the Hohokam, this fact needs still to be established.

Cotton

Cotton (*Gossypium* sp.) is not ordinarily thought of as a food plant, but the seeds do have nutritive values. They were parched and eaten by the Pima and Papago Indians historically (Castetter and Bell 1942: 198). This custom in antiquity probably accounts for the fact that charred cotton seeds, resulting from overparching, found their way into the trash heaps. Fine screening of refuse for carbonized organic residues yielded 22 seeds in nine samples ranging in time from the Sweetwater to the Sacaton phases (Bohrer 1970: 425), and small quantities of seeds were found in houses, all of the Sacaton Phase (Castetter and Bell 1942: 32-33). The presence of cotton at Snaketown in the early centuries of the Christian Era is not inconsistent with data obtained from Tularosa Cave, White Dog Cave, and Tsegi-ot-sosi, as summarized by Kent (1957: 468).

Since cotton has been recognized as a domesticate in the Tehuacán Valley of Mexico as early as the Abejas Phase, 3400–2300 B.C. (MacNeish 1964: 536), it is likely that cotton was accepted everywhere in Mexico where it could be grown at an early enough time so that it could have reached Snaketown with the original settlers. Because the Hohokam inhabited an environment specially favorable to cotton culture and they were skilled in weaving the fiber into cloth, their role in disseminating the plant and the products made from it throughout the Southwest must have been a vital one.

Tobacco

While not a food plant, tobacco is mentioned here because it may have been cultivated in prehistory, as in recent times (Castetter and Bell 1942: 211-215), as a ceremonial crop. For the desert country the archaeological record of tobacco's presence is slim. It does occur in cane cigarettes (Haury 1945a: 194), and Fewkes notes finding some in a bowl at Casa Grande (1912: 143), both dating from about the 14th century. But Snaketown yielded no evidence of it. If tobacco was known to the Hohokam during early times, its dominant use may have been in the form of cigarettes, for pipes are next to absent.

Discussion

Methods of food preparation and eating habits are revealed in part by residual and secondary evidences. Earth-oven cooking, boiling, roasting, and parching are clearly indicated and may have been principally used. Baking may be inferred, since this was a method generally employed in the production of pottery. But heat was not always necessary and consuming certain foods raw, notably meat, may have been more widely practiced than seems apparent.

There is no easy way to determine accurately the nutrient balance in the Hohokam diet. A heavy starch component derived from maize may be assumed, but the small yield of animal bones as previously noted and the apparent low level of bean production suggest that protein may have been in short supply. The most telling evidence that this condition prevailed comes from the finely comminuted bone screened from trash. In each of about 100

Fig. 8.1. Example of crushed bones of small animals indicating unsophisticated eating habits of the Hohokam in times of hardship.

tests, an unexpected amount of tiny bone fragments and crushed fresh water clam shells was recovered.

The smallness of the material, ranging in size from a millimeter to rarely longer than a centimeter (Fig. 8.1), poses a major problem to those who attempt identification. Relatively few of the bones retain sufficiently complete articular ends and other distinctive features to permit specific detection. But enough species and genera have been recognized to demonstrate the range of life forms present. These include mammals, birds, reptiles, fish, and the afore-mentioned clams. A characteristic held in common by these traces of living matter is that only small animals are represented, creatures of a bite-size variety that could be eaten whole (Appendix 6). McKusick called attention to this in connection with her study of the bird bones. Many of the fragments display the effect of fire, ranging from scorching to white calcination.

The question arises as to whether or not this bone residue is to be attributed to animal or human activity. Dogs, owls, and other meat-eaters might produce these relics as evidence of their food habits. But generally speaking the bones would not be so finely broken. The presence of animals that walked, crawled, slithered, flew, and swam points the finger directly to man as the responsible agent.

While there may be several ways to explain these somewhat different traces of animal life, the most likely one is that the Hohokam, driven by a protein-deficient diet, ate anything that would fill the void. Some scorching of bones may have come from roasting, but, more likely, the creatures were eaten raw. This manner of eating cannot be described as gourmet, for the fracturing of the bones must have come about by crunching-up the mass enough to make swallowing possible. The trash mounds give up the residue because they were used as latrines, and the periodic burning of the wastes on the mounds, whether by accident or as a sanitary measure, may account for most of the charring of the bones.

While this characterization may represent the unromantic side of the Hohokam cuisine, what people do when in dire food straits is well documented (Callen 1963; Callen and Cameron 1960). From Mexico to Peru, the examination of human coprolites preserved in dry caves has shown that strange things were eaten uncooked and lightly chewed. Rodents, lizards, snakes, fish, and

pieces of clam shells are among the many items that have been identified. Joseph Och, S. J., a missionary of the mid-eighteenth century in Sonora, Mexico, has the following to say (Treutlein 1965: 179):

When Indians have the desire to eat meat they are half mad, like a pregnant woman, and even if they be threatened with the whip they will kill the first good ox or cow they find to satisfy their craving. This voracity incites them also to gulp down unseemly things such as rats of great size, larger than two fists; snakes of various lengths and thicknesses, as well as finger-long grasshoppers. For all these things they feel no revulsion. I also had a supply of sugar and honey for the Indians. A pot accidentally left uncovered served me as the best mouse-trap, for every day several mice would jump into it and be unable to get out of the honey. Daily my houseboys exerted themselves to see who would be the first to the pot so as to get a sweet breakfast. They took the live, sugared mice, whose heads stuck out of the honey, and pulled them delightedly four or five times through their mouths so as to lick the honey from them.

What happened after that is not related.

Some of the "foods" ingested by the Hohokam must have given them a temporary feeling of fullness, though little nourishment was derived from them. The marvel is that the human digestive system could withstand the harsh treatment inflicted upon it, and that the human mind is capable of erasing any feelings of revulsion about unattractive foods when hunger pangs set in.

Many aspects of Hohokam subsistence will probably never be reconstructed. It would be useful to know what food items, if any, were used as barter in times of plenty and what was obtained by the same means in times of want. We know next to nothing about how animals were taken. Figure 12.92u shows a hunter with drawn bow aimed at a (?) deer; but beyond this we can only surmise. The throwing club was present in the area (Haury 1950: 420-421), and a possible stone model (Gladwin and others 1937: Pl. LXXX) suggests that the Hohokam knew it. The Pimas are said to have had communal rabbit hunts, evidently without the benefit of the long net. Rabbit nets were widely used (Kaemlein 1971), however, and they may be presumed to have been a part of the Hohokam food-getting complex (Haury 1950: 399-400). Snares doubtless served them well for small animals and waterfowl. Fish may have been netted or hand-caught. There is no suggestion in the artifact collection that fishhooks or other fishing gear were used.

Food preservation must have been accomplished mainly by drying and parching, as was done historically by the desert people. Jars and baskets made convenient containers for the storage of seed crops. Small-mouthed pottery vessels were particularly effective because the openings could be sealed to curb invasions by pests. There is no evidence that the Hohokam ever used pit storage in the earth. Corn ears in husks were doubtless strung together and suspended from the roof beams in houses.

Recipes and seasonings are, of course, unknown. There is no direct evidence for the use of salt, but deposits of it near Camp Verde and along the Salt River were known to have been exploited in pre-Spanish times by Indians. The evaporation of ponded water in the environs of Snaketown leaves a salty crust, but the presence of undesirable salts makes it unlikely that the Hohokam depended upon this source. The acquisition of salt from the ocean during shell-collecting expeditions was perhaps the answer to their needs for this seasoning. Elongated pottery dishes with rough inner surfaces provide weak secondary evidence that *Capsicum*, or a similar "hot" plant, may have been known to the Hohokam.

Viewed broadly, the Hohokam relationship with the plants and animals of their world was an intimate one. It was practical where and when food dependence was concerned, and it was of a more esoteric nature when supernatural dimensions intruded. Awe and reverence for certain animals comes through in their art forms, although plants seem not to have been similarly regarded. They benefited early from cotton, from the macaw and the parrot in their economic and sacred but nonfood worlds. The dog was the only animal domesticate, and it appears not to have been abundant. There were no dog burials and there are no hints that the animal was used as food as was the case in Colima of western Mexico. As an adjunct to certain ritual observances, seasonally determined, there are hints that a mildly alcoholic beverage, saguaro fruit wine, was consumed.

Most important to Hohokam survival was cleverly merging the seasonality of grown and gathered crops. Double annual plantings of domesticates were coordinated with the natural harvest times of the saguaro and mesquite. When nature's bounty was about to run out, planted crops began to yield. As time passed, the availability of new races of maize should have, and probably did, lead to an increase in the gross yield of foodstuffs. In spite of the technological advances in irrigation and a respectable roster of edible domesticates, the Hohokam did experience shortages. Their food-producing efficiency could not overcome natural calamities: the drying up of the river, serious flood damage to the canal and field systems, the effects of pests, and the possible though not demonstrable break-down of social or political controls. They were tough enough and adjustable enough, however, to weather adversities and to survive as a viable and identifiable people for more than 1,500 years.

My own subjectively-derived explanation of their exceptional capacity to persist was the simpleness and uncomplicated nature of the social and political systems. Shifts in food dependencies could be made with no more than the temporary trauma of being hungry. Tribal cohesion was not threatened as long as people were willing to move down the food scale to the less desirable resources. Fortunately these resources were always there. The ability to last saw the Hohokam through the greatest crisis of all, the break-up of the large communities, such as Casa Grande, Los Muertos, Pueblo Grande, and many others, at the end of the Classic Period, near A.D. 1450. It was then that the Hohokam-Piman transition became a reality.

CANAL CONSTRUCTION

One of the declared objectives in returning to Snaketown was to delve deeply into the history of Hohokam agriculture. The investigations of 1934–35 established the existence of a formal and advanced canal system in the environs of Snaketown by about A.D. 800, or toward the end of the Colonial Period (Haury 1936a; Gladwin and others 1937: 50-58). Other studies (Judd 1931; Haury 1945: 39-42; Woodbury 1960a, 1961) have focused on the water systems subsequent to that time, notably the achievements of the thirteenth and fourteenth centuries. The goal, therefore, was to extend the record at the early end of the spectrum. The probability that this could be done was predicated on a set of observed conditions: internal stratigraphic evidence pointed to the fact that Snaketown was a stable, relatively large, sedentary community for centuries before A.D. 800, the oldest evidence we had for canal use.

The length of antecedent time, while debatable in the minds of some, nevertheless appeared to me to be the longer part of the village's history, perhaps 1,000 years in contrast with less than 400 years that followed A.D. 800. Widespread trash of the Pioneer Period, architectural remains, and cremations were testimony of established living; the quality of the surviving cultural material signaled a mode of life that was far from the beginning of sedentism. It was unreasonable to believe that a settled village could exist in the desert without some form of water technology. To phrase the proposition in another way: in the arid environment of the Gila valley, a sizable clumping of people could not survive as

a village without farming; farming could not be pursued without an advanced knowledge of arid land agriculture; and arid land agriculture could not be effectively practiced without irrigation. Our projection, therefore, was that in the vicinity of Snaketown traces of a canal or canals should be found that were as old as the founding of the village. This was evidence we bent all efforts to detect.

Having demonstrated in 1934–35 that the later canals hugged the edge of the upper terrace, it was plausible enough to think that the earlier waterways might be there too. Yet, there were lingering doubts for the following reasons: At the time the work began in 1964–65, my concept of Hohokam origins was that people representing a branch of the native Desert Culture were stimulated to pursue other ways of living than food gathering by adopting ideas flowing out of the south. The consequences of this should have produced a recognizable cultural stage introductory to the Vahki Phase which was already well along the path of a settled way of life. Logic suggested that the living floor of this hypothetical pre-Vahki stage with elemental agriculture was probably on the lower terrace where a simple ditch system could have been established and where domestic activities took place close to the fields. With the introduction of more advanced water systems, use of the upper terrace became preferable. However, since the lower terrace was subject to periodic flooding, alluviation would have buried the traces of early canals and other evidence of the initial step toward village existence. The discovery of the same would be good luck.

A long machine-dug trench in the lower terrace revealed subsurface conditions of silts, clay, and sand that held out little hope of finding use or field surfaces (Fig. 8.2). We therefore concentrated the testing on the edge of the upper terrace by a series of trenches ranging over a lateral distance of about 5.5 km (3.5 mi), going 2.5 km (1.5 mi) east and 3 km (3 mi) west of Snaketown (Fig. 8.6). These tests were made through and beyond each edge of the observable surface remains of the fourteenth-century ditch, with the ideas that we would not only learn about it but also, hopefully, pick up traces of older systems on the premise that the courses followed would not have changed much through time.

It soon became apparent that the most complex overlapping of ditches and remodeling of systems took place in Snaketown itself and that perhaps the best prospects of finding the early evidence would be there.

It is worth digressing here to ask why the most extensive remodelings occurred at the terrace edge marking the southern limits of Snaketown. The principal reason was the fact that the largest acreage of arable land on the lower terrace for many miles up and down the river lay directly below the village. Drawing water from the canals through outlets laterally to the lower terrace, an abrupt drop of about 3 m, had at least two side effects that were troublesome. One was erosion, caused either by too much water or by the gradient change, requiring more or less continual maintenance and in some cases realignment of the ditch. The other was the opposite effect, namely, a gradual filling-in of the canal, caused by slowing down the water's velocity at the diversion point where its silt load was dropped. In time this would clog the ditch and require cleaning. There is evidence for both of these seemingly contradictory phenomena, as will be brought out later.

At this time, however, one point needs stressing. If one stands on the lower terrace 0.5 km south and looks directly back, or north, to Snaketown, the eye can trace a gentle rise on the horizon formed by the terrace edge starting at the eastern limit of the village and falling off again on reaching the western boundary. This subtle doming is the product of desilting the ditches, the volume of removed silt having been enough over the years to alter the natural profile of the terrace. The increased silt deposition here was the function of more water management at the village's

Fig. 8.2. Illustrating use of the backhoe to dig long exploratory trenches and in exposing segments of canals. Trench at right started on lower terrace. Canal being cleared is at edge of upper terrace (Four Canal Station).

edge, suggesting that the location was a strategic one both for irrigating fields below and perhaps for drawing domestic water. This hint reinforced the feeling that the oldest canal evidences would be found on the upper terrace.

Having cut a series of trenches with the backhoe, ranging from 8 to 60 m in length, we then carefully examined the trench walls for soil texture and color changes that would signal the presence of disturbances. In most cases, having learned something about the nature of canal morphology from prior work, we had no difficulty in picking up canal profiles. However, we also discovered that natural weathering of trench faces after several months' exposure brought out details not observable after the trenches were freshly cut. Recognition of this phenomenon was fortunate, for it was the decisive factor in delaying the back-filling of the tests.

In the meantime, much energy and time were spent clearing a set of superimposed canals, the Four Canal Station, and the Diversion Area at the east edge of Snaketown, but we were not getting any closer to the detection of the early canal traces we so desperately wanted.

Early in April 1965, only days before the planned end of the operation, trench profile-checking and mapping brought to light some curious surfaces and soil changes that had gone unnoticed. Further investigations led to the discovery of what we had been looking for all along, the Pioneer Period canal. Several weeks of intensive study produced information that amply fulfilled the predicted existence of a water-control technology believed to be the essential underpinning to Hohokam life from the moment they set foot in the Southwest.

Topographic Setting

For an agriculturally dependent people, water and land are the most essential resources. Broadly speaking, two options face the farmer: dry land tillage which takes advantage of natural rain, and cultivation by irrigation in the arid belts where rainfall is inadequate. In the latter instance greater resourcefulness is required for crop production, entailing knowledge of the behavior of water and the technical skills to control it. For the greater effort demanded by the latter system the recompense is a higher assurance

of bountiful and certain harvest than can be expected under dryland cultivation. In addition to land and water, however, another essential ingredient is required for the development of successful waterworks: a land configuration that permits the construction of a canal or canals which lead the water from a living source, usually a river, gradually away from it to cultivable land surfaces. For the development of large canal systems under primitive conditions this means a terrain of low relief and streams shallowly entrenched in the flood plain. Further, natural obstacles as hills and side drainages must be minimal or surmountable by the level of technology possessed by the subjugators.

It is no accident that the Gila and Salt River valleys experienced irrigation achievements unmatched anywhere north of Mexico. They provided an ideal topographic setting, and these advantages did not escape the searching eyes of the Hohokam, already knowledgeable in the methods needed to conquer the desert when they arrived in the Southwest.

Let us look more closely into the land surface and river characteristics that were attractive to the Hohokam. For about 8 km (5 mi) above and below Snaketown the Gila River has established a bed that drops a little more than 2 m per km (about 10 ft per mi) (Fig. 8.3a). Associated with this relatively flat gradient is a broad valley with only now and again a close impingement of the drainage on the low volcanic mountains that dot the area. Locally, where they were developed and not modified subsequently, an upper terrace and a lower terrace are discernible, separated altitudinally from 3 to 5 m. Where best preserved the upper terrace edge falls away sharply to the lower terrace surface. Proceeding south in a course from Snaketown toward the river (Fig. 8.3b), for about 1 km, we reach the edge of the floodplain, marked by an escarpment cut into the lower terrace by past floods. Dropping down about 1.5 m onto the rivulet-creased and silty surface of the floodplain, one soon comes to the river which flows in a channel about 2.0 m in depth, and 20.0 m in width. It is dry now, in the 1970s, except after rains, the waters being impounded by upstream dams. Continuing south for a kilometer, the floodplain gives way to the lower terrace edge again, though here poorly developed, and from this point on the land surface gently rises with no perceptible separation of the lower and upper terraces. This ground is now, and has been for long, under Pima cultivation. Before that it served well the occupants of what is now the large ruin of Casa Blanca.

The land near Snaketown most easily brought under cultivation was on the lower terrace, but the acreage was limited because it was hemmed in by the upper terrace and the floodplain. Water introduced onto the upper terrace would bring a vast additional acreage under cultivation. It is worth noting at this juncture that Pima fields were always on the lower terrace (Castetter and Bell 1942: 17). Hohokam cultivation was certainly there too, but they also mastered upper terrace tillage.

It is not my intention to look closely into Pima irrigation as a modern model of what once might have existed, but a brief inspection of the recent fields is worthwhile if for no other reason than to demonstrate the availability of nearby fertile lands. In Figure 8.4, the field patterns on the lower terrace have been taken from aerial photographs. It is clear that several generations of field systems are represented: older ones with indistinct borders in which the irregularly laid out fields were served by small canals; and later fields, geometrically engineered, with well-preserved borders, served by canals that were laid out by instrument. The older fields must date from the nineteenth century when a number of Pima families settled in Snaketown, and the newer fields date from about the turn of the century when federal assistance was given the Indians in field improvement. The canals serving these acres are shown as not in use on an irrigation map produced by the U.S. Indian Service, based on a survey made in 1914. The

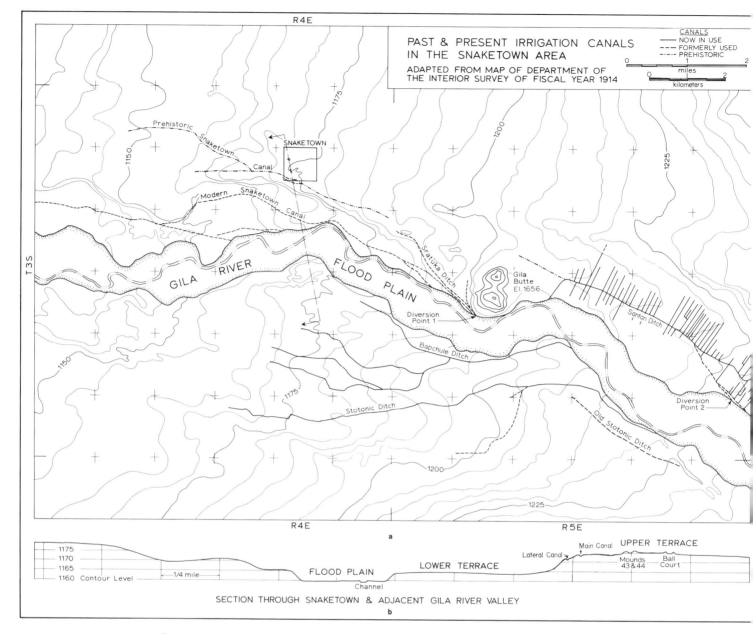

Fig. 8.3. Plan and section of Gila River valley near Snaketown showing land form favorable to canal system development. All recent and modern ditches not indicated; probable diversion points for prehistoric canals are shown.

Hohokam fields probably were much like the older Pima farming plots in general layout.

Pima agricultural activity, together with the periodic flooding suffered by the lower terrace, has effectively erased all obvious traces of Hohokam use of the same acreage. Although Pima cultural materials, as for example pottery, are recoverable from the lower terrace surface, diligent searching failed to reveal any concentrations of pre-1400 Hohokam pottery. If such evidence is present, it is buried under silt, but our machine-dug trenches failed to produce any subsurface indications either of old cultivated land surfaces or of buried cultural vestiges.

Existing Evidence of Canals

We turn now to the evidence of ancient canals in the environs of Snaketown as the basis for the detailed examinations that follow. Ground inspection, aerial photographs, and old maps have been used in preparing Figure 8.3. The principal canal, in fact the only surface evidence of old irrigation, is first picked up about 2 km northwest of Gila Butte on a spur of the upper terrace. To the west it has been washed out by erosion of the terrace edge for several

hundred meters, whence it picks up again in an easily traced trough. In the southwestern environs of Snaketown, the waterway divides to form north and south branches. This fork was trenched in 1934–35 (Gladwin and others 1937: 55-56) and restudied by Woodbury in 1959 (Fig. 8.39). The north branch continues for approximately 4 km in a northwesterly direction where acreage on the upper terrace could have been exploited, and the south branch becomes vague and not certainly traceable 2 km beyond the junction. Both may have been much longer than the evidence indicates.

The main interest now focuses on the point at which river waters were diverted into the canal. For this there is no clear answer and there may never be one due to the extensive natural modifications of the terrain. Nevertheless, two possibilities exist as were noted in 1937 (Gladwin and others: 52), with a few elaborations. The first option is to suggest a diversion system in the floodplain about 6 km (4 mi) east of Gila Butte (Diversion Point 2) where formerly used, but historic, ditches also took water from the river. The present Santan Ditch apparently follows the course of the old one which reappears as a remnant about 1 km east of Gila Butte where the Santan Ditch turns abruptly to the

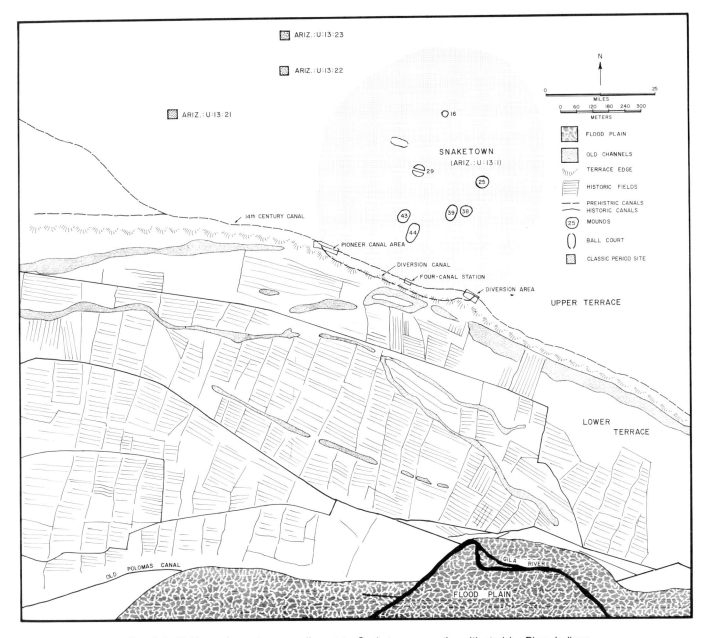

Fig. 8.4. Fields on lower terrace adjacent to Snaketown recently cultivated by Pima Indians. Borders within field plots are not accurately depicted as to spacing, but directions are correct. Meanders in the Gila River (bottom) have destroyed sections of Old Polomas canal and required extensive realignment of other ditches. Based on aerial photograph taken April 14, 1965.

southwest. The stub of the old canal continues northwesterly for more than a kilometer where it vanishes. Projected further, this canal could logically be joined to the old Snaketown Ditch. Contour configuration permits this extension.

A striking feature of the Santan Ditch (Fig. 8.5) is the fact that the water level is well above the ground surface of the adjacent fields. The canal runs on a levee which can only be the product of desilting operations over a long period of time. The unique consequence of this is that laterals depart from the ditch in *both* directions (Fig. 8.3), instead of only on the down side, the usual pattern. The hypothesis that the Santan Ditch is flowing on the course of an ancient canal could be verified, in all probability, by digging one or more sections through it, a difficult feat now because the system is in almost constant use.

The second option is to place the diversion of river water at the foot of Gila Butte (Fig. 8.3, Diversion Point 1). The 1914 survey shows two old canals departing from the river at this point, one going a short distance almost due north on the west side of Gila Butte, the other heading northwest for about 3 km (2 mi), called

the Sratuka Ditch. An extension of about 0.5 km would join it with the old Snaketown canal. The terrain would permit this because in the first 2 km west of Gila Butte the upper-lower terrace configuration is lost and a gentle slope exists. By holding to a gradient less than that of the river, water flow could be directed to the upper terrace at this point.

It may be that both of these diversion points figured in the story of irrigation at Snaketown, the one at Gila Butte being the first one, where the Pioneer Period canal headed; the second one east of Gila Butte being considerably later, perhaps dating from Classic Period times when the system reached its greatest geographic extent. The question should be pursued further by field investigations.

Once on the upper terrace, the course of the canal was relatively free of obstacles, such as depressions or large side drainages. There were, however, a few indentations caused by small drainages that had to be overcome. The evidences of how the Hohokam engineers accomplished this have not survived.

Fig. 8.5. The Santan Ditch, looking west to Gila Butte. Canal runs high on a wide levee permitting field irrigation to left and right.

Scope of Testing

Figure 8.6 is a control map which identifies the locations of about 30 canal-sectioning trenches we made, ranging over a lateral distance of 8 km (5 mi) east and west of Snaketown. Also, those places where intensive work was done are readily singled out. These will be reviewed in detail in the pages that follow. Simple cross-section trenches were useful in plotting the precise location and axis of the ditch, in establishing its morphology, in slope determinations, and in detecting clues as to canal ages. Furthermore, by studying the trench walls carefully for superpositions of one canal on another we could better program the lateral digging for a plan view of the system. In general, the greater the profile complexity, the more horizontal space would be needed to expose the features. We came to refer to this method as profile-plan excavating, the type example being the Pioneer Period canal which was cleared over a distance of about 75 m.

As far as we know, Cushing was the first to open a section of prehistoric canal in 1887–88 by stripping, the results recorded only as a sketch (Haury 1945a: Fig. 25). Trenches were dug at Snaketown in 1934–35, but Woodbury again used the stripping method at the fork west of Snaketown in 1959. The advantages of lateral exposure over a simple trench were so obvious that we employed the method with most productive results. Clearing an entire canal should be the goal in any future work because it would produce details of water control which we do not have now. But time and money are practical limiting factors.

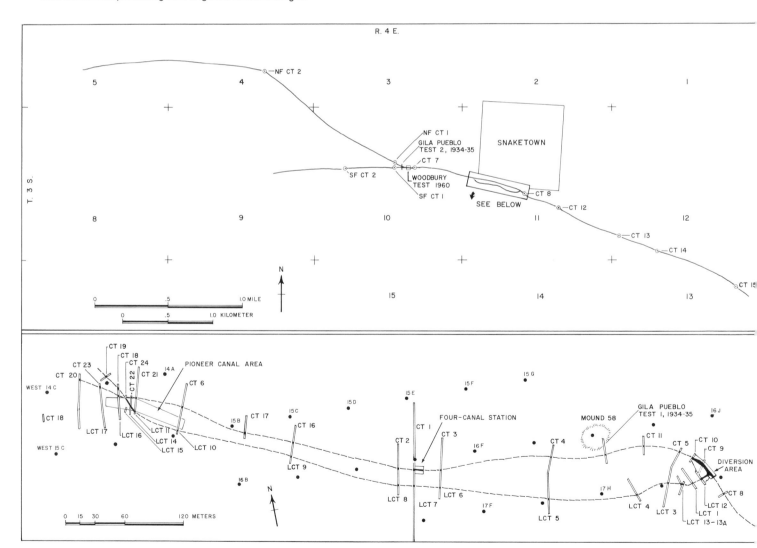

Fig. 8.6. Control map indicating where trench tests intercepted canals and the location of areas of more intensive study. Lower map is enlargement of main and lateral canals at southwest edge of Snaketown. CT = canal test; LTC = lateral canal test; 15 D = grid designation.

Trench walls, as left by the machine, are rough and difficult to read except where the features present radical contrasts with the adjacent natural matrix. For this reason a Pima worker was assigned the task of dressing the walls to a smooth surface with a flattened shovel and trowel. Upon exposure to the air, ground moisture was lost, which was both helpful and detrimental, depending on the nature of the deposits. In the long run, however, except in tight clays, drying hastened a natural etching which revealed nuances in the strata and in the disturbed areas that had escaped detection immediately after the trench was dug. As noted before, several months exposure to the elements led to the identification of the Pioneer Period canal. Light conditions were important also. Diffused light as provided by an overcast sky was found to be better than direct sunlight, and worst of all was an overhead sun. Repeated inspections of the trenches were found to be helpful.

Wherever it became necessary to expand the area under excavation, for example, the Diversion Area, we did not hesitate to put the machine to work provided that projections of a canal course could be made between two points where it had been sectioned. Our backhoe operator, Joe Marrietta, shown the soil conditions as exposed in the cross-sections, could, by color of the soil and "pull" of the machine, nearly always tell whether he was removing canal fill or whether he had reached the matrix layer. An expert shovel man worked with the machine, guiding it as needed, cutting down the risk of "over" excavation. Without the energy provided by the machine to excavate and to haul away the back dirt we would not have dared to undertake the broadside digging we did. With it we learned infinitely more than we lost in the few spots where limited damage was done.

The aggregate length of exploratory trenches in our search for canals was 1,300 m, or well over 1 km (0.8 mi), and the depths ranged from 1 to 3 m. We did not attempt to calculate the volume of dirt removed from the major areas where stripping was done, but it amounted to a respectable percentage of all the dirt moved at Snaketown. Canal studies are costly of machine- and man-time, and displayable specimens are, for the most part, nonexistent. But such information as is recovered relates directly to the heart of Hohokam economic life, ample justification for the total effort.

DIVERSION AREA

In the southeast outskirts of Snaketown exceptionally large piles of silt along the main canal pointed to the existence of a special feature, a spot where more than usual desilting took place. This came to be known as the Diversion Area (Fig. 8.6). Here, in the natural topography, the upper-lower terrace boundary was erased; instead, there was a gentle merging of the two terrace surfaces. The cause, as we learned after testing, was the drainage of water from the upper to the lower terrace on its way to the Gila River. This feature in the terrain did not go unnoticed by the Hohokam, for they saw in it an advantage that suited their needs. Water from the upper terrace canal could be gently lowered by a supply ditch to fields below with less risk of washouts than would have been the case where the gradient was steeper. It remained for us, however, to prove this and to provide the details.

Cleaning off the desert growth clearly delineated the main canal and a break in its embankment on the south or low side. This we assumed to be the location of the diversion canal (Fig. 8.7). It was also anticipated, in view of the extensive silt piles, that we might find a settling basin from which both the main and the lateral canals could draw water with lesser amounts of solids in it, an idea which proved to be erroneous.

The first step was the excavation of a trench by machine at the west end of the area to accurately locate the bed of the main canal. From here on it was a question of groping, always with the knowledge that a trench might remove crucial evidence. This risk was largely overcome by close vigilance as the machine did its work. In time, a number of trenches revealed the gross nature of the

Fig. 8.7. The Diversion Area. Men in row on left stand in main canal. Predicted course of lateral canal is shown by line of workers to right. Looking east, or up-stream.

complex which then let us move in with hand labor. Indistinct soil color and texture changes could not always be read with certainty, a fact which resulted in over-excavation in several spots. This amounted to the removal of old surfaces, but serious damage to canals was avoided. The alternatives in large-scale earth-removal operations are either to dig over-cautiously, covering less area and thereby learning less, or, to be somewhat bolder, taking in more area and learning more. I elected the latter course. The results, in my estimation, justified the choice.

As the area unfolded, we could see that there was no settling basin as predicted but rather a direct turnout of the lateral, leaving the main waterway at somewhat less than a right angle (Figs. 8.8, 8.9). The main canal here had an upper and a lower bed, separated by about 0.5 m (Figs. 8.10, section EE'; 8.11), representing two periods of canal use. These were not clearly datable by contents, but on the basis of collateral evidence coming from the side canal and a washout spot, I infer that the system as we found it was operable at least from the Santa Cruz Phase of the Colonial Period through the Civano Phase of the Classic Period, or through a time span of 600 or 700 years. It may be assumed that the lateral ditch was in service during this period. Many remodelings during six or seven centuries undoubtedly took place, but the evidence was not preserved.

A diversion structure, or structures, are necessary at any canal fork to effectively control the water. Postholes in the floor and in the sides of the lateral bore testimony to the former existence of headgates designed to admit or block water from entering the lateral system. One can imagine that a series of posts were set across the canal at right angles to its axis as supports for horizontal lacings of pliable branches. Either bundles of brush or woven mats could be laid against this structure, thereby creating a temporary dam, confining the water to the main canal, or when open, admitting water into the lateral.

The rebuilding of this structure numerous times has left behind a confusing set of postholes (Figs. 8.10, 8.12). Two post alignments are identifiable, section DD' being one of them, but these do not account for all of the holes present. The structures were set from 1 m to a little more than 4 m back from the south bank of the main canal instead of flush with it. The reason for this is not clear, but it may be easier to control water when the detaining structure is set back from the main flow. The choice of this spot for the device was an unhappy one, however, for it was placed directly in

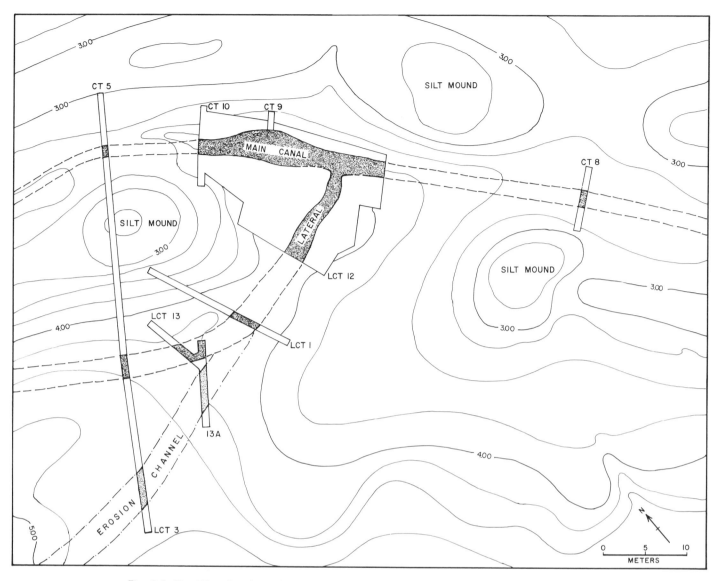

Fig. 8.8. The Diversion Area showing the exposed parts of the main and lateral canals and projections thereof established by tests, the silt mounds, and erosion channel caused by a break in the lateral canal. CT = canal test; LCT = lateral canal test. Contour interval 0.25 m.

Fig. 8.9. General view of Diversion Area at southeast border of Snaketown, looking westerly.

line with an old erosion channel filled with sand and fine gravel. This weakness was revealed when excess water, either spilling over the retaining dam or leaking around it, carved out a meter-deep plunge pool. Uncontrolled, this might have acted as an erosion head and eaten its way back into the main ditch. But corrective measures were taken by filling the hole with several discarded metates and more than 250 kg of broken pottery (Fig. 8.13). Potsherds were obviously selected for their large size, being more resistant to washing away than smaller units.

Hodge reported (1893) postholes in the canal at Los Muertos, though no details of the presumed headgate were given. Woodbury states (Fig. 8.39) that no traces of canal structures were found at the fork in the main system west of Snaketown.

Although a few sherds of late Pioneer and Colonial Period times were present in the afore mentioned erosion repair, 95% of the sample was Sacaton Red-on-buff, probably taken from a nearby trash mound, No. 58, which was composed of Sacaton Phase refuse. Curiously, the ratio of painted to plain pottery was about 100:1 (normal ratio 2:3), further evidence of a selective process at work, but for what reason is not known. The date of the repair, however, must have been later than the Sacaton Phase, for small amounts of Gila Red and Gila Polychrome indicate the Civano Phase, roughly during the fourteenth century, to have been the time the washout occurred, or at least the last time that the repair was made.

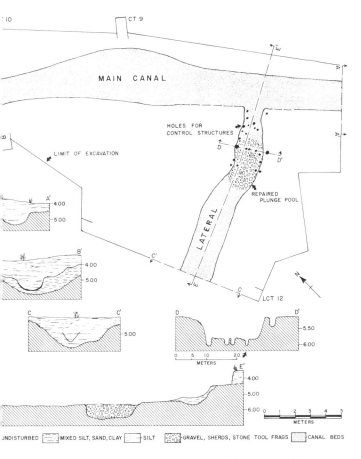

Fig. 8.10. Diversion Area plan and sections: BB′ shows 14th century canal with calcareous lining running in a mixed deposit filling earlier ditch; CC′ has trace of post-1400 "echo" canal.

Fig. 8.12. Postholes in the lateral canal of the Diversion Area are remnants of water control structures. Dotted lines indicated locations of two frameworks. Metates rest in plunge pool.

Fig. 8.11. The main canal in the Diversion Area illustrating two phases of use: older (foreground) and younger (background). Man stands in lateral canal.

Fig. 8.13. Cross-section of the intentional erosion control fill below diversion structure consisting of potsherds and worn-out metates.

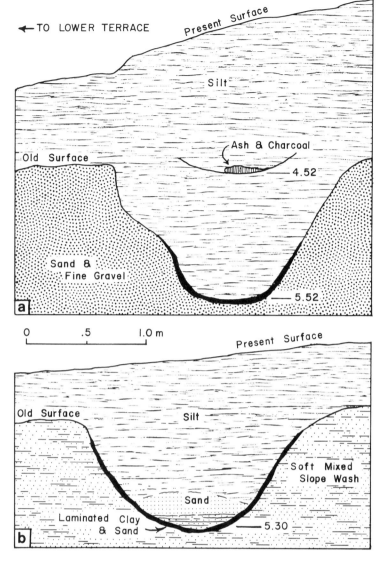

Fig. 8.14. Two north-south sections of a presumed lateral ditch east of the main Diversion Area. Both profiles reveal artificially applied clay linings.

Careful searching in the floor of the main canal failed to reveal any traces whatever of a diversion structure. The absence of post-holes, taken at face value, means that no structure ever existed there. From this one infers that the main ditch always carried water, some of it being let out into the lateral as needed. This parallels modern practices in which the main canal runs constantly, supplying the numerous outlets that are dependent on it, when the time for water delivery has arrived.

While we explored the obvious place where the main canal was split into two, it may be assumed that diversions existed in other places as well. The arable land extends eastward nearly to Gila Butte, and this acreage would not have gone unexploited. Present dendritic erosion channels exposed differences in soils on the downslope from the upper terrace several hundred meters east of the Diversion Area. Limited probing here established the fact that one or more canals in addition to the main one did exist, but time limitation did not allow further study. One ditch, exposed in three cuts, ranged from 1.0 to 1.5 m in width and about 0.75 m in depth (Fig. 8.14). Since the canal here was originally excavated in redeposited slope wash, including some sand and fine gravel and therefore softer and more pervious than the normal first terrace matrix, holding the water presented a problem. To overcome seepage and perhaps erosion, the canal was lined with a clayey material up to 5 cm thick. This was evidently hand applied and was not the result of natural encrustation as was the case in the

main canal. Woodbury has recorded a similar lining (1960a: 269) in a canal near Pueblo Grande, Phoenix, evidently designed to reduce water loss by ground percolation. An "echo" canal, partly ash and charcoal filled, was observed in one section (Fig. 8.14a). Too few potsherds were recovered to suggest the time of use. Further work in this area would be rewarding.

LATERAL CANAL

Sections were cut through the lateral canal in 14 places which provided information about its exact location and details of its shape, size, and grade (Fig. 8.6). Although the downslope of the upper terrace is exposed to continual erosion, once having established where the lateral canal lay, it was possible to detect it in a few places by surface evidence alone: by a slight benching of the slope where it was freshly washed clean, by a soil change from the silt that filled the canal to the harder redder terrace matrix adjacent, and by concentrations of sand and fine gravel next to the canal, probably remnants of cleanings. I doubt that these traces would have been recognized as marking the presence of a canal without first knowing that it was there.

The path of the lateral never took it far from the main canal, and the maximum vertical difference in the two canal floors was only 1.25 m. This was enough to bring the lateral near the average surface level of the lower terrace so water could be drained from it without risk of washouts. While the actual outlets, or head ditches, were not found, the function of the lateral as a supplier of water to the lower fields seems certain. Figure 8.41 illustrates the comparative grades of the main and lateral canals west of the diversion to the point where the two are presumed to have merged again.

Poor engineering or the peculiarity of the terrain resulted in a sharp bend in the lateral near its departure point from the main artery (Fig. 8.8). The unhappy consequence of this was a washout. Too much water, perhaps when the main canal bank on the upslope side was breached by floods, filled the lateral and broke through its side at the bend seeking the shortest path to the river. An arroyo about 2 m deep resulted. This was repaired by filling the gully with soil that contained a liberal amount of pottery, and by restoring the canal bank. Noting once again the youngest potsherds in the sample, Santa Cruz Red-on-buff, it is inferred that this event took place sometime between A.D. 700–900. The episode adds another detail to the general problem of maintenance that perpetually faced the Hohokam.

Although the lateral was about as large as the main ditch, it was somewhat shallower on the whole and flatter bottomed (Figs. 8.15, 8.16). Presumably it never carried the same head of water as did the main ditch, and the shallower bed made the drainouts easier to construct and to control. While the test trenches revealed marked differences in the essentially natural deposits into which the lateral canal was excavated, a few instances were detected where the matrix was the product of earlier human disturbances. For example, the high sand wedge in LCT 8 (Fig. 8.15) was clearly trapped in an earlier ditch of which only a small part remains. Considerable water loss must have been sustained where the lateral passed over sand and gravel zones (Fig. 8.15, LCT 6).

What happened to the lateral canal at its westernmost end is an enigma. Had we been able to clear a larger area where the Pioneer Canal was exposed, the answer might have proven to be a simple one. As it stands, however, the evidence shows that the lateral was directed back on the upper terrace where it sliced through a series of older ditches (Fig. 8.22, Canal 5) and where it may have rejoined the contemporary main canal. If true, returning surplus water to the main artery was a shrewd piece of engineering, thereby avoiding its release on the lower terrace with the attendant risk of starting gully-cutting. Grade separations of two arms of one waterway and their eventual reunion would represent an impressive understanding of fluid mechanics.

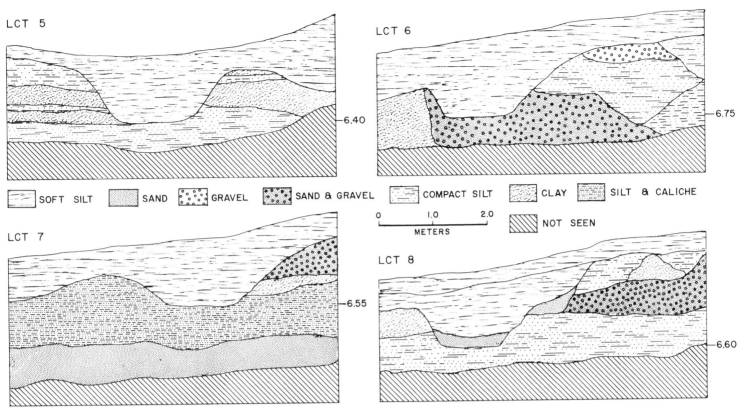

Fig. 8.15. Profiles of four tests in Lateral Canal (looking west), illustrating its shallow and flat-bottomed configuration.

Fig. 8.16. Silt-filled lateral canal as seen in face of Canal Test 1, looking west. Ditch is exposed in foreground.

Reviewing the evidence for the age of the lateral canal we have the arroyo wash-out, mentioned earlier, as an indication of its use in the Santa Cruz Phase, A.D. 700–900, and on the basis of sherd contents, its use extended upward in time to at least 1400 or to the end of the Classic Period. This is a long time, and it may be assumed that during these centuries the lateral was cleaned and repaired many times. Our trenches did not reveal any overlaps or stratification of the lateral indicating that the original grade and configuration were maintained or that the last rehabilitation erased all traces of the former canal if it was present. This fact may account for the absence of a calcareous lining in the lateral, a curious situation because in the main canal this lining was well developed, as is reviewed later.

FOUR CANAL STATION

A hand-dug trench in 1934–35 (Test 1) through Mound 58 and the adjacent canal in Block 16H demonstrated a superposition of ditches, the oldest of which was in use by A.D. 800, and the youngest of which served residents in the area perhaps as late as A.D. 1400 (Gladwin and others 1937: 53-55). Moving west about 200 m to Blocks 15E and 16E (Canal Test 1), our machine sliced through a projection of the canal with the hope of duplicating the earlier findings. This trench, a long one (about 315 m) started on the lower terrace, moved to the upper terrace, and continued northward to Mound 44. This venture produced information about the upper-lower terrace geomorphology, disclosed an unexpected canal bed on the slope of the upper terrace which proved to be the lateral already discussed, a cluster of four superimposed canals which we had hoped for, and a Snaketown Phase house (1:15E), also unexpected (Fig. 8.17). The traces of all of these were first picked up by examining the trench walls. The complexity of each feature was the basis for determining the kind of lateral excavation it would receive.

Turning first to the superimposed canals, it was estimated that a 10 m long exposure would adequately lay bare remaining fragments of the four arteries as seen in the profile (Figs. 8.18, 8.19) so the physical relationships could be understood.

The sequence of events that led to the preservation of this complex of ditches was as follows (Fig. 8.20): Canal 1, the largest and oldest of the group, was about 2.5 m wide and an estimated 2.0 m deep. It was constructed between A.D. 700–900 on the basis of potsherd content. Through extended use, the bed was completely filled with a silty clay deposit, requiring a re-excavation which produced Canal 2 that seems to have been only

Fig. 8.17. Aerial view of Canal Test-Trench 1 (center) which exposed House 1:15E, 4 superimposed canals and the lateral ditch. Looking east.

Fig. 8.18. Four superimposed canals as seen in test trench face. Boundary lines, determined by color, texture, and structure differences in the soils have been accentuated by scoring.

about half as large as the first one, and lying completely within the old bed. The few potsherds recovered from the fill were of the Sacaton Phase. The alluviation cycle was then repeated, necessitating the opening of Canal 3, whose south bank seems to have coincided with the south bank of Canal 1. Remnants of silty clay fill in Canal 3 indicate it was nearly completely filled before a cleaning became necessary. This effort removed about two-thirds of it, forming Canal 4 which retained the general configuration of Canal 3. The last two canals are attributable to the Classic Period, roughly A.D. 1200–1400.

What cannot be determined from a situation like this is how many remodelings there may have been which completely erased a prior canal or canals. Assuming that all the evidence is there in this case, and that the time span represented is about 600 years, it would appear that each canal had an average life of 150 years. This seems altogether too long, though it must be admitted that longevity of use was probably directly connected with the diligence manifested in maintenance. Some presently used Pima canals have been in use at least half that length of time, and there appears to be no reason why this figure cannot be doubled.

From the evidence at hand it may be inferred that the surface adjacent to the canals extant at the time they were in use remained stable. There was, however, an accumulation of silt on both sides nearby, which was added to with each canal cleaning. It was this material, in the main, which filled the wide canal trough created by the embankments and buried Canal 4 with more than 1 m of silt on top of the canal fill left by water flowing in it when the system finally fell into disuse.

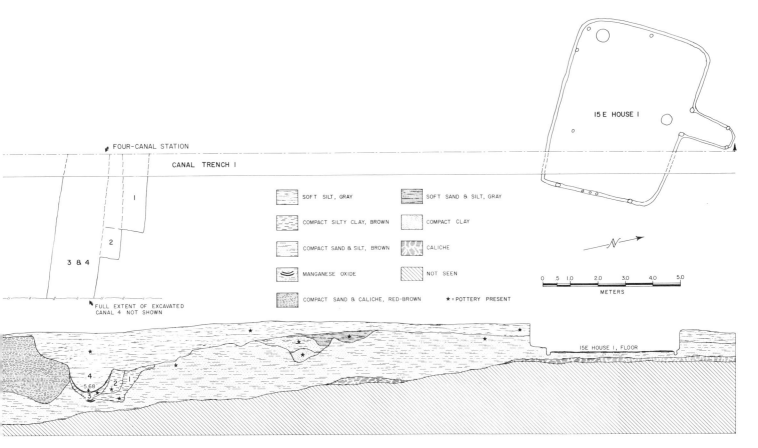

Fig. 8.19. Plan and section of the Four Canal Station and nearby House 1:15E. Canals are numbered in the order of succession.

Fig. 8.20. Segments of ditches in Four Canal Station, constructed in order of numbering. Time span is roughly from A.D. 700 (Canal 1) to 1400 (Canal 4).

It is doubtful if the decrease in canal size, as between Canals 1 and 4, is really meaningful. The oldest canal in the 1934–35 Test 1 excavation (Gladwin and others 1937: Fig. 17) was also the largest there, and it probably is Canal 1. Contemporary and earlier ditches in the Pioneer Canal area are mostly somewhat smaller. The apparent greater width may have been a function of having had to dig the canal deep to maintain grade.

The repeated filling and rehabilitation of the ditches raises the question of the continuity of canal use. Since the record shows that the channels were completely clogged periodically and the old surface grade was nearly reestablished, one wonders whether there were times, and if so, of what duration, when the systems were totally inoperative. This condition could not have been tolerated long under permanent tenure of the village by agriculturists. I would speculate, therefore, that the fillings were perhaps of single flood or slack season origin and that the rejuvenation was done quickly thereafter.

Because the texture of the channel fills differs, a dense silty-clay in Canals 1, 2, and 3, and a soft laminated and sometimes cross-bedded silt and fine sand in Canal 4, one may argue for varying sets of sedimentation conditions as well as for different origins of the filling materials. Solids scoured from canal banks upstream by a high water velocity and redeposited lower down may be projected as the source for the filling material in the first three canals. A lower water velocity would tend to encourage plant growth, which would further reduce water flow and lead to silting. These conclusions are based on modern irrigation experiences. The slower water velocity in Canal 4 may have been a function of its somewhat reduced gradient in relation to the earlier three ditches.

The matrix into which Canal 1 was dug, as well as parts of the later ones, too, where the channels departed from the course of the older ditches, was a compact silty sand, homogeneous over the area exposed (Fig. 8.19). The floor of House 1: 15E, Snaketown Phase, was also intruded into this layer. While a few potsherds were found in the upper 15-20 cm, these were almost certainly intrusive and not indicators, therefore, of man's presence at the time the bed was formed. During the process of clearing House 1:15E, we believed that it was built into canal spoil dirt, suggesting the existence of a canal older than any we had seen. But subsequent probing showed that the house pit penetrated a native deposit. The disturbance midway between the house and the canals was man-caused during the Colonial or Sedentary Period, but no effort was made to determine what it meant.

Within the first 15 cm below the bed of Canal 3 were lenses of black material that contributed measurably to the hardness of the matrix. These black stains proved to be manganese oxide, evidently concentrated during favorable conditions established by long periods of continual wetting of the ground.

As already noted, the approach to the dating problem of the canals was on the basis of the contained pottery. This is not wholly satisfactory because sometimes the samples were too small to be helpful, and it will be readily understood that pottery of any type manufactured up to the time of the canal's use may be expected in it. The youngest pottery, therefore, is likely to be the most accurate indication of the age. In any given sample, however, the newest pottery may not always be present. The latest canal in this series by stratigraphy displayed a unique calcareous lining, up to 2 cm thick, a natural side effect of the minerals carried by the water and other factors. Some potsherds were literally cemented in and became integral parts of the lining (Fig. 8.21). These have special interest, for this phenomenon established beyond a doubt that the pottery was in the canal when it carried water, eliminating the chance intrusion of late potsherds into an older ditch. The diagnostic and late types recovered from the matrix were: Gila Red, Casa Grande Red-on-buff and Gila Polychrome. In round numbers, these spell the fourteenth century, extending possibly somewhat beyond A.D. 1400. By that time Snaketown as a village had been dead for about 300 years, except for the Classic Period settlements in the western suburbs. It was these communities, plus others still farther west and several to the east, that this late canal served.

Fig. 8.21. Fourteenth century potsherds cemented into calcareous lining of Canal 4 in the Four Canal Station.

PIONEER CANAL AREA

The four stratified canals just examined brought us no nearer to the beginnings of Hohokam irrigation than we had known in 1934–35. Yet, we were confident that the traces of older systems were there, if we could only recognize them. Discovery was delayed by two factors: the subtle nature of the evidence which became apparent only after the test trenches had stood open for a while, and one's own preconceived notion, based on prior experience with canals, of what the canal morphology should be.

As it turned out, the shape of the early canal was totally different than that of the canals in the later systems. In fact it took more than a little probing to convince us that a hard surface, concave in the axis exposed, from 3 to 5 m wide and less than 1 m in depth, could be a canal. This uncertainty continued to linger even after a lateral section 10 m long was opened to view. The proof needed, we judged, would come only by opening a much longer expanse of the feature. Additional cross-section trenches told us that it continued both to the east and the west of Canal Test 21, where it was first detected, and that other canals bore a later stratigraphic relationship to it. On the strength of these clues, the work schedule was revised and the total labor force was committed to clearing a 75 m section of what was becoming an ancient waterway with increasing clarity. In addition to that, we were confronted with one of the most perplexing entanglements of canals imaginable.

Pioneer Canal (Canal 1)

The oldest artery in the series was labeled Canal 1 (Fig. 8.22a), not only because it preceded all others stratigraphically but also because the potsherd contents revealed its use to have been during the several phases of the Pioneer Period. The position of the canal on the upper terrace merits note for, unlike all others, it hugged the edge where the surface started to slope toward the lower terrace (Fig. 8.23). This location may have been inspired by the greater convenience it provided in developing turn-outs from the shallow canal so water could reach the fields below. But this advantage may have been offset by making the canal more susceptible to erosion in the normal regression of the terrace edge.

The confusion we encountered at the eastern end of our exposure of the Pioneer Canal may have been the result of this erosion, and there was clear evidence in the west end that the later canals were shifted progressively higher on the terrace with each renovation (Fig. 8.35) thereby avoiding the risk of break-throughs on the low side of the canal. Attrition of the terrace edge since the fourteenth century is indicated by the loss of a part of the canal of that century east of Snaketown. This may be the reason why traces of the Pioneer Canal were not found in our tests eastward, assuming that it headed in the direction of Gila Butte 5 km (about 3 mi) to the east. There appears to be no alternative to getting water on the upper terrace except by going this far upstream in order to meet grade requirements.

In viewing the remnants of the Pioneer Canal, and indeed, others related to it, it must be stated that many details remain unclear. The only satisfactory way of studying canals is large-scale stripping, far exceeding what we were able to do. Even given the chance to view long stretches of canals, both man and nature may have intervened as destructive forces to remove the wanted evidence. Looking at the eastern end of the Pioneer Canal (Fig. 8.22a,b) we see the first of the enigmas exposed in Lateral Canal Test 10. The canal floor ended abruptly, and in its place was an area of undetermined size of mixed sand, silt, and clayey materials heavily impregnated with broken pottery and stone tool fragments. The disturbance went down a little over 1 m below the canal floor. We surmised that this represented damage to the canal by erosion, though the point cannot be established with the data at hand.

The few discarded stone implements and more than 12 kg of potsherds (about 2,000) removed from this area were of the

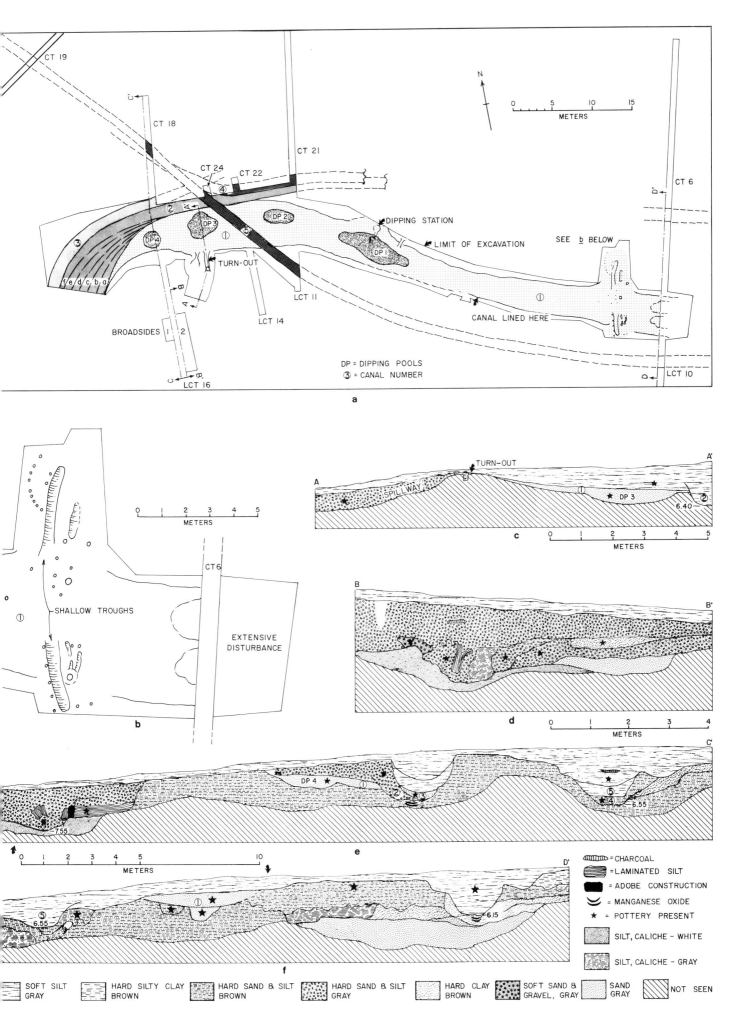

a

b

c

d

e

f

= CHARCOAL

= LAMINATED SILT

= ADOBE CONSTRUCTION

= MANGANESE OXIDE

★ = POTTERY PRESENT

SILT, CALICHE – WHITE

SILT, CALICHE – GRAY

SOFT SILT GRAY | HARD SILTY CLAY BROWN | HARD SAND & SILT BROWN | HARD SAND & SILT GRAY | HARD CLAY BROWN | SOFT SAND & GRAVEL, GRAY | SAND GRAY | NOT SEEN

Fig. 8.22. Plans and sections of Pioneer Canal Area: (a) arrangement of late ditches over Pioneer Canal (No. 1); (b) evidence of water control structure at east end of Pioneer Canal; (c) sections through Canals 2, 1, and turn-out in latter; (d, e) profiles of Broadsides 2 and 1 showing results of excessive erosion by water discharged through turn-out; (f) section through Canals 5, 1, and a canal not identified by number (far right). Non-culture bearing deposits have been simplified.

Fig. 8.23. The broad shallow bed of Pioneer Canal (No. 1), crossed and truncated by later ditches, rides close to upper terrace edge (dashed line, right). Approximate path of later systems indicated on left. Looking east to Gila Butte.

Fig. 8.24. East end of exposed Pioneer Canal showing features related to probable water control structures. Canal in excavated area below tripod was evidently destroyed by erosion during its use.

Pioneer Period. A handful of painted pottery, less than 0.5% of the sample, represented Estrella and Sweetwater Red-on-gray and Snaketown Red-on-buff. The pottery sample recovered from the deeper parts of the tests produced only Vahki Plain and Vahki Red. My speculation is that this presumed washout occurred early in the canal's history and that a by-pass of the trouble zone was effected by going higher on the terrace.

The indications for this are found some 6 m to the west where the canal floor turned north and east but progressively lost its distinctiveness. Also, at this point there were perplexing grooves and series of holes presumed to have housed posts (Figs. 8.22b; 8.24). Some kind of a structure, or structures, to aid in water-control must have stood here. The inability to come up with a clear explanation of what the feature was probably stems from our failure to uncover all the related bits of evidence and from the fact that different generations of structures are represented which cannot be differentiated now. A groove leading from the center of the canal to the south bank, and a faint hint of a bank repair in this locality, together with a series of postholes on the down side of the groove, as though a head gate had stood there, suggest a turn-out at this point.

Between the locus of these features and Lateral Canal Test 10 on the canal floor and in the fill immediately above, potsherds once again were abundant, amounting to 12.6 kg (about 2,000). Roughly 10% of the sample was Snaketown Red-on-buff, the rest Vahki Red and Plain, indicating a Snaketown Phase deposit.

These potsherds were not rolled, as were many found in the canal elsewhere, and the inference may be drawn that refuse was thrown into the canal late in the Pioneer Period. Further, it supports the notion that domestic structures existed close to the canals. A few Colonial and Sedentary Period pottery types occurred high in the canal fill.

Directly west, or down canal, from the grooves and posthole complex for a distance of about 3 m the potsherds from canal floor contact and in the sand up to 0.15 m above were also assignable to the Snaketown Phase. In a 4-kg sample, 10% was Snaketown Red-on-buff, the dominant painted type. An 11-kg sample from the upper fill of the canal at this point showed basically the same distribution of types with, however, slight admixtures of Estrella and Sweetwater Red-on-gray, evidently derived from older nearby rubbish sources. Also, Colonial and Sedentary Period types were more numerous, a predictable situation in view of the intensity of the occupation and the maze of nearby canals of these periods. The conclusion may be drawn that by the end of the Pioneer Period, during the Snaketown Phase, the standard canal form was still broad and shallow, basically the same configuration that it had at the beginning of the period.

As an aside, much of the pottery recovered in clearing the canals represents large jars, shapes suitable for the transport of water to nearby houses. Numerous fragments from the same jar point to the smashing of occasional vessels, perhaps accidentally. While no consistent shape or design differences were recognized between these and the rest of the ceramic output of the village, it may be a little more than an accident that several fragments of a jar showing a person carrying a vessel on the head (Fig. 12.92*l*) were present in the sample of canal sherds.

Dipping Pools

Continuing westward or downstream in the canal, its bed widens, probably to accommodate a series of depressions in the canal bottom. These hollows have been labeled Dipping Pools, number 1 through 4, for reasons that will become apparent. They range in size from 2 to 8 m in greatest diameter, which parallels the canal's axis, and up to 0.5 m in depth (Figs. 8.22a, c; 8.25). Not until related details began to appear at the north edge of Pool 1 was it possible to speculate about their signficance.

Because of the exceptionally hard and characteristic floor of the Pioneer Canal there was no problem whatever in defining a vertically oriented groove and two adjacent, flat, well-worn shelves. Since these were not the products of the excavator's trowel, they had to be the result of work or of intentionally made features on someone's part. It was obvious that the depressions would hold water when it ceased to flow in the canal. It was also clear that the depressions were artificial and that they were put there with a purpose, namely, to provide a limited supply of domestic water for families nearby when the live flow in the ditch dried up.

If this reasoning was correct, then what we saw was evidence of the physical act of drawing water from the pool. Left-foot and right-knee positions were easily established on the flat shelves. Left-handed dipping, reaching down to water level, and the dragging of the dipper against the side of the pool, produced the vertical groove. A larger flattened area just above the right-knee position would have been a suitable place for the water jar to rest (Fig. 8.26). All in all, what was laid out before us here was no more than a common-sense way of obtaining domestic water easily, for, at low water times the chore of carrying it from a more distant point, the river, could be thus delayed.

The dipping pools were important for another reason. They were filled with sand and great quantities of broken pottery and other cultural items, clues to their respective ages. Pool 2 had an intermediate level in it created by a stable period in the accumulation of solids, which provided a measure of stratigraphic differentiation.

The samples retained for analysis, the results of which are given in Figure 8.27, do not represent the total sum of potsherds collected from the various pools. The reason for excluding some is based on the fact that in the early stages of excavation we were not always sure what the feature was, and some mixing of the sherd returns resulted. Once the feature became clear, better control was established. The more than 84 kg analyzed probably amounts to about half of the recovered sherds in the pools, a sufficiently large quantity to be indicative of the time of accumulation.

Pool 1 was the largest yet the poorest in terms of artifactual returns. Perhaps it was cleaned more frequently, because it seems to have been the main source of domestic water. A preponderance of Snaketown Red-on-buff suggests use to the end of the Pioneer Period, duplicating the record to the east near the structure area. The few Colonial Period sherds in the sample may be considered to have been downward intrusions.

Pool 2 had two floors and large amounts of pottery in the respective overlying sand fills. Out of 23.515 kg from the deeper context only three painted sherds, one Estrella Red-on-gray and two Sweetwater Red-on-gray, were recognized. This pool must have been in use during the early part of the Pioneer Period, perhaps from its beginning. Above the second lining, the dominant painted pottery was Snaketown Red-on-buff.

Although Pools 3 and 4 produced relatively small lots of pottery, a total of 21 kg (3,200 sherds), the samples were completely lacking in painted pottery. The time of use of these pools may be attributed to the Vahki Phase. The amounts of pottery recovered

Fig. 8.25. Low cross light brings out the Dipping Pools in the Pioneer Canal. Pool 1 in foreground. Looking west.

Fig. 8.26. Pat Stone, the wife of one of our workers, demonstrates the stance used by Hohokam water carriers in filling a jar from Dipping Pool 1 in the bed of the Pioneer Canal.

POTTERY TYPES / SOURCES	ESTRELLA RED-ON-GRAY	SWEETWATER RED-ON-GRAY	SNAKETOWN RED-ON-GRAY	GILA BUTTE RED-ON-BUFF	SANTA CRUZ RED-ON-BUFF	SACATON RED-ON-BUFF	VAHKI PLAIN	VAHKI RED	TOTALS	NUMBER OF SHERDS (EST.)
POOL 1: FILL	.005	.035	.135	.055	.035		3.915	.635	4.815	750
POOL 2: ABOVE MID-SURFACE	.025	.600	1.800	.025			31.000	1.600	35.050	5,250
BELOW MID-SURFACE	.005	.010					22.000	1.500	23.515	3,500
POOL 3: FILL							11.000	.900	11.900	1,800
OVERFLOW AREA (WEST)							.535	.125	.660	100
POOL 4: LOWER FILL							7.500	1.000	8.500	1,300
TOTALS	.035	.645	1.935	.080	.035	.000	75.950	5.760	84.440	12,700

Fig. 8.27. Pottery frequencies in the Dipping Pools of the Pioneer Canal (No. 1). Values are in kilograms, except right-hand column.

would have yielded painted and grooved examples had the pools been in use when these types were produced.

Most of the pottery in the pools was not rolled. It must have been derived from nearby trash sources, or, from refuse thrown directly into the canal. The latter alternative does not seem likely. Discarded stone implements, as, for example, broken manos, were also found in some quantity. Children may have added to the concentration by responding to the ever-present temptation of throwing rocks into the water. Cast-off stone tools would have been about the only source of stone at hand for them to use. Also, more than usual numbers of shell and turquoise beads and shell bracelet fragments came from the sand filling of the canal bed and the pools. It is tempting to explain this situation by imagining children rough-housing while swimming in the canal and some of the ornaments they were wearing were damaged and lost in the frolicking.

Another point worth mentioning is the fact that Vahki Red in the pool fills was present in a somewhat higher percentage than was normal elsewhere in early Pioneer Period contexts, and there was a much higher proportion of jar vesus bowl sherds as well. I attribute this to the fact that redware jars may have been commonly used to transport water, and some were lost through breakage in the process. The predominance of redware around water sources has also been observed in the Point of Pines area (Haury 1957: 18; Wheat 1952: 194).

The dipping pools are indicators of discontinuous water flow in the canal, occasioned by choice during off-season times and by necessity when the river itself was running low. However, the presence of undamaged fresh water snail shells (*Physa virgata* Gould) in the sands of the Pioneer Canal is evidence of water over a sufficiently long time for the mollusks to become established. The shells are much too fragile to have been washed in with the sand.

Turn-Out

A groove in the canal edge immediately northeast of Pool 1 was considered at first to be a possible turn-out, but the grade is uphill in the groove and the outlet would have been above the water carrying capacity of the canal. Furthermore, it was in the terrace's upslope side of the canal. This feature must represent something other than a discharge point, but what, we do not know.

Farther west, south of Pool 3, our workmen exposed a feature which can, with confidence, be called a turn-out (Figs. 8.22a,c; 8.28). It consists of a groove at the canal's edge 0.2 m wide, and west of it 0.5 m is a fanlike discharge point. Both outlets coincide with the maximum water level the canal could carry. The groove in particular is a made feature and therefore cannot represent an accidental breakthrough of excessively high water. The turn-out bottom drops rapidly on its course down the slope to the lower terrace. It was obvious that erosion was excessive here and that,

from time to time, repairs were necessary. There was no evidence of a check dam or control structure in the main canal below the turn-out. Water flow regulation must have been a matter of constant vigilance. What appears to be a posthole occurs in the groove, possible evidence of a reinforcement for an earth plug when the drain was to be closed.

A projection of the spillway southwesterly for a few meters connects it with an area of exceptionally complicated stratigraphy and disturbances exposed in the south end of Lateral Canal Trench 16 (Fig. 8.22a). Our attention was attracted to this spot by the unnatural bedding of sharply differing materials and by the presence of deep cultural residue, indicating that man had had something to do with it. In an endeavor to understand the situation, the digging was expanded to the west (Broadside 1) and to the east of the trench (Broadside 2). Although we could not absolutely convince ourselves what the physical remains here represented, the weight of the evidence strongly suggested that this was, in fact, a continuation of the turn-out seen above and that it further reflected the chaos that erosion produced when the control of water was lost. Cross sections of the area as given in Figure 8.22d,e, are different on each side of the trench, not too surprising considering how water can undercut banks and produce caving of the sides. Both trench faces reflect this circumstance in the erratic blocks of laminated silt completely dislodged from their original contexts. As noted, cultural remains are present in most of the churned materials; where remains were absent, as in a large block of caliche-silt, we assumed this was original terrace matrix which caved off as a big lump. Between the east and west faces of the

Fig. 8.28. Canal turn-out south of Pool 3 consisting of groove and fanlike discharge area to right. Man stands in flume eroded by cascading water on its way to lower terrace.

trench, a distance of 0.75 m, the bottom of the disturbed area fell 0.3 m, a sharp drop although not inconsistent with the gradient in the turn-out.

Broadside 1, on the west face, exhibits a feature which is of special interest. This is an adobe construction in the shape of a lining 0.15 m thick, an apparent effort to channelize the water and thereby to reduce erosion (Figs. 8.22e; 8.29). The evidence indicates, as does the canal lining noted later, that adobe may have been more generally used to make structures, reinforcements, linings, and repairs than has been suspected. The detection and the full understanding of such features will require a broader and more intensive attack on the irrigation problem than we were able to undertake.

About 4 kg of potsherds were recovered in both broadside excavations. Whether high or low in the disturbed channel areas, the predominant types were Vahki Plain and Vahki Red. The half dozen painted pieces were all of the Pioneer Period, but the frequencies were too low to warrant phase assignments of any of the deposits that yielded culture. It may be stated, however, that the events recorded in this area took place during the Pioneer Period and that they were temporally in harmony, therefore, with the age of the upper part of the turn-out and the Pioneer Canal itself.

Canal Lining

Although the floor of the Pioneer Canal had characteristics not seen in any other ditches, it appears not to have been artificially produced by giving it a special lining. However, there is good evidence that the Hohokam did apply lining mixes in a plastic state locally where canal bank weaknesses appeared, where repairs had to be made, or where efforts became necessary to reduce water loss in soils that were especially pervious. One such place was directly east of the turn-out reviewed above. Here, soft laminated silts represented an unstable bank condition. This was remedied by applying a clay-loam mix from 8 to 10 cm thick (Fig. 8.30). While a relatively minor detail, it nevertheless symbolizes further the early Hohokam mastery of problems associated with waterworks and the measures taken to keep the system operating at an efficient level.

Pioneer Canal Floor

Once the Pioneer Canal floor was identified for what it was, tracing it became a relatively easy matter. The floor was not only hard, much more resistant than the overlying material, but it also had a distinctive red-brown color which contrasted sharply with the tan and buff-colored soils above. Both the color and the texture derived from the qualities of the original terrace matrix and the effects of wetting over a long period of time. Most characteristic of all were small crystal clusters partially imbedded in the canal floor. They even formed on stone artifacts and sometimes on potsherds that were in floor contact. In scraping the bed with a trowel, some of the crystal nodules would pop out leaving a distinctive pitted surface (Fig. 8.31).

R. N. Rogers of Los Alamos, New Mexico, has identified the crystals to be almost pure gypsum by chemical and x-ray diffraction techniques. While the precise circumstances that promoted their formation are not known, they were certainly the result of evaporation and the drying of the canal floor. Crystals of this description were seen in none of the later canals.

Later Canals

Toward the west end of the area under study, the Pioneer Canal suffered serious damage when channel renovations became necessary in later times. These efforts on the part of the Hohokam engineers produced a perplexing maze of arteries that, once unraveled, proved to be a unique asset, for they placed the Pioneer Canal in its chronological position with respect to the others in a most convincing manner.

Figure 8.22a portrays the situation as encountered in plan, and

Fig. 8.29. West face of Lateral Canal Trench 16 (Broadside 1) showing cross-sections of several presumed turn-out channels and an adobe retaining wall (below tip of trowel).

Fig. 8.30. Cross-section of Pioneer Canal bank showing how it was stabilized by application of impervious lining (dark band) on horizontally bedded silts.

Fig. 8.31. The Pioneer Canal floor revealing gypsum crystal clusters as white spots and pits where crystals have been removed by scraping of trowel. Note crystals on stone artifact fragments.

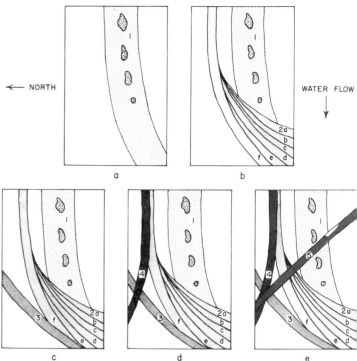

Fig. 8.32. Schematic reconstruction of canals in Pioneer Canal Area. The succession of canals is correct, but physical relationships have been altered slightly for clarity. (a) Canal 1, with dipping pools, Pioneer Period; (b) Canal 2, including 5 modifications, Colonial Period; (c) Canal 3, Sedentary Period; (d) Canal 4, Classic Period; (e) Canal 5, Classic Period. (Canal 6 is not shown, an "echo" ditch riding high in Canal 3.)

Figure 8.32 is offered as a schematic depiction of the succession of events. To appreciate how the area appeared in reality, consult Figures 8.33 and 8.34. These should help in clarifying the following discussion.

The labeling system assigns an Arabic number to a discrete canal which followed a given course, and letter designations refer to modifications of it when its course was not grossly altered. The Pioneer Canal designation is No. 1, and since its path seems not to have been changed throughout its time of use, letter designations are not used, even though dipping pool contents reflected a considerable passage of time.

Canal 2 represents a marked transformation in canal form, being deep and narrow, while Canal 1 is wide and shallow. Also, Canal 2 underwent a series of at least five remodelings, the general trend being, at the point observed, a progressive shifting of the ditch farther away from the edge of the terrace. The course followed brought it into the study area along the north edge of Canal 1, whence it turned rather abruptly southward, truncating Canal 1. The southwestern limits of our test show the sequence of channels in plan and profile (Figs. 8.22a and 8.35). Two conditions complicate the interpretation: It is almost certain that the full record is not there for us to decipher, and the nature of the evidence loses clarity as one moves laterally along the channels from the older to the younger ones. It was no simple task, and in some cases impossible, to isolate every channel through the length of the area exposed. Figure 8.36 is offered as a further effort to record the steps we believe to have been followed in the rebuilding of Canal 2.

With so much evidence of alterations, one naturally thinks of when the events happened and how much time was involved.

Fig. 8.33. Photographic record of Pioneer Canal (No. 1) showing how later canals were related to it stratigraphically; looking east. (See also Fig. 8.34).

Here again we must rely upon the pottery samples recovered from the various channels. The results are tabulated in Figure 8.37. It is reassuring to observe that the general time order of the pottery types, as determined in other excavations, and the physical stratigraphy of the channels are in agreement. Synoptically, the identifications are as follows: Canal 2a—Gila Butte Phase; 2b—no sample available, but by extrapolation it should be Gila Butte or Santa Cruz Phases; 2c—dominantly Santa Cruz Phase, the Sacaton Red-on-buff sherds may have been intruded; 2d—Santa Cruz Phase; 2e—Santa Cruz Phase; 2f—no sample, but most likely Santa Cruz Phase.

Canal 3 joined the channel of 2f, but at a slightly lower level thereby destroying it. Canal 3 made a wide swing from the northeast to the southwest where it entered the Canal 2 maze. At this point, Canal 3 had a wide, relatively flat floor with three closely spaced, shallow, and small depressions which may have been dipping pools as in the case of the Pioneer Canal (1).

Pools 2 and 3 contained fragments of several smashed Sacaton Red-on-buff pots; these fragments, taken with a large sample of the same type from the floor elsewhere, surely establish Canal 3 as of Sacaton Phase vintage. Much of the fill in Canal 3 had a whitish color and a chalky texture. The pottery in this matrix was also Sacaton Red-on-buff. If further confirmation of the age is needed, it comes from the fact that pottery derived from red spoil dirt resting on the chalky deposit was also of the Sacaton Phase. The spoil dirt came from some other undetermined canal excavation. The ratio of Gila Plain to the painted types from Canals 2 and 3 is roughly reversed over the ratios of equivalent types derived from refuse. One concludes that in late times painted pottery was preferred over plain as the container for transporting water.

Fig. 8.35. Sequent channels of Canal 2, as well as Canals 3 and 6, are here seen in cross-section in the southwestern limits of the Pioneer Canal test area. Canals 2 and 3 date from the Colonial and Sedentary Periods.

Fig. 8.34. The Pioneer Canal (No. 1) Area, looking west. (See also Fig. 8.33.)

Canal 4 represents a partial re-excavation of the main trunk of Canal 2, but it veers to the northwest instead of following the old course to the southwest. We were not able to pursue it far, and as a consequence the pottery yield was too small to be of diagnostic value. Because it has a calcareous lining, identical in appearance with that of Canal 4 at the Four Canal Station, the two were probably one and the same. If so, Canal 4 was of the Civano Phase, Classic Period.

Then, swinging in from the southeast and on the low side of all prior waterworks, was Canal 5. It stabbed obliquely across all others except the fanned-out subchannels of Canal 2, sectioning, however, the main stem of the latter (Figs. 8.22, 8.38).

Stratigraphically, Canal 5 was the latest formal canal of all; ceramically (Fig. 8.37) the sample was mixed in the extreme, not surprising in view of the availability of pottery from practically every antecedent phase in the soils adjacent to it. Nonetheless, Canal 5 is assignable to the Classic Period; for reasons of its relationship to Canal 4, it is assumed to have been in use late in the Civano Phase.

Although our limited probing did not verify the circumstance, it was tempting to recognize Canal 5 as the lateral ditch which served the lower terrace fields from its position on the upper terrace slope. This would have meant engineering it back onto the upper terrace, a not impossible feat considering the contours. In favor of the idea was the depth of the floor of Canal 5. Where it intersected the others, it was absolutely lower than any of them, and this would have brought it within range of the lateral canal gradient as it projected from our westernmost section through LCT 10.

The possibility that Canal 5 actually rejoined Canal 4 must be considered. The feat could have been accomplished with only relatively minor adjustments in canal depths. Since our excavations suggested two canal beds (CT 24 and CT 18), I have shown them as separate ditches (Fig. 8.22). However, should future broadscale testing prove this speculated merging to be true, then the reunion of two ditches could represent an ingenious way to

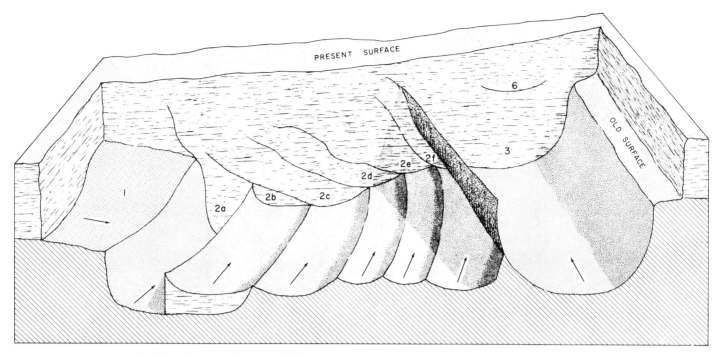

Fig. 8.36. Diagrammatic portrayal of relationships of Canals 1, 2 with its revised channels, 3 and 6, based on actual section and surviving remnants of ditches. Arrows indicate direction of water flow. Color and grain variations in silt channel fills are not shown.

POTTERY TYPES / SOURCES	ESTRELLA RED-ON-GRAY	SWEETWATER RED-ON-GRAY	SNAKETOWN RED-ON-GRAY	GILA BUTTE RED-ON-BUFF	SANTA CRUZ RED-ON-BUFF	SACATON RED-ON-BUFF	VAHKI PLAIN	VAHKI RED	GILA PLAIN	TOTALS	NUMBER OF SHERDS (EST.)
CANAL 2:											
A			.025	.845					.545	1.415	150
B (NO SAMPLE)											
C SAMPLE 1		.005		.110	1.525	.050			.345	2.035	200
SAMPLE 2				.025	.555	.120			.460	1.160	115
D			.025	.025	.370				.175	.595	60
E				.060	.335				.065	.460	50
F (NO SAMPLE)											
CANAL 3:											
FLOOR SW END		.015		.050	.280	4.480		.005	.995	5.825	600
POOL 2		.005		.040	.200	2.320			.205	2.770	275
POOL 3					.030	.730			.035	.795	80
WHITE FILL (UPPER)						.945			.025	.970	100
IN RED SPOIL DIRT ON WHITE FILL					.035	.365			.195	.595	60
CANAL 5:	.025	.015	.070	.220	.110	.520	1.020	.120	.345	2.445	250
TOTALS	.025	.025	.135	1.375	3.440	9.530	1.020	.125	3.390	19.065	1,940

Fig. 8.37. Analysis of pottery by types from Canals 2, 3, and 5. The sample from Canal 4 was inadequate. Values are in kilograms, except in the right-hand column.

Fig. 8.38. Canal 5 lies exposed in the foreground where it cut through the bed of Canal 1. Wall of excavation reveals contrasting nature of fills in Canals 2, 4, and 5.

conserve the water in the lateral not needed on the lower terrace by turning it into the main system for use farther down the line.

High in the silt of Canal 3 was evidence of the "echo" canal (No. 6) seen in several places, apparently a late and futile effort to revive the irrigation system.

Looking back on our discovery of the Pioneer Canal (No. 1) I am impressed anew with the role of chance in the detection of archaeological phenomena. It could have been easily missed except for persistent curiosity, frequent reexamination of trench faces, and a nagging belief that something older had to exist. Without its recognition we would have been little better off in our knowledge of old agricultural practices than we were before the project started. With it we now know that a water-control capability by agriculturally oriented peoples was the basis for inspiring the settlement and subjugation of the arid valleys of the Gila and the Salt rivers probably as early as 300 B.C. And this technical knowledge of fluid mechanics, though at a simple level, was by no means in the incipient stages, because the carriers of the idea already knew the terrain requirements to achieve successful irrigation. They engineered at least a 5-km long ditch and hand dug it; they equipped the canal with the needed structures and turn-outs for effective distribution of the water to fields and, by the use of adobe, to supply canal linings and retaining devices as control measures when maintenance problems developed. The Hohokam, at this early time, had established a sound base for the nearly fifteen centuries of successful tillage that followed.

WEST FORK

A major branching of the Snaketown canal system took place less than a kilometer west of the village. In addition to investigations at this fork by Gila Pueblo in 1934–35 (Gladwin and others 1937: 55-56), Richard B. Woodbury conducted studies in 1959 which substantially amplified the knowledge gained earlier. Because his findings relate directly to the story of irrigation in the Snaketown area, he consented to my invitation to include his analysis in this report.

The Canal Fork West of Snaketown
by Richard B. Woodbury

Investigation of the area of branching of the Snaketown canal system was carried out in December 1959 as a part of the University of Arizona Arid Lands Program, supported partially by the Rockefeller Foundation. The work was planned to amplify the

results reported by Haury from earlier excavation and was confined to the area east of his work [see Fig. 8.39a]. My work was conducted with the permission of the Gila River Indian Community and with the skilled participation of a group of Pima Indian workmen. In spite of the rain and fog which hampered the work, they accomplished a great deal in the time available. The opportunity to summarize results here is greatly appreciated, as they will have more meaning in the context of Haury's much more extensive subsequent work at Snaketown than if presented alone.

The major question to which an answer was sought in 1959 was, "What kinds of controls might have been used to divert water from the main canal to the north and south branches?" Disappointingly, we found no direct evidence for any structure or barrier in the area that was cleared to canal floor just east of the fork. There were no postholes, no boulders or brush, no imprints of materials that might have been in place temporarily and then removed. Therefore, either such a light structure or ephemeral one was used, such as matting weighted with poles, that no traces remain, or no diversion was made and water normally flowed equally into both channels. Without other evidence a choice cannot be made between these alternatives.

The profiles provided by the several trenches just east and west of the fork [Fig. 8.39b-e] agree in general with the information from Haury's earlier report, but in detail there are some differences. For example, Section A-A', about 30 m east of the fork, shows a V-shaped cross section rather than the U shape of this same canal a little more than a kilometer to the east (Gladwin and others 1937: Fig. 17). Section A-A' also lacks successive channels at higher levels, suggesting that it was completely cleaned out rather than only partially, with none of the fill remaining as the floor of a new channel. However, toward the end of its use four

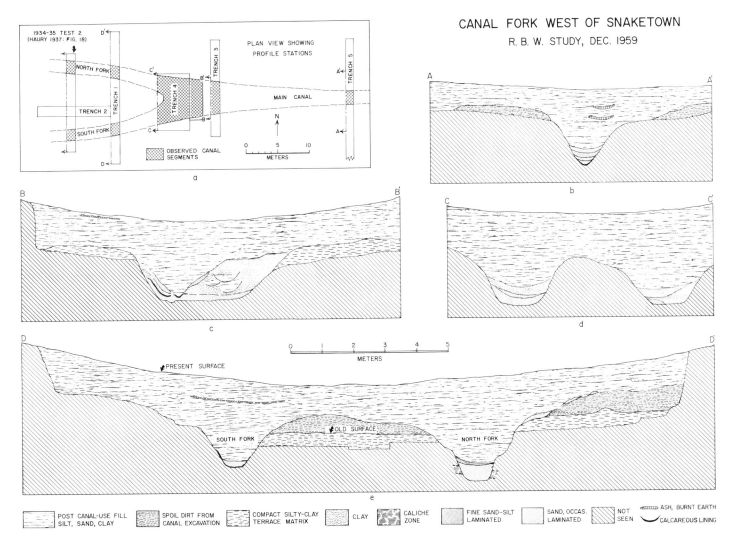

Fig. 8.39. Plan and sections of Richard B. Woodbury's study of the west fork in the Snaketown canal system.

distinguishable layers of sand and silt accumulated and were left undisturbed at the final abandonment of the canal. Just as at several other locations, Section A-A' shows a calcareous lining that had formed on the bottom and lower sides of the channel.

A second question to which we sought an answer was whether the high spoil banks just east of the fork did indeed come from a repeatedly cleared "settling basin," as suggested by Haury previously (Gladwin and others 1937: Pl. XIII). Although with the means at our disposal we could not clear the entire broader portion of the canal, the conformation shown in Section B-B' quite clearly suggests a wide flat-bottomed basin which would have markedly slowed the rate of flow. This would have caused all but the finer sediments to settle, and their periodic removal would account for the conspicuously higher banks at this point along the canal. The profile shows the fine sediments accumulated to a depth of about 1.10 m, with several channels representing possible stages of filling and cleaning. Then a major cleaning resulted in the large V-shaped channel along the south side of the basin, which reached down almost to the original depth. It in turn filled with fine sand and silt to a depth of at least 0.9 m and was almost completely cleaned out.

The dimensions of this settling basin indicate that it had four or five times the capacity of a stretch of canal of comparable length and normal width, and thus could accommodate a substantial quantity of sediment. Repeated cleaning of the basin easily explains the height of the banks, even after centuries of erosion.

Section C-C' shows the beginning of the north and south channels at the diversion point, separated by a rounded nose of the hard native soil. As mentioned, no traces of diversion structures were found here where they might have been expected. Just as in the 1934–35 section farther west (Gladwin and others 1937: Fig. 18) and the 1959 section at an intermediate point [Fig. 8.39e], there is no evidence that these channels, just beyond the settling basin, were repeatedly cleared out to create channels at successively higher levels. Either no cleaning took place, or more probably each cleaning removed completely all previous deposits.

One interesting fact can be noted in Section D-D'. The bottom of the north fork is somewhat lower (about 40 cm) than the south channel. A similar difference is apparent, although less conspicuous, in Haury's Trench 2 (Gladwin and others 1937: Fig. 18). This difference is not due to subsequent silting but to the depths to which the channels were prehistorically excavated. The deeper north channel may have been an error in construction, however, as it appears to have silted fairly rapidly to a point where both channels were of the same depth. Any short stretch of the canal dug a little too deep would collect sediment faster than the rest of the canal and thus equalize the gradient. Finally, it should be noted in Section D-D' that no spoil dirt is shown on the south bank of the south channel. This is because no spoil bank could be distinguished in the field from material attributable to post-canal filling. There is no reason to think that at this particular point the same practice did not obtain as elsewhere, with material dug from the canal piled more or less equally on both sides of the channel.

Other Observations About Canals

GRADE

There now remain several topics which have not been adequately covered in the discussions of the localities studied in detail. The first of these relates to the gradient of the system. This is an important quality because the amount of water deliverable to fields and its control were determined in part by the grade. The present visible surface evidences of a canal range from remnants extending about 2.5 km (1.5 mi) east of Snaketown to a point about 5 km (3 mi) west of the village, for a lateral distance of somewhat less 7.5 km (5 mi). We assumed that the surface traces were of the same ditch and so designed a series of probes to establish grade values. Twenty-one trenches sampled a canal length of roughly 5.8 km (3.6 mi). Where more than one canal in a superimposed sequence was represented, we accepted the highest, or latest, one as the same ditch measured elsewhere.

On the whole, this produced compatible results. However, several curious anomalies appeared which suggest that the method may have been faulty and that our trench separations were too great to warrant this kind of an assumption. As indicated in the Pioneer Canal area, time and space shifts led to complicated canal crossovers, and our efforts may have over-simplified a complicated story. Furthermore, over- or under-excavation, multiple canal floors locally present only, canal bed settlings and slumpage, could all contribute to inconsistent slope measurements.

In future studies it would be advisable to expose long stretches of a canal, making certain by this means that the same canal is always under scrutiny.

Since the project cartographer, Gell, did obtain a series of grade readings, they are presented because a canal quality is described by them which we have not had the privilege of examining heretofore.

Figure 8.6 locates the various numbered tests where the readings were made, including the main and the lateral canals. Depth and distance notations are listed in Figure 8.40 and the results are plotted in Figure 8.41. The main Snaketown canal dropped 6 m in 5.8 km (3.6 mi), a grade of nearly 1 m per km, or a little over 5 ft per mi. This slope value roughly coincided with the surface topography which, of course, it must approximate. For modern earth ditches the recommended grade is 0.1 ft per 100 ft, or about 5 ft per mi (Irrigation Advisers' Guide 1951: 117).

From this it would appear that the Hohokam selected an ideal

STATION	DEPTH	DIFFERENCE	DISTANCE IN METERS	
			BETWEEN STA.	CUMULATIVE
MAIN CANAL				
CT 15	3.28		0.0	0.0
CT 14	3.65	- .37	940.0	940.0
CT 13	4.04	- .39	437.0	1377.0
CT 12	4.79	- .75	735.0	2112.0
CT 8	5.35	- .56	420.0	2532.0
CT 9	5.38	- .03	38.0	2570.0
CT 10 *	5.35	+ .03	9.0	2579.0
CT 5 *	5.30	+ .05	10.5	2589.5
CT 11	5.30	.00	40.5	2630.0
CT 4	5.31	- .01	91.0	2721.0
CT 3	5.56	- .25	107.0	2828.0
CT 1	5.68	- .12	25.5	2853.5
CT 2 *	5.70	- .02	16.0	2869.5
CT 17	6.08	- .38	160.5	3030.0
CT 6	6.15	- .07	65.0	3095.0
CT 21	6.30	- .15	48.0	3143.0
CT 19	6.25	+ .05	36.0	3179.0
CT 20	6.40	- .15	30.0	3209.0
CT 7 (FORK)	7.38	- .98	610.0	3819.0
NF-CT 1	7.68	- .40	218.0	4037.0
NF-CT 2	9.21	-1.53	1762.0	5799.0
--	--	--	--	--
CT 7 (FORK)	7.38	- .98	610.0	3819.0
SF-CT 1	7.53	- .15	218.0	4037.0
SF-CT 2	7.58	- .05	528.0	4565.0
LATERAL CANAL				
CT 8	5.35		0.0	0.0
DIVERSION PT.	5.35	+ .10	31.0	31.0
LCT 12	5.80	- .55	12.0	43.0
LCT 1	5.83	- .03	10.5	53.5
LCT 13	5.80	+ .03	13.0	66.5
LCT 3	5.80	.00	12.0	78.5
LCT 4	6.65	- .85	24.5	103.0
LCT 5	6.40	+ .25	94.5	197.5
LCT 6	6.75	- .35	107.0	304.5
LCT 7	6.55	+ .20	28.5	333.0
LCT 8	6.60	- .05	17.5	350.5
LCT 9	6.25	+ .35	108.0	458.5
CT 17	5.60	+ .65	50.5	509.0
LCT 10	6.55	- .95	63.5	572.5
LCT 11	6.55	.00	47.0	619.5
LCT 24	6.65	- .10	17.0	636.5

Fig. 8.40. Tabulation of grade measurements of main and lateral canals at Snaketown (* not plotted in a, Fig. 8.41).

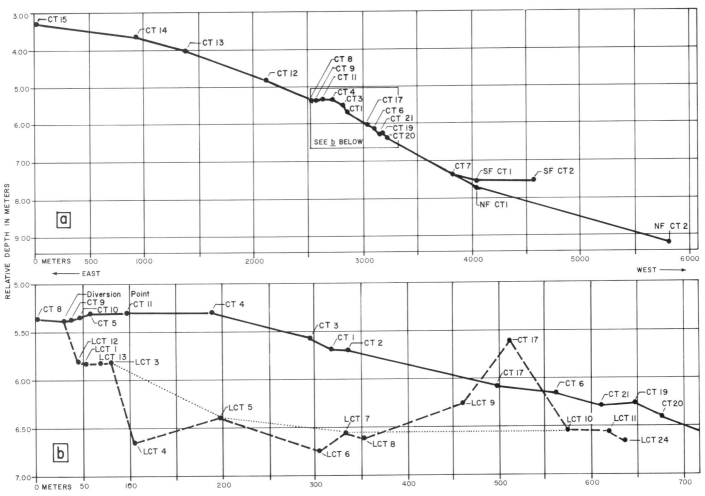

Fig. 8.41. Graphs showing canal gradients: (a) main canal; (b) segment of main canal (solid line) and adjacent lateral canal (dashed line). Dotted lines are projections between stations eliminating apparent errors in profile readings. CT = canal test; LCT = lateral canal test; NF = north fork; SF = south fork.

spot in the Gila valley to test their irrigation skills in a new land. Both east and west of Snaketown the grade was relatively constant, an impression created in part by the greater distance between tests. A series of closely spaced probes at the edge of Snaketown show departures from the norm by holding to a near constant grade over longer stretches than elsewhere, except the south fork. This is particularly noticeable in Stations CT 8, 9, 10, 5, 11, and 4, a distance of about 190 m. Because this section of the ditch was located closest to the heart of Snaketown the flattening of the canal may have been intentional as a means of pooling the water to make it more accessible for domestic use. A natural consequence of ponding the water was the depositing of solids, and this fact is reflected by the excessive build-up of silt along the canal banks.

West of CT 7 the canal divided, the longer north fork maintained the grade exhibited eastward but the grade of the shorter south fork was almost flat, having a measured fall of only 0.06 m in 528 m. A substantial head of water would be required to maintain a flow in this stretch of the canal. Flatness may have been the reason for its shortness.

Figure 8.41b brings us to the Diversion Area and the lateral canal which rides on the apron of the upper terrace for a lateral distance of 635 m. Its slope is compared with that of the main canal. The results emphasize the problem of inconsistencies in grade values. The initial drop in the lateral canal after it leaves the main artery west of CT 8, that is, the diversion point to LCT 12, includes the place of the outlet structure. In addition, it is in the steepest part of the terrace slope. It was here, as noted earlier, that

erosion occurred when the canal was in service. The four check points beyond the diversion itself (LCT 12, 1, 13 and 3) present no problem, but the fall to LCT 4 is too much and is somewhat below LCT 5 farther west. LCT 4 presented a strange and confused profile because it was in a heavily eroded area, the probable reason for a faulty reading. Connecting LCT 3 and LCT 5 directly (dashed line) eliminates the apparent error. Similar corrections are necessary to take care of irregularities between LCT 5, 7, and 10. The worst of these is CT 17. A close examination of the field records provides no clue to explain this discrepancy.

For the total distance of the lateral canal, the drop was 1.40 m in 635.5 m, or about 2.10 per km. This is about double the grade of the main canal, most of it having been accounted for at the diversion point drop. The abrupt fall here underscores the effort the Hohokam made to bring the water closer to the level of the fields on the lower terrace at a point where they had a reasonably good chance to control it.

While the engineering capabilities of the Hohokam evoke admiration, what they accomplished was perhaps no more complicated or involved than the application of a grass-roots experience in water management. By trial and error and trained judgment, problems of intakes, canal routes, grades, shapes, and control points were overcome. The evidences we are privileged to study tend to show the Hohokam did mostly the right things. Yet they had troubles, and they must have made mistakes. Except for those instances mentioned, the other errors we do not know about because nature would have erased most or all of the traces. That so much did survive for us to examine is a near miracle.

CARRYING CAPACITY

In modern agriculture the water requirements of a given plot of arable land determine the size of the ditch that is to serve it. Slope and soil texture are additional factors. For the old earth ditches of the Hohokam, however, the acreage to be irrigated cannot be used as a measure of canal size because this dimension is unknown. Canal characteristics are therefore the sole basis for developing notions of how much water the canals could carry. While ditch profiles differ somewhat in form and size from section to section, on the average, the rounded bottoms are about 1.25 m wide before the sides rise sharply to terminate in the canal's rim or free board. Water depth is not determinable with certainty in all sections, but there is good evidence in the lineations of the calcareous lining in Canal 4 (Four Canal Station) that stream flow reached a depth of 0.6 m for some periods of time. The crust extended upwards to 0.75 m, indicating that wetting went that high even though it may have been sporadic. Since the water level obviously fluctuated in response to water needs, conservative figures will be used to arrive at a conclusion of Canal 4's carrying capacity.

Employing a water depth figure of 0.45 m (about 18 in), a canal base width of 1.0 m (about 40 in), and a slope value of 1 m per km (about 5 ft per mi), the mean water velocity would have been about 0.45 m (1.5 ft) per second. This means that the stream volume was about 0.336 m³ (12.0 ft³) per second. These calculations are based on Kutter's formula as given in the Bureau of Reclamation's "Irrigation Advisers' Guide (1951: 122). Furthermore, given the conditions described, 0.028 m³ (1 ft³) per second will serve from 40 to 70 acres, or an aggregate 480 to 840 acres for the postulated carrying capacity of the canal. But how many acres of tillable land this amount of water could really irrigate by the methods the Hohokam used cannot be determined because we have no data on methods of water application, whether by furrows or by flooding in bordered fields or yet by some other mode of distribution devised by the Hohokam; and we do not know whether they used the tail water system to flush out the salts that tend to concentrate in fields under frequent irrigation. They probably did, because of Snaketown's long life. Otherwise salt concentration might have greatly reduced soil fertility long before the village's end, and the use of water in this way would have cut down on the acreage served by the system. Also, we know nothing about the frequency or the amount of water application. Given these imponderables, any estimate of acreage irrigated must be highly speculative. Nevertheless, it is worth trying.

By its location the lateral canal could only have served the acreage on the lower terrace. Assuming that it was capable of carrying the full stream of the master canal, then, by applying modern standards, up to 840 acres could have been irrigated. Southworth notes (1919: 127) that, at the time of his survey, 1,273 acres of tillable land on the lower terrace below Snaketown were then under cultivation or were previously cultivated. To this figure should be added an estimated 500 acres washed away by floods in the first decade of this century. While it is recognized that the river margin of the lower terrace has been subjected to continuing forces of building or destruction, the probability is that the gross acreage available to the Hohokam in this setting was somewhere near the present (early 1970s) figure. If one assumes that the old irrigators were somewhat more sparing of water than their modern counterparts, then it seems safe to conclude that the carrying capacity of the lateral canal was adequate to supply all the water needed to bring most of the arable land on the lower terrace under cultivation.

The evidence of a structure in the lateral at the diversion point hints that the flow to the lower fields was sporadic, applied only as needed, and that the main flow in full force could be sent far to the west to serve fields on the upper terrace. How many acres

were cultivated there is not known, nor is there any apparent way of calculating the acreage now. But the inference may be drawn that by conservative water application and by watching water wastage, the main canal was capable of supplying water to a substantially greater acreage than the estimated capacity of the ditch indicates. Given the state of our knowledge, I see no basis now for calculating the probable acreage served by the Snaketown system.

Some of the canal profiles show that the first canal in a sequence, excepting the Pioneer Canal, was the largest in terms of depth and breadth of bottom. The Four Canal Station (Fig. 8.19) is a good example. If this dimensional difference is meaningful, then one might speculate that more acreage was watered in the Colonial Period, the probable age of the ditch, than later. But this correlation might be specious since bigness may spell lack of sophistication in canal building or grade problem adjustments. The apparent reduction in canal size through time probably came as a response to more efficient water management.

REGIMEN OF WATER USE

The presence of dipping pools in the Pioneer Canal (No. 1) suggests that there were times of low water. Seasonal fluctuations in river discharge, in demand for water, and damage to the system due to washouts certainly affected water flow in the canals. There may have been times when the canals stood empty for extended periods. Drying cracks (Fig. 8.42) suggest this. Further, the complete silting in of some of the ditches indicates there were also times when the system was inoperative for that reason. Against these lines of evidence, however, there are suggestions of water permanency over long enough periods of time to encourage the establishment of snail colonies and the growth of aquatic vegetation. While fishbones were found in refuse, no fish remains were observed in the canals.

Some characteristics of canal floors lead to the belief that water permanency was normal. The bed hardness and the presence of crystal clusters in the Pioneer Canal have already been noted. Occasionally thin layers of fine reddish-brown clay coated the canal surfaces, which I interpret to be a settling out of near-colloidal particles in a quiet water situation. A similar material was observed by Woodbury in the Salt River valley and was considered by him to have been hand applied to prevent water loss in highly pervious layers below (1960a: 269). The Snaketown

Fig. 8.42. Drying cracks in the floor of Canal 1, Four Canal Station.

Fig. 8.43. Canal 4 in the Four Canal Station showing a calcareous lining precipitated from the hard water it carried.

clay coatings appeared in limited patches only. This, together with the thinness (5 to 8 mm), suggests a natural origin, probably due to the settling of exceptionally fine solids in low pockets as the water in the system dried up.

Calcareous Lining

Most fascinating of all canal floor features was a calcareous lining, prominent in Canal 4 of the Four Canal Station (Fig. 8.43) and Canal 4 in the Pioneer Canal area. Its presence made definition of the ditch a simple task because the lining contrasted sharply with the adjacent materials. The layer was thickest, nearly 2 cm in places, on the canal bottom. It extended one-third the way up the sides as a heavy deposit, then feathered-out to nothing at about two-thirds toward the canal rim. In the absolute bottom the lining was apt to be broken and locally absent, either due to mechanical removal or to other forces. Walking in the floor of the ditch at low water stage might tend to break the crust.

Figure 8.44 illustrates features of the lining in the main canal as exposed in several places. In the Diversion Area it is seen as a crust on silt filling a somewhat older ditch. Subsequently, the upper canal was itself completely clogged with silt when it fell into disuse for the last time. The crust's upper surface is irregular and wavy (Fig. 8.44b), partially in response to rises and hollows in the matrix below and partly the product of foreign materials that reached the canal floor where the precipitate formed around them. The laminated structure of the lining (Fig. 8.44c,e) removes all thoughts that the crust was applied by the Hohokam. Another surface detail of no small interest consists of parallel grooves shallowly etched into the crust precisely following the axis of the canal (Fig. 8.44d). These are the product of the varying amounts of water the ditch carried. At the water's edge, either by solution or by mechanical action, the lines were formed, a phenomenon observable in the Pima canals in the early 1970s (Fig. 8.45).

Let us look more closely into the morphology and probable genesis of the crust. The obvious characteristics are the laminations and the crystalline structure of the laminae. The specimen shown in Figure 8.44e has twelve observable layers, averaging slightly less than 1 mm in thickness. The extremes in thickness variation are from 0.1 to 2.0 mm, and both the number of layers and the thicknesses are highly variable within short distances. Micro-sand layers, either wind or water derived, locally separate the thin stony sheets. These actually have two zones, a dense

layer resting on top of a stringy calcareous structure. The grain of the latter runs at right angles to the surface of the lining, evidently the product of the crystallization process. Although the laminae have a varve-like quality, there is no reason to believe that the accretions in the crust have an annual value. Some kind of cyclical phenomenon, however, is indicated.

The following information is taken from a report by Ray N. Rogers of the Los Alamos Scientific Laboratory, Los Alamos, New Mexico, who was invited to analyze the canal crust. The main mineral component is calcite ($CaCO_3$), amounting to almost 100% of the mass. Contaminants are probably some manganese in solid solution and small amounts of clay and other salts. When the calcite was dissolved in hydrochloric acid, crystals of gypsum ($CaSO_4.2H_2O$) were present in the insoluble residue. The filtrate was found to contain a relatively high concentration of sulfate ions.

Rogers notes that analyses of Gila River water in 1932 showed 3.59 milliequivalents of CaII per liter, and 1.99 me/1 of MgII. Solubility products were: $CaCO_3$, calcite 1×10^{-8}; $MgCO_3$, 3×10^{-5}; and $CaSO_4.2H_2O$, gypsum, 2×10^{-4}. Carbonates would be the first to precipitate and hence the most important in deposits formed by Gila River water. He calculates that the evaporation of a cubic meter of Gila River water would leave a carbonate deposit approximately 0.3 mm thick, a figure consistent with the observed mass of the laminae in the crust. A layer of about this thickness could be laid down by a single filling of the ditch and its subsequent evaporation.

This fact, together with the presence of gypsum ($K_{sp} = 2 \times 10^{-4}$), which has a solubility factor in pure water of 0.24 g/100 ml, convinces Rogers that the crust was not deposited in running water but that the layers were evaporites. The alternation of the layers led to the speculation that the canal saw intermittent use, or more likely, that the deposits were formed after the seasonal disuse of the canal, each layer representing a flood season. This could mean, he notes, that the canal filled with water and evaporated and that the stretch of the canal containing the evaporite should be the lowest part of the ditch in terms of grade. Our observations do indeed show that the best developed crust was in that segment of the ditch with the flattest grade, but the phenomenon was not confined to this stretch because it was also seen in Canal Tests 13, 17, and 19 in the eastern and western environs of Snaketown. Test 13 had a grade value of about 2 m above the level of Tests 17 and 19, indicating that the standing water concept does not meet the physical conditions observed.

It should be noted here that water discharged from Montezuma's Well in the Verde valley left a thick calcareous deposit in the flumes used by pre-Columbian Indians to direct water to their fields. The same phenomenon may be observed today where the well overflows into Beaver Creek. It is evident, therefore, that crusts do form under flowing-water conditions, or, to put it another way, that ditch slope was not the primary controlling factor. Moreover, the water level lines scarring the crust emphatically demonstrate that water did run in the ditch in varying amounts either during or after the formation of the deposit, and hence during the life of the canal. The drying-out of the ditch at the end of an irrigation cycle may have produced some evaporites, but, if so, these were subsequently modified by lineations due to the removal of soluble elements when the system was next put into use.

Another curious circumstance is the fact that the lateral canal which drew water from the main line, and therefore carried the same water, did not show traces of the crust. Obviously, water quality was not the sole condition responsible for the deposit.

Another possible agent contributing to the crust's formation was calcium precipitating algae. Slack water in the flatter grade of the main canal would have encouraged a heavier-than-normal growth of this aquatic plant. To test this idea a sample of the

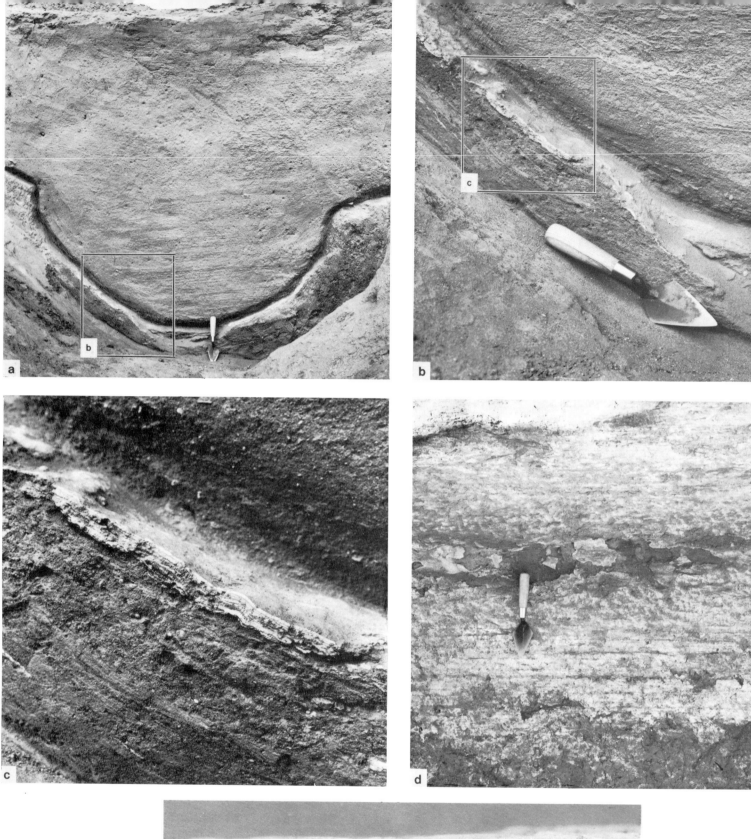

Fig. 8.44. Cross-section of main canal in the Diversion Area showing the calcareous lining. (a) Lining here extends about half-way up sides of ditch, absent behind trowel. (b) Surface of coating is rough and irregular. (c) Close-up reveals laminar structure of lining. (d) The lining as seen from directly above, Canal 4 in Four Canal Station. Faint parallel lines tell of fluctuating water levels. (e) Enlarged cross-section of canal crust. Laminar structure clearly visible. The water-carrying surface is up in photo. Thickness 1.1 cm.

crust was submitted to Robert W. Hoshaw, Professor of Botany, University of Arizona, for analysis. Although he found a single filament, probably organic, 8-10 microns in diameter and 100 microns long, there were no filaments with cells in series attributable to algae. A sample taken from the center of the crust was cultured with the thought, improbable though it was, that any extant spores might generate. The results were negative.

Modern irrigators know that the addition of certain liquid fertilizers to irrigation waters hastens the precipitation of calcium on canal banks. Knowing of this, one of our Pima workers remarked that the Hohokam must have had fertilizers. Leaks in concrete pipelines today are sealed by adding ammonia as a calcium precipitant to water if it carries enough of the mineral and meets pH requirements. In the early days horse manure was added to the water as an ammonia source to achieve the same effect.

These practices raise the interesting question as to whether or not an unusual ammonia source may have existed in the environs of Snaketown resulting from the accumulation of human wastes during fifteen centuries of time. One speculation held that the main canal was used as a latrine, but this is not likely, because by the fourteenth century, when the canal lining was precipitated, urban Snaketown did not exist. The surviving communities in the suburban areas both east and west would probably have had no effect. Why the crust was not present in earlier canals, why the precipitate was heaviest in Snaketown, and precisely what the conditions were that produced it are questions that cannot now be answered with conviction.

The principal indicators of the time of deposition of the lining are the stratigraphic position of the canal and the potsherds cemented in it. A fourteenth century date seems certain on the basis of these controls. A radiocarbon date for the crust is a surprising 1580±60 B.P., or A.D. 370 (Haynes, sample No. TX-891). This high age is indicative of a C^{14} deficiency from which Haynes concluded that "... the Hohokam used for irrigation either ancient water from springs or water that had dissolved ancient carbonates" (Letter dated Oct. 2, 1969). The former alternative seems entirely unlikely because no evidence exists of old or even contemporary springs in the Gila River valley alluvium capable of discharging the large volume of water needed for irrigation. The opportunity was present, however, for water to dissolve old carbonates, witness the prevalence of caliche in the watershed. Whatever the reason, the radiocarbon age is 1,000 years too old.

Canal Morphology

Note has already been made of the shape difference between the Pioneer Canal (No. 1) and those of later dates. The broad, shallow, and low bank standards at the beginning may be indicative of limited experience with water-control problems. A canal of this configuration would be wasteful of water, both through ground absorption and evaporation. There probably was also a smaller safety factor with respect to water breaking over the sides because of the low free board. Minor water level fluctuations could have been disastrous, particularly when the canal was already running to, or near, capacity. Experience may have been the teacher in introducing the deep narrow canal form at the beginning of the Colonial Period. But it may also represent a transmitted idea, coinciding with the appearance of such other elements as the ball court, a change in pottery art, and a shift in the function of figurines.

However generated, the change was for the better because narrow confinement of the water conserved it, greater water level deviation was permitted, control structures could be built more easily, and one may guess that both initial digging and ditch maintenance were easier.

A review of selected canal profiles brings out a few additional noteworthy details. In the first place, the deposits into which the

Fig. 8.45. The modern Santan ditch duplicates phenomena seen in the old Hohokam canals: drying cracks in mud and lineation of the canal bed by fluctuating water level.

canals were dug and those that accumulated later often present perplexing stratigraphic situations, representing discontinuities and reversals. Figure 8.46e, for example, reveals clay within canal fills, evidently the results of slack water deposits, and a high surficial silty-clay deposit that normally lies deeper. It must represent spoil dirt from nearby canal excavation. Adequate explanations of the observed conditions are not always forthcoming from single profile examinations, although the canal morphology in most cases is clear.

It is evident in most sections that the initial canal excavations seldom went deeper than 2 m below the then extant desert surface. Depths up to 3 m below the present surface were measured, but the increase is accounted for by the dumping of silts removed from the canals along the banks. The net effect of this was that canals ran on successively higher beds as the systems were remodeled. The succession of canals in the Four Canal Station was not unique. Multiple canals were visible in most tests east of Snaketown (Fig. 8.46a-e). To the west of Snaketown this situation did not prevail, on the basis of which it may be argued that the westerly extension of the system was a late development. Some of the disturbances, as seen in Figure 8.46g, may represent traces of the Pioneer Canal, but tangible support for this idea was not forthcoming. Few potsherds were found in the canal tests located some distance from Snaketown.

Almost all of the ditch sections revealed a rounded bottom. The

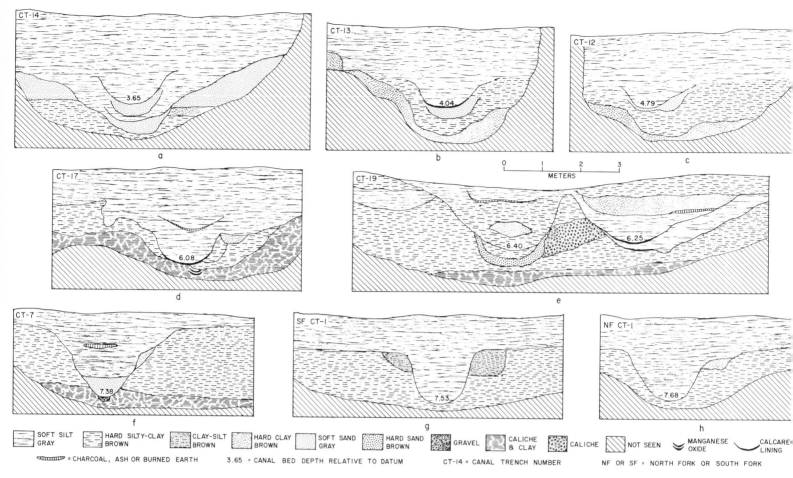

Fig. 8.46. Representative canal profiles. For test locations, see Figure 8.6.

lateral canal, on the other hand, exhibited a flat floor in several places (Fig. 8.16). No apparent significance is attached to these shape differences. In their general configuration the Hohokam canals closely match the Pima ditches of today where construction was not done by ditching machines and cement linings have not been added. Whether old or new, there is little evidence of bed or bank cutting by erosion. The Hohokam were certainly cognizant of this problem and purposefully avoided water velocities that would cause serious damage under normal use conditions.

Cushing noted a small inner canal at Los Muertos presumably intended to confine the water when the flow was low (Haury 1945a: 41). At Snaketown there were a few hints of a similar feature (Figs. 8.44a; 8.46f), but these were on a small scale and seen only over such short lateral distances that we cannot be certain whether they were due to erosion or to construction design.

Measurements showed that some canals carried water up to 1 m in depth, a sizable head of water except in the large primary ditches. Even at this depth, most canals had enough free board to provide adequate safety against breakouts. Canal 4 in the Four Canal Station best illustrates this characteristic (Fig. 8.43).

Maintenance

Keeping the canal system at maximum operating efficiency required constant maintenance. Vulnerable spots along the ditches needed watching against washouts; desilting, weed control, rodent activity and other problems demanded close vigilance. Limited areas of trash along canal banks suggest that small groups lived along the ditch, perhaps a man and his family who was assigned or assumed the task of tending a given section of canal. Most of the pottery in these concentrations dates from the Classic Period although all other periods were represented as well, particularly where canal vestiges were the best preserved. It was, in fact, a relatively high incidence of Pioneer Period pottery along

the canal east of Snaketown that led to the conviction the early canal was on the upper terrace.

Several Classic Period sites are situated about 2.4 km (1.5 mi) east of Snaketown where drainages from the north have heavily eroded the terrain. It would appear that the villages were located here so that an ample labor force was at hand to protect an especially weak spot in the system. Side erosion and the effects of lateral drainages appear to have been greater threats to canal security than the lowering of the Gila River channel as factors in the breakdown of the system.

For the larger tasks, such as repairing the intake weir, canal extensions, desilting, and taking care of major breaks, we may assume that a coordinated effort prevailed on the part of those dependent upon the system or a given canal. Historic Pima practices teach us a valuable lesson in this respect. A picture in the Homer L. Shantz collection (Department of Botany, University of Arizona) taken near Sacaton in 1915, illustrates this point impressively (Fig. 8.47). Flood damage to the weir diverting water into a ditch directly south of Olberg is being repaired. Identifiable in the picture are at least 25 tethered saddle horses and 21 wagons each with a span of horses and a single teamster. Approximately 50 men are engaged in the action. Thirteen wagons are drawn up in tandem on the upstream side of the weir, unloading brush (probably arrowbush, *Pluchea sericea*) for use in establishing a lining of the intake ditch on the downstream side, to counteract erosion of the soft silts of the flood plain. Approximately 10 men are busy near the intake in the flood plain. The uniform orientation of the wagons and the several kinds of activities that are taking place are signs of organized leadership, and indeed there would need to be with a work party of about 50 persons. It is reasonable to believe that, except for wagons and horses, this scene might be turned back a full two millennia.

Whether in old or modern times, users of an irrigation system recognized that a cooperative spirit had to prevail if the system was to be operated successfully. Given this over-riding force, the

Fig. 8.47. At least 50 Pima men with the aid of 21 two-horsepower wagons are repairing intake weir on flood plain of Gila River south of Olberg. Looking downstream with Sacaton in the left distance. Homer L. Shantz photo, 1915.

political or social control to achieve maintenance efficiency need not have been on a highly organized level, perhaps less formal than speculations have indicated, including my own (1956: 8-9). Woodbury (1960b, 1961) has explored this question in greater depth and I see nothing in the record from Snaketown to alter his opinion that the Hohokam did not have a hydraulic bureaucracy, or a central authority over matters related to water management. However, where multiple villages depended upon a single canal, some form of intervillage management, including agreements on water allocation, had to be in effect.

The evidence suggests that houses were deployed along canals, both because of the accessibility of domestic water and as caretaker stations. The dipping pools in the Pioneer Period Canal (No. 1) and the Snaketown Phase house (1:15E) are in support of the former condition; and maintenance houses as indicated by trash concentrations at canal banks suggest the latter. We do not have enough information now to detect a more meaningful pattern with respect to residence-canal relationships.

ADDITIONAL CONSIDERATIONS

Referring once again to Figure 8.43, it will be readily seen that crossing a canal of this dimension presented something of an obstacle to the people living in Snaketown who needed to get to their fields on the lower terrace. It was too wide to jump and too deep to climb in and out of in those places where we saw it in section. Either an easy ford or a foot bridge had to be provided, features to watch for as more canal studies are undertaken.

Many years ago I heard Frank Pinkley of the National Park Service speculate about the use of canals as avenues for the transport of goods. His thought was that the pine timbers in the Casa Grande, perhaps grown in the Pinal Mountains some 135 km (85 mi) to the east, might have been floated down the Gila River and eventually shunted in the canal that served the Casa Grande area. Similarly, one might speculate that the Douglas Fir logs recov-

ered from House 3:10F at Snaketown were introduced in the same way. But there is no evidence to support these ideas. Cushing believed that navigation by balsa boat was known to the Hohokam (Haury 1945a: 41), with the inference that canals were highways of commerce. This contention has not been verified by any of the studies since 1887–88.

Relatively high in the fill of the last canal in a number of sections, we mapped a shallow trough-like depression (Figs. 8.36, 6; 8.39b,e; 8.46d,e,f), previously alluded to as an ''echo'' canal, which often-times contained charcoal and ashes, or pottery, or was filled with material different than the adjacent matrix. The feature was present too persistently to have been accidental, and it was noted in the main and lateral canals. The evidence is clear that a small high ditch did exist, scratched into silts of the older waterway. The frequent presence of charcoal, ashes, and burnt earth suggests clearing the vegetation-clogged channel with fire when it was dry. These traces mean that someone attempted to bring back, though on a minuscule scale, what was once a lifeline of the local populace, literally a ''last-ditch'' and desperate attempt at keeping the system alive. How long after 1400 this happened we do not know.

DISCUSSION

The evidence presented in the preceding pages about the age and nature of Hohokam waterworks supports the conclusion that agriculture by canal irrigation began when Snaketown was founded, about 300 B.C. While it would be folly to believe that no canals existed on the lower terrace as preludes to the Pioneer Period canal on the upper terrace, the fact remains that this waterway, wide and shallow, was the oldest we were privileged to see. Its existence in the Vahki Phase tells us the Hohokam had a mastery of this form of agriculture from the start. As far as is known, the earliest canal did not change shape or location throughout the Pioneer Period, thus indicating that experimental

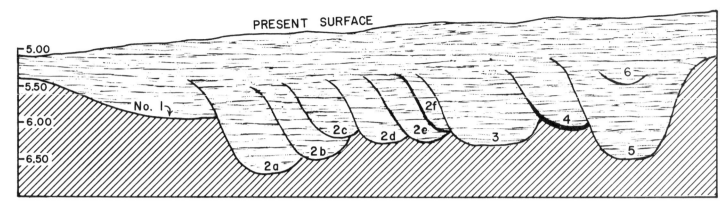

Fig. 8.48. Composite section of Snaketown canals emphasizing sequential relationships, based mainly on data from Pioneer Canal Area (no scale). Pioneer Period: No. 1 (phases not shown). Colonial Period: No. 2a—Gila Butte Phase; No. 2b—(Gila Butte-Santa Cruz Phases by position); No. 2c—Santa Cruz Phase; No. 2d—Santa Cruz Phase; No. 2e—Santa Cruz Phase. Sedentary Period: No. 2f—? Sacaton Phase; No. 3—Sacaton Phase. Classic Period: No. 4—Civano Phase (has calcareous lining); No. 5—Civano Phase. (?)Post-Classic: No. 6.

irrigation was far behind its makers. It also helps to explain the physical nature of the canal's hard and crystal-studded floor, because it was disturbed little or not at all over long periods of time. The canal's take-off point from the river was most likely about 5 km (3 mi) to the east near the foot of Gila Butte.

At about the beginning of the Colonial Period the canal shape changed to a narrow and deep configuration, a geometry which has lasted to the present day. Periodic realignment of canals has given us an unmatched record of a series of ditches dating from practically all phases to the end of the Classic Period. Only the Soho Phase is not represented with certainty. Later, possibly after the close of the Classic Period, we see traces of the "echo" canal. The succession of ditches, as we encountered them in the Pioneer Canal area is shown schematically in Figure 8.48.

This impressively long and evidently continuous record of Hohokam accomplishments in arid-land agriculture raises a number of interesting questions and implications. Foremost is the problem of origins. How did the Hohokam come by their knowledge and skills in the area of water management? My early speculations held that canals were an indigenous invention (Gladwin and others 1937: 57-58; Haury 1945b: 65) in southern Arizona, mainly because the evidence for irrigation in central Mexico before the sixteenth century was lacking. It would have made better logic to say that canals, along with other Mesoamerican elements, were passed northward to shape the nature of the Hohokam society. This claim can now be made, for the recent intensive studies in the Tehuacán and Oaxaca valleys of Mexico have provided the agricultural base needed to give strength to the hypothesis.

For the Tehuacán valley, MacNeish believes that agriculture by canal irrigation started in the Santa Maria Phase, 900-200 B.C. (1964:536), and in Oaxaca ingenious and varying responses to local conditions introduced several agricultural systems, including small-scale canals by the Middle Formative Guadalupe Phase, 900-600 B.C. (Flannery, Kirkby, Kirkby, and Williams 1967: 454). The early Teotihuacános evidently had ditch irrigation by the beginning of the Christian Era (Millón 1967b: 39). Further, Fowler reports well-developed canals at Amalucán, Puebla, dating from Preclassic times, or about 500-200 B.C. (1968: 32).

The adaptability of early farmers to peculiar environmental conditions in the first millennium B.C., already including canal systems, leads to the assumption that the beginnings of water-management systems were earlier still and that the art of irrigation was probably known and practiced throughout Mexico wherever rainfall was inadequate, where man was motivated to pursue it and where the natural resources permitted it. In all likelihood, therefore, the stage was set far enough back in antiquity for the introduction of canal irrigation into the arid Southwest by 300 B.C. Given this condition, and knowing that many other elements of

Hohokam culture had southern beginnings, the spread of a water technology from the Mesoamerican hearth becomes a logical conclusion. The origin of irrigation, therefore, is inseparable from the question of the origin of the Hohokam themselves. Although this problem is reviewed in greater detail in the concluding chapter, suffice it here to note that of several alternative explanations, the present evidence best supports the concept that the Hohokam were a migrated people, having moved out of the south and having been equipped with knowledge and material attributes theretofore unknown in the valleys of the Gila and Salt rivers.

Whatever the cause or causes of the move northward, whether a voluntary search for a better home or whether in response to pressures, the Hohokam seem to have known what they wanted and where they were going. An immediate and practical problem faced them on their arrival in the Southwest, and that was the digging of a canal. At Snaketown nature dictated that this ditch needed to be a minimum of about 5 km (3 mi) in length if it was to be on the upper terrace. The amount and distribution of Vahki Phase refuse indicate that the community was relatively large, although there is no sound basis for accurately estimating how large. For the sake of discussion let us suppose there were 25 families, about 100 souls in all. Could they subsist by living off the land while the canal was being built, the fields cleared, and the first crop matured? Since we have no evidence that they displaced anyone along the banks of the Gila and Salt rivers, they would have found native food at its natural and optimum level. The river environment would have provided the greatest variety of food resources that the desert had to offer. It would appear that a group of people of the size speculated could live off the land for a year without undue hardship.

Because Hohokam farming was not incipient farming, they lost no time in the experimental engineering of the first canal or in the management of their economic plants as they became adjusted to new physical surroundings. Of special interest is the amount of time required to excavate the first canal. Woodbury has shown that, contrary to popular belief, neither a great labor force nor an undue amount of time was needed to dig a canal 3 to 5 km (2 to 3 mi) in length (1961: 556). For the Snaketown canal, assuming that there were fifty able-bodied men and women of the hypothetical migratory group, each capable of excavating one lineal meter of canal per day, using digging sticks and basket, the 5-km long Pioneer Period canal could have been completed in about 100 days. Even with a substantially reduced labor force, the canal could still have been completed in time to mature a crop within the first calendar year of their arrival.

Halseth, for many years a student of Pima Indians, has observed (1947: 252-3) that in each of a dozen villages, averaging roughly from 300 to 350 people, the community was served by a ditch which was dug and maintained by an unspecified number of village "shareholders." The average canal length was 5 km (3 mi), and excavation took about one year; longer, if there were distractions, as for example, Apache wars. Intakes were constructed of logs, poles, and brush, and water ran "knee-deep" most of the year. Ditches were emptied for cleaning, and they had steeply rising sides and were 1 to 1.75 m in width. Pima irrigation is a mirror image of the older Hohokam efforts, though on a less ambitious scale.

As for social and political implications which may be drawn from the Hohokam waterworks, it has often been stated that strong central authority and effective political leadership guided their development. Yet these forces may have been on a somewhat less advanced level than we have been supposing. Woodbury has raised this question (1960a: 492; 1961: 556-7), and the early historic Pima practices once again provide some useful hints in support of a simpler system. Each Pima village did have a headman, an inherited position, whose responsibility it was to initiate the construction of irrigation ditches, to see that they were maintained, and that the diversion dams were kept in order (Hill 1936; Hackenberg 1962: 190). Regulations were few, the important one being that users must contribute labor to launch and maintain the system. The "only coercive weapon was public opinion" (Hill 1936: 587) to enforce the obligation. Survival demanded that the Pimas work together, whether in agriculture or in protecting themselves against aggressor tribes, and it was this mutual feeling that solidified the villages. The Hohokam social and political patterns were probably much the same.

Why the extensive canals in the Gila and Salt river valleys fell into disuse has long been a vexing problem for which no clear answers have been forthcoming. I cannot believe that the breakdown of this major economic advance in pre-Columbian times came as a result of salinization of the fields from over-irrigating, or from a drought, or from the lowering of the river channels by erosion leaving the systems high and dry. These and other forces may have affected some of the systems, but not all of them. The break-up of population centers in the desert valleys came at about the same time as did the population shifts and abandonment of towns and villages in the Hopi and Zuni areas, in a vast region west and south of the White Mountains, in the tributary valleys of the Salt and Gila rivers, as far away as the Mimbres and El Paso on the Rio Grande, in fact in most of the Southwest. This phenomenon serves notice that broadscale forces were at work, cutting across both tribal entities and environmental types that we label as plateau, mountain, and desert. The abandoned canals should be viewed as evidence of this pan-Southwestern shake-up rather than as the producers of it.

It would be a mistake to think that irrigated agriculture came to an end with the death of the big systems. The survivors of the disintegrated "urban" centers in the fourteenth century needed irrigation to exist, and it was they who preserved and connected the tradition as practiced by the Hohokam in prehistory with the farming ways of the Pimas today. It is not likely that all ditches were abandoned or that there was a time when there were no people in the Gila valley to pursue irrigation. The Santan Ditch, cited earlier, is capable, I believe, of supplying the data to demonstrate that this continuity did indeed exist.

That Hohokam irrigation did have an impact on the desert environment has been determined by Bohrer in an interesting study of plant remains from Snaketown and other sources of information (1971). She notes that "... Agricultural activities promoted an increase in ragweed (Ambrosiae) as new land was incorporated into the irrigation system in the earlier phases. Irrigation (also) fostered the extension of many riparian plant communities ..." (1971: 11). Historically, the environment has been rendered harsher and more desert-like than when Snaketown was alive by impounding Gila River waters upstream, thereby exterminating most of the riparian vegetation. If the Hohokam were susceptible to hay fever, one wonders what effect the increase in ragweed growth had upon their general well-being!

In retrospect, some new dimensions and details of Hohokam agriculture have been added by the recent work at Snaketown. But one needs only to write about the topic to realize how much we do not know. A fresh concerted attack on Hohokam farming should be launched. It is already too late to look intimately at the larger systems described by the early investigators in the Salt and Gila river valleys. Reclamation and industrial and urban expansion have taken care of that. The Snaketown system, however, offers the one remaining opportunity to do something in depth. This would entail opening long stretches of the canals, of searching for and examining in great detail turn-outs and control structure placements, slope, and canal morphology studies, identification of field systems through micro-soil analyses, and paying particular attention to climatic, orographic, and hydrographic conditions. The investigation of necessity would include a number of disciplines, and it would be costly. But the cost would be small if compared with the loss we would all sustain should the system be destroyed by fast encroaching developments.

Determinations should also be made as to whether or not the Hohokam engaged in other kinds of agricultural efforts. It would be surprising, indeed, if they did not make use of every food-producing opportunity provided by their environment. Evidence of check dam systems on the run-off slopes of the desert mountain ranges is known, and water detention plots, sometimes called "waffle gardens," exist on the western slopes of the Santan Mountains; but none of these features has been studied in detail. Russell noted (1908: 88-89) such agricultural remains and assumed they were of Hohokam origin, because the Pimas disclaimed them. The answer may not be as simple as that. Dune agriculture, as practiced by the Hopi Indians (Hack 1942), was possible in limited places along the Gila River; but whether or not the Hohokam employed this form of crop production is not known. When the full spectrum of farming activities is better understood, we can discuss more meaningfully than is possible now the cause-and-effect relationship of irrigation on Hohokam society and, vice versa, on population changes and on a host of other problems as touched on in the 1955 Symposium on Irrigation Civilizations (Steward, Adams, Collier, Palerm, Wittfogel, and Beals).

To conclude this long but nevertheless crucial section on Hohokam farming, I wish to reiterate my preference for the idea that brings the Hohokam into the Southwest as a migratory group equipped with a mature food-producing capacity based on irrigation, over several other possible explanations of their origin. This event probably took place near 300 B.C. If future work supports this reconstruction, then it is clear that the formative stages of the Hohokam economic base must be sought in Mexico and that they were in a strategic geographic and temporal position to exert far-reaching effects upon other societies in the Southwest, whether they were agriculturally minded or not.

9. Other Subsistence-related Pursuits

One measure of cultural activity might be based on the amount of digging a people do in the soil beneath their feet. The Hohokam, perhaps as much as, and probably more than, other southwestern groups, were energetic movers of dirt. Admittedly, the construction of canals required the greatest effort, but other basic activities demanded digging in the ground as well, and some of these were closely related to keeping alive, namely, house-building, well-digging, making hearths and roasting pits, quarrying raw materials for pottery-making, acquiring bulk earth for platform and ball court construction, and disposal of the dead. Let us examine some of these.

WELLS

The obvious water available to the Hohokam was in the Gila River which, in their time, must always have been accessible and essentially inexhaustible. Man's inescapable attachment to watering places has been an important factor in determining his residence. Yet, where he built was not always based on the easily seen surface water. Instead, the intimate knowledge that people gain by close observation of their environment sometimes leads to surprises for those of us who are trying to understand what happened in the past. Changes in surface features, alluviation, earth disturbances, and other forces may eliminate water sources that once existed.

This was the case at Snaketown, for, in addition to the water supplied by the river, an immediately local source was also available, the consequence of a special geological condition. To the northeast of Snaketown, Queen Creek debouches from the mountains onto the open flat in a myriad of rivulets before it reaches the bed of the Gila River. Much of this water goes underground where, given the proper aquifer, it may remain fairly close to the surface as it slowly seeps southward toward the river. In effect, this produced underground drainages, marked today by lines of heavier desert vegetation and thicker stands of mesquite. One of these passed through Snaketown, trending roughly north to south just west of Mounds 38 and 39 and under Mound 40.

Our excavations in this area revealed a sandy layer at a depth of about 3 m on top of a hard and massive caliche stratum. Locally, in intermittent lenses, caliche capped the sand. The sand zone, up to 0.75 in depth, served efficiently as the aquifer, the lower caliche holding it to a fairly constant depth.

It was the presence of shallow water, perhaps as much as the nearby arable land, that attracted the Pima families to establish the modern village of Snaketown just before 1880. Remnants of Pima wells are still to be seen near the large ball court. We drew water from one of these in 1934–35 to supply our camp. A Pima visitor, Harvey Allison, during the 1964–65 excavations, told me he grew up in Snaketown and that it was his job to go into the family

well periodically to clean it out. He remembered the depth as being about 3 m, which fits the physical conditions we found. Of all the places in the wide open desert where Snaketown might have been established, the knowledge that potable domestic water could be had by digging shallow wells was certainly a key factor in selecting the site for the old village. No other argument seems quite as convincing. As we will see presently, the digging of wells was a technical skill the Hohokam had from the start, and it is fair to assume that this capacity, together with the knowledge as to where to dig wells, was something learned from long residence in arid country.

Hohokam probing for water resulted in two kinds of excavations: (1) tubelike penetrations to the water table, not unlike our hand-dug wells, and (2) pits with wide mouths and sloping sides, resembling an inverted cone. Access to water in these was by walking into them, whereas in the former type a rope lift appears to have been needed, unless the water table was higher than seems to have been the case.

Well 1: 10F

The best example of the vertical side type was Well 1:10F. It is shown in the course of clearing in Figure 6.10. The profile of the well, its relationship to the surface from which it was dug and to cultural features post-dating its excavation, notably House 5, are given in Figure 6.9.

From the old desert surface, the well's depth was 2.0 m, enough to penetrate the desert soil and the sand aquifer to a depth of 0.75 m. In our reopening of it, the bottom was established by the abrupt change of pottery-bearing trash to clean sand. An auger test showed that the culture-free sand and fine gravel layer continued downward for at least another meter, revealing a thicker aquifer here than in all other tests.

Once wells were abandoned, they became convenient places for dumping trash, a fortunate circumstance for us because the contents help directly in dating them. The results of the analysis of some 35,000 sherds are given elsewhere. All of the available stratigraphic evidence points to the fact that the well was dug, used, abandoned, and filled with refuse during the Vahki Phase. This observation, joined with those that follow, resulting from work in the well area of Block 10G, leads to the conclusions that well-digging was known to the Hohokam and practiced by them from the moment they set foot on the spot called Snaketown.

An alternative to the idea that wells of this kind only served domestic water needs must be considered. It has been demonstrated in Oaxaca that shallow wells in high water table zones were used in "pot-irrigation," that is, a method of individually irrigating plants with water drawn from wells within the fields. This technique seems to have been known at least by 1000 B.C.

(Flannery, Kirkby, Kirkby, and Williams 1967: 450). As for Snaketown, the location of the tube wells and subsequent filling with refuse in the architectural complex favor their use as a source of domestic water rather than for irrigation.

Well Area in Block 10G

An impressively deep cultural deposit below what appeared to be the natural desert floor was detected in a backhoe trench a short distance northeast of Mound 40 (Fig. 1.6). Extensive probing on our part (Fig. 9.1), reaching a depth of about 3 m, revealed the nature of the geological formations and the reason the soil disturbance occurred here.

About 2 m down, a hard, more or less flat-lying caliche layer was encountered ranging from 0.15 to 0.30 m in thickness (Figs. 9.2f, and 9.3j). This capped a sand layer averaging 0.5 m in depth (Figs. 9.2g, 9.3k), which in turn rested on another caliche layer (Figs. 9.2h, 9.3l). In places, the top caliche layer was missing. Where its edge could be detected, the pattern described was usually in arcs, suggesting removal of the deposit by man. Further support for this idea was the fact that where the upper caliche was missing, potsherds extended down into the sand, sometimes as far as the lower caliche stratum. Where the upper caliche cap was intact, no potsherds were found in the sand under it. We may assume, on the basis of all evidence available, that the sand layer was the aquifer and that tapping the water supply was the motive for the digging. Although no groundwater was encountered in our search, enough moisture existed to produce cauliflower-like crystallization of salts on the surface of the lower caliche layer during a single night's exposure to air.

The exact outline of any one well could not be delineated because of the extreme disturbances the area suffered. However, remnants of the penetrations through the top caliche zone were traceable (Figs. 6.12, 9.2). In all probability, the wells were of the walk-in type, that is, pits with a large diameter at the surface, tapering to a small width at the water table, thereby permitting easy access by foot. The fouling and filling of wells of this kind by wind and human action and by the surface water run-off must have been an ongoing process. New wells were doubtless dug frequently, and in the process the old holes were obliterated by dumping freshly excavated earth and trash into them (Figs. 9.2, 9.3). In time the entire area, encompassing some 60 m², became a garbage dump which extended below the desert level instead of above it.

Sensing the stratigraphic importance of this locality, we removed 17 more-or-less adjacent blocks of rubbish either by arbitrary or by natural levels, as required by the circumstances. An analysis of the potsherd yield, about 130,000 fragments, and the implications, are presented elsewhere (pp. 104–106). For the moment it is enough to observe that the deeper levels of all tests produced pottery representative of all Pioneer Period phases, remains of the Estrella Phase being the most notable. Although the evidence for a Vahki Phase use of the wells is not strong, the conclusion seems warranted that the Hohokam knew the art of well-digging at the time of their arrival in the Southwest.

HEARTHS AND WORK AREAS

The hard-baked hearths in houses (Fig. 3.27) leave no doubt about the fact that fires inside the homes supplied warmth, light, and the energy to cook foods. By stripping the desert dust from areas surrounding houses, we have learned that outside fires were also frequently used. Many of these left no more than an oxidized stain on the then extant ground surface, or, at the most, they are marked by shallow depressions. The majority of these, one suspects, were places where the gross firewood was burned to coals which were then transferred to the small hearths inside the houses.

Fig. 9.1. Excavators in the well area (Block 10G) are attempting to delineate early Hohokam efforts to reach the water table.

Fig. 9.2. Stratified deposits (east face of Tests 5 and 6) where Hohokam dug for water: (a) desert surface; (b) floor of House 13:10G, Sacaton Phase; (c) ashy refuse dominantly Sweetwater Phase grading to Estrella Phase in stratum d; (e) nearly sterile waste dirt from early excavations; (f) upper caliche layer, abrupt end at far right representing ancient penetration; (g) sand, sterile where caliche layer is intact above; (h) lower caliche layer.

Fig. 9.3. Profile of irregularly stratified deposits in well area (Block 10G), west face of Test 4: (a, b) mixed Pioneer, Colonial and Sedentary Periods trash; (c, d) Pioneer Period (Sweetwater-Estrella Phases) trash; (e, f, g) mixed refuse and spoildirt in old excavations, Estrella Phase; (h) spoildirt including broken caliche; (i) mixed sand and dirt with some pottery, Estrella Phase; (j) upper caliche layer remnants; (k) sterile sand; (l) lower caliche layer.

This measure would reduce the smoke nuisance and keep to a minimum the danger of setting ablaze the combustible materials in the roof inside the house. We have not seen enough of the outside burning places to determine whether or not a pattern in their placement existed.

An adjunct to some hearths, particularly those in use during the Sacaton Phase, were specially made clay lumps grouped in threes in a fire bed as rests for a jar, keeping it above the live coals. These are generally called trivets. Although most often seen in house fireplaces, it is logical that they should have been used outside as well. The idea survives among the Pima who substitute stones for the clay elements (Russell 1908: 69).

Apart from the isolated firepits adjacent to houses, concentrations of hearths associated with other features were encountered in Block 10G, labeled as Work Areas 1, 2, and 3 (Fig. 1.6). Because Work Area 2 was a pottery manufactory it will be reviewed elsewhere (p. 194). Work Areas 1 and 3 were recognized as separate entities because House 6:10G lay between them. Functionally there may have been no difference, as most of the features were associated with the same walking surface. Some variations in level and overbuilding, however, make it clear that these areas existed for some period of time and that new pits were excavated as needed if the old ones did not serve. Scarcity of pottery makes it impossible to arrange the pits in any meaningful order. Such dating evidence as we have suggests that the most intense use of the area was during the Sacaton Phase, although, not surprisingly, some indications of earlier activity were seen.

Work Area 1

The entry of House 6:10G opened directly on Work Area 1 (Figs. 9.4, 9.5a), and we may suppose that the house occupants made use of at least some of the pits. The level at which they occurred appears to have been somewhat lower than that of the

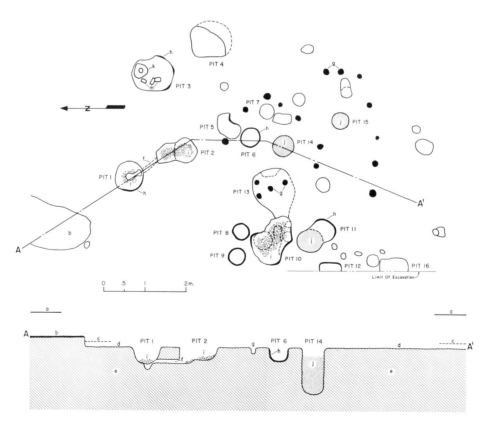

Fig. 9.4. Plan and section of Work Area 1 (10G): (a) present surface level; (b) entrance passage of House 6:10G; (c) probable surface from which most pits were dug; (d) our excavated surface level; (e) native soil; (f) tube leading from Pit 1 to 2; (g) postholes, stippled strips suggest possible configuration of wind breaks; (h) burned pits shown by heavy line; (i) fire-cracked stones; (j) gravel in pits; (k) lava mortar; (m) metate fragments.

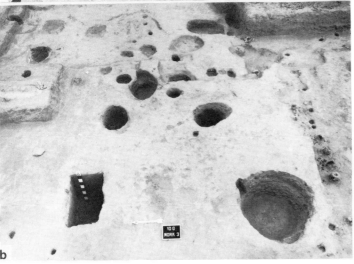

Fig. 9.5. Work Areas 1 (a) and 3 (b) in Block 10G. Meter stick stands in cleared test pit from 1934-35 operation.

in outline, it has a dumbbell-like hole in the bottom and side which connected with a tunnel that extended in a southeasterly direction for 0.5 m, ending at the base of the vertical wall of the north end of Pit 2 (Fig. 9.4). Although we cannot be absolutely certain that this feature was not the work of rodents, the arguments in favor of human design are as follows: the roundness, placement, and size of the holes in the pit and the arrangement of these with respect to the tunnel seem much too formal to assign to the usually capricious nature of rodent runs. Ending as it does at the bottom of the extension of Pit 2 seems a logical placement for the tunnel, if it was functionally related to the pit, and if the whole system was used, as the evidence suggests, as a vent for introducing a draft into the hearth. Unfortunately, there are no other vented hearths at Snaketown, and it cannot be said, therefore, that we have read the evidence properly. No records exist indicating that the Hohokam employed the deep and large pits with flues for corn roasting, as has been noted among the Anasazi (King 1949: 63-65).

As for other features in Work Area 1, Pit 4 apparently was the result of quarrying earth or clay, and Pits 11, 14, and 15 were partially filled with pea-size gravel bespeaking a special but unidentified function. A number of the penetrations made into the subsoil were clearly postholes, notably two series arranged in arcs that probably represent the location of windbreaks. They remind one of the brush-enclosed kitchens widely used by desert tribes, the Pimas included (Russell 1908: 69). Hearths specifically associated with these features could not be identified.

It is evident that various activities took place in areas like this one, a simple observation, but what activities are demonstrable only by the nature of the physical evidence. Surprisingly, the artifactual return from the stripped areas was almost nil.

Work Area 3

Located between Work Area 2 and House 6:10G (Figs. 9.5b, 12.2), this cluster of pits was less instructive than were the other localities. Five of the dozen pits showed burning; none contained fire-cracked rocks, and only one was gravel-filled. Considerable Pima disturbance was noted, for a corral once topped it. Some of the holes accommodated railroad tie fenceposts.

Hearths Below Mound 38

Under the southwest flanks of Mound 38, our explorations revealed a hard-packed and burned floor marked with a series of crematoria (Fig. 10.5d). Noting clues of various kinds that this floor was not resting on natural desert soil, the decision was made to sacrifice it and to search below for whatever prefloor features there might be. This probing exposed several cremations and 23 hearths, most of them in linear arrangements unlike anything heretofore reported in Hohokam villages (Fig. 9.6).

These hearths were circular in outline and surprisingly uniform as to size. Diameters ranged from about 40 to 55 cm, and depths varied from about 25 to 45 cm. Typically the side walls were vertical and the bottoms were flat or slightly concave. Every pit was lined with a thin slurry of clay, hand applied (Fig. 9.7a), and every one was burned though in most cases only lightly. In a few cases the oxidation layer extended deeper than the applied plaster. It would appear that the pits may have been used only once, otherwise repeated fires and certainly fires burning over a long duration would have baked the soil to a greater depth than they exhibit. Hearths in houses establish a useful comparative control in this respect. Clay trivet fragments rested on the bottoms of two pits, and a mano was found in one with two trivet fragments (Fig. 9.7b), designed to support a vessel over the coals without

entrance, a condition not observed elsewhere. From burned clay, plastered walls, the presence of charcoal and thermally fractured rocks, or combinations of these features as evidence of hearth use, we may recognize several pit forms in this work area. Pits 6, 8, and 9 are similar in size (diameter range 0.37-0.39 m, depth range 0.22-0.29 m) and in having vertical sides and flat bottoms. These clearly conform to some cultural standard. They compare favorably with the banks of hearths that predated the large pyral floor partially covered by Mound 38. If these pits ever had clay rims, they were lost either by erosion or by our own excavating. Pit content was mostly a silty soil containing a few potsherds but no charcoal. Only Pit 6 had plastered walls.

Another category of hearth, sometimes round but more often of irregular outline, is considerably larger than the preceding. Pits 1, 2, 3, 5, 10, 11, and 12 answer to this description in varying degrees. Pits, 1, 2, 3, and 10 contained fire-cracked rock, including thermally altered metate fragments and a mortar (Pit 3, Fig. 9.4) broken into a number of pieces by heat. Only Pit 2 in this group, though containing heat fractured stones, evidenced no baking of the clay side-walls.

The presence of the rocks as well as shape variations hint at some functional differences between the foregoing two sets of pits. Heated rocks were an accessory to cooking, best seen in the large roasting pits discussed later. The vertical-sided round pits must also have been used in food preparation, but just what was cooked or how we do not know. Pit contents provided no suggestions of specific uses.

Pit 1 must be singled out as having special properties. Circular

Fig. 9.6. Hearths in linear arrangements under Mound 38 and the crematory floor (11H), Gila Butte Phase. Raised rims represent level from which hearths were originally dug.

Fig. 9.7. Details of hearths under Mound 38 (11H): (a) vertical side showing smeared clay lining; (b) mano and two clay trivet fragments amidst mesquite charcoal.

smothering them. Charcoal, when present, was of mesquite wood.

In three of the five sets of hearths a shallow oval excavation was first made into which the pits were then dug. Johnson, who worked in this area, thought he detected evidence that the oblong pits were originally deeper, that they were filled with earth, and the hearths were then put into the artificially established matrix. This point was not definitely settled between us. It should be noted that digging stick marks were preserved in the soil under the plaster lining in several instances, indicating that it was well compacted.

Slight variations in the surface level from which the pits were dug were detected, but the time difference could not have been great. All associated material, principally pottery, indicates that these hearths date from the Gila Butte Phase, possibly extending into the Santa Cruz Phase. The overlying crematory floor was of Sacaton Phase age.

I have been unable to produce any references in ethnological accounts that would help directly in explaining these curious groups of hearths. Russell refers to "mesquite meal, roasted in mud-lined pits" by the Pima (1908: 94), but no description of the pits is provided. The circumstantial evidence indicates that these hearths were employed in some way in the preparation of food or drink; but the form, size uniformity, light burning, linear arrangement, consistent directional orientation and the mode of construction raise suspicions that they were of a rather special nature. It is tempting to think of the pits as the original cafeteria-type of service, but this idea goes beyond the realm of probability and is too simple.

The light burning of the pits leads to a thought about possible function. We know from the occurrences of charred seeds that the Hohokam collected the fruit of the saguaro, just as the Pima and the Papago still do in the 1970s. We also know that sea shell was etched, presumably with the vinegar derived from fermented saguaro fruit juice. Until packaged liquors became common, the modern desert Indians made a wine, mildly alcoholic, from saguaro fruit by burying the juice in earthen jars to control fermentation (Underhill 1946: 44). Papago informants have told me that they sometimes built a fire in the pit to warm the earth. This suggests the possibility that the Snaketown pits, large enough to accommodate jars with capacities of 10 to 15 liters, were pre-warmed to speed the production of the wanted liquor. The lack of charcoal in most hearths may mean that the embers were removed to prevent over-heating of the product. We saw no evidence of lining the holes with grass, as has been done historically.

ROASTING PITS

It has long been known that large roasting pits, or earth ovens employing the principle of the fireless cooker, are an attribute of Hohokam sites. Cushing was the first to recognize them in the Salt River valley, and he even named a village after them, "Los Hornos"—The Ovens (Haury 1945a: 179-180). Trischka described a number of unique ovens in the Sulphur Spring valley of southeastern Arizona (1933), and they have also been noted in the Tonto Basin, in the northeastern part of the Hohokam range (Haury 1932: 57-61). It was something of a surprise, therefore, that the work of 1934-35 in Snaketown did not produce the feature. Several test pits of that time were within a meter or so of three pits described in the following paragraphs, but their presence was not detected. If we need to be reminded how the vagaries of digging may influence conclusions, these instances will serve well.

Six large pits, more or less rock-filled, were found in 1964–65. Fortunately, they occurred under varying conditions from which useful information about age, longevity, and use may be inferred. The inventory of roasting pits follows:

Roasting Pit 1: 9E

Encountered during the course of stripping operations, this feature was in an area where there were numerous borrow pits but few house remains. The rim was approximately 0.5 m below the present surface, and we surmised that the old surface which gave access to the pit was at about the rim level. The overlying sheet trash formed during the Colonial Period, indicating that the pit was at least that old and most likely older.

At the rim line, the pit's diameter was 1.6 m, and its depth measured slightly over 1.0 m (Figs. 9.8A; 9.9a, b). The sloping sides, joining a flat bottom, consisted of a heavy coating of applied clay burned to a depth of 5 to 10 cm. Three large blocks of mica-schist, the largest 0.4 m long, rested in the bottom tripod fashion. The body of the pit was filled with fire-cracked rocks, predominantly granite, mica-schist, and river cobbles.

Pottery from the pit, analyzed by weight, produced the following results:

Fig. 9.9. Roasting pits: (a) Pit 1:9E as initially exposed and (b) after removal of the rock content; (c) Pit 1:11I with large thermally fractured rocks on the floor.

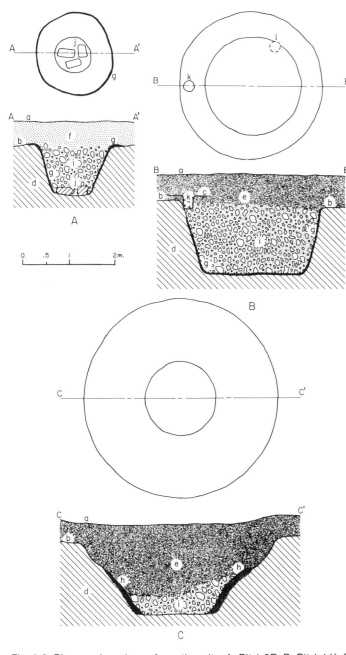

Fig. 9.8. Plans and sections of roasting pits: A, Pit 1:9E; B, Pit 1:11I; C, Pit 1:16L. (a) present surface; (b) old surface from which pits were dug; (c) surface at time Cremation 3:11I was buried; (d) native soil; (e) sandy-silt overburden containing some culture; (f) Santa Cruz Phase trash; (g) applied clay pit lining; (h) burned natural soil; (i) firecracked rocks; (j) stone trivets; (k-l) Cremations 2 and 3:11I.

Santa Cruz Red-on-buff	0.019 kg
Vahki Red	0.029
Vahki Plain	2.024

Since the overlying trash was principally of the Santa Cruz Phase, the few painted sherds of this horizon are accounted for easily. The predominance of older pottery types tells us that the pit probably dates from the early Pioneer Period and most likely from the Vahki Phase.

Roasting Pit 1: 11 I

During magnetometer testing by Rainey and Bergh (Appendix 3), the instrument registered an anomaly in Block 11 I. Test excavations immediately encountered a large, heavily burned, roasting pit, the cause of the machine's abnormal behavior (Figs. 9.8B; 9.9c). It was 3 m in diameter at the rim line and 1.2 m in depth, measured from the old surface which was approximately 0.5 m below the present desert level. The hard burned sides sloped gently toward a flat bottom. Sintered rocks, mostly granite and mica-schist, filled the pit to the rim; the larger individual stones rested near or on the pit's floor. Lumps of mesquite charcoal were scattered among the rocks, the fuel used in the heating process. Other organic remains or the residue of substances cooked in the pit, such as animal bones, were lacking.

Dating this pit is dependent upon three lines of evidence. First was the pottery content, consisting of a meager 82 sherds. Of these, 78 were Vahki Plain, 3 were Vahki Red, and 1 was Santa Cruz Red-on-buff. The latter can be ruled out as meaningful because the sheet trash above was of Santa Cruz Phase vintage and the sherd may have come from the contact zone close to the rim of the pit or it may have been intruded downward. On the basis of the other pottery types the pit may be assigned to the Vahki Phase or, more conservatively, to the early Pioneer Period.

The second line of evidence is a radiocarbon date derived from the mesquite charcoal in the pit. The sample tested (No. 873) yielded a date of A.D. 60±220, corrected to A.D. 170±220. This information is entirely consistent with the ceramic evidence. Finally, a pre-Santa Cruz Phase date for the pit is demonstrable by the presence of Cremations 2 and 3: 11 I in the top fill. A Santa Cruz Red-on-buff jar was associated with Cremation 3. The record is clear that Pit 1: 11 I is an old one and closely parallels Pit 1: 9E in age.

Roasting Pit 1: 16 L

Located near the southeastern outskirts of Snaketown, this hearth was marked by a low annular dirt mound sprinkled with gravel. The central depression was only about 0.25 m in depth, while the diameter of the mound crest was about 5.0 m. Before excavation, this was thought to be an old Pima well, the gravel suggesting penetration to the aquifer. The remains of a Pima house dating from the early decades of this century were nearby. However, digging soon revealed the feature to be a roasting pit.

The initial excavation for this pit was larger than any of the others investigated at Snaketown. The rim diameter at the old surface level was 4.2 m and the depth reached 1.6 m (Fig. 9.8C). The sides sloped rapidly toward the flat bottom, which had a diameter of 1.5 m. Hard burning of the natural clay-silt sides extended upward from the floor for about 1.0 m, leaving the wider flared part of the pit essentially unmodified.

The bottom third of the pit was filled with a heavy concentration of fire-broken stones, mostly granite and mica-schist. A little ash was present, but bones, charcoal, and plant remains were lacking. Of approximately 210 potsherds recovered from among the rocks, 60 were Santa Cruz Red-on-buff and 8 were Gila Butte Red-on-buff, the rest being Gila Plain. Higher in the fill and above the rock line, pottery was somewhat more abundant, still predominantly Santa Cruz Red-on-buff but with some Sacaton Red-on-buff added. On the ceramic evidence, the use of the pit may be assigned to the Colonial Period. Scraps of iron and stock manure noted as deep as 0.75 m indicate disturbances by the Pimas.

Roasting Pits in 11F
PIT 1

Roasting pits seldom occur in circumstances that permit definitive placement in relation to other features. Pit 1 was a most welcome exception to this apparent rule. It was located under the southern margin of Mound 40, a component in an impressive stratigraphic situation (Fig. 9.10). Pit 1 was a funnel-shaped excavation into sterile subsoil from a surface level not clearly definable but presumably close to the highest surviving remnants of the rim. Diameter and depth measured 2.5 m and 1.3 m respectively. The specially applied clay lining, up to 0.1 m in thickness, was more heavily burned than were the sides of any other pits investigated. Areas reached by little oxygen were deeply impregnated with carbon as though produced by drippings of grease or other

Fig. 9.10. Roasting Pit 1:11F, Sweetwater Phase, was buried under a prepared surface of Snaketown Phase times and the trash of Mound 40, deposited during the Snaketown and Gila Butte Phases. Man is standing in Pit 2, Snaketown Phase.

organic substances. Ralph W. G. Wyckoff, Department of Physics, University of Arizona, was unable, however, to extract any fatty materials from lining samples examined in the laboratory.

Details of pit contents and the order of overlying deposits are given in Figure 9.11, and a visual portrayal of the profile is seen in Figure 9.12. Worthy of special note was the compacted layer of

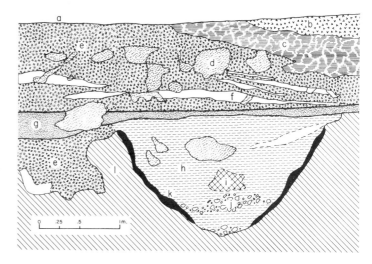

Fig. 9.11. Cross-section of Roasting Pit 1:11F capped by trash of Mound 40. (a) existing surface; (b) Gila Butte Phase trash; (c) structureless, disturbed trash; (d) areas disturbed by rodents; (e) Snaketown Phase trash; (f) ash lenses; (g) introduced desert soil with floor-like surface; (h) Sweetwater Phase trash; (i) charcoal concentration; (j) lens of fire-cracked rock; (k) hard-baked applied clay lining; (l) native soil.

clean soil which extended over the pit. The significance of this hard surface is associated with the use of certain trash mounds as platforms.

The only organic remains from the pit other than charcoal was the carbonized basal portion of a monocot leaf. Charles T. Mason, Curator of the Herbarium, University of Arizona, believes it to be *Nolina microcarpa,* commonly known as beargrass or Sacahuista. Although not outstanding for its food value, the caudex and emerging flower stalk are reported to have been used as food by Indians (Kearny and Peebles 1960: 189). Prevalent in the desert grassland flora, *Nolina m.* generally grows above the 1,000 m level today, and we may assume that there has been no appreciable change in its lower range since the Hohokam occupation of the Gila valley. Because Snaketown lies slightly less than 400 m above sea level, well below the natural range of beargrass, it may be inferred that the plant was brought into the village from the higher terrain in the distant mountains. The expenditure of this kind of effort suggests that it was used for food and not as insulating material to prevent foods from coming into direct contact with heated stones. Nearby plants would have served this purpose, as they did for the Pimas in their pit cooking (Russell 1908: 71).

Other cultural material in the pit was limited to potsherds. The sample, aggregating about 1,200 fragments, was classified by weight as follows:

Snaketown Red-on-buff	0.085 kg
Sweetwater Red-on-gray	0.400
Vahki Red	0.025
Vahki Plain	4.580

A Sweetwater Phase placement for Pit 1 is suggested by the pottery content as well as by the related stratigraphic evidence which has been reviewed elsewhere (Fig. 6.6).

PIT 2

By size, shape and contents, Pit 2 was not a roasting pit of the kind examined in the preceding pages, but it is included here because it retained the effects of an intense fire within it. Actually, the oblong shape of this pit and its extraordinary size, maximum diameter about 6 m (Fig. 6.6), may have been due to the joining of two adjacent borrow pits. Finishing the side walls evidently was not a part of the plan because digging stick marks were well preserved in the south face where Pit 2 intersected Pit 1 (Fig. 9.13). This unusual trace of earth-moving activity was preserved by the heat generated when what appears to have been an unusually thick mat of grass and small plants in the bottom of the pit was set afire. Fine white ash, some of it retaining the plant form, and a total absence of lump charcoal as might be derived from wood, characterize the fuel residue. In all probability the open-standing pit trapped wind-driven herbage which may have been set burning to clear it. Burning as a nonintentional part of the pit's use seems all the more likely when one considers the difficulty of exercising any effective control over a blaze 6 m across.

That part of the fill of Pit 2 removed under controlled conditions contained pottery as listed in Table 9.1.

This pottery sample, aggregating some 60,000 units, clearly establishes the Snaketown Phase as the time of filling of the pit. Because it post-dated Pit 1 assigned to the Sweetwater Phase and

Fig. 9.12. Roasting Pit 1:11F, Mound 40, emptied of most of its contents. Rocks at left were removed from the pit.

Fig. 9.13. Digging stick marks in the side wall of Pit 2:11F preserved by baking.

TABLE 9.1

Pottery Content in Pit 2:11F

Level	Sweetwater Red-on-gray	Snaketown Red-on-buff	Vahki-Gila Plain
1		0.845 kg	2.375 kg
2	0.340 kg	4.800	16.400
3		3.470	5.600
Total	0.340	9.115	24.375

was itself capped by the sterile layer making the walking surface on top of which more Snaketown Phase trash lay (Fig. 6.6), the time of Pit 2's use can only have been the Snaketown Phase. The small sample of Sweetwater Red-on-gray in Level 2 had to be intruded by rodent or human action. Patches of redeposited trash, distinguishable from primary rubbish by color and structure, were observed in the course of removing the contents of Pit 2.

PIT 3

Located southwest of Mound 40 (Fig. 1.6), in general configuration Pit 3 resembled Pit 1:9E, but it differed in not having a prepared lining. The native soil served this purpose, and it was baked to a depth of 10 cm or more. Evidently the pit was well cleaned of its contents after the last use, for it held only a few fire-fractured rocks and no charcoal. Potsherds in the fill, roughly 5 kg, were mainly Vahki Plain, and a few pieces of Snaketown Red-on-buff and Sweetwater Red-on-gray. A late Pioneer Period time assignment is indicated.

Discussion

From the information now at hand we may draw the conclusion that pit-roasting, or the earth oven, in which extensive use was made of heated rocks, was known to the Hohokam from the time of Snaketown's founding. Indeed, it was a trait that extended deep into antiquity and was, perhaps, the only significant feature shared by the indigenous Cochise culture gatherers and the farming Hohokam. Furthermore, the utility of this method of cooking is demonstrated by the fact that it survived into modern times among the Pimas (Russell 1908: 70) and other Southwestern tribes.

All of the pits noted here, excluding Pit 1:16L, are assignable to the Pioneer Period, the exception being of Colonial Period vintage. This one, joined with those reported from the Grewe site (Woodward 1931: 15) and Roosevelt 9:6 (Haury 1932: 57-61), also of Colonial Period times, suggests that there was some increase in size and depth of roasting pits as time passed and a tendency to flare the rims. The absence of Sedentary and Classic Periods roasting pits at Snaketown and vicinity is attributable to sampling rather than to changes in customs of food preparation.

Successful pit-oven roasting was dependent on the use of stone. The absence of stone at Snaketown demanded that it be imported if cooking was to take place in the village. The rock species in the pits described were almost wholly granite and mica-schist, traceable to Gila Butte some 5 km (3 mi) to the east. The transport of stone over this distance and the probability that the food to be cooked was brought in from some distance as well, represent a considerable expenditure of energy. We do not see this among the contemporary tribes who depended on the earth oven, for they dug the pits in the hills close to the supply of food. Evidently the Hohokam placed a high premium on large-scale "cook-outs," motivated either by the level of sedentism they had reached or to social factors not now recognized.

Pits with large rim diameters, from 2 to 3 m, raise the puzzling problem of how cooking was managed. Removal of heated rocks for placement on top of the food layer was generally entailed, and one wonders how the rocks were reached and handled while at a high heat. The question also remains as to how the food was introduced in the lower part of the funnel-shaped pit without getting pretty well scorched in the act. High temperatures are attested by the vitrification of some stone and by the observed reduction of some lava metate fragments to a plastic state. Most basalt softens between 962° and 1020° C (Clarke 1924: 298) or 1763° and 1868° F, a respectable temperature without the benefit of forced draft. It was far in excess of the degree of heat needed for ordinary pit-oven cooking.

MISCELLANEOUS PITS

Borrow Pits

Most of Snaketown is underlain by a layer of mixed caliche and clay, variable in thickness and occurring at depths ranging from 0.5 to 3.0 m below the present surface. This deposit was exploited for caliche to make house floors, probably for potter's clay and for other uses where soil was needed. Greater or lesser amounts in the clayey matrix evidently influenced the extent to which certain spots were utilized, and convenience of location, no doubt, played a part too. Figure 9.14 illustrates a plot in Block 11G, which was heavily quarried.

Where large quantities of dirt were needed, as in constructing the sides of the ball court, Mound 16, and capping material for mounds, the borrow pits grew to large dimensions with irregular outlines and sloping rather than vertical sides. The smaller pits, varying from 1 to 3 m in diameter, generally had nearly vertical side walls, though undercutting and inward sloping sides were observed. No changes in quarrying patterns through time were detected. The actual excavation was done mainly with a digging stick, as already noted, although flat hand-held stones would also have served well.

As far as we could determine, there was no direct or functional relationship of pits to mounds. However, when large borrow pits were used as refuse dumps, the discarding of material sometimes continued after the pit was filled, resulting in a mound. Mound 11, tested in 1934–35 (Gladwin and others 1937: 34-35), illustrates this point well.

Fig. 9.14. Borrow pits in Block 11G. See Figure 9.19 for identification of pit contents.

Fig. 9.15. Pit 1:9G, filled with sorted pea-size gravel.

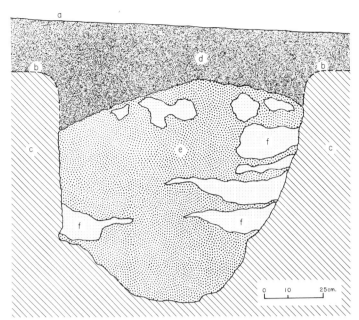

Fig. 9.16. Sectional view of Pit 1:9G: (a) present surface; (b) probable surface from which pit was dug; (c) native soil; (d) sandy-silt overburden; (e) pea-size gravel containing a few small water-rolled sherds; (f) silt lenses and irregular deposits.

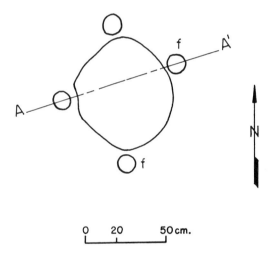

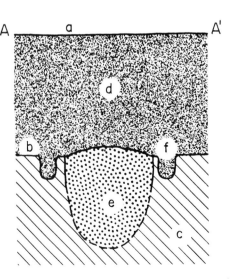

Fig. 9.17. Pit 3:9G with adjacent holes: (a) present surface; (b) probable old surface; (c) native soil; (d) sand-silt overburden; (e) gravel; (f) adjacent holes.

Gravel-Filled Pits

In a number of instances, holes in the floors of houses were found to have been filled with small gravel. At the time of excavation, the gravel was believed to have been nothing more than a special tamping material in setting the post, although there were no apparent reasons why gravel instead of soil should have been used only occasionally. The discovery of gravel-filled pits, not architecturally related, raised the question as to whether or not those that had been seen in houses were actually a part of the structure. A review of the problem did not produce definitive results because the cases examined were too few, but it did become clear that most of them did not relate to the plan established by the posts that supported the superstructure. These pits were from 0.25 to 0.40 m in diameter and 0.25 m or more in depth. There is no assurance that they did not post-date the life of the house.

The larger gravel-filled pits, with diameters averaging about 1 m, appeared to be completely independent of architectural units. Three of these, Pits 11, 14, and 15, occurred in Work Area 1 (Fig. 9.4) among hearths. It was noted that pits with evidence of burning never held gravel and the pits with gravel showed no signs of fire.

Three closely spaced pits in Block 9G, along with those in Work Area 1, suggest that they tend to occur in multiples, which may have some bearing on their function. Pit 1 of this group illustrates the nature of the contained gravel (Fig. 9.15). Curiously, the gravel was intercalated with lenses and masses of unstructured silt grading to sand (Fig. 9.16). The lenses of silt in the lower half of the deposit could conceivably represent washed-in material from the surface if the gravel was added by stages and stood higher in the central part of the pit than at the edges, a profile maintained by the gravel surface. The lump-like masses of

Fig. 9.18. Sample of gravel from Pit 1:9G; about half actual size.

Secondary Use of Pits

Once a pit had served its primary purpose of supplying caliche, clay, or water, it became something of a hazard to human traffic. A gaping hole was an invitation to throw refuse into it, thereby getting rid of garbage while eliminating a nuisance in the inhabited area. Through the centuries, thousands of pits became trash depositories. These, for the following reasons, are of interest to the archaeologists:

1. Usually pits were filled in a short time. Cultural remains recovered from them accordingly represent a narrow time range. Broken pottery, which the pits yield in great abundance, may reflect the handiwork of only a few potters and for only short moments in their productive careers. Inter-pit comparisons show typological nuances in painting styles that may be explained either as records of individual differences among potters or as evidence of ceramic evolution through time.

2. Once tossed in a pit, rubbish was less subject to mixing and contamination with the residue from other periods than was the refuse thrown on mounds. Rodent activity was limited because they preferred to burrow in the soft mounds rather than the hard natural layers into which the pits were dug. The net effect was about equivalent to storing trash in a large, sealed jar.

3. Pit relationships to other site features, such as houses, set up stratigraphic situations essential for chronology building. The complex of pits illustrated in Figure 9.14 provided little stratigraphic data because they were not associated with other datable features. Ceramic typology was the criterion for determining the ages of the deposits, complicated by pit shallowness, and by an unusual amount of human disturbance (Fig. 9.19). In contrast, pits sealed by house floors and floors penetrated by pits (Fig. 9.20a, b) are certain indicators of the sequence of events. In either case, the pit contents may be of the same age as the house, but more likely the time difference will be greater than that. Figure 6.17A and the related text clearly demonstrate how importantly pits have contributed to building Snaketown's long history, reason enough why so many of them were cleared.

Incidental Notes on Pits

The method of excavating pits varied according to their characteristics and the circumstances of discovery. A pit sliced through by the backhoe was examined in profile for clues of age and trash structure. It was either cleared as a unit or the refuse was taken out by layers, arbitrarily established if no depositional lines were present, or by natural levels if structure lines were observed. Pits discovered in stripping operations were emptied as a unit if small, and by arbitrary screened levels if large.

As noted elsewhere, the mounding of rubbish was a late Pioneer Period innovation at Snaketown. Refuse of earlier vintage was either spread over the inhabited areas as a sheet of variable thickness or it was concentrated in pits. Comparative volumetric studies were not made, but extensive digging provided the distinct impression that pit trash far outstripped refuse scattered over the surface. When pottery of pre-Snaketown Phase age appears in mounds, it could only have gotten there by human or animal transport from the original resting place below the desert floor.

Pits containing refuse of the Sweetwater and earlier phases usually exhibited faint stratification lines, while those of later times showed pronounced bedding zones. The chief marking material was wood ash. There is no obvious explanation why ash was separated from other trash during the older phases.

Finally, on the average, potsherds coming from pit trash were smaller than those in mound rubbish. A weight-count comparison

silt may be attributed to rodent disturbances. I have no explanation for these phenomena, but they are noted as possible aids in future studies of similar features.

Pit 3: 9G provided details of related features not seen in any of the other pits holding gravel. These consisted of four holes more or less symmetrically placed around the perimeter of the pit (Fig. 9.17). Whether these held posts as supports for a platform or some kind of superstructure is not known.

In all instances, whether the pits were large or small, the filling material was pea-sized gravel of surprising uniformity (Fig. 9.18), sorted from stream bed aggregate. The basis for this statement is the fact that small water-rolled potsherds are mixed with the gravel. Where typable, the latest sherds are Sacaton Red-on-buff of the Sedentary Period.

As of now, information is lacking to interpret the role gravel-filled pits played at Snaketown. The conscious selection of the gravel, a hint of installment filling of the pits, and of a related structure whet one's curiousity. Smiley notes (1949: 168) a cist filled with coarse gravel in a Mesa Verde pit house dating from about A.D. 700, but the phenomenon appears not to have been common. What few dating controls we have indicate Sedentary Period usage.

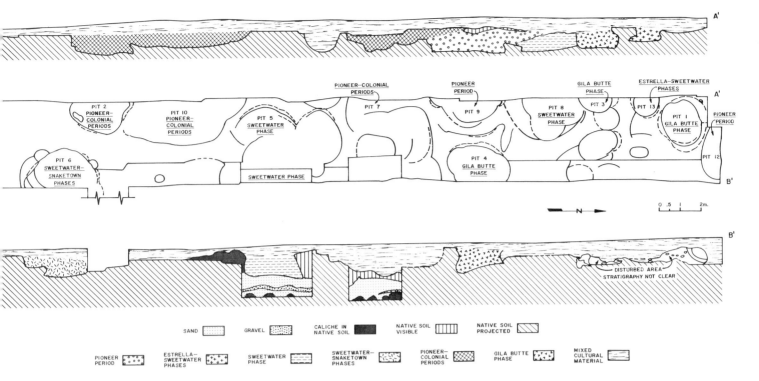

Fig. 9.19. Plan and sections of a cluster of borrow pits in Block 11G (see also Fig. 9.14). Trash period or phase assignments are given.

expresses this difference quantitatively. Sherds from pits numbered from 150 to 250 per kilogram compared with 75 to 150 units per kilogram derived from mounds. Paste hardness remained about the same from beginning to end, but vessel walls did become thicker as time passed. In all probability the thinness of early pottery rendered it more friable, enough so to account for the difference noted.

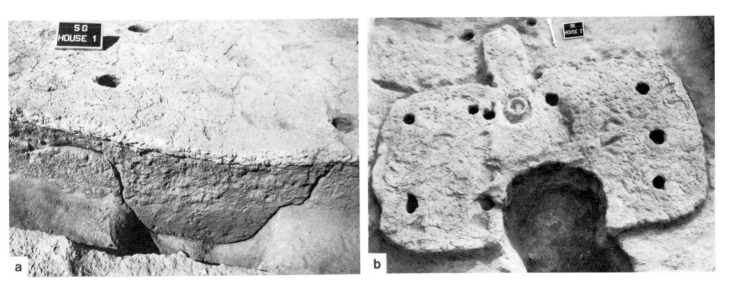

Fig. 9.20. Examples of floor-pit relationships: (a) thick caliche floor of a Sacaton Phase house (1:5G) seals a pit with Santa Cruz (upper third) and Estrella Phase trash (lower two-thirds); (b) Sweetwater Phase house (2:9E) partially destroyed by pit filled with Gila Butte Phase trash.

10. Care of the Dead

Before A.D. 1200, the Hohokam in the Gila valley traditionally disposed of their dead by cremation. Earth burial was infrequently practiced before that date, but with the beginning of the Classic Period inhumation met with increasing favor. By the mid-fifteenth century burning of the dead had about vanished as a burial custom.

Much of the effort in 1934–35 at Snaketown was devoted to systematic excavations in the cremation plots (Fig. 1.6). From the 530 deposits of human ashes recovered, Sayles established the methods and temporal changes in the manner of ash disposal (Gladwin and others 1937: 91-100). Ten inhumations were also reported. In 1964–65 the goals of the excavation emphasized architectural studies, stratigraphic testing, and canal explorations, resulting in a low yield of evidence of the dead. Cremations totaled only 94, and most of these were encountered incidental to other work. Three inhumations must also be recorded in Snaketown proper. Sixteen cremations and four earth burials came from the Classic Period sites in the western outskirts of Snaketown.

CREMATION

Figure 10.1 summarizes the cremations recovered during both operations by location and by phase assignment. When cremation frequencies are compared with house distributions by grid blocks (Fig. 1.6), it becomes immediately apparent that densities of each trait were largely mutually exclusive. Residence areas and plots for human ash disposal appear to have been differentiated in the minds of the Hohokam. Such overlaps as did occur represent isolated departures from the apparent rule when a cremation was deposited indiscriminately in the village and in the process penetrated the floor of an abandoned house, or was built over by the construction of a late house.

Accurate identification of cremations to phase is dependent on associated diagnostic cultural materials or on a physical context that clearly relates the bone deposit to other features which are datable. As an example, Figure 10.1 carries no entries for cremation in the Estrella Phase. The scarcity of painted pottery at that time reduced the chances that any of it might have been included as offerings with bones. Lacking it, a Vahki Phase or an "Unplaced" assignment would have been made.

The "Unplaced" cremations amount to about 30% of the total sample. Had it been possible to date more of these, the low frequency counts of Pioneer Period cremations would have been substantially augmented. There is no doubt, however, that burning the dead was the custom at all times.

While the 1964–65 sample is small, trends in the manner of ash disposal are suggested. A comprehensive typology of cremation forms, to my knowledge, has not been made, and Snaketown by no means yielded all the kinds of deposits known in the area occupied by the Hohokam. Broadly speaking, three forms may be

recognized: (1) pit depositories, round or oval in shape, holding both bones and offerings, if present; sometimes with ancillary pits containing bones and artifacts in a manner reminiscent of Yuma customs, that is, the ashes of a single person divided four ways and separately buried (Spier 1933: 303); (2) trenches of variable length with bones and smashed artifacts well mixed; and (3) urn disposal. Using these categories, the new lot of cremations may be tabulated as in Table 10.1.

Information given by Sayles (Gladwin and others 1937: 95) for the Pioneer Period indicates that pit (Fig. 10.2a, d) and trench disposal (Fig. 10.2b) were early practices and that the former method survived commonly throughout the time cremation was the vogue. Trench disposal lost in favor in later times, and although the earliest example of urn burial was in the Snaketown Phase, enshrining bones in jars (Fig. 10.2c) was not common until the Classic Period (Haury 1945a: 43-48; Johnson 1964).

Insofar as funerary offerings are concerned, the excessive smashing of pottery in Pioneer Period cremations was noted by Sayles (*ibid.*), and until late in the period little else accompanied the bones. Unfortunately, the custom did not die in the Pioneer Period (Fig. 10.3). About 65% of the bone lots have associated cultural materials, not counting the urn as an offering when the ashes were entombed in that way. Needless to say, material goods that passed through the pyral fire suffered external damage, and as a rule we see only the inorganic accompaniments, and oftentimes no more than tantalizing fragments. Occasional quirks of preservation tell us that perishable objects also were associated with the dead. For the most part, these may have been articles of dress. Sandal and textile fragments have been reported (Gladwin and others 1937: 159-162; King 1965).

A tabulation of the kinds of cultural goods associated with the 94 cremations reads as follows (numbers indicate times of occurrence rather than numbers of specimens): pottery vessels, 21;

TABLE 10.1

Categories of Cremations

Phase	Pit	Trench	Urn	Total
Civano	9		7	16
Soho				
Sacaton	23	1	4	28
Santa Cruz	20			20
Gila Butte	3			3
Snaketown	4	1		5
Sweetwater				
Estrella				
Vahki				
Unplaced	37	1		38
Total	96	3	11	110

[164]

PHASE	3C	3D	3F	3H	3I	4H	4I	5F	5J	6A	6F	6G	7A	7F	7I	7J	8A	8E	8F	8G	8H	9D	9E	9F	9G	9H	9I	10D	10E	10F	10I	10J	10L	10M	10N	11F	11G	11H	11I	11J	11M	12G	12J	12K	AZ U:13:21	AZ U:13:22	AZ U:13:24	SUB-TOTAL	GRAND TOTAL
CIVANO																																													39	36	16	75 / 16	91
SOHO																																																	
SACATON	1	15	1	2	9	1	2	2 / 10	1	10	2	8	2	11	4	2			1			1	1		1	1			4	2				1	6	7	2		7	1	3	22	1	4				123 / 28	151
SANTA CRUZ		1							1		15	3		2	1				1			1	2	1	2			8	63	12	1	36	2	1			3		10	5	1	8	1					163 / 20	183
GILA BUTTE								1						1											6	1		3										1		1		1						12 / 3	15
SNAKETOWN								2											1			1	1	1	3								1					2				3						10 / 5	15
SWEETWATER																									2	2																						4 / 0	4
ESTRELLA																																																0 / 0	0
VAHKI																							5		1	3									2													11 / 0	11
UNPLACED	4		1	2	3			2 / 7			12		2	3	2			2	2			3	3				5	4	22	4	32			5	4	2	1	13	4	1		11	1	2	1	11	9	142 / 38	180
SUB-TOTAL	1	20	1	3	11	4	2	4 / 21	1	37	5	10	7	15	4	2		4	2			11	6	1	2	1	6	1	14	98	25	1	74	2	1	14	13	5	1	32	11	5	45	3	6	50	45	540 / 110	650
GRAND TOTAL	1	20	1	3	11	4	2	21	4	1	37	5	10	7	15	4	2	4	2	4	2	11	6	2	8	2	14	98	25	1	75	2	1	1	14	13	5	1	32	11	5	45	5	6	1	50	45	16	650

GRID BLOCK

2 =1934-'35 — 2 =1964-'65

Fig. 10.1. Distribution of cremations by grid block and phase. The 1934-35 figures are from Gladwin and others 1937: Fig. 38, and they include 10 burials from grid blocks as follows: 3D (2); 5J (1); 6F (1); 6G (4); 10E (2); and by time, Sacaton Phase (6), unplaced (4). This tabulation reassigns the Soho Phase sites to the Civano Phase of the Classic Period.

Fig. 10.2. Some variations in the disposal of human ashes: (a) Cremation 1:11I, pit type, Sacaton Phase; (b) Cremation 5:11H, trench type, Snaketown Phase; (c) Cremation 2, Arizona U:13:22, urn type, Civano Phase; (d) Cremation 18:5F, with pottery vessel resting on palette, bones in pit below, Sacaton Phase.

Fig. 10.3. Offerings of finely shattered clay vessels accompany some deposits of human ashes. Gila Butte Phase. About actual size.

shell bracelets, 21; shell beads, 17; stone palettes, 16; bone hair ornaments, 15; stone projectile points, 7; whole shells, 7; miscellaneous stone tools as manos, scrapers, reamers, 12; substantial amounts of shell wastage, 2; stone bowls, 2; pottery censers, 2; shell ring, bone tube, clay figurine, antler tool, turquoise pendant, 1 occurrence each.

Several categories of ash-associated specimens may be identified: (1) objects worn at the time of cremation, namely, shell bracelets, beads, hair ornaments; (2) stone tools as manos, projectile points, scrapers and pottery vessels, which are subsistence-related objects and may have been personally owned or may have been a reflection of the idea that the deceased were in need of tools; (3) inclusions of shell wastage, suggesting the craft specialty of the dead person; (4) esoterica, namely, stone palettes, clay figurines and incense burners.

The latter class of goods, particularly the palettes, had special meaning for the Hohokam in life and death. The custom that called for their use may have been hazardous to health, for almost all palettes that have been tested for lead show traces of it. In spite of the high incidence of palette and human ash association, I do not believe we are entitled as yet to assume the relationship was lethal.

When pottery accompanied the ashes, vessels were sometimes broken before interment, and occasionally only large vessel fragments were used, the kinds that might have been retrieved from trash mounds to serve as token offerings. Burial furniture was often deposited in the pit after the bones had been well covered with earth (Fig. 10.2a). Unless the excavator digs deeply enough to locate the ashes, such objects might be identified as "strays." During the Civano Phase redware jars seem to have been preferred over other pottery types (Fig. 10.2c).

A number of questions related to Hohokam cremation practices have not received much attention. Our information is sketchy about regional differences in modes of bone disposal and, in fact, about temporal variations in any part of the Hohokam domain except in the most general terms. A detailed examination of cremation accompaniments might well reveal some social and attitudinal values. Unexplained are the meanings of caches and the mass destruction of cultural goods, in both of which fire played an obvious part. These customs appear to be connected in some way to cremation as such. But I strongly suspect that the relationships of many activities derive from fire as a revered and sacred agent, essential in death, in making sacrifices and in ritual. Particular questions about cremations should be examined in this larger context.

Crematoria

The actual burning of the dead took place over, or in, shallow elongated pits. These were specially constructed as a planned part of the funeral pyre. Only four isolated crematoria and a group of eight, associated with the large crematory floor, were found. Three of the single pits, in Blocks 10D and 11G, varied from 1 to 2 m in length, but they had a surprisingly uniform width of 0.5 m. Depths below the surface at the time of use did not exceed 0.5 m. The fourth example, Crematorium 1:8E, was different in form. A large pit, 1.5 by 2 m and 1 m deep, it contained an abundance of mesquite charcoal derived from a number of logs 10 to 15 cm in diameter that served as fuel. Although the human ashes removed from the pit were small in volume, three persons, two adults and one adolescent, were represented (Appendix 9). There is no way of knowing whether these ashes resulted from a single or from several burnings. A broken Vahki Red pottery bowl rested on the floor of the pit.

Stratigraphically, the pit was later than a house floor through which it was intruded (Fig. 10.4a). The house lacked dating materials, but by form and floor composition a Pioneer Period age was indicated. The Vahki Red bowl suggests early Pioneer Period use

of the crematory. A radiocarbon date derived from the charred mesquite (our No. 16, University of Arizona Lab. No. A-689) yielded a date of A.D. 920±120. This is an unlikely value because it would place the crematory either in the Santa Cruz or Sacaton Phases, far too late. By that time Vahki Red pottery had been out of style for half a millennium. A second sample (our No. 17, University of Arizona Lab. No. 1072) dated A.D. 410±70, an acceptable value for the Pioneer Period when all other dating controls are considered.

The more conventional crematoria (Fig. 10.4b) showed burned bottoms and sides, and remnants of human ash were present in all of them. These have not been included in the tabulation of cremations because they most likely represent the incomplete recovery of bones after the fire had cooled. The ages of these pits were determined as early Pioneer Period (10F) and Colonial Period (11G). Crematorium 1:10D, on the basis of an associated Sacaton Red bowl, was attributed to the Sedentary Period. Mesquite charcoal from this pit (our No. 4, University of Arizona Lab. No. 598) dated A.D. 1660±100.

Once again, something is drastically amiss with this value. Beyond the fact that we have no evidence that Sacaton Red lasted later than about A.D. 1200, the bones in the pit, those of a child, rested at a depth of about 1.5 m under undisturbed trash of the Sacaton Phase. The probability that this was a late intrusion is ruled out by the physical evidence. The reoccupation of Snaketown by the Pimas did not take place until more than 200 years after this date, and historically they did not cremate except when warriors were killed away from home. Furthermore, they did not make Sacaton Red pottery. The unacceptability of the two radiocarbon dates derived from crematory charcoal raises the disconcerting question about the reliability of other age values based on radiocarbon assays.

The Big Floor

The eight crematoria previously alluded to, integral parts of a large prepared earthen floor, are somewhat more revealing of the existence of a formalized pyral ritual among the Hohokam than the isolated burning pits indicate. The discovery of the floor under the southwestern flanks of Mound 38 came as a by-product of a machine-dug trench probing the contents of the mound (Fig. 10.5a). The hard, heavily trampled, and fire-stained floor appeared as the base of the mound was reached, particularly at the point where it flattened out to meet the old desert surface. The ease with which the floor could be traced over an inordinately large distance in the east-west trench ruled out the thought that it was a house floor.

EXPLORATION OF THE FLOOR

The novelty of the feature was a persuasive factor in deciding that it should be fully explored, even though this necessitated the removal of an awesome amount of overburden. Only in this way could a notion of the floor's function be developed. After viewing the profiles of the trenches made to determine the floor edges and studying the pottery recovered in the process, it was decided little or nothing could be gained by stripping the overlying mass in levels or by blocks. Accordingly, the backhoe was brought in to do as expeditious a dirt removal job as possible (Fig. 10.5b,c). The floor was cleared without suffering injury and without loss, we believe, of significant information.

Absolute pinpointing of the floor edges was not possible because it tended to feather out and lose itself in the surrounding soil; but it can be said that the area encompassed was approximately square and about 400 m² in extent. The floor's surface was surprisingly level and hard packed, especially near the center, where five of the eight crematoria were located (Fig. 10.5d) and where most of the human activity seems to have taken place. The

Fig. 10.4. Crematoria and burials. (a) Crematorium 1:8E (with meter stick) intruded through floor of House 1, Pioneer Period; (b) Crematorium 1:11G, heavily burned, Colonial Period; (c) burials under the deep trash of Mound 44; (d) Burials 1a and b (reading clockwise), 2 and 3. Heads to east, Sacaton Phase.

floor was made of introduced material, mostly a silty clay, which stood well the trampling of feet and effectively sealed and protected preexisting features.

The crematoria were easily detected during the floor-cleaning process by the baked clay edges and the ashy contents (Fig. 10.6). They averaged only 1.5 m in length, 0.75 m in width, and a mere 0.2 m in depth. Although large enough to gather together most of the human ashes during a cremation, the pits represent only a fraction of the area over which a fire was built, accounting, in the main, for the extensive fire staining of the floor. The possibility must also be entertained that cremation of the dead took place on the floor without benefit of a pit, or that fires were built on the floor as a normal part of cremation-related death rites.

Four crematoria contained no bones in the remaining fill, meaning they were well cleaned out after the last use. The other four held bones in some quantity, and in three funerary offerings were

Fig. 10.5. Crematory Floor under Mound 38. (a) A machine-dug trench probes the mound's west side. Mound 39 lies beyond the backhoe. (b) Removing part of Mound 38. Heavy equipment worked on cushion of earth to prevent floor damage. (c) Stripping of overburden nears completion. Hand scraping of floor revealed crematoria, here being cleared of contents. (d) Crematory floor from Mound 38, looking southwest. Central elongated depressions are crematoria.

c

d

Fig. 10.6. Color and hardness differences aid the excavator in locating and outlining a crematory pit.

still present. With one exception, all crematoria uncovered at Snaketown were oriented east-to-west. Crematorium 2, associated with the large floor, produced skull remnants in the east end, duplicating the conditions encountered near Gila Bend by Wasley and Johnson (1965: 66) in a Classic Period site and the custom of the historic Yumas (Spier 1933: 302).

The purpose of several round pits about 0.25 cm in diameter, visible in Figure 10.5d, could not be determined with certainty.

Two of these, situated near the east ends of crematoria, call to mind the Yuma manner of constructing a funeral pyre in which a meter-high post was set in the ground as the initial step in pyre construction (Spier 1933: 301-302). The post arrangement around a pit which so clearly revealed details of the burning process at the Fortified Hill Site near Gila Bend (Wasley and Johnson 1965: 66-67) was not seen at Snaketown at all. Other breaks in the floor near the eastern margin represented two cremations deposited in holes dug through the floor from a higher surface, and a large irregular pit near the northeast corner was caused by the crumbling of the floor over loosely packed trash.

DATING THE FLOOR

Features present before the floor was built included the following: (1) a notable series of hearths of Gila Butte Phase; (2) several pits filled with Gila Butte-Snaketown Phase trash; (3) several cremations of Santa Cruz Phase age or older; and (4) House 1: 11H of the Santa Cruz Phase superimposed on an older structure of probable Snaketown Phase age, under the southwest corner of the floor. In sum, nothing later than the Santa Cruz Phase was encountered during the subfloor probing, which prompts the inference that the feature under study was of Santa Cruz Phase age or later. Inspection of the sherds taken from the floor, but more significantly, the broken vessels associated with the bones of the last people cremated, represent a late form of Santa Cruz Red-on-buff. The pottery content of that portion of Mound 38 which spread over the floor was Sacaton Red-on-buff.

On the basis of the foregoing evidence, the floor was last in use during the end of the Santa Cruz Phase, as the pottery of that time was shifting stylistically toward the attributes that became the hallmarks of Sacaton Red-on buff. Because the refuse of Mound 38 extended over the floor, we know it fell into disuse before Snaketown was abandoned.

The closeness of the crematory floor to Mound 39 with its succession of cappings probably represents a planned and functionally related religious complex. Seen from above (Fig. 10.7),

Fig. 10.7. Aerial view of Mounds 38, 39 and the crematory floor. Nos. 1 and 2 are remnants of prepared surfaces on an old mound most of which has been moved eastward (to the right) to make Mound 39 with its own hard surface (No. 3).

Mound 39

1 2

3

Crematory Floor

Mound

the floor and the mound make an imposing pair of features, which, for the most part, were in simultaneous use. The last capping (No. 3) on Mound 39 appears to have outlived the floor but not by much, and the pre-floor hearths tend to extend the ritual use of the area as far back as the Gila Butte Phase. If any part of Snaketown in its deployment of features recalls the planned religious centers of Mesoamerica, it has to be Mound 39 and the adjacent crematory floor. The juxtaposition of the two provides a strong hint that the dance was a part of the death ritual.

Although cremation was one of the distinguishing attributes of the Hohokam from the moment of their arrival in the Southwest, they were not the initiators of the custom. The practice had early beginnings in the New World, for it has been noted in the Renier Site, northeastern Wisconsin (Mason and Irwin 1960), with an estimated age of 6500 to 4000 B.C.,and in the El Riego Phase of the Tehuacán Valley, Mexico, between 7200 and 5200 B.C. (MacNeish 1964: 41). Later occurrences are known in Mesoamerica, as, for example, at Chupícuaro (Porter 1956), suggesting that the custom was part and parcel of the Hohokam southern inheritance. However, the story may not be as simple as it seems, because cremations have been noted in the mountain environment of the San Carlos Indian Reservation dating from about 500 B.C. (Haury 1957: 26). This evidence, in the Cienega Site near Point of Pines, led to an inference, though improbable, that an ancestral stage of diffusion without pottery but with certain other Hohokam attributes, reached a highland mountain habitat before the main migrants established residence in the desert environment of southern Arizona.

Crematory Mounds

In 1934–35, several localities were encountered in Snaketown which produced large quantities of incinerated materials. Sayles referred to these as Crematory Mounds (Gladwin and others 1937: 95-96) because he believed the deposits represented the periodic accumulation of goods, including some bone which had been burned in other localities. The mounds themselves show no direct trace of fire. Thousands of projectile points and large quantities of calcined shell, including bracelet fragments, mosaic elements, and whole shells, were recovered. We did not encounter anything like this during the 1964–65 excavations, but it is worthwhile recalling the existence of the deposits because they may represent the only physical evidence that links an ancient custom with one that has been observed historically among some of the Gila and Colorado River Indian tribes.

Mourning rites, particularly those associated with the anniversary of a death, called for the burning of much personal property (Spier 1933: 305-309). The residual ashes were buried separately, sometimes in several places. In antiquity, the unburnable parts of personal property sacrificed during mourning rites may have been collected and thrown on the same spot, which, in time, developed into the low crematory mounds. Burning the blankets and other possessions of a deceased person among the Pimas (Russell 1908: 195) may be a holdover from an earlier custom.

Analysis of Cremated Bones

The excessive comminution of human ashes in Hohokam cremations has markedly reduced their value as a source of information about the physical make-up of the people. It has been amply demonstrated, however, that examination of ashes does provide useful information of several kinds (Gejvall 1963). Birkby's report (Appendix 9) shows that age and sex determinations can be made in some instances and that morphological observations are possible also. The problem, of course, is that the sample is too small to permit inferences about population, morbidity, and other like questions. But a few notes on the cremation custom can be made.

The smallness of the bones, seldom more than 3 cm in size, suggests the possibility of mechanical breaking of the bones after burning, or, stirring the ashes as the pyre burned itself out. It may also mean that the desert hardwoods generated hotter than usual fires to achieve more complete combustion. On this point, lumps of slag-like material occasionally occur with the ashes. Qualitative analysis shows the substance to be sodium aluminum silicate with minor amounts of calcium, magnesium and iron, suggesting that the slag was derived from the desert soil into which the crematory pit was dug. Heated to 850° C (1,562° F) (by George H. Roseveare, Metallurgist, Arizona Bureau of Mines), a sample did not soften; but it was pointed out that initially the components may have reached the plastic stage at a much lower temperature, in the order of 400° C (752° F). The heat-warped obsidian projectile points suggest that temperatures of about 800° C (1,472° F) were reached.

Birkby notes that in only one instance were bones of more than one person observed (Cremation 4: 11 I) in the same lot of ashes. A single fire for a single person seems to have been the rule. The inclusion of an occasional calcined rodent bone with the human ashes may be due either to accidental association or to the presence of ingested rodent parts in the alimentary tract of the deceased. Of more importance is the observation that ash quantities varied enormously, from a few fragments to a number of double handfuls of an adult.

The weight range, as recorded by Birkby, is from 9.1 gr (Cremation 2:8E) to 2,353 gr (Cremation 4:11 F). The latter figure approaches the normal skeletal weight, 2,882±365 gr of Asiatic adult males and females. While this difference might be attributed to a lack of care in collecting the bones from a crematory or to post-interment loss, it is far more likely to be a reflection of a mortuary custom that specified the ashes of a single person were to be split into a number of small lots for separate burial, not unlike the practices of the Colorado River Yumans (Spier 1933: 303).

Clearly, the likelihood that this did indeed happen among the Hohokam immediately places constraints on how cremation data are used. Ordinarily, the archaeologist inventories ash lots as though each one represented a single person, but this may be far from the truth. The quantities expressed in Figure 10.1 are best interpreted, then, as numbers of ash samples rather than numbers of people. Future investigators of ash plots should watch particularly for evidence of multiple disposal, for example, recovery of parts of the same artifact in two or more ash lots; and the clearing of crematoria should be carried well beyond the limits of the pit itself to detect possible associated ash deposits.

INHUMATION

In the extensive excavations of Snaketown, stray unburned human bones were not encountered. A comparable amount of earth turned in Anasazi or Mogollon sites would produce many scattered bones, mostly derived from disturbed burials. The low yield of burials during both Snaketown operations does indeed emphasize the infrequency of inhumation.

Before turning to the burials, note must be made of a fragmentary burned human skull resting nearly 2 m down in a large pit (Pit 3: 10E) filled with Pioneer Period rubbish. The skull parts rested on water-deposited sediments representing a period of time when the pit stood open to the weather. Directly associated material included two hammerstones, a quartzite core, a metate fragment, and a few potsherds, giving the impression that a basketload of trash had been dumped into the pit. Unbroken depositional lines in the refuse above indicated these materials were not given the treatment accorded incinerated bones, and for that reason it was not included in the inventory of cremations. The apparent lack of respect for the dead in this case was exceptional.

The 1934–35 excavations netted ten inhumations, six of which were of Sacaton Phase age, and the others were unassigned (Gladwin and others 1937: 91, 93). These included the remains of four infants and six adults. Where the bones were sufficiently articulated to judge burial position, the bodies were extended, supine, with heads oriented to the east, except for one which was flexed. Two of the interments had red-on-buff pottery associated as grave furniture.

In the main village of Snaketown, the 1964–65 work produced only three nearly complete and one highly fragmentary skeletons, all occurring in a tight cluster under 2.5 m of trash in Mound 44 (Fig. 10.4c, d). The grave pits were shallow penetrations into the sterile subsoil underlying the mound. While the surface from which the burials were made could not be identified, the supposition is that some accumulation of refuse had already taken place, otherwise there would not have been enough soil to cover the cadavers. That part of the trash through which the interments were made, and the great depth of refuse that developed later, were all of Sacaton Phase age. The graves are therefore of Sacaton Phase times as well. Burial accompaniments were lacking, except for a single shell pendant under the chin of Burial 1a (Fig. 15.17b), which was of no real diagnostic value.

Drawing upon Bennett's study of the bones (Appendix 10) the primary information about these individuals is as follows: Burial 1a, probably male, age 12-15 years, prone, head east. Burial 1b, disoriented remnants of a youth, 5-8 years, probably disturbed when 1a was buried. Burial 2, nearly complete skeleton of a female, supine, age 25-35 years, head east. Burial 3, male, supine, age 17-20 years, head east but skull missing, evidently removed when Burial 2 was made (Fig. 10.4d). The occipitally deformed skull of Burial 1a and the undeformed skull of Burial 2 suggest that some cranial diversity existed, a condition noted also for the human remains in Ventana Cave (Gabel 1950: 519). The skulls recovered during the 1934-35 Snaketown work were undeformed (Gladwin and others 1937: 246).

The main consistent features of the Snaketown burials are extended body position, head oriented toward the east, and a Sacaton Phase age. At first glance, the burials under Mound 44 would appear to be a group interment, but this view may be discounted because of the disturbances of Burials 1b and 3. While it is tempting to think of these as "foreigners" who were not accorded the usual Hohokam cremation, burial at intervals of both sexes, with a considerable age spread, suggests these individuals were Hohokam as well. There is no obvious answer as to why these graves were so closely clustered.

The pre-Classic Period earth burials at Snaketown, those attributed to the early Classic Period (Soho Phase) in a village 5 km (3 mi) east of Snaketown (Johnson 1964: 151), two flexed inhumations in a Vahki Phase site on the south bank of the Salt River west of Granite Reef dam (Morris 1969b) and the bodies recovered in Ventana Cave where earth burial was the normal practice (Haury 1950: 460–468), suggest that personal preference and regional differences may have been more common among the Hohokam than we have heretofore thought.

In the Classic Period sites, Arizona U:13:21 and 22 (Gila Butte 1:2 and Gila Butte 1:3, respectively, in the Gila Pueblo numbering system), the field notes record one and three burials, respectively, of fetal or newborn infants (Bennett, Appendix 10). These same two villages yielded 50 and 45 cremations during the 1934–35 work. In Arizona U:13:22 the infant remains were buried below house floors, a phenomenon not seen in a single house in Snaketown. The inference may be drawn that infant disposal below house floors was foreign to Hohokam custom and that it related to the intruded complex of cultural elements along with adobe-walled surface buildings and polychrome pottery, hallmarks of the Salado people. In Los Muertos, Cushing noted (1890: 169-172) that infants were buried near house hearths, suggesting that the Civano Phase Salado-inspired practice was common.

PART FIVE

MATERIAL CULTURE

The nature of the archaeologist's sources of information demands that he place a high priority on the examination of the cultural goods available to him. It is mainly through artifacts and the by-products of certain human activities that inferences may be drawn which bear on the life and the time of the people under study. Technical details of objects, such as the materials of which they are made, the manner of construction, the form and art styles they reflect, become space and time markers while simultaneously illuminating the customs and attitudes, the patterned behavior, the unfolding or the retracting, and the borrowing or the giving of the elements that identify a people.

Unhappily, the personal factor, the names, ages, sex, and roles of the makers and users of the artifacts remain anonymous. These limitations, and our ignorance of beliefs associated with the making of objects and the details of their ultimate uses, impose a special burden on the student of prehistory.

Furthermore, there are other handicaps. First, the archaeologist deals only with those elements which have survived the destructive forces of man himself and, most importantly, those of nature. Wide ranging classes of objects made of plant fibers and wood, organic animal products such as skin, fur, and feathers, have long since returned to dust except where special circumstances preserved fragments of them. Second, the vagaries of excavation, and even the particular interests of the archaeologist, may skew what he finds in a direction which is not necessarily a fair portrayal of what was once there.

The following pages bring out the wealth and the scope of Hohokam material remains, but the account is one-sided. We are given hints of the riches in the area of perishable goods by the occasionally preserved fragment of textile or basket, by rare recoveries in caves, as, for example, in Ventana Cave (Haury 1950); by the depictions on pottery of elaborate headdresses, flutes, and rattles; and by the indirect evidence supplied by neighboring tribes, notably the Anasazi, who possessed things which certainly were passed on to them by the Hohokam. Textile techniques and cotton itself are examples. Access to the full range of goods that have been destroyed would vastly illuminate the Hohokam life style and the tribe's origin.

But we must work with what is at hand. The 1934–35 effort produced a disproportionate amount of the "fine" class of goods, palettes, sculptured stone, carved shell and bone, because many cremations were found, and these are the producers of imperishable material wealth. Less attention was paid, perhaps, to the recovery of work-a-day tools, though they were not ignored. In 1964–65, on the other hand, the cremation plots were not sought out and more care was taken with the recovery of utilitarian tools. The combined collections we believe to be the most representative sample of Hohokam products available.

In analyzing these materials, about 3,150 catalogued items from the most recent excavations, the system employed in the 1930s will be generally followed. We are still in need of confirmation of what the Hohokam had at any one time and what transformations their possessions underwent as a function of normal change or due to the effects of outside forces. Reasoning back from the artifact to societal behavior is not ignored, but the deep insights we would like to have are not forthcoming at the present time. A conscious effort has been made to maintain simplicity in classifying artifacts and to avoid the pitfalls of a complex typology stemming from excessive subdivision of categories. If the error lies in the direction of generalizing, then someone has the reason to pick up the "ball" and coax it in the opposite direction.

In making time assignments of artifacts, prime dependence has been placed on stratigraphic position and on relationship to an identified cultural layer. Where these dimensions were not apparent, the association of specimens with other materials of known sequential position was relied upon. Repetitive occurrences of association as, for example, a given palette type with Sacaton Red-on-buff, have been accepted as reliable evidence of equivalent age. Where none of these conditions prevailed, time placement was made solely on typology if the requisite criteria were recognizable.

The small-scale excavations in the Classic Period sites, Ariz. U:13:21, 22, and 23, produced a limited number of specimens. Rather than to examine these separately, they have been considered as a part of the Snaketown sample, providing in some cases revealing extensions in the form trends of objects.

11. Caches

In nearly all places and times, man has resorted to hiding treasures in the ground or in secluded spots. Hoards of gold coins in Europe, the Dead Sea Scrolls secreted in the caves of Palestine, and the caches of esoterica so frequently reported in the pyramids of the Maya come to mind as examples. The motives for these acts were not always the same. Sometimes it was a matter of safeguarding personal wealth; or concealing cultural items which had served their purpose but could not be otherwise destroyed because they were infused with power; or to propitiate the gods during especially sacred events. The common denominator was the idea that the earth was the safest keeper of secrets.

For the archaeologist, whatever their reason for being, treasure troves have a special meaning that extends far beyond the aesthetic or intrinsic values the objects may manifest. The contemporaneity of different kinds of articles is usually established by the fact that they occur together. Exceptions to this assumption can be demonstrated: witness the jolting contrast provided by an aboriginal three-quarter grooved axe in a historic Pima cache of milled boards from a modern box, tin cans, and an iron shovel (Fig. 12.7). But, by and large, goods that are associated may be regarded as being of the same age.

The Hohokam had their own custom which impelled them to dispose of items by burial, but with a notable added characteristic: the objects destined for burial were first demolished by force, or by fire if burnable. These destructive actions have robbed us of much useful information while at the same time revealing a possible motive, sacrifice. During both operations at Snaketown a number of caches were found, randomly disposed and having no apparent functional relationship to houses or other features. No connection with cremations could be established. The following examination of the caches keeps the assemblages together, representing a departure from the more usual category approach to artifact description and thereby also emphasizing the importance of association as a means of establishing phase hallmarks.

CACHE 1:9F

House 3: 9F was one of many tightly clustered near the geographical center of Snaketown. Although the floor was not well preserved, the rounded ends and the stepped entry, as well as the meager pottery sample in the fill above the floor, indicated the structure dated from the Sacaton Phase. Less than a meter south of the hearth the workers encountered a deposit of 18 censers and a giant-sized palette (Fig. 11.1). All specimens, except the palette, were mutilated. Hard blows, most often delivered on the bottoms of the censers, were enough to shatter them. Because a

number of them were incomplete it may be assumed that the breakage was not done at the burial site. It was clear that subsequent to the destruction of the house and the filling of the house pit to a depth of about 0.5 m, a hole was made into the soil which reached and slightly penetrated the house floor. The objects were tossed into the pit, the palette lying a few centimeters away from the main mass of fragments on the southeast side. The separation of the palette from the censers left some doubt as to whether or not it was truly a part of the cache. This fear was allayed when it was established that the two human effigy censers in the collection were functionally related to the palette. The location of the cache near the center of House 3 may be presumed to have been accidental.

Two of the 18 censers were anthropomorphic, the faces executed in relief and with paint on "shields" rising from the body of the container (Fig. 11.2a and b). It was these two specimens whose imprints are visible on the palette (Fig. 11.3m). Two other

Fig. 11.1. Cache 1:9F, consisting of 18 clay censers, all intentionally broken, and a stone palette. Length of palette, 31.1 cm.

Fig. 11.2. Human and animal effigy censers in Cache 1:9F.
Diameter of b, 10.9 cm.

censers incorporated animal characteristics (Fig. 11.2c and d), the
former not identifiable with certainty, the latter a horned lizard.
Twelve of the 14 remaining specimens are shown in Figure
11.3a-1. Most of them manifest the pulley-shape, the flaring of
tops and bottoms, so typical of the censers of the Sacaton Phase.
The palette (Fig. 11.3m), similarly, is assignable to the same
phase. Since all objects in the cache, the house, and the soil that
filled it were of the same time period, it must be concluded that
the use of the house and its destruction took place early in the
Sacaton Phase and that the artifacts were buried late in that
horizon, perhaps not long before the main part of Snaketown was
abandoned. This sequence of events is not unreasonable if the life
of the Sacaton Phase, an estimated 300 years, is correct.

CACHE 2:9F

Immediately to the west of House 3 lay the floor of House 7, a
rectangular structure not clearly assignable to phase but certainly
of the Pioneer Period (Fig. 1.6). While searching for the western
edge of House 3, a workman's shovel exposed the bodies of three
clay animal figurines. Inspection showed that he had broken into
the edge of a pit which was packed with cultural materials.
Approaching the pit from above, its outline was picked up 20.0
cm below the existing ground surface, and it had a diameter of
about 0.8 m. As it turned out, the pit was located entirely within
the fill of House 7, and its excavator stopped at the hard-burned
floor line except in the central portion which penetrated the floor
for about 0.1 m.

Fragments of broken vessels, censers, and animal figurine parts
were encountered at the upper limits of the pit (Fig. 11.4), and
they continued to the bottom, an almost solid jumble of specimens
over a vertical distance of 0.65 m. There was no evident difference in the distribution of the materials except that shell bracelets
and carbonized perishable goods as, for example, baskets, matting and cordage, were limited to the lower half of the pit. With
few exceptions, objects were extensively broken, a willful act.
Direct evidence of burning in the pit was not observed, but the
fragile nature of the perishable materials, and the suffocation of
the fire before complete combustion of the organic materials was
achieved, make burning in the pit seem likely. Adjacent fragments of the same pottery vessel often showed no fire stain and

Fig. 11.3. Clay censers (all restored) and a large stone palette from
Cache 1:9F. Length of palette, 31.1 cm.

heavy fire-blackening. The total assemblage gave the impression
of being the residue of a sacrificial act. The absence of cremated
human bones eliminates the idea that the materials were directly
associated with the disposal of the deceased.

Altogether 97 catalogued objects were removed from the pit.
They are especially significant in demonstrating the kinds of
goods and the shapes of vessels that may be presumed to have
been contemporaneous.

During restoration, a task of considerable proportions, it was
noted that all fragments of vessels and figurines were not always
present. This duplicates the situation noted in Cache 1 and once
again raises the question whether or not destruction took place in
the pit or elsewhere. At the moment, there is no sure answer, but
on the basis of the remnants of carbonized substances it appears
likely that the pit was the place of demolition. Because pieces of
the same vessel were widely scattered, one can imagine someone
standing at the edge of the pit, breaking the vessels and letting the
fragments fall at random, an act most likely accomplished with a
hammerstone found with the rest of the materials. Three animal
figurines escaped this fate, as did a large effigy jar which lay on
its side in the bottom of the pit, though it was cracked by earth
pressure (Figs. 11.5 and 11.10c). Missing pieces of broken units

had some value in the mind of the maker. If connected with productive magic, the greater the number of figures, the more potent and coercive the plea.

A comparable deposit of 15 animal figurines, though somewhat different stylistically, was found by Cushing in Los Guanacos in 1887 (Haury 1945a: 174-5). These two instances of massed figures, in both cases associated with other objects, as, for example, censers and pigments, tend to establish a pattern of Hohokam behavior. What animal was being portrayed is a matter of speculation. Cushing's identification of them as guanacos (1890: 178-179) may be discounted as unrealistic. More probably, they represent deer, the female of the species, which, if correct, would fit the idea that they were fertility rite objects.

The collection also includes a single hollow animal figure, not identifiable as to kind (Fig. 11.8j) because of its fragmentary nature. The hollow treatment for animals seems never to have been common among the Hohokam.

Figures 11.7—11.10 illustrate all but a few of the pottery vessels included in the cache. There were a number of small vessels (Fig. 11.7), no different in form from other examples retrieved during the general digging. Of special note are Figures 11.7r, s, the first, a bird effigy, and the second, a bi-lobed vessel, which lend some distinction to the lot. Other standard forms of intermediate size are shown in Figure 11.8a-h, plates, bowls, and jars; k is a rectangular vessel, and l and m are hollow-handled pieces which may have been incense burners, based on the bottle gourd as a model. Large jars and a fine example of a cauldron are shown in Figure 11.9. Of particular note are three human effigy jars (Fig. 11.10), a shape concept which had a long history among the Hohokam, though examples are rare at all times. Specimens a and b, because of form and design similarities, must have been the products of the same potter. While sex characteristics are not emphasized, breasts on a and the more robust nature of b suggest male and female portrayals. Both have painted faces and pierced ears, and the presumed male figure has a large perforated nose and bands on the upper arms. Figurine c has suffered extensively from exfoliation, but it was originally painted. The head fillet has not been observed on other effigy vessels.

Fig. 11.4. Cache 2:9F. The uppermost layer of broken and mutilated objects.

Fig. 11.5. Cache 2:9F. A few pieces escaped breakage and earth pressure cracked the effigy jar, upper center. Note abundance of charcoal and black stains on specimens.

must be accounted for by careless scattering of fragments outside the pit's limits at the time of breakage, or to subsequent removal from the pit by rodents.

Turning to a review of the specimens, attention is called first to an outstanding array of solid clay animal figurines, 19 in all, and so much alike that they could only have been made by a single craftsman (Fig. 11.6). After modeling in potter's clay, the figures were swabbed with a light-buff colored creamy wash followed by slight hand rubbing. A hollow grass stem or sharp instrument served in making eye and anus; mouths and nostrils are shown by slits and punctations. The repetiveness of the form seems to have

Fig. 11.6. Cache 2:9F. Solid animal figurines, probably representing deer. Average length, 13 cm.

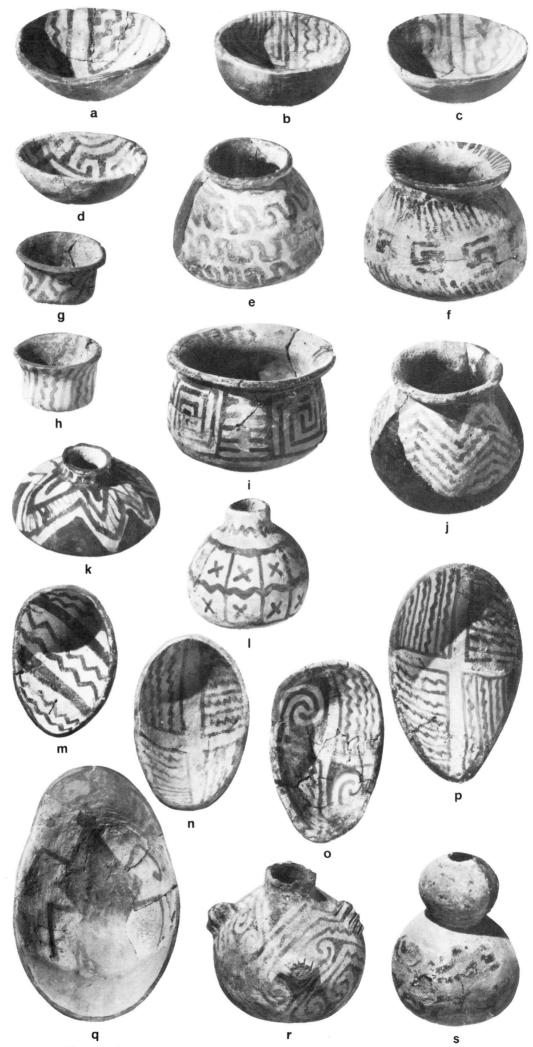

a

b

c

d

g

e

f

h

i

j

k

l

m

n

o

p

q

r

s

Fig. 11.7. Cache 2:9F. Small vessels of Sacaton Red-on-buff. Length of *q*, 13.9 cm.

Fig. 11.8. Cache 2:9F. (a-c) plates; (d-f) bowls; (g-h) small mouthed jars; (i) redware jar; (j) hollow animal effigy; (k) rectangular bowl; (l-m) (?) incense burners; (n) solid clay cone, unfired; (o-p) censers. All painted pottery is Sacaton Red-on-buff. Length of *k*, 25.9 cm.

Fig. 11.9. Large vessels from Cache 2:9F. (a) Santa Cruz Red-on-buff; the others, Sacaton Red-on-buff. Diameter of *f*, 56.5 m.

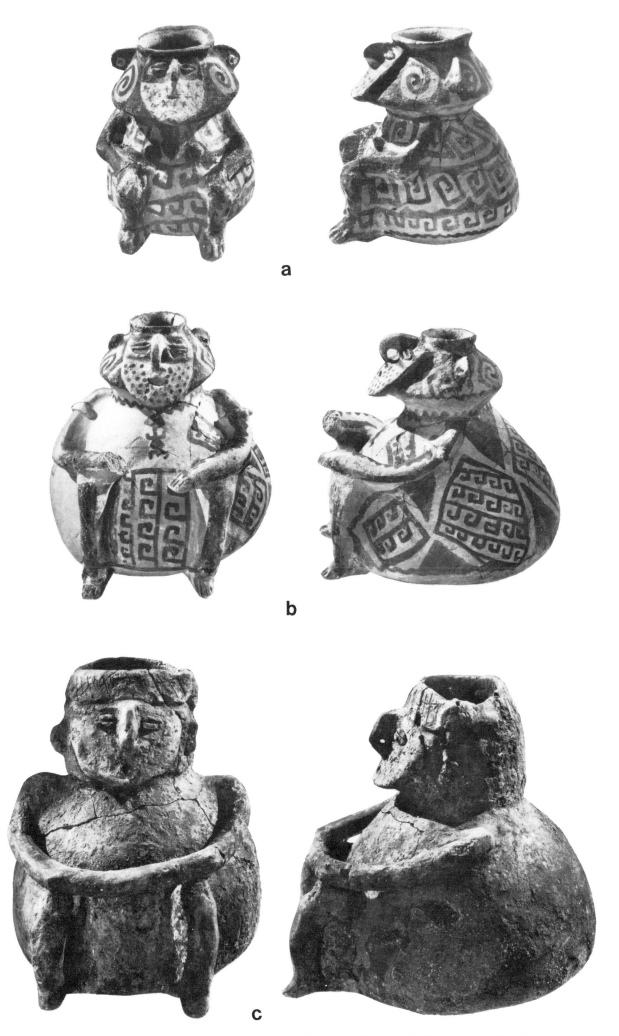

Fig. 11.10. Human effigy pots from Cache 2:9F, Sacaton Red-on-buff. Diameter of *c*, 17.8 cm.

Two solid female figurines (Fig. 11.11) are unlike others of the period because of curious posterior bumps.

It should be noted that all pottery vessels except one in the cache were painted. The exception is a small polished red shouldered jar (Fig. 11.8i), possibly Sacaton Red, although it does not conform fully to the characteristics of this type in color or finish; in the general sherd collection, the jar form is not represented. Additionally among the clay products were two censers (Fig. 11.8 o and p) and an unfired solid clay cone with blunted end (Fig. 11.8n). Its function is not known. The apex is not pitted as is usually the case with *pahoe* or feather holders among the Pueblos.

Before leaving the category of pottery, attention is called to a plate (Fig. 11.8c), the surface of which is smeared with a white incrustation. At one stage this material was plastic, as is evidenced by smears and impressions of other substances that came in contact with it. The crust is readily soluble in water and it reacts to hydrochloric acid. Ralph W. G. Wyckoff says the following about it: ''This residue gave strong x-ray patterns for quartz and calcite, with weaker patterns for clay and probably some plagioclase feldspar. An x-ray spectroscopic scan was in accord with this result and showed only some manganese and titanium as accessory elements. ...'' (Letter June 9, 1967). Although the components of the substance have been identified, what prompted its mixing remains unanswered.

Shell artifacts included at least a dozen bracelets and a large *Laevicardium elatum* shell, which, with some of the bracelets, reflected the effects of burning (Fig. 11.12).

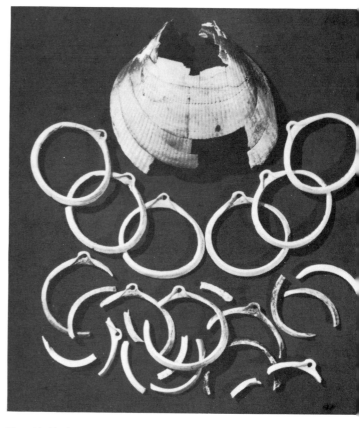

Fig. 11.12. *Laevicardium* valve and shell bracelets associated with Cache 2:9F. Average bracelet diameter, 6 cm.

Not illustrated among the pit contents are: a battered egg-sized hammerstone, a cobble quartzite rubbing stone which also saw service as a hammerstone, a nondescript flake of micaceous schist, several lumps of red hematite pigment mixed with earth, and a small Colonial Period palette fragment. Because no more of this palette was found, and its lime incrustation differed from that of the other artifacts in the pit, one suspects that it was in the soil and not a part of the cache.

Salvagable among the perishable goods, preserved by carbonization, were: a coiled basket fragment (Fig. 11.13); remnants of one or more sandals of the sewed type (Haury 1950: 435–439); plain weave cotton cloth with weft-wrap openwork (Kent 1957:

Fig. 11.11. Female figurines from Cache 2:9F. Height of *a*, 12 cm.

Fig. 11.13. Carbonized coiled basket fragment, from Cache 2:9F. Length 10 cm.

501–505); cordage of various types not clearly referable to specific artifacts; and cotton twill textile too fragmentary to yield the weave rhythm. Plant parts include: two corncob fragments and male corn florets; bottle gourd fragments probably from artifacts; mesquite seeds; a leaf base, probably agave; what appear to be yucca leaves carrying the impressions of cross elements, indication they came from matting; rods from coiled basketry foundation, not identified; lumps of mesquite charcoal, either fuel remnants or artifact parts as suggested by one fragment 9 cm long by 1.7 cm thick, having a rounded edge which could be from a potter's paddle; miscellaneous matted plant remains including horse purslane (*Trianthema* sp). Vorsila Bohrer, who made the identifications, reports that capsules rather than seeds were present. This suggested to her that the sacrificial deposit was made after August and before the first hard frost in the fall. The corn and mesquite evidence, though less definitive, is consistent with the temporal hint provided by the horse purslane.

The tabulation in Figure 11.14 compares the kinds and quantities of objects in Cache 2: 9F and Cremation 2:6G, uncovered in 1934–35. The latter deposit, though designated as a cremation, had no human ash associated with it. In the light of the more recent findings it should be classed as a cache. Most of the material in the two caches was pottery. Paint, solid figurines, and shell were unique to Cache 2: 9F, and only a Mountain Sheep horn core represents a different category among the objects in "Cremation" 2:6G. The former cache contained more than twice as many specimens, suggesting that the greater form range in this deposit is attributable to that fact rather than to a selective process.

The significance of these caches remains to be worked out; but a pattern is beginning to emerge with respect to content and to time. Caches with a predominance of pottery appear to be of Sedentary Period age and those consisting mostly of sculptured stone derive from the Colonial Period.

Looking at Cache 2: 9F as a whole, much of the material was run-of-the-mill, objects that might be expected in other secular contexts, as for example on house floors; but the animal and human figurines, the anthropomorphic and other eccentric vessels, the clay cone, and associated plant remains suggest something more than a routine disposal of hardware. Ritual motivation is implied, but what this was cannot now be stated.

The age of the cache can be assessed with certainty. Most distinctive as time markers are the pottery vessels, which, by design and shape, derive from the Sacaton Phase, the terminal horizon of Snaketown proper. But a closer typological inspection indicates that the deposit was made early in that phase. This is predicated principally on the large vessels(Fig. 11.9b-e) in which the jar necks are shortened over what they were typically in the Santa Cruz Phase, but they have not yet reached the complete loss of necks and the sharply out-turned rims so characteristic of vessels in the final stage of the Sacaton Phase. The presence of a Santa Cruz Phase vessel (Fig. 11.9a) supports this view, as do the patterns on jars *b* and *c*, which are carry-overs from Santa Cruz Red-on-buff. Whether an heirloom piece or made contemporaneously with the others, jar *a* serves as a bridge between the two phases concerned. Hazarding a guess as to a calendrical date for the act which accounted for the cache, the tenth century seems reasonable.

CACHE 1:10G

A remarkable collection of carved stone vessels and other objects came to light near the northwestern margin of House 13:10G. This house, of Sacaton Phase age, was constructed in a solid matrix of predominantly Pioneer Period trash which blanketed an area where early penetrations into the subsoil were made in search of water. Cache 1 was deposited in a pit dug into the older trash sometime during the Colonial Period. Happily, it was not disturbed when the house was built.

Pit dimensions could be established only by the distribution of

CATEGORY	CACHE 2:9F (1964-65)	CREMATION 2:6G (1934-35)
CLAY		
SACATON RED-ON-BUFF		
BOWLS	13	7
Flare-rimmed	5	6
Deep	5	6
Outcurved	6	
Deep	4	
Shallow	2	
Shouldered	1	1
Deep	1	1
Rectangular	1	
Flared sides	1	
JARS	14	2
Shouldered	9	2
Sharply returned rim	4	1
Open returned rim	5	
Without returned rim		1
Globular-bodied	3	
Vertical neck	1	
Open, flare-rimmed	1	
Open returned rim	1	
Bi-lobed	1	
Without neck	1	
Flat-bottomed	1	
Vertical neck	1	
PLATES	3	
SCOOPS	6	1
THREE-LEGGED VESSELS		7
Circular bowl		6
Square bowl		1
CENSERS	2	9
EFFIGIES	7	
Human	3	
Male	2	
Female	1	
Bird	1	
Mammal	1	
Plant (Gourd)	2	
Incense burner (?)	2	
FIGURINES	2	
Human	2	
Female	2	
SACATON RED (?)		
JARS	1	
Shouldered	1	
Short vertical neck	1	
SACATON BUFF		
FIGURINES	19	
Deer	19	
SANTA CRUZ RED-ON-BUFF		
JARS	1	
Elliptical-bodied	1	
Open, flare-rimmed	1	
GILA PLAIN		
PLATES		1
WORKED SHERDS	1	1
Disc-shaped	1	1
FIRED-CLAY		
TRIVETS		7
CONES	1	
STONE		
PALETTES	1	
HOES	1	
HAMMERSTONES	2	
METATES		1
MINERAL		
HEMATITE	1	
HORN		
HORN CORES		1
Mountain sheep		1
SHELL		
PLAIN SHELL BRACELETS	12	
LAEVICARDIUM SHELL	1	
CHARRED ORGANIC MATERIAL		
WOOD FRAGMENTS	1	1
GOURD FRAGMENTS	1	
GRASS		1
YUCCA	1	
Sandal fragments	1	
BASKET FRAGMENTS	1	
SEEDS	1	
COTTON TEXTILES	3	
Weft-wrap openwork	1	
Yarn	1	
Unidentified	1	
CORN COBS	1	
TOTAL	97	39

Fig. 11.14. Comparison of specimens in two Sacaton Phase caches.

Fig. 11.15. Cache 1:10G. (a) broken stone and clay artifacts as initially exposed. Clustering of fragments reveals nature of the receiving pit. (b) the same, after some of the upper fragments were removed.

the artifacts because the soft trash retained no evidence of the excavation. On this basis, its depth was 0.7 m below the existing surface, extending some 0.3 m below the level of the house floor, and it was 0.45 m in width. Into this hole were indiscriminately dumped the shattered fragments of items which, from our point of view, were cultural treasures, articles of high artistic merit (Fig. 11.15).

Breakage of the specimens appears to be attributable to two forces: physical, as with a hammerstone, and thermal. The former is seen in impact marks and fractures radiating from them. Discoloration by heat is evident, as is the spalling caused by the same energy source. The effect of fire is seen most clearly in the mirror backs, not only in the breakage, but in the loss of the mosaic pyrite units that made the reflecting surface. Shattering of specimens ranged from halving a piece to such extensive disintegration that restoration was difficult or impossible. Contributing to the problem of restoring was the fact that all fragments of a unit were not always recovered. Once again it seems that destruction took place somewhere other than the locus of the pit. No burning was evident in the pit. A contributory factor to the loss of fragments was rodent action. By carefully stripping the area, we recovered a number of pieces in rodent burrows, sometimes as much as 3.0 m away, and several fragments were found under the entrance passage of House 13. The restoration of missing parts of specimens was done only when details were demonstrably certain. By this device some of the aesthetic qualities of the stone carvings have been recovered.

In all, the inventory of pit contents notes 95 catalogued specimens, almost the same number as in Cache 2: 9F. No organic remains are included in the lot. Because the repetition of motifs and the range of forms are deemed to be important in establishing the styles of contemporaneous materials, the collection is liberally illustrated. Frequencies are given in Figure 11.31.

Among the clay products are a number of censers, most of them plain and unpainted (Fig. 11.16a and b, d-f); three are solidly covered with a deep maroon colored slip, characterized also by a smaller diameter and shallowness as compared with the others (Fig. 11.16c); one is reversible in that the bottom has a receptacle too (Fig. 11.16g) and one is zoomorphic, having a triad of frogs

modeled in high relief (Fig. 11.16h). To emphasize temporal form differences, these censers dating from the Colonial Period should be compared with those shown in Figure 11.3 of the Sedentary Period.

Other clay objects include a fragmentary figurine head (Fig. 11.17a), a rim piece of a heavy-walled vessel (Fig. 11.17b), a curious, crudely fashioned semicylindrical unit unlike anything else in the collection (Fig. 11.17c), and a fragment of a thick-walled vessel of unreconstructible form (not shown).

Fig. 11.16. Clay censers, Cache 1:10G. Diameter of b, 9.5 cm.

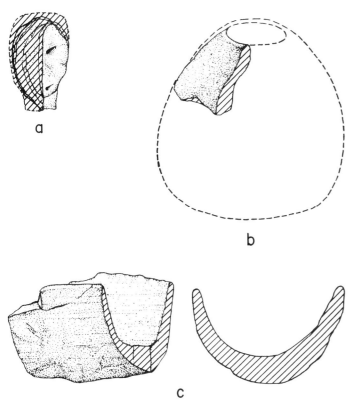

Fig. 11.17. Clay objects from Cache 1:10G. (a) human figurine; (b) heavy-walled vessel; (c) unidentified. Diameter of c, 6.7 cm.

The collection of small stone vessels, fifty in number, is doubtless one of the finest yet found in a Hohokam site in a single context. It calls attention, by sheer number, by range of subject matter and by illustrating sculptors' skills and their aesthetic standards, to the importance of the element in Hohokam society. Although the function of these objects is not clear, a few show slightly blackened interiors suggesting censer-use. At the same time, employment as medicine cups is not improbable.

Materials used, in order of dominance, are small-pored scoriaceous basalt, a deep red-colored argillaceous stone, sandstone, a tufaceous stone, and basalt. The scoria was most easily worked, but fine detail was difficult to achieve. To offset this deficiency, the pores were filled with a pinkish colored pasty material to produce a smooth and more attractive surface (Fig. 11.18). Where greater detail was needed, the denser harder stones were selected.

Reviewing the finished products, the plainest units are shown in Figure 11.19 a-g. Only f reveals any effort at decoration in the form of faintly scratched lizards. Simple side-grooving (Fig. 11.19h-j) was a form of decoration that extended back into the Vahki Phase. Of these three, h has cross-hatched incisions covering the bottom, and being of scoria, it was coated with a pale red mastic to produce a smooth surface. Lizards, including the easily recognized horned "toad," were favorite subjects, peering over the rim of the receptacle either in threes or fours, and in low or high relief (Fig. 11.20).

The snake motif takes several forms: alone, as a circumambient figure on an otherwise simple receptacle (Fig. 11.21a and b), in the act of catching a frog (Fig. 11.21c and d), and a type in which the coiled body constitutes the receptacle with head and tail as extensions therefrom (Fig. 11.21e). Another variation is seen in the twisted body of a snake which serves as a handle to the receptacle (Fig. 11.22 a-a', d-d'). In the case of the former, the deeply pitted and rimmed eyes may have accommodated settings of contrasting material. The serpent's body envelops a pointed rod, an integral part of the carving.

Fig. 11.18. Censer fragments made of volcanic scoria. Porous texture of stone has been treated with a thin, inorganic paste to produce a smooth surface. Length of a, 5.1 cm.

A whole rod with tapered ends of duplicate size and several fragments of others also occurred in the cache (Fig. 11.22b and c). They are included at this point as probable cult objects which were intimately related to snake symbolism. As in shell carvings, when portrayed, the serpent is always a rattler, sometimes specifically identifiable as a sidewinder. Emphasis on the reptile by the Hohokam artist is within the traditional Mexican art pattern.

Another broad category of stone vessels are those made in the image of an animal, true effigies except that the receptacle lies in the back of the creature. This usage contrasts sharply with most other stone vessels in which animals were employed as relief embellishments. Figure 11.23 illustrates this difference as applied to lizards (a-c) and mammals (d-e).

Three-dimensional sculpture reached its peak in the portrayal of the human form. The dominant theme appears to have been one in

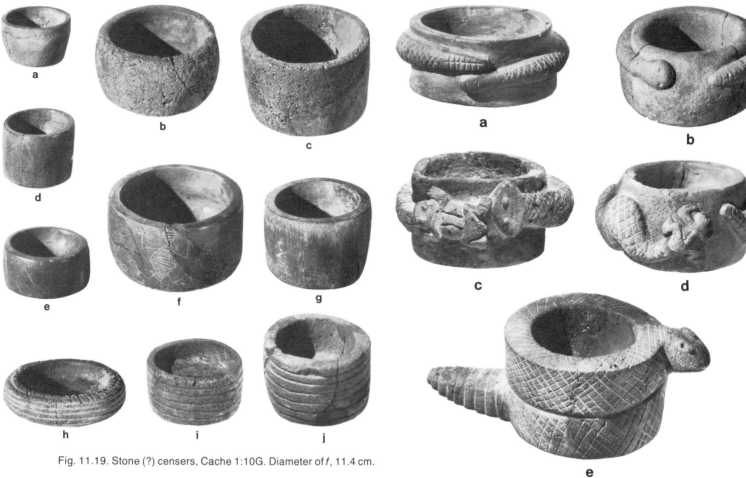

Fig. 11.19. Stone (?) censers, Cache 1:10G. Diameter of *f*, 11.4 cm.

Fig. 11.21. Stone (?) censers, snake and snake-frog motifs, Cache 1:10G. Length of *e*, 15.8 cm.

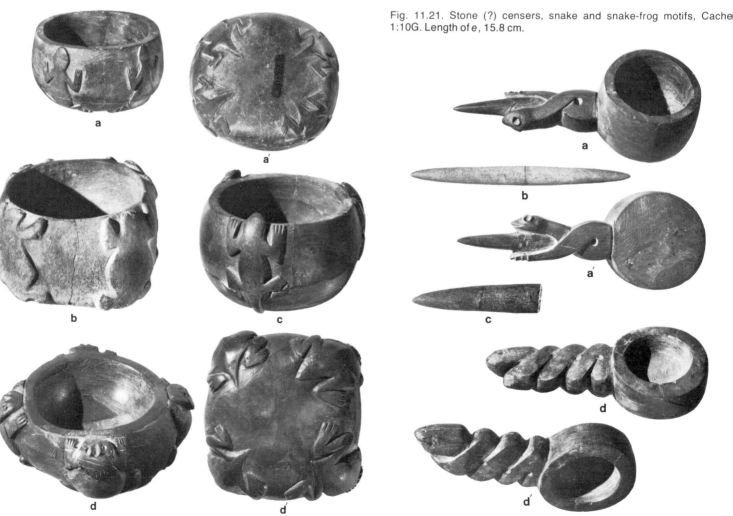

Fig. 11.20. Stone (?) censers, with lizard motif, Cache 1:10G. Diameter of *d*, 11.1 cm.

Fig. 11.22. Stone (?) censers with snake handles and related stone rods (b, c), Cache 1:10G. Length of *a*, 16.8 cm.

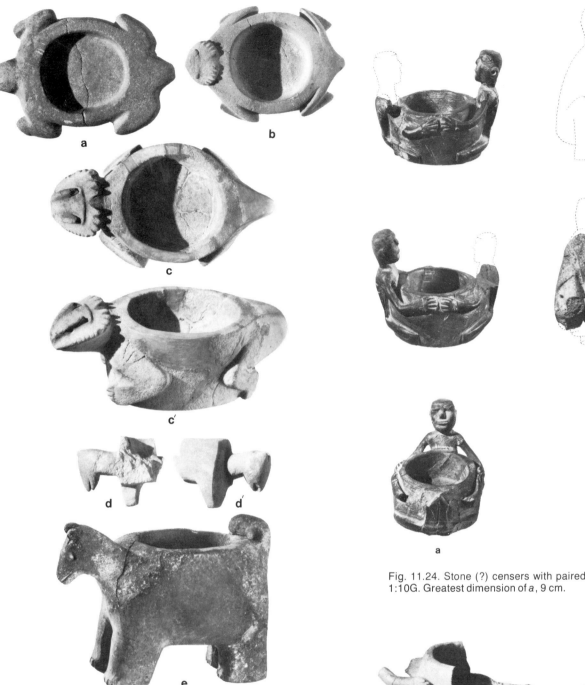

Fig. 11.23. Stone (?) censers of the effigy type, Cache 1:10G. Length of c, 15.4 cm.

Fig. 11.24. Stone (?) censers with paired human figures, Cache 1:10G. Greatest dimension of a, 9 cm.

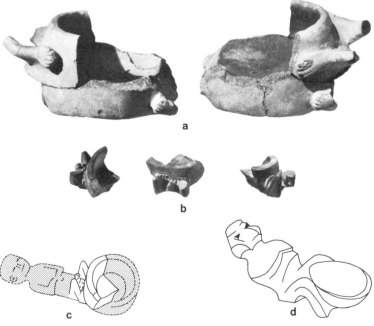

Fig. 11.25. Fragments of stone (?) censers with human figures, Cache 1:10G. Reconstruction of b as given in c is based on specimen d from Guerrero, Mexico. Maximum width of a, 11.5 cm.

which paired figures, facing each other, clutch a bowl between them with arms and legs (Fig. 11.24a and b and Fig. 11.25a). The position of the arms and legs varies, but the concept remains the same. In Figure 11.24a, the head, chest, and upper arms are treated in full-round, and Figure 11.25a suggests, from the fragments available, that the body was free, attached to the bowl only by hands and feet.

Unhappily, all specimens of this configuration from Snaketown are so fragmentary that it is impossible to say whether or not both sexes were represented. The probability that this was so is indicated by Figure 11.24b, lower, male, and by a female figure on a specimen recovered in 1934 (Gladwin and others 1937: Pl. LXIIIa).

A small but delicately carved specimen of red mud-rock (Fig. 11.25b) shows human feet attached to the receptacle with knees tightly flexed. The male sex organ and scrotum are realistically

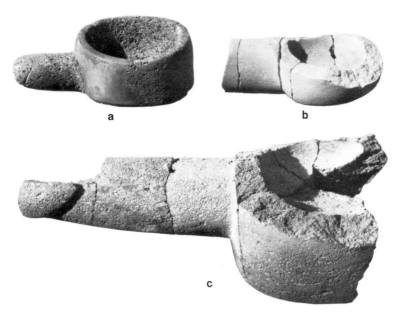

Fig. 11.26. Stone (?) censers with phallic handles, Cache 1:10G. Length of c, 23.7 cm.

depicted. The probable original form of this piece is reconstructed in Figure 11.25c in which the human body served as a handle. A similar concept occurs in a stone carving from Guerrero (Fig. 11.25d; Borbolla 1964: 15, center).

The sexual theme in the cache materials is best illustrated by three stone vessels with phallic handles, two of which are severely damaged (Fig. 11.26).

Sculptures in the full-round without the receptacle also occur although infrequently. Figure 11.27 shows half of what must have been a horned lizard. It compares favorably with two specimens recovered in 1934 (Gladwin and others: 1937: Pl. LXXV).

The cache collection also contains fragments of three mirror backs (Fig. 11.28), all of which have suffered extensive damage from burning. The material in each case is a fine-grained indurated sandstone, unlike the material seen in any other artifacts at Snaketown but comparable in nature to mirror backs from Jalisco, Mexico. None of the pyrites platelets constituting the reflecting surfaces have survived, although hematite stains remain and there are traces of the mastic with which the mosaic elements were fastened to the base.

The mirror diameters are 10, 14, and 24 cm, the latter being an especially large one (Fig. 11.28c). In each specimen, the edge is beveled toward the under surface, and the entire upper surface was covered with mosaic, the characteristic form of the early type as recognized at Snaketown in the previous work (Gladwin and others 1937: Pl. CIX, CX). There can be little doubt about the fact that these were actual imports from Mexico.

Two objects, sometimes referred to as "medicine" stones, must also be noted (Fig. 11.29). Both are made of scoria, the first (a) being more or less cylindrical with one squared end, the other rounded. It has a shallow oblique groove in which the cutting marks are preserved, but most interesting is its greenish glazed coating which fills most of the pores in the scoria. By color and texture it resembles the slag-like siliceous material sometimes found as lumps in burned houses or associated with cremated bones. It would appear that this piece was submitted to a high temperature at some stage in its use. The other specimen (b), a tapered cylinder with a central groove, does not evidence the heat treatment.

Thus far the items described from Cache 1: 10G may be regarded as esoterica. It is a matter of some interest, therefore, to note that fragments of utilitarian objects should also have been included. Pieces of manos and metates, and a set of other tools, in

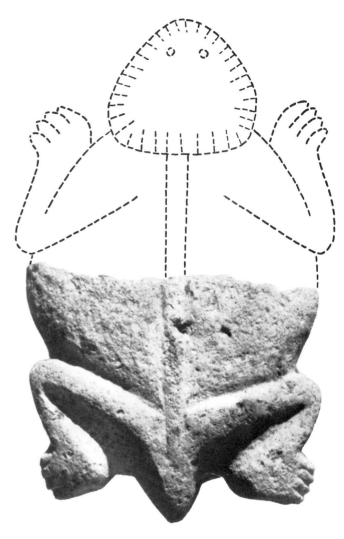

Fig. 11.27. Fragment of lizard sculpture, Cache 1:10G. Maximum width, 10.3 cm.

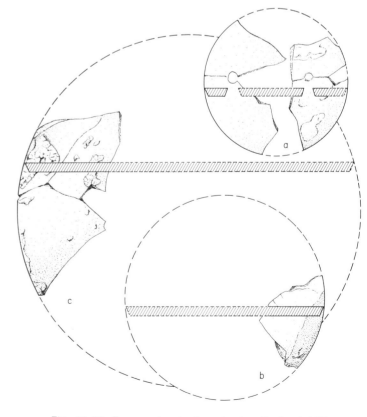

Fig. 11.28. Fragments of mirror backs, Cache 1:10G. Diameter of c, 24 cm.

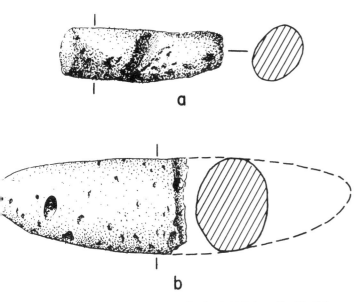

Fig. 11.29. "Medicine" stones from Cache 1:10G. Length of *b*, 5.4 cm.

all probability those used in fashioning the stone carvings, are represented. These, along with the rest of the specimens, were intentionally broken.

It is doubtful whether or not the two metate parts were from milling stones that were whole at the time the "sacrifice" was made. The pieces are small solitary units, hinting they may have been picked up on a dump and symbolically added to the lot as a way of recognizing the importance of tools associated with food preparation. Of the three manos, one was complete and the others may have been whole at the time of burial. Milling-stone typology is not critical by phase for Snaketown. The most one can say is that the shaped block metates and the fat single-faced manos represented by the fragments were normal for the late Pioneer Period and subsequent times.

Figure 11.30 illustrates the best of the stone working tools recovered in the cache. Although a variety of activities is represented by them one suspects that instruments not included must also have been employed in achieving some of the more delicate carvings. Reviewing the specimens, the cylindrical hammerstone (*a*) carries red paint stains on both ends, suggesting that it was also used as a pestle and that some of the stone cups may have served as mortars, though no evidence for this has survived; in succession, the other specimens include a triangular-sectioned hammerstone (*b*), one of several sandstone tablets the flat surfaces of which were used as sandpaper and the corner as a reamer (*c*), a wedge-shaped fine-grained sandstone file coming to a chisel-like edge (*d*), a polisher of metamorphic rock (*e*), a chalcedony flake with the retouched edge blunted by the work done with it (*f*), a thin phyllite flake whose rounded edge has scars from sawlike action (*g*), and two large specimens, one of slate (*h*) and the other of mud rock (*i*) which carry grooves and depressions resulting from use as abraders.

The absence of diagnostic pottery types in this cache requires dependence upon other criteria for reaching some conclusion about the age of the deposit. Though not absolutely definitive, the relationship of Cache 1 to House 13:1G suggested that the latter was constructed during the Sacaton Phase and after the objects were buried. Clay censer, mirror back, and figurine types, when related to the known sequence of form changes in these elements, dictate a Colonial Period assignment. In general, the subject matter and the style exhibited in the execution of the carvings confirm this placement. In all probability, the cache was made during the Santa Cruz Phase, the terminal one in the period.

The excavations of 1934–35 produced a cache (15:6F) which was similar to the one under discussion in that it contained only

stone articles, although only about a third as many. The contents of the two caches are compared in Figure 11.31. Zoomorphic themes are similar but not duplicative; mirror backs are lacking in 15:6F, as are also the tools to work stone, even though both caches had utility stone objects. Willful breaking and burning were evident in both. Sculpturing excellence is better in Cache 1:10G, and more hard stone was used. All units in Cache 15:6F were in soft stone. Future investigators, given enough caches to analyze, may derive meaningful conclusions about them on the basis of subjects, style, and other factors, but with the evidence now at hand, about all that can be said is that a Hohokam behavior pattern is beginning to emerge which was built around the idea that certain kinds of cultural wealth stood in a special relationship to a person or persons, and these had to be destroyed and disposed of in set situations.

What those situations were are not clear, but a few speculations may be made, stimulated by Dozier's plea for a better understanding of socio-political and ceremonial units in the Southwest as recovered from archaeological evidence (1965). Some thought was given to the nature of the ownership of the objects in a specific cache, whether they were the possessions of an individual or of a group of people, as, for example, a clan. Judgments of Pima-Papago practices are ambiguous in that Strong (1927:45)

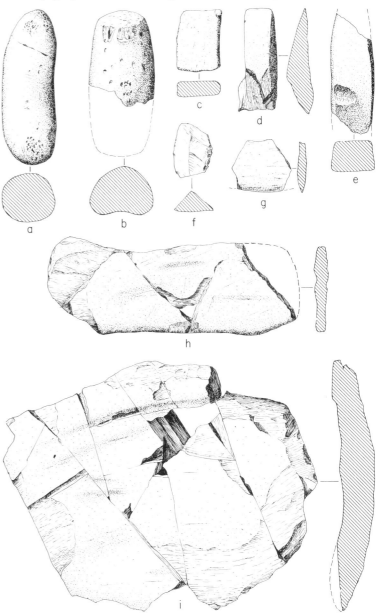

Fig. 11.30. A stone sculptor's tool kit, consisting of pounding, abrading, cutting, reaming and polishing implements found with Cache 1:10G. Length of *h*, 18 cm.

CATEGORY	CACHE 1:10G (1964-65)	CACHE 15:6F (1934-35)
CLAY		
CENSERS	10	
Plain	6	
Single receptacle	5	
Dual receptacle	1	
Slipped red	3	
Zoomorphic relief	1	
Frog	1	
HALF-CYLINDERS		1
"LAMPS"		1
FIGURINES		1
SHERDS		1
STONE		
CENSERS	50	20
Plain	10	1
Incised	1	1
Lizard	1	
Cross-hatching		1
Grooved	3	1
Zoomorphic relief	20	6
Snake	8	2
Horned toad	2	
Snake with toad	2	
Lizard	3	
Frog		1
Bird		1
Mountain sheep		1
Human	3	
Unidentifiable	2	1
Zoomorphic effigy	9	11
Snake	3	2
Horned toad	4	
Tortoise		2
Bird		2
Pelican		2
Duck		1
Bear (Dog?)	2	1
Unidentifiable		1
Zoomorphic handle	7	
Snake	2	
Human	1	
Phallic	3	
Unidentifiable	1	
EFFIGIES	1	
Horned toad	1	
TAPERED RODS	4	
MEDICINE STONES	2	
MIRROR BACKS	3	
MILLING STONES	5	
Mano	3	
Metate	2	
STONE-WORKING TOOLS	15	
Hammerstone	3	
Abrading slab	8	
Saw	1	
Chipped scraper	1	
Polishing stone	2	
AXES		7
3/4-grooved		6
Full-grooved		1
MORTARS		2
PESTLES		1
DISCOIDAL STONES		1
CHERT CHIPS	1(33)	
TOTAL	95	31

Fig. 11.31. Comparison of specimens in two Colonial Period caches.

characterizes them as having a "clan house-priest-fetish complex" and Underhill (1939: 71-72) makes it clear that Papago villages owned supernaturally-acquired sacred objects which were kept in secret hiding places away from the settlement; but Spier (1936: 11) believes that ceremonial equipment was individually rather than clan-owned. Burial of the objects within the village of Snaketown tends to support the idea of individual ownership. If it could be established that all objects in one lot were made by the same craftsman, further credence might be lent to this judgment; but variations in sculpturing techniques and styles indicate that the objects in stone caches were made by more than one artist.

At this time the following alternative explanations of the Snaketown caches may be given: if individually owned by a person of special note, for example, a shaman, as appurtenances needed in his profession, custom may have dictated that they be destroyed at the owner's death because they were possessed of too much personal power to be passed on to someone else. If clan possessions, made by various of its members, the items could have been destroyed and disposed of upon the extinction of the clan, once again because they could not be reused by another group.

The following generalizations about caches are in order: (1) Specialization in the kinds of things that were buried is apparent, some are predominantly of stone, others of pottery. (2) No human cremated remains have been associated with them. (3) Mutilation by force and by fire was standard practice. (4) No plan is apparent as to the place of burial. (5) Zoomorphic themes were derived from local fauna. Assuming that these had potency, as in curing or in other forms of magic, and were not merely aesthetic embellishments, we may recognize the close relationship that existed between the Hohokam and components of their environment.

The role of fire in the use of presumed ritual gear recovered in caches, exemplified by censers, should not be minimized, and especially the dependence on fire as a destructive agent for paraphernalia that was no longer usable. The burning of masks and other ceremonial gear after ritual use is commonly practiced by the Cora, Huichol, and Yaqui Indians of northwestern Mexico.

Although clay censers and animal figures sculptured in stone antedate the Colonial Period, the data available indicate that the idea of the cache was an innovation of that period, sometime between A.D. 500-900. Depositories of worked stone pieces appear to be limited to that time while the caches predominantly consisting of pottery were made after A.D. 900 during the Sedentary Period. A shift in the kinds of artifacts used esoterically appears to be indicated. The survival of the cache idea into recent times is suggested by a deposit of a dozen stone pipes in San Cayetano (Di Peso 1956: Pl. 115, 430), perhaps of eighteenth century age, and by the Pima caches at Snaketown made since about 1875.

12. Pottery

Most agricultural people in the ancient world found clay to be an indispensable raw material. The Hohokam were no exception. Among them, the knowledge that clay, if moistened, kneaded, shaped, dried, and baked, could be converted into accessories that would enhance the quality of life, was a legacy from the Indians of Mexico. While the details of this transfer of cultural knowledge are yet to be determined, we can say that clay was used in a technologically advanced way from the moment of Snaketown's founding several centuries before the beginning of the Christian era.

Variously mixed with other substances, caliche, as an example, clay was favored in making house floors and, in purer form, for daubing and plastering house sidings as a weather-proofing. In these cases, baking was not foreseen, although the disastrous fires that destroyed many homes hardened the clay so as to make the detection of the original form an easy task. Also, in many residences, a clay of fine quality was used to make the hearths around which so much of a family's activities centered. From similar clay were also fashioned the trivets, or "fire dogs," designed to give tripodal support for pots over live coals. In both of these instances hardening by fire was a function of use and not an intentional pre-use treatment. Except for house floors and walls, we were not confronted with the problem of uncovering and preserving many articles of unfired clay. The occasional unbaked figurine retained its shape after slow drying.

We were not able to determine with certainty where the better quality clays were quarried. Caliche in a clayey matrix, suitable for house floors, was obtainable almost everywhere underfoot in Snaketown, as indicated by the ever-present pits. Clay suitable for pottery production was probably similarly found and the texturally fine silty-clay needed to achieve details in figurines appears to have been river mud. The point to be noted is that clay types were recognized and that there was a conscious selection of the kind of clay best suited for the product that was in the maker's mind. The lavish use of clay in architecture and pottery-making indicates the availability of a limitless supply. No evidence of raw clay importation was seen.

The immediate task ahead is to make rhyme and reason out of the numerous whole vessels and the 1.5 million potsherds that passed over the analyzing tables in our field laboratory. What is it we really want to learn from this class of material, and how far can we go in extracting from it information about the role of pottery in Hohokam society? Traditionally, pottery studies have occupied a key position as a means of ordering certain information about past peoples. The present effort is no exception, and the length of this chapter is an open recognition of the importance of the potter's craft. But nowhere in archaeological reporting does the inadequacy of the written word show up more strongly than when one begins to talk about pottery. Working with enormous quantities of it brings out subtle qualities which cannot be as sensitively expressed by word as they are felt, qualities that speak of distinctions growing from the passage of time, the nuances in form, design, and use that bind the products together like the links of a chain into a continuous and harmonious whole. Because of this, photographs have been heavily depended on to illustrate the incomparable succession of Hohokam pottery forms.

Discounting the use of clay in house construction, pottery production called for its most consistent tonnage utilization. The sheer quantity of broken pottery bids close inspection. Potsherd density in refuse is measurable on a volume-unit basis. A cubic meter of trash, whether in mounds above the desert floor or in pits beneath it, produced from 2,000 to 8,000 sherds. A single pit 2 m in diameter and 3 m deep yielded 20,000 units. Large as our study collection of pottery is, what fraction does it represent of the total sample that might be recovered in the 300-acre site if all of it were excavated? An estimate can be made, though it probably errs in being too conservative.

The three screened stratigraphic columns in Mound 39, aggregating about 44 m³ of trash, produced roughly 100,000 sherds. To remove these columns in the soft unstable refuse and to understand the structure of the mound, it was necessary to cut a wide trench through it by machine. The area ratio of column tests to trench was about 1:10. Using the pottery density from the controlled tests as a base for calculations, we can say that had all pottery from the trench excavation been saved, the return would have been close to 1,000,000 sherds. The volume ratio of trench-to-mound was in the order of 1:10 so the total potsherd content of the mound may be estimated at 10,000,000.

There are 60 mounds on the site, a few larger than Mound 39 and the rest smaller. Adjusting for this by using a factor of 50 mounds, one can guess that the pottery content of all mounds approaches a half-billion units. Remembering that probably as much trash exists below the desert floor in pits as above it in mounds, this figure can be doubled, to bring it to a billion. Not taken into account is the pottery that exists in the many acres of sheet trash and in the fill of hundreds of unexcavated houses. This is an astronomic amount of cultural evidence representing only one aspect of the society. Surfeited with potsherds as we were, it is something of a shock to learn that we were dealing with only a probable 0.0015% of the available pottery!

What did this bulk of pottery mean in terms of invested human energy? Why was so much of it broken? What were the effects of a high replacement rate on the development of the potter's art? Collaterally, can the archaeologist evaluate the history of pottery through more than a thousand years of time by seeing so little of it?

Excepting a minuscule amount of pottery obviously foreign to the site, it is safe to conclude that the potsherds recoverable at Snaketown came from pots made in Snaketown. Evidence for pottery production, if only late in the history of the village, will be discussed later. Extension of this activity into earlier periods may be assumed.

To return to the question of man-hours invested in pottery production, one must again engage in speculation in seeking an answer. An acceptable fragment-per-vessel factor after breakage is not easily established. Vessel diameters varied from a few centimeters to nearly a meter for the larger storage jars. Actual counts range from two pieces to the pot to over 200 for the larger ones that have been restored. Striking an average, a factor of 50 will be used.

If we now consider the life of Snaketown to have been 1,400 years, how many vessels would have had to be produced per year, or per day, to yield the volume of fragments we have calculated? The figure comes out to 14,288 vessels per year, or nearly 40 every day of the year. This is assumed to represent the amount needed to maintain the domestic supply and does not recognize possible export or trade reserves. A 40-vessel output per day is not an overly impressive number for a village of Snaketown's size.

It must be remembered, however, that pottery-making was not a daily occupation, that it had a seasonality about it, that the weather and the inclination of the potters were important factors. Useful time studies of pottery manufacturing today among the Pima and Papago Indians who employ the paddle-and-anvil method, as did the Hohokam, are not available; but by whatever guidelines one uses, it is clear that the total activity related to pottery production, quarrying the clay, gathering tempering materials from Gila Butte 5 km distant, preparing the clay, shaping the vessels, drying time, painting time for decorated vessels and preparing the paint therefore, collecting the fuel, and firing time, required the full effort of few people relative to the size of the village. If the average village population over the years was 500 persons, perhaps no more than 10% of them, 10 or so families, could have produced the pottery needs of the community.

However erroneous this calculation may be, the fact remains that the abundance of broken pottery gives us an illusory feeling of an inordinately high energy investment in its manufacture. Nevertheless, the potter's art may be regarded as a prime ingredient in Hohokam life, basic to the full realization of the advantages of an agricultural economy.

We do not know whether or not the producers of pottery occupied a prestigious position in the community. Judging from accounts of contemporary Pima and Papago potters, the answer is no. On the other hand, the celebrated Maricopa potter, the late Ida Redbird, enjoyed special acclaim as a producer of collectors' items in our modern economy. But this condition did not prevail in early times, even though certain individuals may have been known for the excellence of their products.

Returning to an earlier question bearing on the apparent high replacement factor in pottery making, it must be noted that Hohokam pottery was not of superior quality. Vessels of good tensile strength were never produced at Snaketown because of the low grade of the clay. The Hohokam, while good potters, were poor ceramists. Frequent breakage required equally frequent replacement. From the cultural historian's point of view this was a happy situation, for the never-ending need to produce new vessels provided a continuing challenge to the potter to do something different, to experiment with a new form, to modify slightly the standard canons of motifs and composition.

Boredom in making the same thing over and over must have been a potent but subtle moving force in leading to change in pottery. Shifting social customs and pressures, adaptive adjustments required by nature, borrowing, and the like, do lead to modifications, but I believe that the archaeologist has not adequately recognized boredom in a repetitious activity as a taproot of change.

The never-ending need to replenish the pottery supply contributed to the gradual improvement in the dexterity and in the artistic expressions of the craftsmen and out of it emerged a cultural "stamp," a ceramic "nationality," which distinguishes Hohokam pottery from that of all other groups. This quality, however, was some time in developing, for early Pioneer Period pottery shared a number of characteristics with the pottery of the Mogollon people.

Facing the question of sample adequacy, I hold firmly to the notion that the 1.5 million fragments we have seen are truly representative of the site's ceramic history and that they are adequate in quantity and quality to provide the bases for inferences of a broader nature. Were it not for the fact that the working sample is so large, so duplicative of the pottery recovered in 1934–35, and so internally consistent in illuminating a long ceramic tradition, some hesitation might be expressed in putting much faith in it. However, I find the repetitive nature of the stratigraphic-typological record in so many different situations in widely separated parts of the village thoroughly convincing. This does not mean that the employment of other methods of pottery recovery would not yield additional details. These will surely come as future investigations are pursued.

ORIGIN OF HOHOKAM POTTERY

How and when the Hohokam acquired pottery are questions directly related to the origin of the Hohokam themselves. As stated elsewhere, my belief is that these people appeared as a migrant group in southern Arizona. They were characterized by a number of attributes new to the region, the making of pottery being one of them. We may speculate that the homeland was to the south and that they derived their cultural advantages from the more advanced people of Mesoamerica.

Identification of the precise spot in Mexico which gave rise to the Hohokam and their pottery may never be achieved. Wasley's search in Sonora has not produced connecting links, and it is doubtful if they will be found in a manner we desire even farther to the south. On a broad comparative base we see that the use by the Hohokam of an oxidizing atmosphere, leading to a brown-to-gray utility ware, and a slipped and polished redware, produced the elemental types that underride practically all early Mexican ceramics. The thinness of their pottery, and the graceful forms, speak of a control over clay and therefore of a point in pottery history far removed from the moment of its invention. The introductory stages from which Vahki Plain and Vahki Red were evolved are not to be sought in the Southwest but, instead, far to the south.

Within this framework, then, how far back in time pottery-making may be ascribed to the Hohokam is directly dependent upon one's willingness to accept or reject the chronological data presented herein. Since I favor the "long count," for reasons stated in the chapter on Dating, I hold that the Hohokam possessed the ceramic art when they arrived about 300 B.C. This antiquity is not inconsistent with either the internal ceramic sequence or the information we now have for the age of pottery from other parts of the Southwest.

With respect to the former problem, we can evaluate style changes during centuries which are reasonably well dated, from A.D. 700 to 1400, spanning the time when Santa Cruz, Sacaton, and Casa Grande Red-on buffs were produced. In other words, three sequent pottery types, easily segregated from each other, are identified with a time span of 700 years. A "splitter" could, it is true, point to intermediate forms between those listed which would serve to make the evolutionary changes smoother but would not materially alter the idea that stylistic change was slow. The differences between the Santa Cruz, Sacaton, and Casa Grande types are no greater than those between antecedent types, namely, Estrella and Sweetwater Red-on-gray and Snaketown and Gila Butte Red-on-buff. Using the yardstick for post A.D. 700 changes, the extension backwards to 300 B.C. does not seem unreasonable to accommodate five cultural phases and their related pottery types. I admit that this approach is risky business in chronology building, but a long span of time is also indicated by radiocarbon and archaeomagnetism as noncultural means of dating. The slowness of style changes in later centuries, when the society was at climax, calls for adequate time to fit in the presumed slower changes that we see during the nascent period. The almost imperceptible modifications of Pima pottery since the moment of European contact fit the prehistoric trend. Hence, on internal evidence alone, it seems to me that time is needed to account for the growth we recognize in Hohokam pottery and that the estimated beginning date of 300 B.C. is consistent with all aspects of the problem.

The oldest pottery recognized elsewhere in the Southwest is from the Pine Lawn Phase of the Mogollon Culture in west-central New Mexico with a radiocarbon date of 150 B.C. (Martin and others 1952: 496) and a projected introductory date of 300 B.C. (Martin 1959: 80). The types present are Alma Plain, Alma Rough, and San Francisco Red (Martin and others 1952: 56). Excepting the texturing of Alma Rough, the basic ceramic fabric of the Mogollon tradition is like that of Vahki Phase Hohokam, a similarity which I believe to be no accident. Broadly speaking, both had plain brown-to-gray ware and a slipped and polished redware; yet the methods of manufacture were somewhat different: paddle-and-anvil for Hohokam versus coil-scrape for Mogollon. But perhaps more important as indicators of a longer familiarity with the art among the Hohokam were a higher degree of technological perfection and a greater roster of forms. To say that because of these the Hohokam had the edge on the Mogollon, and the latter learned the art from their western neighbors, is a possible solution, but it is also most likely an over-simplification of what did take place.

The two ceramic manifestations may actually represent a two-pronged movement of people from the south who were already adapted to desertic and mountainous living, respectively, but who drew their basic elements from a common Mesoamerican reservoir. Regardless of what the mechanics of transmission were, the complexity of the early Hohokam society tends to give them some measure of dominance over the simpler early Mogollon people. If the reconstruction is correct that the Hohokam and Mogollon were village living, agriculturally oriented, and pottery producing by 300 B.C., then some explanation is needed to account for the 700-year lag in the adoption of the plastic art by the Anasazi (Basketmakers) whose oldest pottery appears to date from about A.D. 400 in the Four Corners area.

CYCLICAL DESTRUCTION OF POTTERY?

Mindful of the Mesoamerican impact on the Hohokam, the question must be raised as to whether or not the enormous quantity of fragmented pottery in Snaketown's mounds was due in part to forces other than the inferior quality of the clay, to normal day-to-day breakage from use or accident. Was deliberate destruction a factor? It was noted during the testing of trash mounds that, in addition to a general saturation of the refuse, locally heavy deposits of sherds occurred, amounting in some cases to lenses 10 to 20 cm thick (Fig. 12.1). Could these represent house cleansings, starting life anew with fresh utensils at the end of a calendrical cycle, as reportedly was done in Mexico (Vaillant 1938: 552-553)?

If this custom was actually practiced in Arizona, it would be logical to assume that fragments of the same vessel, in fact restorable vessels, might be sorted out of a massed deposit. To test this idea, many thousands of fragments were examined from a heavy deposit in Mound 40, but to no avail. Clearly, a few pieces were noted that came from the same vessel, but the number of

Fig. 12.1. Section in Mound 40 showing massed sherd deposit, Gila Butte Phase.

matches was too small to lend much credence to the idea. We do not know to what extent post-depositional scattering took place, a factor which might have some bearing on the conclusions. It must also be observed that the phenomenon of layered pottery did not occur in a sequential system, a requisite, if cyclical destruction was an established custom. Until new evidence is forthcoming, the broken pottery at Snaketown may be attributed to normal wear and tear.

THE HOHOKAM POTTER

A number of general topics should be touched on before embarking on the analysis of pottery types *per se*. Is there any evidence in the ceramic record to tell us that pottery-making was woman's or man's work, or both? Directly, no. Perhaps the most satisfactory approach to the question is to look at the existing and early historic attitudes of the Pima and Papago Indians. In a valuable ethnohistoric study of Papago pottery, which also includes many references to the Pima (Fontana and others 1962: 5 ff), the fact becomes clear that among these desert tribes, potting was woman's work. The primary sources for information on the art as practiced by the Maricopa, Yuma, Cocopa and Seri, ably reviewed by Fontana and others (1962: 117-122) indicate that the women were the workers in clay among these tribes as well. Since some, or all of them, have roots that dip into prehistory, and the likelihood that there has not been a shift in the custom of pottery making through time, we may infer that historic practices reflect aboriginal ones as well. The ethnological analogy appears to have meaning in this case. This is not the precise answer one would like, but until sex-differences in dermatoglyphics, or some other means of identification of pottery authorship are found, we will have to be content with this conclusion.

The clay employed by the Hohokam potter, either for the plain cooking and storage vessels or for the more dressy painted pieces, was relatively soft and low in tensile strength. Obsolescence by wearing out, exfoliation from repeated heatings over the cooking fire, and easy breakage were the results. Other defects, equally as damaging to the pottery, were attrition of the clay by contained salts and the development of popouts, or craterlike pits, caused by the differential expansion during firing of temper particles and the clay matrix. Further, the impermanence of the painted patterns resulted in design loss during the life of the vessel; because of this the scrubbing of potsherds was avoided in the laboratory processing of them.

Pottery was made either by employing the continuous coil or the paddle-and-anvil thinned unit coil techniques. The former was limited in time to the Vahki and Estrella phases mainly, though a few instances of it were noted in the Sweetwater Phase. Further, vessels produced by it were small, and it was never used to the exclusion of the paddle-and-anvil. This curious blend of methods suggests that the laying up of vessel walls by continuous coiling may have been the older way of making pottery.

For all the experience the Hohokam had in the making of pottery, both in time and quantity, it is a wonder they did not hit eventually on a better quality product. The potter's genius came to the fore in the production of new and interesting forms and, most of all, in the versatility in creating involved painted designs. But these are not qualities that add to the life of the pot. Perhaps as archaeologists, we should be thankful that frequent replenishment was necessary, for it provided continuing challenges for the expression of new artistic ideas and as a result, a wealth of material for us to study.

POTTERY MANUFACTURING AT SNAKETOWN

The methods used by the Hohokam for the production of pottery have been reviewed in a number of places (Woodward 1931: 15-16; Haury 1932: 72-86; Gladwin, W. and H. S. 1933; Gladwin and others 1937: 171 ff; Haury 1945a: 51 ff), making further description in depth unnecessary here. Anyone with special interest in this problem should look into the modern methods of pottery manufacture by the Papago and Pima Indians, because these probably come closest to replicating what the Hohokam actually did (Russell 1908: 126 ff; Fontana and others 1962: 49 ff). There remain, however, several topics which merit discussion.

Place of Manufacture

To my knowledge, the actual place of manufacture of pottery has not been identified in the villages of the Hohokam. We have assumed that this was probably done in the vicinity of the potters' households and that few, if any, detectable signs of the activity were left. What was given a field designation of Work Area 2 in Block 10G proved to be a place devoted to the production of pottery, and the physical remains of several steps in the process were there for us to see (Figs. 12.2, 12.3). Clearly attributable to the Sacaton Phase, the last horizon in the village's history, it is surprising that no other places like it of the same age or earlier were discovered. Stripping the soil from wide areas is, of course, the answer to the discovery of such remains.

First, with respect to placement, the pottery-making features occupy the empty elongate space framed by Houses 3, 4, 6, 8, 10, and 18 in Block 10G. All of these are of Sacaton Phase age, and all of them, save one, have outward facing entrances, or with the backs of the houses turned toward the pottery-making area. Only the entrance of House 4 fronts, or leads directly into, the area. This house too was late, probably later than the others noted. The logical question follows as to which of the houses were most likely occupied by the potters who made use of the adjacent facilities.

No absolute answer is forthcoming, but a guess may be made. The arrangement of the five houses formed an enclosure which would have provided some protection against wind, a not inconsiderable factor in the making and the baking of pottery. But more impressive is the fact that there were five elongated clay-lined mixing bowls, as though there was one for a potter in each of the households. Firing pits, numbering six or seven, depending on the manner of counting, suggest use by several potters.

The deployment of the houses leads to the question as to whether or not pottery making was an extended family occupation or whether the complex is evidence of the existence of a guild where the place of work determined the location of the residence. In either case it is assumed that all the features were contemporary, an assumption that is probably correct. Although we cannot be sure of the sociological implications of Work Area 2, some kind of organization revolving around a craft activity seems logical. However, I do not believe that all of the pottery of the Sacaton Phase was made here, or that all of the pottery of the time was made by complex social units. The probability that there was a total shift of pottery making from a household craft to an industry in late Hohokam times appears to me to have been unlikely. Stylistic diversity points to the conclusion that many families manufactured pottery to fill their own needs, even though the trend may have been towards mass production.

Looking at the area now in more detail, there is a recognizable division between the clay preparation and the firing areas, the latter being to the northeast of the former (Fig. 12.3). This may have an environmental explanation in that the prevailing winds are out of the southwest. If, therefore, clay preparation and firing were simultaneously carried on, smoke and heat would not bother those working with the clay. Too few posthole arrangements were detected to suggest the presence of a shade, or structure, in the area. Yet, considering practices among modern potters generally and the Papago, as a representative group of Desert Indians in particular, molding the vessels is preferably done in the shade so the clay does not dry too quickly and because it is more comfortable for the workers (Fontana and others 1962: 58).

Clay Mixing Basins

In Figure 12.2, features numbered 1 through 5 are remnants of north-south-oriented caliche-clay-lined basins. Where measurements were possible, the lengths were about 1 m and the widths 0.3 to 0.4 m. These basins were made by excavating a shallow elongated pit below the extant surface and lining it with a mixture of caliche and clay having an average thickness of 5 cm (Fig. 12.4). The basin was then lightly burned to set the clay, but the heat did not penetrate the full thickness of the lining.

The identification of these features as basins for kneading moistened clay, to wet it thoroughly and also to improve its plasticity, is seen in the thin (average thickness 1 cm) veneer of pottery clay, dried but not fired, adhering to the surface of the basins (Fig. 12.5). This would be the natural consequence of working wet clay. Furthermore, at the southwest edge of basin No. 5 lay a weathered lump of prepared clay which was never reclaimed after the last time the feature was used.

No ethnological equivalent for these bowls is recorded among the Desert tribes. If their use was widespread in space and time, the data to support this claim are still to be gathered. There is no immediate explanation for the consistent north-south orientation, and we could not come up with any clues indicating whether the persons using them faced north or south.

Feature No. 6 (Fig. 12.2) differs from the others in that it was a shallow bilobed pit, the western unit having had built into its bottom a large, slightly concave, potsherd roughed-out from the basal portion of a Gila Plainware jar. This probably served as a support for a vessel under construction, facilitating turning it and keeping the under side of the vessel clean, a precaution still current among modern potters, although different materials are used (Fontana and others 1962: 59).

"Kilns"

Adjacent to the clay bins on the east were a series of pit "kilns," consisting of simple, more-or-less circular excavations into the ground (Fig. 12.6). Pits 3 to 6 were about 1 m in diameter

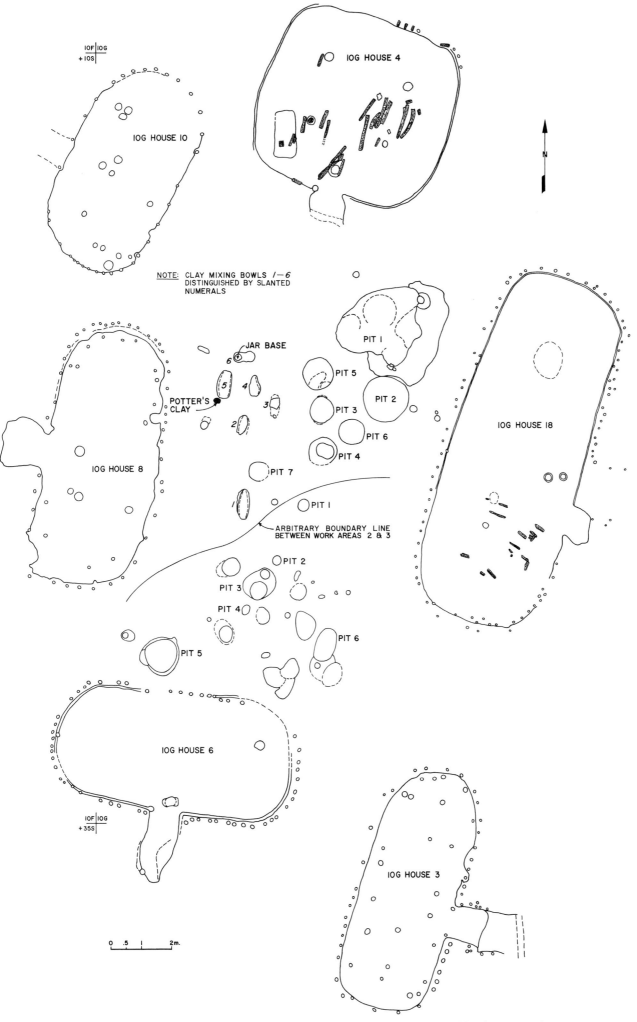

IOF|IOG
+IOS

IOG HOUSE IO

IOG HOUSE 4

N

NOTE: CLAY MIXING BOWLS *1—6*
DISTINGUISHED BY SLANTED
NUMERALS

JAR BASE

6

5 *4*

POTTER'S
CLAY

3

2

PIT 1

PIT 5

PIT 3

PIT 2

PIT 6

PIT 4

IOG HOUSE 8

PIT 7

1

PIT 1

ARBITRARY BOUNDARY LINE
BETWEEN WORK AREAS 2 & 3

IOG HOUSE 18

PIT 2

PIT 3

PIT 4

PIT 6

PIT 5

IOG HOUSE 6

IOF|IOG
+35S

0   .5   1   2m.

IOG HOUSE 3

Fig. 12.2. Map of Work Area 2 (10G), showing the relationship of pottery-making features to the
immediately adjacent houses. Elimination of other nearby houses of same age artificially
heightens the "unity" effect of the complex.

Fig. 12.3. Work Area 2 in 10G devoted to pottery making. Clay mixing basins lie to the west (left) of the shallow central trench.

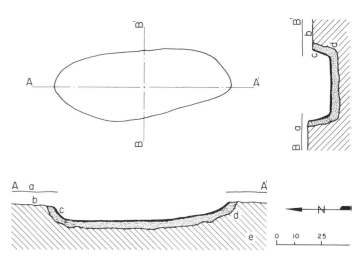

Fig. 12.5. Plan and sections of pottery clay mixing basin (10G No. 1): (a present surface; (b) surface at time basin was used; (c) residual potter's clay; (d) caliche-clay lining, stabilized by burning; (e) native soil.

Fig. 12.6. Pottery firing pits in Work Area 2. (a) Pits 1 and 2 dominate picture. Thermally fractured stones (in pile) were originally scattered among re-fired potsherds; (b) Pit 1, partially cleared. Dirt and ash core is heavily packed with pottery.

Fig. 12.4. Mixing basin No. 1 in Work Area 2 (10G). Potter's clay was prepared here. Length, about 1 m.

and 0.3 m deep, except Pit 6 which was shallow (0.15 m). Pit 2 was half again as large as those already listed. Pit 1 not only was the largest (3 m in diameter) but also had the most irregular outline and the most variable depth. Clearly, it was the product of repeated use in which only parts of it would see service at any one time. Pits 1 and 2 penetrated what was left of an older house floor, age not determined. Pit 7, close to mixing bowl No. 1, suggests that all features were not in simultaneous use because the two separate functions could not readily have been performed at the same time.

Pit contents provided the clues as to how they were used. In addition to some reddening of the soil, ashy material made up a large part of the matrix, and most importantly, were the quantities of potsherds, many of them large, and all of them heavily burned (Fig. 12.6b). Most of the pottery was Gila Plainware, and when painted pottery occurred, it was consistently Sacaton Red-on-buff. The function of this pottery was that of insulating material, to protect the pottery being fired from coming into direct contact with the fuel and thereby avoiding blemishes. This was done most likely by "shingling" the sherds around the batch to be baked, perhaps much as modern potters use tin to make an oven. Only Pit 6 did not contain sherds, though it had a few heat-fractured stones. The occasional burned stones elsewhere among the sherds suggest they may have been used as props in loading the "kiln" with raw vessels.

Examination of fragments of charcoal recovered from the pits showed the fuel to have been mesquite wood. No doubt other woods also were used, as is the case presently, in the early 1970s (Fontana and others 1962: 68; see also Russell 1908: 127).

A point-by-point comparison between Hohokam and modern practices of Pima and Papago potters can be made, and, where comparable data exist, the differences are in details rather than in basic methodological principles. For example, Hohokam firing pits were deeper and larger than their modern counterparts, possibly the function of multiple pot baking in old times versus single vessel baking today. In short, technological elements strongly hint that continuity in the ceramic art from ancient times to the present exists.

Hand tools associated with pottery production might be expected in an area devoted to ceramic art. Yet, the record is disappointingly slim in this respect. Stray potsherds which permeate the soil everywhere were present, and the catalog refers to a lone fragment of a mano. Perhaps most significant was a mortar and pestle located near the clay mixing bins (Fig. 14.12b and c). Careful examination of the soil in the pores of the mortar failed to support the notion that it might have been used to grind either clay or paint. Wooden paddles probably were used to thin the vessel walls by hammering, but these would not have survived in an open site except under ideal conditions. Small cobbles, often used as anvils, were not noted by the excavators. Neither the scraping tool nor the polishing stone for finishing vessel surfaces were ever much used by the Hohokam, and none were found.

The floor artifacts in the houses circling the pottery work area, averaging only a little more than one per house, were not the tools normally associated with pottery making. There were no recurrent assemblages, or even single tools, to support the idea that the houses were the residences of potters. Furthermore, the architectural form of the five houses was no different than the usual Sacaton Phase house. If the status of potters differed from that of nonpotters in Hohokam society, nothing in the remains we encountered would suggest it.

ANALYTICAL PROCEDURES AND JUDGMENTS
Field Analysis

The sheer bulk of pottery from Snaketown demanded a cursory analysis of the day-to-day returns during the field operation. This step had two immediate effects: (1) On the practical side, it re-duced the volume of pottery to manageable proportions. (2) Knowing what was coming out of the ground as the work progressed provided the guidelines for more efficient and productive excavations.

After washing, gross analysis was accomplished by sorting the sherds on the typological basis established in 1937 and arriving at quantity values either by weighing or by counting.

It must be said at the outset that the use of the 1937 typological structure may appear to have biased the case for an independent analysis of the pottery yield, but it provided all project personnel with an immediate starting point. At the same time, we were continually mindful of the fact that the original system may have had its flaws and that a fresh look was necessary. As time progressed and increasing familiarity with the samples was developed, it became clear to everyone's satisfaction that while refinements were possible, there was no need to introduce fundamental changes in the taxonomic system. Feasible improvements were specifically related to expanding the details of design and shape characteristics of specific pottery types, leading to their sharper delineation and to a better understanding of the gradations between types, thereby underscoring the smooth continuum of Hohokam ceramics. These points will be noted later.

Sample evaluation by weighing has the advantage of speeding up the process over counting without loss of relative quantitative data. An experiment (unpublished) by Alfred E. Johnson on a moderately large sample of potsherds, in which counting and weighing were compared, indicated that the relative values were essentially the same. Periodic checks of the number of sherds per kilogram were made at Snaketown, with the interesting result that considerable difference was detected between early and late samples. Sherds in Pioneer Period deposits tended to be small, perhaps a function of thinner vessel walls and a somewhat softer paste than later on. It may also be that the unmounded rubbish of this time was subject to more human traffic, a possible factor in breaking sherds into smaller units. Colonial, Sedentary, and Classic Period pottery was somewhat thicker and slightly harder and the average vessel size was larger, resulting in larger sherds. Tossed on mounded trash with a good amount of cushioning organic material, these stood a good chance of escaping further breakage. The quantitative difference between the older and the younger potsherds per kilogram is in the order of 2:1, or from about 200-300 to 100-150.

For most of the analyzed samples, liberal fractions of them were kept, representing pieces best calculated to reveal details of vessel shape, design, and technology. Certain lots, notably those from pits which were freest of admixtures of types from other phases, were kept en toto for seriational studies, leading to a better understanding of the nuances in style trends.

The broken pottery used in the following typological examination, aggregating close to 0.5 million units, came from a number of sources. Most of them derived from trash, either in mounds or in pits, from house fills, as cremation accompaniments, and from caches. Whole, or nearly whole, vessels used in the study came from house floors, cremations, caches, and in a few instances as isolated occurrences. These number about 140 specimens.

The chronological evidence for Snaketown ceramics, based primarily on stratigraphic relationships, has been presented in Figure 6.17. The typological entities are drawn from the smooth and uniform unfolding of a long pottery tradition. To be understood, a slowly evolving cultural attribute must be fractioned into meaningful subunits by identifying changes in observable characteristics. Adherence to strict canons of the art on the part of the potters led to a patterned behavior which makes the typological approach possible. Yet, typing of pottery has its drawbacks because it introduces the feeling that the development was halting or jerking, when, in all probability, it was an even-tenored progression. To appreciate Hohokam ceramics as seen at Snaketown, it is well, after achieving some mastery of the fractions, to forget the names of types and look at the total pottery fabric for what it was. Our chief aim is to comprehend the history of ceramic development by identifying the chain of ideas and thereby to seek to understand the total culture the better.

At the same time, while we are forced to look at the smaller parts of a culture before generalizing, I want to emphasize the fact that these have chronological as well as taxonomic validity. The reason for mentioning this stems from the fact that opposing points of view have been expressed in the literature.

Gladwin's revised version (1948) of his first revision (1942) of the original Snaketown study (1937) literally "threw the baby out with the bath." He contended that several mistakes were made, the principal one being that variations in pottery styles were overweighted (1948: 61) which led to a compounding of other errors. To pick only a few of the better known pottery types, he asserted that Santa Cruz Red-on-buff was present in the "lowest and earliest levels of the site" and similarly that Gila Butte Red-on-buff "has now been shown to have had the longest life of any local pottery type, beginning in the earliest levels and lasting almost, if not quite, to the end of Mound 29"; and that Snaketown Red-on-buff, Sweetwater Red-on-gray, and Estrella Red-on-gray "possessed minor values as cultural criteria and even less as dating mediums because of contemporaneity with each other and also with Sacaton, Santa Cruz and Gila Butte Red-on-buff" (1948: 54).

In effect, the typological structure was deemed worthless except for Sacaton and Santa Cruz Red-on-buff. Had these deductions been based on a sound reevaluation of the stratigraphic evidence, the chronological picture at Snaketown as given in 1937 would have been a gross misreading of the data. But I do not think that archaeological procedures were as bad as all that, even in the mid-1930s. The new evidence at hand shows the above conclusions were ill-advised and that the "old" system was essentially correct.

As an apparent by-product of Gladwin's 1948 work, the notion has arisen and has been often repeated in the active oral tradition of the archaeological fraternity that the Snaketown pottery types were not found in discrete stratigraphically related trash units but instead were synthesized from the total pottery sample as it went over the analyzing table by applying typological principles. In short, the sequence as published, save for Santa Cruz and Sacaton Red-on-buff, was an artificial contrivance. Actually, nothing could be farther from the truth. In approaching the descriptive section in which the pottery recovered during the most recent effort at Snaketown is reviewed in detail, it must be understood that the sequence is verifiable and therefore viable. Time and unique attribute values are credited to them, and it is these that distinguish pottery as the single most useful hallmark in identifying the smaller time segments in the Hohokam record.

However, two factors bearing on type discreteness, the phenomena of mixing and overlapping, must be discussed before continuing.

Problems of Mixing and Overlapping

It is axiomatic in archaeology that the objects found together belong together and that they may therefore be assumed to be of the same age. Yet, we know from experience that there are many instances in which physical togetherness does not spell contemporaneity. We do not hesitate to adjust for mixed cultural attributes when the elements are obviously incongruous, for example, porcelain or glass associated with Indian-produced pottery a thousand years old, because we connect porcelain and glass as materials introduced by Europeans. But what of less obvious materials? We cannot so easily make this discrimination when dealing with pottery that was produced by the same people but is several hundred years different in age, and because of that, it also is typologically different. Because mixing is present at Snaketown, and particularly since data, objectively quantified, have been misused, it is worth looking at the problem in more detail.

In a vast site like Snaketown, which had an exceptionally long history and a subsoil that, in the main, was soft and easily disturbed, the opportunities were ripe for objects of different ages to become mixed. The agencies that produced mixing are attributable to man, animal, and natural forces. As examples of man's work I can cite two obvious cases from Snaketown: The first was a cache of historic Pima materials, including indigenous pottery, an iron trivet, an enamel coffee pot, and a sawed beef bone, resting directly on the floor of a Vahki Phase house dating from about 300 B.C. The usual principle of dating the house by the objects found on the floor does not apply here. It is obvious that within the last hundred years a Pima Indian became discouraged while burying the goods, probably belonging to a deceased relative, when the hard house floor was struck.

Another Pima cache had a three-quarter grooved axe, certainly archaeological, where it was associated with sawed boards from a box, tin cans, and a round point shovel head (Fig. 12.7). The axe, although Pima-used was not Pima-made, and there is no evidence that they ever produced tools like it. As an object salvaged from the ancient villages nearby, it must be given a different value than would be assigned to native-produced goods or even to the contemporary commercial products of our culture. It would be unreasonable, on the basis of this occurrence, to claim that the three-quarter grooved axe enjoyed a life, meaning time of production, from some indefinite time in the past to A.D. 1900.

In clearing the floor of House 3:10G, a Sacaton Phase structure, several fragmentary Snaketown Red-on-buff vessels were encountered in contact with it. This was a perplexing situation, not easily explained, until work was done in the environs of the house. It then became clear that the initial excavation for the house penetrated Snaketown Phase deposits and that the vessel fragments must have been found, possibly with a cremation, and kept as curiosities or as evidence of something strange to the contemporary potter. Once again, man was responsible in bringing together objects that were out of phase. Further, one needs

Fig. 12.7. A Pima cache at Snaketown with mixed historic white-derived cultural objects and a prehistoric stone axe probably dating from the Sedentary Period.

Fig. 12.8. Portals to rodent dens on the crest of Mound 10. Note pottery scattered about, much of it brought up from below.

Fig. 12.9. Face of cut in Mound 40 showing orderly stratified deposits extensively disturbed by rodent action. Note the unstructured character of the refuse in the rodent tubes. Large hole in what may have been a badger hole was opened by a burrowing owl after our excavation was made.

only to think of the eastern half of Mound 39, which represented the willful transport of material from a pre-existing mound and the attendant mixture of Santa Cruz and Sacaton Phase trash.

The less obvious cases of mixture are those involving excavations into older deposits which produced melding of refuse of different periods, but such materials are not easily distinguished because the diagnostic criteria are few. Instances of this can be cited. Most easily mixed of all occupational wastes is sheet trash where throwing new material on old, human traffic, and continual digging produced unexpected blends. The ability to determine that mixing has taken place, whether by man or animal, is dependent on the recovery of unmixed samples which provide the base line, or the standard for understanding what truly characterized a given phase.

Animal disturbances constitute a real force for churning cultural deposits, notable phenomena in the soft refuse of the mounds. Here the situation is intensified by the fact that mounds have been subject to rodent activity from the time they were formed. Given hundreds of years for rodents, owls, and larger animals to burrow, it is a marvel that much refuse is left in mounds at all that is capable of giving meaningful stratigraphic data. Unhappily, those mounds with the "purest" trash, and therefore capable of telling us the most, were subject to the greatest activity, perhaps because of their softness. In contrast, mounds composed mostly of silt and soil, and therefore more compact, (Mound 16) displayed little rodent activity.

The evidence of animal disturbance is visible on mound surfaces (Fig. 12.8) and in excavated profiles (Fig. 12.9). In the former instance, the ground is honeycombed near the surface with tunnel openings ringed with dirt and pottery brought up from below. This material eventually falls back into the holes as the burrows are abandoned from rain action or as man or animal walks across the ground and breaks through the surface crust.

The three-meter deep profile in Mound 40 reveals clearly the depth of the burrowing and the complexity of the underground network of runways. Except for the gaping hole (top, center), exploited by a burrowing owl after the test was dug, the tubes are plugged with drifted refuse. This must have come from adjacent or higher matrices, including the contained cultural materials. Occasionally, evidences of water-laid silt layers are found in the

tunnels, derived from surface drainage. So, opportunities existed for late pottery to drop down into older contexts. But in the initial digging of the burrows, the material had to go somewhere, and much of it was taken up to the surface. In this process, early pottery was mixed with late high in the mound.

In screening trash deposits like the one depicted, it is not practical or even possible always to distinguish disturbed versus undisturbed refuse when digging down from above. Noting the fact that there was rodent interference when recognized is about all one can do. Separating the disturbed materials and eliminating them from the sample is not feasible except rarely. In short, one comes to expect a certain amount of mixture, and adjustments must be made for it, using as guidelines the less mixed samples derived from trash-filled pits as indicators of normalcy.

Burrowing animals can also disperse cultural objects horizontally when not in a mound. Cache 1:10G is a case in point. Fragments of carved stone vessels were found as much as 3 m away from the cache in Pioneer Period trash when the material itself was of Colonial Period age. Had we not found the cache, the interpretation might have been that the fragments of sculptured stone were earlier than they actually were.

Natural forces leading to mixing are erosion, slumpage in

mounds due to decomposition of organic components and consequent reduction in volume, and possibly other causes. At Snaketown these were unimportant; at least no convincing examples of the phenomena can be given.

I have gone into some detail to emphasize field conditions which are commonplace in the experience of an archaeologist but which are all too easily forgotten or ignored when someone looks at frequency or distribution figures and interprets them in the quiet of his study. All of this would have been redundant were it not for the fact that in the re-analysis of Snaketown data by several authors the problems described above were ignored or the information derived from analyses was wrongfully used. Groundless interpretations resulted. Let us look into the situation a little further.

The greatest upheaval of the original Snaketown analysis was Gladwin's own restudy published in 1948. Unfortunately he limited himself only to the stratigraphic tests made in Mound 29, avoiding equally, and even more important, data from other excavations that would have produced at least alternative interpretations to those he made. His particular use of the information from Mound 29 brings us into a direct confrontation with the phenomenon of mixing, a concept to which I must give a high priority when attempting archaeological reconstructions.

Gladwin properly credits me as using this concept in my analysis of Mound 29 (1948: 213) and then goes on to say: "Any two types of pottery which are associated provide a mixture, but it is the conditions under which such mixtures occur that constitute the essence of stratigraphic testing. In the case of Mound 29, the associations occurred in one-half cubic meter of rubbish and were removed under conditions which were controlled with the greatest care. Once the importance of these associations was realized, they provided evidence of the utmost value and significance." This is to say that because the digging was done with precision, the associations are validated thereby. Certainly "good" digging practices inspire confidence, but no matter how well the testing is done, pitfalls still exist, and this fact must be recognized. Mound 29 is an excellent example.

To illustrate the nature of the co-occurrence of pottery types, Gladwin selected Section F.5, Trench 1 of Mound 29 and gave the actual counts as follows: 1 Sweetwater Red-on-gray, 3 Snaketown Red-on-buff, 10 Gila Butte Red-on-buff, 771 Santa Cruz Red-on-buff, 1 Sacaton Red-on-buff, 1 Kana-a Black-on-white, and 1,057 Plain. For purposes of the present discussion, the last two entries may be omitted. According to my inference, the overwhelming dominance of Santa Cruz Red-on-buff is the most significant single element in identifying the time the trash was laid down. My position, furthermore, was that the types other than Santa Cruz Red-on-buff found their way somehow into the artificially determined block of trash where they were "out of phase." The basis for this belief was the clear-cut evidence we had in 1934–35, and duplicated many times over in 1964–65, of the valid statigraphic order of these types, that there was no appreciable overlapping of types and concomitantly, that there was a time difference between them.

Gladwin paid no heed to the information given in his Figure 9 (1948: 35) and proceeded to use the Mound 29 data in another way. To him "All six types were associated with one another in one-half cubic meter of rubbish and consequently each possess the same correlative value as any other type of intrusive pottery ..." (1948: 35). This would be tantamount to saying that all automobiles found in a car graveyard are contemporary, that is, made in the same year, by virtue of the fact that they physically occur in the same lot! The value of relative frequencies and physical differences, both functions of time, were ignored.

Extending this concept to all of the screened blocks of Mound 29, Gladwin developed a numerical basis for a series of conclusions which cannot be supported by either the old evidence, seen in totality, or the products of the new digging. He has detailed these over many pages (1948: 36-81). To answer every conclusion would result in a tedious replay now; but a few cannot go unheeded to show the enormous disparity in our respective points of view.

Having plotted pottery type occurrences and frequencies on the Mound 29 stratigraphic profile grid of Trench 1 (1948: 32-33, Fig. 8), Gladwin found Gila Butte Red-on-buff in varying amounts in almost all test blocks, but the frequencies were always far below the dominant associated types, either Sacaton or Santa Cruz Red-on-buff which, between them, demonstrated a clear stratigraphic relationship. This prompted him to observe: "Instead of Gila Butte being earlier than Santa Cruz, as had been claimed in 1937, the stratified positions (Fig. 8) and the evidence of associations (Fig. 9) both show unmistakably that Gila Butte was not only contemporaneous with Santa Cruz throughout the early half of Mound 29—the two types being associated in 56 sections—but that Gila Butte Red-on-buff actually reached its greatest density in Trench 1 during the Sacaton Phase, having been associated with Sacaton Red-on-buff in 63 sections" (1948: 39). A little farther on he notes that "... Gila Butte Red-on-buff was present during most of the occupation of Snaketown" and still later, the distribution of Gila Butte Red-on-buff throughout the mound provided a "... convincing demonstration of the fact that the whole span of culture at Snaketown, from first to last, must have been very much shorter than anyone heretofore has thought to have been possible."

The answers to these statements seem to me to rest in the hard core data presented elsewhere which clearly establish: (1) the validity of Gila Butte Red-on-buff as a type, (2) the correctness of its stratigraphic position, (3) its discreteness as a time marker, of equal value with other types, and (4) its position in the measured time scale of years.

That Gila Butte Red-on-buff was so widely distributed throughout Mound 29 does raise an interesting question as to why. I think we may have a partial answer as the result of the recent work. Adjacent to Mound 29 to the west and northwest was an area intensively used during the Gila Butte Phase, particularly for dumping refuse in normal pits and especially in an extraordinarily large borrow pit which probably supplied material for the ball court embankments. The volume of trash of this phase aggregates many hundreds of cubic meters. Sheet trash here also, which includes the nearby ball court environs, has a heavy Gila Butte Red-on-buff component. Disposal of earth on the mound from late Colonial and Sedentary Period house construction could well account for some of this mixture, although I would not assume that this was the only mechanism at work. Since we know now that the Hohokam purposefully added to mounds to gain height or size, this factor cannot be ruled out in the growth of Mound 29. Bullard (1962: 91) recognized this as a possibility in his recent review. It suits my sense of logic better to think of ways whereby the state of affairs we see was accomplished rather than to accept the association of disparate types as valid evidence of contemporaneity. In other circumstances, why Sacaton and Santa Cruz Red-on-buff can be found without Gila Butte Red-on-buff, and deposits of the latter can be found without the former, needs to be recognized too. These phenomena are far more relevant to understanding prehistory than are the other associations resulting from forces that cloud the record.

Having written at some length about mixing, the question follows naturally that, if this factor plagues and confuses the record in the ground at Snaketown, how can we be sure that any of the data are sound and usable? The extremist view would be that one does not have the right to be selective, using some information and ignoring, or, at least discounting other data. To this I would say that the archaeologist is obliged to make these judgments, that he must evaluate ground conditions, that what he does is still mostly an art strengthened by the use of some scientific procedures but which, by their use, do not guarantee accuracy. The subjective judgment, a feeling of rightness or wrongness, does play a part in what we do, though we constantly strive to reduce this weakness by achieving a higher order of objectivity by employing improved methodologies.

To return to the example of the block in Mound 29 quoted previously, there was also listed a single foreign sherd, Kana-a Black-on-white from northern Arizona. The response might be that since you have discounted the indigenous types other than Santa Cruz Red-on-buff as having had any chronological meaning within the context of the block tested, you must also treat the intrusive sherd in the same way. This might or might not be so. Looking at the situation in more detail, one finds that this is not the only time Kana-a Black-on-white has been found in a Santa Cruz Phase matrix, that the evidence is repeated a dozen times and that a whole vessel has been found in a Santa Cruz Phase cremation. Repetition of association in this case is more indicative of contemporaneity than was true for the repeated occurrences of Gila Butte Red-on-buff with every other indigenous type in varying intensities. Furthermore, Kana-a Black-on-white also is associated, but to a lesser degree, with Sacaton Red-on-buff, the sequel to Santa Cruz Red-on-buff, indicating that its life spanned the transition from one to the other of the two Hohokam types. Kana-a Black-on-white, in its home base, was followed by Black Mesa Black-on-white, which is associated with Sacaton Phase materials. In other words, it is not merely the repetition of evidence that tends to build confidence in the data, but of value also is the compatibility of the internal and external records.

A logical correlate of the phenomenon of mixing is the idea of overlapping, of the continuation of a pottery type once established into later times when it was made concurrently with a new type which had evolved in the same ceramic tradition. Thus, pottery thought to have been restricted to one horizon, or phase, lost its diagnostic value because it was produced in several. Much has been made of this problem in the literature as the basis for sequence revision, particularly as it refers to Snaketown. Why overlapping should apply more to the Hohokam than to the Anasazi, or even to other archaeological areas, is not clear. Observations among present day craftsmen as to the extent to which the form and style of established products are retained while new ones come into being seem not to have been made, so no help can be expected from that quarter. On empirical grounds, however, the several facets of the problem may be reviewed.

First, let us see what was done with the old data. On the basis of pottery counts from various tests in Mound 29, Gladwin concluded that Gila Butte Red-on-buff was produced during practically the whole life of Snaketown, that "... it showed little, if any change from first to last ..." (1948: 81). In other words, because Gila Butte Red-on-buff was noted as present in tests, the aggregate of which produced all the other pottery types in the sequence, it was judged to be useless as a hallmark of time. Further, he held that "... Estrella Red-on-gray overlapped on Vahki Red; Sweetwater Red-on-gray overlapped on Vahki and Estrella; and Snaketown Red-on-buff overlapped on Vahki, Estrella, and Sweetwater. Instead of a succession of three clearly differentiated decorated types of pottery, the record of association show(s) ... that the three decorated types were partly or wholly contemporaneous ..." (1948: 220). To say that Vahki Red was overlapped by the Pioneer painted type is meaningless because Vahki Red was a natural associate of them, though decreasing in frequency through time. His further reference to the fact that "... all three types shared the same style and design" is correct, but he failed to note the ascending typological complexity and most of all that discrete samples of Estrella, Sweetwater Red-on-gray, and Snaketown Red-on-buff were found in stratigraphic contexts.

Di Peso (1956: 346 ff) relied heavily on overlapping in his reevaluation of the Hohokam sequence partly because "... all the types which constituted the Hohokam wares (at San Cayetano) were in association with one another." It is worth mentioning that San Cayetano had no piling-up of refuse, rather, mainly sheet trash which would have been subject to greater disturbances than mounded trash. While he found no physical evidence in support of a long occupancy, his red-on buff and red-on-gray pottery sample for the Gila Butte Phase and for all Pioneer Period phases is so small (59 sherds) that it seems too thin a basis for drawing such an important conclusion. Finally, Bullard (1962: 93) also invokes the concept of type overlap in his own revision of the Hohokam chronology.

Now, there is no doubt that some overlapping occurs in cultural attributes which are slowly changing as time passes. What has been labeled as one type may embody elements that forecast dominances and useful identifiers in the next emergent type; similarly a type may retain traits of a previous one as a reminder of the ancestral form. These properties do complicate classification, ever a problem for the taxonomist who is trying to understand an evolving element by segmentation, be it in the animal or the cultural world. I take the position, however, on practical grounds, that it is extremely unlikely Gila Butte Red-on-buff would have been made in the Sacaton Phase or that even Santa Cruz Red-on-buff in its most typical form would have been made as a contemporary of full-fledged Sacaton Red-on-buff.

Cogent arguments against overlapping as a significant factor in affecting the one-line growth in Hohokam ceramics as exemplified at Snaketown may be made. Except for the notably static utility types and conscious efforts to replicate old kinds of pottery, I think world-wide ceramic history would support the generalization that the retention of old types along with the new was not the rule, particularly before well-developed commerce set in. In other words, change, resulting in identifiably different products as a function of the passage of time, was normal. Practically all ceramic taxonomies have been built on this demonstrable phenomenon, whether guided by stratigraphy or seriation.

When dealing with discrete pottery sherd samples, coming from trash deposits quickly formed and which were not subjected to later disturbances as, for example, pit contents, overlap is not seen. The "purity" phenomenon comes into clear focus in the analysis of such deposits. On the basis of this evidence alone one must take the position that the probability Santa Cruz Red-on-buff only was made in the Santa Cruz Phase is far greater than that some selective factor was working to remove from the sample all other kinds of pottery. The many instances of "pure" samples assignable to specific phases or time units establish what I regard to be a norm, and this norm largely eliminates the reason to believe in the overlap factor.

Another line of reasoning holds that if overlapping was indeed a significant factor, then large lots of whole or restorable vessels, as those directly associated in caches, cremations, or on house floors, should show this phenomenon in a most convincing manner. Such samples are normally believed to be truly contemporaneous and reflect the vogue of the day. Reference to examples from Snaketown is in order. House 8:6G, uncovered in 1934–35 (Gladwin and others 1937: Fig. 21), terminally used for storage, produced 33 painted pots, all Sacaton Red-on-buff; of the 10 vessels on the floor of House 2: 9E, 7 were painted, all identifiable as Sweetwater Red-on-gray. The tabulation of the contents of two caches (Fig. 11.14) indicates a total of 74 painted vessels, all except one being Sacaton Red-on-buff. The exception was a Santa Cruz Red-on-buff jar (Fig. 11.9a) in Cache 2:9F, which was judged to be early Sacaton Phase on typological grounds. Examined in aggregate, the four cases of association listed above, produced only *one* vessel out of 117 which mirrored the form and decorative style of the prior period. I do not believe it was made by the potters who produced the associated Sacaton Red-on-buff because it does not seem likely that the subtle differences in color, brush use, design organization, vessel wall thickness, and form could have been so faithfully reproduced. Its status as an heirloom is the most logical answer.

Further light is shed on the ceramic developmental process when one examines the numerically large number of small sites which were occupied for short periods of time only. The original Gila Pueblo survey collections from the Hohokam country show many sites to be 100% of a given stage or horizon (Gladwin and Gladwin 1929a and b, 1930a). While the pottery analysis was not made as critically then as now, reference to the collections, presently housed in the Arizona State Museum, shows that multiple types do not occur in many sites.

Following this point up with an excavated site, the Buttes Dam site (Ariz. U:16:4) east of Florence deserves mention. Not only did the survey show this site to straddle the Santa Cruz-Sacaton Red-on-buff transition, but the excavations by Sciscenti amply confirmed the initial interpretation (Wasley and Benham 1968: 278).

It is possible that the pattern of pottery growth in Hohokam communities elsewhere did not exactly duplicate that at Snaketown, either in style or time. Yet the best comparative sequence available from the Hodges Ruin near Tucson (Kelly and Officer, in preparation) displays an impressive parallelism. Once again I must express my skepticism that even the factor of unequal rate of change dealt the kind of a blow to the Hohokam cultural sequence often claimed to render it so strongly suspect. It does not seem methodologically sound to destroy the Snaketown pottery sequence, supported by numerically large sherd samples and repetitive stratigraphic relationships, by invoking the association in a distant village of numerically small lots of discrete types in thin and largely unstratified deposits.

To reiterate my position, I do not believe that the attributes of a pottery type which were the vogue of one day became frozen and immutable while the main stream of pottery production moved on slowly and subtly to emerge as another type. The conscious production of an older type by imitation is not an impossibility, though I cannot produce a good example in archaeology. Nampeyo's imitation of old Hopi pottery excavated by Hopi workmen on Fewkes' crew at Sikyatki is an example from recent times; yet the product was not a carbon copy, and therefore, it was distinguishable from the archaeological prototype.

The wide scale retention of the patterned behavior of potters that produced one standard form while yet another was coming into being does not fit the generally accepted rule of cultural dynamics where attributes appear, enjoy a period of popularity, fade, and are replaced by some descendant form. In other words, change is the product most often of "evolutionary" forces at work. These changes affected not only the art but also the artist. The chances are that the irreversibility of evolution in the biological field also held for cultural change, that by and large there was seldom a return to a set of attributes that once characterized a social group.

I see the painted pottery of the Hohokam at Snaketown slowly undergoing changes in color, form, motif, layout, vessel size and quantity produced in relation to the total ceramic output which, in varying combinations, are usable as identifiers to separate one type from another. In general the change was unilineal, and there was no appreciable return to or retention of older forms in younger times. Furthermore, these entities, recognizable and quantifiable, have a demonstrable stratigraphic, or time, order; most important of all, the types have proven useful as tools to mark segments of Hohokam history for detailed examination of other cultural phenomena.

POTTERY TYPES

The availability of the original report on the material culture of Snaketown (Gladwin and others 1937) renders it unnecessary now to describe in detail the pottery types listed then. While this may work a hardship on some readers, duplication of text seems unjustified at this time, particularly since there is no change in the

basic taxonomy. I propose to build upon the old report by illustrating new and additional examples of each type, thereby expanding our appreciation for the distinctness of the categories, while at the same time underscoring the nuances in style that bind the formally conceived types together. Attention will also be given to the synoptical aspects of key elements in the Snaketown pottery fabric. Non-Hohokam ceramics and the historic pottery of the Pima Indians will be discussed separately.

Ignored in the 1937 study were any of the types diagnostic of the Classic Period. Excavations in three Civano Phase sites situated near the western periphery of Snaketown proper (Ariz. U:13:21, 22 and 24) yielded the material which is now added to round out the picture. The following review takes up the types in a time order, from recent to early.

CLASSIC PERIOD SITES (Ariz. U:13:21,22, and 24)

Civano Phase

CASA GRANDE RED-ON-BUFF (GLADWIN AND GLADWIN 1933: 22-24; HAURY 1945a: 51—62)

Even though Casa Grande Red-on-buff pottery was the diagnostic type for sites of the Classic Period, little of it was made. No significant new details can be added to extant descriptions on the basis of the present sample. Figure 12.10a-i illustrates representative sherds for comparison with painted categories from other time horizons, and Figure 12.11 emphasizes

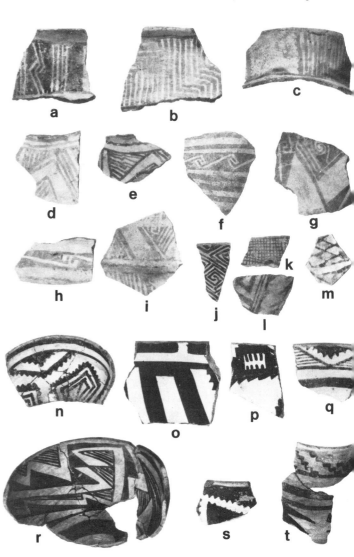

Fig. 12.10. Painted pottery types from Ariz. U:13:21, 22 and 24: (a-i) Casa Grande Red-on-buff; (j-l) Tanque Verde Red-on-brown; (m) unplaced black-on-white; (n-q, s-t) Gila Polychrome; (r) Pinto Polychrome. Width of r, 18.3 cm.

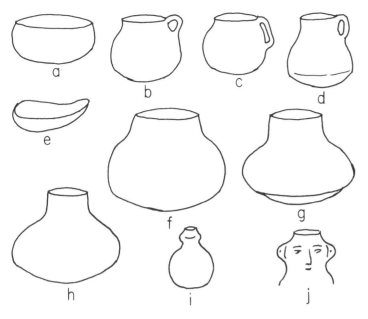

Fig. 12.11. Inventory of the main Casa Grande Red-on-buff vessel forms. (a) bowl; (b-d) pitchers; (e) scoop; (f-h) jars; (i) canteen; (j) effigy vessel.

the limited repertoire of vessel shapes as contrasted with earlier phases.

The style changes from Sacaton Red-on-buff to Casa Grande Red-on-buff were more marked than between any other two phases. The flare-rimmed bowl passed out of existence, in fact almost no painted bowls were made; the typical jars were characterized by a tall cylindrical neck as compared with the low, sharply returned rim of Sacaton Phase times, and the Gila shoulder was placed higher on the vessel and was much less acute than before. Vessel sizes were greatly reduced. The handled pitcher came in as a new form, and the scoop, a canteen, and the effigy vessel were rare indeed. Painted decoration is derivable from the Sacaton Phase pottery, notably the plaited or "woven" type of pattern, but it became stereotyped along simpler lines, and there was an almost complete loss of the life form and the small repeated elements. The thin, often faded, and yellowish paint adds to the loss of crispness in the patterns.

Of the 6,700 analyzed sherds from the three Classic Period sites, only about 5% were Casa Grande Red-on-buff. This small fraction underscores the observation made by Hayden (1957: 191) that the quantity of painted pottery was greatly reduced between the Sedentary and Classic Periods. Decorated pottery aggregated about 40% of all ceramics produced during the Sacaton Phase. Assuming that a continuity existed between Classic Period Hohokam and historic Pima, the diminishing attention to painting of pottery continued, and typologically the transition from Casa Grande Red-on-buff to Pima Red-on-buff is no greater than that between Casa Grande Red-on-buff and Sacaton Red-on-buff.

The reasons for the fading Hohokam pottery tradition, affecting painting and the roster of forms, have not been adequately explored. A few possibilities suggest themselves. Reduction in painting may have resulted from the increasing attention given to the lavish production of highly polished red and smudged pottery. Or, it may reflect internal changes in the social system arising from the association of the Hohokam with the puebloid Saladoans, authors of a polychrome pottery, and other attributes new to them. On the other hand, the shifts we think we see may be a product of gaps in our investigations. If large comparative collections of Soho Phase material were available, and if the postulated Santan Phase, following the Sacaton Phase, could be established with the same firmness that characterizes other phases, the abrupt changes in pottery noted might prove to be more apparent than real. The best candidate for a Santan Phase, or at least

for the time period that phase would occupy, is the material excavated by Hammack at Las Colinas, Phoenix (1969). By time and type, this collection, not yet reported on in full, renders the transition from Sacaton to Casa Grande Red-on-buff intelligible.

GILA POLYCHROME (GLADWIN AND GLADWIN 1930c: 6-7; HAURY 1945a: 64-80)

There is some question as to whether or not consideration should be given here to Gila Polychrome (Fig. 12.10n-q, s-t) as an indigenous ware, or elsewhere under the heading of intrusive pottery. Because this Salado culture attribute holds a somewhat unique position in the Hohokam area, there having been more of it than any other foreign type, and its appearance is marked by other associated elements, treatment here seems desirable.

The presence of Gila and Tonto Polychromes is one of the distinguishing features of the Civano Phase. Unfortunately, the quantity recovered from the Classic Period sites adjacent to Snaketown was so small as to be of no help in technological studies but useful only as an aid in placing the occupation of the sites in the appropriate time horizon.

Only about 0.5% of the total pottery sample was Gila Polychrome, a meager 35 sherds. This frequency was far lower than the 6.5 to 4.1% of Gila Polychrome in the larger villages in the Salt River valley and those farther south (Hayden 1957: 122). The answer may lie in the fact that the villages tested by us were small outlying farming communities and that the occupants were less subject to the impact of the Saladoans who were concentrated in the larger communities. Proveniences of Gila Polychrome within the sites revealed no meaningful concentrations in houses or in general trash. Two fragmentary vessels were noted as accompaniments with Cremations 11 and 14 (Arizona U:13:24), and the evidence is clear that they passed through the crematory fire.

A megascopic examination of the clay in the Gila Polychrome fragments suggests this pottery was not locally produced, but we do not yet have sufficient knowledge of regional variations in clay and temper in this far-flung type to make reasonable guesses as to where it was actually made.

A single sherd of Tonto Polychrome and a fragmentary Pinto Polychrome bowl (Fig. 12.10r) were noted. Pinto Polychrome is ancestral to Gila Polychrome in the Tonto Basin, but the painting style of the former, somewhat modified, survived into the later time period, and its presence, therefore, is not necessarily indicative of an older date in the valleys of the Gila and Salt rivers. A time assignment of about A.D. 1350 to 1400 appears acceptable for the Classic Period sites tested near Snaketown on the basis of the associated Gila Polychrome.

GILA RED AND GILA SMUDGED; SALT RED AND SALT SMUDGED (SCHROEDER 1940: 183-86; HAURY 1945a: 80-100)

A useful diagnostic for Classic Period sites is the presence of red pottery, often with smudged interiors. Gila Red and Gila Smudged are antecedent to Salt Red and Salt Smudged, the latter an indicator of the Civano Phase. Comparative frequencies for these kinds of pottery in the two principal sites studied are given in Table 12.1. Percentages are calculated on the total sample of unpainted pottery.

TABLE 12.1

Comparative Frequencies of Pottery From Two Sites

	Ariz. U:13:21 (3,594 sherds)	Ariz. U:13:22 (2,351 sherds)
Salt Red	7.8%	8.5%
Salt Smudged	7.6	9.1
Gila Red	1.6	3.1
Gila Smudged	3.5	4.2
Gila Plain	79.5	75.1

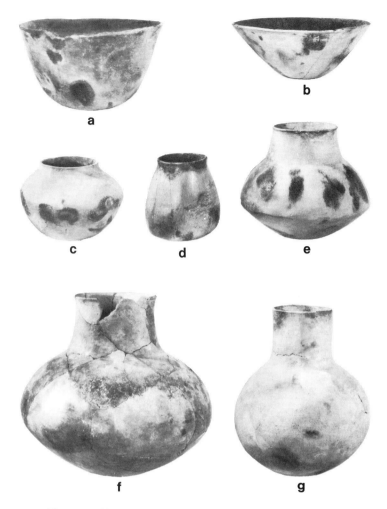

Fig. 12.13. Salt Red beaker severely warped by the crematory fire. Ariz. U:13:24. Height, 17 cm.

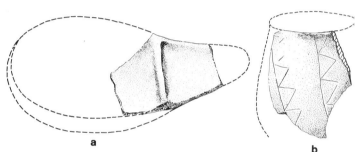

Fig. 12.12. Red and smudged vessels of the Civano Phase: (a-e, g) Gila Red; (f) Salt Red. All from either Ariz. U:13:21 or Ariz. U:13:22. Diameter of f, 35 cm.

Fig. 12.14. (a) Gila Red scoop fragment with thumb protector; (b) sherd of egg-shaped Salt Red jar with scratched pattern. Both from Ariz. U:13:22. Length of b, 6.4 cm.

The dominance of Salt Red and Salt Smudged, taken with other criteria, such as Gila Polychrome and the architectural form, determines placement of the sites in the Civano Phase.

Figure 12.12 illustrates some of the better preserved vessels as a sample lot for comparison with the pottery of earlier times. Both forms and finish are unique to the Classic Period. All of these were either urns for cremated bones or were associated with cremations. Fragment yields from mounds and house fills make it clear that cremation urns were drawn from the normal inventory of household vessels and that they were not especially made for the enshrinement of bones. Not infrequently the vessels passed through the funeral pyre, the high heat of which cracked and warped the vessels. An extreme case of this phenomenon is shown in Figure 12.13.

No effort has been made to analyze the smudged and red types in detail, because little would be added thereby to the existing literature. Generally speaking, the types are indistinguishable from their counterparts found in the ruins of the Salt River valley, as for example, at Los Muertos. Two minor features may be noted. The pottery scoop, an oblong bowl with a slightly elevated and constricted handle end, a standard form among the Hohokam from at least the Snaketown Phase onward, in painted form, continued to be made in Salt or Gila Red. A feature seen only in the Classic Period was the addition of a partition at the handle end to protect the thumb from immersion in whatever liquids were being transferred by it (Fig. 12.14a). I doubt if this was inspired by sanitary motives.

A dimly scratched pattern on Salt Red was seen in only one piece (Fig. 12.14b). This was formal enough to be more than an idle act, but the idea seems never to have caught on, and it does not merit a type distinction, though a Salt Red sherd with a scratched pattern has also been reported from Las Acequias (Haury 1945a: 166).

GILA PLAIN (GLADWIN AND OTHERS 1937: 205-11; HAURY 1945a: 101-06)

Table 12.1 indicates that from about 75 to 80% of the potsherds were of Gila Plain type. Both clay and shape characteristics show Classic Period Gila Plain to be an extension of earlier Gila Plain, from which most of it is indistinguishable. For many hundreds of years the common utility pottery appears to have been exceptionally stable. More than that, except for minor temper differences, the Gila Plain of the Gila valley and that of the Salt River valley are also remarkably similar. Some of the smudging, notably on bowl interiors, must certainly have been intentional, not a surprising extension of the technique which was so well developed on Gila and Salt Smudged.

Intrusive Pottery
TANQUE VERDE RED-ON-BROWN (DANSON IN HAYDEN 1957: 220-24)

Tanque Verde Red-on-brown (7 sherds) was the temporal equivalent of Casa Grande Red-on-buff and was dominant between about A.D. 1200-1400 from Tucson westerly deep into Papaguería. Recent work in the Gila Bend area shows it to be relatively common there as well (Wasley and Johnson 1965: 88-89). It is not surprising to see this type show up in the Classic Period villages near Snaketown, inasmuch as its makers were kinsmen and a close relationship was maintained. Representative pieces are illustrated in Figure 12.10j-l.

BLACK-ON-WHITE

Figure 12.10m is a carbon-paint black-on-white bowl fragment unplaced as to origin, although its pattern characteristics suggest lateness. By the fourteenth century few communities in what was to become Arizona were producing the traditional black-on-white, and these survival areas have not been clearly defined. The specimen in question probably came from the western or southern fringes of the White Mountains and is a hint of Hohokam-Western Pueblo contacts.

Comment

Before we leave the subject of Classic Period pottery, several observations are in order. Gila Plain and Casa Grande Red-on-buff are obvious extensions of Hohokam ceramics. The polished red and smudged types and Gila Polychrome were new to the complex, attributable to an infusion of either new ideas or new people, a problem that begs attention. The combinations of types, particularly Casa Grande Red-on-buff and Gila Polychrome, serve as excellent time indicators because they are not readily confused with other pottery and their life spans are reasonably well known.

The Classic Period villages at the edge of Snaketown explain the occasional Classic Period sherds that came from Snaketown itself. The greatest concentration of these was noted in the canal diversion area where maintenance and gate tending were vital activities. From the Classic Period pottery cemented into the calcareous lining of the last canal, we know that it was in service during that time. It is no surprise therefore that a family or two probably lived at the diversion point, accounting for the refuse in that sector.

With constant human traffic over the abandoned main village, it is difficult to explain why more pottery from it did not find its way into the Classic Period settlements. Only three sherds, of Colonial and Sedentary Period ages, were noted in the collection. Nothing about these was distinctive enough to encourage even children to pick them up. One wonders whether or not there was a conscious avoidance of anything that related to the old settlement. This clean separation of pottery assemblages of different ages encourages reliance on horizontal stratification, a condition noted even over short distances within Snaketown itself.

Snaketown Painted Pottery

SEDENTARY PERIOD

The period-phase classification given in the original Snaketown volume (Gladwin and others 1937: 170) takes note of a Santan Phase in the Sedentary Period. Into the 1970s, the Santan Phase is still largely a hypothetical construct. We were unable in the current work to produce evidence to validate it. As noted previously, a phase is needed in the classification at the Sedentary-Classic Periods interface to make the transition more understandable. If evidence for it exists it must be sought elsewhere than Snaketown. This being the case, the Sedentary Period types listed below refer explicitly to the Sacaton Phase. The order of treatment will be, first, painted and closely related types, followed by redwares and finally plainware.

Sacaton Phase

SACATON RED-ON-BUFF (GLADWIN AND GLADWIN 1933: 16-20; GLADWIN AND OTHERS 1937: 171-78)

In a number of respects, the Sedentary Period for which the hallmark pottery was Sacaton Red-on-buff was a time of "firsts."

Painted pottery in comparison with all other kinds was produced at a ratio of 2:5, a figure based on a perhaps not-too-reliable sherd count. Comparatively, however, values similarly derived for all types (Gladwin and others 1937: Fig. 107) probably have validity. Sacaton Red-on-buff was also the most robust ever produced by the Hohokam in terms of vessel wall thickness, a characteristic having a range of 0.4 to 1.0 cm and an average of 0.6 cm. Thickness may have been a function of another fact, namely, that the largest painted vessels ever produced at Snaketown were of this type. Jars and bowls with diameters of 0.6 to 0.7 m are not unusual.

Sacaton Red-on-buff also exhibited the greatest variety in vessel forms (Fig. 12.15), some of them bizarre, and a boldness and flamboyance in design that was undisciplined in both concept and execution. The over-all impression is that the ceramic fabric was undergoing change, that quality was giving way to quantity as a prelude to the disintegration of a long and distinguished tradition. What followed was Casa Grande Red-on-buff of the Classic Period which, by its low level of production, limited range of form, and stilted painting, is the culmination of the anticipated decline.

A few technical details of Sacaton Red-on-buff are worth noting. All Hohokam pottery was paddle-and-anvil made unless otherwise noted. The soft buff-colored paste of this type usually carries mica-schist temper with resultant free mica that shows in varying amounts on the surface, rounded or angular quartz pebbles, and some other heterogeneous substances. Surface pores are common, derived from some evanescent substance that apparently was lost in firing or afterward. Pores are seen also in vessel wall sections, many of them elongated and oriented more or less parallel to the surfaces. This character appears to be connected with wall thinning by paddling, and it established a built-in weakness, for extensive exfoliation of surface plaques appears to be the consequence (Fig. 12.16a). Occasional cratering was caused by the differential expansion of the temper elements and the paste (Fig. 12.16b). Anvil marks are common on jar interiors, but all exposed surfaces were generally hand smoothed, almost never tool-finished. Though paddle-and-anvil produced, Sacaton Red-on-buff was constructed by broad unit coils which were hammered out to a width of 5 to 6 cm. Coil joints were not always sound, and separations along these lines are observable, as is the rounded edge of the preceding coils, where the welds were poor (Fig. 12.16c). Surfaces, including many jar interiors, were covered with a cream-colored wash, apparently swabbed on with a rag, the marks of which often clearly remain (Fig. 12.16d). When the covering material was thick, the bonding with the base was generally poor (Fig. 12.16e).

The red paint used in designs was occasionally applied as a wash, producing an over-all red vessel lacking polish or other alterations. This treatment appears to have been limited to bowls. It has not been deemed significant enough to warrant separate classification. Vessel conformation and rim finish were often careless, leading to profile irregularities to a much higher degree than is seen among the products of Anasazi potters.

An interesting detail, so far seen only on some Sacaton Red-on-buff, is a faint line scratched in the decorative surfaces under the painted patterns (Fig. 12.16f). The first impression is that these lines represent a pre-painting blocking out of the pattern. However, close study shows this not to have been the case; rather, the line was the product of the nature of the brush. Evidently brushes were made by tying hair or some other suitable fiber to a sharpened stick. When the brush bristles wore short or heavy pressure was applied by the painter, the stick scratched the surface. The proof for this idea lies in the fact that the painted line irregularities match those of the scratched line in a way that would be impossible if the paint was applied on a sketch of the pattern. The length of strokes indicates the brushes had a good paint-carrying capacity. Notwithstanding, the brush work on Sacaton

Fig. 12.15. Inventory of Sacaton Red-on-buff vessel shapes: (a-m) bowls of various kinds; (n-r) oval and rectangular vessels; (s-t) cauldrons; (u) plate; (v-y) scoops; (z) beaker; (a'-c') legged vessels; (d'-l') jars; (m'-n') handled vessels; (o'-p') eccentric shapes; (q'-u') effigies—gourd, bird, human, shell and fish; (v') knobbed vessel; (w'-b") simple censers; (c") legged censer; (d"-e") effigy censers; (f"-g") censers with human motifs; (h") hollow censer with clay pellets. Sizes are relative within categories. Total size range not shown.

Red-on-buff was poorer than at any other time in the history of Hohokam ceramics. The lack of precision in layout and execution, poor line junctures, and paint dribbles, give the impression that the potters were hurried or did not care, further symptoms of a declining craft.

The iron oxide pigment, standard for all Hohokam painted types, was heavier and denser in Sacaton Red-on-buff than at other times, but it was also the most impermanent because the paint-wash-paste bond was weak. For this reason, brush scrub-

bing of most Hohokam pottery in the laboratory should be avoided. Paradoxically, in some instances the paint appears to have acted as a protective coating, preventing the background from eroding where it was applied. In advanced cases a false relief effect was achieved, reminding one of a mechanically altered surface (Fig. 12.16g).

Appliqued or relief elements were rare, appearing mostly as knobs or nonlife forms, and as anatomic features, such as ears, noses, arms, wings, and feet when life forms were depicted. The

Fig. 12.16. Technological details observed on Sacaton Red-on-buff: (a) surface exfoliation; (b) cratering; (c) coil joint; (d) swab marks from wash application; (e) exfoliation of heavy surface coating; (f) paint brush scoring marks; (g) erosion of unpainted surfaces. Width of a, 20 cm.

Fig. 12.17. Sacaton Red-on-buff flared bowls. Diameter of a, 31.6 cm.

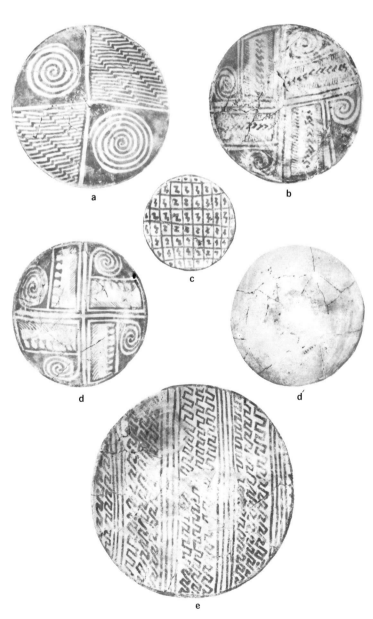

Fig. 12.18. Sacaton Red-on-buff plates. Diameter of e, 28.7 cm.

use of handles appears to have been limited to an occasional figurine, serving as a grip on a scoop, or a rodlike extension serving the same purpose, but most often small bowls were equipped with a basket-type handle.

Vessel forms of Sacaton Red-on-buff that recur most commonly and which are, therefore, the most typical, include the flare-rimmed bowl (Fig. 12.17), out-curved bowl (Fig. 12.15g-h), plate (Fig. 12.18), shouldered jar (Fig. 12.19a-c), and cauldron (Fig. 12.19d). All except the plate have an uncommonly large size range. The emphasis on bigness, while not provable with the data at hand, was probably related to a period of crop surpluses and a time of greatest village population as well. We know that large painted jars, as well as plain ones, were used for storage (Gladwin and others 1937: Pl. XVIIb).

Although all vessel shapes seen in Sacaton Red-on-buff were anticipated by the pottery of earlier phases, demonstrating the continuance of a tradition, a few elaborations assume primary diagnostic value. The sharp shoulder on jars and the associated acutely everted rim, the shouldered cauldron, the scalloped rim treatment on certain vessels (Fig. 12.15p), the sharply concave-sided censer (Fig. 11.3), the effigy censer and the hollow rattle censer (Fig. 12.15g″ and h″) are examples. Additional examples of Sacaton Red-on-buff recovered in 1964–65 are illustrated in Figures 12.20 and 12.21 to expand the inventory of those now available in the literature.

While it would be feasible to examine in extensive detail the painting on Sacaton Red-on-buff, a task that someday will be done, the emphasis now will be on the study of certain traits as they appeared and were transformed through time, such as the

Fig. 12.19. Sacaton Red-on-buff. (a-c) shouldered jars; (d) cauldron. Diameter of c, 61 cm.

Fig. 12.21. Sacaton Red-on-buff: (a) open vessel; (b-b') rectangular vessel. Diameter of a, 25.3 cm. Length of b, 14.5 cm.

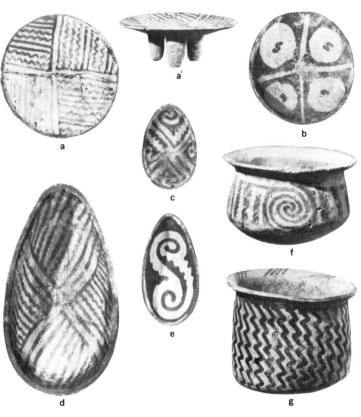

Fig. 12.20. Sacaton Red-on-buff: (a-a') legged vessel; (b) shallow bowl; (c-e) scoops; (f-g) small open vessels. Diameter of g, 14 cm.

scroll, life forms and repeated elements. A section is devoted to these considerations later in this chapter. Some artistic renderings which were specific for the Sacaton Phase will be recognized in this way. There is, however, another aspect of pottery development that deserves attention at this time.

In a continuing pottery tradition, it must be accepted that gradually changing properties will produce recognizable differences in decorative treatments as a function of time. The establishment of types is based on this principle. But it is also possible, because of the length of the phases, somewhat arbitrarily required by the taxonomic system in use, to observe variations between lots of pottery coming from different proveniences but still at-

tributable to the same phase. This is a matter of no small interest theoretically, because it essentially clinches the idea that we *are* dealing with a continuum when we look at pottery and that the phase and type boundaries are artificial indeed. Although these shades of "earliness" and "lateness" within a type, stylistically placed, are observable in all Snaketown painted types, Sacaton Red-on-buff demonstrates the phenomenon particularly well.

An alternative position to the one just expressed is that the variations noted, while possibly time-related, could also be the product of individual potters, of guilds, or schools. This factor cannot be denied, but adequate controls of the material, temporally and otherwise, are not available now to shed light on the issue.

Reference is made once again to Cache 2:9F (Chap. 11) as an example of a collection of specimens believed to date early in the Sacaton Phase, a judgment made on the retention of an earlier rim characteristic and certain carry-over design properties. Other departures from the "standard" can best be illustrated by potsherds coming from single proveniences where they were in actual association. For none of these, however, are there close enough time controls to declare the relative order of progression, and it must be recognized that there are contradictions. For example, the less acute jar rim eversion and shoulder treatment and a tendency toward the retention of the outside trailing line on flare-rimmed bowls suggest closeness to Santa Cruz Red-on-buff in time, but the designs are large, bold, and flamboyant, and far removed from the painting style of the Santa Cruz Phase. The samples from Mounds 39 and 44 (Figs. 12.22, 12.23) illustrate this point, as does also the material recovered from House 5:8F (not shown). A quick degeneration of the Santa Cruz style of painting, or more conservatism in the modification of form than in design seems to be implied; but this does not agree with what was said above concerning Cache 2: 9F.

A contrasting sample, drawn from House 5:10J (Fig. 12.24) exhibits a lightness and laciness of pattern, with few solid masses, and an emphasis on rectilinearity. These characteristics together with the near absence of flare-rimmed bowls suggest lateness because they are the qualities that appear in the Classic Period. This somewhat confusing situation is presented with the idea of stimulating further attention to the problem. At the moment I do not think that the differences we see are the bases for talking about further divisions in the classification. It does mean, however, that a considerable typological range for Sacaton Red-on-buff must be admitted as it is now described.

Fig. 12.22. Sacaton Red-on-buff. Actual associated potsherds from Mound 39, Strat. Test 1, Column 3, Levels 2 and 3. Width of a, 12.5 cm.

Fig. 12.24. Sacaton Red-on-buff. Associated potsherds from House 5:10J, floor and fill. Emphasis on rectilinear designs and near loss of bell-shaped bowls suggest late Sacaton Phase. Maximum dimension of a, 11.3 cm.

SACATON BUFF (GLADWIN AND OTHERS 1937: 178-79)

Omission of the paint on Sacaton Red-on-buff, a rare event, produced a few examples of Sacaton Buff. Shapes unique to this type, as is the case with Santa Cruz Buff, have not been detected. Forms represented include the flared, outcurved, and incurved bowls, plates, ladles (Fig. 12.25a), jars with necks and without (Fig. 12.25b), and legged vessels. Sacaton Buff does not appear to have much diagnostic value, but its presence is noted as the probable result of potters' whims.

Fig. 12.23. Sacaton Red-on-buff. Closely associated units from Mound 44. Width of a, 14.5 cm.

Fig. 12.25. Sacaton Buff. (a) ladle; (b) neckless jar. Diameter of b, 23.8 cm.

COLONIAL PERIOD

Santa Cruz Phase

SANTA CRUZ RED-ON-BUFF (HAURY 1932: 75-88 (NOT NAMED); GLADWIN AND GLADWIN 1933: 8-14; GLADWIN AND OTHERS 1937: 179-85)

A little experience teaches the examiner to differentiate between Santa Cruz Red-on-buff and the type derived from it, Sacaton Red-on-buff. Crystal clear distinctions, however, are not always possible because, as has been noted, in an evolving tradition there must be moments in the succession when the old characteristics had not been completely supplanted by the innovations that were advancing the product toward a new mode. It is these transitional pieces that act as the "connective tissue" between our formalized types and that make the unfolding of the craft real and believable.

In general, the level of production of Santa Cruz Red-on-buff seems to have been slightly below that of Sacaton Red-on-buff. Using Sacaton Red-on-buff as the comparative base, in the type under discussion the background color is somewhat darker, trending towards a pinkish hue; vessel walls average slightly thinner (5 mm), and gross vessel sizes were smaller, seldom exceeding 0.50 m in diameter. Although the basic forms carry through (Fig. 12.26), the repertoire of vessel forms shows a smaller range. The sharp shoulder seen on later jars was absent, and jar rims were more open and gently curved, not acutely turned back. The prevailing vessels were the flared bowl and the jar with a vertically compressed body.

Decorative treatment is the surest way of identifying Santa Cruz Red-on-buff. Examples previously illustrated (Gladwin and others 1937: Pls. CLIV-CLXX) portray those qualities that are thought of as modal for the type. Additional pieces are shown in Figures 12.27-12.30, recovered in 1964–65 (see also Fig. 12.68ff showing life form and repeated element treatment on Santa Cruz Red-on-buff). A representative sample of sherds found in actual association in a single small pit, and therefore probably closely contemporaneous, is given in Figure 12.31. Occurrences of this kind are basic to developing one's ideas about the range in variations of characteristics of any given type. The examples illustrated in Figure 12.32 have purposely been highly selected to emphasize the quality of the brushwork in Santa Cruz Red-on-buff painting. The themes shown, more than any others, characterize the type. The Santa Cruz Phase artist was given to executing thin lines, scanty use of solids, and a tight packing of motifs. Radical departures from these modes in Sacaton Red-on-buff are seen in the heavy and sloppily executed linework, massive solids, and openness of patterns.

While it is recognized that value judgments of artistic merit are highly subjective, I believe a case can be made for identifying the Santa Cruz Phase potter as the best in the line. Grace in form, and imagination and skill in composing the painted line, were never exceeded.

SANTA CRUZ BUFF (GLADWIN AND OTHERS 1937: 185)

Unlike Sacaton Buff which was no more than unpainted Sacaton Red-on-buff, this type appears to have been limited to a particular form, a small (11-13 cm diameter) thin-walled jar with one or two vertical strap handles emerging from the rim and

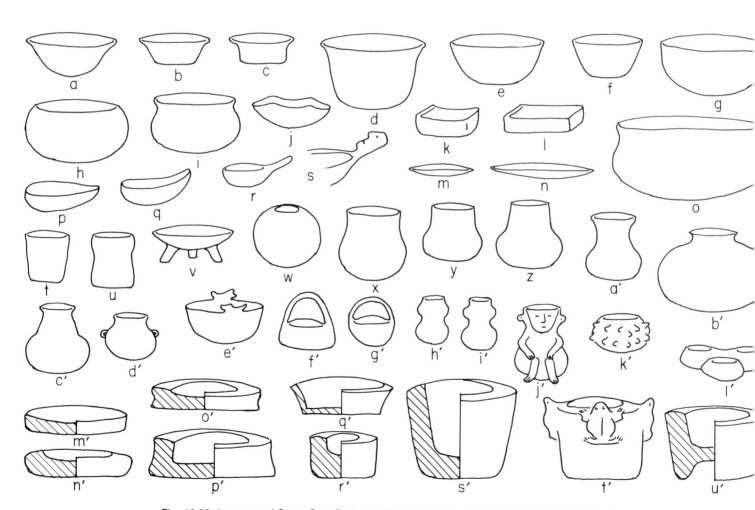

Fig. 12.26. Inventory of Santa Cruz Red-on-buff vessel forms. (a-j) bowls; (k-l) rectangular vessels; (m-n) plates; (o) cauldron; (p-s) scoops and ladles; (t-u) beakers; (v) legged vessel; (w-d') jars; (e') bowl with animal rim ornaments; (f'-g') handled vessels; (h'-i', l') eccentric forms; (j') human effigy; (k') knobbed vessel; (m'-u') censers.

Fig. 12.27. Santa Cruz Red-on-buff. (a-c) bowls; (f) jar; (g-g')
rectangular dish; (h) scoop. Diameter of a, 18.2 cm.

Fig. 12.29. Santa Cruz Red-on-buff. Small bowls and jars including two
handled vessels, i and j. Diameter of g, 12.6 cm.

Fig. 12.28. Santa Cruz Red-on-buff plates. Diameter of a, 23 cm.

Fig. 12.30. Santa Cruz Red-on-buff jars. Diameter of a, 52 cm.

Fig. 12.31. Santa Cruz Red-on-buff. Actual associated potsherds from Pit 4:8E. Similarity of *b* and *e* suggests work of same potter. Width of *a*, 23.3 cm.

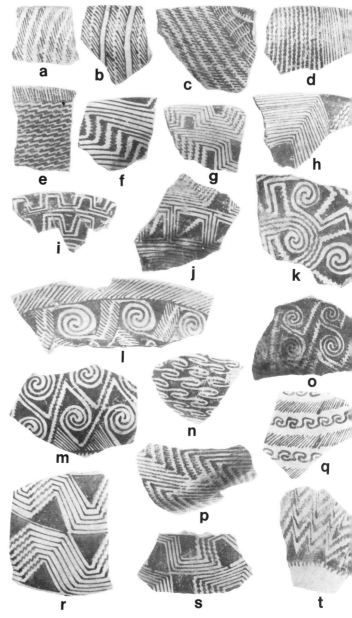

Fig. 12.32. Santa Cruz Red-on-buff. Selected pieces to illustrate the typical use of linear, solid, and scroll motifs. Length of *l*, 25 cm.

fastening to the upper part of the body (Gladwin and others 1937: Pl. CLXXI). No equivalent shape occurred in the associated painted pottery. These vessels must have fulfilled a special function and though infrequent, when found they are associated with cremations.

Gila Butte Phase

GILA BUTTE RED-ON-BUFF (GLADWIN AND OTHERS 1937: 185-89)

The stratigraphic position of deposits that produce Gila Butte Red-on-buff and the vast amount of trash that produce it are clear indicators there was a time of no short duration when the type was in vogue. Gila Butte Red-on-buff has a rightful value in the pottery sequence that differs in no way from all other types. By all criteria, stratigraphic and chronologic placement, typological considerations, the detection of Gila Butte Phase houses and cremations, it is indeed the derivative of Snaketown Red-on-buff and the progenitor of Santa Cruz Red-on-buff, claims to the contrary notwithstanding. The time of production was somewhere between A.D. 550 and 700.

More than any other type, Gila Butte Red-on-buff represents the moment in the sequence when a stylized and conservative mode of decoration was converted into one that provided great freedom of expression and embodied infinitely more motifs and new ways of organizing the fields to be painted. The fetters that bound the artists to a universal hachure style during the Snaketown Phase were broken.

Generally speaking, the paste in this type was more heavily tempered than in the later types, mostly with quartz and mica schist, resulting in fewer pores and a harder pottery. This difference was observed with a hand lense but independently confirmed by a wholly different kind of ceramic examination. In

1968, R. N. Rogers of Alamos, New Mexico, then a student in the University of Arizona, undertook a feasibility study of x-ray fluorescence spectrometry of pottery samples supplied him. One set of potsherds was from Snaketown. Tested for minor or trace elements, such as strontium, rubidium, and barium, a change was detected in the clay or the relative amount of clay and temper between the Snaketown and Gila Butte Red-on-buff types. While Rogers' studies were only exploratory, the utility of the technique is promising, not only to detect differences within a ceramic series but between sets drawn from diverse geographical sources.

To return to Gila Butte Red-on-buff, the near absence of fire clouds is normal in later painted types. While the lightening of the background color began as a trend in Snaketown Red-on-buff, the final step in this direction was really taken by the potters of the Gila Butte Phase. One suspects that it was due to a combination of changing clay sources and of improved firing control. Support for this idea comes from the following test: If the pottery with the lightest background is grouped together by design elements and less attention to painting the outside of the vessel, it is close to Santa Cruz Red-on-buff (Fig. 12.33a); if the darker sherds are grouped, the patterns, notable for the retention of hachure, dis-

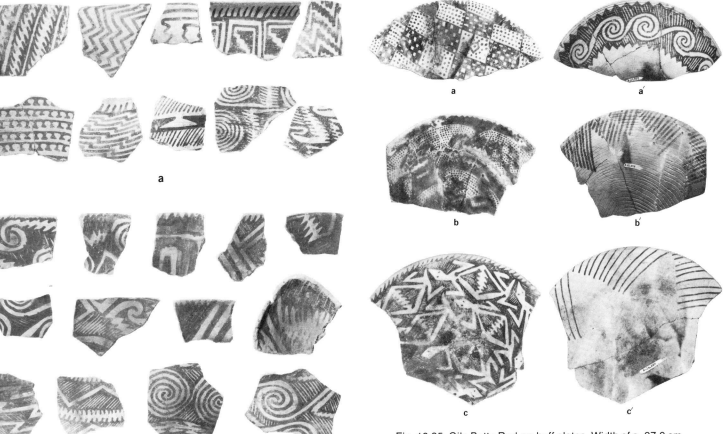

Fig. 12.33. Gila Butte Red-on-buff. Typologically sorted sets suggesting lateness (a) and earliness (b) by background color and design.

Fig. 12.35. Gila Butte Red-on-buff plates. Width of a, 27.9 cm.

tinctly favor Snaketown Red-on-buff (Fig. 12.33b). On these also the paint often assumes a purplish metallic cast and is not fugitive, the possible function of a hotter fire than was used later.

A before-painting scoring of vessel exteriors, to the extent of about 85% of the pots produced, is one of the prime diagnostics of Gila Butte Red-on-buff. It was done haphazardly with a stick or bone awl and represents the terminal stage of a trait which had a long history (Fig. 12.35a′–b′).

The inventory of vessel shapes is noticeably simpler than in the later types (Fig. 12.34), the principal difference being in the smaller range of variation within each shape category. The flared bowl, rectangular vessel, plate, cauldron, scoop, legged vessels,

and jars with gracefully everted rims were present. A newcomer was the pedestal vessel (Fig. 12.34s). Although fragments of human and bird effigy vessels have not been seen, they may be presumed to have been present, because earlier and later examples are known. Censers have simple profiles and usually are embellished with the grooving of the phase (Fig. 12.34a′).

Previous illustrations (Gladwin and others 1937: Pls. CLXXII-CLXXX) are helpful in establishing the characteristics of Gila Butte Red-on-buff. Additional examples follow: The fragmentary plates in Figure 12.35 emphasize the retention of Snaketown Red-on-buff hachure style and dots and the massing of negatively portrayed life forms in b and c, resulting in a tightly-packed decorative field. They also provide good examples of exterior decoration which occasionally became elaborate (a′). Notable in Figure 12.36 is a scoop (a) with a solitary life form, an uncommon usage at this early time but diagnostic of Sacaton

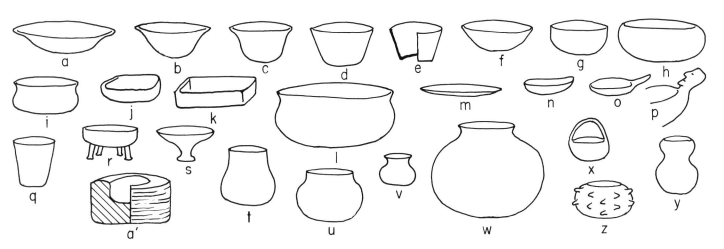

Fig. 12.34. Inventory of Gila Butte Red-on-buff vessel shapes: (a-i) bowls; (j-k) rectangular vessels; (l) cauldron; (m) plate; (n-p) scoop and ladles; (q) beaker; (r) legged vessel; (s) pedestal vessel; (t-w) jars; (x) basket-handled vessel; (y) eccentric vessel; (z) knobbed vessel; (a′) censer.

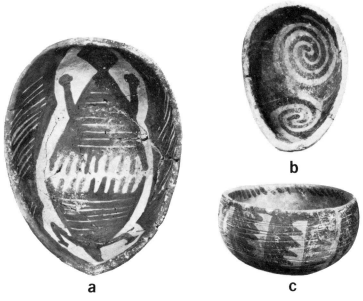

Fig. 12.36. Gila Butte Red-on-buff: (a-b) scoops, (c) bowl. Length of *a*, 13 cm.

Red-on-buff. Sherds from a single provenience, Pit 6: 8E (Fig. 12.37), are useful in showing the range of patterns on pottery that was directly associated. This lot is typologically closer to Santa Cruz Red-on-buff than to Snaketown Red-on-buff.

As evidence of relaxing decorative standards in the Gila Butte Phase were the proliferation in the ways of using the scroll and the burgeoning of the small unit elements and life forms. These subjects are reviewed later in this chapter.

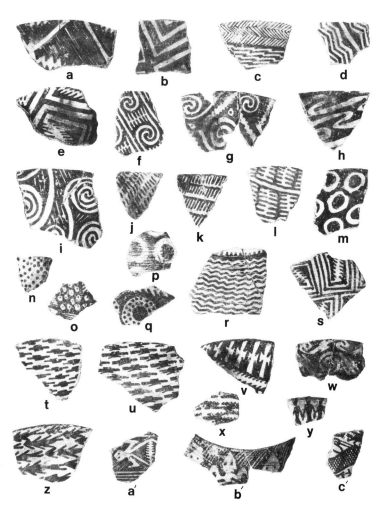

Fig. 12.37. Gila Butte Red-on-buff: Actual associated potsherds from Pit 6:8E. Retention of hachure principle of Snaketown Red-on-buff is seen in *a*, *b*, *i*, *o*, *a'* and *b'*. Width of *a*, 12.8 cm.

PIONEER PERIOD

Snaketown Phase

SNAKETOWN RED-ON-BUFF (GLADWIN AND OTHERS 1937: 189-92)

Two main characteristics distinguish Snaketown Red-on-buff from earlier types: a shift in background color from the prior predominantly gray to buff color and the formalization of a design style consisting of hachure-filled patterns that speaks of a rigidity of expression unique in the long record of Hohokam ceramic development.

The crushed mica-schist and quartz temper components, mostly angular, and the clay quality are about the same as in Gila Butte Red-on-buff. Few of the impermanent solids that created the pores in later types were included in the paste. The methods of manufacture appear to have been unchanged, although in addition to hand-smoothing, evidence of tool-smoothing of surfaces exists. Vessel walls of bowls average 5 mm in thickness.

The dark backgrounds, providing a low-key contrast with the red painted patterns, are mainly the result of fire clouding, generally more pronounced in the interior than on the exterior surfaces. In section, bowl fragments typically show a grading from buff to gray, as one ranges from the exterior to the interior surfaces. Obviously, less oxygen reached the insides of vessels, permitting either the deposition of carbon, or preventing its oxidation, if present.

Although modifications in the firing methods are partly responsible for reducing the amount of fire-clouding, a condition that persisted throughout the rest of Hohokam pottery production, another important technological innovation took place. This was the application of a light-colored wash over the surfaces to be decorated, a reasonably clear indication that the effort to achieve a brighter pottery was intentional. The wash was not consistently used, and it is best recognized in the late variants of the type.

The background color gradation is clearly brought out in Figure 12.38 between lots *a* and *b*. That this change was the function of time is demonstrated by shifts in associated features. For example, group *a*, the lightest in color and therefore typologically the latest, is closest also to group *b* in Figure 12.33, the early variant of Gila Butte Red-on-buff. In the painting the linework tends to be more tightly packed, and tips of scrolls and triangles are usually solid, forecasting the solid line that was to become the mode later. Similarly, exterior painting lies midway between full-fledged Gila Butte Red-on-buff and the older variant of Snaketown Red-on-buff as seen in lot *b* (Fig. 12.38). The same holds true for texturing in which there is a gradual shallowing and less precise spacing of the grooves. In lot *b* (Fig. 12.38) the hachure is done in excellent draftsmanship with slightly wider spacing of the lines than was the custom later on, representing the mastery of the style that was already taking shape in Sweetwater Red-on-gray (Fig. 12.44). In sequence, then, tracing the development through two variants of two phases, the order from early to late is: Figure 12.38b, a; Figure 12.33b, a. While this series has been selected from a large general sample to illustrate gradation, actual ground collections from pits and other sources can be produced to support these differences. An example of late Snaketown Red-on-buff from a single provenience is shown in Figure 12.39.

Departures from the hachure style were rare. Cross hachure and the use of dots appear to have been venturesome, and only occasionally did a piece leave the rigid tradition to be different if only slightly (Fig. 12.40d). Opposed serrated figures took shape at this time (Fig. 12.40a), although the idea had beginnings in Sweetwater Red-on-gray. Most interesting as a new invention in painting was the depiction of life forms and other figures in negative fashion (Fig. 12.41), a topic reviewed more fully later on.

The nearest analogue in Anasazi painting to the Snaketown Phase hachure style was the black-on-white pottery of Chaco

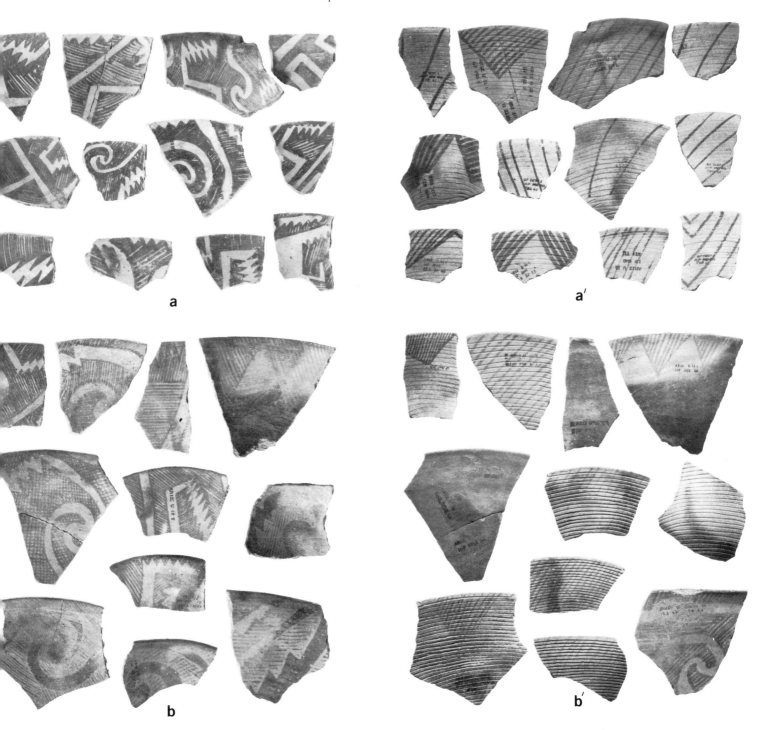

Fig. 12.38. Snaketown Red-on-buff: (a) late variant characterized by light backgrounds and closely spaced hachure lines; (a') simply painted and grooved exteriors; (b) early variant with dark backgrounds and open hachure; (b') more complicated outside painting when used, and precise deep grooving. Length of upper left in *a*, 9 cm.

Canyon, New Mexico (Judd 1954: 180, Plates 54-57). The age of this pottery, between A.D. 1050 and 1200 (Breternitz 1966:71) was more than a half millennium later than the Hohokam manifestation, dated at about A.D. 350 to 550. Apparently the Chaco Canyon potters hit upon the older Hohokam style of decoration independently, since there are no obvious connecting links.

The predominant shapes in Snaketown Red-on-buff (Fig. 12.42) in open forms were bowls with moderately flared rims and of medium depth and plates which put in their first appearance at this time (Fig. 12.41). The standard jar had a body somewhat vertically compressed and a neck slightly longer with a more accentuated rim than was typical of Gila Butte Red-on-buff (Fig. 12.40e-g). Although the scoop, a conventional vessel of later times, was present, the handled dipper was the more prevalent.

An ellipsoid-shaped bowl (Fig. 12.40b) is recognized in the Snaketown Phase for the first time, although it probably had earlier beginnings. The existence of eccentric forms is indicated by a few fragments, but the shapes cannot be reconstructed with the pieces at hand other than those illustrated in Figure 12.42. Scalloped rims and knobs on vessels were apparently not a part of the complex. There is no certain evidence of tripod or tetrapod vessels that were not of an effigy nature. Human and bird effigy vessels were present (Fig. 12.43), shapes that had still earlier beginnings. Censers, though for the most part simple in profile, also occurred in the form of quadrupeds. Vessels with handles, other than dippers, seem not to have been used. The handled bowl was not represented in the collection, but it was doubtless made because earlier and later examples are known.

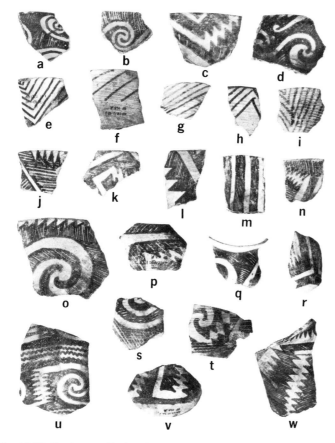

Fig. 12.39. Snaketown Red-on-buff. Actual associated potsherds from the fill of House 8:5F. Lateness in phase is indicated by frequent massing of hatching lines to produce a solid effect as in c, d, r, s, u, and v. Width of o, 11 cm.

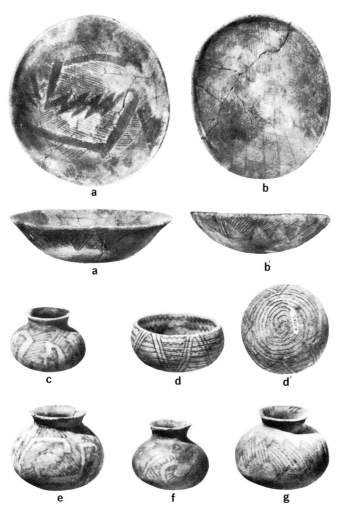

Fig. 12.40. Snaketown Red-on-buff: (a) incipient flared bowl; (b) oval bowl; (d) incurved bowl; (c, e-g) small jars. Diameter of a, 19.4 cm.

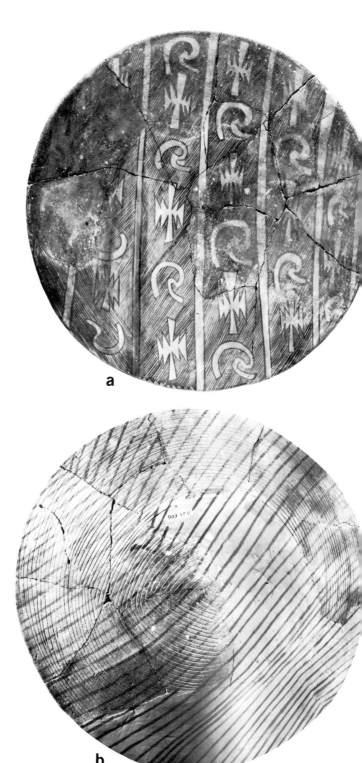

Fig. 12.41. Snaketown Red-on-buff plate: (a) interior and (b) exterior views. Diameter, 35.2 cm.

More than half of the potsherds of the Snaketown Red-on-buff exhibit surface grooving, more often applied to bowls than to jars. The quality of grooving, that is its regularity and depth, clearly places it in a declining scale of excellence between Sweetwater Red-on-gray and Gila Butte Red-on-buff.

Snaketown Red-on-buff presents us with few aesthetic surprises. It comes closer than any other type in fulfilling the requirements of a taxonomic ideal. Fortunately the gradations in decoration between early and late variants fit the total scheme of pottery development, removing the temptation from labeling it as an intrusive tradition. The adoption of strict standards by the potters in the Snaketown Phase must somehow be related to the maturing of an art style. All methods of testing the time indicate that this took place between A.D. 350 and 550.

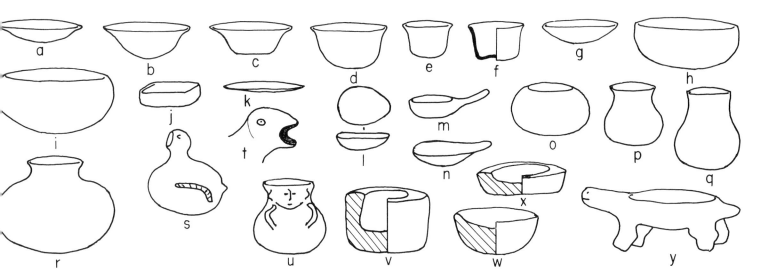

Fig. 12.42. Inventory of Snaketown Red-on-buff vessel forms: (a-i) bowls; (j) rectangular vessel; (k) plate; (l-m) scoop and ladle; (o-r) jars; (s-t) bird effigies; (u) human effigy; (v-x) censers; (y) animal effigy censer.

Fig. 12.43. Snaketown Red-on-buff effigy vessels: (a) human, restored; (b) bird. Diameter of b, 13 cm.

Sweetwater Phase

SWEETWATER RED-ON-GRAY (GLADWIN AND OTHERS 1937: 192-98)

The descriptive adjective gray, replacing the usual buff, denotes the dominant but not universal color of the above-named type. On many fragments with the darker tones, the applied red pigment is difficult to see, in fact one wonders why the Hohokam bothered to decorate the pots at all. It may have been this question, asked by them, which led to the steady brightening of the backgrounds, beginning in the Snaketown Phase.

The clay in Sweetwater Red-on-gray was liberally tempered with mica schist and angular quartz grains which fired to a slightly harder pottery than was true later on. Surfaces were hand smoothed, although jar interiors were not so treated, and only a few examples of red-slipped surfaces were observed. Finely comminuted mica is liberally seen on all surfaces and fire clouds are prominent.

Like other types, in both shapes and decoration, Sweetwater Red-on-gray "fits" between Estrella Red-on-gray, its antecedent, and Snaketown Red-on-buff, its successor. The stratigraphic position held by it fully supports this typological placement. A simple comparison of painted and unpainted sherds suggests a value of about 5% for decorated pot production. The exact figure is not as important as is the trend established by it, for from a low quantity of about 2% in the Estrella Phase, the amount here was more than doubled, showing that the idea was meeting with favor among the potters.

It is not surprising therefore that with this increasing opportunity to decorate vessel surfaces, a certain maturing effect should be observed. It is noticeable, for example, that in some associated lots of sherds, simple patterns in medium broad lines resemble Estrella Red-on-gray (Fig. 12.44b, Pit 10:10E), while other groups (Fig. 12.44a, Pit 9:10E, and Fig. 12.45, Pit 2:10D) reflect the adoption of a hachure technique to fill gross elements forecasting the Snaketown Phase mode. The scroll took form at this time, shown with terraced or serrated roots, and producing, in effect, the beginning of the stepped greque. It was this artistic innovation that makes Sweetwater Red-on-gray stand out, and it set the tone for so much of the subsequent Hohokam painting. The previous examples of pottery illustrated were derived from individual refuse-filled pits. While lending credence to the typological succession, they are somewhat lacking in numbers of painted pieces. It seems worthwhile to offer additional examples, drawn at large from the study collection, to further underscore the difference between early and late variants of Sweetwater Red-on-gray (Fig. 12.46).

An early effort to produce small unit elements is shown in Figure 12.47. The disorganized nature of the visible parts of the design suggests an experiment in painting.

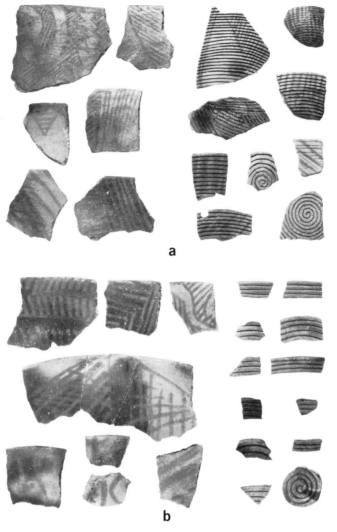

Fig. 12.44. Sweetwater Red-on-gray: (a) late variant, from Pit 9:10E; (b) early variant, from Pit 10:9E. Width of upper left, 10.8 cm.

Fig. 12.46. Sweetwater Red-on-gray. Typological variants: (a) early; (b) late. Width of upper left, 9.9 cm.

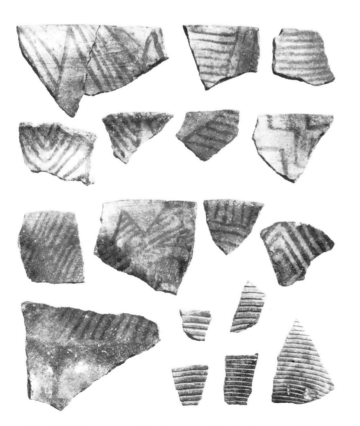

Fig. 12.45. Sweetwater Red-on-gray. Sherds from a single association, Pit 2:10D. Width of upper left, 12.5 cm.

Fig. 12.47. Sweetwater Red-on-gray bowl with isolated geometric design units. Diameter, 24 cm.

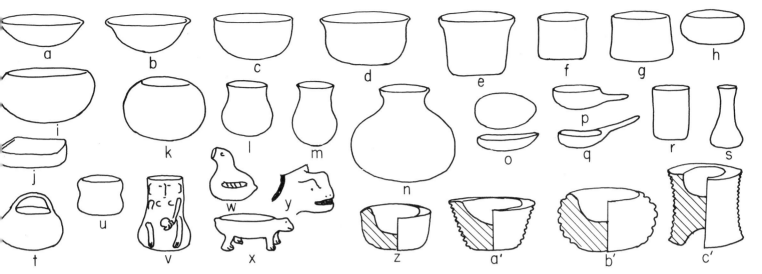

Fig. 12.48. Inventory of Sweetwater Red-on-gray vessel shapes: (a-i) bowls; (j) rectangular vessel; (k-n) jars; (o-q) scoop and ladles; (r) beaker; (s) bottle; (t) basket-handled vessel; (u) eccentric vessel; (v-y) human, bird, and animal effigy vessels; (z-c') censers.

The vessel shape inventory (Fig. 12.48) does not parallel the simplicity of the painted treatment. In Hohokam pottery it becomes increasingly clear that the aesthetic value of form exceeded that of surface painting. The flared bowl begins to come into prominence in Sweetwater Red-on-gray, and it takes on the shallowness so popular in later times.

Other basic bowl forms were known as well, the outcurved, incurved, and vertical rim types. Jars were generally medium large-mouthed with longer necks, more flaring of rims, and more vertical elongation of the body than exhibited by later jars. The standard dipping vessel was the handled ladle which was eventually replaced by the scoop. But the more eccentric vessels were present too, the basket-handled vessel, a rectangular shallow dish, bottles, a weakly developed bilobed vessel, and both human and animal effigy vessels. Censers, also, were a part of the complex, and they usually carried the grooving associated with the other vessels of the type. The oldest example of double-decked censers is noted at this time (Fig. 12.48c').

About one vessel in five was given a grooved exterior, and the kind of grooving is a useful diagnostic for Sweetwater Red-on-gray. The two handsome bowls shown in Figure 12.51 illustrate the oldest form which began in the Estrella Phase and extended into the Sweetwater Phase. The spacing and the regularity of the grooving were determined by the coiling technique employed in the production of the vessels. Within the phase, however, grooving was freed from the effects of the coils leading to a closer spacing, a narrower groove and the introduction of patterns in the textured surface (Figs. 12.49 and 12.67). The net result of this was the production of a class of pottery that lies outside the central theme seen in most Southwestern ceramics, namely, the smooth-surfaced and the corrugated-surfaced vessels. Most Sweetwater Red-on-gray open-formed vessels were painted outside as well as inside.

In many samples of Sweetwater Red-on-gray, derived from general trash or house fills, jars are rare. Except for small specimens, there are no whole jars in the collection. Fragments, however, were common in the broken pottery yield from the Pioneer Period canal fill and particularly from depressions in it used as dipping pools during the Sweetwater Phase. This suggests that the primary function of the painted jar was for water transport and storage.

Finally, after reviewing potsherds of Sweetwater Red-on-gray, if doubts linger about its discreteness as a type, they should be dispelled by the collection of vessels from the floor of a house (House 2:9E) which was razed by fire during occupancy. These

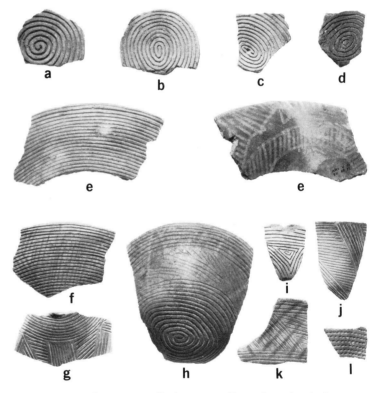

Fig. 12.49. Sweetwater Red-on-gray. Examples of exterior grooving: (a-d) bowl bottoms; (e-e') exterior-interior of same sherd; (f) bowl; (g) jar, patterned; (h-k) bowls, patterned; (l) bowl with linear punctate decoration. Width of e, 17.2 cm.

are shown in Figures 12.47, 12.50 (except specimen f) and 12.51. The eight vessels match the criteria developed for Sweetwater Red-on-gray painting and add the additional notes of refinement in forms and control of plastic clay achieved by the potters of the time. Adherence to a decorative norm in all pieces is reassuring to see.

SWEETWATER POLYCHROME (GLADWIN AND OTHERS 1937: 198)

It may have been the experimental nature of the potters during the Sweetwater Phase that led to the development of a pottery type with two applied colors, red and yellow, derived respectively from hematite and limonite. A firing atmosphere low in oxygen would insure the retention of these two colors, for in a rich oxygen

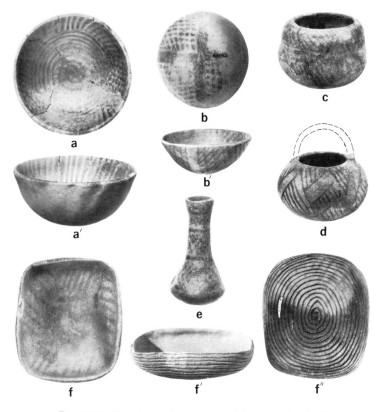

Fig. 12.50. Sweetwater Red-on-gray. Diameter of *a*, 13.7 cm.

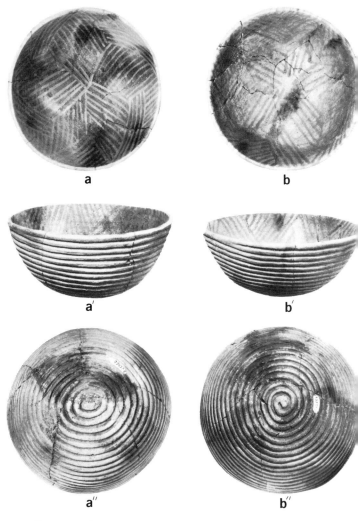

Fig. 12.51. Sweetwater Red-on-gray. Diameter of *b*, 16.8 cm.

atmosphere with reasonably high firing temperatures the yellow would turn red. However, considering the age of this pottery, between A.D. 200-350, and the apparent derivation of other ceramic elements in the complex from Mexico, it may be more reasonable to believe that the polychrome idea came from the south as well. By that time polychrome painting was already well established there.

Not much Sweetwater Polychrome was ever produced, as the collection numbers only one vessel (Gladwin and others 1937: Fig. 90) and a half-dozen fragments. Alternation of red and yellow lines and yellow bands with red edges appear to have been the only ways of combining the colors. The type remains as a curiosity and occurs too infrequently to have much diagnostic value.

Estrella Phase

ESTRELLA RED-ON-GRAY (GLADWIN AND OTHERS 1937: 199-202)

This type brings us to the beginning of painted pottery in the Hohokam series. Before turning to the question of how painting may have originated, some attention must be paid to technological points.

The basic clay and its treatment was about the same for all the pottery produced at this time: early Gila Plain, Vahki Red, and Estrella Red-on-gray. Tempering materials were angular chunks of mica schist, and some pieces show liberal inclusions of quartz as well. Variation in the total amount of temper particles is noticeable. While most of the pottery was paddle-and-anvil produced, the continuous coiling method was also known, as evidenced by the small amount of associated grooved pottery. Surfaces were hand-smoothed, and vessel wall thicknesses range from 2 to 7 mm, averaging 4 mm. The thinner pieces are excellently made, exhibiting a high degree of skill in the control of clay. The differences in the three types named above stemmed primarily from firing and surface treatments. Vahki Red was slipped and lightly polished and burned in an oxygen-rich atmosphere with little opportunity for fire-clouding. Gila Plain and Estrella Red-on-gray, on the other hand, were baked in less-well-managed atmospheres, producing dominantly gray to nearly black tones and abundant fire-cloud blemishes.

It was the technological treatment of Vahki Red, the skilled use of a red slip and its polishing, that appears to me to have kindled the idea of applying painted designs to vessel walls. Let us examine the evidence. A review of a number of trash deposits which produced Estrella Red-on-gray demonstrated that differences in treatment and in decorative effect could be established in separate lots, lending to the supposition that the variations were most likely the product of differences in age. Although the stratigraphic record is clear with respect to the position of Estrella Red-on-gray in the sequence, it is of no help in drawing fine time differences within the phase. This is attributable to the fact that the best Estrella Phase samples were recovered from pits which were filled too fast to reflect any changes in decorative treatment. The approach, therefore, must be through typology, which has proven so useful in calling attention to early and late variants of practically all previous types discussed.

What I consider to be the oldest form of Estrella Red-on-gray, and therefore the earliest effort at decorating, was recovered from Pit 17: 9E (Fig. 12.52). The pit produced some 1,500 sherds, of which about 3% were decorated. What we see in these predominantly is an exterior red slip, polished, and a carry-over to interior surfaces of the slip material as broad lines directed toward the center of the field from the rim. These lines may have been finger-applied. The potters, accustomed to polishing the slip, applied this treatment to the painted lines as well, and polishing-over-the-paint resulted. This act obliterated any sharp edges the paint lines may have had, making detection more difficult, but conversely, the polishing streaks make identification a little bit easier.

If this reconstruction is correct, then one may postulate that a hundred or so years before Christ the innovation took place. It

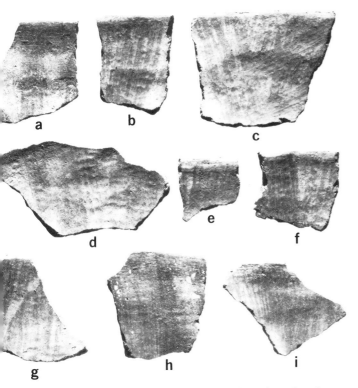

Fig. 12.52. Estrella Red-on-gray. A typologically early variant from a single deposit, Pit 17:9E. Note especially the pebble polishing marks over painted bands. Width of left center, 11 cm.

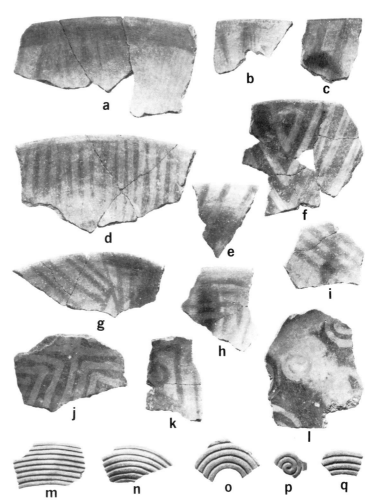

Fig. 12.53. Estrella Red-on-gray. (a-c) early variant, polished over decoration; (d-l) late variant, not polished over decoration; (m-q) exterior grooving. Width of a, 19.1 cm.

was a simple technological step to convert Vahki Red, which had already been produced for several hundred years, to effect the change by applying stripes or wedges of color instead of wholly covering inner bowl surfaces. In some examples, an inside rim line was applied amounting only to bringing the slip from the outside to below the inner rim (Fig. 12.53a). Breadth of lines and simplicity of design layout further support the idea that the pieces under discussion do indeed represent an early variant of Estrella Red-on-gray.

The late variant of the type is shown in Figure 12.53 d-l. Although these units were selected from the type collection, a number of Estrella Phase rubbish deposits, notably in the well area of Block 10G, produced this variant to the near exclusion of the presumed older form. The diagnostic features here are brush-applied lines, narrower than the other variant, but still having an average width of 8 mm; no polishing over the paint; decoration to the rim, that is, no rim-line; and a high percentage of bowl exteriors revealing no red slip. In other words, it looks as though either Vahki Red or the contemporary plainwares were painted, that a special kind of pottery with the intent to paint it was not being made. The brightest red paint occurs on those pieces, a minority, which were most heavily oxidized. For the most part backgrounds are dark and the designs are difficult to see.

Too few large sherds were found to say much about pattern details, but a quartered scheme appears to have been a favorite layout (Fig. 12.53j), the quarters chevron-filled; and there are a few hints of crude hachure-filled units. Most of the linework was rectilinear, but a few simple noninterlocking spirals were noted. The relatively small independent unit seems to have had its birth at this time. While painted jars were not common, the inner rim surfaces were sometimes painted well below the point where they were visible.

Grooving seems to have been restricted to small bowls, clearly the product of mechanically altering the troughs between coils to a deep U-shaped channel. Fractures along these lines often show the coil interfaces where the welds were poor. On the average the grooves are wider than in Sweetwater Red-on-gray, and no cases of patterning were observed, not likely anyway because the coil joints established where the grooves were to be.

The inventory of vessel profiles is small as compared with later types, and, for the most part, the shapes were simple. An out-curved bowl of medium depth was the dominant form (Fig. 12.54a). It, together with deeper bowls with rounded or flattened

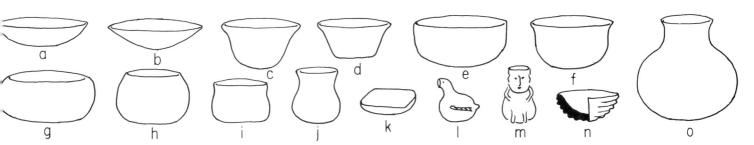

Fig. 12.54. Inventory of Estrella Red-on-gray vessel shapes. (a-i) bowls; (j, o) jars; (k) rectangular vessel; (l-m) bird and human effigies; (n) censer. All determinations based on potsherds.

bottoms, begins to develop a slight flare to the rim (Fig. 12.54c and d). Bowl rim fragments indicate that diameters reached 40 cm. Jars tended to have larger mouths in relation to the maximum body diameter than at any other time (Fig. 12.54o), and variations away from the mode were few. While no ladle fragments were found, this container may be presumed to have been present. Traces of legged vessels were not found, but hints of the rectangular dish do occur, and most surprising of all are fragments of human and bird effigy vessels, the exact shapes of which are not restorable from the fragments at hand. Censers were rare, being bowl-like and thin-walled (Fig. 12.54n). They probably appeared for the first time in the Estrella Phase.

Although Estrella Red-on-gray was the first and clumsiest painted type the Hohokam undertook to make, the technical excellence of the wares of the phase, including Vahki Red, leaves no doubt about the fact that pottery production was a long way from the adoption of the craft by them.

Snaketown Unpainted Pottery Redware

SEDENTARY PERIOD

Sacaton Phase

SACATON RED (GLADWIN AND OTHERS 1937: 202-04)

Not much new information can be added to the discussion cited above. The 1964–65 collection consists only of about 150 sherds and 2 restored pieces of Sacaton Red. Where the associations were clear, which was true for the majority of the units, the phase was always the Sacaton. Proveniences about cover the range of excavations, from trash mounds to houses. Cremations, however, have not yielded specimens of the type. There is no basis for assigning a special function to Sacaton Red. Yet, because petrographic analysis has shown it to have been locally made, one must conclude that its low level of production means either it did serve a special and limited purpose, or the potters never favored it.

Sacaton Red departs in several respects from other contemporary wares. The inner surfaces carry a heavy red slip, well polished with a tool, as compared to the more usual washed and hand-smoothed surfaces; outside surfaces were hand finished, and some pieces show a number of careless strokes with the polishing tool. Mottled surfaces resulting from firing blemishes are usual. Other differences include thicker vessel walls (average 6 mm) and a restricted number of shapes. Typical is the bowl with a slightly out-turned rim (Fig. 12.55a). Out-curved, subhemispherical in-curved bowls (Fig. 12.55c and d), a plate (Fig. 12.55e), and a small jar (Fig. 12.55f) complete the shape roster. Bowls reached a diameter up to about 40 cm, but the average was nearer 20 cm.

Sacaton Red carries a heavy amount of temper, both angular and rounded quartz grains, and much mica, probably derived by crushing mica schist.

Thoughts about the position of Sacaton Red in Hohokam ceramics will be delayed until after a review of Vahki Red which follows.

PIONEER PERIOD

All Phases

VAHKI RED (GLADWIN AND OTHERS 1937: 204-05)

Vahki Red, with Vahki Plain, constituted the total repertoire of the Hohokam potter at the time Snaketown was founded. Perhaps less than 4% of all pottery made at the start was Vahki Red, and it continued to survive in diminishing amounts throughout the Pioneer Period. By the beginning of the Colonial Period it was no longer being made. Its distinguishing features are: a paste generally firing to a buff color, tempered with fine grains of quartz and micaceous schist; thin vessel walls, average 4 mm, range 3 to 9 mm; a thin red-brown slip sometimes trending toward magenta, usually applied over all exposed surfaces, tool polished and much mica showing through; vessel shapes as illustrated in Figure 12.56. Sizes for both bowls and jars reached diameters of 40 cm.

Although the clay had a low tensile strength, form aesthetics and surface treatment show that the potters were a long way from the first experimental stages of pottery production. The small-mouthed bottle (Fig. 12.56m) and hints of eccentric forms, including the human effigy vase, may be singled out particularly in support of this view. It is worth noting that the flaring of the rim on bowls is first detected here, a shape that was eventually to become exaggerated and to stand out as one of several distinctive hallmarks of Hohokam pottery. A few censer fragments, probably of Vahki Red, were found in Sweetwater and Snaketown Phase trash.

Grooving has not been detected in Vahki Phase contexts, but it does appear in the Estrella Phase to a limited extent on Vahki Red. The grooves are deep and widely spaced. Subsequently there was a transfer of the grooving idea to painted types inasmuch as the feature is lacking in Vahki Red from late Pioneer Period contexts.

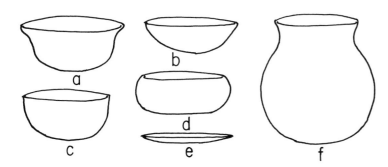

Fig. 12.55. Inventory of Sacaton Red vessel forms: (a-d) bowls; (e) plate; (f) jar.

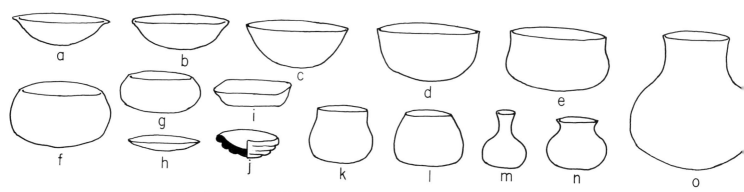

Fig. 12.56. Inventory of Vahki Red vessel shapes: (a-g) bowls; (h) plate; (i) rectangular vessel; (j) censer; (k, l, n, o) jars; (m) bottle. Human effigy not shown but probably present.

DISCUSSION OF HOHOKAM REDWARES

If the idea is accepted that the oldest pottery in the Southwest is traceable to a Mesoamerican origin, then it is easy to understand why redware was a component of the initial ceramic fabrics of the Hohokam and Mogollon traditions. With few exceptions, the earliest Mesoamerican pottery complexes include good slipped and polished red types which, by virtue of their age, would have been the prototypes for the kinds seen in the Southwest.

A plausible explanation is that red pottery was diffused northward along two lines: the first west of the Sierra Madre, the route most likely followed by the Hohokam, as leading to the production of Vahki Red; the second, a route through or along the eastern margins of the Sierra Madre, which resulted in the making of San Francisco Red in the Mogollon territory. The time of entry for both was about coeval. Technically they had much in common, and the companion pottery in each case was a brown or gray ware.

Early contemporaneity of the two redwares is indicated by dates derived by several time measuring methods and by the appearance of San Francisco Red as an intrusive type in the Vahki Phase. In the light of the above interpretation, my original thought that Vahki was a derivative of San Francisco Red (Gladwin and others 1937: 217-18) no longer stands.

Insofar as the history of red pottery within the Hohokam sequence is concerned, the following points should be noted. Though technically excellent, Vahki Red was never produced in quantity. Perhaps no more than 5% of the total ceramic output was of this kind at the start, and its frequency slowly diminished thereafter, the last of it having been made in the Snaketown Phase. This information supersedes that given earlier (Gladwin and others 1937: Fig. 107) in which the Sweetwater Phase was believed to have been the terminal date. During the Colonial Period red pottery was absent altogether and sometime during the Sedentary Period Sacaton Red came into existence. Its beginnings are obscure, but because the smudging of interiors was completely foreign to the type, a treatment almost universally seen in the red pottery to the north and east, it would appear that Sacaton Red was derived from or related to red pottery that occurs in abundance along the northwest Mexican coast, as at Guasave (Ekholm 1942: 74-77). The trend was altered, however, in the Classic Period, with the abundant production of Gila and Salt Reds with which smudging of interiors was heavily associated. Whether an all red pottery made historically by the Pima Indians is in any way related to Sacaton Red remains to be established.

While red pottery appears never to have been strongly favored, it did play an important role in generating the painting of pottery. The long-standing facility in the use of a slip was a technical antecedent to the creation of patterns, whether invented by the Hohokam or whether the idea was borrowed from elsewhere.

Snaketown Unpainted Pottery Plainware

ALL PERIODS

All Phases Except Vahki

GILA PLAIN (GLADWIN AND OTHERS 1937: 205-11)

The notable fact about the plainware the Hohokam produced over a millennium and a half of time, from the Estrella Phase to the end of the Civano Phase, is that it underwent so little change in those characteristics which one must employ to detect phase or even period differences to render the task almost impossible. For this reason, the common utility pottery designated Gila Plain is not a useful diagnostic for close dating, but when seen in large quantities certain details, mostly related to shape, are helpful in identifying samples as early or late and as having come from the Gila Basin or some other source.

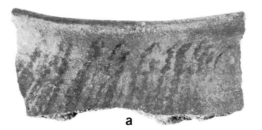

Fig. 12.57. Gila Plain jar rim (a) and body sherd (b) showing marks resulting from use of polishing tool. Length of a, 10.6 cm.

While some variation in temper is observable, most likely the result of individual choices, the normal tempering material was crushed mica schist, liberally mixed with the clay. Both angular and rounded quartz grains are also often present. Mica platelets and temper particles cover the surface, sometimes amounting up to 30 to 40% of the surface area. Vessels were brought to form with the paddle and anvil, and frequent cracking visible on jar interiors where the rims were sharply everted indicates the paste was dry when being laid up. Interior surfaces of jars were not modified, showing the anvil depressions; but outer surfaces, after hand-finishing, were usually given a few casual strokes with a polishing tool, trending from the rim downward. This act certainly did nothing for the quality of the pottery or to enhance it aesthetically, although polishing strokes have been mistaken for painted decoration (Fig. 12.57). Casual polishing may reflect a feeling on the part of the potters that surfaces *should* be treated in that manner because that was the way it was once done. Vahki Plain, on the whole, and early Gila Plain, were smoother surfaced than the later products.

Fire clouds are common, revealing direct contact of the fuel with the pots and related variations in the firing atmosphere which produced color ranges from brown to gray, the former predominating. Vessel wall thicknesses are highly variable, depending on the kind and size of the vessel and whether the measurements are made at the rim, midwall or bottom of the vessel. A reasonable average thickness figure is 8 mm for Gila Plain of the Sedentary Period, twice that of Vahki Plain; but the Gila Plain of the late Pioneer Period was thinner, averaging around 6 mm. In stratified deposits, particularly those in which the test levels spanned the Pioneer and Colonial Periods, the most pronounced change in vessel wall thickness came at the Snaketown-Gila Butte Phase transition. Although not tested, the strengthening of vessel walls may have been a function of a steadily increasing vessel size.

The collection does not have enough whole or restorable examples in it to provide the base for evaluating trends in size differences through time. The strong impression prevails, nevertheless, that although jars were large in Vahki Plain, a doubling in size of storage jars took place by Sedentary Period times. One restored vessel of this age measures 85 cm in diameter and has an estimated capacity of about 200 liters. This apparent size increase could be associated with a presumed greater crop yield and a higher population in Snaketown during the Sedentary Period.

Figure 12.58 provides an inventory of Gila Plain shapes, the examples being drawn from all phases, and Figures 12.59 and 12.60 illustrate a few actual pots. The bodies of jars were typically somewhat vertically compressed at all times. There were, however, noteworthy changes in the nature of the neck and rim. These became progressively shortened through time beginning in Vahki Plain as a slight eversion on a tall neck (Fig. 12.61g), reaching minimum neck height and sharpest rim eversion in the Sedentary Period (Fig. 12.61b), whereupon there was a return again to a taller neck in the Classic Period (Fig. 12.61a). Associated with this trend was also a slight reduction in orifice diameter in relation to maximum vessel diameter. Greater ease in sealing a jar to protect

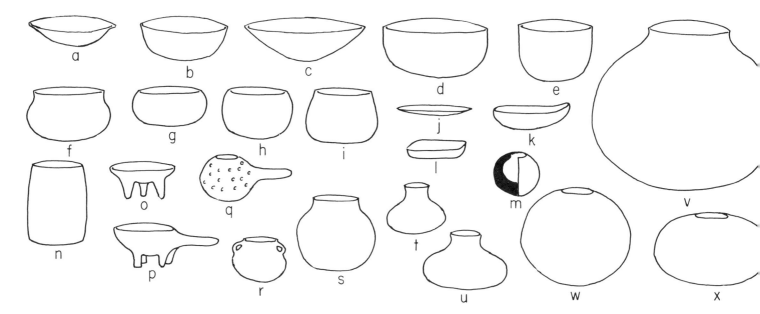

Fig. 12.58. Gila Plain vessel shapes: (a-i) bowls; (j) plate; (k) scoop; (l) rectangular vessel; (m) heavy-walled vessel; (n) beaker; (o-p) legged vessels; (q) colander; (r) handled vessel; (s-x) jars.

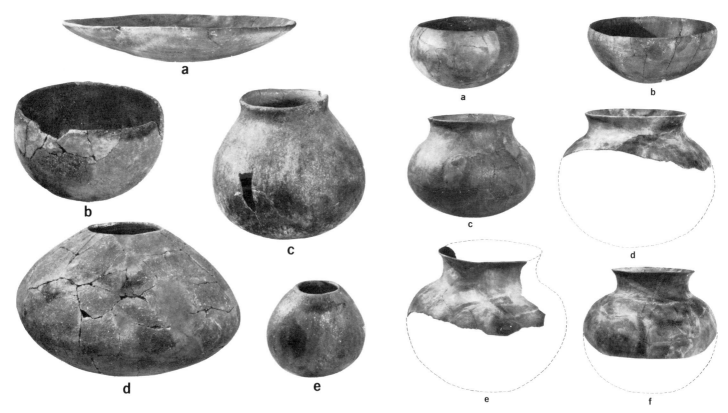

Fig. 12.59. Gila Plain: (a) plate; (b) bowl with smudged interior; (c-e) jars; e is Sweetwater Phase, all others Sacaton Phase. Diameter of d, 30 cm.

Fig. 12.60. Gila Plain of the Pioneer Period. (a-b) Sweetwater Phase bowls; (c-f) jars, Sweetwater Phase except c, Pioneer Period. Diameter of c, 43 cm.

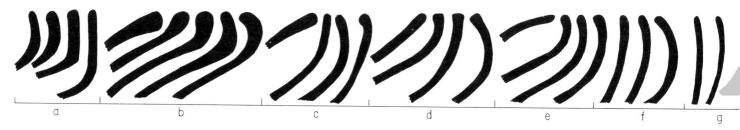

Fig. 12.61. Representative jar rim and neck profiles of Gila Plain (a-f) and Vahki Plain (g): (a) Classic Period; (b) Sedentary Period; (c-d) Colonial Period (Santa Cruz and Gila Butte phases respectively); (e-f) Pioneer Period (Snaketown and Sweetwater-Estrella phases respectively); (g) Pioneer Period (Vahki Phase).

Fig. 12.62. Stucco on Gila Plain. Width, 9.5 cm.

its contents may be offered as a reason for the shrinking mouth diameter.

Jars without everted rims were also typical of the Sedentary Period (Fig. 12.59d) though they had a somewhat earlier beginning. The Gila shoulder, so common in painted pottery, is rarely seen in Gila Plain. When present the specimens date from the Sacaton Phase.

Plates (Fig. 12.59a), scoops (Fig. 12.58k), legged vessels (o), beakers (n), handled vessels (r), and thick-walled vessels (m and Fig. 12.66) were never abundant but, when present, are of Colonial Period age or later. An unexpected shape is a colander (Fig. 12.58q). What appear to be parts of human effigy vessels do occur, but all of them are too fragmentary for reconstruction.

The use of handles in Gila Plain was rare indeed. The few examples noted not only are late but are undistinguished rodlike loops attached vertically below the rims of small jars.

Exterior stucco on jar bottoms (Fig. 12.62), a character associated with aboriginal Yuman pottery, Lower Colorado Buffware (Schroeder 1958) was seen in only one instance, fragments of a single jar of Santa Cruz Phase age. Because the paste and all other characteristics suggested this to have been a locally produced pot, one may infer that it was the result of an idea borrowed from the Yuma neighbors to the west.

On the basis of comparative potsherd counts, plain to painted, Gila Plain in the Estrella Phase may have amounted to 95% of the total pottery output, a figure which steadily diminished to 60% in the Sacaton Phase. A concomitant increase in painted pottery is noted.

The presence of large blackened areas on Gila Plain introduces the question as to whether or not the Hohokam endeavored purposely to achieve smudged surfaces. This intent can be ruled out, I believe, as far as vessel exterior surfaces are concerned, since the observable fire clouds are erratic and placed with no suggestion of a plan. Interior surfaces of bowls, however, are another matter. A small percentage of bowls have all-over blackened interiors which may be presumed to have been intentional. With few exceptions, vessels showing this characteristic dated from the Sacaton Phase, a time when smudging was a common practice among neighboring potters, especially to the northeast. Missing, however, was the polishing which brought the surfaces to a gloss.

It is tempting to establish a new type, Gila Plain Smudged, or Sacaton Smudged, but it seems better, because of its infrequency, to accept smudging as within the range of variation of Gila Plain. A generalization that can be made is that intentional smudging of pottery among the Hohokam was not one of their strengths before the Classic Period when the technique came to them as one of a number of new attributes. Failure during earlier times to make much use of smudging seems to fit the broader ceramic tradition of contemporary western Mexico.

PIONEER PERIOD

Vahki Phase

VAHKI PLAIN (GLADWIN AND OTHERS 1937: 211-12)

The designation of the oldest Hohokam utility pottery as Vahki Plain introduces the question as to whether or not the category is justifiable on taxonomic grounds. In 1937 it was believed the division was worth making because it called attention to the qualities in form, thinness, better finish, more uniform color, and the more finely divided mica temper in which Vahki Plain differs from Gila Plain. Limiting the type to the Vahki Phase also called attention to its precursory position in Hohokam ceramics and to its qualitative excellence. Even though the difficulty of separating Vahki Plain from Gila Plain, except in large lots, is recognized, I see no reason at this time to restructure the classification, because nothing really new would be gained by it.

Shapes were limited to bowls and jars (Fig. 12.63), and a single sherd of a small-mouthed, neckless spheroidal vessel suggests that there may have been a wider range than seems apparent. Fragments of scoops, plates, flared bowls, effigies, and legged vessels have not been seen, and there are no examples of handles.

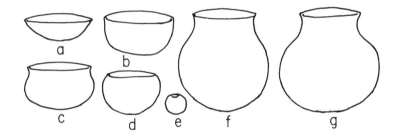

Fig. 12.63. Vahki Plain vessel shapes: (a-d) bowls; (e) spheroidal vessel; (f-g) jars.

Generally speaking, jar rims were only slightly everted on a relatively tall neck (Fig. 12.61g). Jar diameters up to 0.45 cm have been measured. The average vessel size was probably somewhat smaller at this time than it was in later periods, a difference possibly attributable to more bountiful crops resulting from the mastery of agricultural techniques.

The outstanding character of Vahki Plain is its thinness. Even in the largest vessels, body walls were only 3 to 5 mm thick with an average of about 4 mm. That vessels of such fragile nature could satisfy domestic needs is evident, but it is also clear that, because of thinness and low tensile strength of the clay, the mortality rate was high. Refuse deposits of early Pioneer Period phases carry an especially high count of sherds per unit of trash volume. Furthermore, because of the tenderness of the clay, potsherds are small, averaging 200-300 per kg as compared with 100-150 in the late deposits that produced Gila Plain.

OTHER CERAMIC CONSIDERATIONS

So far we have been mainly concerned with the typological approach to pottery, looking at it in terms of the kinds that were produced at any one time, with the idea of establishing the ceramic components useful in distinguishing phases. Furthermore, this has been done in the reverse order of development, that is, beginning with the recent and ending with the oldest manifestations. Attention should now be paid to a review of certain elements in an evolutionary sense, looking at items and changes in them in the natural order of events, or to identify traits for other reasons. To limit this section, I have made arbitrary judgments as to what should be included, using those subjects which appear to me to be most meaningful and helpful in understanding pottery in Hohokam culture.

Most of the points made in the discussion of 1937 (Gladwin and others: 220-29) still apply, and they will not be repeated here. More important are observations possible now after the recent new work, or, which for some reason, were not included then.

Technology

Hohokam pottery, seen over about a 1,700-year span, exhibits remarkable stability in basic methods of construction, surface treatment, and firing. At the beginning both painted and plain-wares were made of essentially the same paste. Toward the end of the Pioneer Period minor modifications in the paste of painted pottery led to a lighter background, coupled also with the application of a wash resulting in a crisper and more sharply delineated painted decoration. Associated with the brightening of the patterns was a marked increase in the range of motifs and in design organization. It was then that the most distinctive of all Hohokam painted elements, the small geometric units and life forms, found their maximum levels of expression.

Shapes

Inventories of vessel forms given for each type made clear a gradual proliferation of shapes through time, probably in response to the needs of society expanding in both numbers and complexity of organization, and to a continuing flow of stimuli out of the south. The greatest range came in the Sedentary Period. It is worth noting that human and animal effigy vessels were present in the ceramics of the Hohokam practically from the beginning and that they therefore might have served as the prototypes for similar forms among the Anasazi of later times. Models of effigy vessels in Mexico abound in great variety, extending into Pre-Classic times, and varying in style from place to place and time to time. Close analogies with Hohokam products can be found by searching the literature (compare Fig. 11.10 with Porter 1956: Fig. 7h and Fig. 9q), but specific relationships cannot be identified because the data are lacking.

Shapes distinctive to the Hohokam, as compared with other Southwestern groups, were: the flare-rimmed bowl with modestly everted rim at first and accentuated in the Sedentary Period; the shouldered jar, a hallmark of the Sedentary Period; plates, having had a history about as long as Hohokam pottery itself, legged vessels, usually tripod, but sometimes tetrapod and even more legs, Colonial Period and later; the cauldron, an unusually large, wide-mouthed vessel of Colonial-Sedentary Periods; rectangular vessels with rounded bottoms (early) and flat bottoms in late times; and probably related elongated dishes in plainware with eroded inner surfaces; the so-called "lamps" or heavy-walled vessels, unique to the Colonial and Sedentary Periods; finally censers. The predilection to produce eccentric forms appears to have been strongest in the Sedentary Period.

While there was appreciable duplication in forms between Hohokam, Anasazi, and Mogollon ceramics, there are enough shapes unique to the Hohokam to warrant considering their pottery as the product of a different tradition than the others, even Mogollon, which, in terms of age or longevity, was closely parallel to Hohokam. The probability is that Hohokam and Mogollon, although both Mexican derived, sprang from different sources and that lines of contact with the south remained open to the Hohokam, less so to the Mogollon.

In spite of the specific analogies that can be pointed to between Hohokam and Mexican pottery, there are many other elements in Mesoamerica that did not enter the Southwest. These include a vast array of shapes of ceramic products, and specific traits as the annular base, the use of molds, champlevé, engraving and negative painting, to mention but a few. What this suggests, of course, is a weakening of the complex of transmitted elements as a function of distance, a recognized phenomenon in cultural diffusion. This does not deny the possibility of other controlling factors as well.

Note has been taken of vessel size increase with the passage of time, both in plain and painted wares. Quantification has not been attempted, though the topic is an interesting one and should be pursued because of the light that such a study might shed on social changes.

The use of handles on vessels by the Hohokam was not one of their strengths. Loop handles, vertically set, were seldom employed and late when present. The basket handle on bowls was commonest of all, with some use of it in the Pioneer Period but most often in the Sedentary Period. A single anomaly was the sticking of two lumps of clay 10 cm in diameter to the opposite sides of a Gila Butte Red-on-buff jar after it was made to provide a better grip. Although secondarily fired, it was a precarious way of attaching handles, witnessed by the fact that both of them broke off when the vessel itself was crushed. The minimal use of handles by the Hohokam may prove to be a helpful dimension in relating their pottery to southern traditions as the latter become better known.

CENSERS

Heavy-walled clay vessels, whose most likely function was that of holding and burning incense, were first detected in the Estrella Phase. The probability is, however, that they were known and used from the beginning and that they were a component of the ceramic complex that the Hohokam brought with them. The early examples usually carry the grooved surface treatment of the Pioneer Period, and they are typable either as Vahki Red or as the painted pottery of the phase (Fig. 12.64a). Double receptacled censers were first noted in the Snaketown phase (Fig. 12.64b).

Form changes through time included transitions from a simple outcurved bowl type, through outward slanted or vertical-sided units (Fig. 11.16), to a pronounced pinched-waist type (Fig. 11.3). The latter were typical during the Sedentary Period. Censers with false-bottoms, providing a void for gravel or pellets, thereby making a rattle, were also confined to the latter period. Censers in the form of animals were first detected in the Snaketown Phase, although the best of them date from the Sacaton Phase, a time to which the human effigy censers must also be

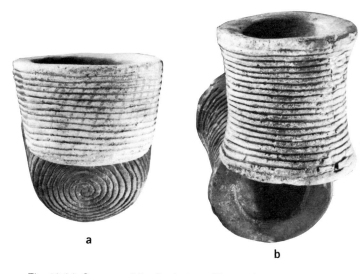

a   b

Fig. 12.64. Censers of the Snaketown Phase, photographed on a mirror. Height of b, 6.6 cm.

ascribed. Bas-relief decoration is generally a late characteristic. Little or no use appears to have been made of the censer during the Classic Period.

Specific analogies of Hohokam type censers in the cultures of Mexico are not easily found. But incense burners of great variety were widely used there and for a long time. All of the Hohokam examples do not show the effects of burning substances in them, and it may be that their use was symbolic. Others, however, are fire- and carbon-stained, extending even to outside surfaces in one case (Fig. 14.23). The sacrifice of censers, as in the case of Cache 1: 9F, adds to the likelihood that the idea of the objects and practices related to them were imports from the south. Evidently the complex did not find a receptive home in the neighboring cultures of the Southwest. Two specimens illustrated by Pepper (1920: Figs. 91, 143) are altogether different than those the Hohokam used.

ELONGATE VESSELS

Apart from the rectangular containers in the painted pottery category which date principally from the Colonial (Gladwin and others 1937: Plate CLVI, d, f-i) and Sedentary Periods (Fig. 11.3), there are eleven whole and fragmentary vessels of plainware which are shallow, round-ended and about twice as long as they are wide. Sizes range from 13.2 to 19.1 cm in length. A detail common to all of them is an abraded interior bottom, a post firing condition, derived evidently from the use to which the vessels were put (Fig. 12.65). Nine of the specimens date from the Pioneer Period, representing all but the Estrella Phase, and two are assignable to the Colonial Period.

A specialized vessel type of wide distribution in ancient Mexico is the chili grater, or *molcajete*. Generally bowl-shaped, the floors were mechanically incised when the clay was plastic, to provide the rough surface needed to abrade chili peppers. The Snaketown specimens do not show this, but there can be no reasonable doubt about the fact that the rough bottoms were the result of rubbing

Fig. 12.65. Elongate vessels of Gila Plain with abraded bottoms. Length of *e*, 19.1 cm.

something on them, a function for which the vessel's shape was well suited.

Although we have no ethnobotanical proof that chili peppers were known to the Hohokam, or even anywhere in the Southwest in pre-Spanish times, the likelihood nevertheless exists that they did. The acid juice of the *Capsicum* plant together with the effects of the physical rubbing of the fruit could well have etched the vessel bottoms that we see. Kelly (1945a: 9) made an interesting observation with respect to her work at Culiacan, namely, that chili graters were minimally present in her Early I and II horizons and absent thereafter. The specimens under consideration from Snaketown are early as well with no traces of the artifact type after about A.D. 900. The time equivalency between the Culiacan and Snaketown chronologies has not been established, but the patterns of occurrence match.

HEAVY-WALLED VESSELS

An interesting shape category that deserves attention consists of 56 fragments and two whole specimens of heavy-walled small-mouthed containers that obviously met a special need. The paste is that of Gila Plain, course and heavily laden with mica. The outer surfaces were accorded no more treatment than hand smoothing. Paddle marks on some are still detectable. Inner surfaces are rough, sometimes showing finger indentations and smears left by forming the cavity through the small aperture, usually only big enough to accommodate the largest finger.

The sizes of these specimens are surprisingly uniform. Where measurable, the approximate ranges are as follows: diameters, 9.5 to 11.5 cm; heights, 7.2 to 11.0 cm; wall thicknesses, 1.0 to 3.0 cm, and orifice diameters, 2.6 to 3.8 cm. Figure 12.66 illustrates the shape range, the dominant characters being the vertically compressed body, sometimes with a slight shoulder, and a flattened bottom. In a few instances the orifices have slightly extended or everted rims.

The high incidence of breakage and the nature of the fracturing suggest they may have been intentionally broken. Although there are many body fragments, 25% of the lot are broken vertically, that is, from orifice to bottom, making literally a vertical cross-section. Shatter lines indicate the pieces were given a heavy blow on the bottom to produce this effect. Once broken, the pieces were tossed out with other refuse, since most of them were recovered in trash mounds. The two whole examples were associated with cremations (18: 5F, Fig. 10.2d; 5: 11H) both of the Sacaton Phase.

The nine vessels reported from the earlier work (Gladwin and others 1937: 207) were assigned to the Santa Cruz and Sacaton Phases. The present lot was distributed as follows: Sacaton Phase 18, Sacaton-Santa Cruz Transition 7, Santa Cruz Phase 11, Gila

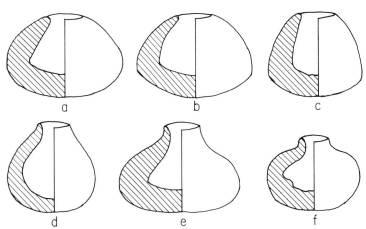

Fig. 12.66. Heavy-walled vessels of Gila Plain: (a) Santa Cruz-Sacaton Phase transition; (b-e) Sacaton Phase; (f) Gila Butte Phase. Diameter of *b*, 10.5 cm.

Butte Phase 1, Colonial-Sedentary 13, Unplaced 8, making a total of 58. There can be no doubt about the lateness of this trait, none was earlier than the Colonial Period, and dominance was reached evidently in the Sedentary Period. Reports on Classic Period sites make no note of them, so the element seems to have died out by that time. No shape change through time is detectable.

The principal interest connected with these is the use to which they may have been put. Interiors show one of two conditions: either highly oxidized, brick-red surfaces, indicating exposure to intense heat generated by abundant oxygen, and fuel, an uncommon condition in small-mouthed vessels, or, dense black surfaces, including the lip of the orifice, derived from incomplete combustion of organic materials. In fact organic residue has been recovered from one of the two unbroken specimens (A-27, 136). Identification of the brownish caked material has not been made. When ignited it glows like punk, and the smoke has a pleasant incense quality about it. Some years ago, a heavy-walled vessel found during road construction near Sacaton yielded a lump of pitch about 6.5 cm in diameter and 1.5 cm thick. It burns readily and the odor reminds one of pinyon pitch (Information from David J. Jones; pitch specimen donated to Arizona State Museum No A-41,157). It may be concluded that these containers did function as a sort of crucible, either for incense or highly combustible substances, to give off light, heat, or aroma. Association with cremations suggests death rite uses. The specimen resting on a palette (Fig. 10.2d) is evidence of the same concept as is manifested by the effigy censer and the large palette recovered in Cache 1:9F (Fig. 11.1). The plainness of the objects and the common occurrence of fragments in trash hint also of more secular uses.

Kelly (1945a: 99) reports identical heavy vessels from Culiacan, Sinaloa, the only instances I have been able to find in the literature outside of the Hohokam area. She makes the following interesting observation "... Five of the twelve (show) evidence of thin interior coating of black, pitchy substance; on one specimen this has run down the exterior from the mouth, as though contents had boiled over. At the risk of being fantastic, one may suggest tentatively that these vessels were used for working rubber. At least, a ball game is reported in early sources for neighboring districts ..." These presumably date from Kelly's Middle Culiacan horizon. Though difficult to correlate specifically with the Hohokam chronology, they are probably of about the same age.

Surface Texturing

The grooving and incising of both bowl and jar exteriors during the earlier stages of Hohokam pottery history remains one of the enigmas of the art. The question is: What prompted the technique? Was it a truly local invention or was it borrowed? The pottery of the oldest horizon, the Vahki Phase, clearly indicates that grooving was not practiced from the start. Tests 10G-12A, B, and C, Levels 1-4, on an aggregate of 16,500 sherds produced no grooving. But Estrella Phase deposits show a low percentage, less than 1%, of grooving on either Estrella Red-on-gray or Vahki Red. It consists of mechanically deepening and widening the joint lines between the spirally laid up coils by which the vessels were made. The tool used was evidently a blunt stylus. While this style of texturing persisted into the Sweetwater Phase, during that time free incising also was introduced. Coil joints no longer imposed restrictions on the craftsmen, and as a result patterned incising became an innovation (Fig. 12.67). From the Sweetwater Phase on, incising became more prevalent, coupled, however, with a steady decrease in the quality or precision of the texturing. The technique died at the end of the Gila Butte Phase, a time when only token scoring of surfaces was practiced.

Although the conditions were present for the local innovation of grooving, namely the spiral coiling of pottery which needed only the tracing of the coil joints with a blunt instrument, the fact

Fig. 12.67. Sweetwater Red-on-gray bowl, inverted to show the incised pattern. Diameter, 17.2 cm.

remains that surface texturing by incising, channeling, and grooving was both so widespread and early in Mexico that, in all probability, the idea spread from there as an integral part of the pottery-making complex. Without implying direct connections but as evidence of similar textured pottery to the south, reference is made to type K-2 of Epoc I in Monte Alban (Caso, Bernal, and Acosta 1967: 47, 193) dated at about 700 B.C. (ibid., 267), to channeled decoration in Chupícuaro Black Ware (Porter 1956: Fig. 4t, Fig. 6j) and to an impressively similar tradition at Tlatilco (Piña Chan 1958: Fig. 47). Whatever the origin of Hohokam grooving and incising may have been, they employed the techniques more often than did any other groups of southwestern potters, and peculiarly theirs was the fact that the quality of the work steadily degenerated from a high precision beginning to token scoring and complete loss in 600 or 700 years. This represents an unusual case of what may be called the devolution of a trait. If developmental steps leading to the oldest manifestation of grooving exist, the evidence is not to be found at Snaketown.

Painting

Applied pigment on exposed vessel surfaces was preferred by the Hohokam over modeled or surface-textured pottery. Expectably, most attention was given to the readily visible surfaces, but, curiously, on some Estrella Red-on-gray jar interiors, decoration was extended well below the visibility line. Flared bowl and flat exteriors, unseen when the vessels were resting in their natural position, carried complicated patterns, in the Snaketown and Gila Butte Phases. This custom persisted as a few widely spaced trailing lines in the Santa Cruz Phase, after which exterior decoration on bowls passed out of existence (Gladwin and others 1937: Fig. 111).

If the previously discussed types have been examined, the unfolding of Hohokam pottery painting will have become apparent. In synopsis, the art began probably as the manipulation of the red slip which made Vahki Red by reducing it to bands and lines, polished over the pigment at first, unpolished later. The standard early linework was rectilinear and the first formal subdivision of the decorative field in bowls was quartering. Chevron-filled units evidently led to the development of hachured patterns, the linework becoming progressively narrower and more closely spaced with the passage of time. By the end of the Pioneer Period an exceptional degree of formalization had been reached and the art canons imposed a straightjacket upon the artist. Technically the work was good, but except for the rare use of life forms the repertoire was nearly limited to large interlocking scrolls and opposed stepped elements, always hatch-filled.

Renouncing the monotony of this style of painting ushered in the beginning of the Colonial Period. There were marked changes, not so much in the basic elements but in the virtuosity with which they were treated individually and as components in complex compositions. Hachure was replaced by solid linework. The peak of excellence in layout and in execution is seen in Santa Cruz Red-on-buff at the end of the Colonial Period.

Then started a trend toward grossness of vessel size and coarseness of linework and layout, which was unmatched before or after, phenomena probably coupled with a higher level of production of pottery than at any other time. All of this took place in the Sedentary Period.

As though having burned themselves out, the Classic Period potters produced only a small fraction of the red-on-buff that issued from the hands of the artists before, and the forms were limited and the patterns stiffly rectilinear. By jumping the little-known "interregnum" of A.D. 1400–1700, we see the thread faintly carried on by the historic red-on-buff pottery of the Pima Indians (Fig. 12.112). What remain for someone to determine are the reasons for the shifts in style and trend.

Hohokam pottery painting has the earmarks of an essentially internal evolutionary tradition, though with occasional infusions from the outside. Furthermore, the tradition was peculiarly Hohokam. Leavitt's detailed comparison (1962) of Hohokam and Mesa Verde Anasazi painted decoration led him to conclude that there was no relationship between the two traditions.

LIFE FORMS

Much of the uniqueness and charm of Hohokam pottery arises from the emphasis the artists put on the simple but dynamic rendering of life forms: birds, reptiles, mammals, and human figures. They also devised a bewildering array of small geometric figures, often repeated over and over again. The latter have been frivolously called the "Hohokam alphabet." Amsden (1936:43-44) noted these distinctive aspects of Hohokam pottery when he referred to the decorator as a "... master of the extemporaneous stroke, using her brush in truly creative delineation, whereas the Pueblo decorator used hers as a methodical generator of prim lines in formal geometric figures. The latter is a well-schooled draughtsman, the former an unschooled artist."

In the life form category, modes of portrayal, associated elements and details related to the representation of the human form, are hints of Hohokam customs. In fact, cultural elements can be added to the inventory on the basis of "pictures" when the objects themselves have not survived, as, for example, flutes and fancy headdresses. Art style changes and shifts in emphasis on specific animals through time make life forms a topic worthy of separate treatment. In the same way, the repeated small geometric elements add an interesting footnote to artistic endeavors.

The following type-frequency study of life forms is based on the total sample of potsherds and whole vessels recovered during the 1964–65 operation. Later, in reviewing the subject matter repertoire, the collection of 1934–35 has also been drawn on. Were one to examine the pottery from other sites, the range of portrayals could no doubt be much expanded; but time and space factors have limited this assessment to the resources from Snaketown alone. The sample is a large one, consisting of 1,347 fragments and 7 whole or restored vessels. The quantitative results are tabulated in Figure 12.93. Time assignments were made on a typological basis from the Snaketown through the Sacaton Phases. The phases of the Classic Period have been omitted, because by that time the life form had all but died out in Hohokam art (Haury 1945a: 62).

A primary distinction has been made between positive and negative portrayals because they have both chronological and topical values. Within each of these categories, the subjects are looked at separately, employing criteria as, for example, layout, best judged to bring out differences. The significant analyzable features in the various lots are not always the same. Inspection of Figure 12.93 quickly reveals the fact that the first animal depictions were in negative painting, an interesting point in Hohokam art history. This means that the artist thought of the form as unpainted background, the effect being achieved by treating the space around it.

Although depictions of life forms are known in media other than pottery, for example, carvings in shell and modeled effigy vessels in clay from early phases of the Pioneer Period, it is not until the Snaketown Phase that the first painted animal forms appear. Close examination of a large sample of Sweetwater Red-on-gray provides no hints whatsoever of animals, even though a few geometric elements do occur and the modeled effigy jar was known. The first efforts are seen in Snaketown Red-on-buff, and, without exception in the collection at hand, the figures are in negative. Furthermore the creatures reveal a finesse in depiction that seems incompatible with what appear to be first efforts at animal drawing. Only rarely used at this time, the subject matter was evidently restricted to lizards and birds (Gladwin and others 1937: Pl. CLXXXII, i-k; Fig. 246r-t). If this departure from the strict geometric canons of the times was not a spontaneous creation, then one must look to the pottery of Mexico for the inspiration because highly decorated earthenware was not yet being made elsewhere in the Southwest. It appears that the distinctive geometric figure best described as a serrated cross (Fig. 12.98) could be a derivative from Chupícuaro pottery. If true, then a similar explanation may account for the animals. Although extensive comparative studies of Chupícuaro materials have not been made, it is known that life forms do occur. The alternatives are to believe that life form painting was indigenous to the Hohokam, or that other forces were at work.

That the mode of expression took the form of negative representations may be related to the outlook of the decorators. The close packing of hachure lines, particularly when 60 to 70% of the background was covered in this way, called attention to the unpainted zones. What came through as untouched spaces may have been thought of as the prime decorative elements. In support of this idea is a negatively shown S-like figure (Fig. 12.41a) which has no apparent prototypes and was not obviously representative or symbolic of anything we know. Its genesis is traceable to the weak interlock of two scrolls.

Birds in Positive

What motivated the Hohokam to favor the bird in painting, stone and shell carving, we do not know; but the fact remains that various species were shown in numerous poses sometimes in combination with other creatures, in positive or negative painted fashion, and occasionally in a manner which suggests the reenactment of a story or an idea. Russell notes that the bird played prominent roles in Pima myths and songs, the quail, raven, humming bird and roadrunner among them, and that four birds were the causes of diseases: the vulture, eagle, hawk and owl (1908: 263). These modern practices and beliefs may be survivals from ancient times, and the Hohokam depictions may have been inspired by still older concepts. Stylistic changes through time make these subjects both interesting and useful as period markers.

Quail. The identification of bird species drawn by the Hohokam cannot always be made with certainty. Among those that leave little doubt as to what they had in mind is the quail, one of the preferred avian subjects (Fig. 12.68). The top-knot feather has been interpreted by some to be the beak of a parrot, but in viewing scores of examples, the intent seems certain.

Using the sample of about 150 potsherds on which the quail is found (Fig. 12.73) the following observations are in order: The earliest depiction of the quail was in the Gila Butte Phase, reaching dominance numerically in the Santa Cruz, and it was little used in the Sacaton Phase. It was never shown in negative as were many other birds.

Preference in basic layout was not the same through time, the emphasis going from massed figures to series between free fringes to single figures framed in the three successive phases. Birds shown in bands established by lines (Fig. 12.28e) were seldom used. The working habits of the artist probably determined the orientation of the birds, that is, whether the feet or the heads were directed toward the rim of the vessel. If painting proceeded from rim toward the center of the field, one might expect the heads at the rim. A start in the center of the field might produce the reverse. At any rate, there appears to be little utility in this feature as a time marker. With few exceptions, the birds are right-facing, again probably the result of right-handedness or the acquired working habits of the painters. Bodies for the most part are filled-in solid, although hatching is seen more often in the Gila Butte Phase than later, a carry-over from the dominance of hachuring in the Snaketown Phase.

While other birds were frequently shown with outstretched wings, the convention in showing the quail was with wings folded. One exception (Fig. 12.68j) was noted. Greatest variability in eye-depiction was in the Gila Butte Phase. An elongated

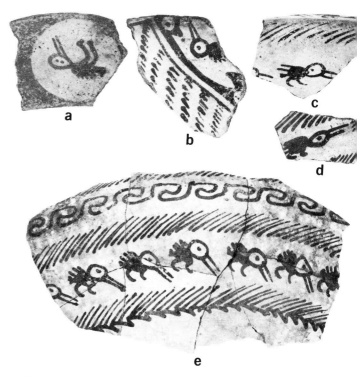

Fig. 12.69. Santa Cruz Red-on-buff with humming bird motif (?). Width of *e*, 27 cm.

body, spike tail, portrayal of toes, and occasional association with X's (?tracks) and solid circles (?eggs) are other features typical of the Gila Butte Phase. In the Santa Cruz Phase, the head was often larger than the body, the body being plump, often with a triangular tail; the top-knot feather and the beak were often made by a single curved line. Toes and associated geometric figures were not shown. The few examples of the quail on Sacaton Red-on-buff are somewhat larger than earlier forms, and generally heavier-lined in execution.

?Humming Bird. A bird with the body configuration of a quail but with a long open bill, and no topknot feather suggests attempt to portray a humming bird (Fig. 12.69). This figure seems never to have been popular, since there are only nine examples of it and all are limited to Santa Cruz Red-on-buff. One of these (Fig. 12.69a), although a profile view, shows the two-eye distortion. The humming bird is mentioned frequently in varying versions of the Pima flood myth (Bahr 1971: 248 ff).

Water Bird. About as prevalent as the quail and in many ways duplicating the portrayal of the quail was a long-necked, long-billed water bird. The heron or crane appears to have been the model for this group, represented by 157 examples in the positive. The subject also is shown infrequently in the negative, reviewed elsewhere.

Figure 12.73 summarizes the details. It should be noted that in the layout category the single figure that covers the whole decorative field, limited to the Sacaton Phase, was not included.

In general, the changes in orientation and body treatment parallel the characteristics already noted for the quail. Bills agape appear to have been more prevalent in late than in early times, and left-facing birds were more common than among quail. Figure 12.70 shows a typical series of sherds bearing this subject matter.

?Cormorant. Figure 12.71 illustrates four of nine sherds that show a bird with elongated body and in *a* a forward directed crest. The others lack this feature, but they appear to be abstractions of the same bird. The general profile of a cormorant is suggested, but this identification is sheer speculation.

It should be noted that all specimens with this motif are Gila Butte Red-on-buff bowl fragments and that in every case the bird is presented in massed layouts. In Figure 12.71a, the bird is

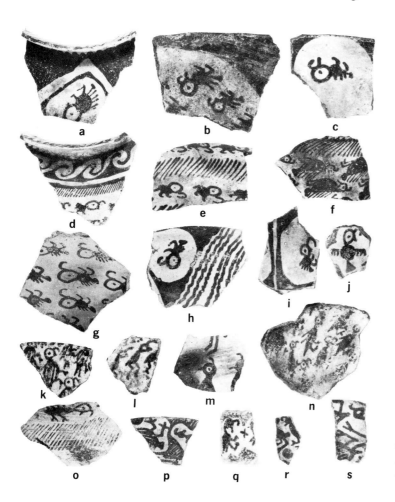

Fig. 12.68. Quail, painted in positive: (a-c) Sacaton Red-on-buff; (d-j) Santa Cruz Red-on-buff; (k-s) Gila Butte Red-on-buff. Width of *a*, 11.5 cm.

associated with a lizard occupying a central position in the field of decoration.

Parrot. The Hohokam seldom painted the parrot, strange enough considering the bird was well known at least from the time of Christ and the probable importance the feathers held for them. No examples of the parrot painted in the positive exist in the collection; there is only one instance of a negative representation. The outstanding characteristic of the bird, the beak, was accentuated, leaving no doubt of the artist's intent (Fig. 12.72m).

Birds in Negative

We next come to the depiction of birds in negative fashion, that is, in which the unpainted background color of the vessel constitutes the figure by blocking in the space around it (Fig. 12.72). This treatment is unique in two respects: First, the oldest bird painting among the Hohokam, in the Snaketown Phase, was exclusively in the negative manner; second, most of those shown were species associated with water. Sixty-seven fragments make up the collection, distributed as indicated in Figure 12.73. Apart from the negative approach, another basic difference distinguishes these from the quails and water birds already discussed. With five exceptions, wings are outstretched and heads are turned aside in contrast to the silhouette treatment of the others. Three of the five exceptions were Sacaton Red-on-buff, the entire sample from that phase (Fig. 12.72a). It would be interesting to know why these differences in attitude existed.

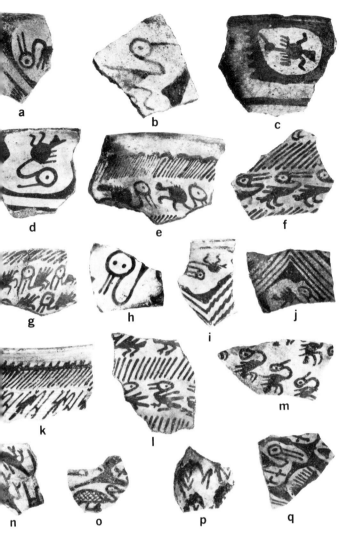

Fig. 12.70. Water birds, painted in positive: (a-c) Sacaton Red-on-buff; (d-j) Santa Cruz Red-on-buff; (k-q) Gila Butte Red-on-buff. Width of c, 11 cm.

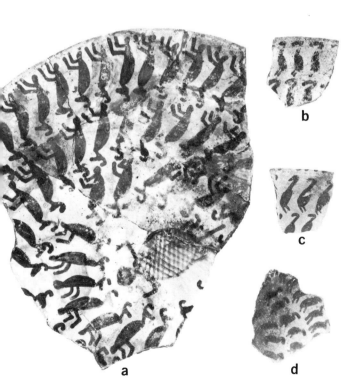

Fig. 12.71. Unidentified birds (? cormorant) on Gila Butte Red-on-buff. Width of a, 22 cm.

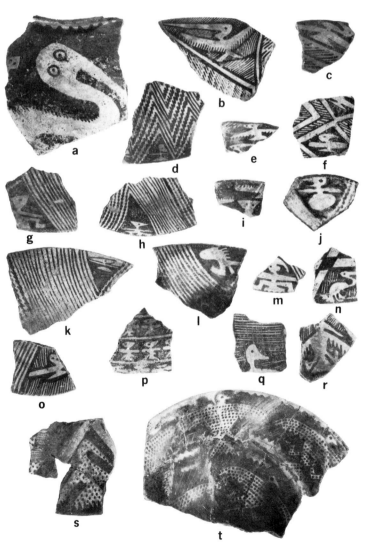

Fig. 12.72. Birds shown in negative. Rim orientation of vessels adjusted to place subjects in natural viewing position: (a) Sacaton Red-on-buff; (b-m) Santa Cruz Red-on-buff; (n-r) Gila Butte Red-on-buff; (s, t) Snaketown Red-on-buff. Width of t, 25 cm.

PHASE	Quail – Massed	Quail – Fringed	Quail – Framed	Quail – Banded	Quail – Sub-total	Orient. Head to rim	Orient. Feet to rim	Orient. Do not know	Facing Right	Facing Left	Body Hatched	Body Solid	Wings Folded	Wings Outstretched	Wings Not shown	Eyes Neg. circle	Eyes Dot	Eyes Do not know	Hummingbird Various	Water – Massed	Water – Fringed	Water – Framed	Water – Banded	Water – Do not know	Water – Sub-total	Orient. Head to rim	Orient. Feet to rim	Orient. Do not know	Facing Right	Facing Left	Body Hatched	Body Solid	Wings Folded	Wings Outstretched	Wings Not shown	Eyes Neg. circle	Eyes Dot	Eyes Double dot	Eyes Do not know	Neg. Massed	Neg. Framed	Neg. Solitary	Neg. Do not know	Neg. Sub-total
SACATON	2	0	6	1	9	2	4	3	9	0	0	9	9	0	0	0	9	0	0	0	0	6	0	4	10	2	3	6	8	2	0	10	10	0	0	0	6	0	4	0	0	1	3	4
SANTA CRUZ	23	53	39	6	121	42	31	48	120	1	3	118	120	1	0	1	100	20	9	7	45	23	6	21	103	37	28	38	86	17	1	102	102	1	1	1	75	2	24	9	19	0	4	32
GILA BUTTE	15	3	3	0	21	8	4	9	19	2	5	16	21	0	4	2	12	3	0	21	11	7	2	3	44	22	13	9	29	15	9	35	44	0	8	1	30	0	5	5	10	0	6	21
SNAKETOWN	0	0	0	0	0	0	0	0	0	0	0	0	0	0	0	0	0	0	0	0	0	0	0	0	0	0	0	0	0	0	0	0	0	0	0	0	0	0	0	6	5	0	0	11
TOTAL	40	56	48	7	151														9	28	57	36	8	28	157															20	34	1	13	68

Fig. 12.73. Quantitative and stylistic study of bird forms in Hohokam pottery. Birds in combination with other life forms not shown.

It appears that painting zoomorphic figures was an innovation late in the Snaketown Phase. Birds and lizards were evidently the sole subjects, and often associated with them was the liberal use of dots as fillers in the body areas. Subjects at this time were a short-billed bird (?eagle) (Fig. 12.72t) but dominantly a long-billed bird (Fig. 12.72r,s). The latter was apparently in the minds of the artists also in Gila Butte Red-on-buff (Fig. 12.72n), although a departure from that theme is evident in the image of a duck (Fig. 12.72q) and a probable pelican (Fig. 12.72b). A trend toward abridgement of the bird form is seen in examples g-l (Fig. 12.72), some of which are intermediate steps between realism and the complete abstract representations that also were highly popular. Figure 12.72k is a rare instance of an artist's slip in failing to complete blocking out the background. In Sacaton Red-on-buff, both quantity and quality suffered, and bigness of the bird figure was the vogue, matching the trend in other life form renderings.

Birds in Combination With Other Creatures

When birds were combined with other life forms, positive painting was employed almost exclusively. Two examples in the collection show the bird with the lizard, one in Snaketown Red-on-buff, the other in Gila Butte Red-on-buff. When bird and snake were joined, an action scene resulted in which the bird vigorously pecked at the reptile. Variations on this theme range from a single bird to a series of them strung out along the snake's body, working on it from head to tail. The body of the snake is usually represented by plain or cross-hachure, sometimes as a solid line, straight or sinuous. No whole examples were recovered at Snaketown, but a plate of Rillito Red-on-brown found in a site near Tucson (Ariz. BB:13:43) and equivalent in age to Santa Cruz

Fig. 12.74. Rillito Red-on-brown plate associated with Cremation 1 in Ariz. BB:13:43 near San Xavier Mission. The scene represents a snake under attack by a series of birds. Central hole may represent ritual "killing." Diameter, 34.5 cm.

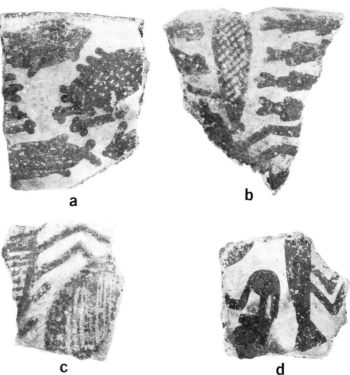

Fig. 12.75. Bird-serpent patterns: (a, b) Sacaton Red-on-buff; (c-f) Santa Cruz Red-on-buff; (g-i) Gila Butte Red-on-buff. Width of *a*, 13.5 cm.

Fig. 12.77. Gila Butte Red-on-buff showing bird and fish. Width of *a*, 6 cm.

Red-on-buff dramatically illustrates the pictorial quality of the theme (Fig. 12.74). Fragments selected from the Snaketown sample are illustrated in Figure 12.75. Frequencies were as follows: Gila Butte Red-on-buff 7; Santa Cruz Red-on-buff 34 (one of which was in negative, Fig. 12.75f); Sacaton Red-on-buff 2.

The bird involved in this act was either a long-billed long-necked water bird, or a long-billed stubby-necked type which fits the profile of the one suggested to be a humming bird; but the association of these two creatures appears to have no basis in nature. The roadrunner would be the likely subject, known for its skill in overcoming snakes. When identifying characteristics are given or are preserved on the sherds, the reptile is always the rattlesnake. The combining of the bird and serpent, also frequently depicted in shell, was probably much more than a diverting art style. For the origin of the concept, we must look to the south (Chap. 18).

The fish in Hohokam art was both rare and stylized, but its identity seems certain in a simple story-telling scene of a water bird with one in its beak (Fig. 12.76). Only five Gila Butte Red-on-buff and one Sacaton Red-on-buff sherds show the bird and fish together, and they are so fragmentary that the exact relationship cannot be recovered. Four are illustrated in Figure 12.77.

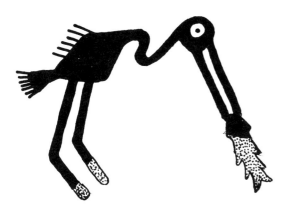

Fig. 12.76. Water bird with fish in beak, Sacaton Red-on-buff. Stippled parts represent reconstructions. Actual size of bird about 5 cm high. (See also Fig. 12.92u).

Reptiles in Positive

Except in a broad way, the identifying characteristics of reptiles in the painted form were less clearly shown than in carved stone or etched shell. In the latter two media, the sidewinder and horned toad were unmistakably represented. But on pottery, the painted reptiles cannot always be certainly separated as to turtles or lizards, although the serpent, sometimes with rattles, and rarely the horned toad, possibly the Gila Monster, can be distinguished. Although the technique provided the opportunity to depict more identifying marks, the artists neglected in most cases to take advantage of it.

Turtles and Lizards. In the following analysis no serious effort has been made to separate turtles and lizards, and fewer categories have been used than in the bird analyses because, in general, the trends duplicate each other. Specific departures will be noted. Turning first to positive-painted forms: None occur in the collection dating from the Snaketown Phase, although subjects in negative were shown. Numerically, the sample of 152 units was heavy in Gila Butte Red-on-buff (63), heaviest in Santa Cruz Red-on-buff (82), and nearly extinct in Sacaton Red-on-buff (7). The progression in layout was from massed to fringed forms with framed figures strong in both phases of the Colonial Period (Fig. 12.86). No examples of the banded layout were seen. For a Sacaton Phase treatment, see Gladwin and others 1937: Plate CXLIX*e*.

Whatever the layout or orientation systems were, the figures always trend head-to-tail on the same vessel, well exemplified by Figure 12.30a, and an arrangement that even holds true in negative painting where orientation was dictated by the canon of tightly packing the field of decoration (Fig. 12.79). Bodies, especially of presumed turtles, were almost always hatched in the Gila Butte Phase, less commonly so treated later, and eyes were seldom shown at any time. Figure 12.78a-p illustrates typical reptile treatment in the positive during the Colonial Period.

Snakes. Serpents treated in the positive are seen on only 30 sherds, barely enough to reveal any style changes through time. The usual layout criteria have been set aside in favor of body treatment as the more significant indicator of style trends (Fig. 12.78q-v). The "cross-over" coil (s) appears to be limited to the Gila Butte Phase, and the circle thus formed was dotted, perhaps having had some ideologic meaning. Solid body painting and lack

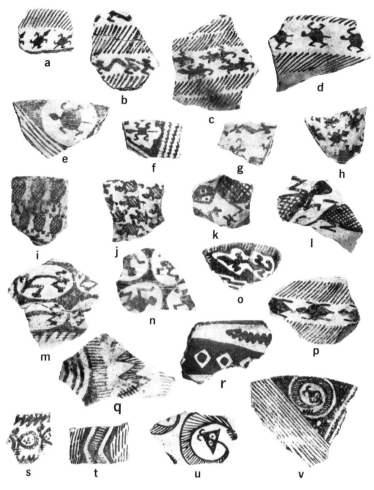

Fig. 12.78. Reptilian forms painted in positive: Lizards and turtles (a-p); snakes (q-v); (a-h) Santa Cruz Red-on-buff; (i-p) Gila Butte Red-on-buff; (q-r) Sacaton Red-on-buff; (s-t) Gila Butte Red-on-buff; (u, v) Santa Cruz Red-on-buff. Width of d, 11.5 cm.

of details, as for example eye and tongue portrayal, were also typical of this phase. During the Santa Cruz Phase, hatched bodies, eyes, and forked tongue were the rule (u-v). By the Sacaton Phase, individual snakes were large, and bodies were textured in a way reminiscent of the diamond-back rattler. A few examples are illustrated in Figure 12.78q-r.

Reptiles in Negative

The story of reptilian painting in the negative is somewhat at variance with the preceding account of positive depictions. The notable differences are: The beginnings were earlier, in the Snaketown Phase rather than in the Gila Butte Phase; although the numbers of samples are about the same in negative and positive representations, in negative painting the big production time was the Gila Butte Phase with a sharp tapering off in the Santa Cruz Phase while the reverse trend was true in the positive painting category. Also more ingenuity was displayed in organizing the units in the field of decoration, and the turtle gave way in favor to the lizard, in a few instances the horned variety. The extensive use of body dots suggests that the artist had the Gila Monster in mind. Some examples are illustrated in Figure 12.81a-p.

In Figure 12.86 where layout types have been tabulated, the principal treatment was massing the figures during all phases except the Sacaton, where framing seems to have been the rule. Arranging the creatures in bands, as noted in the Santa Cruz Phase, was probably influenced by the vessel form, a rectangular dish on whose vertical sides lizards were painted in an endless chain (See also Gladwin and others 1937: Pl. CLVI, f-i). Filling the decorative field with massed figures appears to have been a complicated process and most demanding of the artist's skills in utilizing space. As is usually the case, close study reduces what seems to be a hopeless tangle to an end product that made sense because the artist observed a simple formula.

Figure 12.79 illustrates fragments of two plates of Gila Butte Red-on-buff for which full field reconstructions have been suggested. Inspection of the linework in a, using differences in paint intensity and apparent starting and ending points in

a   b

Fig. 12.79. Gila Butte Red-on-buff plates with negative lizards in massed layouts, circular in a, parallel in b. Width of fragment a, 20 cm.

brushwork, indicates that the painter began at the rim and worked toward the center and that the first move may have been the establishment of dots as guides for the art work that was to follow. Some evidence for these exists. Since the Hohokam often quartered the decorative field when concave, as in bowls, it may be that the artist thought first of the quadrant lines as a basic way of controlling the field. On or close to these imaginary lines paired dots were put equidistant from the rim (Fig. 12.80). Additional paired dots could then be added, two pairs between sets already there, so spaced that distances between dots were alternately greater and smaller. With these guides established, open-ended diamonds drawn between the more distant quartets of dots blocked out the body configuration of the lizard, six in all as allowed by the twelve sets of dots. After this came the adding of legs, tail and head, skewing them as demanded by the space available. In the next tier, the number of units was reduced to four, and finally the central two were added to complete the composition. While we cannot be certain that this principle was used, some kind of a simple progression system must have been followed to avoid chaos and the production of odd unfilled spaces or the creation of units of vastly different sizes.

Figure 12.79b presents a somewhat different and simpler problem in which two large opposing central figures were first painted with others added at the sides to fill the field in what appears to have been a free or "ad lib" manner. Dislike for large solid painted areas is indicated by the addition of negative "V's" between the hind legs (top figure) and a zig-zag (right margin).

Preferred filler elements in lizard bodies were dots, seen in all phases, although no treatment at all was also favored. Opposed fringed wedges (Fig. 12.79), not only most common but most varied in the Gila Butte Phase and the interlocked key (Fig. 12.81e), are limited in the present collection to Santa Cruz Red-on-buff of the same phase.

Reptiles, other than snakes, occur only with birds when subjects were mixed, and then not often: three times with realistic bird figures in Gila Butte Red-on-buff and twice with the conventional bird symbol in the same type. Far more freedom in orientation is detected in negative reptiles than in any other form

Fig. 12.81. Reptiles shown in negative. Lizards: (a-d) Sacaton Red-on-buff; (e-m) Gila Butte Red-on-buff; (n-p) Snaketown Red-on-buff. Snakes: (q, r) Sacaton Red-on-buff; (s) Santa Cruz Red-on-buff; (t) ? Gila Butte Red-on-buff. Width of c, 22 cm.

of life form depictions, probably more attributable to differences in artist brush-use characteristics than to art canons. Interior bowl and plate surfaces were preferred as decorative fields over jar surfaces, though the latter were not spurned.

Only nine sherds preserve negative characterizations of serpents, and the repertoire of styles seems to have been equally limited. Perhaps the mode of portrayal was responsible for the difference, but the layout categories used in positively depicted snakes could not be applied here. Massed snakes, easily made by drawing adjacent zig-zag lines and providing head and tails, were favored (Fig. 12.86). Body details, except for eyes and occasional dotting, were omitted (see also Fig. 12.81q-t).

Of special interest on a single Santa Cruz Red-on-buff sherd is a horned snake (Fig. 12.81s), indicated by elements trailing backward from each side of the head. A serpent with horns or plumes was widely shown, both archaeologically and by contemporary tribes, in Mexico and the Southwest. The Snaketown occurrence places the usage as early as A.D. 700–900, roughly contemporary with horned snake drawings in the Ayala Phase of the Chalchihuites complex in Mexico (Kelley and Abbott 1966: 17). (See also Johnson, 1958, for further trait comparisons between Hohokam and Chalchihuites).

Fish in Positive

The Hohokam had ample opportunity to observe fish because the perennial water in the Gila River supported a fish population, and, in fact, they probably also abounded in the irrigation canals. We know from bones in the refuse that fish were taken and presumably eaten. Yet, they were seldom delineated by the pot-

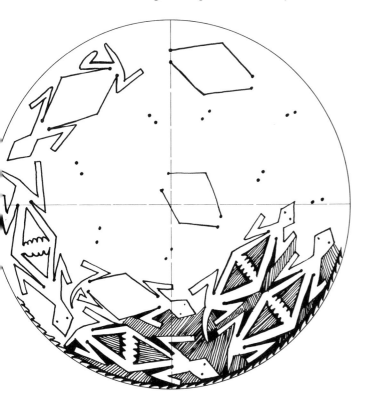

Fig. 12.80. Suggested scheme followed by Hohokam artist in establishing control points in decorative field for massed lizard pattern on Gila Butte Red-on-buff plate in Fig. 12.79a. Quadrant lines imaginary.

ter's brush. As noted before, fish were shown being devoured by water birds. There are only sherds showing the fish alone (Fig. 12.82a-j) and most of these were Santa Cruz Red-on-buff, the rest Gila Butte Red-on-buff. Layout dominances, as with other subjects, shifted from massed to fringed treatments as time passed. In spite of the few sherds, it is apparent that the earliest versions of the fish were the more realistic (Fig. 12.86) and that later renditions were abstract. Fish by themselves are not represented in Sacaton Red-on-buff, and at no time, apparently, were they shown in negative fashion.

Scorpions in Positive and Negative

The only invertebrate in the Hohokam art repertoire recognizable by us is the scorpion. Even then, one cannot be sure that all of the 32 pieces of pottery so identified really fit the category, because many of the depictions have only four legs and with or without two forward projections from the head. The general appearance, however, suggests arachnids. Figure 12.86 once again makes it clear that the mode in the Gila Butte Phase was the massed portrayal giving way to the fringed treatment later. Figure 12.82k-q illustrates good examples. There is only one instance of a negative scorpion (Fig. 12.82q), a possible derivative from a curious abstract pattern seen rarely in Snaketown Red-on-buff (Fig. 12.82r).

Scorpions must have been something of a scourge to a people living on the ground and in whose houses the brushwork of the roofs made ideal hiding places. Our excavations repeatedly brought them to light, and we had to exercise care when removing protective covers from archaeological features.

Mammals in Positive

Bones in refuse deposits indicate that deer and antelope formed a relatively important part of Hohokam diet. However, four-footed animals figured only moderately in the potter's art. Paintings in positive aggregate only 132 sherds, most of them assignable to the Santa Cruz Phase, next abundantly in the Gila Butte Phase, and, finally, a few from the Sacaton Phase (Fig. 12.86). The disparity in abundance between birds and reptiles on the one hand and mammals on the other, leads to the idea that economic importance had little to do with determining what was painted. The artistic merits of the creature, the fun of painting them, or awe, may have been the more telling stimuli.

Identification of quadrupeds is not a simple matter. Variations in head configuration, tail length, and posture suggest deer, antelope, and coyote, or dog. Figure 12.83 illustrates the range, and the reader is privileged to draw his own conclusions as to what was in the minds of the artists. The rabbit, the commonest food animal by numbers taken, appears not to be among them.

The following characteristics should be noted: Snaketown Phase painters did not make use of the mammal as a subject; four legs, rather than two, were more often painted in the Gila Butte Phase, with a curious recurrence of the same theme in the Sacaton Phase; and during the Gila Butte Phase animal bodies were rectangular, replaced by more cursive and fluid representations later to achieve a far greater feeling of motion. Continuous lines of animals between fringes were favored throughout the Colonial period, contrasting with the more normal massing of other kinds of life forms in the Gila Butte Phase. Head or feet orientation to the rim was in about the same ratio as among birds (not tabulated). In one instance, (Santa Cruz Red-on-buff), quadrupeds appear with birds and a deer (?) in the line of fire of a man with drawn bow and arrow (Fig. 12.92u).

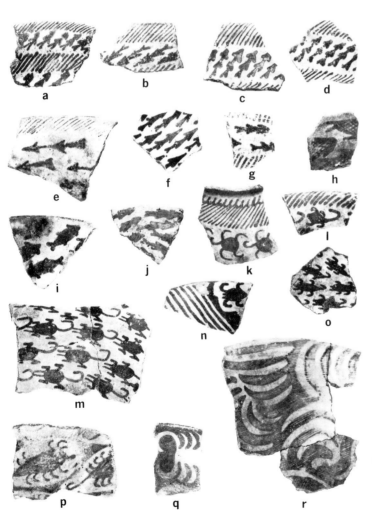

Fig. 12.82. More life forms. Fish: (a-g) Santa Cruz Red-on-buff; (h-j) Gila Butte Red-on-buff. Scorpions: (k-n) Santa Cruz Red-on-buff; (o-q) Gila Butte Red-on-buff; (r) abstract design in negative suggesting an *arachnid* on Snaketown Red-on-buff. Width of *m*, 13.5 cm.

Fig. 12.83. Mammals painted in positive and negative: (a-k) Santa Cruz Red-on-buff; (l-v) Gila Butte Red-on-buff. Width of *j*, 19.5 cm.

Fig. 12.84. Rillito Red-on-brown bowl with depiction of a quadruped probably inspired by a southern art form. Diameter, 24.2 cm.

Mammals in Negative

It is a curious fact of selection that the mammal was seldom depicted in negative. When shown, principally in Gila Butte Red-on-buff, with a faint carry-over into Santa Cruz Red-on-buff, it appears as the same kind of creature (Fig. 12.83t-v). If the two extensions on the head, a standard pattern, are equated with the two-pronged treatment of many positive paintings, then the animal might be a deer or antelope; yet there is something about it, in spite of its short muzzle, that suggests linkage with *cipactli*, the mythical monster of Mexico, as has been noted later in connection with Hohokam shell carvings (Fig. 15.28). The special treatment this creature was given is shown in Figure 12.84, a vessel from a village southwest of Tucson dating from about A.D. 700–900.

Flowers

Preoccupation with animals was almost complete, for only four sherds bear patterns reminiscent of flowers (Fig. 12.85). Three of these are Gila Butte Red-on-buff; the fourth is Sacaton Red-on-buff, and it is the least convincing. I do not think it is fair to conclude from this imbalance that the plant kingdom was less important to the Hohokam than were animals. The simple truth probably is that the artists found the animal world a far more stimulating reservoir of subjects and hence turned to it.

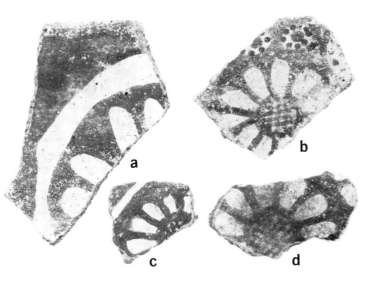

Fig. 12.85. Floral patterns: (a) Sacaton Red-on-buff; (b-d) Gila Butte Red-on-buff. Height of a, 10 cm.

Human Figures

The most interesting, and in some ways the most informative of life form topics, are the human figures. These, more than all others, come closer to telling a story. Even in the simplest representations they tend to reveal facets of Hohokam life not recoverable in any other way. Actions such as dancing, or packing burdens on the back, and perishable paraphernalia such as headdresses, rattles, and baskets with tumplines, are revealed with sufficient clarity to make further inferences possible. Painting of human figures began in the Gila Butte Phase of the Colonial Period and faded sharply by the end of the Sedentary Period. Some stylistic shifts are detectable as time passed. It is a curious fact that the human form seems never to have been shown in the negative. Figure 12.87 summarizes the range and phase differences in human subject matter and related gear.

Dancers. Hand-holding figures in dance postures were the commonest mode of showing the human form in all phases. The emphasis placed on this art motif strongly reflects not only the Hohokam fondness for dancing but the nature of their dancing, a group or circle type. Russell's observations of Pima dancing appear to fit the aboriginal situation well (1908: 170): "The dancers stood in a circle with arms extended across the shoulders of those adjoining. This position did not permit much freedom, and movements were confined to stamping the feet and bending the body."

To the Hohokam artists, dancers were to be shown as stylized figures, lacking details of sex or dress, moving in circles around the decorative field or diagonally through it in bands, arms connected, legs bent, and bodies slanted. Massed or recurrent bands seldom occur, and the favorite manner of depiction was a string of dancers between fringes, particularly in the Santa Cruz Phase. Generally the figures are small, closely spaced, and stiff in Gila Butte Red-on-buff, giving way to larger, more openly-spaced, and fluid arrangements in Santa Cruz Red-on-buff. Finally, in Sacaton Red-on-buff, the dancer theme was little painted but the figures were large when used.

Body form, whether a solid oval or an hour-glass, has some time value, as indicated in Figure 12.87. Differences in posture, head form, neck length, and arm configuration are shown in Figure 12.88. These examples made it clear that bending the body, a forward or backward lean, was a significant means of dramatizing the same movements.

In most cases the orientation of the figures with respect to the vessel rim is a "heads-up" position, while in other life forms the up-side-down position was common. With two exceptions (in Gila Butte Red-on-buff), the figures are right-facing. Dancers and birds occur on the same vessel once (Fig. 12.88m).

Burden Carriers. Without beasts of burden, man himself becomes the carrier of goods. This common activity found expression on Hohokam pottery through the repeated depiction of a figure in a most stereotyped fashion: a slightly hunched-over person with a basket or bag on the back supported by a tumpline to the forehead. One hand, presumably the left, is on the tumpline; the other holds a staff with a forward directed crook (Fig. 12.89). The figure is always right-facing, and the silhouette of the individual is much the same in all examples, pot-bellied and noncommittal as to sex. The preferred way of depiction was in massed groups, and, according to our sample, the theme was used more in the Santa Cruz Phase than at any other time (Fig. 12.87). It started without developmental antecedents in the Gila Butte Phase.

The greatest variation is seen in the apparatus on the back. The near standard cross-hatching of the equipment suggests efforts to reproduce netting, and one suspects, therefore, that the item was a bag, or a unit with netting stretched over a rigid frame similar to the Pima and Papago *kiaha*. In Figure 12.87 the container has been categorized on the basis of shape. Most often shown was the flat-topped round-bottomed variety indicating it to have been

Fig. 12.86 — Quantitative and stylistic study of reptile, fish, insect, mammal, and flower subjects.

Column group key:
- REPTILES › LIZARDS & TURTLES › POSITIVE › LAYOUT (Massed, Fringed, Framed, Banded, Solitary, Do Not Know, Sub-Total)
- REPTILES › LIZARDS & TURTLES › NEGATIVE › LAYOUT (Massed, Fringed, Framed, Banded, Solitary, Do Not Know, Sub-Total)
- REPTILES › SNAKES › POSITIVE › BODY TREATMENT (Straight, Sinuous, Scroll Coil, Cross-Over Coil, Do Not Know, Sub-Total) ; LAYOUT (Massed, Framed, Sub-Total) ; NEG. (Sub-Total)
- FISH › POS. › LAYOUT (Massed, Fringed, Sub-Total)
- INSECTS › SCORPION › POSITIVE › LAYOUT (Massed, Fringed, Framed, Do Not Know, Sub-Total)
- MAMMALS › QUADRUPEDS › POSITIVE › LAYOUT (Massed, Fringed, Framed, Solitary, Do Not Know, Sub-Total) ; DETAILS (4 Legs, 2 Legs, Right Facing, Left Facing) ; NEGATIVE › LAYOUT (Massed, Framed, Do Not Know, Sub-Total)
- FLOWERS › NEG.
- MISCL.-TOO FRAGMENTARY TO ID.

PHASE	LT+ Ma	LT+ Fr	LT+ Fm	LT+ Ba	LT+ So	LT+ DNK	LT+ ST	LT- Ma	LT- Fr	LT- Fm	LT- Ba	LT- So	LT- DNK	LT- ST	Sn Str	Sn Sin	Sn ScC	Sn CoC	Sn DNK	Sn BodyST	Sn Ma	Sn Fm	Sn LayST	Sn NegST	Fi Ma	Fi Fr	Fi ST	Sc Ma	Sc Fr	Sc Fm	Sc DNK	Sc ST	Q+ Ma	Q+ Fr	Q+ Fm	Q+ So	Q+ DNK	Q+ ST	4 Legs	2 Legs	R Facing	L Facing	Q- Ma	Q- Fm	Q- DNK	Q- ST	Fl Neg	Miscl
SACATON	0	0	1	0	1	5	7	0	0	6	0	1	4	11	0	2	4	0	1	7	4	1	5		0	0	0	0	0	0	0	0	0	0	0	1	1	2	2	0	2	0	0	0	0	0	1	7
SANTA CRUZ	6	38	30	0	0	8	82	11	0	4	5	0	1	21	0	0	15	0	0	15	2	1	3		6	17	23	7	9	1	0	17	5	77	0	0	8	90	1	89	86	4	9	3	2	14	0	21
GILA BUTTE	39	4	17	0	0	2	63	79	1	11	0	0	10	101	1	2	1	4	0	8	1	0	1		8	2	10	11	2	1	1	15	11	26	2	0	1	40	7	33	38	2	0	2	0	2	3	22
SNAKETOWN	0	0	0	0	0	0	0	4	0	0	0	0	8	12	0	0	0	0	0	0	0	0	0		0	0	0	0	0	0	0	0	0	0	0	0	0	0	0	0	0	0	0	0	0	0	0	1
TOTAL	45	42	48	0	2	15	152	94	1	21	5	1	23	145	1	4	20	4	1	30	7	2	9		14	19	33	18	11	2	1	32	16	103	2	1	10	132					9	5	2	16	4	51

Fig. 12.86. Quantitative and stylistic study of reptile, fish, insect, mammal, and flower subjects.

Fig. 12.87 — HUMAN FIGURES

Column group key:
- DANCERS › BODY TYPE (Elliptical, Hour Glass, Do Not Know, Total)
- BURDEN CARRIERS › LAYOUT (Massed, Fringed, Framed, Do Not Know, Total) ; CONTAINER TYPE (Flat Rim, Concave Rim, Triangular, Elliptical, Inverted Pear, Circular)
- FLUTE PLAYER › LAYOUT (Massed, Framed, Fringed, Do Not Know, Total) ; FLUTE (End Bulb, No Bulb, Do Not Know) ; HEAD-DRESS (Present, Absent, Do Not Know)
- MISCELLANEOUS › POSTURE (With Shepherd's Crook, Splayed, Hands On Head, Hands On Head And Hip, Hands On Hips, Seated Knees Up, Total) ; REGALIA (Footgear, Head-Dress, Hand-Held Wands, Leg/Hand Rattles, Total) ; OTHER (Jar On Head, Bowman, Large Solitary Figure, Human Foot-Print, Total) ; Too Fragmentary To ID ; Grand Total

PHASE	D Ell	D HrG	D DNK	D Tot	B Ma	B Fr	B Fm	B DNK	B Tot	C FlatRim	C ConcRim	C Tri	C Ell	C InvPear	C Circ	Fl Ma	Fl Fm	Fl Fr	Fl DNK	Fl Tot	EndBulb	NoBulb	Fl DNK2	HD Pres	HD Abs	HD DNK	P Crook	P Splay	P HdHead	P HdHeadHip	P HdHips	P Seated	P Tot	R Foot	R HdDr	R Wands	R Rattles	R Tot	O Jar	O Bow	O LgSolo	O FootPr	O Tot	TooFrag	Grand
SACATON	2	5	2	9	1	0	2	0	3	1	0	0	0	0	2	0	0	0	0	0	0	0	0	0	0	0	0	0	1	0	1	0	2	0	0	0	0	0	0	1	3	1	5	2	21
SANTA CRUZ	80	19	16	115	21	0	0	23	44	24	1	1	3	0	0	1	5	2	6	14	0	9	5	3	1	10	8	3	5	0	0	1	17	1	9	2	1	13	0	0	0	0	0	14	217
GILA BUTTE	7	21	4	32	2	0	3	5	10	8	0	0	1	1	0	11	3	0	0	14	7	6	1	9	0	5	2	0	0	1	1	0	4	0	3	1	0	4	1	1	0	0	2	4	70
TOTAL	89	45	22	156	24	0	5	28	57							12	8	2	6	28	7	15	6	12	1	15	10	3	6	1	2	1	23	1	12	3	1	17	1	2	3	1	7	20	308

Fig. 12.87. Summary chart of the Hohokam way of showing the human form at Snaketown. Frequency figures are based on 1964-65 sample only; for the illustrations, the 1934-35 collection was drawn upon as well.

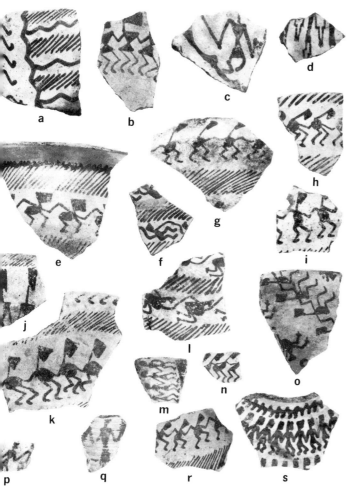

Fig. 12.88. Dancing figures: (a-d) Sacaton Red-on-buff; (e-l, o) Santa Cruz Red-on-buff; (m, n, p-s) Gila Butte Red-on-buff. Width of e, 14.5 cm.

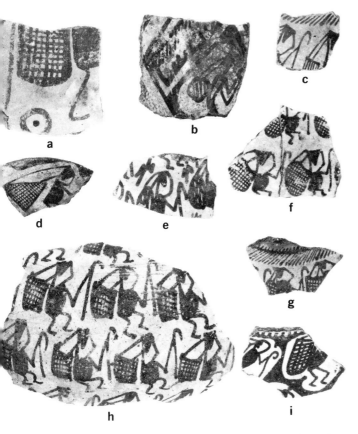

Fig. 12.89. Burden carriers: (a, b) Sacaton Red-on-buff; (c-f) Santa Cruz Red-on-buff; (g-i) Gila Butte Red-on-buff. Width of h, 23 cm.

open. Closed forms, bags with purse strings, are suggested by the oval or circular types. The triangular, or conical form, shown only once (Fig. 12.89d) is most tantalizing because it duplicated the shape of the historically used *kiaha* (Russell 1908: 140-143), although the protruding four framework sticks are not indicated. The Pimas used a forked helping stick in contrast to the crook in the Hohokam version. The likeness and the custom of backpacking are consistent with other lines of evidence supporting the idea of prehistoric to historic continuity in culture traits, if not people, in the Gila River country.

Among the Pima, the carrying of burdens was woman's work (Russell 1908: 140), and it was up to her to make and care for the *kiaha*. Unhappily, the Hohokam did not think it important to make the sexual division of labor clear to us by indicating male or female characteristics in the figures.

The point of all this becomes apparent when one begins to ponder about the inspiration for the theme. Could it be calling attention to the existence of "foreign trade," to the southern traders known as the *pochtecas* which have gained attention in the recent literature, or, was it purely a decorative motif drawn from everyday experience? According to the present time calculation, the burden carrier was already being painted perhaps by A.D. 600, a little early for the systematic and exploitive pursuits of the merchant men working out of Casas Grandes, identified as a frontier trading center after A.D. 1000 (Di Peso 1968).

In one case (Fig. 12.89e) the conventional bird symbol fills the empty spaces between burden carriers. The question arises as to whether or not this association was meaningful, whether it was a hint that birds (? macaw) were being transported and that the closed containers on the backs of some figures, including those on the specimen mentioned, were indeed cages. Traffic in macaws has been well documented, and the idea may have some merit. The macaw bones identified among the faunal remains from Snaketown tell us that the Hohokam had access to the bird as early as about A.D. 1, at least 500 years before the earliest depictions of burden bearers.

Flute Player. Another figure that deserves to be singled out of the Hohokam repertoire of life-form paintings is the flute player. Unlike the burden-basket carrier, a Hohokam trademark, the flute player had a wide distribution and a long history extending from remote antiquity into modern times. The theme, more than any other in the ceramic art, brings archaeology and ethnology together, as Hawley has so well noted (1937).

Generally the Hohokam showed the figure alone, right facing, often with arched body but not with an unmistakable humpback, and holding in both hands a straight object slanting downward from what would be the face on the stylized head. The identification of this object as a flute is based on the fact that most North American Indians knew the flute for a long time, dipping back at least to the time of Christ in the Southwest (Brown 1967: 82). It was present among the Pima historically as the only tone-producing musical instrument they had (Russell 1908: 166-67). Archaeological specimens of flutes from the Hohokam territory have not been reported.

The Snaketown sample of 28 pottery fragments (1964-65) bearing the flute player clearly indicates that the theme was restricted to the Colonial Period (Figs. 12.87, 12.90), its earliest occurrence being on Gila Butte Red-on-buff. The well-established trend through time, from massed to fringed to framed portrayals, which has been noted in other themes is repeated in the small sample of flute players as well. The dominant body configuration is a bent hour-glass supporting a roundish head on a short neck in Gila Butte Red-on-buff. Later, in Santa Cruz Red-on-buff, a squarish head was attached to a somewhat longer neck.

Judging from the paintings, the transverse flute was not known. The archaeological flutes from the San Juan country (Morris 1959: 408) were end-blown, without mouthpiece. The column of air in the instrument was set in vibration by blowing obliquely across the open end. The Hohokam flute was probably of the

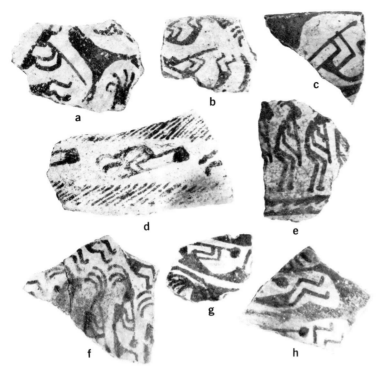

Fig. 12.90. Flute players: (a-d) Santa Cruz Red-on-buff; (e-h) Gila Butte Red-on-buff. Width of *d*, 14 cm.

same type. Interestingly, in the oldest depictions (Gila Butte Phase), the flute was commonly equipped with a bulb at the distal end (Fig. 12.90f-h), although in one case the bulb is shown proximally (Fig. 12.90b), possibly an error in draftsmanship. The bulb may represent a resonating chamber, but no proof of this can be adduced from Southwestern archaeological remains. The end swelling is noted as a feature of some Mexican flutes (Salvidar 1934: Fig. 70-77; Martí 1955: 84), whence the idea likely emanated in the first place. Neither Snaketown nor any other related sites have produced evidence of clay flutes, flutes made of human femora or the Pan pipe as were known to the Indians of Mexico.

Usually the Hohokam outfitted the flute player with a headdress (Fig. 12.87), indicated by three to seven backward directed lines, presumably representing feathers. This detail, together with the flute and the hunched figure, hints at the nonsecular role the flute player had in Hohokam society. It is clear that they thought of him as a human being, at least most of the time. Only once in the collection of 28 sherds with the figure, does the body configuration and the two forward antennas suggest the features of an insect (Fig. 12.91). This painting also comes closest to showing the humpbacked character. In the Anasazi country the humpbacked flutist of early times is said to have been an insect (Parsons 1938: 337), and the one depicted by Hawley (1937: Fig. 1b) on a Pueblo I sherd from Chaco Canyon does indeed look like one. What this does is to increase the likelihood that the Hohokam and Anasazi expressions of the figure were somehow related, though the meaning of the linkage remains to be worked out. The Snaketown example is early Gila Butte Red-on-buff, which indicates an awareness of the element possibly as early as A.D. 550. Evidently the flutist of the Anasazi eventually became the humpbacked but fluteless Kokopelli with strong erotic overtones (Parsons 1938; Titiev 1939). The Hohokam flutist is not associated pictorially with phallicism.

Lambert may well be correct in saying that the flute player was one of the earliest depictions of a supernatural being in the Southwest (1966: 24-25). Knowledge of the figure and related concepts, and the time depth in two adjacent but different peoples, support the idea. Speculating as to how it may have happened, I would postulate that the Hohokam drew the idea from Mexican antecedents by A.D. 550, or before if they brought the theme with

them; that it was diffused to the Anasazi by Pueblo 1, about A.D. 700–800, where strong phallic aspects became associated with the figure and where the transfer to Kokopelli took place probably in late pre-Spanish times. The theme appears to have been lost among the Hohokam by 1200.

Snaketown produced the widely exhibited and illustrated plate of Santa Cruz Red-on-buff showing the humpbacked flute player with a supporting figure behind him, hands on the back as if holding the personage up (Gladwin and others 1937: Pl. CLVIII i).

Miscellaneous. A variety of human subject matter remains to be considered. While the number of examples in each category is small, the ideas depicted are, nevertheless, interesting and instructive. Figure 12.87 tabulates the themes and representative specimens are illustrated in Figure 12.92.

First, we see a person with a hump back, bent over, supporting himself with a staff reminiscent of a shepherd's crook. The composition suggests the idea of age. The theme appears in the Gila Butte Phase (Fig. 12.92c), becomes dominant and formalized in the Santa Cruz Phase (Fig. 12.92b, see also Gladwin and others 1937: Pl. CLXVIII a-c), and seems to have been forgotten thereafter. Rarely, a supporting figure at the back is shown (Fig. 12.92a), not unlike the pair noted in the flute player theme. The deformed figure, the companion, and the crook, matching the one held by the burden carrier, tend to lift the subject from a purely artistic expression to one that had mythological, or at best, nonsecular meaning. The staff as a badge of office was a concept widely held before Spanish times (Parsons 1939: 1021-1022), and even the god-figure Quetzalcoatl had a shepherd's staff sceptre, according to Sahagun (Bandalier 1932: 26).

Next follows a group of figures in various stances (Fig. 12.92d-i) expressed in different positions of the legs and arms, and then figures equipped with items of dress and regalia. While fragmentary, Figure 12.92m, apparently represents footgear of a leg length type, unusual for the hot country, and Figures 12.87 and 12.92 j, k, n-q bring together various forms of headdresses by phases. No archaeological traces of headgear have survived, but one may gather from the paintings that elaborate inventions, presumably with feathers and other trappings, were known. There

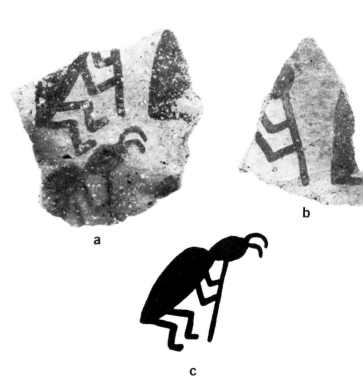

Fig. 12.91. Flute player in form of insect as seen on two sherds (a,b) from the same jar of Gila Butte Red-on-buff; (c) reconstruction. Maximum dimension of *a*, 7 cm.

Fig. 12.92. Various attributes of human life forms: (e, h, u, w) Sacaton Red-on-buff; (a, b, d, f, j, k, n, o, r, s) Santa Cruz Red-on-buff; (c, g, i, l, m, p, q, t, v) Gila Butte Red-on-buff. Width of d, 12 cm.

beliefs, and attitudes that inspired it all. These are lost beyond certain retrieval.

The fact that the Hohokam life form painters were in the beginning stages of a story-telling art has already been alluded to. The most complicated narrative, yet simple as compared with the achievements of the classic period Mimbrenos, is a bowman directing his weapon against what may be a deer, seen on a jar sherd of Sacaton Red-on-buff. The theme is repeated evidently in a band (Fig. 12.92u). A lower band depicts a series of waterbirds with the head of a fish showing in the beak of one. Close examination of the bow reveals two vertical lines crossing the arrow in front of the bow. This same idea is duplicated in a Gila Butte Red-on-buff pattern (Fig. 12.92v).

During the Sacaton Phase, human figures not only were absolutely large as compared with earlier versions but were more apt to occur as solitary figures (Fig. 12.92w and Fig. 12.21b). While the figures may show complicated headdresses (Gladwin and others 1937: Pl. CLII n), the bodies usually are hour-glass shaped, leg and arm bends are angular, and the phallus is more apt to be shown than at any other time. The human footprint occurs only once (Fig. 11.8a), and spoors of other animals are not recognizable as such if they were painted. No examples of the human handprint are known in Hohokam art.

Some sherds are too fragmentary to extract the thematic material even though it is clear that the human form was shown. These reveal just enough, however, to provide notice of the fact that the inventory of subject matter has been far from exhausted. We can be certain that, in their simple and direct way, the Hohokam were depicting far more topical material than we have been able to note from the sample at hand.

Discussion

The analysis of zoomorphic elements was done by typing sherds from all sources in Snaketown in accordance with the criteria established for pottery in 1937 and which have been reaffirmed by the present work. As a check, the three stratigraphic tests made in Mound 39, sampling refuse that ranged through the three major periods, Pioneer, Colonial, and Sedentary, and encompassing the time when life form painting was in vogue, produced 185 sherds with life figures. These verify the essential trends noted in the types collected. Additionally, stratigraphic placement and the dominance of associated materials were used wherever possible. A good example of the latter circumstance was Pit 6:8E, which produced a "pure" sample of Gila Butte Phase material (Fig. 12.37). In the lot were 28 zoomorphic figures representing as many vessels, and these accurately reflect the conclusions drawn about style and subject matter from the review of the total sample. The approach to this problem I regard as valid and adequate for the recovery of the kind of information which was of special interest to me.

The quantitative information is brought together in Figure 12.93. The 1,347 sherds and 7 whole vessels reviewed represent

is no hint in the depictions that certainly suggests the use of the mask, though this may have been a part of some of the headgear types.

Occasionally associated with headdresses are hand-held multi-toothed wands, spheroidal rattles, doubtless representing gourds, and what appear to be rattles worn on the calves of the legs, both types having been known to the Pima Indians (Russell 1908: 168–69). The latter formerly were made of deer dewclaws or cacoons and were evidently shared widely by desert dwelling tribes in the Greater Southwest. These glimpses of articles not found directly in archaeological contexts signal a richness of Hohokam culture that challenges the imagination. And it is not only the material goods that must be thought of, but the concepts,

PERIOD AND PHASE	BIRDS				BIRDS WITH OTHER FORMS		REPTILES				FISH	INSECTS	MAMMALS		HUMAN					FLOWERS	MISC. FRAGMENTS	TOTAL
	POSITIVE			NEGATIVE	POSITIVE		POSITIVE		NEGATIVE		POS.	POS.	POS.	NEG.	POSITIVE							
	QUAIL	(?) HUMMING	WATER	ALL KINDS	REPTILE	FISH	LIZARDS & TURTLES	SNAKES	LIZARDS & TURTLES	SNAKES					DANCERS	BURDEN CARRIER	FLUTE PLAYER	REGALIA	POSTURE & OTHER			
SED. SACATON	9	0	10	4	2	1	7	7	11	5	0	0	2	0	9	3	0	0	7	1	9	87
COL. SANTA CRUZ	121	9	103	32	34	0	82	15	21	3	23	17	90	2	115	44	14	13	17	0	35	790
COL. GILA BUTTE	21	0	44	21	8	5	63	8	101	1	10	15	40	14	32	10	14	4	6	3	26	446
PION. SNAKETOWN	0	0	0	11	0	0	0	0	12	0	0	0	0	0	0	0	0	0	0	0	1	24
TOTAL	151	9	157	68	44	6	152	30	145	9	33	32	132	16	156	57	28	17	30	4	71	1347

Fig. 12.93. Summary tabulation of zoomorphic paintings seen on potsherds by phase and subject. Whole vessels not included.

the total sample from the 1964–65 excavations. I believe that the frequency values acceptably reflect both theme and style changes. In descending order the topical interest scale went as follows: birds, reptiles, man, quadrupeds, fish and insects, and flowers. There were some shifts in emphasis on these topics as time passed, as already noted. While life-form painting began in the Snaketown Phase in the negative vernacular, the big time of production was in the Santa Cruz Phase when positive portrayal dominated over the negative.

Attention was given to the proveniences of zoomorphic figures within the various sectors of Snaketown. This study came up with no meaningful concentrations within the site or any repetitive topical samples with geographic limits. In other words, wherever trash or houses were examined that were of the right age, life form depictions could be expected, and when that happened, the topical material was predictably wide-ranging if the sample was large. I see no hints that clans or residence units had a monopoly on particular art styles or motifs. The most that might be expected would be the detection of artists' idiosyncrasies, and this would be dependent on the concentration of the products of one person on a house floor or in a unit of trash, but such collections were not identifiable with certainty.

How the Hohokam came to develop the zoomorphic vernacular is not readily explained. Certainly it is no accident that similar, though stylistically distinct, life-form painting sequences existed in Durango, Jalisco, and Nayarit in western Mexico. Somehow, these must all have been generated through mutual or linear stimuli. Kelley and Abbott note (1966: 9-12) that in the Chalchihuites Culture of the northern Mesoamerican frontier, life forms in rich variety appear during the Alta Vista Phase, circa A.D. 300–500. This phenomenon, with others, is seen as evidence of a wave of Mesoamerican influence moving northward from Teotihuacan and as yet unidentified west Mexican sources during Classic Teotihuacan (III) times. A study of Chalchihuites and Hohokam life forms (Johnson 1958) points up the fact that the traditions have similarities and differences in style and topic, a not surprising situation. One notable difference is the complete absence of anthropomorphized animals in Hohokam art. What is of interest especially is the fact that the introduction of life forms in the Alta Vista Phase of the Chalchihuites Culture roughly coincides with the first appearance of them in the Snaketown Phase, about A.D. 350–550.

I would note further that Chupícuaro, even though imprecisely known, may have been a contributing influence also. It is usually given an early time assignment, early enough to have been in a position to pass on elements of its rich pottery tradition to other societies. One format of a bird figure in Chupícuaro pottery (Solorzano Collection, Guadalajara) closely parallels the earliest rendering of the bird by the Hohokam, even though the comparison is based on positive (polychrome) and negative (monochrome) depictions respectively (Fig. 12.94a and b). Other life forms were shown as well (Fig. 12.94c-e) in a style more reminiscent of Chalchihuites than Hohokam, although there was a matching of the fluid, dynamic quality of the animals. A detailed examination of Chupícuaro pottery collections might prove to be rewarding.

My feeling has been that these two modes of artistic expression were linked and that, viewed together, they might be further indicative of origins. Perhaps the following speculation is far fetched, but I note it with the thought that someone may test it further as new evidences come to light.

In varying degrees throughout Mesoamerica, the isolated element, geometric or animal, portrayed in whole or in abbreviated fashion, stood as a symbol for a cosmological, calendrical, or numerical value. Initially, most of these were expressed on stone or native paper, less frequently on pottery. However, a mode of communication was established in which the unit element was thought of as a vehicle for expressing an idea. As this concept spread northward to the Mesoamerican frontier, it is likely that the

symbolic meaning and the precise form of elements were lost or modified as functions of the distance over which they were diffused. The orientation of the recipient culture would also have had its effect.

A statement of Kelley and Abbott (1966: 11) is worthy of note, for in addition to life forms, in the Alta Vista Phase of the Chalchihuites Culture, they see small geometric elements appearing as "almost certainly" derived from Mesoamerican symbolism. Pursuing this line of reasoning further, by the time the Hohokam domain was reached, little was left but the impulse to fill spaces with small elements, and the original abbreviated life form was converted to a simple silhouette of the whole creature. Calendrical or numerical values were most likely completely lost in the process, and any attached meanings could perhaps be best explained as mythological and secular inspirations.

A review of the synoptical charts (Figs. 12.73, 12.86, and 12.87) demonstrates a phenomenon which deserves mention. This was the fact that after feeble beginnings in late Snaketown Phase times, a notable spurt in the repertoire of themes and styles of rendering ushered in the Colonial Period, beginning about A.D. 550. This was a time of extensive overhauling of the strict canons of the ceramic painting that characterized the Snaketown Phase. Because of the carry-through of many of the art motifs, it impresses one more as the consequence of an internal rebellion against tradition than it does to a new thrust from the outside. The latter idea cannot, however, be totally ruled out. Kelley (1960: 571) has suggested that the Chalchihuites Culture of Durango influenced the Hohokam "... changing almost overnight the simple Pioneer Hohokam into the efflorescent Hohokam of the Colonial Period." This, he believes, took place at about the Classic-Post Classic break, which would be roughly between A.D. 500–600. The possibility of such influence must be kept in mind, whether from Chalchihuites or some other Mexican source but the abruptness and depth of the change require further attention.

The claim has been made that the earliest Hohokam zoomorphic patterns were forms of fauna not found in Arizona and the Southwest but rather were drawn from a marine environment. Turtles, fish, and water birds are given as examples (Gritzner, C. F., paper read before the Society for American Archaeology, Santa Fe, May, 1968). Later, it is said, the Hohokam gradually trended toward the rendering of the local desert fauna. This interpretation is introduced as evidence in support of a Hohokam migration from South America to the Southwest by sea. The Snaketown sample of life-form paintings, the largest and temporally the longest sequence we have yet had to study in detail, does not support these statements. Turtles were endemic to the desert and to the watery environment of the Gila River, as were also fish and water birds, including the pelican. We know the

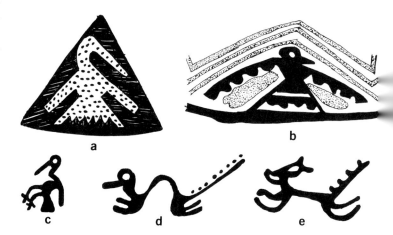

Fig. 12.94. Animal depictions: (a) Hohokam, negative bird, Snaketown Red-on-buff (plate); (b) Chupícuaro (Michoacán), positive painted bird in black-on-white and red (stippled) (jar); (c-e) Chupícuaro white-on-red; (b-e) from Solórzano Collection, Guadalajara.

Hohokam took fish from the river, but even so its depiction was never common. The topknotted quail was a favorite subject almost from the beginning, and one of the two initial zoomorphic elements was the lizard. It is doubtful that the life-form art of the Hohokam, painted or sculptured, will help much in establishing exact points of origin in Mexico or the means of travel from a distant homeland even when a migratory situation is indicated.

As for the achievements of the Hohokam artists in their zoomorphic efforts in relation to others in the Southwest, the case is clear that they were far and away ahead, both in time and in the range of subject matter. The occasional life forms in Basketmaker III pottery were exceptions, and in the Mogollon area there were literally no early attempts at this kind of art, but once the idea caught on it was carried by the Classic Mimbrenos to a degree of perfection in draftsmanship and subject complexity never reached by the Hohokam. There is evidence, chronological and stylistic in nature, that the Mimbres artists were inspired by the Hohokam. This happened late in the history of life-form depiction among the Hohokam, and the Mimbres climax came after the concept was literally dead in the west.

"FLYING BIRD"

A distinctive trademark of the Hohokam artist is a motif which lies somewhere between the life form and the abstract geometric element. It is an oft-repeated pattern which, with deft changes in brush stroke, could be altered to produce a great variety of form (Fig. 12.95). It was a simple unit consisting of a short line with additions at the sides, and when shown in massed arrangements, often oblique to the vessel rim, the effect was that of a flock of

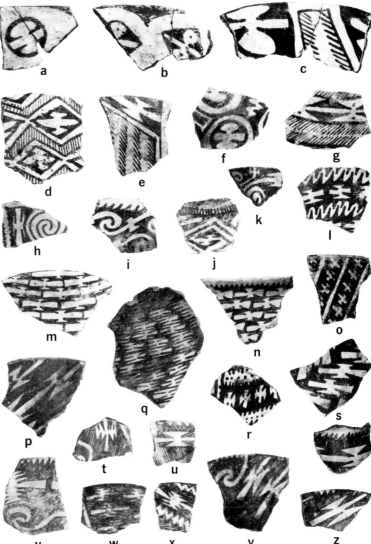

Fig. 12.96. "Flying bird" motif shown in negative: (a-d) Sacaton Red-on-buff; (e-h) Santa Cruz Red-on-buff; (i-s) Gila Butte Red-on-buff; (t-z) Snaketown Red-on-buff. Width of c, 18 cm.

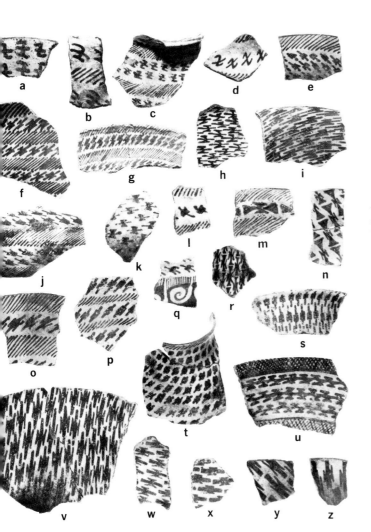

Fig. 12.95. "Flying bird" motif, painted in positive: (a, b) Sacaton Red-on-buff; (c-q) Santa Cruz Red-on-buff; (r-z) Gila Butte Red-on-buff. Width of g, 14 cm.

birds in flight, hence the label. But tracing the long and curious history of the convention indicates that the first depictions, in the Snaketown Phase, consisting predominantly of serrated figures (Fig. 12.96t, v, w, x), may have stood for something different, as is suggested later. The avian meaning, if indeed this was in the minds of the artists, comes through strongest in the Santa Cruz Phase.

Figures 12.95 and 12.96 illustrate the motif in a number of its variations in both positive and negative portrayal. In the simpler forms, angular lines in the shape of Z, M, or H, executed at right angles to the "body," altered the nature of the pattern. These traits, plus more carefully delineated figures and the layout, constitute the bases for the typological distinctions in this study. It is evident that the repetitious strokes required to make hundreds of the figures led to boredom and a consequent loss of precision and quality of the product.

The sherd sample used in the study was drawn from all proveniences within Snaketown. Positive renderings total 548 and negative 122 units for a total of 670 sherds. Only three whole or restored vessels carry the pattern. I have not considered it worth while to do meticulous quantitative analysis of both form and layout, although this could be done. The following observations are based, therefore, on a quick survey in which developmental trends and dominances have been noted and transferred to a synoptic chart (Fig. 12.97).

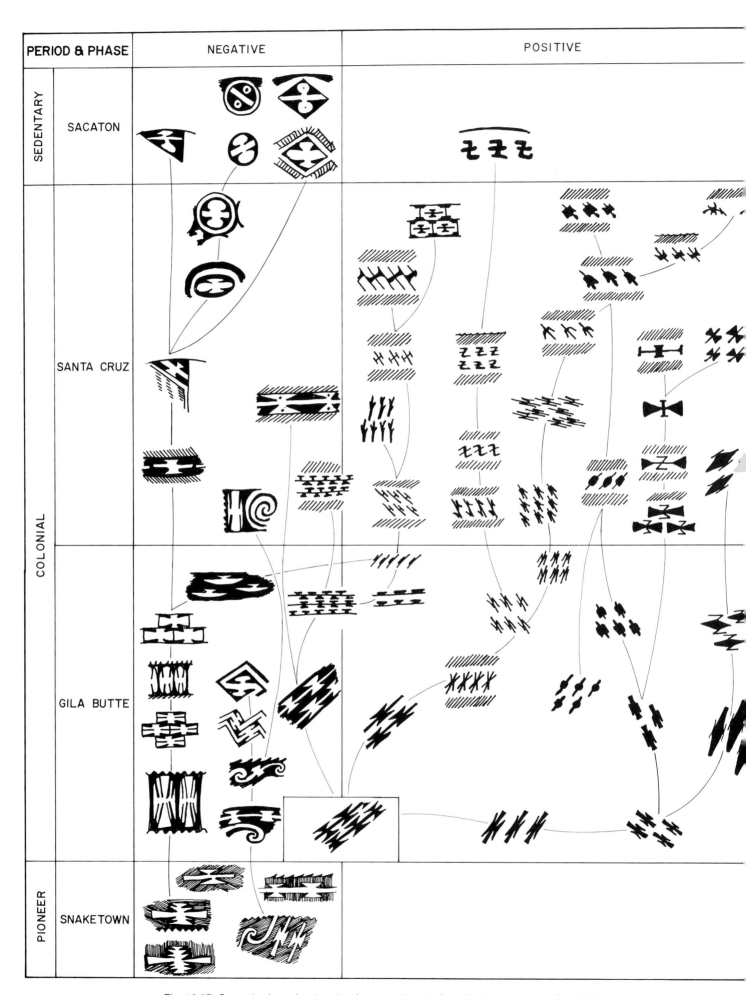

Fig. 12.97. Synoptic chart showing developmental trends from beginning to end of the Hohokam "flying bird" convention. Descent lines are suggestions only. All form variations have not been used.

PERIOD & PHASE		NEGATIVE	POSITIVE
SEDENTARY	SACATON		
COLONIAL	SANTA CRUZ		
	GILA BUTTE		
PIONEER	SNAKETOWN		

The following points are noteworthy:

1. The symbol was given first expression on Snaketown Red-on-buff, always in the negative, set against closely packed hatched backgrounds, and in its most elaborate form might be called a foliated cross.

2. The negative tradition continued prominently into the Gila Butte Phase, usually in massed arrangements, became simplified and numerically weak in the Santa Cruz Phase, and degenerated into large clumsily drawn and framed figures in the Sacaton Phase.

3. The loosely interlocked scroll, seen in negative as a flared S figure, accompanies the "bird" in several instances (Fig. 12.96y, i, k) joined in cursive, grading to angular, expressions in the Gila Butte Phase, losing favor thereafter.

4. On pottery typologically transitional between Snaketown and Gila Butte Red-on-buffs, two things happened to set the course for further changes: (a) A positive-negative figure was produced (Fig. 12.96p) which can be read either way, and (b) positive, precisely painted, elements appear (Fig. 12.95w-y).

5. From this point on, great proliferation took place, dominantly as massed layouts in the Gila Butte Phase and as rows between free fringes in the Santa Cruz Phase, although these were not mutually exclusive.

6. Numerically in the sample of 670 sherds studied, only 30 carrying the design are Snaketown Red-on-buff and 20 are Sacaton Red-on-buff, signifying that the element was slow in being accepted and fast at becoming obsolete at the end of its cycle. The convention was clearly a Colonial Period attribute.

It would be surprising if, on the thousands of Anasazi black-on-white pots to be found in museums, this distinctive figure did not appear, but I cannot recall seeing any. In its classical form, the "flying bird" appears to have been a Hohokam monopoly. Yet, its beginnings present another kind of a problem. It appeared, as has been noted, during the Snaketown Phase with no recognized local antecedents in pottery, as a negative figure in its most complicated form. A simpler version was produced as pendants of shell (Fig. 15.17 h-l). As Hohokam lines of contact with other peoples were south, it is natural to turn there for a possible source for the element. But the answer does not emerge clearly. As a speculation, since some of the life-form inspirations may have come from the Chupícuaro tradition of Michoacán and Guanajuato, the figure in question may have been derived from there too. If we consider the Snaketown Phase dates to be valid, about A.D. 350–550, this stage in Hohokam development would equate roughly with Porter's Chupícuaro Late Phase (1956: 572-75). In the Chupícuaro Early Phase tradition is a figure somewhat suggestive of, but not identical with, the one the Hohokam first used. It appears in polychrome and could be an abstract zoomorphic element, painted between modeled human faces (Porter 1956: Fig. 14t; Covarrubias 1957: Pl. VIII lower right; Piña Chan 1960: 127). The "head" part (Fig. 12.98) most closely resembles the Snaketown form, although the shapes are not identical. The Chupícuaro renderings have two centrally located shallow drilled pits not seen in the Hohokam version. This source, or another one similar, I believe to best explain the first use of the element among the Hohokam.

As noted earlier, the serrated figure may not have been thought of initially as a bird; indeed, even for the later renderings, this association may be ours rather than that of the Hohokam. Yet, the probability that this interpretation is correct is supported by the subtle trend toward the portrayal of typological birds. During our work at Snaketown we were greatly impressed by the huge flocks of lark buntings, locally called snowbirds, that winter in the temperate climate of the Gila and Salt River valleys. These flocks, on taking wings, may have provided the natural model the Hohokam artists endeavored to capture.

Fig. 12.98. Element on Chupícuaro Early Phase black, red (heavy stipple) and buff polychrome pottery from Guanajuato, Mexico (after Porter 1956: Fig. 14t).

GEOMETRIC ELEMENTS

Small geometric elements, shown either as massed groups in a large field of decoration, in series between free running fringes, or singly as fillers in "bullseyes," are found in approximately 25% of Hohokam painted pottery. This figure is based on a review of 200 whole vessels from Snaketown representing all phases except Vahki, a better basis for making the calculation than would be provided by a review of potsherds. However, reference to many thousands of potsherds has been necessary to develop an inventory of the motifs. The list consists of 129 entries which is representative, though not exhaustive, of this aspect of Hohokam painting. In this study the goals were to gain an understanding of the history of geometric element painting, the time of appearance or disappearance of specific motifs, changes in form and usages, and shifts in trends or emphases through time. While draftsmanship in most cases was clumsy, the ingenuity demonstrated in coming up with variations on a theme was almost limitless.

The information derived from the survey has been brought together in Figure 12.99. Convergences in characteristics lead to difficulties in classifying because one form may be catalogued under two different headings. For example, dotted negative circles, Categories 19-20, also fit in Category 1 illustrating the use of dots. Actually, this possible source for confusion does not make much difference because the trend, in which the interest lies, comes out about the same in the end.

There is also the question: How small is small? While most of the elements are small by any standards applied to pottery painting, some forms did change through time, becoming larger, but they were still shown as free units. This is best seen in Sacaton Red-on-buff (Fig. 12.104v). In the analysis the position was taken that if a motif started out small but grew in size and in refinements over prototypes, it should be considered as a free-unit design and hence a part of the story.

It is not my intention to review stylistic changes in detail, category by category, though some specific points and gross differences should be noted. Figures 12.100 to 12.105 attempt to capture the "moods" of Hohokam geometric elements in the different phases. These, examined with Figure 12.99, will provide the reader with the salient features.

Categories 1–20

PERIOD	PHASE	1	2	3	4	5	6	7	8	9	10	11	12	13	14	15	16	17	18	19	20
SED.	SACATON	4		9	1	12	4	2	2	29	3	2	1	2	13	2	3	1			
COLONIAL	SANTA CRUZ	4	4	18		17			3	31	1	3			14		2				1
COLONIAL	GILA BUTTE	19	8	5		1	1		8	31	2	4			3		9	4	1	2	
PIONEER	SNAKE-TOWN	11					2		1	2											
PIONEER	SWEET-WATER	1		2				1													
PIONEER	ESTRELLA																				

Categories 22–41

PERIOD	PHASE	22	23	24	25	26	27	28	29	30	31	32	33	34	35	36	37	38	39	40	41
SED.	SACATON	1		1	4		1			4	8	7	1	6	12		1	1			
COLONIAL	SANTA CRUZ	3		5	13		3			3				4	1	2				1	
COLONIAL	GILA BUTTE	2	2	4	9	1	4	3	1										5	2	1
PIONEER	SNAKE-TOWN																				
PIONEER	SWEET-WATER																				
PIONEER	ESTRELLA																				

Categories 43–62

PERIOD	PHASE	43	44	45	46	47	48	49	50	51	52	53	54	55	56	57	58	59	60	61	62
SED.	SACATON	3			1	5	6	4	8	3	7	3	2	25			12	23	13	6	
COLONIAL	SANTA CRUZ		1	2		35				1	22	1	1	56	3	4		8	1		
COLONIAL	GILA BUTTE					11					6			7							1
PIONEER	SNAKE-TOWN																				
PIONEER	SWEET-WATER																				
PIONEER	ESTRELLA																				

Fig. 12.99. Inventory of geometric elements in Hohokam pottery painting as seen at Snaketown. Vertical placement of figures in categories denotes passage of time, bottom to top, or the range of variation within a single phase. Orientation of figures is with vessel rim at top where determinable. Frequency values based on nearly the whole sherd sample and complete vessels from the 1964-65 excavation. Classic Period phases not shown because unit elements were minimally used and the Vahki Phase has been omitted because pottery was not painted at that time. Elements surrounded by black, other than triangles, have been lifted out of a massed arrangement.

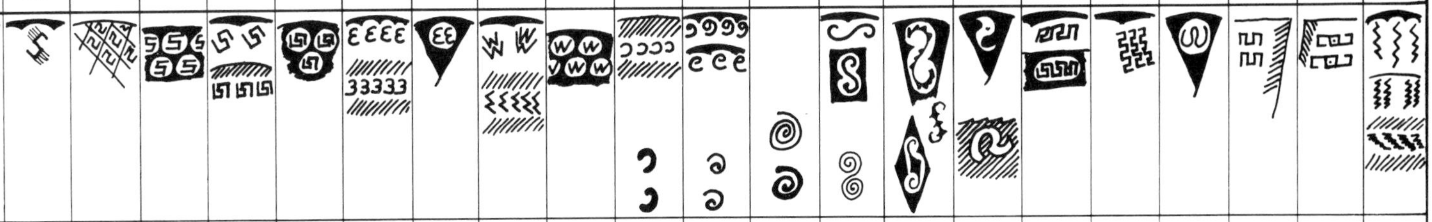

Table block 1

65	66	67	68	69	70	71	72	73	74	75	76	77	78	79	80	81	82	83	84	85
1	3	8	19	3	7	2	2	3	1	5		6	4	2	3	2	1	1	1	10
					12		5	2				2								18
														1						
										2				3						
									1	3	2	1								
									1	1	3									

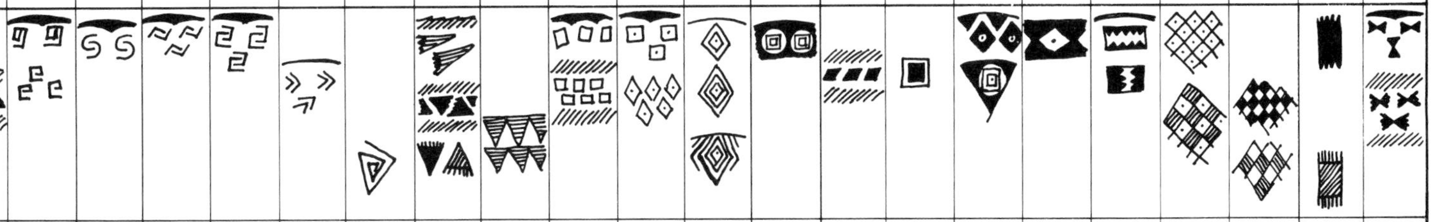

Table block 2

87	88	89	90	91	92	93	94	95	96	97	98	99	100	101	102	103	104	105	106	107
2	5	1	9			1		4	9	5	1	1		3	1	5	4		1	1
1				1		4		1	7	2		4	1		1	1				1
						2				6							5	13		
							1										1	18	2	
					1															

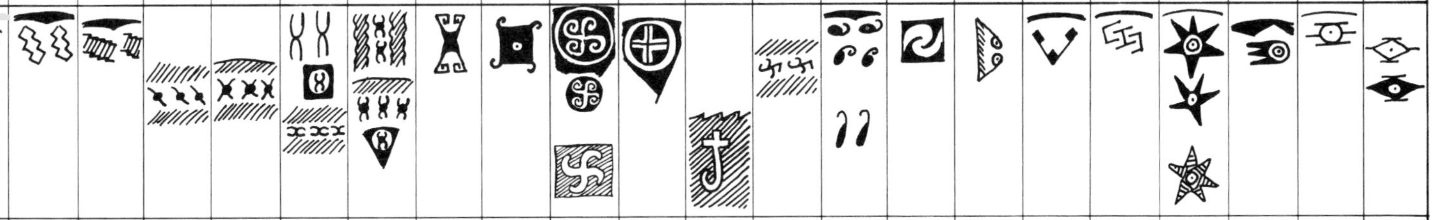

Table block 3

109	110	111	112	113	114	115	116	117	118	119	120	121	122	123	124	125	126	127	128	129
1	2			3	6	1	1	3	1			7	1	1	1	1	2		2	
		1	2	6	22			1		2	4							1		4
												1								
								1		1							1			

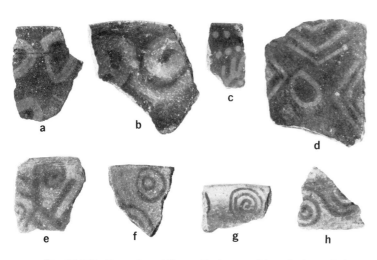

Fig. 12.100. Examples of the earliest geometric unit elements in Pioneer Period pottery: (a, b) Estrella Red-on-gray; (c-h) Sweetwater Red-on-gray. Width of *d*, 8.9 cm.

Fig. 12.101. Unit design elements on Snaketown Red-on-buff ranging from positive to negative treatments. Width of *b*, 13.3 cm.

Fig. 12.102. Examples of unit geometric elements on Gila Butte Red-on-buff, Colonial Period. Width of *a*, 11.3 cm.

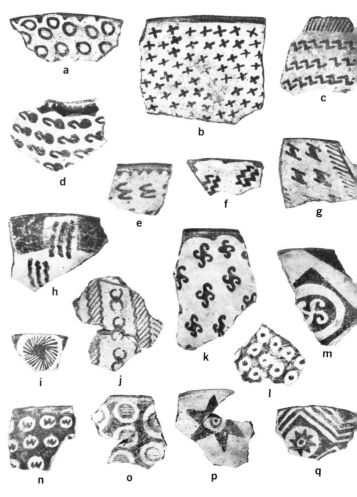

Fig. 12.103. Examples of unit geometric elements on Sacaton Red-on-buff, Sedentary Period, that also appeared on earlier types. Width of *b*, 15.0 cm.

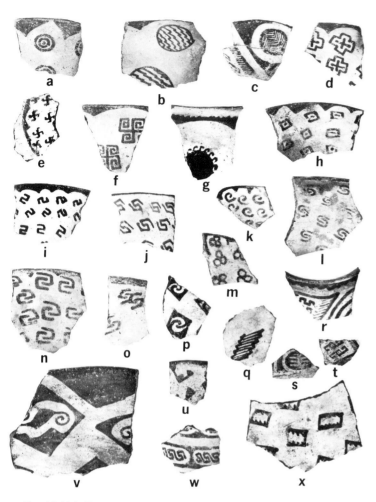

Fig. 12.104. Examples of unit geometric elements found only on Sacaton Red-on-buff, Sedentary Period. Width of *v*, 15.8 cm.

1, dots, here considered when used in groups or in series, had a long life with the greatest preference shown toward them during the Snaketown and Gila Butte Phases. The repeated short line, Category 2, was not thoroughly analyzed, and the noted frequencies are misleading. More will be said about this in connection with the development of the fringe in Hohokam painting. Generally speaking, those elements with the longest life were also the most favored or most often repeated (Categories 3, 8, 9, 14, 25, 47, 52 and 55). Not surprisingly, the circle in its various forms was perhaps the favorite and was treated with the greatest variations. Most common among the alphabet-type elements were X (Category 47), I or H (52), N or Z (55), a rectilinear S (64), and a cursive E (70). Category 127 (Fig. 12.105v) reminds one of the "weeping eye" element of the southeastern United States, but since only a single occurrence was noted, it may mean no more than the chance product arising from an effort to achieve variety.

Elements spanning several phases are shown in Figure 12.103. Because of the thematic increases noted above, it is natural to find elements that were limited to and diagnostic of a single phase. In this respect the Sacaton Phase is the most outstanding. Recognition of specific elements, or a particular way of treating them (Fig. 12.104), aids in the identification of Sacaton Red-on-buff. In general the units are largest and most elaborate at this time. The use of the small element as a filler in a negative circle, or a "bullseye," while having early beginnings, reached its most intense application during the Colonial and Sedentary Periods. Closely packed small units are hallmarks of the Colonial Period (Fig. 12.102a-h), although late in the period the repeated unit in bands between free fringes is a good, though not exclusive, diagnostic (Fig. 12.105k-u).

There is little evidence in the oldest painted pottery, Estrella Red-on-gray, to forecast the emphasis placed on geometric elements in later times. What examples there are may be accepted as the likely origin for the mode. Small "blobs" and wide-lined simple scrolls are present (Categories 74, 75, 76 and Fig. 12.100a and b). For Sweetwater Red-on gray, the next sequent type, a few more forms appear: dots (1), simple circle (3), concentric circles (7), scrolls (74, 75, 76), the reverse or S-scroll (77) and a rectilinear reducing triangle (92 and Fig. 12.100c-h). For all forms in the Sweetwater Phase frequencies are low, from which one concludes that the unit element was still not popular. In Snaketown Red-on-buff, when formalization of the hachured style was effected, there were some innovations, and most importantly, a new concept in their portrayal was launched, the negative form of expression (1, 8, 9, 104, 105, 117, 119). Most often shown at this time were the negatively treated life forms. The dot as a filler element (1, and Fig. 12.72s and t) was prominent, and new figures were the negative circle (8, 9), an S-figure (79), triangles (94), joined squares in checkerboard (104, 105), a curious fringed element (106), curvilinear swastika (117), an unidentified T-figure (119), and the star (126) (see also Fig. 12.101h).

Although not common during the Pioneer Period, unit elements nevertheless were present, and I see no reason to doubt the fact that they were the prototypes for an idea that was to flourish with great vigor later on.

A steady enrichment of motifs took place after the Snaketown Phase. Using only the sample at hand, the increases in the number of categories by phase may be listed as follows: Estrella 3, Sweetwater 8, Snaketown 13, Gila Butte 36, Santa Cruz 62, and Sacaton 97. By Classic Period times the idea was essentially dead (Haury 1945a: 60), a fate that also befell the life forms.

Comments about a few particular motifs are in order. Category

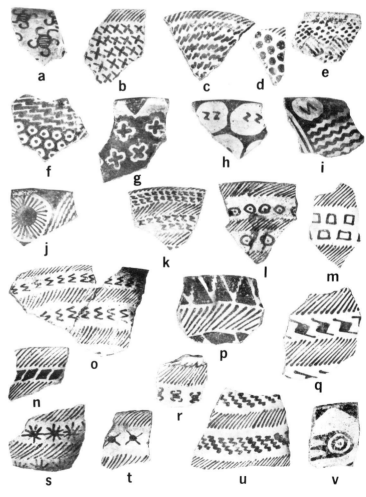

Fig. 12.105. Examples of unit geometric elements on Santa Cruz Red-on-buff, Colonial Period. Width of *o*, 14.8 cm.

Fig. 12.106. Developmental chart showing how the scroll was treated by the Hohokam potter. Taken from a study by Jon Czaplicki.

THE SCROLL AND THE STEPPED GREQUE

To the person interested in the unfolding of the scroll as a motif, Hohokam pottery presents a special challenge. From simple beginnings it passed through a succession of transformations both bold and subtle. With life forms and repeated geometric elements, the scroll is a Hohokam hallmark, not because it was unique to them but because nowhere in the Southwest was it used more. It is not my intent to analyze the scroll as a decorative element in detail, though this could be pursued with profit, and useful phase and period criteria could be established. A start has been made in this direction by a senior student (1969–70) in the University's Honors Program, Jon Czaplicki. This study, done under my direction, utilized only the type sherd collection representing a small fraction of the total sample, and it was concerned only with the scroll as a motif, not in the manner in which it was organized within the total field of decoration. The approach was stylistic, and the time order of the units in the sample was determined by stratigraphy.

Czaplicki's summarizing chart is reproduced in Figure 12.106, and the following information is excerpted from his paper. First, although examples of the rectilinear treatment of the scroll were noted in each phase, the preferred mode of depiction was curvilinear, excepting in the Classic Period when the emphasis was reversed.

A free-floating curled element appears sparingly as the first feeble effort at showing the scroll in the Estrella Phase, the moment when the painting of pottery began. In the Sweetwater Phase, the earlier solid line portrayal was converted to a hachure-filled unit, often interlocked, large in relation to the total decorative field. The basal part from which the scroll rose was often saw-toothed, introducing the concept of the stepped greque. During the Snaketown Phase, the hachure was refined, the lines became increasingly closely spaced so that by the end of the phase the solid scroll was again emerging. Edge-terracing became more prevalent, and the scroll size, on the average, was somewhat reduced over the preceding phase. The solid line scroll in increasing manners of portrayal became dominant in the Gila Butte Phase, and saw-toothed, or terraced edges were converted often to parallel lines resembling a fringe. Scroll size was further reduced and organization was in complex assemblies. The trend toward variability of use continued into the Santa Cruz Phase, fringed edges being dominant over saw-toothing and cursive noninterlocking forms appended to a line became more prevalent. Some increase in size over immediately earlier treatment is noted also. During the Sacaton Phase the trend was toward larger scrolls with more volutes, possibly associated with increase in vessel size. On the average, scrolls were used more as fillers in panels and solid triangles than in the complicated total field layouts of the Colonial Period. Rectilinearity became more prevalent. And finally, in the Classic Period, Soho and Civano Phases, the mode was the rectilinear scroll, seldom shown in any way other than in a simple band arrangement. Edge-fringing was lost.

The stepped greque is a widespread motif in the arts of the Americas, seen most often in pottery. The usual distinguishing feature is a saw-toothed or terraced element from which the scroll, rectilinear or curvilinear, arises. It is sometimes referred to as the bird-wing design in the Southwest, because on bird-effigy vessels, the element is often painted in the wing position. The history of the motif is a long one, dating from the Sweetwater Phase in the early centuries of the Christian Era among the Hohokam; in Pre-Classic Mexico it occurs earlier, as in Monte Alban II (Caso, Bernal and Acosta 1967: Lám. IV, *c*), and perhaps even before that among the Olmecs. Tracing the American development of the motif as suggested by Braniff (1970), and even making comparisons with Asiatic forms, should be a challenge to students of art history.

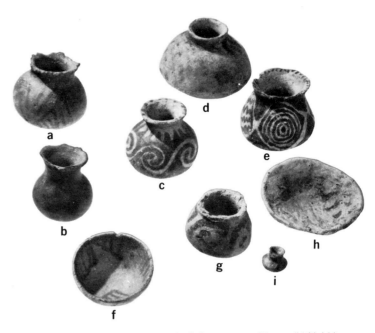

Fig. 12.107. Miniature vessels: (a-f) Sweetwater Phase; (b) Vahki Phase; (c) Santa Cruz Phase; all others Sacaton Phase; (h) bears mat impression on under side. Diameter of *i*, 15 mm.

Miscellaneous Ceramics

MINIATURE VESSELS

Small copies of large vessels were evidently sparingly produced at all times (Fig. 12.107). For the most part they are well made, the products of accomplished potters and not the experiments of novices. Most of the specimens were recovered during probes in trash deposits, although one specimen (Fig. 12.107d) was in a posthole of House 13:5G. Snaketown produced no helpful clues as to the use of mini-vessels.

CLAY TUBE

A Sacaton Phase house floor (House 3:10I) produced the fired clay tube illustrated in Figure 12.108. Crudely made of the clay used for painted pottery, its one end is tapered, the other slightly flared. Its use remains unknown.

WORKED POTSHERDS

In spite of the almost inexhaustible supply of broken pottery, relatively little use was made of the resource by reshaping pieces for specific purposes. A sample of the kinds of specimens recovered is illustrated in Figure 12.109, and the distribution and frequencies are noted in Figure 12.110. Small discs, both plain

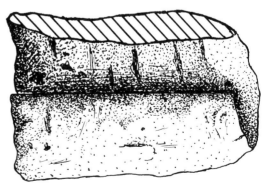

Fig. 12.108. Clay tube, Sacaton Phase. Length, 6.7 cm.

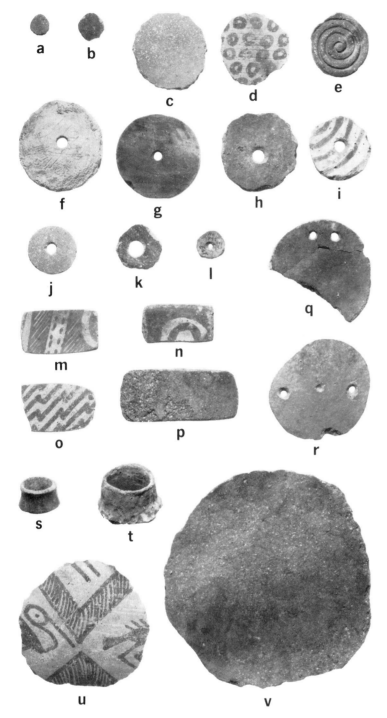

Fig. 12.109. Worked potsherds: Unperforated discs: (a) Sweetwater Phase; (b) Gila Butte Phase; (c, e) Estrella Phase. Perforated discs: (f, i) Sacaton Phase; (g, h) Gila Butte Phase; (j) Vahki Phase; (k) Snaketown Phase; (l) Estrella Phase. Rectangular units: (m) Snaketown Phase; (n, o) Gila Butte Phase; (p) Sacaton Phase. (?) Mirror backs: (q) Santa Cruz Phase; (r) Gila Butte Phase. Worked jar necks: (s) unplaced; (t) Sacaton Phase. Large discs: (u) Santa Cruz Phase; (v) Gila Butte Phase. Diameter of v, 16.4 cm.

PHASES / TYPES	DISCS SMALL UNPERFORATED	PERFORATED	LARGE	? MIRROR BACKS	RECTANGULAR UNITS	JAR NECK RINGS	MISCELLANEOUS	TOTALS
CIVANO		2					1	3
SACATON	37	17	5		6	1	1	67
SANTA CRUZ	40	17	6	1	1		1	66
GILA BUTTE	14	12	1	1	14	2	1	45
SNAKETOWN	30	16	4		22	1		73
SWEETWATER	25	31	1			1	6	64
ESTRELLA	9	9			1		3	22
VAHKI	26	37	1		1		3	68
PIONEER P.	1	3	3				3	10
NOT PLACED	11	12				1	1	25
TOTALS	193	156	21	2	45	6	20	44

Fig. 12.110. Type and time distribution of worked potsherds.

and centrally drilled, are omnipresent, as they are most everywhere. Diameters vary from 1.5 to 7.5 cm, workmanship ranges from good edge trimming, including grinding, to no more than rough shaping. The numbers made of plain or painted pottery are about even. Speculations about their uses have varied widely, from spindle whorls to gaming pieces. We do know that symbolic use has been made of them when tied together in pairs and deposited in caves (Fulton 1941: 24-25) and placed singly in the bottom of major Great Kiva roof supports at Point of Pines (Ariz. W:10:78, Turkey Creek Ruin). The latter references are to unperforated pieces. Proveniences at Snaketown shed no light on possible uses.

The perforated discs average 5 cm in diameter, the biconically drilled holes averaging about 8 mm in size. In general, these discs were better shaped than the unperforated ones. Those with grossly off-centered holes might rule out spindle-whorl use. As for the better ones, they may have served spinning needs because the specially made Mexican-derived clay whorl did not become a part of the cultural complex until late in the Sedentary Period. Whorls of other materials may also have been used.

The few large discs in the collection, from 10 to 20 cm in diameter, were most often fashioned of painted pottery, as seen variously on the concave or convex surfaces. They must have served as plates.

The two specimens listed as mirror backs (Fig. 12.109q and r) are conjectural, but the disc size and the placement of the holes are indicative. A mica-covered disc found earlier (Gladwin and others 1937: Pl. CCIXj), together with the aforementioned specimens, could represent Hohokam efforts to duplicate the mosaic plaques coming to them from Mexico with the materials they had available.

Two other classes of worked sherds deserve mention. The first is a relatively numerous lot of roughly rectangular units from 4.5 to 7.7 cm long (Fig. 12.109m-p). Widths are usually one-half the length. Ends were squared or rounded, edges were well trimmed, and even some faces were worn down to reduce the convexity. Alterations were intentional and not the result from work, as scraping, done with the pieces. These objects were most prevalent during the Snaketown and Gila Butte Phases.

The second group consists of small jar necks (Fig. 12.109s-t) with edges finely fractured or ground smooth. They remind one of ear spools, and indeed they may have served as such, as some figurines show ear ornamentation. If this is the case, however, it is strange that so few exist and that ear spools were not made for the purpose, given the skill the Hohokam had with clay.

Finally, there is a single potsherd of Snaketown Phase age which was modified in the form of a miniature palette (Fig. 12.111). The back, as well as the edges, was shaped; the face, naturally slightly concave because the fragment is from a jar rim, was further marked with the characteristic rectangular area of a palette.

Fig. 12.111. Miniature palette made from a pot-sherd, Snaketown Phase. Actual size.

INTRUSIVE POTTERY

Because the main value of trade pottery lies in its usefulness as a tool for correlating the Hohokam sequence with the histories of other people, the creators of the trade items, this topic is discussed later in the section entitled "How Old is Snaketown?"

PIMA POTTERY

The reoccupation of Snaketown by a number of Pima families late in the nineteenth century introduced their pottery into the site. Although most of the containers used by these families were of glass, porcelain, and metal, the Pimas nevertheless still made use of their own pottery, a plainware, red-on-buff, a slipped and well-polished redware, and a redware carrying weak black designs. While most of the vessels were clearly for storage, smaller containers, presumably for holding and serving prepared food, also appear in the collection. All contemporary Pima pottery was sufficiently different from the old Hohokam types so as to cause no real confusion in identification. Even though the Pimas settled on or next to existing refuse mounds in some cases, they did not add their trash to the old heaps.

The principal sources for Pima wares were the caches randomly scattered over the site and found by accident in the course of our excavations. These deposits represent the possessions of deceased Pimas which were buried apart from the owner's mortal remains, a custom that in itself is worthy of study. It is not the intent here to do that or to review in detail the Pima pottery and associated objects recovered in the caches. However, Figures 12.112 and 12.113 are included to provide an impression of the main types of local historic ceramics. Documentation for this kind of material does exist (Russell 1908: 124-131; Hayden 1959: 10-16; Fontana, Robinson, Cormack, and Leavitt 1962).

A question most closely bearing on the objectives of this report is the relationship between Pima Red-on-buff and the types produced by the Hohokam. The materials, the manufacturing techniques, and the colors are basically the same; the forms and the designs differ. This is not surprising, considering the centuries that separate the latest formal identified Hohokam pottery and late nineteenth century Pima products. The tradition appears to be one and the same. This question will not be convincingly resolved until a continuity can be demonstrated by the recovery of materials datable to the span of years between 1400 and 1800.

Fig. 12.112. Historic Pima pottery recovered from caches at Snaketown. (a, b) plainware, the latter a bean pot; (c-h) Pima Red-on-buff. Diameter of g, 39.5 cm.

Fig. 12.113. Historic Pima pottery recovered from caches: (a) redware; (b-e) black-on-red. Diameter of e, 29.3 cm.

CONCLUDING THOUGHTS
ABOUT POTTERY

No two people devoted to studying the vast collection of pottery from Snaketown would produce exactly the same kind of descriptive and interpretive results. In reviewing what has been said here and in later pages, it is immediately apparent that top priority has been given to ceramics as a vehicle for chronology building. Such a thrust has a number of facets. Moments of stability in style are accepted as hallmarks of a phase, while at the same time the changes in style provide the connective tissue of a tradition; associated trade pieces are looked upon as indicators of coevality with neighboring tribes, and local pottery is seen as a resource for highly particular studies of changes in the paleomagnetic intensities of the earth's magnetic field (Bucha, Taylor, Berger, and Haury 1970). Next in importance was using pottery as a reflector of intercultural connections, the societies of Mexico being an example.

Not as much has been done with this subject as it deserves, but the "southern look" of Hohokam ceramics is unmistakable. While the role of pottery in Hohokam society has been touched on, little dependence has been placed on it as a way of measuring social change. I consider this aspect of pottery analysis to lead to unsure results, which explains my neglect of the subject area. However, I do not consider efforts in this direction necessarily wasted, for problem formulation and ways of data collecting and processing are steadily improving. These advances will eventually lead to far better insights than we are now capable of developing.

A speculation about the changes that have been noted in the stream of Hohokam pottery is in order. I see little or no basis for believing that the physical environment exerted any influences leading to modifications in ceramics directly. It may be reasoned that abundant crops grown in a favorable environment called for an increase in storage container size during late times. Mainly, however, the basic needs of cooking, serving, and storing of foodstuffs were not affected, and adverse natural conditions left no recognizable stamp on the ceramics. Clay supplies and fuel for firing appear to have been constants.

Two moments in the life of the Hohokam may be identified when societal pressures apparently left imprints on the pottery. The first was in the Sedentary Period when the suggested population upswing called for a higher ceramic productivity, attended by a proliferation of vessel shapes and a decline in the quality of the painted decoration, a forerunner of the scourge of mass production. The second was the major shift from many to a restricted number of vessel forms, a complete reorientation of the painted regimen and a vastly reduced level of production, all of which happened in the Classic Period. These losses may be related somehow to the intercultural contacts with the Salado people, which, if one reads the pottery correctly, did have some effects on the resident Hohokam.

By and large, however, looking beyond the situations noted above and those additions to the pottery inventory which were required by religious and magical practices—the censer, as an example—I see Hohokam ceramics as a naturally evolving fabric, an unplanned blossoming of a craft. The change-producing forces were inherent in the medium because the duplicating factor was high. Furthermore, the relative social tranquility, unbroken for many centuries, provided the seed bed in which the potter's art could flourish.

13. Figurines and Miscellaneous Clay Objects

One of the activities dictated by Hohokam custom was the production of clay human figurines. Some of the miscellaneous other clay products may have had a direct relationship to the figurines.

FIGURINES
Human Forms

Remnants of figurines were associated with every time horizon of the village. Their frequency and formalization suggest that they were not made as toys or to pacify the baby at the potter's side. The meaning is clearly deeper than that, although, as of now, it is impossible to say what purpose they served.

A well-developed figurine complex is one of the distinguishing marks of the Hohokam, and it was more firmly imbedded here than among any other archaeological groups north of Mexico. Important also is the fact that the figurines were present from the time of founding of Snaketown. Their use continued uninterrupted for at least a thousand years. Considered quantitatively, the Hohokam produced far less than were made in the high centers of culture in Mesoamerica but far more than their neighbors to the north and east, the Anasazi and the Mogollon. The origin of the idea, along with the other elements that characterize the early Hohokam, such as canal irrigation, a sophisticated agricultural economy, pottery-making, and stable architecture, must be attributed to the south. But in the transmission of the idea, time and distance did much to filter out certain aspects associated with the southern figurine assemblages: the range of subject matter, the imagination and the detail seen in the finished products, variability in posture, use of pigment, and the quantity needed to fulfill their intended purpose.

The present sample, numbering 1,072 whole and fragmentary specimens, approximately triples the resources of the excavations in 1934–35. It is heavily weighted in favor of specimens from Pioneer Period contexts. This is the product of our more intensive digging in the earlier deposits of the site than in later accumulations. Two additional circumstances are also responsible. First, Pioneer Period figurines occur in the trash where they were thrown with other unwanted refuse. Their recovery came through the screening of numerous stratigraphic tests. Beginning in the Colonial Period, figurines in trash were rare; instead they are usually associated with cremations. This relationship reached climax in the Sedentary Period. Because no systematic effort was made to uncover cremations, the opportunity to recover the later figurines was therefore limited. Second, with this apparent change in function, there seems also to have been a change in the quantity produced, fewer after the Pioneer Period, unless there was a switch from clay to perishable substances. The scarcity of

figurines in Classic Period sites hints that the figurine complex, including the motives for producing them, was on the path to extinction.

Clay for figurine-making and a group of other objects associated with them, all of Pioneer Period age, was specially gathered, and it differed from the clay used in the production of pottery. Its fine consistency was well suited for the execution of details and the application of slender arms and ornaments. The high organic content of the clay, indicated by the blackness of the products when lightly fired, its basic consistency and occasional rounded sand grain inclusions, suggests that the clay may have been gathered as river mud. Bearing out this supposition is a broken figurine of probable Snaketown Phase age which contains a cast and a shell of fresh water snails. The finished figures at best are soft and are easily scarred by brushing. Colonial and Sedentary Period figurines tend to be made of a coarser clay, more nearly approaching the type used in pottery, and they were also better fired.

The mould for figurine-making was unknown to the Hohokam. They were hand modeled and unpolished, frequently showing the imprints of fingers. Sticks or bone splinters, blunted or sharp, finger squeezes, and fingernails were used to produce anatomic details, body incising, and occasional elements of dress. Applique was sparingly used. Armatures, consisting of grass stems or thin twigs, were occasionally used to reinforce limb and head attachment to the body (Fig. 13.19).

Typically, Pioneer Period figurines were made by a two-piece method. Two rods of clay were pressed together, the upper segment being modeled into head and torso and the lower section being separated to form the legs (Fig. 13.1). Anatomic details were then added by squeezing the clay or by applique and by indentations. The welding of the two rods was not always well done, and many have come apart, accounting for a sizable number of half-heads and torsos in the collection. The smaller figurines were fashioned from a single rod.

After the Pioneer Period the technique changed to a dominant single piece method of production. During the Sedentary Period notable departures were the use of clay for the head and face only, the rest of the body being made of perishable material, and there was a break from the earlier canons of a stiff style to greater realism in facial modeling.

Most of the figurines were little more than scorched by the fire. A few are unfired, and some are hard-baked to a light buff color due to the oxidation of the organic matter in the clay. This variability in firing raises the question as to whether or not baking was a function of use rather than a step for use, a subject which will be examined later.

With few exceptions all figurines recovered were fragmentary. Some significance may be read into this, for I believe it means

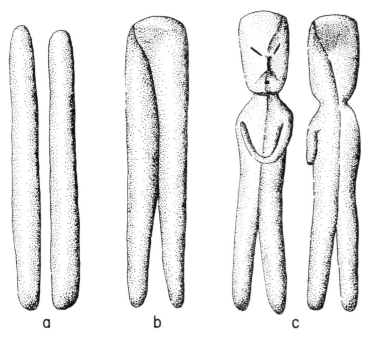

Fig. 13.1. The two-piece method of making Pioneer Period figurines: (a) two rods of clay; (b) partly welded; (c) finished by hand modeling with appliqued arm.

PARTS	PIONEER PERIOD										COLONIAL		SED.	TOTAL	
	PIONEER PERIOD	VAHKI	ESTRELLA	V-E	V-SW	SW	E-SW	SW-ST	ST	ST-GB	GB	SC	SAC.		
LIMBS	14 / 80	10 / 67	17 / 112	5	10	25 / 75	11 / 94	2 / 32	3 / 24	3 / 30	1 / 10	6	2	88 / 545	633
HEADS (SOME W/ TORSO)	21 / 4	21 / 3	24 / 5			38 / 3	6 / 9	12 / 4	7 / 1	6 / 1	8	2	7	152 / 30	182
TORSOS	12 / 12	13 / 8	18 / 11			24 / 13	5 / 13	6 / 1	8 / 1	5 / 4	6		1	98 / 63	161
MISCL. FRAGS.	13	16	16		1	15	25	4		6				96	96
TOTAL	47 / 109	44 / 94	59 / 144	5	11	87 / 106	22 / 141	20 / 41	18 / 26	14 / 41	15 / 10	2 / 6	10	338 / 734	
	156	138	203	5	11	193	163	61	44	55	25	8	10	1072	GRAND TOTAL

5 = TOO FRAGMENTARY TO CLASSIFY ACCURATELY   V = VAHKI   SW = SWEETWATER   GB = GILA BUTTE
5 = CLASSIFIABLE   E = ESTRELLA   ST = SNAKETOWN   SC = SANTA CRUZ   SAC.= SACATON

Fig. 13.2. Tabulation of human figurines in Snaketown sample.

that there was willful breakage following their utilization, perhaps to discourage recovery as playthings by children. This act, together with disposal in trash, reveals an attitude of complete uselessness toward them, once the purpose for which they were made was fulfilled.

On the whole, the new collection agrees with the previously established developmental sequence (Gladwin and others 1937: 233ff). Some new details have been added. These, together with the typology and the observable trends in style, will emerge in the phase analysis that follows. Two analytical procedures might be pursued in studying figurines. The first would be strictly typological, paying no attention at the start to provenience, and through this approach to develop a hypothetical sequence to be tested against the stratigraphic record. However, with the firm establishment of the phase sequence it is more realistic to tackle the problem from the known contextual point of view. Phase assignment of the majority of the specimens was not difficult; but in case of badly mixed trash samples, the most one can do is to relate the figurines to a period. Some extreme mixing, as Pioneer Period figurines in Sedentary Period trash, is seen, and in these cases the separation is made on typological grounds. This is considered a safe procedure because of the different typology of Sacaton Phase figurines and because the mixing was not limited to figurines but included pottery as well. In "pure" Sacaton Phase contexts Pioneer Period type figurines did not appear.

The quantitative distribution of figurines through time is given in Figure 13.2. It is tempting to establish an elaborate typology, recognizing the minor details that are exhibited by the figurines in the collection. But this would complicate what is really a fairly simple picture. Instead, sample lots selected to portray kind and range for each phase will be shown. Stylistic details and other relevant facts will be noted in summary fashion.

PIONEER PERIOD

Vahki Phase (Figs. 13.3 and 13.4)

Nearly every phase has some figurines in the collection which are no more than clay rods with pinched clay for a nose and indented dots for eyes and mouth (Fig. 13.3b and c), about as simple a portrayal of the human face as is possible. The female figurine (a) is a simple abstraction with only enough detail to

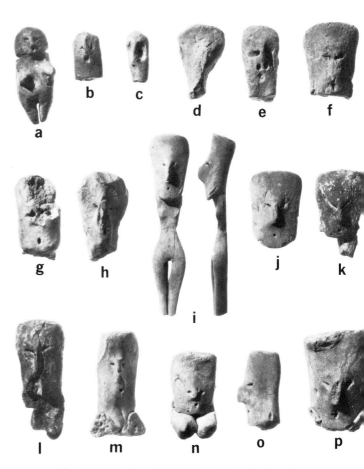

Fig. 13.3. Figurines, Vahki Phase. Length of i, 7.4 cm.

show the sex of the subject. Typically, in indicating the female form, the breasts are emphasized, genitals are not. The rest of the heads in Figure 13.3 establish the headform characteristic of all Pioneer Period figurines: slightly wedge-shaped in frontal outline with tops rounded or flat but generally sloping backward toward a concavity in the back of the head when seen in section. On the facial surface the nose was pinched up from the basal clay (o), and pits or slits, often oblique, sufficed to show the eyes. Mouths are almost always shown as pits, and nostrils (e) are seldom portrayed. Specimen d lacks all facial marks except the nose.

In some instances, pinches of clay along the lower cheek borders of the face (f, k, o) may represent ears, but it is more likely that these are simplifications of the chin ornaments seen as indented appliqued clay pellets in p (see also Fig. 13.15j). This head also shows remnants of red paint, wavy lines radiating outward from the nose.

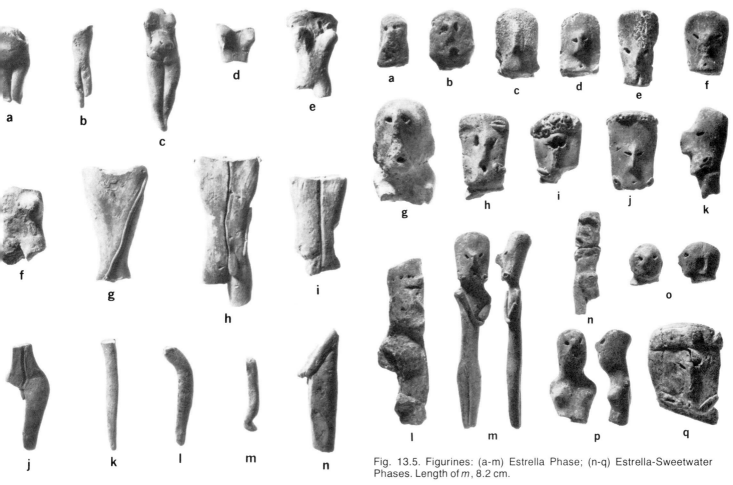

Fig. 13.4. Torsos and limbs, Vahki Phase. Length of h, 5.7 cm.

Fig. 13.5. Figurines: (a-m) Estrella Phase; (n-q) Estrella-Sweetwater Phases. Length of m, 8.2 cm.

Figure 13.4 illustrates torso treatments, the most common form being the hourglass, or "Mae West," type. This is seen to best advantage in the nearly complete specimen shown in Figure 13.3i. When sex is determinable, about half of the figures are female in the Vahki Phase sample, and one (Fig. 13.4c) portrays pregnancy with hands under the abdomen. Some male torsos show a curious longitudinal scoring on the anterior surface reaching from the pubes to the neck (Fig. 13.4h-j). These were made while the clay was still plastic and before the application of arms and genitals. There is no hint as to what this feature means. Slender strings of clay were attached to the torso as arms. The hands, not represented as such, generally cross over the pubes "September Morn" fashion. Legs most often are slender and peglike (Fig. 13.4k and l) as though designed for sticking the figure in the ground. Foot representations and heavy blunt-ended legs also occur (Fig. 13.4m and n).

Although the Vahki Phase collection of figurines shows only bodies in an extended position, there is no reason to doubt that the seated posture was also known. Sitting figures are present in the Estrella Phase.

Estrella Phase (Figs. 13.5 and 13.6)

The general style of Pioneer Period figurines as established in the Vahki Phase continues in the Estrella Phase. The crude and featureless faces (Fig. 13.5a-c) are present, and on the others in the same illustration, attention is called to a "coffee-bean" eyebrow (h) and to appliqued and pitted head bands (i, j). Figurine l is a clear example of the medial splitting arising from the two-piece method of construction while at the same time illustrating punctate eyebrows, the earliest occurrence of this feature. Specimen m, lacking only the leg-ends and an arm, is the most nearly whole early figurine recovered. The right arm apparently

came down over the pelvic region while the left one is folded back up over the right shoulder. A curious patch, seen in a few other examples, is stuck on the upper arm as a separate piece.

Some figurines are not clearly assignable to phase as they came from mixed contexts. Specimens n-q are in this category, having been found in Estrella-Sweetwater phase trash; o and p are simple but show a more realistic head form than was usual; n, a pregnant female figure, is included because of the mutilation in the eye area, seen also in i. Specimen q is another example with head band.

Estrella Phase torsos and limbs are shown in Figure 13.6. Male torsos outnumber female by ratio of 2.5:1. The hourglass form (a-c) appears to be standard; pregnant figures are seen in d-f, e being in a seated position. Arm positions are given in f, g, and h, the first one having a broad lower arm "guard" and h is equipped with what probably represents a series of bracelets. Ventral incising shows on h, i, and m, all male figures. Specimen j reveals a dented pellet omphalos, rarely shown at any time, and what may be presumed to be a long pubic apron. Male seated torsos (k-m) and leg types complete the survey. Leg t has an applied anklet, and u-v show a delicate incised and punctate pattern on the lower limb (see also Fig. 13.14h and i).

Details present in this phase and not in the Vahki Phase are doubtless due to sampling and not to innovations.

Sweetwater Phase (Figs. 13.7, 13.8, and 13.9)

The Sweetwater Phase collection is larger than that of any other phase, attributable to more extensive digging in trash deposits of this phase rather than to an intensification of figurine production. Of special interest in Figure 13.7 are: a, a head, featureless except for the nose, which is a complete unit and was never attached to a body; g, manifesting a profile unlike all others and curiously, has

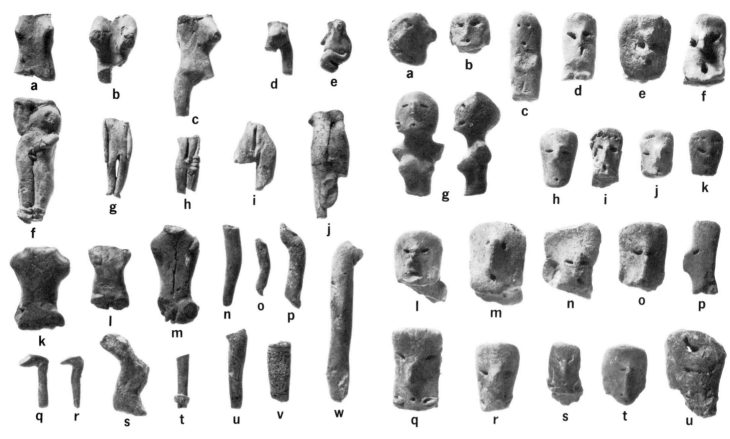

Fig. 13.6. Torsos and limbs, Estrella Phase. Length of *f*, 5.6 cm.

Fig. 13.7. Figurines, Sweetwater Phase. Length of *g*, 4.5 cm.

a sand grain stuck in the tip of the nose as though to simulate a nose plug; *i, j* and *k,* with punctate eyebrows; *t,* with nostrils portrayed; and *u,* a badly damaged specimen but having a hole through the forehead made while the clay was plastic, possibly a manifestation of ''black'' magic.

Sweetwater Phase torso types follow the pattern already set with the following additional notes: In Figure 13.8, *g* and *h* indicate chest decorations, probably necklaces, either as dented pellets or clay fillets, and the latter also repeats the upper arm decorations seen in other examples; ventral incising is seen in *e, f,* and punctate in *g*; and *o* and *p* are indubitable pregnancies.

Limbs of this phase (Fig. 13.9*a*-*l*) indicate that in some figurines they sometimes extended from the body (*a, b, h, i*) instead of as applied thin fillets and that figurine size varied greatly (*e, f*); *k* is another example of an incised-punctate decorated thigh, and *l* introduces a new theme for a figurine base, an egg-shaped foot or basal weight. A similar handling of the base is observed in a few Prescott figurines (Gladwin and others 1937: Pl. CCVII *c*; Scott 1960: Fig. 2 *g, i*), and curiously, something similar appears in a small group of figurines from Bee Cave, Brewster County, Texas (Coffin 1932: Fig. 17).

Figurines from mixed Sweetwater-Snaketown Phase deposits are shown in Figure 13.9 *m*-*v*. Of special interest are *r*-*u* because they were not baked; *r* retains black paint representing hair; *s* and *t* clearly show an incrustation of wood ash, a detail seen on numerous other figurines as well; *u* is an incised and punctate leg fragment; and *v* is a phallus fragment which, with those of stone, reflects the relatively minor preoccupation by the Hohokam in the realistic portrayal of sex organs.

Once again in moving up the time scale, the Sweetwater collection of figurines amplifies but does not alter the formalized tradition established in earlier phases of what surely was cult paraphernalia.

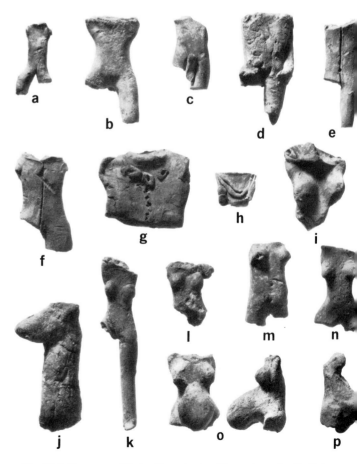

Fig. 13.8. Torsos and limbs, Sweetwater Phase. Length of *k*, 7.1 cm.

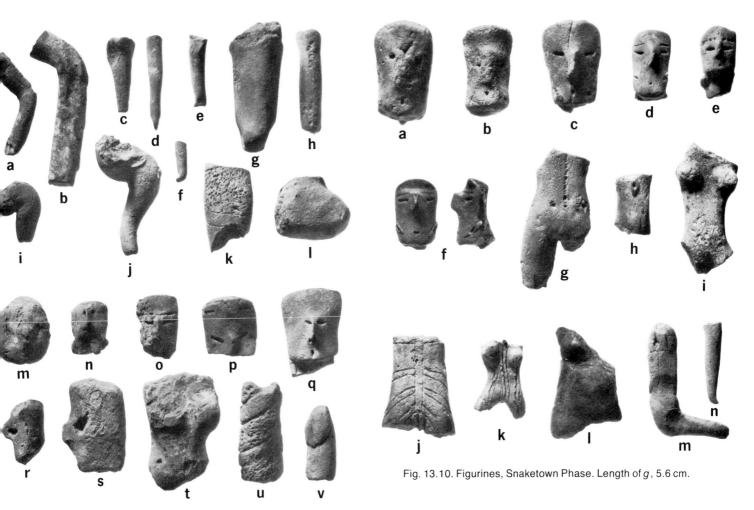

Fig. 13.9. Figurine fragments: (a-l) Sweetwater Phase; (m-v) Sweetwater-Snaketown Phases. Length of *b*, 6.3 cm.

Fig. 13.10. Figurines, Snaketown Phase. Length of *g*, 5.6 cm.

Snaketown Phase (Fig. 13.10)

Though small, the Snaketown Phase sample reveals no sharp changes over earlier times. Head painting to represent hair (*f*), a ventral scar by punctation (*g*), and a chest ornament (*h*) are worthy of attention, as are also *j* and *k*, both female torsos which indicate different kinds of body incising. The latter has a small black pebble pressed in the clay between the breasts, apparently an intentional addition as foreign materials of this kind are not visible in the rest of the object. It is reminiscent of the small quartz crystal in the heart position of an unfired figurine from Ventana Cave (Haury 1950: Fig. 84*g*).

Pioneer Period Unplaced as to Phase (Fig. 13.11)

Inevitably there is a residue of figurines assignable by type to a period but whose provenience in churned trash precluded assignment to phase. As often happens, some of these add details which are new. For example, *a* is one of the smallest heads in the collection, raising the question as to whether smallness was intended to represent infants. The collection is notably lacking in clearcut examples of these. The portrayal of all ages and sexes might have some bearing on conclusions as to figurine function. Figure 13.11*j* again shows a headdress and ventral incising. Among the torso types, *k* departs from the hourglass norm, and *l* is limbless, ending bluntly as though designed to set up in soft earth; *o,* a torso with pendulous breasts, in sitting position, is unfired; *p* and *q* show pregnancies, the former also seated; *r,* a male torso with folded right arm, has patches on both upper arms; and *s* hints at the use of a waist band.

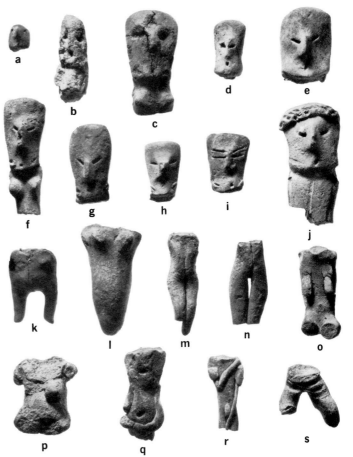

Fig. 13.11. Figurines, Pioneer Period, unplaced as to phase. Length of *l*, 4.9 cm.

Fig. 13.12. Figurines: (a-g) Snaketown-Gila Butte Phases; (h-q) Gila Butte Phase. Length of c, 7.4 cm.

COLONIAL PERIOD

Snaketown-Gila Butte and Gila Butte Phases (Fig. 13.12)

The tiny example (*a*) may represent an infant, though ear-punctures are shown; *b* is featureless except for nose; and *d* is a lantern-jawed head duplicating one found by Gila Pueblo (Gladwin and others 1937: Pl. CXCIX*h*) assigned to the Gila Butte Phase, where this one also probably "fits." Torso *f* is of the stub variety, an uncommon treatment but presumably not accidental.

More accurately placed Gila Butte Phase figurines are shown in *h* to *q*. The mode of the Pioneer Period style is still present, but a trend to a different form is setting in: Consistent use of eyebrow slits, crude as they may be, but culminating in greater realism including better face modeling, a diamond-shaped eye with pupil and slit mouth, are exemplified by *l* (see also Gladwin and others 1937: Pl. CXCIX). Leg *q* clearly shows the imprint of a grass stem used as an armature (see also Fig. 13.19).

Santa Cruz Phase (Fig. 13.13a-d)

The Santa Cruz Phase collection numbers only a few units but enough to show the "coffee-bean" eye (*a, b*) (see also Gladwin and others 1937: Pls. CXCVII and CXCVIII) as well as a carry-over of the earlier style (*c, d*). Along with the form change, a functional change may also have taken place, for most Santa Cruz Phase figurines have been found with cremations although those shown here came from trash.

SEDENTARY PERIOD

Sacaton Phase (Fig. 13.13e-h)

Several marked changes took place in the figurine tradition during the Sacaton Phase. First, in certain ones ultimate simplicity was achieved by pressing out at the top of a clay rod an oblique discoidal area representing the face carrying no more than a

pinched ridge for a nose (*e*). This style is evidently a late one, as close parallels have been reported from the Prescott area (Scott 1960), from the Sinagua culture of Flagstaff (McGregor 1941: Fig. 23f), and Los Muertos (Haury 1945a: Fig. 69a). All are Sedentary and Classic Period productions. Second, in direct contrast to the above, is a group of heads in which maximum realism was achieved. These are no more than faces, cleverly modeled in clay around a stem of perishable material. The original Snaketown volume (Gladwin and others 1937, Plate CXCV) illustrates these superbly. The current work produced only two examples, associated with Cremation 20:5F. Both were subjected to such intense heat in the crematory fire that the clay became viscous and bubbly. The better of the two is shown in Figure 13.13f. The idea of putting a clay face on a perishable body, as far as we now know, is a Sacaton Phase hallmark.

Third, two leg fragments, one of them illustrated (*g*), suggest that the idea of making figurines with movable limbs was not foreign to the Hohokam. Actually this fits the general concept of composite figurines, as does adding a clay face to a perishable body. If the identification of these pieces is correct, it underscores the closeness of the tie between the Hohokam and the figurine-makers of Mexico who occasionally produced the assembled type (Borhegyi 1966; Séjourné 1966: Pl. 56).

Fourth, a large seated figure, supporting a vessel on top of the

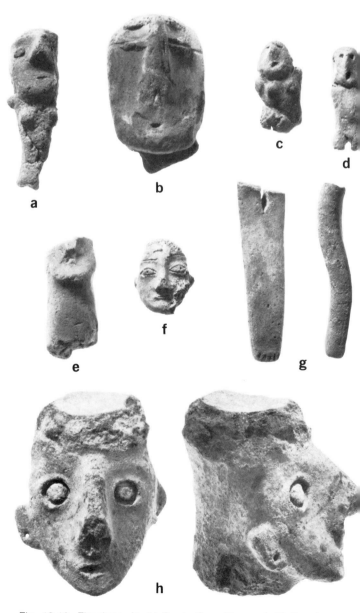

Fig. 13.13. Figurines: (a, b) Santa Cruz Phase; (c-h) Sacaton Phase. Height of *h*, 7.1 cm.

head (Gladwin and others 1937: Pl. CXCVIa), is represented by a battered head (*h*). This figure, along with those referred to next, is washed with a buff coating. Painting in red, mostly faded, is visible on the face. Deeply incised eye circles, pierced ears, a prodigious nose with nostrils and mouth complete the facial details. Actually the theme of a vessel on the head of a figure is at least as early as the Snaketown Phase (Gladwin and others 1937: Fig. 113), but the monumental nature of the figure appears to be of Sedentary Period age.

Finally, two solid, essentially identical figures found with Cache 2:9F (Fig. 11.11) deserve a special note. Judged by the nature of the associated material, these probably fit somewhere in the early part of the Sacaton Phase, perhaps about A.D. 900–1000.

In both cases a seated female is portrayed with upturned face, hands on the knees and arms akimbo on the better preserved of the two. A bulky apron appears on both, as does a curious posterior protuberance. What this represents is not clear. If it shows a body abnormality it may help to explain the apparent facial anguish; on the other hand, if a part of costume, it might be no more than the gathering-up of a voluminous string apron known to have been worn by the Hohokam (Haury 1950: 429, Pl. 40). The argument against this alternative is the fact that the apron appears to terminate in front, as would be the case with a free-hanging type.

CLASSIC PERIOD

Our limited work in Classic Period sites produced no figurines, not surprising since the complex appears to have been on the way out after the Sedentary Period. Morss (1954: 27*ff*) reviews what is known about figurines in a development he calls the Southern Tradition.

ANALYSIS

In open sites where organic goods are subject to the destructive effect of moisture, the archaeologist is deprived of the opportunity to study an important class of materials, the elements which often tell so much about customs and costumes. Figurines provide a little help in this direction, but considering the number of units found, revelations about the Hohokam are actually disappointing. Nevertheless it is worthwhile to examine the figurines again from the trait-like standpoint.

Manufacture

The early two-piece method of figurine production has been described (Fig. 13.1), and note was made of the fact that this technique was supplanted by the one-piece, or rod, method at about the beginning of the Colonial Period. Correlated with the change was the occasional use of a wooden pin or armature to better secure the limbs to the body. The Snaketown collection shows this in the most fragmentary form only; but a Santa Cruz Phase figurine from a site near Winkelman close to the junction of the Gila and San Pedro Rivers illustrates the principle well (Fig. 13.19a). This specimen is in the Arizona State Museum collections by courtesy of Alice Carpenter of Oracle, Arizona. Penetration of the stick armatures into the torso was about 1 cm, a little more than that into the head.

Subject Matter

During all phases, the subject matter was equally divided between adult male and female portrayals. When female, breasts were often accentuated but sex organs were not. The pregnant female figure, extended or seated, is prevalent throughout the Pioneer Period, less so during subsequent periods, which suggests that they may have been inspired by increase rites, the importance of which may have waned with the passage of time. Arms in the act of supporting the extended abdomen are the rule when pregnancy is shown and arms are preserved. Male portrayals show subdued masculine features.

Looking at all the opportunities the Hohokam had to depict sex, by painting on pottery, clay modeling, stone and shell carving, one concludes that they were not pornographically minded and that when sexual characteristics were shown, they were both natural and incidental to the subject matter. There was no preoccupation with eroticism as in Peru. Infant portrayals are not certainly identified, and the "babe-in-cradle" theme appears to be absent. Depictions of deformities and the consequence of diseases have not been recognized.

Posture

The function of figurines in the culture may have had something to do with body posture, but at best the Hohokam repertoire was limited to either extended or seated figures, the former predominating. Both postures occur in all phases, with no observable emphasis of one over the other at any time. Although dancing figures were often painted on pottery, this theme, and stances suggesting sports activities, were not shown. The versatility of postures seen in so many parts of Mexico did not extend to the Hohokam.

For the most part, leg positions were stereotyped extensions of the trunk; if in a seated figure, the knees were drawn up usually serving as supports for the arms or hands. Figures with splayed legs are seen only occasionally. The arrangement of arms, when more than stumps, appears to have had explicit meaning to the Hohokam. Arms at the side (Fig. 13.14a) was not the mode, but hands crossed over the pubic area was (Fig. 13.14b). Flexed arms, the hand clasping the opposite shoulder (Fig. 13.14c and d) was a Pioneer Period trait.

Torso and Leg Incising

Incising the trunk ventrally with a single scar was restricted to the Pioneer Period (Fig. 13.14e), occasionally expanded to multiple scorings (Fig. 13.14f). Less frequent are incised patterns covering the entire trunk and legs (Fig. 13.14g-i). Facial incising, except for anatomic details, does not occur. Whether incising imitated body tattooing or some other form of decoration is not known.

Painting

Generally speaking, details of body painting and dress are not lavishly shown. In the early Pioneer Period, face paint is present in only one figurine (Fig. 13.14j), a Vahki Phase product. A more common form was the use of paint to accentuate the hair (Fig. 13.14k and l), which was never simulated by modeling, and for emphasizing the eyes. The foregoing specimens are Snaketown and Gila Butte Phase pieces, respectively. Figure 13.14m is a Gila Butte Phase figurine with face painting, taken from the 1934–35 collection. The larger Sacaton Phase figures provided large surface areas for the artist's brush (Gladwin and others 1937: Pl. CXCVIa), and the ultimate in paint application is seen in the effigy vessels of this phase (Fig. 11.10a and b).

Head Dress

Forehead decoration is seen on a small percentage of the figures, ranging upward in time from the Estrella Phase to the Colonial Period. That the trait eventually will be found in Vahki Phase figurines may be predicted. The decorations consist either of simple punctations or appliqued bands and fillets, variously incised and dented (Fig. 13.15a). The Snaketown collection does not have examples of the more intricate headdresses which the Hohokam sometimes portrayed. A cache of figurines found near the north end of the Tucson Mountains illustrates the point. These are in the possession of Mrs. Ralph G. Vaughan of Tucson who has kindly permitted the use of the illustration used in Figure 13.16, exemplifying the turbanlike head piece with which a number of the figurines are endowed. The greatest elaboration in the clay headdress was reached in the Colonial Period,

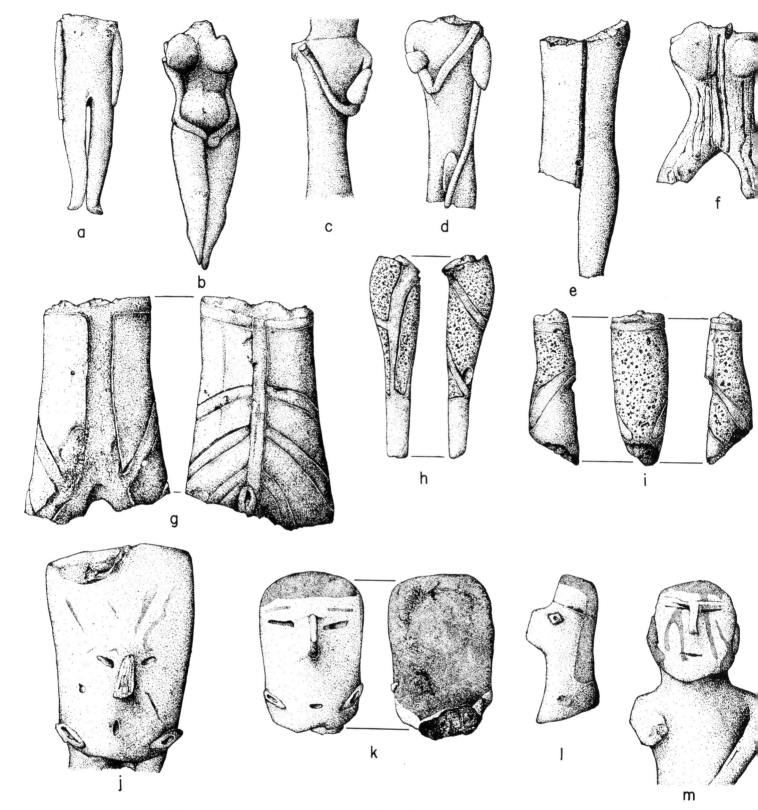

Fig. 13.14. Figurines from various phases illustrating: (a-d) arm positions; (e-i) body incising and decorating; (j-m) face or head painting (*k*, *l* black; *j*, *m* red). Length of *j*, 4.1 cm.

probably in the Santa Cruz Phase, where the specimens in this cache may be confidently assigned.

Another figurine (Arizona State Museum collection GP-46159), said to have been found in a village 2.5 km north of Sacaton, also illustrates a well-developed head piece (Fig. 13.17). A rope-like head cover, with long side appendages, suggests a turban. It is a fully modeled seated figure wrapped in a blanket that passes over the left shoulder and under the right armpit. The age is probably Sacaton Phase.

Beginning in the Colonial Period, another change took place, representing a sharp shift away from the appliqued headdress. This was the making of a hollow head and a shallow, broad

encircling groove at the forehead level, seen in the clay faces of the Sacaton Phase which were modeled around perishable stems (Gladwin and others 1937: Pl. CXCV). In the new Snaketown collection a good example dating this trait to the Santa Cruz Phase does not exist, although two specimens were found earlier (Gladwin and others 1937: Pl. CXCVIIe). For further substantiation, it is desirable at this point to introduce a specimen from the Van Liere site near Liberty Station about 65 km down-river (west north-west) from Snaketown (Fig. 13.18). In the possession of J. W. Evans of Phoenix who has kindly allowed its reproduction here, this image shows clearly what the head configuration meant. There can be no reasonable doubt that the hole engaged

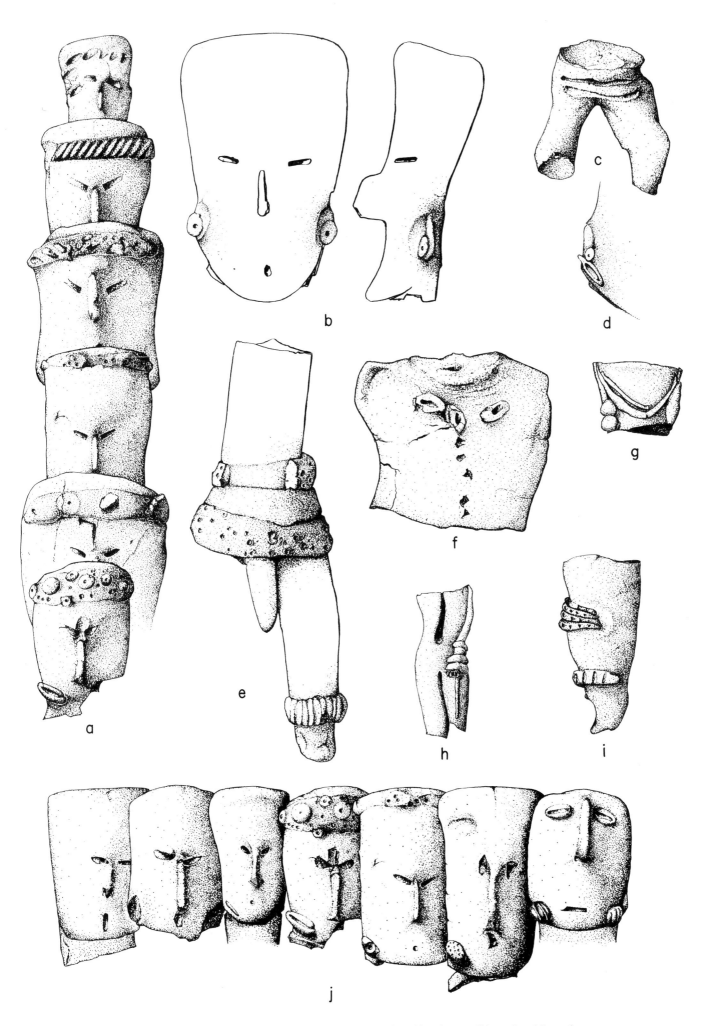

Fig. 13.15. Figurines from various phases illustrating: (a) head band types; (b) earplug; (d) earplug and chin ornament; (c, e) belts and breech clout; (f, g) chest decoration or necklace; (e, h, i) leg and arm ornaments; (j) variations in chin ornaments. Length of *e*, 7.7 cm.

Fig. 13.16. Figurine with elaborate headdress, Santa Cruz Phase. From the Mrs. Ralph G. Vaughan collection, found northwest of Tucson. Height of head about 4 cm.

(Arizona State Museum photo by Sayles).

Fig. 13.18. The Van Liere site figurine, Santa Cruz Phase. Found in 1936 in a cremation with four Santa Cruz Red-on-buff vessels, a stone palette and a small stone vessel. Height, 7.6 cm. Courtesy J. W. Evans.

(Arizona State Museum photo).

hair, that it was brought down over the head and tied, the band being kept in place by the head groove. The ethnological model for this interpretation is drawn from the method the Yuma Indians employed in making dolls just before the turn of the century (Kaemlein 1955: 5).

However, hair may not have been the only material used to lend more realism to these lumps of clay shaped in the human image. A hole in the top of the Winkelman figurine, made while the clay was soft and therefore before firing, carries the imprints of what appear to be small sticks. In other words, the edge of the hole is rough as though designed to retain elements in it by friction. The supposition is that feathers were inserted in the hole, as shown in Figure 13.19b, making a most impressive display as assembled by Alice Carpenter. Since headdresses, presumably of feathers, are depicted on human figures in the simple painted style employed in decorating pottery, the idea of stuffing feathers in a clay head is not out of reason.

Fig. 13.17. Seated figurine wrapped in blanket and with turban. Probably Sacaton Phase. Height, 9.9 cm.

Fig. 13.19. Santa Cruz Phase figurine from near Winkelman, Arizona, showing use of armatures (a) here supplied, and suggested use of feathers (b). Length of head, 6.5 cm.

Face Ornaments

More than half of the heads in the collection display a curious chin ornament. These are present in all phases of the Pioneer and Colonial Periods, lacking only in the Sedentary Period. Typologically they range from a pinched-out portion of the cheek to applied pellets without punctation, or with a dot, slit, or multiple dots or slits for accent (Fig. 13.15j). Generally, the latter are the later forms, though there is no observable difference in type during the Pioneer Period. What these chin decorations mean is a matter for speculation, as the only hint of actual artifacts that might have been worn as cheek plugs were reported in 1937 (Gladwin and others: Pl. CVIIIf). The low-level recovery of articles of this kind would suggest that the custom was not as prevalent as the figurines themselves indicate. This feature appears to be peculiarly Hohokam, as examples do not occur elsewhere in the Southwest and no analogies have been detected on Mexican figurines.

Nose plugs are never depicted, but the large nasal perforations in the effigy jar in Figure 11.10b and the figurine in Figure 13.19 suggest the use of some form of nose decoration. An undoubted representation of ear spools is shown in Figure 13.15b. Example d in the same illustration establishes the separateness of the ear spool and the chin ornament. Actual ear spools are rare (Gladwin and others 1937: Pl. CVIIId). The two specimens in the collection date from the Sacaton Phase while the above-referenced figurine is of early Pioneer Period age. Perforation of the ears was a late phenomenon, probably beginning in the Colonial Period, and became standard procedure during the Sedentary Period.

Clothing and Body Decoration

Clothing was seldom shown on Hohokam figurines. The blanket and turban have been referred to (Fig. 13.17), and in the Snaketown collection the only specimen that adds a new detail is a figurine with a breech cloth (Fig. 13.15e), representing the front-to-back belted type, actual examples of which have been found on mummies in Ventana Cave (Haury 1950: Pl. 40). Other attachments to trunk and limbs may be considered in the nature of decorations. Necklaces (Fig. 13.15f and g), bracelets (Fig. 13.15h), and both anklets and bands high on the leg (Fig. 13.15i) about cover the range of forms. Peculiar upper arm pads are seen in a number of instances (Fig. 13.14c and d). This feature is well represented in the Vaughan collection of Colonial Period age from near Tucson, demonstrating thereby that the trait was thought of as necessary equipment on some figures throughout the Hohokam domain. What it was intended to represent is not known, but it is reminiscent of arm guards on some west Mexican figures portraying ball players. A similar "shield" with a centrally mounted pellet is seen on the left leg of the Van Liere figurine (Fig. 13.18). Generalizing, although all the traits listed above occur early in the Pioneer Period, their depiction climaxed in the Colonial Period and then waned as clay modeling of solid human figurines itself began to decline.

CONCLUSIONS

Obeying the rigid artistic canons of the Pioneer Period, the Hohokam produced a myriad of monotonously similar human figures in clay. Although simple in form and embellishment, the absence of observable changes in style during the period suggests that they were not the initial efforts in a figurine-making tradition. Rather, it appears that the idea was established and had become stabilized in a pre-Vahki horizon in some place not yet identified. Beyond the obvious connection with Mexico, the origin is indelibly linked with the source for all the other traits that made the Vahki Phase what it was, the introductory stage at Snaketown but not the beginning of Hohokam. Only in the Colonial and Sedentary periods, when the Hohokam rose to their "golden age," are stylistic changes seen, perhaps related to a shift in function, from an as yet vaguely understood initial use to one which associated

them with funeral rites and led to their burial with the incinerated bones of the deceased. Even this custom was subject to further modifications during the Classic Period when figurines all but died out. At that time, the Hohokam were exposed to outside influences, those of the Salado-puebloid people, which may have been the unsettling force responsible for bringing down the curtain on the formal figurine tradition, reducing the images to the status of dolls or toys.

A key question that now arises is whether or not the typological changes noted in the Colonial and Sedentary Periods were introduced by an immigrant group, the Hohokam, into the indigenous pattern of figurine-making by the Ootam, as argued by Di Peso (1956: 434). My personal position with respect to the nature of Hohokam culture history, an essentially unilineal unfolding, should be well known to the reader by this time. Nevertheless, the problem deserves attention with respect to the figurine complex alone. It is only fair to point out that at stake, basically, are the different weights and values two archaeologists place on the same evidence. At stake also is the willingness or unwillingness to accept the history of a single trait as indicative of the group's history as a whole. My choice is to see how the figurine story agrees, or disagrees, with the trends seen in the totality of cultural remains available to us.

Let us first review the typological changes through time. An important baseline here is the fact that Snaketown has produced more figurines than any site in the Southwest, about 1,500 whole and fragmentary specimens. The majority of these are firmly placed as to phase and the typological evidence has repeated itself often enough to inspire confidence in its validity. In general, the developmental chart published in 1937 (Gladwin and others: Fig. 114) still stands, and I therefore see no need to repeat the evidence again here. Careful study of all the plates of figurines in both volumes will serve this purpose.

Except for an increase in size, body treatment undergoes minor changes through time. A notable exception is the appearance of the hollow head in the Santa Cruz Phase which became common in the Sacaton Phase, a clay head modeled on organic material extending from a presumed perishable body. Indeed, this was a new departure, but one wonders whether or not this may have been inspired by the use of grass stalks and slender twigs as armatures. Since no analogies for perishable bodies are reported from Mexico, I would accept this development to be a typically Hohokam innovation.

Realism in face modeling in the hollow Sacaton Phase heads is at its best, yet the trend toward it is already recognizable in the Gila Butte Phase. With better face portrayal one also sees changes in the eye treatment, from slits or dots in the Pioneer Period to half circles appended to a horizontal line, dotted diamonds, sometimes painted, in the Gila Butte Phase, to an extension of the diamond eye and the "coffee-bean" type in the Santa Cruz Phase. In the Sacaton Phase the "coffee-bean" type persisted, as it does even into the Classic Period (Haury 1945a: Fig. 69b); but the more common form was a raised bump with lenticular incision centrally dotted. In connection with the "coffee-bean" eye it should be noted that the dented appliqued pellet was present from the beginning, the Vahki Phase, as chin ornaments, and that it persisted into the Santa Cruz Phase. Their use as eyes represented only a minor shift. Arm shields or patches, a rather distinctive and uncommon trait, appear early in the Estrella Phase and were still present in the Santa Cruz Phase figures. The same is true for turbans, though those on figurines of the Colonial Period, especially the Santa Cruz Phase, are the most elaborate.

These typological unfoldings, in my judgment, signify an even and steady internal evolution. Innovations are more rationally explained as a function of normal change, with probably some reinforcement from Mexico through stimulus diffusion as time went on, than they are as the introductions of an immigrant group. Santa Cruz and Sacaton style figurines flow smoothly out of the old antecedent line.

It should be noted that San Cayetano and Ramanote Cave together produced only seven figurines, on which Di Peso relied heavily. Of these only two could be equated with the so-called Pioneer type and one with the Santa Cruz type (Di Peso 1956: 436). The rest were "... so badly broken that the style identification would be hazardous."

The Snaketown figurine complex provides a clear record of a continuing tradition, a tradition indubitably present from the moment of the village's founding, the figurines having been made locally during all phases and responding primarily to internal impulses to modify them. The Ootam-Hohokam-Ootam hypothesis, as an alternative explanation, has little support from the data.

Morss (1954) has given us an able and useful synthesis of anthropomorphic figures in the Southwest, relieving the necessity for extensive comparative efforts now or a broad search for ideas as to the purposes for which figurines were made. On the latter point, however, it is worthwhile to look a little more closely into the internal evidence than has been done. A hint as to how figurines may have been used during Pioneer Period times comes from both their form and the nature of the baking. Peg, or pin-type, legs are common, suggesting the images may have been stuck in the ground; blunt-edged legs and stump trunks also occur which would have served as well in setting them in upright position. In one instance involving a head, the side and back surface shows three parallel reed impressions (Fig. 13.25f), the kind of reed known to have been used to line house interiors. Other clay objects, possibly associated with the figurine complex, also have reed or grass impressions (Fig. 13.25a-c). As noted earlier, some figures are unfired, although the majority were scorched enough to set the clay and carbonize the organic matter in the matrix. Coupled with this is the fact that a number of specimens have the eye and mouth slits filled with white wood ash and occasional flecks of charcoal. It may be speculated that these images served as household "gods" or adjuncts to house-blessing and fertility rites. If the objects were assembled near the hearth, the heat might have been enough to effect the degree of burning noted and also to provide the opportunity for the figures to come into contact with ashes. A few may have been stuck to the reeds lining the house interior.

Other clay objects recovered from Pioneer Period trash, always in association with images and made of figurine-type clay similarly burned, may be helpful in shedding further light on the topic of use. These specimens, less numerous than the humans representations, consist of miniature vessels with incised designs, possible miniature metates, sundry "blobs," and curious coarse-coiled arcs (Fig. 13.25g-j) which appear to have been broken from circular elements with a bottom and a side wall two to three coils high. It is tempting to think of these as parts of the figurine assemblage, a diluted northern extension of the "activity" or group scenes which are present in western Mexico. At the conclusion of the rite, one may surmise, all units were broken and swept out with the other trash to be deposited where we found them.

The fire-associated aspect of figurines was retained in the Colonial and Sedentary Periods when they customarily passed through the pyral fire. A Sedentary Period specimen in the collections of the Southwest Museum (Bryan 1963:85) illustrates still another application of the fire idea. This is a supine figure of a pregnant female with bowl mounted on the back, likely used as an incense burner.

In regard to Pioneer Period images, does the monotony of form mean that they were made by a "clan head," a shaman or priest, or are we to believe that persons or families in need of them made their own? The first alternative would help to explain the uniformity; on the other hand the style may have been so indelibly imprinted on the minds of the people so that any one making them followed the canons automatically. The consistent figurine occurrence in Pioneer Period trash makes it look as though most everyone threw them away and that their use was general. While answers to these questions are not clear, I favor the latter alternative as the best interpretation possible now. There is no evidence of seasonally-oriented production of figurines.

Specific attachment of the figurine complex to agricultural productivity seems not to be warranted, although we know that the figurine and maize culture were associated at an early time. If they were seasonally produced, the evidence seems to be beyond recovery. To place figurines in a meaningful cultural context, the following hypothesis is offered. Because of their general occurrence in the village, their uniformity, the assumption they do not portray deities, and the physical properties of light firing, peglegs and presumed connection with other clay objects, I suggest they were the tangible objects associated with a system of worship, or a means of supplication, which affected everyone in the culture. Most likely they were a form of house blessing, a means of insuring increase, of the family, of crops, and through these, securing the fulfillment of the society's needs. A deep-seated conviction of their efficacy may well have restrained morphological changes over so long a period of time.

It is doubtful that figurines played a significant role, if any role at all, in the art of "black" magic. The Snaketown material fails to produce clear evidence of transfixion or the kind of mutilation that indicates evil intent. A single pierced head (Fig. 13.7u) could be an accidental occurrence. The few planned extraneous inclusions known, best illustrated by the tiny quartz crystal pressed in the heart position of a Ventana Cave figurine (Haury 1950: Fig. 84g), are not enough evidences on which to build a case. How then should the intentional breakage and in some cases face mutilation, especially by disfiguring the eyes, of Snaketown figurines be explained? The logical interpretation is that this was a normal part of the disposal act after figurine use. Destruction of cultural "treasures," seen best in the cases of caches, of heavy-walled vessels, of carved stone bowls, and the excessive smashing of pottery with cremation, are clear demonstrations of Hohokam attitudes toward hardware when, for some reason or other, it was to be buried. And this behavior carried over to figurines as well. Having served their purpose, they were useless, and fracturing was in a sense the *coup de grâce with the* not impractical objective of preventing reuse by having them fall into the hands of children as playthings.

The general topic of relationships between the Hohokam and other Southwestern figurines has been reviewed by Morss (1954) in an extended discourse on what he calls the "northern" and "southern" figurine traditions. His conclusion that Basketmaker II and III figurines of the Anasazi were stimulated by those of the earlier Southern tradition is supported by two conditions, namely, the abundance of clay images in the Hohokam, relatively more than are known for any other archaeological group north of Mexico and, more meaningfully, the new data on the Hohokam chronology which permit the confident recognition of a pre-Christian Era Vahki Phase when the figurine complex was already firmly established. As far as our dating records now go, this would have been three to five centuries earlier than terminal Basketmaker II.

Another figurine complex that deserves passing mention is the one associated with the area now inhabited by the Seri Indians of coastal Sonora. A large collection of these, all surface "finds," owned by Mr. and Mrs. Ed Moser, highlights the existence of a figurine "cult" in the Greater Southwest which had an impressive vitality. Unfortunately we have practically no data on age, on associated material culture except a thin, hard pottery, and no reliable information on tribal authorship (Owen 1956; Manson 1961). The connection with the Seri is based mainly on a similarity of subject matter between the old ones and those now being made by them, which they frankly admit are copies. A review of the collection (Moser and White 1968) revealed little in the nature of attributes that could be used in establishing a link between the coastal Sonoran and Hohokam complexes. Incising of the torso and the pregnant female figure are common treatments, but the style is altogether different than that of the Hohokam.

It is appropriate to ask whether or not echoes of the ancient custom of making figurines have survived to the present day. This is a difficult question to answer because ethnological records for the desert tribes, in post-Conquest time to the turn of the twentieth century, are meager. The likelihood that any viable tradition lasted is somewhat reduced by the apparent loss of the importance of figurines beginning at least as early as the Classic Period. Figurines are not known to occur as paraphernalia in medicine men's kits or in other circumstances which would suggest any form of sacred attachment.

The idea of modeling clay figures, both human and animal, does survive among the Pima and Papago, but this is most likely an expression of the idea that they were toys, or even as a response to tourist demand. Vivian (1965: 106) records fragments of figurines found in a dump dating from the nineteenth century, located at the mouth of Castle Dome Wash. These may be of Papago manufacture. Subject matter includes a probable cowboy, cows, and horses. The clearest case of a possible survival is the Yuma doll (Kaemlein 1955) which typologically retains some of the elements of the Sedentary Period figurines. However, I do not think that a good case for continuance of the Hohokam tradition to Yuma can be made.

Finally, we come to the question of the derivation of Hohokam figurines and developing the justification for the position taken. The question really reduces itself to talking about generalities because of the voids that exist in the available comparative data. References have already been made to a Mexican or Mesoamerican source. This is predicated on the abundance and the earliness of figurines in Mexico and their scarcity in all areas adjacent to the Hohokam domain. Further, the chief attributes that made early Hohokam what it was, water technology, agriculture, the domestic plant complex, pottery-making, a shell industry, along with figurines, constitute a core of traits that all point to a southern origin.

In reality it should be possible to pinpoint specific analogies with the figurines of the South, particularly of western Mexico; but a search of the literature leads only to the broadest comparisons and tantalizing clues. For example, Ekholm (1939: 10) states that Huatabampo figurines from southern Sonora "... bear a striking resemblance to a type from Snaketown ... which is dated there before A.D. 900." He goes on to say that the Huatabampo complex "... appears to be basically Southwestern, and, if this is true, we have found a cultural connection between the Southwest and Mexico...." There are indeed a number of correspondences between the Huatabampo materials and that of the Hohokam, especially in pottery form and shell products, as well as the figurines, to bear out his contention. Ekholm's estimate of the age of the complex is A.D. 1000–1250 (personally related). One implication to be drawn is that Huatabampo may be a late surviving manifestation of a cultural pattern in Mexico from which the Hohokam were originally derived.

A somewhat more specific similarity may be seen in the upward inclination of the face which Kelly reports from Culiacan (1945a: Figs. 61h and i; 64; 65c and e), probably of post-Aztatlan age. This configuration is late in the Snaketown series, not seen before the Sacaton Phase. The best examples are the solid figures from Cache 2:9F (Fig. 11.11) and the effigy vessels from the same cache (Fig. 11.10). The Sonoran and Snaketown figures are probably of about equal age, and there doubtless was some connection between the two complexes.

Speaking more broadly, however, to the point of vagueness, two alternative conclusions seem inevitable: either the comparative data do not strike deeply enough in time and we therefore do not have the wanted information to make valid comparisons, or, the figurine complex as noted in the oldest Hohokam horizons has already undergone such extensive transformations from the parent complex that relationships to a specific source in space and time may never be established. At the present time—the early 1970s—the case must rest on the general statement that Hohokam figurines are a northern outlier of the firmly rooted and widespread Mesoamerican pattern.

Animal Forms

Animal effigy production in clay did not receive the emphasis given to the making of human figures. Yet they do occur and they had a much longer history than was supposed in 1937 (Gladwin and others: 238) when it was believed that none antedated the Santa Cruz Phase. Considering only the solid figure form, ten fragmentary specimens are assignable to the Pioneer Period with specific associations to all phases but Snaketown, and the absence in this phase is surely a matter of incomplete recovery. Three examples extend the theme into the Gila Butte and Santa Cruz Phases of the Colonial Period. Discussion of Sedentary Period figures will be momentarily delayed because a radical shift in style took place at that time.

Quadruped portrayals apparently were standard, as birds and reptiles are not included although these are commonly shown in stone. Attempts to identify specific animals lead, in most cases, to uncertain results. During all the phases of the Pioneer and Colonial Periods the style and crudeness of execution were essentially the same. Figures range from 3.0 to 6.0 cm in length and were carelessly modeled of a clay type similar to that used in human figurines. They were unpolished and only occasionally dignified by supplying anatomic details. Figure 13.20 illustrates representative examples.

The scarcity and careless work in the figures from the Vahki through the Santa Cruz Phase do not suggest they were fetishes or were given the same significance that seems to have been attached to the human images. At the Santa Cruz-Sacaton Phase transition something happened to elevate the animal effigy from a probable level as a toy to one which gave it a higher order of meaning. Clay animals became much more abundant, they were better executed and were large, 15 to 20 cm in length. Furthermore, the clay type was the same as in pottery, and painting the animals was not uncommon.

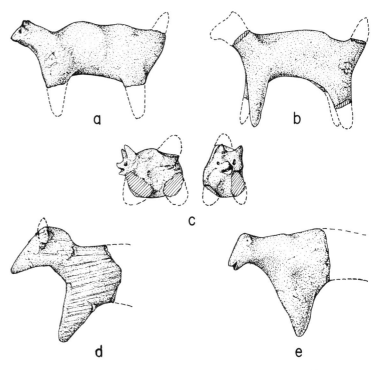

Fig. 13.20. Clay animal figurines: (a, b) Vahki Phase; (c, d) Pioneer Period; (e) Santa Cruz Phase. Length of a, 5.9 cm.

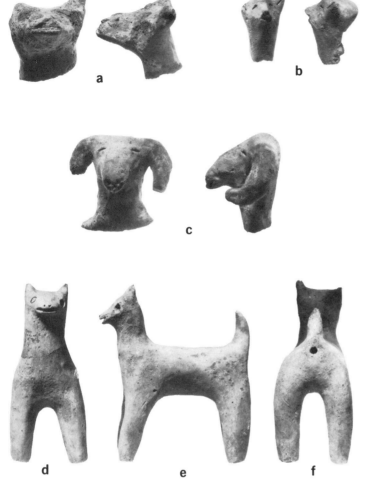

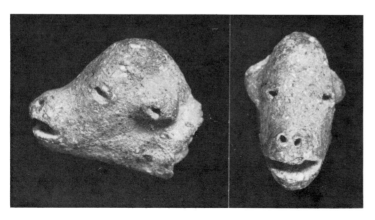

Fig. 13.21. Heads and whole animal effigies, Sacaton Phase. Width of *c* at horns, 6.7 cm. Length of *e*, 11.6 cm.

The best evidence in support of the idea that Sacaton Phase animal effigies were accorded a special functional niche comes from their occurrence in groups as caches. Two cases of this are now documented: the first, Cushing's discovery in Los Guanacos in the Salt River Valley (Haury 1945a: 174–176), and the second, from Snaketown, discussed more fully in the chapter on Caches (Fig. 11.6). In both instances other articles, such as censers, pottery vessels, and paint, were found with them. The circumstances of burial clearly show intentional disposal, accompanied by the use of fire, and, for some of the figures, what appears to be willful breakage. Stylistically, the animals of both caches are similar in size and in finish. They are unpainted and

Fig. 13.22. Clay head of Mountain Sheep ewe. Probably Sacaton Phase. Length, 3.5 cm.

portray the same animal, most likely deer. The chief difference is in the position of the tail, erect in the Snaketown group (Fig. 13.21e) and directed back (except one) in the lot from Los Guanacos. The most plausible explanation for these figures is that they were associated with magical increase rites for which there are ethnological models (Parsons 1919: 279-286) in the Southwest, though not among the Pima or Papago.

Figure 13.21 illustrates several animal heads: *a* and *c*, deer and mountain sheep respectively, and *b*, a creature of curious configuration. Figure 13.22 illustrates the head of a well-modeled mountain sheep ewe. By and large, animals played a prominent role in Hohokam art during the Sacaton Phase, but less in the painted form in pottery than in modeled expressions, either as full figure animals or as effigy vessels.

By Classic Period times, notably the Civano Phase, animal figurine production appears to have reverted to the earlier casual form. Our excavations in Classic Period sites (Ariz. U:13:21, 22 and 24) produced only a few fragments, and those illustrated from Los Muertos (Haury 1945a: 114-115) may be taken as typical.

MISCELLANEOUS CLAY OBJECTS

Approximately 176 miscellaneous fragmentary objects have been found. Many of these are not specifically identifiable, but it seems advisable to include a representative sample so that possible future recoveries may bring them into focus. The clay in nearly all specimens is the same as in the figurines, and the degree of baking also matches that of the figurines. Temporal distributions and frequencies are shown in Figure 13.27.

(?) Leg Fragments. The first group consists of more or less cylindrical units with flat, concave, or bifurcate ends (Fig. 13.23a-e); *b* has a punctate pattern on the flat end. If figurine legs, these might have been designed for images intended to be set on the surface of the ground, but they impress me as being something other than parts of figurines. All units in the collection came from Pioneer Period contexts.

(?) Body Fragments with Bands. Another group of generally tabular pieces shows that clay strips or bands have been wrapped around the "body" either as decoration or as a means to attach something else (Fig. 13.23f-k). Specimen *k* might represent a highly stylized babe-in-cradle motif, but to be certain, more specific characteristics would be needed. It is strange that all of these units are too fragmentary to give a clearcut notion of their original form. Once again they are, with one exception, assignable to the Pioneer Period.

Armature Base. Figure 13.23*l* is a fat Y-shaped piece showing stick impressions in the two branches as though armatures supported extensions. The main stem is broken. It could be the basal portion of a seated figure.

Miniature Vessels. These are not to be confused with the miniature vessels treated earlier, which are made of conventional pottery clay and often painted. Those now discussed were made of the finer clay used in figurine production and, when decorated, were incised. Figure 13.24a-i illustrates a ladle, jar, and bowl fragments, the latter usually decorated. Articles of this kind occur frequently enough and are consistent enough as a group to warrant considering them as having fulfilled a special purpose. This has led to the supposition that they were connected with the figurine complex, as elements in assemblies which included the common objects about the house as well as the human forms. A detail inconsistent with this reconstruction, however, is the fact that the designs are incised on vessel interiors not conventionally done in pottery, and the patterns do not imitate the painted designs on pottery of equivalent age. These objects come from all phases of the Pioneer Period.

Miniature (?) Metates. Two clay lumps have the form of metates (Fig. 13.24j and k), one having a hole through the bottom made while the clay was plastic. There is no evidence that these

Fig. 13.23. Miscellaneous clay objects: (b) Sacaton Phase; all others various phases of the Pioneer Period. Length of *h*, 6.4 cm.

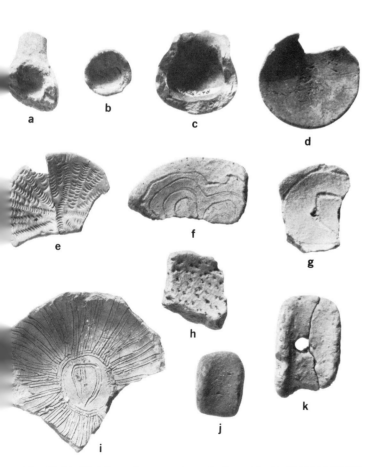

Fig. 13.24. Miniature clay vessels and other objects. Pioneer Period, various phases. Width of *i*, 7.0 cm.

were ever a part of anything as, for example, the figure of a person grinding on a metate, a depiction sometimes seen in western Mexico. They may, however, have the same relationship to Hohokam figurines as the miniature vessels discussed above. Both specimens date from the Pioneer Period.

Reed- or Grass-Impressed Pieces. Clay fragments with reed or grass impressions occur often enough to suggest that they acquired the imprints from the specific use to which they were put. Shapes vary from round to rectangular where enough of the form survives (Fig. 13.25a-c). The obverse of *c* retains two limbs of an appliqued figure. Fragment *d*, in addition to reed impressions, has holes punched into the clay, not unlike the shape and size of the pin-type legs of figurines; *e* carries a random impression except for the parallel horizontal lines that probably were made manually. Specimen *f* (also Fig. 13.3h) is illustrated again to show the three parallel reed impressions oblique to the long axis of the head, possibly the result of pressing the head into the reed lining of the house while the clay was soft. All units in this group are of Pioneer Period age except the plaque with an applied figure (*c*), which is assignable to the Gila Butte Phase.

Coiled Pieces. A sizable number of pieces, from all phases of the Pioneer Period, involve the use of a coarse-coiling technique with apparently never more than three coils superimposed (Fig. 13.25g-j). The general form seems to have been circular with diameters as much as 25 cm. One fragment (*i*) retains a portion of the bottom disc to which the coils were attached. Coils were pressed together, clearly showing the fingermarks, and there was no smoothing either inside or outside. The degree of baking matches that of the figurines. Once again, the fragmentary nature of these objects leaves us little chance to reconstruct probable use. Yet the feeling persists they were somehow related to the figurine "cult," perhaps as a component in an assembly of a number of articles required by ritual practices.

Spindle Whorls. The especially made clay spindle whorl, as distinct from perforated potsherds, is not plentiful at Snaketown. Only four were recovered in the present operation and two during the first work in 1934–35. Subspheroidal and pulley-shaped types (Fig. 13.26a-d) are the only forms represented. Diameters vary from 2.1 to 2.4 cm, and the apertures are a consistent 0.4 cm in diameter. The clay is somewhat finer in quality than that in contemporary pottery, but surfaces are unpolished and unslipped. The four specimens reported on here are all from undoubted Sacaton Phase associations; the two earlier ones were surface finds but were presumed to be late (Gladwin and others 1937: Pl. CCXIII l and m), probably Sedentary Period.

Evidence from numerous ruins in southern Arizona clearly places the red-slipped and polished whorl, often of turbinate and biconical form, in the Classic Period (Haury 1945a: 119-121). It may be concluded with a fair degree of certainty that the specialized spindle whorl reached the Hohokam during the Sedentary Period and that it reached its fullest use and most refined forms in the Classic Period. The derivation is most likely out of western Mexico where the simpler kinds in an otherwise sophisticated tradition (Kelly 1938: Fig. 24a-i; Ekholm 1942: Fig. 17q and r; Kelly 1949: Fig. 85a-f) could have served as prototypes. Yet it is strange that the more elaborate forms with incised patterns did not influence the north and that direct imports were evidently not made. Absent in the Mexican whorl inventories is the pronounced pulley-shaped type which is so common in the southern Arizona sites.

I do not believe that the introduction of the specialized whorl signalled the appearance of cotton as a companion element. The Sedentary Period is much too late for that. Good loom cloth was a Hohokam hallmark, known from actual pieces (Gladwin and others 1937: 162; Tanner 1950) by A.D. 1000, which means that weaving technology can assuredly be extended into far earlier horizons.

Cylinders and "Pillows." A group of about twenty fired clay

Fig. 13.25. Miscellaneous clay objects. (c) Gila Butte Phase; all others various phases of the Pioneer Period. Length of *g*, 7.1 cm.

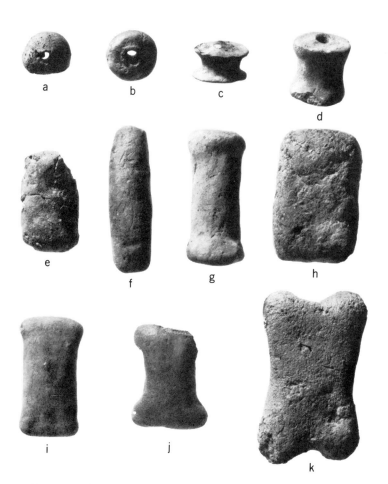

Fig. 13.26. Spindle whorls and other clay objects: (a-d) Sacaton Phase; (e, f) Snaketown Phase; (g, j) probably Colonial Period; (h, i) Santa Cruz Phase; (k) probably Sacaton Phase. Length of *k*, 7.1 cm.

objects appear to be variations on a single theme, ranging from cylinders, some with faintly swollen ends, to pillows, to units with flared corners (Fig. 13.26e-k). Lengths range from about 3 to 7 cm, and a few fragments suggest some were larger. These were classed as reel-shaped objects previously (Gladwin and others 1937: 243). The quality of the clay is poor, which, with weak firing, led to easy breakage. Chronologically, these objects range the full scale from the Vahki to the Sacaton Phases. The only typological differences to be noted are an increase in size and greater accentuation of the "ears" through time.

All but two were found in trash, indicating that, like figurines, once they served their purpose they were thrown away. The two exceptions were in the fill of Crematorium 7:11H of Gila Butte Phase. This association is not enough to justify the conclusion that the objects were connected with death rites, but their use over a long period of time does indicate that they symbolized some cultural value in a specific way. Although specimens of this kind are unreported in the literature, I do not believe them to be unique to Snaketown.

Miscellaneous Unidentified Units. There are more than forty pieces of clay in the collection, consisting of lumps, squeezes, and fragments that defy identification or classification. Since they are baked, it may be assumed that the makers had some purpose in mind. A few may be ceramists' efforts to test the quality of clay for pot production.

Pot Supports. In the discussion of architecture, reference has been made to the use of clay trivets in sets of three around hearths for supporting cooking pots above the coals. A few additional notes are in order here. These were always made of a poor-quality clay, which means that replacement was frequently necessary. The discarded fragments were plentiful in the rubbish, and the evidence at hand indicates that the idea of using this device was as early as the Sweetwater Phase, considerably earlier than was previously known (Gladwin and others 1937: 244). Typological differences are not determinable, although an impression prevails that the earlier ones were generally small.

In their production, the clay was sometimes formed on matting (Fig. 13.28a) or basketry (Gladwin and others 1937: Pl. CCXIIa), leaving impressions on the bottoms and sometimes on

PHASE OR PERIOD	"LEGS"- FLAT OR CONCAVE	"LEGS"- BIFURCATE	BANDED "BODIES"	ARMATURE BASES	MINIATURE VESSELS	MINIATURE (?) METATES	REED OR GRASS IMPRESSED	COILED PIECES	SPINDLE (?) WHORLS	CYLINDERS	"PILLOWS"	MISCL. UNIDENT.	TOTALS
SACATON	1								4		1	2	8
SANTA CRUZ											4		4
GILA BUTTE			1				1				3	5	10
COLONIAL											4	8	12
SNAKETOWN	2		2				3	10		2		2	21
SWEETWATER	4	2	1	1	9	1	1	8			1	9	37
ESTRELLA	1		2		3		1	16			2	11	36
VAHKI		1	1		7	1	2	11			1	5	29
PIONEER	1		1		8			8			1		19
TOTALS	9	3	8	1	27	2	8	53	4	2	17	42	176

Fig. 13.27. Kinds, numbers, and phase associations of miscellaneous clay artifacts from Snaketown.

the sides. Baking was presumably a function of use. Diameters vary from 15 to 30 cm and heights from 15 to 25 cm. The standard shape in section was oval but some were also quadrangular.

Jar Stoppers. To safeguard jar contents, such as food surpluses, clay was packed into the mouth of the jar usually against grass or a fragment of matting (Fig. 15.1) to separate the plug from the contents. The clay has a much lighter color, specific gravity, and finer texture than potter's clay; judging from inclusions of small pieces of charcoal, wood ash may have been mixed with the matrix. Specimens of this kind survive only when the house burned in which vessels were stored; otherwise the breaking of the seal to recover jar contents would have destroyed them.

Drawing on samples from the 1934–35 work and those now at hand, jar seal types are of two classes, those lapping the rim and extending over on the outside of jars (Fig. 13.29a, b, and c) and those fitted inside the jar's mouth (Fig. 13.29d). Examples are

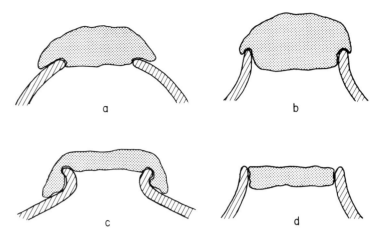

a   b

c   d

Fig. 13.29. Jar stoppers shown in section.

known from most phases and the custom probably extends backward in time to the beginning of pottery-making.

Pipe. Whether of stone or clay, pipes were never a trademark of the Hohokam, although a few show up in late times (Haury 1945a: Fig. 112h; Vivian 1965: 139-40, Fig. 8b; Morris and El-Najjar 1971: 32). The most definitive evidence of both the formality of the pipe and its late survival, possibly as late as 1751 among the Upper Pimas, is the cache reported by Di Peso (1956: 426-430) in San Cayetano in southern Hohokam territory.

In the combined Snaketown operations only one pipe was recovered from a Sacaton Phase context (House 1:10F). Made of clay, gray in color, and tempered with angular quartz particles, this pipe tapers slightly toward the bit end as do most Southwestern "cloud-blowers." The surface is rough and unpolished and the form lacks symmetry (Fig. 13.30). There is no trace of dottle or bowl-smudging.

It would be surprising indeed if tobacco-use was foreign to the Hohokam during the early stages of the tribe's history. Admittedly, the presence of pipes does not automatically spell tobacco as the plant used in them, nor does absence of pipes mean that tobacco was not smoked. The more durable pipes may have been replaced by something that was consumed in the smoking process, as for example, cane cigarettes, the presence of which in the Hohokam territory has been cited (Haury 1945a: 194-96). The use of tobacco as early as the 7th century A.D. has been demonstrated (Morris and Jones 1960) for the Anasazi. Since tobacco, like the useful food plants, originally came out of Mexico, one may infer that it was available to the Hohokam as early or earlier than it was to the Anasazi. On the basis of censers, the idea of making ritual smoke-and-smell extended into the early phases of the Pioneer Period. If this was an alternative to producing mouth-drawn smoke, the early absence of pipes may be explained.

a

b

Fig. 13.28. Clay pot supports: (a) bottom aspect showing impression of a *petate*; (b) a trivet with petate impressions on sides, quadrangular section, restored. Both Santa Cruz Phase. Height of *b*, 21 cm.

Fig. 13.30. Clay pipe, Sacaton Phase. Length, 5 cm.

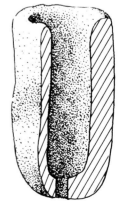

Considering the elaboration and abundance of elbow pipes as far north as Guasave (Ekholm 1942: 83-85) and Culiacan (Kelly 1945a: 133-37) in Sinaloa, western Mexico, it is interesting that this trait did not diffuse northward to the Hohokam, particularly since other elements as spindle whorls, comales, and figurine-style analogies do exist. The fact that elbow pipes, often of effigy form, did not spread northward may reflect Hohokam selectivity and their preference of holding to the use of censers, not infrequently of effigy form.

Clay Cone. To conclude the study of clay products from Snaketown, reference is made to the solid clay cone found with Cache 2:9F (Fig. 11.8n) which may have served as a feather holder.

14. Stone, Mineral and Metal Products

Long stretches of the Gila and Salt River valleys once under Hohokam domination are free of stone. River alluvium and the soils of the geologically ancient terraces dominate the landscape. Yet, distant mountain ranges are in sight everywhere, and these beckoned whenever stone was needed. The problem of transport on human back, the distance and the kinds of stone available, were limiting factors in determining how much and what kinds of stone were imported to Snaketown.

Whenever the excavator's shovel struck a stone, we could be sure that man had introduced it into the site. The nearest outcrop, 5 km (3 mi) to the east, is Gila Butte, a twin-peaked elevation rising about 140 m (460 ft) above the desert floor. The mica schist and granite exposed on its flanks were carried to Snaketown primarily for two purposes: the schist to be crushed and used as pottery temper, and the granite for hearth stones and occasional tools. For basalt, chippable stone, fine grained stones for carving, and semiprecious minerals, the Hohokam had to go much farther afield or to acquire them by trading with other tribes.

It should be asked whether or not the scarcity of stone near many Hohokam sites influenced the trend of the architectural development. Was stone not used because it was difficult to obtain, or was the mode of house construction culturally determined and stone would not have been used even though handy? Except for the few cases where stone was used as risers in house entrances and notched supports embedded in the floor, it would appear that the latter alternative is probably the correct one. Villages near available stone, like Roosevelt 9: 6 (Haury 1932), used stone in houses only in specialized ways; many Classic Period sites, even though close to rock supplies, did not use it regularly (Johnson 1964). One wonders, therefore, whether the Hohokam may have originated as a tribal entity in an alluvial environment largely free of stone and that cultural conditioning against the use of stone architecturally was of long standing.

The hard labor required to import good stone for sculpturing did, I believe, influence the products of the stone carver. He certainly was capable of fashioning monumental objects, and contacts with Mexico might have given him the needed inspiration as well as models. But instead, his skills and energy were spent on small objects, in producing finely polished surfaces and decorations in bas- and full-relief. The choice of material was made having in mind the nature of the finished product and size was a function of stone availability.

The value of stone as a commodity at Snaketown had another side effect which is seldom encountered in the ruins of the Southwest. Worn-out stone objects were habitually reshaped and used as something else. It is significant that of 167 houses excavated in 1964–65 and in the vast amount of other work, only seven unbroken metates were found; even worn-out ones were rare. Fragments were more common, some remodeled into other kinds of artifacts. Final use of the basalt of which most metates were made was as hearth stones.

The energy needed to transport a large block of basalt to the site for metate production and the use of the available material in it when worn out create the impression that the metate was the single most prized item the Hohokam had. These factors, plus its basic relationship to existence itself as the means of preparing corn for consumption, must account for the few found at Snaketown. Salvage from old houses, and removal from the site at the time of abandonment, appear to have been normal procedures.

BASIC USE CATEGORIES FOR STONE
Stone and Fire

The heat-holding property of stone was well understood. The giant hearths in which food was prepared always yield varying amounts of thermally fractured rocks, a clear indication that the principle of the fireless cooker was employed. Metamorphic and igneous rocks were preferred for this use over sedimentary rock types because they were less prone to disintegrate. Even so, prolonged heating eventually reduced large blocks to worthless fist-sized or smaller angular chunks. Although worn-out metates often found their way into hearths, much stone was brought to Snaketown specifically as a cooking aid.

The use of stone trivets in small fireplaces was seen only occasionally. Pot supports made of clay seem to have been preferred. Flat slabs used as hearth liners or deflectors were not observed.

A unique reason for bringing stone and fire together has been noted by Crabtree and Butler (1964). Heat improves the chipping quality of certain kinds of stone, notably chert, which was commonly used by the Hohokam. Crabtree believes that without preheating they could not have made many of the long, elegant projectile points that so distinguish their stone work.

Stone in Architecture

As already noted, the Hohokam were not dependent on stone in house construction. Discounting the lithic artifacts sometimes found on house floors, in only six instances were shaped stones incorporated visibly in the architectural units.

Four of these instances were Sacaton Phase structures, House 1:6H (Gladwin and others 1937: Pl. XXIIId) and House 4:9E, House 1:10J, and House 3:9G of the 1964–65 operation. In these, thin slabs of mica schist were used as risers in the midsection of the entrance (Fig. 14.1a). Houses earlier than the Sacaton Phase did not have the stepped entry, but even so it seems strange that more use of stone slabs was not made as a protection against wear at a step, whether in or at the end of the entryway.

The other two instances deserve somewhat fuller treatment. In clearing the floor of House 15:10F, our workmen came across a flat-lying notched stone (Fig. 14.1b) resting in a broken section of the floor. Since notched stones imbedded in the floors of Hohokam houses have been noted before (Haury 1932: 38-40), it was believed that this one originally stood upright also. Why there should have been only one remains a puzzle.

Nearby, House 19:10F produced more definitive evidence. In this case there were three stones. Two were complete, though they were damaged by the fire that destroyed the house (Fig. 14.3a and b). The root of the third was buried in the floor, its upper part missing (Fig. 14.3c). The two specimens retaining the tops show excellent workmanship in shaping the concavity, the slightly tapered edges and the shoulders giving way to the stem which was planted in the floor. All three were made of fine vesicular basalt, and they represent the largest worked stone specimens from Snaketown. In functional position, the bottom of the curved notch was 25 cm above the floor. Their deployment symmetrically about the hearth (Figs. 14.1c, 14.2) is not readily explained. It would have been possible to use the two at the sides of the hearth as spit rests because the arcs were properly oriented and anything thus supported would have been almost directly over the coals at a good height for broiling. The third stone near the center of the house does not fit this functional pattern. Unfortunately its top was gone so we do not know how it was oriented. Whether associated with cooking or not, it is reasonable to believe that notched devices were used as supports for something to be held above the floor.

In the case of Roosevelt 9:6, the notched stones supported an elevated floor above the earth base of the pit house (Haury 1932: *op. cit.*). Sayles (Gladwin and others 1937: Pl. XXIIb) illustrates a charred forked post still holding a cross beam 45 cm above the floor. Other examples of notched stones in areas adjacent to the Hohokam are in the Mimbres valley (Cosgrove 1932: 49-50) and northward toward Prescott (Simmons, Arizona State Museum Archives, A-39, A-49, A-50).

House 1:5G, of Sacaton Phase age and built over trash, employed stone in a concealed manner. In the bottoms of three of the four holes for the roof supports, flat sections of metates served as footings to prevent the roof's weight from pushing the uprights into the soft refuse. The vertical sides of troughed metates were removed by percussion (Fig. 14.4).

In sum, all instances of the architectural use of stone date from the Sacaton Phase, apparently a relatively late adoption of non-organic building materials.

Stone in Agriculture

Except for stone hand-tools used in digging canals, in the cultivation of the soil, and possibly in the harvesting of certain crops, stone seems to have been of little or no importance in Hohokam agricultural pursuits. In those sections of canals exposed by us, rocks were noted only once, along with pottery, as coarse materials dumped into a hole to repair erosion damage. Rock water-control structures in the main canal systems appear not to have

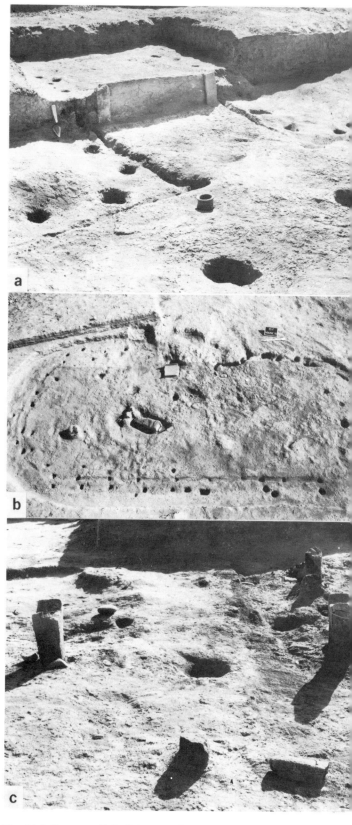

Fig. 14.1. Houses with built-in stone features: (a) House 3:9G, Sacaton Phase, with mica schist riser in entry, pinned in place by long slivers of stone; (b) House 15:10F, Sacaton Phase, displaced notched stone, probably near original position; (c) House 19:10F, Sacaton Phase, notched stones in place near hearth.

been favored or thought necessary, as they were, for example, elsewhere in the Southwest (Vivian, 1974). The small check dams in the mountain foothill drainages adjacent to the Gila River, and the apparently related "waffle" gardens were doubtless built by the Hohokam. These may represent their most ambitious excursion into the use of stone as related to agriculture.

A further use, though not detected at Snaketown, bids mention.

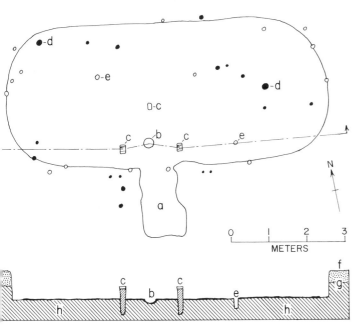

Fig. 14.2. Plan and section of House 19:10F with notched stones near hearth: (a) entry; (b) hearth; (c) notched stones; (d) burned post ends in situ; (e) postholes; (f) present surface; (g) probable surface at time house was built; (h) native soil.

Fig. 14.4. Modified metate fragment used as post rest, House 1:5G, Sacaton Phase. Width, 27.7 cm.

Fig. 14.3. Notched stones: (a-c) imbedded in floor of House 19:10F; (d) House 15:10F. Length of a, 0.74 m.

This was the erection of elongated water-worn cobbles in cultivated areas, presumed to have been field or property line markers. These have been observed in the Salt River valley (Haury 1956: 8) and evidently dated from the Classic Period. The practice may well have extended into the Gila valley, but traces thereof have been destroyed by modern land-reclamation activities.

MINERALS AND METALS

People heavily dependent on the resources of nature inevitably became acquainted with the properties of available minerals and adapted them to specific uses. Many of the common minerals and species of rock were adequate for the workaday tools; the rarer and more spectacular forms were more sparingly and artistically used for jewelry and other purposes. The questions one really

wants answered are: What kinds and to what extent were minerals used by the Hohokam? Were there any changes in preferences through time, and, if so, why? Answers do not come easily. Recognizing the fact that fire, through which many of the Hohokam artifacts passed, tends to destroy or alter the original form of some minerals, and that specimens recovered from cremations might represent a selectivity of cultural items which do not fairly reflect the true situation, it was felt that the most representative samples of minerals might come from the refuse dumps. The presence of minerals in the living debris would indicate that man had something to do with putting them in that environment. It was also believed that these minerals would appear as small pieces and bits, representing the wastage of working with minerals, therefore reflecting Hohokam dependence upon them.

Recovery was achieved by fine-wire screening. The inorganic fraction consisted mostly of sand, fine gravel, and fragments of the common stones of the region used in tool manufacture. From this bulk, by hand-sorting, the less commonly used and more easily identifiable minerals, either because of color or texture, were removed for analysis. Identifications were made by Robert T. O'Haire, Associate Mineralogist, of the Arizona Bureau of Mines. The results of his examination of forty lots of minerals in a micro-state are given in Figure 14.5. Few samples for the Estrella Phase were taken and none was recovered from Civano (Classic Period) Phase trash. Most of the minerals listed were undoubtedly imported to Snaketown, although a few of them could have been a part of the native alluvial matrix. In general, except for the Estrella Phase, the number of minerals attributable to any one phase is surprisingly constant, although the species vary. For the commonest minerals, clear quartz, specular hematite, and muscovite, I do not believe that the temporal differences mean anything, and this probably is true also for rose quartz, biotite, schist, and chalcedony.

However, the most distinctive and colorful forms, as amethyst, asbestos (actinolite), malachite, azurite, chrysocolla, rhodochrosite, and opal, are generally late, of Colonial and Sedentary Period ages. This could be a manifestation either of increasing familiarity with the resources of the mountains around or of expanding trade relationships with neighbors who had access to the sources. The shell listed in the inventory represents finely comminuted fresh water clams, possibly attributable to the use of clams as food.

PHASE	NO. OF SAMPLES	QUARTZ-CLEAR	QUARTZ-WHITE	QUARTZ-GREEN	QUARTZ-ROSE	AMETHYST	SPECULAR HEMATITE	MUSCOVITE	BIOTITE (DARK MICA)	SCHIST	ORTHOCLASE	EPIDOTE	FELDSPAR	GRANITE	CALCITE	GYPSUM	CHERT	CHALCEDONY	OBSIDIAN	JASPER	ASBESTOS	MALACHITE	AZURITE	CHRYSOCOLLA	RHODOCHROSITE	MANGANESE OXIDE	MAGNATITE	OPAL	SHELL	NO. OF OCCURRENCES
SACATON	4	4				1	2	2			1	1	1	1	1			5	1	2				2	1	1				15
SANTA CRUZ	7	3			3		6	5	1	3		5	1					4	3	1	2	3	2	3				2	5	17
GILA BUTTE	7	4	3	1	2		7	6	2	1	3	2			2			2	3	1									4	15
SNAKETOWN	6	2	2		4		4	3	1	3	1	1				1	1	2	1			2							3	15
SWEETWATER	8	6	1		2		2	8	4	4		2	2		1			2	1	3		1							3	15
ESTRELLA	2	2					1	1	1		1				1			1						1						8
VAHKI	6	6	1	1	2		2	3	1	1	2			1		1		1									1			13
TOTAL	40	27	7	2	13	1	24	28	10	12	8	11	4	2	4	3	1	12	12	7	2	6	2	8	1	1	1	2	15	98

Fig. 14.5. Distribution of micro-minerals recovered from trash by kind and phase.

There are no finished artifacts from a number of these minerals, as, for example, amethyst, opal, rose, and green quartz, but they may well have existed.

The negative evidence provided by this exercise is also of interest because certain expectable elements are missing. Turquoise and argillite were absent, not surprising, since shaping them into items of jewelry usually leaves no more than dust. There was essentially a complete lack of chipping debris of the kind that would result from production of pressure flaked points, a problem reviewed later. Wastage from working marine shell was also missing. Most of this was caught in the quarter-inch mesh screen, and the final attrition of shell was normally by grinding which would have left only powder.

The information derived during trash sampling needs now to be augmented by minerals recovered in other circumstances.

Pigment Minerals

Few of the mineral pigments available to the Hohokam could be put to use as found in nature. Copper ores which provided blues and greens were found in the raw state, but derivatives as prepared pigments, and articles painted with them have seldom survived. In general, the incidences of raw copper ore were more frequent in the Sedentary and Colonial Periods (Fig. 14.5).

Prepared red pigments were made by grinding hematite and mixing the powder with clay or other substances and shaping the mass into loaf-like lumps. The amount and kind of additive evidently was responsible for producing reds of different shades.

Most of the prepared red ochre cakes do not appear to have yielded fine enough pigment for pottery painting because the latter is not granular. Instead, caked paints were probably earmarked for body decoration. There are a few instances of prepared pigments in the Pioneer and Colonial Periods, but eight of the recovered samples are of Sedentary Period age. Although the rubbish tests showed specular hematite to be a common mineral, few examples of it were found in lump or ground form, and specularite appears not to have been the form of hematite used in pottery decoration. Only a single instance of yellow ochre, limonite, (Sacaton Phase) was recorded.

In 1697, at a place along the Gila River not far from Snaketown (11 leagues downstream from Casa Grande ruin), Captain Manje observed Indians painted with mercury ore, cinnabar, reportedly obtained four days journey to the northwest. Ives has convincingly established the Dome Rock cinnabar deposits in northern Yuma County to be the source of this pigment (1965). In view of the evident widespread use of cinnabar in early historic times by Indians along the Gila River, it is strange that no samples of the mercury ore were found at Snaketown.

Other Minerals

Most numerous of the non-paint-producing minerals were those which lent themselves to chipping. Large flakes of clear quartz up to 10 cm in greatest dimension testify to the availability of large crystals. The best known source for these is in the Huachuca Mountains of southeastern Arizona. Small quartz crystals were also collected, obviously for other uses than as chipping material. Of the five recovered, three came from Sacaton Phase contexts, one from Santa Cruz Phase, and one from Pioneer Period trash. The naturally pointed ends of the crystals are blunted as though used as gravers. Underhill (1946: 271) notes that quartz crystals are used by Papago shamans for divination.

Amethystine quartz appeared in six different contexts, either on house floors or in trash, ranging in age from the Pioneer to the Sedentary Periods. Three instances are referable to the latter. The amethyst probably came from the Four Peaks area in the Mazatzal Mountains of central Arizona, visible from Snaketown. A large fragment with two crystal faces preserved indicates it came from a crystal at least 9 cm in diameter, an exceptionally large one for the Four Peaks source. Finished artifacts of amethyst have not been found, but one may speculate that had so many of the quartz projectile points in the collection not been subjected to fire, specimens of this material could be detected.

Although obsidian projectile points are not uncommon, raw obsidian and even chipping wastage are scarce. Nodular obsidian appears to have been the form of the stone that was exploited. These are the so-called "Apache tears," prevalent in several places in the Southwest, the nearest one to Snaketown being at Superior. Of the eleven nodules recovered, all but one were of jet-black obsidian. The exception was brown mottled, possibly having come from an exposure between Bagdad and Seligman, Arizona. Six of the nodules were assignable to the Sacaton Phase, one to the Santa Cruz Phase, one to the Snaketown Phase, and three unplaced. Obsidian nodules seldom exceed 6 cm in diameter, a factor which limited the size of the projectile points manufacturable from them. Two fragments of block obsidian were recovered, indicative of exploiting other than nodule sources, and the collection included one chip of green obsidian, a probable import from Mexico where it is abundant.

Chalcedony was a preferred material for chipping. Numerous outcroppings of it occur in the volcanic ranges of southern Arizona, some of which yield large enough chunks for the purpose. Small concretions, known as Desert Roses, were gathered because of their appealing shapes. A group of eleven pieces from the floor of House 10:11F shows someone's penchant for them. All were tested for quality, or, in two cases, to expose crystal clusters within. A hand-sized specimen of a botryoidal chalcedonic formation (Fig. 14.6b) would pass as a prized collector's item today.

Much chert also was used by the Hohokam, but its source has not been identified.

Asbestos was obtainable in the Sierra Ancha and other mountains along the Salt River to the east of Snaketown. Its occasional use, as yet undetermined, appears to have been limited to the Colonial and Sedentary Periods. Muscovite was exploited at all times, at least it found its way into the rubbish during all phases (Fig. 14.5), and large plates, sometimes as much as 15 cm across, were shaped by cutting. Examples of this treatment from the Snaketown Phase show that it was a technique of long standing, lasting through the Sacaton Phase. Mica was one of the elements used in overlay, as demonstrated by a pottery disc recovered in 1934–35 (Gladwin and others 1937: Pl. CCIX,j).

All firmly associated pieces of argillite place its use in the Colonial Period or later. Efforts to link it with catlinite from Minnesota have met with negative results (Gladwin and others 1937: 130). A single fragment of a worked object from Snaketown (No. A-26,252) appeared to have a strong resemblance to catlinite; but John S. Sigstad of the Department of Anthropology, University of Missouri, reports it to have the wrong color, and more importantly that its hardness is about 6.5 as compared with 2.5 for catlinite (letter 8 April 1969). The Snaketown argillite most likely came from extensive exposures in the Mazatzal Mountains at the north end of the Tonto Basin. These outcroppings are known to have been exploited by the Indians (Krieger 1965: 25).

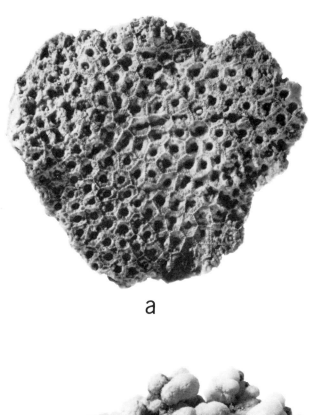

a

b

Fig. 14.6. A Hohokam collector's treasure: (a) fossil coral, *Hexagonaria davidsoni* (identification by Donald L. Bryant); (b) chalcedony, length 11.7 cm.

Oddly weathered formations, concretions, and the unusual stony items in nature were attractive to the Hohokam just as they are to the "rock hound" of today. A Snaketown Phase collector of the fourth or fifth century brought together a fossil coral colony of Devonian age, probably from the Ray area (Fig. 14.6a), and the previously noted chalcedony formation (Fig. 14.6b), leaving them on the floor of his house (House 1: 9G).

TURQUOISE

Since there are no known natural occurrences of turquoise nearer than 120 km (75 mi) to Snaketown, considerable interest is connected with its source because the mineral was acquired by the inhabitants throughout the village's life (See frequency table with Fig. 14.42). Anne Colberg-Sigleo, of the University of Arizona's Laboratory of Isotope Geochemistry, has the following to say about trace-element analyses of turquoise artifacts made by her:

Fourteen turquoise beads and a pendant fragment were chemically analyzed by Neutron Activation Analysis in order to determine the geographic provenience of the mine which supplied the mineral. The samples were subjected to a series of short and long irradiations in a TRIGA reactor with a flux of 10^{12} neutrons/cm^2, and the resultant activity counted in a Li(Ge) detector (see Gordon and others 1968 for the method). The results obtained by this procedure were compared with chemical analyses of turquoise samples from 27 mines in the southwestern United States most of which were reportedly exploited prehistorically (Colberg-Sigleo 1970). These comparisons indicate that the Snaketown artifacts came from the Himalaya, or East Camp, group of claims near Baker, California, about 140 km (90 mi) west of Kingman, Arizona. Descriptions of the prehistoric mines appear in Murdoch and Webb (1966).

Statistical analyses of the data using computer techniques are being developed and, it is hoped, they will confirm the present chemical indications. (See also Colberg-Sigleo 1975:459–460.)

The specimens examined were either of Colonial or Sedentary Period ages. The random selection from the collection as a whole suggests that the area known as the East Camp group of mines in California was the main supplier of turquoise in the later stages of Hohokam prehistory. Follow-up studies in this region to detect direct evidences of Indian activity, and further testing of Pioneer Period turquoise samples to see if early stones came from there as well, could lead to helpful information about Hohokam commercial and mining efforts.

COPPER

The 1964–65 excavations produced no copper objects, a reasonably good indication that products of this metal were never prevalent at Snaketown. The 28 copper bells (Gladwin and others 1937: 163-65) recovered in 1934–35 were components of a single necklace. At that time I speculated that "... the source for Southwestern bells was local and that the bells were made somewhere in the region" (164). In the light of the accumulated information of the last thirty years about copper bells, this idea is no longer tenable, and all evidence points to production in centers well down into Mexico. Sprague and Signori (1963) have given us a useful inventory of the more than 450 known Southwestern bells as the basis for typological studies, probably the most satisfactory way to establish the connections with the south. For those wishing to pursue this subject further, the aforementioned source also provides a good reference list of writings about copper bells. As far as the Hohokam are concerned, it can be stated with certainty that they themselves did not work in copper and that such copper objects they had were acquired at least by A.D. 1100 from west coast Mexican sources. Further clarification of this concept will be found in Pendergast's writings (1962).

LEAD

The presence of lead on palette surfaces was established after the first investigation of Snaketown (Gladwin and others 1937: 165-67). The time has come to look anew at the general question of how much the Hohokam really knew about the element. A crust composed principally of lead oxide and some globules of metallic lead was observed on the inner surface of pottery vessels by F. G. Hawley in 1937 (282-283). Believing that these reflected a conscious activity rather than accidents, a search was made of the pottery collection for additional examples. Two were found from the 1934–35 excavations and two (one fragmentary) from the 1964–65 work that revealed the same type of crust (Fig. 14.7). Of the six units available for study, two were associated with cremations and the rest came from general testing, a circumstance of more than passing interest.

In every instance the pottery vessel is a scoop or ladle, hinting that the shape of the container was a deliberate selection based on its efficiency during the heating process. This is particularly true of specimens b and d (Fig. 14.7) which were handled ladles, an uncommon shape for pottery of the Sedentary Period. The crust in the latter specimen contains some galena, as determined by Ralph W. G. Wyckoff. The vessel forms and the places of discovery raise the question as to whether or not these objects served as crucibles during experiments leading to the extraction of metallic lead from ores, or whether another purpose was being

Fig. 14.7. Pottery ladles and scoops exhibiting a lead-containing crust. Length of e, 15.5 cm.

served. In any event the containers were discarded without ceremony. Although masses of lead or artifacts thereof have not been recovered, the evidence suggests that certain reactions in lead ores induced by heat were understood. What was going on in the minds of the Hohokam when they heated the lead is not clear.

That these crucibles were substitutes for palettes in ritual moments cannot be ruled out; but the idea that the Hohokam may have been at the threshold of knowingly producing metallic lead cannot be ruled out either. The use of ladles and scoops for this purpose represents a conscious decision ruled by functional requirements, an act not so clearly demonstrable for the palettes. The pottery types used place these efforts in the Colonial and Sedentary Periods.

PECKED AND POLISHED IMPLEMENTS

This broad category of stone artifacts includes tools willfully shaped by mechanical acts of pecking, abrading, and polishing, and also those stones whose forms were modified by the work done with them, that is, they were shaped by use and not for use. It should be apparent that many rocks employed momentarily, as for example a hammer in breaking a nut, may retain no identifying marks of having served man. By force, therefore, we are limited in our studies to examining only those pieces which are identifiable artifacts.

Among the simplest of these were blocks of almost any suitable material, waterworn or not, which served as anvils against which other kinds of work could be done. Smaller anvils have been called lap stones, thereby bringing the work close to the body of the operator. These stones show only pitting, as from hammerstroke impacts, or scratches, as might be expected if leather was cut against them. We made no effort to inventory anvils at Snaketown since they were assumed to have little or no meaning in a taxonomic sense. Actually, not many were found, partly because of the scarcity of stone, and most likely because other large stones, as metates, probably served this purpose.

Hammerstones

Hammerstones were plentiful in all horizons at Snaketown, and they testify to the dependence the Hohokam placed on this elementary tool. Weight and form differences are recognizable, deriving largely from the form and size of the original rock when it was put to use and the length of time it was employed. It is not, however, an element that has lent itself to the kinds of typological treatments that might be expected to yield meaningful information. Experience with other collections has shown that time spent in the meticulous weighing, measuring, and classifying of hammers, for the most part, is time lost. Intrasite comparisons are less meaningful at this moment than intersite or regional comparisons. Provenience studies are of little help either, as hammerstones occurred in just about every conceivable circumstance in a site.

Although the hammerstone reported with Cache 2:9F apparently was the one used to demolish the goods in the cache, most of those in the collection were associated with houses, trash, hearths, and random situations revealing no specific uses. Note should be taken, however, that some trash-filled pits, as for example Pit 14:11F of Sweetwater Phase age, produced 14 hammerstones. There was no apparent explanation for this situation. Parts of the Pioneer Canal also contained many hammerstones along with other tool fragments. One suspects that these may have been thrown into the canal by playful children.

The observations of the nearly 450 hammerstones collected will be kept general. Angular, spheroid, and discoid shapes are the norm. Angularity derives from removing flakes from a suitable rock by percussion to produce sharp working edges (Fig. 14.8a and b). Prolonged use produced spheroid or discoid forms, generally with noticeable facets (Fig. 14.8c and 14.8d). Whole specimens and flakes indicate that some rounded stones were resharpened. Nevertheless, it appears that the sharp edges on angular stone and the softer contours of a rounded one may have been preferred for different kinds of work. The latter was probably best adapted for reducing bulk by pecking, as in shaping a mano, while the former was best suited for coarse work where irregular scarring was not a factor or was desirable, as in the sharpening of a metate.

Most hammerstones were made of diorite or andesite; a few are of quartzite, granite, or other crystalline rocks. Sizes range from 4 to 12 cm in diameter. It should be noted that many handstones, and some cobbles, larger and heavier than the hammerstones, show edge abrasions, some of which may result from blade-making as demonstrated by Crabtree (Crabtree and Swanson 1968). Just about any manageable rock of dense material could be used, and often was, as a hammer when the need arose. Multiple use is evident on many of the specimens in the collection. Hammers with grooves are axe fragments. There is no evidence that they were ever intentionally grooved.

In addition to these common hammerstones are several specialty forms that clearly derived from or were designed for particular functions. One group of 21 consists of finger-shaped stream pebbles, 5 to 10 cm long, with heavily abraded ends (Fig. 14.8e and f). Faceting occurs, indicating sustained use of the tool in one position. As in polishers, the material is always dense and fine-grained. Lightness of weight and smallness may mean that these were adapted to delicate work, such as roughing out the sculptured stone bowls. While relatively few of these were found, they appear to have been used during all periods.

A relative of the foregoing in form, but not in material and time, is a kind of tool consisting of 23 specimens made of gneiss, schist, or siltstone, all abrasive rocks. They are large, from 11 to 17 cm in length, and they combine the functions of a file and a

PHASE	a-d	e,f	g,h	i,j	TOTALS
CIVANO	19	1		1	21
SACATON	65	7	10	18	95
SANTA CRUZ	20	3		4	27
GILA BUTTE	39	2		1	42
SNAKETOWN	25	4			29
SWEETWATER	107			2	109
ESTRELLA	15	1			16
VAHKI	64			1	65
PIONEER P.	13				13
UNPLACED	22	3	2	1	28
TOTALS	389	21	12	23	445

Fig. 14.8. Hammerstones: (a, b) angular (diorite and andesite); (c) spheroid (quartzite); (d) discoid (diorite); (e, f) end-abraded pebbles (diorite and quartzite); (g, h) file-hammers (gneiss); (i, j) pebbles with face or edge scarring (quartzite and diorite). Length of g, 13.3 cm.

Note: Frequency charts accompanying figures, as above and hereafter, are keyed to the specimens in the illustrations. The Soho Phase (preceding the Civano Phase) has been omitted because our excavations did not sample this horizon.

hammer by using the sides and the ends respectively (Fig. 14.8g and h). This was a specialty tool associated most likely with the production of shell jewelry, notably bracelets. Since we know that both rasping and chipping were work patterns in the reduction of shell, this implement was admirably designed to serve both needs. Of the 12 specimens, 10 were in undisputed Sacaton Phase associations, and 2 were unplaced. It appears that this tool was a Sedentary Period invention, coinciding with the time of high bracelet production.

Finally, there are 21 stream pebbles, generally somewhat elongated, always of hard fine-grained minerals, 5.5 to 15 cm in length, that show near the end, either on the face or edge, clusters of pit marks (Fig. 14.8i and j). One may presume that these resulted from a series of similar blows directed at some sharp resistant object. All time periods are represented by the lot.

Metates

Considering the large number of houses cleared of debris and the extent of the general excavations, the number of whole metates recovered was unusually small, only seven. In developing the metate typology and the temporal distribution, large fragments with reliable associations were also used. This brings the number of specimens in the sample to 111. The scarcity of the most important stone tool the Hohokam had, equipment used daily by families for grinding corn, requires a word of explanation. Metates were the largest rock artifacts used in the village. This means that when they were broken or worn out the residual stone still could be adapted to many other uses. Native stone on the site, it will be remembered, was nonexistent. Some metate fragments were recovered in refuse, but most of them came as hearth stones, in canal wash-out repairs, and other situations. Only two were found in what appeared to be their use-positions on house floors. These conditions suggest that the metate was highly prized and that it was generally removed from the house on abandonment, except in those cases when the domicile was overcome by a tragedy as, for example, a surprise fire.

The typology of Snaketown metates is simple. There were three main kinds: Type 1, a flat-surfaced form, was made of a granite or basalt block, and exhibiting some edge shaping and slightly concave grinding area in longitudinal section (Fig. 14.9a). The length of manos used on these must have matched the metate width. Chronologically the three examples span the Sacaton and Gila Butte phases. Numerically the type seems not to have been important.

Type 2 consisted of shallow basin metates in which a short handstone was used (Type 1 b) predominantly in a reciprocal, though also in a slightly arcing, motion. Materials in the two at hand are rhyolite and sandstone (Fig. 14.9b and c). Some edge shaping is apparent. The Colonial and Sedentary Periods are represented.

Type 3, full-troughed and open at both ends, is by far the most numerous and interesting metate form and represents the highest degree of workmanship lavished on grinding equipment anywhere north of Mexico. These are generally rectangular in shape with carefully trimmed edges producing near vertical or slightly rounded edges (Fig. 14.9d and e). Bottoms also have been flattened with a pecking stone. There is no trace of the presence of legged metates.

Numerous fragments in the 1964–65 sample indicate that Type 3 metates were employed by the Hohokam from the beginning of their settlement in the Gila River valley, though the 1934–35 collection did not reveal this (Gladwin and others 1937: Pls. XLVII, XLVIII). The present sample is small, and one might be inclined to discount the evidence were it not for the fact that the material in the early Pioneer Period specimens is dominantly quartzite, less often basalt, matching the kind of stone used in the early manos and different, therefore, from metates of later phases in which the material is consistently vesicular basalt. In other words, the associations appear to be dependable. Close exami-

PHASE	a	b,c	d,e	TOTALS
CIVANO			3	3
SACATON	2	1	20	23
SANTA CRUZ			7	7
GILA BUTTE	1	1	14	16
SNAKETOWN			6	6
SWEETWATER			19	19
ESTRELLA			9	9
VAHKI			18	18
PIONEER P.			8	8
UNPLACED			2	2
TOTALS	3	2	106	111

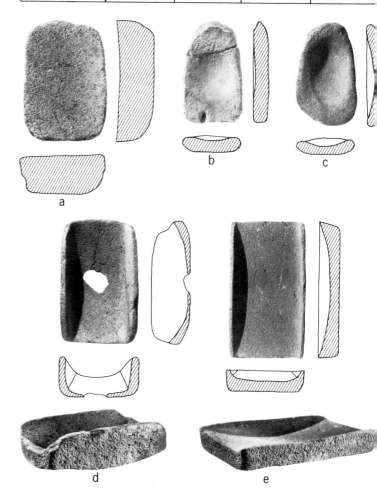

Fig. 14.9. Metates: (a) Type 1, granite; (b, c) Type 2, sandstone and rhyolite; (d, e) Type 3, vesicular basalt. Length of e, 53.5 cm.

nation of the early fragments suggests that, though shaped as the later ones were, the geometry may have been somewhat less angular and the original metate blocks thinner, resulting in a shallower trough.

Long manos rode in the trough of Type 3 metates, resulting, as wear increased, in thin risers or edges. In worn-out specimens a maximum height of edges of 13 cm, above the metate floor, has been noted indicating the extent to which the corn meal was "enriched" by stone meal. But more surprising is the fact that as the bulk of the metate was worn away, the attrition on the mano must also have been heavy on grinding surface and ends, thereby shortening it. Slight ridging on the inner faces of some metate edges probably signifies mano substitutions, apparently a conscious effort to keep the trough width uniform. This is evidence of a "tidiness" of mind and motor habit that goes with the rest of the equipment.

The grinding surface is concave in transverse and longitudinal axes, more so in the latter and most pronounced on those metates which were worn out. In short, the concavity lengthwise increased with the age of the tool. It has not been possible with any degree of certainty to establish the near or far ends of the metates with respect to the user. Sharpening the grinding surface by pecking is evident in the early quartzite metates, but this treatment was unnecessary for the most part in the porous lava specimens, which were "self-sharpening."

We do not have consistent evidence or enough instances to declare in what part of the house the metate was normally used, if the Hohokam followed a pattern. The flat bottom required no propping-up and permitted flexibility in its placement. There is no indication that the slab-lined bin in which metates were permanently set, as among the Anasazi, was ever employed by the Hohokam.

The three metate types noted do not represent a developmental series. The differences in form are probably ascribable to functional differences, as may have been dictated by the varying physical properties of seeds ground on them. Of major importance is the knowledge that the shaped troughed metate was standard equipment from the beginning of the Hohokam record and that it survived through the Classic Period (Haury 1945a: 126-27).

Accepting the present dating criteria, this means that there was no significant change in the metate type for perhaps 1,700 years, making it the most stable element in the Hohokam cultural complex of which we now have knowledge. Since the grinding tools of the San Pedro Stage of the Cochise Culture represent the end of a seven- or eight-millennia-long tradition of grinding stone use, it is worthwhile assessing the relationshp between the old indigenous tools and those of the Hohokam. Although some San Pedro Stage grinders were contemporaneous with early Hohokam metates, they were totally different (Sayles and Antevs 1941: Pl. XV g). The Hohokam open-ended trough cannot be drawn out of the San Pedro deep basin or any of the antecedent types. The best explanation is that the metate was introduced into southern Arizona when the Hohokam arrived from the south and that it represents the superposition of an alien grinding stone tradition on an ancient and less formalized local tradition of food processing stones.

Finally, not included in the typology and not illustrated are four flattish quartzite river boulders, up to 25 cm in diameter, which have worn facets probably from handstone application. They are neither flat-surfaced nor basin metates, but rather a nondescript kind of nether stone altered by use. Three are of Sacaton Phase age and one is Civano Phase (Ariz. U:13:22).

Manos

The mobile stone in the grinding tool combination is the unit held in the hand by the operator. It is moved back and forth in a reciprocal motion or in a slightly arcing motion in relation to an imagined central axis, depending on the nature of the nether stone. A rotary motion was not used, and could not have been used, on metates and milling stones with elongate basins. For our purposes, the terminology and typology of the tool in question are simple. Though meaning the same thing, the terms handstone and mano will be used. Handstone applies to a natural cobble with one or more wear facets, with no or little shaping to alter its natural form, and adapted for use in one hand. A mano may have uni- or bi-facial wear facets over its full length, it has been carefully trimmed to elliptical or rectangular forms or close variants thereof, and it was best operated with both hands. In general, the motion with which the handstones were used was relatively unrestrained because the basin- or flat-surfaced nether stone imposed few limits. The mano, on the other hand, was limited in its use to the rigidly defined area of the trough of a metate. Minor subtypes in these two main categories of tools are recognized. Figure 14.10 offers a synopsis of handstone-mano typology and temporal distributions by type and material.

PHASE	a	b,c	d	e	TOTALS
CIVANO	11	6 ◇△		2 ⑪	32
SACATON	18 ①③	9 ①	1	3 ㊷	78
SANTA CRUZ	1	4		1 ⑤	11
GILA BUTTE	2	2		⑲	23
SNAKETOWN	1	2	1 ④	7 ②	17
SWEETWATER	1	3	7 ⑤☐		17
ESTRELLA	2	1	4 ①		8
VAHKI	5	2	14 ③		24
PIONEER P.			11 ③		14
UNPLACED	2	2	1	3 ⑧◇	17
TOTALS	43 ①③	31 ◇△①	39 ⑯☐	16 ㊼◇	241

2=quartzite ②=basalt ☐=diorite ◇=granite △=tuff

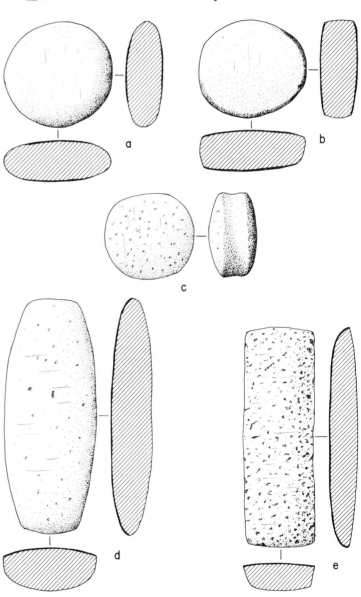

Fig. 14.10. Handstone and metate types. (a) Type 1a; (b) Type 1b; (c) Type 1b (from Ariz. U:13:21); (d) Type 2a; (e) Type 2b. Extent of grinding surface in sections is shown by thickened line. Length of *d*, 25.5 cm.

Natural cobbles, almost exclusively of quartz collected from stream beds, constitute Type 1a, the simplest of the handstones (Fig. 14.10a). Sizes range from 7 to 18.7 cm in diameter, averaging about 11 cm. They are circular or elliptical in outline and naturally flattened. No shaping is evident and wear facets are seen on one or both flat surfaces. Multiple use as anvils and hammers is often evident. These handstones were suited for use on flat or shallow basin metates.

Type 1b handstones share all the characteristics of the preceding kind, and additionally they show edge shaping to bring them to a symmetrical form and to provide a better surface for finger gripping (Fig. 14.10b). Occasionally, the edge trim produced a pulley effect (Fig. 14.10c) which appears to be limited to the Sedentary and Classic Periods. Both handstone types were present in all phases, though numerically they were most heavily represented in the late periods.

Type 2a and 2b manos exhibit all-over shaping by pecking, and both were specifically designed for use in the troughed metate. Shape and material differences distinguish the two, and most significantly, there is also a pronounced time difference. Type 2a manos have convex sides producing a midwidth about 30% greater than the end widths. Generally unifacial, the grinding face in transverse section is convex, though the longitudinal section tends to be relatively flat, with the wear surface curving to include the ends (Fig. 14.10d). There are few whole examples in the collection, but the projected average length was near 25 cm. Quartzite was the favored material, as it was also for the metates in the Pioneer Period, the time to which Type 2a manos may be assigned. Since quartzite and the occasional other dense stones used did not have the self-sharpening qualities evident in vesicular basalt, surfaces of both metates and manos of this time were roughened by pecking to improve grinding efficiency.

The preferred material for Type 2b manos was vesicular basalt. Little-used or unused manos reveal they were preshaped as rectangular blocks. In plan view they are rectangular, no matter how extensively worn. The usual single-wear surface is flat transversely and nearly flat lengthwise with the grinding surface extending well up on the ends (Fig. 14.10e). Typically the sides are slightly beveled toward the back or upper surface, which helped in gripping, but well-defined finger grooves, as often seen in Anasazi manos, do not occur. A variant treatment of the back was a symmetrical convexity, especially pronounced in the Classic Period Type 2b manos. The average length of Type 2b manos was reduced from about 20 cm in the Colonial and Sedentary Periods to 15 cm in the Classic Period. This change should be reflected in the metates as well, but the collection is too small to verify the fact.

The contrasting influences on subsistence patterns and related food processing tools by desert and riverine environments, both occupied by the Hohokam, are sharply brought out by comparing the milling equipment of the agriculturally dependent Snaketown residents and the grinding tools used by fellow tribesmen given to food collecting as evidenced in Ventana Cave (Haury 1950: 305-20). It appears that the formalized trough metate was indeed a correlate of maize culture and that the simple basin mill was totally adequate for processing naturally grown foods. The desert and river Hohokam were in contact with each other, and their preferences for different tool assemblages cannot be attributed to the fact that they did not know what the others had.

Mortars and Pestles

The mortar and the pestle, being bulky in nature, evidently suffered the same fate as the metates, namely, reuse of the stone when they had served their original purpose. The recovered sample is far smaller than might be expected for such practical tools in an economy where seed gathering played a significant role. Wood may well have been substituted for stone. The Pima ethnographic record shows that mortars of wood were "... first in importance among the utensils ..." of the household (Russell 1908: 99).

There is a single large basalt boulder mortar found in a pit filled with hearth stones in Work Area 1 (Figs. 14.11, 9.5a). Since the bottom of the mortar was broken out and it had been heated along with the other stones, the presumption is that it was discarded. However, the edges of the perforation are moderately rounded,

Fig. 14.11. Gyratory crusher, basalt. Sacaton Phase. Maximum diameter, 37 cm.

indicating that the hole was not a break-through from over-use. The specimen was undoubtedly a gyratory crusher, described by Hayden (1969) and so identified by him. Its age is Sacaton Phase.

A second mortar of dense basalt is a well-fashioned cylinder 17 cm high and 15.5 cm in diameter (Fig. 14.12c). The depression is 4.5 cm deep. It was found in Work Area 2 and next to it lay the companion pestle (Fig. 14.12b), also of basalt. Soil from the mortar cavity was tested for pollen, but it gave negative results. Work Area 2 was last used in the Sacaton Phase. A rim of a similar mortar from a Sweetwater Phase context suggests the type had a long life.

The third and last mortar is on the underside of a troughed metate block from Arizona U:13:21 of the Civano Phase. I doubt that the metate-mortar combination has any patterned meaning.

Detailed typing of pestles will not be attempted. A small number were selected from stream cobbles because of their elongated form and put to use without modification (Fig. 14.12a). They are remarkably uniform as to length, 20-23 cm, weighing from 2 to 2.5 kg. Quartzite and schist were preferred.

Shaped pestles are somewhat more common, larger than the unshaped ones by an average of 10 cm, and weighing up to 7.5 kg, a respectable weight to handle. They are either cylindrical in form or somewhat tapered (Fig. 14.12b, d, and e). Granite, gneiss, quartzite, and schist are the materials. The work done with them produced rounded wear surfaces, usually on both ends. Although in our sample most of the specimens are late, the tool is known to have been used widely by preagricultural food gatherers (Haury 1950: 324).

The long pestle illustrated in Figure 14.12e is of special interest because it was found in a Pima cache which appeared in Canal Trench 11. Accompanying the pestle were a number of plain and painted Pima pottery jars, a string of blue glass beads, and several glass whiskey or wine bottles of about 1880 vintage. The pestle is of a type that had a long history, and while it cannot be demonstrated with certainty, one may suppose that the Pimas salvaged it from Snaketown or elsewhere in the area and put it to current use. It duplicates in this respect the three-quarter grooved axe found with an iron shovel and other objects (Fig. 12.7), examples of the human introduction of old artifacts into a modern cultural context.

PHASE	a	b,d,e	TOTALS
CIVANO	2	3	5
SACATON	4	3	7
SANTA CRUZ		1	1
GILA BUTTE		1	1
SNAKETOWN			
SWEETWATER		1	1
ESTRELLA			
VAHKI			
PIONEER P.			
UNPLACED		1	1
TOTALS	6	10	16

served as a simple kind of palette. Fine-grained rock types, as siltstone and andesite, predominate. Like the matching units, these were present in all periods.

Polishing Stones

Stream pebbles of hard, fine-grained minerals, notably andesite, quartzite, and jasper were selected and used as polishers when smooth surfaces were desired. These pebbles vary in size from 3.5 to 18 cm, the average being about 6 cm. The preference of the user determined the original shape of the pebble, and the subsequent mode of use produced the modification seen today. It is clear from studying the wear facets that varying kinds of work was done with them (Fig. 14.13). Most of the 44 specimens were probably used in polishing pottery, though the emphasis on this treatment varied with time, being more consistently practiced in the Pioneer Period than later on. End abrasions on some units indicate hammerstone use also.

The cultural context for about 70% of the specimens was reasonably certain, and these data show only that the element was employed at all times.

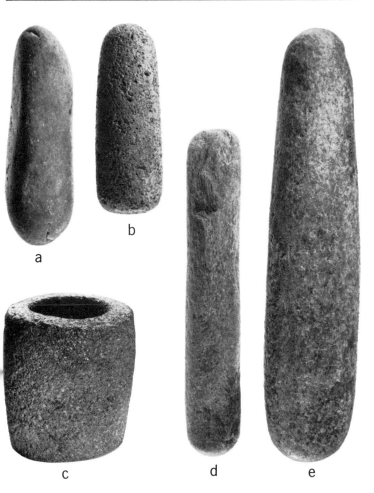

Fig. 14.12. Mortar and pestles: (a) unshaped quartzite, Sacaton Phase; (b, c) Mortar-pestle set found together, both basalt, Sacaton Phase; (d) shaped, cylindrical, schist, Civano Phase; (e) shaped, tapered, quartzite, found in Pima cache of about 1880. Length of e, 45.5 cm.

Rubbing Stones

Nine specimens are best labeled rubbing stones because they have clear wear facets on the midsection of the flattest surfaces. They range from 5 to 11.5 cm in greatest dimension and are therefore smaller than handstones and manos. Andesite, quartzite, and other hard fine-textured rock types were selected for these. Red paint adhering to one suggests use in pigment preparation. Temporally the small sample ranges through all periods.

The probable nether stones for these are predominantly hand-sized, thin, river-worn cobbles. One or both flat surfaces evidence wear as though from use by the stones described above, and several of the 13 in the lot reveal red paint stains. They apparently

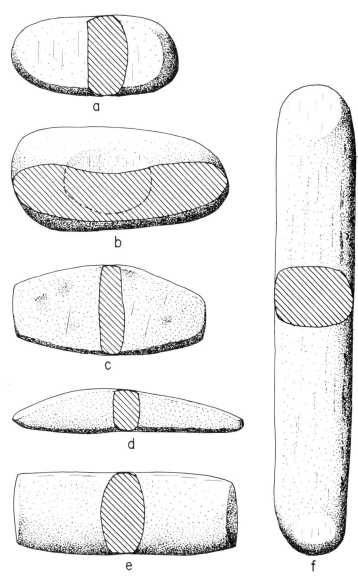

Fig. 14.13. Polishing stones: (a) flat wear surface, Sacaton Phase; (b) concave wear surface, Sacaton Phase; (c) edge wear surfaces, unplaced; (d) edge worn, ends abraded from hammering, unplaced; (e) edge and end worn surfaces, unplaced; (f) wear facets near ends, Sacaton Phase.

Abrading Stones

There are a number of tool types designed to work on other stones or materials either by percussion blows or by friction. Depending on the nature of the work to be done, several specific and interesting tools resulted. The actions include pounding, as reducing mass by pecking with a hammerstone; rubbing, as shaping a shell or a bone awl on an abrasive rock; sawing, as with a thin sheet of abrasive stone on stone, wood, or shell; filing and reaming, as with a rasp or reamer in shell ring and bracelet production; and drilling, as producing perforations by the rotary motion of a cutting tool. A good example of the single association of a number of these tools occurred in Cache 1:10G, a rich deposit of sculptured stone pieces and the tools used to make them. The main categories follow.

Abrading Palettes

These are generally flat tabular pieces, occasionally chunky, of gritty stones, such as sandstone, siltstone, schist, and gneiss. Most were hand-held, and the object to be shaped was drawn across the surface. Wear facets tend to be irregular depressions, partly determined by the form of the original stone. Grooves developed from sharpening such artifacts as awls. The 25 specimens, all different in form, derive from contexts attributable to all phases except Estrella.

Files

Hand-held tools drawn against the surface or material to be modified were analogous to our files and sanding blocks. The preferred materials for the former were gneiss, schist, siltstone, and rarely granite. They are generally elongate in plan and ovate in section (Fig. 14.14a-d) having an average length of about 10 cm.

The artifact was most prevalent during the Sacaton Phase according to the frequency table, a time of high shell-jewelry production for which these were used. But it is important to note that the tool was present as early as the Vahki Phase, a longevity which was not brought out in the findings of 1934–35 (Gladwin and others 1937: Pl. XXXVIII). Since the shell industry had a long life, it is natural to expect shell-working tools to be present as well.

The abrasive blocks are tabular pieces of fine sandstone (Fig. 14.14e and f) or irregular lumps of abrasive materials, averaging about 6 cm across. They too had a long history and were probably put to work in finishing stone sculptures or shell products.

Reamers

This term is limited to those tools which were used in a rotary motion while producing large perforations, as in shell ring-making. The resultant wear on the implement left a blunt cylindrical or tapered projection (Fig. 14.14g–i). Abrasive fine sandstone and gneiss seem to have been favored. The tools themselves vary greatly in gross size, but the perforations ground round with them differed only from 1 to 2 cm in diameter. Although rings were made in all phases, the greatest variety was attributable to the Sacaton Phase, and most of the reamers date from that time (Gladwin and others 1937: Pl. XXXVIII).

Saws

A series of 32 artifacts were employed as cutting tools in a to-and-fro motion, as with a saw; but these implements are toothless (Fig. 14.14j-l). These have rounded edges, and the evidence suggests that they were used against a hard substance like stone. Thin sheets of stone, 3 to 5 mm thick and 6 to 21 cm in greatest dimensions, were selected. The material is predominantly

PHASE	a–d	e,f	g–i	j–l	TOTALS
CIVANO					
SACATON	17	5	5	13	40
SANTA CRUZ	2	2	1	4	9
GILA BUTTE	2	2	1	3	8
SNAKETOWN	1	2	2	2	7
SWEETWATER	2	3		2	7
ESTRELLA	1			2	3
VAHKI	2	1			3
PIONEER P.	1			1	2
UNPLACED	6	3	3	5	17
TOTALS	34	18	12	32	96

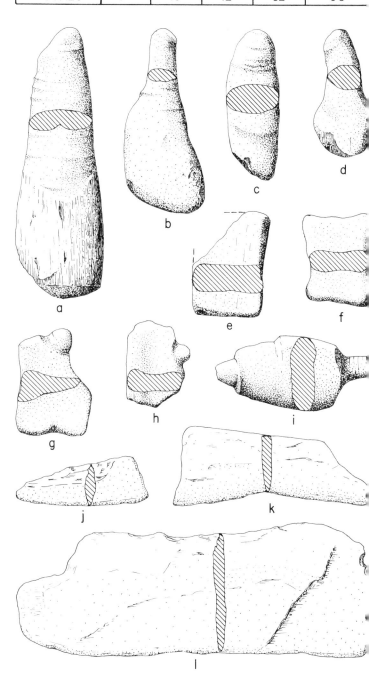

Fig. 14.14. Abrading tools of various types: (a-d) files of schist and siltstone; (e-f) abrasive blocks, sandstone; (g-i) reamers, sandstone; (j-l) saws, phyllite. Length of *l*, 18.3 cm.

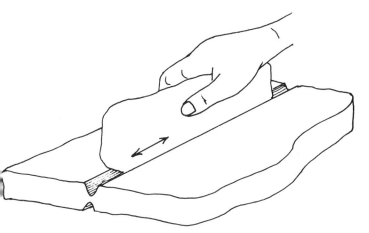

Fig. 14.15. One method of using phyllite saws.

phyllite, and a few other gritty rock types were also selected. No attention was given to form or edge dressing. Edges sometimes show a sinuous quality which would result when the tool was used for making short cuts. Longer cuts, as in trimming a slab of slate for a palette, would produce a more uniform edge. Fragments of slate in the collection show how it was parted by cutting opposing grooves and snapping the piece in two when it was safe to do so (Fig. 14.15). Since the saw edges fit the grooves, it seems certain that the use of this tool can be properly identified.

The temporal range of the artifacts appears to span the life of Snaketown except for the Classic Period. No examples were found in the three Civano Phase sites adjacent to Snaketown. While this tool type can easily go unnoticed, it is not likely that it would have escaped detection in the extensive work in Casa Grande, Los Muertos, and other late villages. Its scarcity may be associated with the dying out of palette production during the Classic Period.

Scoria Rasps

A dozen specimens of vesicular basalt, trimmed to fit the hand but not consistent as to gross form, have flat to slightly concave working surfaces. One of the best shaped units is shown in Figure 14.16a. Diameters range from 5 to 13 cm. A clue as to the probable use of these stones comes from their proveniences. Ten of the 12 were found in houses, and half of the sample dates from the Civano Phase, the others being about equally divided between the Colonial and Sedentary Periods. By actual tests, these implements are highly efficient in rasping wood. Shaping beam ends, wooden mortars, or many other wooden products, would tend to produce the concave surfaces. The need for more precise dimensions of ceiling beams in the adobe-walled dwellings of the Civano Phase may account for their greater prevalence at that time.

One specimen differs from all others in shape (Fig. 14.16b), having two extensions or horns, both broken. These could have provided the needed grip because the worn nether surface shows that it was a working tool. Similar objects have been noted as associated with seed grinding by the Indians in northeastern California (Miles 1963: 45), and Kidder illustrates one from Pecos Ruin where it was found with a cache of shrine materials (1932: 100). Analogous artifacts appear to be relatively common in the Chapala Basin of Jalisco and Michoacan, Mexico (Meighan and Foote 1968: 154, Plate 26A). The Snaketown specimen came from a Sacaton Phase house.

Hoes

Thin sheets of rock, naturally spalled from bedrock deposits, were used as hand-held digging tools. Mostly of rhyolite and andesite, the pieces were given varying attention as to form. The

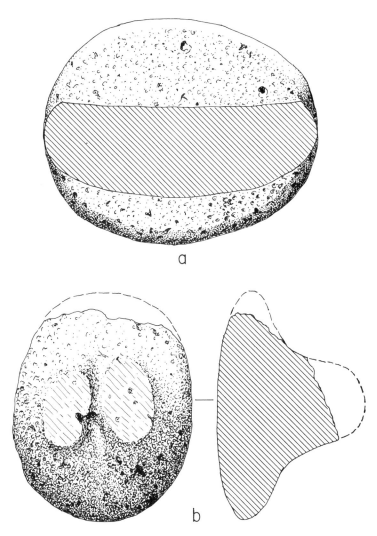

Fig. 14.16. Scoria rasps: (a) Civano Phase (Ariz. U:13:21); (b) Sacaton Phase. Greatest diameter of b, 9.1 cm.

sharpest edge, resulting from prismatic fracturing, was sometimes further improved by grinding and chipping, or a combination of both. Striations running with the edge do occur, the results of sharpening rather than from use. Wear from digging in the ground is best seen on the chipped edges in which the harshness of the flaked surfaces has been softened. Figure 14.17 illustrates two examples from the small collection of 14 (see Haury 1945a: 134-37 for a fuller discussion). Ten of these came from two Classic Period sites, Civano Phase, and only four came from Snaketown itself, all assignable to the Sacaton Phase. The trait was essentially a Classic Period hallmark.

An earlier statement that "... irrigation and the hoe persist more or less together ..." (Haury 1945a: 136) needs correcting because it is now clear that the beginning of irrigation preceded the common use of the stone hoe by more than a thousand years. Wood may have anticipated the use of stone for this all important tool.

Arrow Shaft Polisher

Ridged and grooved tools used to straighten and polish arrow shafts are common in the Pueblo IV ruins of central Arizona and east into New Mexico. Before about A.D. 1200, or the beginning of the Classic Period, the Hohokam did not make use of this implement. Not a single one was recovered in the main Snaketown village during both operations, but one was recovered in a suburban village (Ariz. U:13:21) of the Civano Phase. The

a

b

Fig. 14.17. Stone hoes: (upper) rough edges chipped, working edge sharpened by grinding, Sacaton Phase; (lower) working edge ground and subsequently improved by chipping, Civano Phase (Ariz. U:13:22). Length of *b*, 22.3 cm.

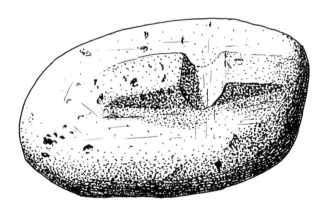

Fig. 14.18. Arrow shaft polisher from Ariz. U:13:21, Civano Phase. Length, 7.8 cm.

material appears to be a gritty compacted volcanic ash. All surfaces have been modified, and the top has a medial ridge with a single transverse groove designed to accommodate an arrow shaft about 8 mm in diameter (Fig. 14.18).

This element was found by Cushing in Los Muertos (Haury 1945a: 139), but it appears never to have been a common-place tool in the Gila-Salt River area. It was a part of the complex of puebloid traits that moved into the desert after about A.D. 1200.

Stones of Unknown Use

Three shaped stones that fit none of the categories established here are illustrated in Figure 14.19. They appear not to have been "working" rocks in the usual sense of the word but perhaps they

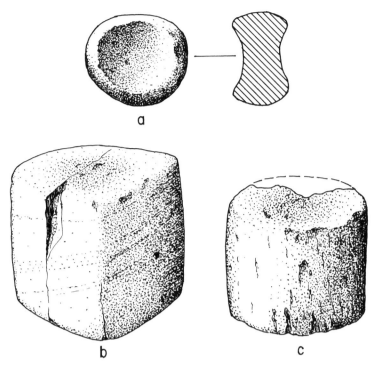

a

b   c

Fig. 14.19. Shaped stones of unknown use: (a) hard, crystalline rock, probably Santa Cruz Phase. (b) quartzite, Santa Cruz Phase. (c) porphyry, Santa Cruz Phase. Width of *b*, 8.5 cm.

fulfilled some special need not now identifiable. Made of hard stone, and differing somewhat in form, they share concave ends. They were associated with Colonial Period remains.

Palettes

The stone palette was one of the outstanding Hohokam hallmarks. Although the present sample is small compared with the 1934–35 recovery, 63 as against 262, the typological range and developmental trend exhibited by the new sample support the conclusions reached in 1937 (Gladwin and others 1937: 121-26). To recapitulate those findings, the palette sequence started in the Pioneer Period, probably as early as the Vahki Phase, with the use of flat tabular stones which soon were modified into rectangular form with a pronounced rim and depressed central portion. These were usually made of a hard crystalline stone. During the Colonial Period both the form and material changed. Shapes included effigy palettes, either human or reptilian, not infrequently with sculptured life forms projecting from the edges; but most often they exhibit a simple rectangular shape having slightly concave margins, square corners, and high incised borders. The material was slate-like, specifically Pinal schist. This was the time when relatively more palettes were made than either before or after. During the Sedentary Period, while the material remained much the same, the manufacturing precision declined, life form additions were almost completely lost, and decorations were mostly simple running patterns lightly incised or occasionally painted on the borders. By Classic Period times the palette was essentially lost as an element in the culture.

Figure 14.20 and the related frequency chart brings the palette record of the recent excavations into accord with the 1937 report. The relatively low level of palette recovery is attributable to the fact that little work was done in the cremation areas which have always been the consistent producers of the element.

Not surprisingly, the undifferentiated types, the simple tabular slabs and those with raised borders (Fig. 14.20a and b), occur spottily through nearly all phases; but the border decorated, edge-grooved, effigy, and sculptured forms (Fig. 14.20e, g, and h-j) dominant in the Colonial and Sedentary Periods do not appear

Fig. 14.20. Synoptic series of stone palettes: (a) shaped metamorphic rock, undecorated, House 2:7H, Sweetwater Phase; (b) crystalline rock, test in Block 5F, Sweetwater Phase; (c) mud rock, Cremation 5:11H, Snaketown Phase; (d) schist, deep edge groove, Mound 40, Gila Butte Phase; (e) schist, edge grooved, Cremation 2:11H, Santa Cruz Phase; (f) schist, not decorated, in trash west of House 3:10D, Sacaton Phase; (g) schist, faintly incised border design, Cremation 13:11H, Sacaton Phase; (h) schist, round palette, Mound 39, Sacaton Phase; (i) schist, horned lizard effigy, Cremation 21:11H, Santa Cruz Phase; (j) schist, pelican, stripping in Block 5F, probably Santa Cruz Phase. Length of f, 22.9 cm.

PHASE	a	b	c	d	e	f-g	h	i-j	TOTALS
CIVANO									
SACATON	1	1				17	1		20
SANTA CRUZ	1				13			1	15
GILA BUTTE		2		1	2				5
SNAKETOWN		2	1						3
SWEETWATER	2	2							4
ESTRELLA									
VAHKI		1							1
PIONEER P.		1							1
UNPLACED	1	2	1	1	5	3		1	14
TOTALS	5	11	2	2	20	20	1	2	63

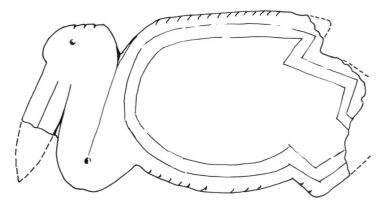

Fig. 14.21. Sketch tracing the light surface engraving of palette *j* in Fig. 14.20.

Fig. 14.22. Fire stains reveal how censers were arranged on a palette platform. Length of palette, 31.1 cm.

in the Pioneer Period, thereby giving meaning to the developmental trend. A fragment of a palette (A-27, 065) of the type shown in Figure 14.20b, was found on the floor of a burned Vahki Phase house (House 1: 7H). Since this house was in an area without late overbuilding, and all floor contact materials were consistent with Vahki associated goods elsewhere, I am inclined to accept the evidence as suggestive of palette use from the beginning of the Hohokam record as we now know it.

The effigy palettes, which may take the outline of an animal (Fig. 14.20i and j), or with sculptured edge elements, or other variations of animal depictions (Gladwin and others 1937: Pl. CI, CII), are clearly diagnostic of the Colonial Period and specifically of the Santa Cruz Phase. Generally, the animal characteristics are emphatically shown leaving no doubt as to what was in the mind of the maker. The pelican (Fig. 14.20j), however, was lightly treated, and the faint scratches not visible photographically are given in Figure 14.21. The Santa Cruz Phase animal emphasis in palettes is duplicated in at least two other products: the carved stone cups and life form painting on pottery. Why this preoccupation existed, whether no more than an artistic flare or fad, or whether there was a deeper devotion to the creatures depicted for magical or other reasons, cannot now be stated.

The common association of palettes with the bones of the cremated dead and the fact that they themselves usually passed through the pyral fire, often with the disastrous consequences of shattering them, is responsible for the notion that palettes were functionally related to an undefined role in the death ritual.

Relatively few palettes exhibit depressions that might have resulted from grinding pigments in them. The raised borders and the heavy incrustation on many specimens suggest that they may have been used as holders of pigments or other substances. Fire appears to have been an important related phenomenon, perhaps going beyond the sheer act of cremation, for burning may have produced effects vital in fulfilling ritual requirements that were achievable in no other way.

Hawley (1937: 282-89) has given us an excellent analysis of palette crusts with a reasoned speculation as to what the Hohokam did to produce them. While the sintered material must originally have been a mixture of things, the most surprising and consistent element is lead, including in some cases small pellets of metallic lead, probably accidentally produced. The question arises as to the original form of the lead. Since metallic lead is not easily released from ores in an open fire except from lead carbonate, Hawley believed that this might have been the form of lead used. But lead carbonate in itself is a whitish uninteresting material. By heating in an open fire, however, it is changed to lead oxide, a chemical alteration accompanied by a color change from white to a strong red. This phenomenon may have been the magical effect desired by Hohokam medicine men. Prolonged heating fluxed the materials on the palettes, producing caked slag-like substances which include some droplets of lead. This incrustation occurs

predominantly on palette faces, but it appears also on the borders and sometimes even on the under surfaces.

Black and greenish glazed surfaces on palettes have also been noted. Thinking that these might represent other minerals, I submitted several samples to Ralph Wyckoff's laboratory for examination. Tests by Philip Matter may be summarized as follows: The x-ray diffraction powder picture shows the black glaze on palette A-26,564 to have, in addition to the minerals in the rock itself, strong lead lines and moderate intensity lines for magnetite (Fe_3O_4) and quartz (SiO_2). Trace amounts of copper and manganese were also present. Matter believes that the incrustation on the specimens studied "... represents a lead slag or glaze which has been colored black by the inclusion of possibly iron, as the mineral magnetite, or small amounts of manganese or copper."

The enormous range in palette sizes suggests that the precise function of the equipment may have varied. It is difficult to see how a palette only 6 cm long served the same purpose as one 38.5 cm in length. A use heretofore not reported is reconstructible after close examination of an exceptionally large palette found in association with 18 incense burners in Cache 1:9F (Figs. 11.1-11.3). Two irregular roundish areas in opposite corners of the palette surface were lighter in color than the surrounding rock, which was darkened by what appears to be soot (Fig. 11.3m). These gave rise to the feeling that two objects were sitting on the palette face while in use and that the contact areas were protected from the general smudging effect. Searching through the 18 censers associated with the palette for bottom configurations that would match the spots, two appeared to be likely candidates. Both of these had modeled human faces on the sides, and they were the only ones so decorated in the cache (Fig. 11.2). The best fit, censer-to-spot, indicates that the faces were looking outwardly (Fig. 14.22). The two palette corners behind them were heavily smudged, leading to the conclusion that something, probably incense, was burned there. Virtual proof of this is seen on the back of the larger of the two censers which carries a flame scar and a smudged area reaching up to and including the rim. The "hotspot" matches precisely the heaviest carbonized patch on the palette (Fig. 14.23). What we have here, then, is an indication that larger palettes served as pediments, or "altar pieces," as supports for other objects. In this instance the palette-censer association, in what appears to be a sacrificial deposit, predicates joint ritual use.

Palettes among the Hohokam still remain something of an enigma. Neighboring tribes did not appear to make much use of them, and the origin of the idea is obscure. The long-standing use of the trait and an evident local developmental sequence suggest that it was a Hohokam creation. Yet, the feeling lingers that the inspiration lies somewhere to the south, perhaps because the older examples were made of the harder materials, the shaping of which had been mastered by the stone craftsmen of ancient Mexico. But

Fig. 14.23. Effigy censer fitted on palette as indicated by pattern of smudging on both.

Bowls

Hohokam artistry in stone is well illustrated by the sculpturing of small stone bowls. They may be plain, ornamented with incised geometric figures, animals in bas-relief, or the whole objects may be made in the form of an animal. The best pieces in the collection, 50 in number, have been discussed in the consideration of Cache 1:10G (Chap. 11). To that list we must now add 28 additional specimens, whole and fragmentary, which came mostly from the general excavations. The 1964–65 sample totaled 78 examples as against 103 in 1934–35.

The randomly recovered pieces are useful, for they give a somewhat wider time range than do the units from caches. Reference to Figure 14.25 and the related frequency table is particularly helpful because it shows the distribution of stone vessels through nearly all phases, even though in low numbers. This is consistent with the 1934–35 results (Gladwin and others 1937: 115, Fig. 45). Of special note is the fact that ornamented specimens were present in the Vahki Phase (Fig. 14.25f, and 14.26). The grooved surface configuration brings to mind the same treatment on pottery, introduced in the Estrella Phase. Stone vessels of hard crystalline rocks were generally early, as was true in palettes, and the stone ladle with a handle, a phallus in some cases (Fig. 14.25g), was at least as old as the Snaketown Phase. Geometric incising (Fig. 14.25c), in general, was a Sedentary Period trait, and relief life forms (Fig. 14.25e) apparently were an innovation during the Colonial Period. Our excavations in the

more importantly, the idea of incense burning, and the concept of sacrifice are southern in terms of the Southwest, and the palettes are connected with these two patterns. On a more specific form level of comparison, the treatment of the human figure as a palette during the Classic Period in Guerrero (Flor y Canto del Arte Prehispánico de Mexico 1964: illustration no. 11) and during the Colonial Period of Hohokam (Gladwin and others 1937: Pl. CII, e) is certainly more than accidental (Fig. 14.24).

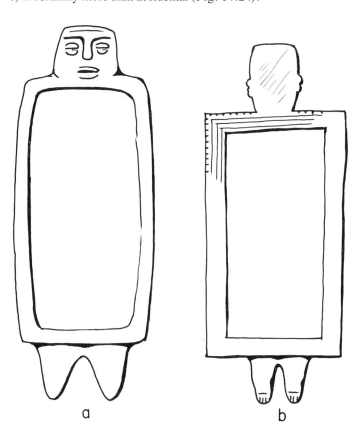

Fig. 14.24. Comparison of stone palettes in the human form: (a) Guerrero, Mexico; Classic Period. Length 29 cm; (b) Snaketown; Colonial Period, Santa Cruz Phase. Length 26.8 cm.

PHASE	a,b	c,d	e	f	g	TOTALS
CIVANO						
SACATON	I	3				4
SANTA CRUZ	I					I
GILA BUTTE	4	I	I			6
SNAKETOWN	3				2	5
SWEETWATER						
ESTRELLA	3					3
VAHKI				2		2
PIONEER P.						
UNPLACED	5	2				7
TOTALS	I7	6	I	2	2	28

Fig. 14.25. Stone vessels: (a) tuff, unplaced; (b) quartzite pebble, Estrella Phase; (c) tuff, Cremation 2:11H, probably Santa Cruz Phase; (d) tuff, Sacaton Phase (unusually small); (e) scoria, snake in high relief, Gila Butte Phase; (f) sandstone, Vahki Phase; (g) indurated sandstone, phallus handle fragment with depression in superior surface, Snaketown Phase. Diameter of a, 7.5 cm.

Fig. 14.26. Restoration of Vahki Phase sculptured vessel of calcareous sandstone. Length of fragment, 7 cm; original diameter about 12 cm.

three Classic Period sites in Snaketown's suburbs produced no examples of stone vessels. This negative evidence, together with the lack of the trait in other contemporary villages, indicates that after the Sedentary Period it lost favor and that by the fourteenth century little, if any, use was made of it.

Collections of sculptured stone from western Mexico yield few pieces that seem to be truly comparable in type and concept to the Hohokam stone vessels. Curiously, closer parallels are drawn from the Pacific northwest (Wingert 1952: e.g. illustration 40). Hohokam emphasis on this trait may have been unique to them, springing, possibly, from deep-seated beliefs connected with magic or curing. When animals were shown, they were the kinds that shared the desert environment with them. The answer may lie in the historic Pima practices, for they believed that the rattlesnake caused kidney and stomach trouble in children, that the horned lizard was responsible for rheumatism. Singing the rattlesnake song or the horned lizard song and pressing an image of the creature on the patients was an effective cure (Russell 1908: 264). The Hohokam stone vessels, suitable for holding potent concoctions, or for the burning of incense, and decorated with the aforementioned and other creatures, could have been used in curing.

Rings

The purpose of stone rings resembling doughnuts has long been the subject of speculation in the Southwest. Vesicular basalt was the preferred material for making them, and most of them appear to have been produced from broken mano halves. Biconical perforations were made before the objects were rounded. Sizes of the lava rings vary from 3.4 to 8.6 cm in diameter. Plain rings (Fig. 14.27a) appear to be late, while the pulley type (Fig. 14.27b) shows occurrences in several early phases. This is at variance with the findings in 1934–35 (Gladwin and others 1937: Pl. LXXXII). I would be inclined to doubt the validity of the early phase associations, but the circumstances under which they were found are convincing. For example, the Vahki specimen (A-26,273) came from Pit 3:10F, Level 4, north test. The potsherd yield from a number of tests was over 14,000 units, all Vahki Plain and Vahki Red except for a few fragments of late painted pottery near the top of the pit. While evidence of late disturbance in the pit was not observed, verification of this long life for the stone ring should be sought.

A specimen distinguished by its size, material, and excellent workmanship (Fig. 14.27c and Fig. 14.28) deserves a special note. Made of dense, dark greenish diorite, weighing 3.49 kg, it measures 18.1 cm in diameter and 5.6 cm in greatest thickness. The outer edge is nearly flat, and the surface is rough and scratched. Both faces show uniform concavities about 1 cm deep, beginning 2.0 cm from the edge, thereby leaving a flat-surfaced

PHASE	a	b	c	blanks	TOTALS
CIVANO				2	2
SACATON	4	2		9	15
SANTA CRUZ		1		1	2
GILA BUTTE		2			2
SNAKETOWN					
SWEETWATER		1			1
ESTRELLA				1	1
VAHKI		1			1
PIONEER P.					
UNPLACED		1	1	2	4
TOTALS	4	8	1	15	28

a

b

c

Fig. 14.27. Stone rings: (a) plain type, basalt, Sacaton Phase; (b) pulley type, basalt, Sacaton Phase; (c) bi-concave type, diorite, unplaced. Diameter of c, 18.1 cm.

band next to the edge. The central perforation is biconical, tapering from a diameter of 5 to 3.7 cm. The greatest wear is evident on the crest of the biconical perforation, a smoothness that could have come only from contact with another object. Discernible striations in the aperture are at right-angles to the ring's faces, suggesting that something was thrust through it. Close examination of the cupped surfaces reveals abrasion marks as might have come from hard objects smashed against the ring. This is more evident on one side than on the other. These dents, the direction of wear in the perforation, the biconcave form, and the scratched and rough outer edge lead to the speculation that this was a chunkee stone, the target element in the hoop and pole game. The

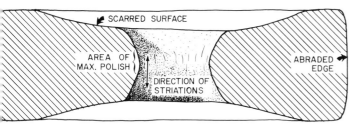

Fig. 14.28. Cross-section of (?) chunkee stone (Fig. 14.27c).

weight of the ring and its wide edge were necessary to achieve any length of roll in the soft desert soil. Biconcave chunkee stones up to 13 cm in diameter are illustrated by Culin (1907: 510) from South Carolina, indicating that large-sized stones were not strange to the players of the hoop and pole game. The Arizona State Museum collections contain at least three additional specimens similar in size to the Snaketown ring. All are biconcave, though two are not perforated. One was found near Tucson; the others probably came from Arivaca northwest of Nogales near the Mexican border. Evidently the element has a wider distribution in the Southwest than has been thought. Unfortunately the age of the specimens is uncertain. In all likelihood, this version of the chunkee stone was of Sedentary Period age and later. The Snaketown specimen was found during stripping operations near Sacaton Phase houses in Block 10G.

The smaller lava rings could also have been used in this fashion, as Culin notes for tribes of the Pacific Northwest (1907: 490, 521). However, the smallest specimens, less than 4 cm in diameter, are surely something else. A use for the lava ring of doughnut size, not generally thought of, is as a sheller of corn. Dried corn kernels on the cob can be quickly and easily removed by swiveling the implement around the cob as it comes up through the hole. An archaeological association that suggests this interpretation to be a sound one occurred in the Point of Pines ruin (Ariz. W:10:50). A burned thirteenth-century storeroom produced many bushels of shelled and unshelled carbonized corn. On the floor lay a well-worn lava ring, the only artifact of any consequence in the room. I doubt that its presence was accidental.

Axes

A stone tool well known to the Hohokam, designed for hard work but which required more care in shaping than any other, was the stone axe. Considering the almost constant need for it in the utilization of wood, notably in house-building, it is surprising that the stone axe collection from Snaketown is not larger. Twenty-one were recovered in 1934–35, and only 12 more were added in the recent work. In addition there are 19 axe fragments, some of which were ultimately used as hammerstones. By Classic Period times the relative abundances of axes had greatly increased, as excavations in Los Muertos, Las Acequias (Haury 1945a: 130, 167), and Casa Grande (Fewkes 1912: 123-24) testify. While the order of the increases is difficult to assess accurately, it may have been as much as a factor of three. An architectural change, from detached shallow pit houses to contiguous adobe-walled surface rooms, took place at about this time. The need for more axes may be linked with this architectural shift, for the flat roofs of pueblo type rooms required more precisely dimensioned logs and relatively more of them per area covered than did the flimsy roofs of huts.

Even though small, the Snaketown collection of axes reflects a form sequence which has interesting and meaningful implications, as noted later. Almost all are made of dioritic material, and all have the three-quarter groove to facilitate hafting with a J-shaped handle. This was the standard haft for central and southern Arizona as contrasted with the spiral groove of the Rio Grande in

New Mexico and the full groove axe of the Four Corners area, both requiring wrapped hafting.

Broadly speaking, two axe types are distinguishable. Type 1 has ridges flanking the hafting grooves on two sides and one edge of the blade and a wedge groove on the nether edge. Type 2, a simple axe with three-quarter groove, lacks the ridges and wedge groove. This typological difference was recognized during the 1934–35 excavations (Gladwin and others 1937: Pls. LXXVII and LXXVIII; Fig. 48). For our purposes, sketches of the two types will suffice (Fig. 14.29). Proveniences, as summarized in the chart accompanying Figure 14.29, provide significant information. On the basis of the 1934–35 work, it was believed that the ridged axe appeared during the Snaketown Phase, late in the Pioneer Period (Gladwin and others 1937: 118, Fig. 48). It now seems clear, however, that the type was well established in the Sweetwater Phase and that it occurred even earlier, on the basis of several associations. Because the Hohokam were skilled workers of stone from the start, it is likely that the implement was one of the original components they introduced into the Southwest, having gained knowledge of it in western Mexico along with other elements that distinguish them. While the three-quarter grooved axe was well known aboriginally in western Mexico, neither typological variations nor time positions are understood as yet, a fact which renders the establishment of specific connections with west Mexico difficult.

A typological change in the nonridged axe of a minor order took place after the Sedentary Period. This amounted to the lengthening of the bit. Medium- and short-bitted axes, of course, persisted. Long-bitted axes reached dimensions of 25 to 30 cm and usually were exceptionally well made. Several of this type, alleged to be from Snaketown, are in the E. H. Parker collection located in the Claremont Colleges Museum, California (Sedat 1972: Fig. 13). If these axes did indeed come from Snaketown, they were recovered from nearby Classic Period sites and not from the older village.

Woodbury has given us a useful summary of the history of the

PHASE	TYPE I			TYPE 2			TOTALS
CIVANO					5	I*	6
SACATON				3	3	3*	9
SANTA CRUZ	I	I		9			II
GILA BUTTE	2		I*		I		4
SNAKETOWN	4		2*				6
SWEETWATER	4						4
ESTRELLA		I*					I
VAHKI	I						I
PIONEER P.	I	4*					5
UNPLACED	3			2			5
TOTALS	7	10	8*	14	9	4*	52

2 = Typable fragments   2* = Whole axes   2 = 1934–35 Collection

Civano Phase axes from Ariz. U:13:21 & 22

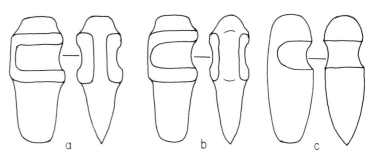

Fig. 14.29. Stone axe types: (a, b) Type 1, ridged; (c) Type 2, without ridges.

three-quarter grooved axe in the Southwest (1954: 29-31), and it must be admitted that since his study little new information has been added to the story, except for one important point: namely, that the beginnings of the axe were even earlier than originally believed. As noted by Sayles (Gladwin and others 1937: 115), the finished form of the axe, its age, and the absence of local prototypes lead to the conclusion that the idea came from the outside. If the trait was already well established in Arizona in the centuries immediately preceding the time of Christ, then, on hypothetical grounds, the only source could have been Mexico where the Olmecs and other groups already had a high mastery of stone sculpturing. The ridged axe in terms of workmanship and age must somehow be linked with the southern technological achievement.

The premium put upon stone at Snaketown is seen once again in the collection of axes. A bit snapped off left a grooved axe head which made a convenient hammerstone, and the bit lent itself to similar use. Fifteen pieces that saw this secondary use have been included in the type frequency and association studies, with the belief that this information was more significant than to recognize them as a separate class of grooved hammerstones.

During each of the two field seasons, one miniature axe was found (Gladwin and others 1937: Pl. LXXVIIIa; herein, Fig. 14.30). Both are of the ridged type. They were well made and embodied all the salient features of normal axes. Assignable to the Pioneer Period, these axes could not have been functional in the usual sense. They may be hints of a custom in which axe symbols played a part.

Fig. 14.31. Three-quarter grooved axe, probably made during the Classic Period but found and later used by the Pima Indians and eventually buried by them in a cache of historic age. Length 14 cm.

Fig. 14.30. Miniature axe, Pioneer Period. Length 7.2 cm.

Russell notes that the Pima Indians obtained their axes from the ruins that dot the Gila and Salt River valleys and that they were especially prized as tools to sharpen the household metates (1908: 110). Evidence for this at Snaketown came from a Pima cache which contained a three-quarter grooved axe (Fig. 12.7) along with an iron shovel head and a machine-sawed board from a box. The practice of salvaging ancient artifacts has doubtless been going on for millennia, and it constitutes a scourge for the archaeologist because it has led to more than one erroneous conclusion. The axe in question, a good example of the Classic Period non-ridged type, has a rounded and heavily battered bit (Fig. 14.31), the kind of attrition it would have suffered if used as an instrument to sharpen a metate.

Balls

The collection includes five stone spheres which have been purposefully rounded, perhaps for use in games. The diameters, materials, and time placements are as follows:

1.6 cm, indurated sandstone, Sacaton Phase
3.1 cm, caliche, Sacaton Phase
3.5 cm, indurated sandstone, Civano Phase (Ariz. U:13:22)
6.5 cm, scoriaceous basalt, Civano Phase (Ariz. U:13:22)
15.8 cm, diorite, Gila Butte Phase

The last specimen listed is the most interesting because of its exceptionally good finish and size. Stone balls of this dimension are not common in the Southwest. It weighs 5.637 kg (12.427 lb) and reminds one of a shot-put. However, this one reveals no scarring resulting from the implied use. Instead there are several pitted areas, each a few centimeters in diameter, the possible result of the use of the ball as an anvil and most likely, therefore, unrelated to the original purpose for which the ball was made. A comprehensive review of stone spheres states that most of them were gaming pieces and that they may have been in more-or-less continuous use for 6,000 years (Broms and Moriarty 1967).

Rubber balls, though rarely preserved (Haury 1937), undoubtedly were associated with a game.

"Medicine," Effigy, and Other Stones

For want of a better term a number of small sculptures, with few exceptions made of scoriaceous lava, have been referred to as "medicine" stones. The recurrent forms are illustrated in Figure 14.32 (compare also with Gladwin and others 1937: Pl. LXXXI). The related distribution table emphasizes the fact that these elements are chiefly assignable to the Colonial and Sedentary periods with minimal survival into the Classic Period and a hint of beginnings in the Pioneer Period.

Perhaps related to the foregoing are effigy figures, both animal and probably human (Fig. 14.33b and d), of which the former are the most realistic and the latter stylized. Pregnancy may be indicated in one of those shown (d). Apart from the difference in subject matter between these and the "medicine" stones is the fact that four of the five in the collection were associated with

PHASE	a	b	c	d	e	f	g	h	TOTALS
CIVANO									
SACATON	2	4			I		I	I	9
SANTA CRUZ	I				I				2
GILA BUTTE				I					I
SNAKETOWN		I							I
SWEETWATER		I		I					2
ESTRELLA									
VAHKI									
PIONEER P.									
UNPLACED		2	I						3
TOTALS	3	8	I	2	I	I	I	I	18

Fig. 14.32. "Medicine" stones of volcanic scoria: (a, b) ungrooved and grooved plummets; (c) cylinder with slightly swollen ends, bifurcated at right angles to each other; (d) four-pointed object, concavo-convex; (e) four-pointed, grooved object; (f) crescentic, grooved; (g) three-pointed; (h) "tuning fork," (fragmentary). Length of *h*, 12.3 cm.

pottery assignable to several phases of the Pioneer Period, the oldest one being Estrella. The fifth specimen was unplaced. If the time placements are correct, then sculptures in miniature have early beginnings. Three of five similar pieces recovered in 1934–35 (Gladwin and others 1937: Pl. LXXIV) were also of Pioneer Period age, nearly duplicating the current findings. The purpose of the three-pronged object (Fig. 14.33e) is not known.

Fig. 14.33. Effigies and other stones of porous lava: (a, c) animals, Pioneer Period and unplaced respectively; (b, d) (?) human, Snaketown and Estrella Phases; (e) three-pronged object, Pioneer Period. Height of *e*, 11.3 cm.

CHIPPED IMPLEMENTS

Proficiency in chipping as a means of bringing stone to desired forms reached its peak in the making of projectile points. For their bizarre arrowhead shapes, the Hohokam have long been noted; but at the other end of the spectrum are a number of practical though clumsily chipped tool classes which do little for the imagination. In between these two extremes there is next to nothing to provide a sense of continuity in the chipper's art.

Even so, the Hohokam were in command of a technique for detaching large primary flakes from tough quartzite, andesite, or other crystalline stream cobbles that has evoked the respect of modern flint knappers, notably Don Crabtree, who has so skillfully learned and duplicated the varied techniques of controlling stone used by the American aborigines. The method in question, described as cone-splitting, entailed the use of a heavy hammer with which a hard blow was struck on a selected point on a cobble, thereby removing a large flake without benefit of a striking platform. The point of impact is easily recognized by what appears to be a section of a subconical pit up to 1 cm in depth. The pit is actually the shatter zone at the point of impact where the stone was pulverized. The resulting flakes, either side- or end-struck (Fig. 14.34) are thin for their sizes, and they preserve the cobble cortex on one face. The scar face is relatively flat with poorly developed features normally associated with percussion flaking, namely, bulb, ripple marks, and fissures. Flakes up to 19 cm in length have been observed. Once detached, the flake was ready for use directly, as a hoe, or for a number of other uses by edge trimming.

Generally speaking, the tools produced by the simple removal of one or more flakes from a cobble, a core, or a thick flake, do not lend themselves readily to typing; yet the use marks are there in the nature of worn or finely chipped edges. The impression one gains after looking over hundreds of specimens, is that the simple tasks of cutting, scraping, crushing, and the like were done with the nearest rock at hand, modified as needed, and then discarded. It does not appear that the Hohokam were thinking along formalized lines when they produced work-a-day tools. In fact the chipped implement categories were far less numerous and more vague in form than were the chipped tools of the Desert Culture Gatherers who preceded them. In the following analysis, no effort

Fig. 14.34. Primary flakes derived by employing a cobble-splitting technique (a, b) and a cobble showing a negative flake scar (c). Length of *a*, 16.5 cm.

has been made to develop a systematic or detailed typology; instead, broad differences only are noted, whether in function or form.

Primary Flake Tools

Edge trimming was the chief way of altering primary flakes. Those with flat flaking served as digging tools as evidenced by the wear on the flake scars; those with a steep edge treatment, producing a generally ragged edge, were better suited as scrapers. Edge abrasions suggest some of the flakes were used as hammerstones, perhaps to wear away stone in narrow grooves of a sculpture. But a number of flakes showing hammer abrasions were digging tools, and one may conclude that the gripping edge was dulled for increased comfort. Since there is no obvious patterning as to size, shape, or edge modification, those illustrated in Figure 14.35 attempt only to show the range.

The 56 specimens in this category were recovered mainly from trash deposits, and all phases are represented. One set of seven was found on the floor of a Sweetwater Phase house (House 1: 9E). It is apparent that cobble splitting was practiced throughout Snaketown's life. Yet, the technique, if known by the Cochise Culture antecedents, has not been reported.

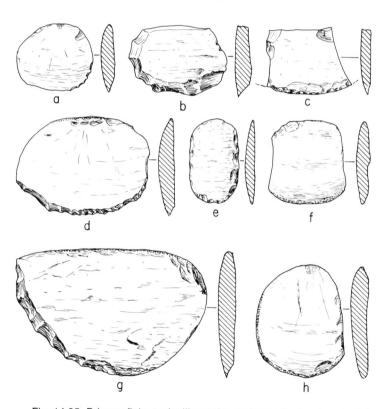

Fig. 14.35. Primary flake tools, illustrating various edge treatments: (a) limited flaking, mostly from work done with it; (b) steep edge trimming, coarse; (c) flat edge trimming, fine; (d, g) lower edge flaked, upper edge smoothed; (e) limited bi-facial trimming; (f, h) edge dulled by hammering. Length of *g*, 19.5 cm.

Choppers

Next to hammerstones, choppers were the simplest to make. A stream pebble of suitable size and material needed only to be edge- or end-trimmed by the delivery of a few hammerstone blows from one side only. The hard crystalline rocks, such as andesite, diorite, and quartzite, were preferred. Because extent of the trimmed edges range from 2 to 19 cm, it was decided to sort the specimens into two groups; large, from 8 to 19 cm in edge length (Fig. 14.36a-c), and, small, from 2 to 7 cm in edge length (Fig. 14.36d-f). It seemed obvious that the smaller stones were

PHASE	a-c	d-f	g,h	i	TOTALS
CIVANO	8		5	1	14
SACATON	20	2	4	4	30
SANTA CRUZ	5	1			6
GILA BUTTE	8	4	5		17
SNAKETOWN	2	4	2	1	9
SWEETWATER	12	3	3	1	19
ESTRELLA	4	1			5
VAHKI	9	3	5	2	19
PIONEER P.	6	2	1		9
UNPLACED	10	3	7	1	21
TOTALS	84	23	32	10	149

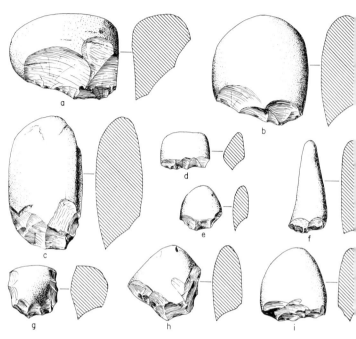

Fig. 14.36. Pebble choppers: (a-c) uni-face, large; (d-f) uni-face, small; (g,h) uni-face, extensive edge trim; (i) bi-facial trimming. Length of *c*, 15.2 cm.

designed for lighter work than the bulkier ones. The frequency table shows a long life for both kinds, but a subjective impression was gained during the analysis that small pebble trimming was given more emphasis in early than in late times. Of particular interest, however, is the fact that the simple chopper, an efficient tool for crushing and coarse cutting, was shared by the Desert Gatherers and the Hohokam, spanning many thousands of years. The presence of choppers, taken by themselves, cannot be used as an index of earliness.

A second group of choppers, smaller numerically than the foregoing, are those with extensive edge trimming, extending around one-half or more of the pebble's perimeter (Fig. 14.36g and h). No meaningful temporal differences are apparent.

Taken as a whole, choppers of all kinds were present at all times at Snaketown. The occasionally heard postulate that the simple tools, like the chopper, went out of use with increasing dependence upon agriculture, is not entirely borne out by the Snaketown record. What we do not know at this stage is the extent of dependence the Hohokam put on the chopper as a tool related to food-getting or to other activities.

It is worth observing that the simpler implements, as choppers and scrapers, were given less attention in manufacture than earlier people accorded the same tools. A review of the flaked implements from the midden deposit in Ventana Cave makes this difference clear (Haury 1950: 206*ff*). The plane (*op. cit.* Fig. 28)

Fig. 14.37. Half-pebble chopper. Diorite, probably Sacaton Phase. Maximum length, 18.5 cm.

PHASE	a	b	c	d	e	f	g-i	j	k	l-n	TOTALS
CIVANO			1					1		1	3
SACATON	1	1	4				3	2	3	1	15
SANTA CRUZ			3	2	1		2	2	3		13
GILA BUTTE	3	1	1		2	1	1	2	2	4	17
SNAKETOWN	3	1	5	1	1		5	2	2	3	23
SWEETWATER		1	2	3		1	3	5	3	4	22
ESTRELLA	3						2	1			6
VAHKI	4	1	3	1		1	4	3	1	1	19
PIONEER P.	1		2						2	2	7
UNPLACED	2		2		1	1	1	1	2	1	11
TOTALS	17	5	23	7	5	4	21	19	18	17	136

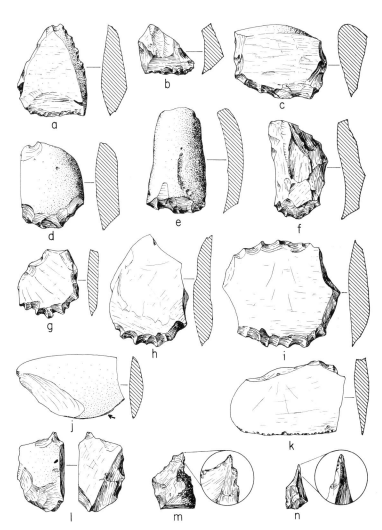

Fig. 14.38. Chipped tools: (a-c) steep-edged side scrapers; (d, e) steep-edged end scrapers, cortex side up; (f) pseudo-keeled scraper; (g-i) serrated scrapers; (j) ground-edge scraper; (k) flake knife; (l, m) gravers. Maximum diameter of i, 7.6 cm.

in Ventana Cave, to which the Snaketown choppers are somewhat analogous, was more finished, on the average, and made from cores rather than from pebbles.

Choppers with a bi-facially trimmed edge are not common (Fig. 14.36i). One suspects that these were mostly treated in this way as a preliminary step to making a sharp hammerstone. In examining stones of this kind, if they showed any use as a hammer they were classified in that category.

Seven tools that may be called half-pebble choppers depart in manufacturing procedure from all the others in that the fractured face of a split cobble was further percussion flaked over most of the whole surface. The edges thus sharpened show some wear. The prime example in this small group is shown in Figure 14.37. The Vahki, Sacaton, and a few intermediate phases are represented.

Scrapers

Implements designed for scraping are neither numerous nor particularly distinguished in workmanship. A few simple categories may be recognized, but typing cannot be done along purist lines because of merging characteristics and the manifest lack of attention to finish on the part of the maker. Production of a scraper demanded no more care than was needed to fashion it for the work intended, a steep edge trim, all blows delivered from one face.

Side-scrapers of amorphous form by size and material separate into two groups: those 3 to 4 cm in length and made of chert and similar tool stone (Fig. 14.38b) numbering only five and widely scattered as to time; and those of andesite and other dense rock, 4 to 7.5 cm in size (average 6 cm) (Fig. 14.38a). These rarely show pebble cortex, and the working edge, percussion produced, ranges from convex to concave. Although the sample is small, it appears that tools of this form were generally early.

Flakes from pebbles that preserve the cortex were trimmed in two ways: with cortex down (Fig. 14.38c), or cortex up (Fig. 14.38d), when the tool is held in its working position. Sizes range from 3.1 to 8.8 cm, the average being about 5 cm.

Five of the nine end scrapers were made of pebble edge flakes,

the cortex side up (Fig. 14.38e), and the rest were pseudo keeled (Fig. 14.38f). Dimensions range from 4.8 to 6.8 cm.

Scrapers that were made with a somewhat more certain intent are a group of 21 with serrate edges (Fig. 14.38g-i). Materials are the familiar andesite, quartzite, rhyolite, and one is of chert, while the initial form of the stone was a pebble flake or almost any suitable lump, thick or thin, ranging in size from 3.5 to 7.7 cm. The edge treatment was achieved by percussion, and the spacing of the teeth varies from 0.8 to 1.5 cm. Microscopic examination of the fine chipping resulting from use and wear on the teeth shows use marks to be limited chiefly to the underside, suggesting that the tool was drawn toward the user. By actual experiment they are effective in the initial stages of shaping wood. The tool as a type appears to have been in use for a long time.

Finally, in the scraper category, are those whose edges have been dulled and rounded by drawing across a hard abrasive surface, or by working other hard materials. Pebble flakes, generally thin, and ranging from 4.3 to 7.8 cm in maximum dimension, were selected (Fig. 14.38j). The ground edges may be convex, straight, or undulating, hinting that they were used on different classes of materials. When visible, striations tend to run at right angles to the axis of the edge. Temporally, the ground-edge scraper appears to have been known for a long time at Snaketown.

Flake Knives

Almost any convenient thin flake could be used as a knife by virtue of its natural sharp cutting edge. Fine chipping along the edge generally resulted from use (Fig. 14.38k), but some intentional sharpening also is noted. Sizes range from 3.5 to 8.5 cm in greatest dimension, and about one-third of the lot of 18 were of the better tool stone, as obsidian, chert, and jasper. The rest are of dense crystalline stone. The majority of these were struck from cores or pebbles with striking platforms.

The puzzling aspect about flake knives and scrapers is why so few were found. The tools of the simplest construction for performing the commonest labors of cutting and scraping appear to have been in shortest supply. There is no obvious answer as to why this was so.

Gravers

Two kinds of gravers are evident in the small collection of 17 specimens: those made of andesite and similar materials with relatively large and strong graving points (Fig. 14.38*l*) and those with small engraving points, designed for delicate work and made of the finer tool stones (Fig. 14.38 m and n). The latter would have been well adapted for decorating bone tubes and working out details on carved shell bracelets. The spotty frequencies indicated in the table are most likely due to sampling differences.

Projectile Points

Numerically, the projectile point yield in 1964–65 was far below that of the mid-1930 effort: 142 as compared with 2,017 classifiable units. Opening canals, clearing house floors, and stratigraphic testing are not the kinds of diggings that produce arrowheads in quantity. Cremations are the prime source, and we made no effort to search out new cremation areas.

Crabtree's informative report (1973) on Hohokam projectile point technology eliminates the need for any extensive discussion of this problem here. He makes the interesting observation that the small points of simple form, made of a wide range of materials, were functional and could have been produced by almost anyone. The long, elaborate, often barbed and serrated points, mostly fashioned of chert and chalcedony, represent a specialized industry, known to perhaps only a few craftsmen. He further believes that the products were intended to fulfill needs other than day-to-day hunting and self-protection. The latter category of artifacts distinguish the Hohokam as master toolmakers.

It is obvious, after reviewing the collection of projectile points from Snaketown, that the Hohokam did not lack good tool stone. Clear quartz, obsidian, and jasper may have been in short supply, but they must have had ready access to supplies or suppliers of chalcedony and chert. The chert-rich Naco Formation of Pennsylvanian age, broadly exposed in east-central Arizona (Brew 1970), is a possible source. Some of the projectile points reveal fine laminations in the material superficially matching the chert available in great quantity along the east rim rock of Canyon Creek. Andesite was almost never used, as indicated by only

three points of this material in the collection, a sharp contrast with the evidence from Ventana Cave where about 80% of the projectile points were produced from this fine-grained volcanic stone in all periods (Haury 1950: 260-62).

The need for liberal quantities of good chippable material is underscored by the fact that large percussion flakes or core nuclei were used in making a preform from which the long points were next fashioned. Long thin blades were not suitable. The steps in the production are clearly demonstrated by Crabtree's skillful replication of the Hohokam flint knappers' achievements (1973). Considering the large numbers of points sometimes associated with cremations and sacrificial deposits, numbering in the hundreds to several thousand fragments respectively (Gladwin and others 1937: 95; see also Wasley and Johnson 1965: Figs. 60 and 78), the need for ample' stocks of raw stone becomes even more impressive. The great effort in fabricating hundreds of long points must have resulted in accumulations of debitage of no small extent. Paradoxically no concentrations of wastage were encountered anywhere in our diggings, and there was only a nominal recovery of small pressure-chipped flakes in the residue when fine screens were employed.

The dearth of chipping evidence leads to the question of whether the fancy long projectile points were made at Snaketown. If there were other areas outside of the Hohokam heartland where these types were common, this idea could be entertained seriously. But no such place is known, and the logic of the situation dictates that they were made at Snaketown. Crabtree's notion that the flamboyant points were produced by specialists should be expanded to say that most, if not all, of the fine chipping was done by specialists. This would limit the number of people so occupied and consequently reduce the number of places where flaking debris in quantity might be expected. If this is correct, then we must conclude that our excavations missed the spots where the work was done, a more likely alternative than to believe that production was elsewhere.

Figure 14.39 and the related frequency table presents the main categories of projectile points. In general the type-phase dominances are the same as determined in the initial excavation in 1934–35: for example Figure 14.39b, d, f, and l are mainly of Sedentary Period age, while the barbed specimens (*m*) are Colonial Period in age (Gladwin and others 1937: Fig. 43). The glaring omission in the record is any meaningful information about Pioneer Period types. While much use may have been made of wooden points, the dependency upon stone both before and after the Pioneer Period makes the use of stone during that time reasonably certain. In all probability the kinds of projectiles used were simple typologically, perhaps like Figure 14.39n and o (also Gladwin and others 1937: Pl. XCIV b, e, f, and g).

The conclusion that emerges from the projectile point study is that with the beginning of the Colonial Period a new tradition in their production arose. This thrust was either developed at Snaketown or reached the village from the outside. The flamboyancy exhibited by the points, exemplified by the long barbed forms, may have been accompanied by new concepts of their use. At the same time one gains the feeling that a kind of competitive exhibitionism among the chippers of stone contributed to their elaborateness. This trend died out during the Classic Period.

As noted earlier the small collection of projectile points was partly due to the fact that so few cremations were encountered. Even so, 50% of the present sample came from cremations, and of the 91 cremations found only 9 had associated projectile points. Unfortunately, the calcined bones in most cremations were too scanty to make even crude age and sex determinations of the individuals involved. We cannot say, therefore, that points occur with adult males or any other age or sex group. There is no evident pattern either in the associated artifacts. These range from utility objects, such as manos and pottery, to palettes, figurines, and shell ornaments. In only one instance were projectile points the sole

PHASE	a	b	c	d	e	f	g	h	i	j	k	l	m	n,o	TOTALS
CIVANO		1	2												3
SACATON	1	32	1	18	10	9			4			8			83
SANTA CRUZ	1	2		2	9	1		1	1				3		20
GILA BUTTE		1		9					2				3		15
SNAKETOWN														2	2
SWEETWATER															
ESTRELLA															
VAHKI															
PIONEER P.															
UNPLACED		1	1	3	3	1	1	1	5	1	1		1		19
TOTALS	2	36	5	23	31	11	1	2	12	1	1	8	7	2	142

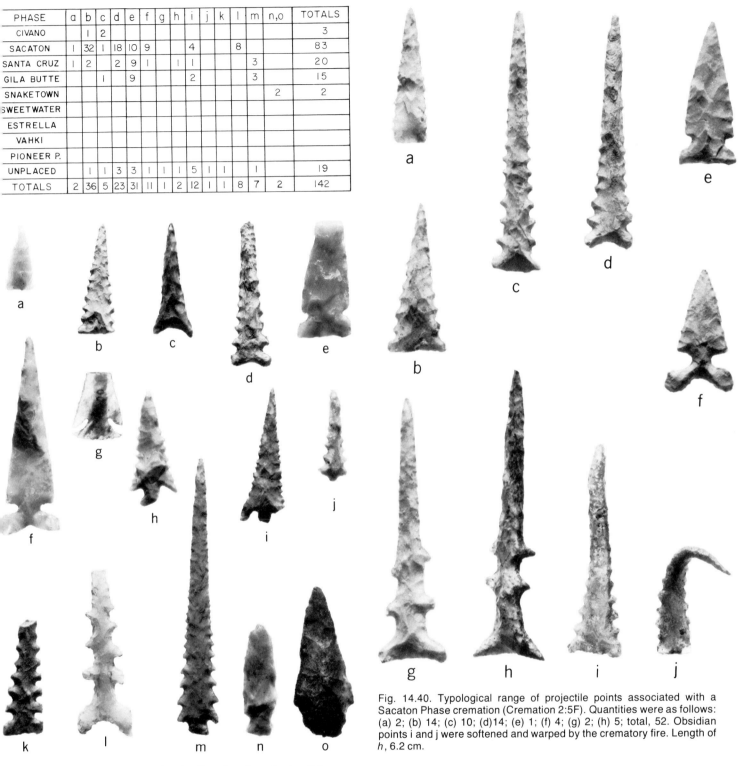

Fig. 14.39. Synoptic series of projectile points. Length of *m*, 7.6 cm.

Fig. 14.40. Typological range of projectile points associated with a Sacaton Phase cremation (Cremation 2:5F). Quantities were as follows: (a) 2; (b) 14; (c) 10; (d)14; (e) 1; (f) 4; (g) 2; (h) 5; total, 52. Obsidian points i and j were softened and warped by the crematory fire. Length of *h*, 6.2 cm.

offerings. It can be said, however, that the bizarre points have come from cremations, almost without exception, a reflection of a special cultural outlook.

The chief value to be drawn from these objects as cremation accompaniments is to demonstrate the contemporaneity of types. Sometimes only a single type occurs with bones, but more often there is a range, as in the case of Cremation 2:5F (Fig. 14.40). Form variations were greatest in the Sacaton Phase, and these tend to de-emphasize temporal differences.

Both cremations and the crematory mounds (Gladwin and others 1937: 95) sometimes produce projectile points in astonishing numbers, running into the hundreds and even thousands. But more impressive than numbers is the duplication of shapes, down to the minutest details (Wasley and Johnson 1965: Figs. 60 and 78) and the identical nature of the material. This must mean that a given lot of points was made by the same knapper, for only he could exercise the tight control over material, form, and the chipping characteristics indicated. I believe this is the most convincing evidence we have that specialty craftsmen existed among the Hohokam. To what extent they may have been organized as guilds and whether or not status values were associated with skills are unknowns.

A few final technological notes are in order. Whether the raw chipping materials were preheated to improve workability cannot be determined with certainty. Those points associated with cremations passed through the fire that consumed the dead, thereby concealing possible earlier thermal treatment. Projectiles from scattered sources other than cremations do not reveal any clear evidence of preheating.

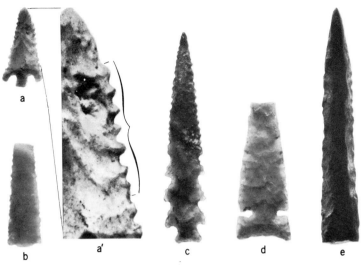

Fig. 14.41. Technological details of serrating, notching, and grinding. Length of e, 6.45 cm; bracketed segment of a', about 1 cm.

Barbing and lateral extensions from the trunk of points add to the elaborateness of Hohokam projectiles. About 50% of them also have serrated edges, a treatment that had a long history in American lithics. But not many people matched or surpassed the Hohokam in fineness of serration (Fig. 14.41a, a', and b). The most closely spaced serrations are eight teeth per centimeter. The height of accomplishment in this area, whimsical in nature to a twentieth century mind, was the serrating of barbs (Fig. 14.41c)! The fine marginal retouch most likely was done with rodent incisor teeth as chipping tools. Their presence in the Hohokam territory has been noted (Haury 1950: 383).

Side or corner notching, straight or curved (Fig. 14.41d and Fig. 14.39g), also reached a state of perfection, if narrowness is used as the criterion. A notch width of 0.8 mm is the minimum observed. Again, rodent teeth were the most likely instruments to achieve this degree of refinement.

Crabtree (1973: 32-33) notes what he termed "basal edge polish" on some specimens and recognizes that this effect may either be mechanical or alterations resulting from the heat of the crematory fire. A kind of surface glazing, not limited to the base, has been observed on cremation-associated points. Examination of unheated points does not reveal this phenomenon. Intentional basal edge grinding appears to be lacking.

There is, however, one specimen in the collection that shows post-chipping grinding (Fig. 14.41e), the tip portion of a long slender point unlike anything seen among Hohokam stone products. The material is a dense black mineral, probably andesite. It was recovered from Gila Butte Phase trash.

Lacking in the 1964–65 collection of chipped stone are large bifacially chipped blades and crescents (Gladwin and others 1937: Pls. XCIII, XCIV and XCII). Implements identifiable as drills were not recovered in either season of our work.

Before leaving the chipped stone category, the contrast between the workmanship in projectile points and the other categories needs to be stressed once again. The mastery of stone chipping was there, but the heavy work tools were given not one bit more attention than was needed to make them effective. The consequence of this was the fact that Hohokam choppers, scrapers, knives, and similar tools were far less formalized than were the similar implements made by the Desert Gatherers. Furthermore, the numbers of specimens recovered in each category, excepting projectile points, were small. For the amount of excavation we did at Snaketown, the fewer than 350 chipped tools is a meager return indeed, a sharp contrast with the high frequency of over 4,000 artifacts in the rubbish of Ventana Cave (Haury 1950: 206). I do not believe this difference was due to the shortage of tool stone; instead it is most likely attributed to the reduced needs for tools of the simpler kinds because of the advanced nature of the agricultural economy. Simplicity of form and the low number of types may be attributable to this factor as well.

ORNAMENTS AND MISCELLANEOUS STONE

While marine shell was the preferred material for ornament production, attractive minerals were not spurned. Turquoise was popular, though perhaps one of the most difficult semiprecious stones to obtain. A variety of fine-grained minerals, as argillite, serpentine, and shale were also shaped. The following resumé of stone ornaments should be augmented by the account of the 1934–35 sample (Gladwin and others 1937: 126-130), which was far more representative than the present lot.

Beads

Eighty occurrences of stone beads were observed, about two-thirds of them being of turquoise (Table with Fig. 14.42). The most useful information to be drawn from disc beads is the fact that they were present in all phases, that even during the Vahki Phase beads with diameters as small as 1.8 mm were skillfully made. The current data support the 1934–35 findings that turquoise was known and used throughout Snaketown's long life (Gladwin and others 1937: 129).

Pendants

Pendants of whatever material and whether geometric or effigy in form were generally late (Fig. 14.42a-c). The exception is a pebble pendant carrying a roughly incised pattern from Sweetwater Phase times (Fig. 14.42e). A clue that explains the large shale pendants, not particularly attractive in themselves, are the traces on one (Fig. 14.42d) of what appears to be a mastic which might have been used as a cement to hold mosaic pieces in place. The red argillite bird (Fig. 14.42g) is notable for its smallness. Wear facets indicate it was worn with beads, and perhaps it would be more accurate to recognize it as an effigy bead.

Nose Plug?

A Ventana Cave mummy documents the fact that the aboriginal inhabitants of southern Arizona wore cylindrical wooden plugs in the nasal septum (Haury 1950: 421). The steatite cylinder, with scored ends and notched middle, illustrated in Figure 14.42f, probably served the same purpose. It was associated with mixed trash of the Estrella and Sweetwater Phases which, if correct, would place the trait much earlier than has been recognized heretofore.

Finger Rings

When stone replaced shell as a material for ring-making, steatite seems to have been preferred. While most stone rings were copies of those of shell, two fragments in the collection depart from this pattern, and they therefore have special interest. The rings are of the broad band type, 1.4 and 0.9 cm wide respectively (Fig. 14.42h and i). Both are exteriorly grooved in a manner that is reminiscent of the grooving on Sweetwater Red-on-gray pottery. The larger of the two pieces came from a trash pit of the Sweetwater Phase, and the other was found in mixed Pioneer-Colonial Period refuse. It is noteworthy that personal jewelry of such elaborateness should appear so early. This matches the Hohokam accomplishments in the making of mosaics and the carving of shell.

Mosaic Work

Complete assemblies of mosaic work were not recovered at Snaketown, but 36 instances were noted of the association of small shaped units that once were a part of mosaics in the refuse or

PHASE	Beads		a,b	c-e	g	f	h,i	j	TOTALS
	Turq.	Other							
CIVANO	1	3						2	6
SACATON	18		4	2	1		1	5	31
SANTA CRUZ	4	1	2	4				2	13
GILA BUTTE	9	6	1	1				8	25
SNAKETOWN	6	2						6	14
SWEETWATER	4	5		1		1	1	6	18
ESTRELLA	4		1					2	7
VAHKI	2	3						2	7
PIONEER P.	4	3						1	8
UNPLACED	2	3					1	2	8
TOTALS	54	26	8	8	1	1	3	36	137

Not Shown

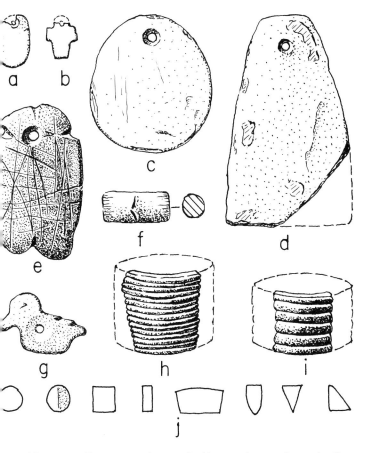

Fig. 14.42. Ornaments of stone: (a, b) turquoise pendants; (c, d) shale pendants; (e) mud rock; (f) serpentine nose plug; (g) argillite bird; (h, i) serpentine rings; (j) shape range of turquoise units. Length of d, 6.6 cm; g-i, x2.

on the house floors of all phases (Fig. 14.42). Both the earliness of the trait and the persistence of it are worthy of note. Figure 14.42j inventories the range in shapes of the pieces, all turquoise, providing reasonable evidence that some of the compositions displayed intricate patterns. Other materials were doubtless introduced for color contrast, as for example, pink shell. But the use of any shell in this way appears not to have predated the Santa Cruz Phase (Gladwin and others 1937: 127). Typically, elements were carefully beveled on the edges so as to provide a better fit on the exposed surface and space for the adhesive material between pieces to hold them firmly in place. Sizes range from 0.3 to 1.6 cm in greatest dimensions.

Mason (1929: 163), in speaking of mosaics of northern Mexico, observed that turquoise "... is sometimes employed in the form of mosaics, and this is the real tie which closely binds the American Southwest with southern Mexico of the time of the Conquest." Mason's observation of more than forty years ago should now be revised to indicate that the Southwestern-Mexican bond, as evidenced by mosaics, and the use of turquoise, existed nearly two millennia before the Conquest. Vaillant records the presence of turquoise mosaic elements at El Arbolillo in the Valley of Mexico (1935: 245), the age of which was probably close to that of the Vahki Phase in the Hohokam sequence. The list of elements that characterized the earliest Hohokam is lengthened by the addition of mosaics, thus further strengthening the implication of their close connections with the South. In all probability the Hohokam introduced the mosaic art to other Southwestern tribes, for nowhere else were mosaic assemblies made as early as in the valleys of the Gila and Salt Rivers.

Mosaic Plaques

The first discovery in Arizona of a stone disc in pristine condition, one face of which was covered with closely-fitted pieces of marcasite (iron pyrites), was in 1922 (Gladwin and others 1937: 131). Subsequently, fire-damaged specimens were discovered in the Grewe site (Woodward 1941: 7-11) and in Snaketown (Gladwin and others 1937: 130-134). These have attracted special attention because identical pieces have been recovered from sites in Jalisco, Mexico, and stretching far to the south to Guatemala in the ruins of the Maya.

It is an interesting footnote to the history of our understanding of these so-called "mirrors" that the relative time order of two types, the older ones with pyrite plates carried to the edge of the upper surface and an inward bevel on the underside, and the younger ones with a beveled margin on the upper face, thereby limiting the surface covered with pyrite, was first established at Snaketown and later duplicated in Nebaj, Guatemala (Smith and Kidder 1951: 44-50). My own speculation in 1937 (Gladwin and others 1937) that these plaques may have been made by the Hohokam now needs revision in the light of more information that has accumulated in the interim. Woodward's restorations of the patterns in the pseudo-cloisonné which decorates the back of the late models are clearly of Mexican derivation in both style and technique (1941).

Although there is still no certain evidence as to where in Mexico and Mesoamerica mirrors were made, the southwest can certainly be ruled out as the place of origin. That they were actively traded for a long time, at least from A.D. 600 to 1100, is indicated by their Gila Butte to Sacaton Phase associations, ages not inconsistent with the data from Mexico. Wherever found, they usually accompany the dead, with burials in Mexico and south, and with cremations among the Hohokam. Ritual meaning is also indicated by caches of burned or broken units in what have been termed sacrificial deposits in both Guatemala (Smith and Kidder 1951: 50) and Arizona (Gladwin and others 1937: 130). This parallelism is not inconsistent with all the other information that points to southern connections.

The number of mirror bases recovered in 1964–65 was small. Three burned and broken specimens were associated with Cache 1:10G (p. 188) of Colonial Period age. The fourth, and only other fragment, unburned, came from stripping operations in Blocks 9E and 10E. It represents a piece of plaque base of calcareous sandstone from near the edge of the late type with upper surface bevel. Happily, paired edge holes, drilled from the back, help in establishing the identification (Smith and Kidder 1951: Fig. 65d) (Fig. 14.43). Being unburned, several details are seen that were usually erased by the fires that damaged them. The back surface was painted red and the beveled area of the upper face carries a stucco-like veneer 0.5 mm thick, also painted red. I have seen mirrors in the collection of Federico Solórzano in Guadalajara from which this fragment might have come.

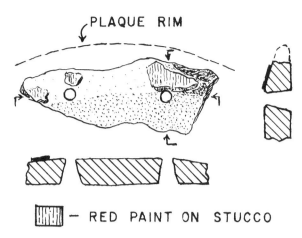

PLAQUE RIM

▓▓▓ — RED PAINT ON STUCCO

Fig. 14.43. Fragment of mosaic plaque base. Length 5.2 cm.

The presence of this specimen in the trash may be a hint that mirror use was somewhat more prevalent than the death- and sacrifice-connected proveniences indicate.

Miscellaneous

Two specimens not readily fitted in elsewhere are a bird head, probably duck, broken from the body, and an unidentified geometrical unit, possibly used in mosaic work (Fig. 14.44). The Sacaton and Santa Cruz Phases are represented respectively.

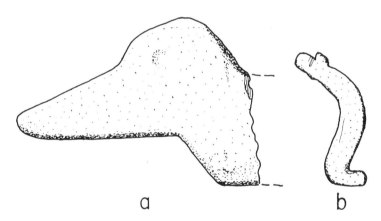

a   b

Fig. 14.44. Miscellaneous worked stone. (a) duck head, flat piece of silt-stone; (b) unidentified, shale, 1.5 mm thick. Length of a, 7.1 cm.

DISCUSSION

Considerable space has been given to describing the kinds of stone tools the Hohokam had, in what amounts they were recovered, and at what times they were used. Although it is not my intent to enter into a detailed comparison between Hohokam, Anasazi, and Mogollon lithics, the following major differences should be noted.

The greatest range of stone artifact types among the three old tribes belongs to the Anasazi tradition. The most elaborate, distinctive, and refined sculptured products distinguished the Hohokam pattern. As a generality, the Mogollon were the least outstanding in both categories. This subject might be pursued further with profit.

Within the Hohokam stone industry, several conditions stand out. First, there was a degree of control over the material which was not manifested in the earlier products of the Desert Culture. An advanced metate and mano combination, stone cups, axes, and turquoise mosaics may be cited as examples. Specifically, hard stone was no deterrent to shaping it. Second, as might be expected in a long village occupation, certain categories of stone objects, notably palettes, axes, stone cups, and projectile points do demonstrate temporal changes; the more common tools do not reflect these shifts and refinements. Third, implements related to agriculture and food preparation exhibit no drastic form alteration or even additions of new types, except the formal hand-held hoe, during a 1500-year long period. This suggests that the agricultural base was well established from the beginning of Snaketown's occupancy and that the Hohokam were not initiating something new when they settled in southern Arizona.

The over-all evaluation of Hohokam stone-working capabilities leads to the recognition of a paradox: on the one hand, intimate knowledge of the physical properties of stone and the skill to shape it are shown by the sculptured pieces and the better of the chipped objects. On the other hand, common tools used to cut, chop, crush, and scrape, were so randomly made that simple typing becomes a problem. A patterning in the baser tools is not easily detected. The polarity in the mastery of working stone prompts the question as to whether or not the merging of two traditions is represented. One of these would have been the "finished" artifacts, the sculptured, polished, and expertly chipped objects, for which no local prototypes existed; and the lack-lustre utility tools, either a carry-through of the typologically undistinguished tradition of the Desert Culture, or the evidence of Hohokam responses to work requirements by making tools of kinds relatively new to them. For a stone age people, the Hohokam, as seen at Snaketown, carved out a good life for themselves without ever having used much stone.

15. Perishable, Bone and Antler, and Shell Products

In an open site like Snaketown, the principal opportunities to examine the fragile goods made of plant and animal products arise from three circumstances of preservation: first, those objects which were carbonized by fire but were not reduced to ashes; second, the impressions of textiles and other materials in clay; and third, mineral replacement, a phenomenon associated with burning. None of these types of preservation happened frequently, thereby limiting our glimpse of what must have been a rich and varied perishable culture. Plant identifications through seeds and other parts have been treated by Bohrer (1970, 1971). The concern now relates to manufactured products. Because fiber and technique identification are not always precisely possible, the following entries should be read with these limitations in mind.

PERISHABLE PRODUCTS
Cordage

Bast fiber: 2-yarn strand, Z-twist (left), 1 mm diameter; Cache 2:9F.
Yucca fiber: 2- and 3-yarn strands, Z-twist, 1 to 4 mm diameter; Cache 2:9F and House 4:10G.
Cotton: 1-ply simple yarn, loose Z-twist, 1 mm diameter; Cache 2:9F.

Much of the cordage came as matted bunches. There are no surviving hints as to the nature of the original objects. Reasonable inferences are that the bast fiber may have come from string skirts or breech clouts (Haury 1950: 429); the cotton yarn, resembling weftage material, may have come from a skein. All Cache 2:9F specimens date from the Sacaton Phase.

Textiles
CLOTH

Cotton, plain weave, about 20 warp per cm; Cache 2:9F.
Cotton, weft-wrap openwork (Tanner 1950: 452-456; Kent 1957: 501-505); Cache 2:9F.
Cotton, twill tapestry, apparently 2-1 rhythm; Cache 2:9F.
Cotton, twill, weaving formula appears irregular, not recoverable; Cache 2:9F.

MATTING

Probably narrow-leaf yucca, element width 4 to 5 mm; twill, 2-2 rhythm. Five examples, all impressions: one on inner surface of clay jar-stopper (Fig. 15.1), two on miscellaneous lumps of clay, one impression on side wall of House 2:10J. These four occurrences date from the Santa Cruz and Sacaton Phases. The fifth occurrence was an impression over a large area, at least 2 m in maximum dimension, on the floor of a Vahki Phase house (House 1:9F) where it probably served as a sleeping mat.

A second type, also twill in 2-2 pattern, was made of elements laid side-by-side, creating units about 3 cm wide; occurs as impressions on trivet bottoms (Fig. 13.28a) and under surfaces of griddles (comales) (Haury 1945a: 109-111). A charred mat of this type was found on the floor of House 4:10G where it probably

Fig. 15.1. Clay jar stopper with mat impression on inner surface. Mound 55, Sacaton Phase. Diameter, 11.8 cm.

served as a sleeping mat (Fig. 3.15f). Civano and Sacaton Phases are represented.

A Pima workman reported that his mother-in-law told him mats of this kind were made of the peelings of screw bean roots. Modern examples are also seen in the *petates* woven by the Yaqui Indians of western Mexico.

Sandals

Carbonized fragments from Cache 2:9F and a small piece in which there has been mineral replacement of fibers (Mound 40, Tier 1, Level 7) are from sewn sandals of a kind that appears to be unique to the Hohokam (Haury 1950: 435-39).

Basketry

Coiled and sewn: two-rod-and-bundle, stitches not interlocked and not split, 6 per cm; coils 2.3 per cm: (Fig. 11.13); Cache 2:9F, Sacaton Phase. There is also a coiled basket impression in clay, 3 stitches and 1 coil per cm; Sacaton Phase association.

Miscellaneous

Charred fragments of what appear to be a mesquite wood paddle and a gourd rind vessel also were related to the Cache 2:9F materials.

Discussion

The inventory of perishable goods from Snaketown, taking into account the 1934–35 returns (Gladwin and others 1937: 159-62), is sparse indeed. There is enough material, however, to suggest the former riches in this category of cultural possessions, particularly when the objects recovered in Ventana Cave (Haury 1950: 390ff; Tanner 1950: 443ff) are added to the list. Although this cave was inhabited by the environmentally restricted Desert Hohokam, the range of remains was broad and the excellent preservation permitted thorough analysis. All natural resources useful to the Hohokam were exploited with inspired ingenuity. One needs only to think of the adaptation of cactus spines as a modern type of needle, or better still, the spike of an agave leaf that served as a needle, attached by nature to the fibers composing the thread.

An observation with respect to the textile arts is in order before leaving this section of the report. Kent, in her monumental treatise on prehistoric cotton textiles in the Southwest (1957: 467) speculated that the cotton present in Tularosa Cave in a 300 B.C.–A.D. horizon (Martin and others 1952: 207) might have reached the Mogollon people via the Hohokam but that traces of cotton among the Hohokam at this early time did not exist. Happily, we now have evidence for cotton at Snaketown in the Sweetwater Phase (Bohrer 1970: 425), A.D. 200–350, in the presence of carbonized seeds from trash. While this is still not early enough to explain the Tularosa Cave occurrence in a precise chronological reconstruction, I believe that inferences can be drawn which are logical explanations of what happened.

Considering the advanced nature of Hohokam culture in the Vahki Phase and particularly the developed irrigation technology, one may postulate that economic plants were also a part of the complex. Cotton was one of these. Under this plan, it would have arrived by about 300 B.C., reaching the Mogollon people soon thereafter as suggested by the evidence in Tularosa Cave. However, the spread of the fiber to the Anasazi lagged by many centuries.

An additional element in the diffusion complex was the loom which, according to my postulate, arrived concurrently with cotton on the Hohokam scene but did not spread elsewhere in the Southwest until some centuries later. By the same token, complex textile weaving techniques, such as twills, gauze, slit tapestry, and weft-wrap openwork were passed on by the Hohokam to other Southwestern groups, having received them from southern sources (see Kent 1957: 639ff for an extended discussion of this problem).

BONE AND ANTLER PRODUCTS

For reasons unclear to us today, the Hohokam did not look on bone and antler as preferred materials for the quantity production of artifacts. Their dependence on stone and shell did not carry over to equally useful animal bone. This was not because of the lack of it, as the larger animals, deer and antelope, were available to them and were hunted. The widely available desert hardwoods probably were viewed as a substitute material for bone, particularly for the more functional types of artifacts. Some inkling of this is seen in the Ventana Cave inventory (Haury 1950: 414-24) of worked wood.

The total return of catalogable items from both operations at Snaketown was only about 200 units, not counting the highly fragmented pieces from some cremations and the cremation mound studied in 1934–35. The 1964–65 excavations yielded a meager 75 items, including two awls from Ariz. U:13:22. Not only was the range of products limited but so also was the number of units fitting the few categories which seem to have been preferred. Yet, the craftsman's artistry and mastery of the medium was extraordinarily high (Fig. 15.5). The conspicuous scarcity of bone artifacts is not limited to Snaketown, as a perusal of the literature quickly demonstrates. Since it was not the inability to work bone or the lack of it that suppressed use, one must conclude that a cultural attitude is reflected.

Another characteristic which distinguishes Hohokam bonework from that of the Anasazi is the high frequency of burned artifacts. This feature is attributable to two kinds of activities, one easily explained, the other not. Most heavily calcined are the hair ornaments. These, with few exceptions, accompany cremation remains and were obvious accoutrements of the deceased. Other artifacts, such as awls and bone tubes, show about a 50% incidence of darkening by scorching, too high a frequency to believe it was accidental. Much of the recovered unworked animal bone residue also shows scorching, perhaps partly related to the method used in cooking the meat but possibly also connected with the practice of throwing bone scraps into the fire to add a modicum of fuel to the flame.

The usual processes for shaping bone were sawing, grinding, drilling, incising, and carving. Chipping bone, while not common, was an effective way of quickly reducing mass, particularly on the shafts of long bones. Two examples are shown in Figure 15.2, both blunt-ended bone pieces of unknown use. Specimen a

b

a

Fig. 15.2. Shaft fragments of (?) deer long bones reduced by chipping: (a) Gila Butte Phase; (b) from mixed Sweetwater-Snaketown Phase trash. Length of a, 11.5 cm.

has a scorched end which may have come from using the tool as a poker or to rake coals from the fire. Chipping was mainly directed from the outer surface inward.

Awls

The collection of awls is too small to allow a typological or chronological analysis. Figure 15.3 provides a sample of those recovered, ranging from splinter awls (*a, b*), units with basal ends lost and therefore not easily typable (*c*), long awls with extensively modified articular ends of the bone (*d*), short stubby notched awls made of split deer or antelope metapodials (*e, f*), and a variant thereof that shows a hacking-away of bone tissue immediately above the articulation (*g*). The articular end of an ulna awl (*h*) carries an incised X.

The distribution chart (Fig. 15.3), compared with the one previously published (Gladwin and others 1937: Pl. CCXV), shows a somewhat earlier appearance of the awl. It was present at least as early as the Sweetwater Phase, and absences earlier are most likely attributable to sampling.

The sturdy notched awl (Fig. 15.3e and f), an attribute of the Mogollon people (Haury 1936c: 110-11), we now know was also shared by the Hohokam. On the slim evidence of a single specimen, the trait appears to have been known as early as the Estrella Phase, an age compatible with the chronological information for the Mogollon (Martin and others 1952: 185).

Hair Ornaments

Bone objects easily confused with awls, at least when in fragmentary form, are hair ornaments. Figure 15.3i and j illustrates the basal ends of two associated with Sacaton Phase cremations. Justification for identifying them as hair ornaments is drawn from their position in relation to the heads of burials (Di Peso 1956: 76, Plate 11). Furthermore, the elaborateness of the articular end, either by carving or by incrusting with turquoise overlay, emphasizes their ornamental nature.

For the most part, the articular ends of hair ornaments from Snaketown were unaltered. What could be done with them, however, is illustrated by the delightful miniature carving shown in Figure 15.4. This animal, possibly a mountain sheep, was delicately fashioned of the cancelous tissue of the bone by a craftsman during the Santa Cruz Phase. A second example (Fig. 15.5) leaves no doubt about the subject matter. The artist took full advantage of the natural shape of the bone to create the horn of a mountain sheep. This specimen was associated with six additional hair ornaments, all plain, with the ashes of Cremation 2: 11H, an adult male, of probable Santa Cruz Phase age. Fifteen projectile

PHASE	a-b	c	d	e-f	g	h	i-j	TOTALS
CIVANO			2					2
SACATON	1	6			2		7	16
SANTA CRUZ		2	2	1			1	6
GILA BUTTE								
SNAKETOWN			1					1
SWEETWATER		2						2
ESTRELLA				1				1
VAHKI								
PIONEER P.	1	1						2
UNPLACED	1	1	2	1		1		6
TOTALS	3	12	7	3	2	1	8	36

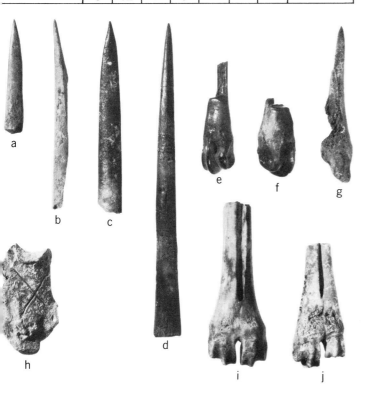

Fig. 15.3. Bone artifacts: (a-h) awls; (i, j) articular ends of hair ornaments. Length of *d*, 15.6 cm.

Fig. 15.4. Carved hair ornament, probably deer leg bone. From Crematorium 4:11H, Santa Cruz Phase. Illustration on right, actual size.

Fig. 15.5. This Bighorn sheep ornamented the end of a bone hair pin. Cremation 2:11H, probably Santa Cruz Phase. Enlarged about x3, actual width 1.6 cm.

points and an incised stone bowl (Fig. 14.25c) also accompanied the ashes. Similar examples have been recovered in the Grewe site and in the Mimbres area (Cosgrove 1932: Plate 59), the latter certainly attributable to Hohokam influence.

Hair ornaments in various stages of completeness occurred with 15 cremations. Birkby's data indicate that 12 of the individuals were adults, the rest infants. Of the 12 adults, the sex determinations show that four were certain males, two uncertain males, one uncertain female, and five adults of indeterminate sex. It would appear that the bone daggerlike hair ornament was predominantly a masculine attribute, indirect evidence for the manner in which the hair was worn, knotted on top of the head. Perhaps of equal importance, however, is the inference that the bone may have been held in esteem less to satisfy vanity than as a useful weapon carried in a convenient place. The man with seven specimens (Cremation 2: 11H), one of which was beautifully carved, may be presumed to have been a dagger maker.

The Snaketown evidence indicates that the bone hair ornament was first known to the Hohokam toward the end of the Colonial Period, in the Santa Cruz Phase. During the Sedentary Period it was common, and its use diminished thereafter. The element occurs over a relatively wide geographic area (Di Peso 1956: 77), but nowhere in the Southwest was it in vogue as early as among the Hohokam. One suspects that, like so many other traits of Hohokam culture, the homeland was to the south. Without implying the existence of a direct connection, the bone carvings of the Maya include ornate objects that probably were hair pins dating at least as early as the Classic Period (Trik 1963: Fig. 8).

Tubes

The most characteristic of all Hohokam bone products appears to have been the tube, produced from the nearly cylindrical shaft of deer or antelope femora. Separation from the articular ends was done by circumferential incisions of sufficient depth to allow a clean break. Exterior bone surfaces were then smoothed to remove traces of the pilaster, and in most cases inner surfaces were also scoured. Lengths range from about 6.0 to 9.6 cm and diameters from 2.0 to 2.5 cm.

Two types, plain and decorated, are definable (Fig. 15.6a-f), the latter carrying incised patterns, sometimes with paint added (Gladwin and others 1937: 155). Contrary to the conclusions reached after the first season's work that the undecorated tube was late and that all early tubes were incised, it now seems certain that the plain tube ranged throughout the total span of Snaketown. However, the fact that the incised tube was a Pioneer Period characteristic and did not persist through the Colonial and Sedentary Phases is confirmed (Fig. 15.6). The normal pattern was geometric in nature with cross-hachured figures, though one example of a life form was noted (Gladwin and others 1937: Pl. CXXVII j). The style of decoration most closely approximates what one sees in painted pottery of the Sweetwater Phase, but

PHASE	a	b–f	TOTALS
CIVANO			
SACATON	1		1
SANTA CRUZ			
GILA BUTTE	1		1
SNAKETOWN			
SWEETWATER	3	4	7
ESTRELLA	1	1	2
VAHKI	2	1	3
PIONEER P.		4	4
UNPLACED	1		1
TOTALS	9	10	19

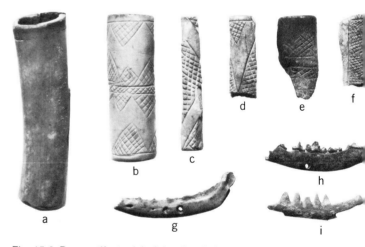

Fig. 15.6. Bone artifacts: (a) plain tube; (b-f) incised tubes; (g-h) pierced jaws; (i) imitation jaw. Length of a, 9.6 cm.

single occurrences of incised tubes in the Vahki and Estrella Phases hint at earlier beginnings. There seems little doubt about the fact that the formalized bone tube, like pottery-making, figurines, and a water technology, was an integral element in the Hohokam complex from the start, possibly extending back into the pre-pottery times (Haury 1950: 381).

Proveniences of the specimens at hand provide no good clues as to use: two were found on house floors, and the rest, all fragmentary, came from trash deposits. It would appear that the tube was a relatively common household article and that when broken it was tossed out with other refuse. A noticeable characteristic of tubes is the smoothly worn surface on the inner margins of the lips, sometimes a distinct bevel directed toward the outer surface. The worn incised patterns provide evidence of much handling. Use by healers as sucking tubes is not improbable.

Bone tubes with incised patterns of the kind described here are not common elsewhere in the Southwest, although decorated tubes, shorter and smaller in diameter and usually labeled as beads, do occur thinly but widely. Carved tubes from Pecos of historic vintage (Kidder 1932: 263) resembling those from Snaketown represent a curious case of convergence. As with hair ornaments, one suspects that the Hohokam incised tube owes its origin to Mesoamerica. Caso describes three tubes bearing Zapotec glyphs from Monte Alban (1932: 475-76).

Miscellaneous

Figure 15.6g and h illustrates two perforated jaws (possibly Gray Fox), both assignable to the Sacaton Phase. Similar units, though with the dental margins modified, were previously recorded (Gladwin and others 1937: Pl. CXXIX d and e). A specimen probably intended to represent a jaw, cut from a flat plate of bone, is shown in Figure 15.6i. It also dated to the Sacaton Phase. Generally speaking, bone products worn ornamentally, such as rings, pendants, and carved pieces, were Colonial and Sedentary Period attributes. Although long bone shafts showing cuts for the removal of segments to make rings were relatively common, only one bone ring fragment was recovered.

No emphasis seems to have been put on antler as a useful material. A single occurrence of a deer antler tine from the Vahki Phase was evidently a flaking tool; but beyond that, the few antler objects in the collection suggest ornamental usages. Painted antler was reported from the previous work (Gladwin and others 1937: 155), and pieces of what may have been a composite necklace came from the ashes of Cremation 2:5F, an adult male, assignable to the Sacaton Phase. In addition to shell fragments, a stone reamer and abrader, and two bone hair ornaments (Fig. 15.7a and b), there were two classes of worked antler. The first lot consists of at least 32 rodlike pieces (Fig. 15.7c) varying in length from 2.7 to 5.3 cm; the second is represented by at least four elongated flat pieces reaching 9 cm (Fig. 15.7d). There are no hints as to how these units were put together if, indeed, they were parts of a necklace.

In concluding this brief account of Hohokam bonework as seen at Snaketown, it is worth reiterating that except for tubes and hair ornaments, bone and antler were unimportant materials. The heavy reliance on bone and the wide range of objects produced from it by the Anasazi make the dearth of bone among the Hohokam all the more enigmatic. The possible existence in antiquity of a cultural restriction which discouraged the use of bone cannot be discounted. According to Antonio Azul, former head chief of the Pimas, hunters had special places where they deposited the horns of mountain sheep that fell before their bows so they would "exert no evil influence upon the winds or rains" (Russell 1908: 82). While this ethnological example is far removed from the Hohokam in time, it might be a surviving echo of an ancient custom that extended to other parts of the animal, and other animals as well. The alternative explanation, which I favor for practical reasons, was that desert hardwoods were substituted for bone. Wood was readily available, more easily shaped and equally serviceable for the production of items like awls, skewers, picks, and musical rasps.

SHELL PRODUCTS

The Hohokam regarded shell as a commodity of more than ordinary importance. It was, in fact, the basis for an industry in which many people in the society had a hand and in which some craftsmen seem to have achieved the level of specialists. The Hohokam have frequently been characterized in the archaeological literature as the shell merchants in the Southwest, and the evidence of their influence on far-flung groups has often been based on the presence of shell artifacts in the distinctive Hohokam

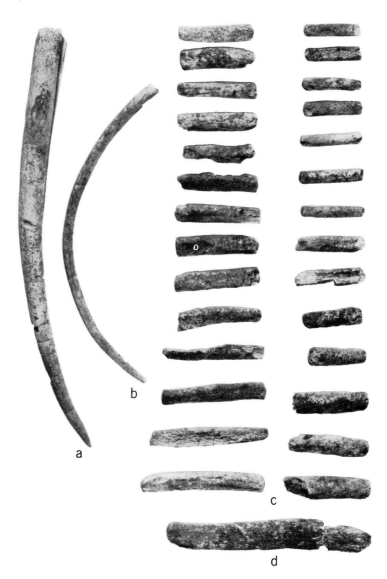

Fig. 15.7. Bone and antler objects from Cremation 2:5F, Sacaton Phase. (For associated projectile points, see Fig. 14.40.) (a, b) Hair ornaments, warped by heat; (c, d) pieces of worked antler. Length of a, 17.8 cm.

idiom. It is well to remember, however, that shell also reached the northern and eastern parts of the Southwest via routes not connected with the Hohokam (Brand 1938; Tower 1945), to complicate what has sometimes been painted as a simple picture.

If the generalization is true that coastal people who are dependent on shellfish for a substantial part of their diet use shell in a variety of ways, functionally and decoratively, then the question should be raised as to whether or not the Hohokam predilection for shell, extending back to the beginning of their tribal history as we now know it, may reflect a maritime origin. I doubt that this idea has much merit, because a counter-argument can be made to the effect that the early possession of a water control technology which arose as a response to arid environment living would more accurately reflect the kind of region the Hohokam originally called home. Nonetheless, it may be assumed that an early acquaintance with shell was made, that its potentiality for jewelry-making and as a commercial material was recognized. Furthermore, a ready source was also known and exploited. If the original homeland was along the western flanks of the Sierra Madre in northern Mexico, the sea would have been within relatively easy reach.

We can be sure that the great quantity of marine shell in Hohokam sites had nothing to do directly with the food quest. The Gila Basin lies inland much too far for the successful transport by foot of quick-to-spoil seafoods. The nature of the shell itself, selected by species best suited for conversion into preconceived products but not noted for food values, the clear evidence that dead material was collected, seen in beach-rolling, fading, and fossil shell in some instances, mean that beaches were combed for the main supply (Haury 1950: 369). The limited use of freshwater clams from the Gila River shows a willingness to employ local materials as well, though the delicate nature of clam shells was not conducive to the production of many ornaments.

Several other broad questions need attention before turning to the analysis of the shell collection at hand. The first one concerns the authorship of the objects found in Hohokam sites. Were they indeed made by them? In 1931 Sauer and Brand (94, 113-14) called attention to the abundance of shell in the villages in northern and western Sonora. By implication (Brand 1937: 300) these were considered to be bracelet manufacturing centers from which the products were passed to northern consumers such as the Hohokam. This position was restated by Brand (1935: 203-4) and further amplified by Woodward (1936). Johnson (1960: 186-88) expresses some doubts about this interpretation after a thorough review of the Boquillas (La Playa) site in northern Sonora.

The basis for the notion of manufacturing centers in Mexico is the presence of large quantities of shell "blanks," or cores, removed from the central portion of the *Glycymeris* shell. A circular groove enclosing the most convex part of the shell facilitated its removal from the remaining circular part, the bracelet-to-be. The villagers of northern Mexico followed this technological process in a surprisingly consistent manner, a point to which considerable importance must be attached. While some finished products may have been acquired by the Hohokam which, in the simpler unornamented forms, would be indistinguishable from those made by them, abundant information is at hand to demonstrate that the Hohokam themselves made the production of shell objects an industry. They were dependent on outside sources only for raw materials.

The justification of this statement is seen in the fact that all parts of Snaketown, whether house-fill or trash, regardless of age, are saturated with shell manufacturing residue of various kinds. In the collection there are 630 samples from controlled excavation units, aggregating more than 3,200 pieces. An examination of these materials establishes what I regard to be the necessary requisites for on-the-spot shell manufacture: (1) raw resources, consisting of unmodified whole shells occurring singly and in caches; (2) specimens broken in the process of manufacture; (3) wastage, or the leftover bits and pieces deriving from shell production activities; (4) the finished products, often in a style peculiarly Hohokam; (5) limited use of local or freshwater shell; (6) the stone tools used in working shell (Chap. 14), and (7) a technology with particular reference to bracelet production which is different than that of northern Sonora.

The last point needs further elaboration. Not a single "blank" or core of the kind so abundant in northern Sonora (Woodward 1936: Pl. 8, Fig. 1) was found at Snaketown, and only five were found at Ventana Cave (Haury 1950: 368). Examination of shell fragments demonstrates the absence to be related to the work pattern. The highest part of the convex surface of a *Glycymeris* valve, preferred for bracelet production, was worn down on an abrasive surface until a small hole could be punched through it. The diameter of the opening was then expanded by chipping. If the valve wall became too thick for successful chipping, more grinding thinned the shell and provided the edge which made further chipping easy. Roughed out in this way the shell circle could then be finished by rasping and reaming. Figure 15.8 illustrates the evidence for this technique, including the wastage from chipping. In places where a shell craftsman had been working or where waste products were dumped, considerable amounts of residue were recovered by screening. Shaping shell by the method described above resulted in frequent breakage because chipped bracelet fragments are among the most common units in the collection. The reason why "blanks" do not occur is now clear,

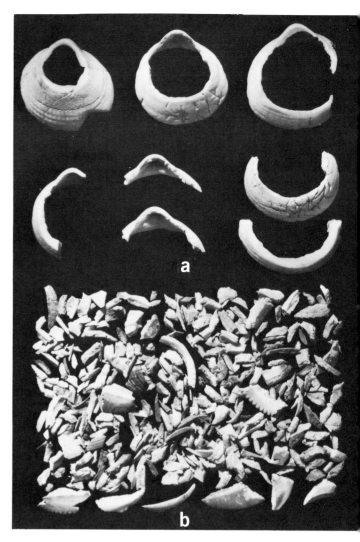

Fig. 15.8. By-products of shell bracelet manufacturing: (a) *Glycymeris* valves discarded because of imperfections or broken during work; (b) wastage, most of which resulted from the chipping method of roughing out the bracelet. Diameter of shells in *a*, 6-8 cm.

attributable to a technological quirk peculiar to the Hohokam. The chipping method was used as early as the Vahki Phase. This may prove to be a useful bit of information when efforts are made to connect the Hohokam shell industry with that of southwestern Mexico, as for example, the Rio Balsas country where a developed shell industry also existed.

Although shell trade has been discussed a number of times (Brand 1938, Colton 1941 and Tower 1945), a few additional points need emphasis. With few exceptions, the raw shells used by the Hohokam came from the Gulf of California. How they were acquired is a question of some interest. It may be assumed that people close to the gulf, such as the Trincheras Culture of northwestern Sonora, themselves elaborators of shell, were active as middlemen. The presence of Trincheras pottery in Snaketown suggests that contacts existed. It is also probable, however, that the Hohokam indulged in collecting trips, providing them with the opportunity of exercising a high level of selection of the material they wanted. At the same time they would be attracted to the strange or rare type of shell which might account for the single or infrequent occurrences of some species.

Note should be taken of the wide but sparse scattering of Hohokam pottery along the eastern shore of the Gulf of California (Gifford 1946: 219-21). Ruppé has shown me potsherds of Sedentary and Colonial Period age which he collected on shell heaps in the vicinity of Rocky Point, Sonora. Bowen called my attention to a Sacaton Red-on-buff sherd from a shell midden (Sonora B:11:1) in an estuary about 15 km up the coast. While these could be the result of trade, perhaps better testimony of Hohokam movements is the presence of their pottery and petroglyphs along the ancient trails in southwestern Arizona and northwestern Sonora leading to the shell collecting grounds (Hayden 1972). Treks to the coast may also have been coupled with the acquisition of salt, or other marine resources of which we know nothing.

In spite of the probable direct gathering of shell, it is apparent that no great surplus stocks were maintained or, if extant, they were not found in either of the two operations. Caches of shell did exist at Snaketown, and they have been recorded elsewhere (Stanislawski 1961), but the volume in all was far below a single individual's carrying capacity. The human figure often painted on pottery with tumpline-supported burden basket on the back may be a depiction of a shell importer in action.

Just as the modern marine conchologist searches for good collecting areas, so the Hohokam must have explored the beaches nearest their domain for localities where shells were abundant. S. S. Berry writes most informatively (1956: 81-84) about collecting conditions in Cholla Cove, the southern indentation of Adair Bay on the northern Sonoran coast about 300 km southwest of Snaketown. Cholla Cove is a great tidal flat several miles in extent with plant-covered sloughs in the higher reaches, then black mud, sandy mud, clean sand, and finally the outer strand in successive zones. At extremely low tide, fossiliferous reefs are exposed. He notes especially the rich and varied fauna associated with these zones, and to read his list is almost like reading the inventory of shell species collected by the Hohokam, though many species exist in Cholla Cove which do not occur in the ancient villages. We may be reasonably certain that the Adair Bay region was the prime source for Hohokam shell.

Reference was made earlier to the use of fossil shell. A number of specimens, particularly *Glycymeris,* are caked with shell breccia. Some finished bracelets retain the breccia matrix on the inside of the umbo, worn smooth with the rest of the shell. These shells may have been pried out of the cemented layers of marine debris exposed during extreme low tides or from uplifted marine deposits of late Pleistocene age near Punta la Cholla (Gifford 1946: 216), probably when the free material along the beaches became scarce from constant exploitation. The fossil material was far less desirable than the fresher shells because it was darker in color and brittle, making it more difficult to shape and resulting in a higher rate of breakage. Figure 15.9 illustrates the evidence on which the above determinations are based. It is probably no accident that most of the fossil shell in the collection dates from the Sedentary Period, the time when shell utilization was at its peak.

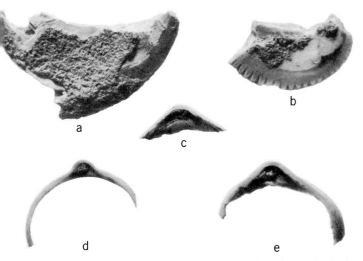

Fig. 15.9. Fossil *Glycymeris* shells with cemented breccia matrix: (a, b) inner surfaces near outer margin; (c-e) bracelet fragments with breccia in umbonal recesses. Width of *a*, 8.5 cm.

Species

In the list of species in Table 15.1, the order of presentation roughly expresses the relative frequency of occurrence. The difficulty of accurately identifying much of the material, either highly fragmented or beach-worn, substantially reduces the value of a unit count. *Olivella* and other whole shell beads were given a frequency value of one, even though there may have been multiple units in any lot. Identification of a type series of marine shells was made by L. G. Hertlein of the California Academy of Sciences. The rest of the collection was identified by me using Hertlein's set as a guide. Freshwater and land shells were identified by Joseph C. Bequaert, Department of Biological Sciences, University of Arizona.

In the list of marine shells, *Haliotis* is the only one native to Pacific waters, while the rest are at home in the Gulf of California. *Haliotis* must have reached the Hohokam domain by an overland desert route not directly associated with the trade corridors to the Gulf. Evidence of some reciprocal relationships between the Hohokam and the California coast is seen in the occasional occurrence of red-on-buff pottery and other Hohokam artifacts in coastal sites.

The list in Table 15.1, compared with the one compiled after the first work at Snaketown, reveals many duplications and some species that are unique to each list. What emerges is the impression that the Hohokam were collecting or otherwise acquiring not only preferred shell types but also species which appealed to them and could be tested for ornamental values.

TABLE 15.1

Species of Shells Used by the Hohokam*

Marine Shells
   Glycymeris gigantea REEVE
   Glycymeris maculata BRODERIP
   Laevicardium elatum SOWERBY
   Olivella cf. *dama* MAWE (and probably others)
   Pecten circularis SOWERBY
   Pecten vogdesi ARNOLD
   Turritella sp. (possibly *T. leucostoma* VALENCIENNES)
   Cerithidea albonodosa CARPENTER
   Cerithidea cf. *C. monteguei* d'ORBIGNY
   Cerithium menkei CARPENTER
   Spondylus cf. *S. princeps* BRODERIP
   Haliotis, probably *H. cracherodii* LEACH and *H. fulgens* PHILIPPI
   Pteria sterna GOULD
   Pyrene strombiformis LAMARK
   Trivia solandri SOWERBY
   Argaronia sp.
   Cypraea annettae DALL
   Nerita cf. *N. scabricosta* LAMARK
   Neritina luteofasciata MILLER
   Nassarius iodes DALL
   Conus fergusoni SOWERBY
   Nomaeopelta stanfordiana BERRY
   Dosinia ponderosa GRAY
   Vermetus sp.
   Anachis sp.

Freshwater Shells
   Amnicola longingua GOULD
   Anadonta dejecta LEWIS
   Lymnaea (Fossaria) dalli F. C. BAKER
   Physa virgata GOULD
   Helisoma tenue sinuosum BONNET

Land Shells
   Catinella avara SAY
   Gastrocopta cristata PILSBRY and VANATTA
   Succinea avara SAY

*Listed roughly in order of frequency of occurrence.

Fig. 15.10. (distribution of shell genera by phase)

PERIOD	PHASE	GLYCYMERIS	LAEVICARDIUM	OLIVELLA	PECTEN	TURRITELLA	CERITHIDEA	CERITHIUM	SPONDYLUS	HALIOTIS	PTERIA	PYRENE	TRIVIA	AGARONIA	CYPRAEA	NERITA	NERITINA	NASSARIUS	CONUS	NOMAEOPELTA	DOSINIA	VERMETUS
SED. CLASS	CIVANO	•	•	•	⊙	⊙	•	⊙	•	⊙		⊙	•					•	•		⊙	•
COL.	SACATON	•	•	•	•	•	•	•	•	•	•	•	•	•	•		•				•	
COL.	SANTA CRUZ	•	•	•	•	•	•			•	•							•	•		•	
	GILA BUTTE	•	•	•	•	•				•	•	•										
PIONEER	SNAKETOWN	•	•	•	•	•				•											•	
PIONEER	SWEETWATER	•	•	•	•		•			•								•			•	
PIONEER	ESTRELLA	•	•	•	•		•			•		•										
PIONEER	VAHKI	•		•	•					•	•		•									

Fig. 15.10. The distribution of shell genera by phase. The Soho Phase, preceding the Civano, has been omitted since it was not detected in the Snaketown work. Circled dots denote presences at Los Muertos. Otherwise the incidences are based on the 1964-65 Snaketown collection only.

Fig. 15.11. (occurrences of nacreous shell)

PERIOD	PHASE	NACREOUS SHELL						TOTALS		
		HALIOTIS		PTERIA		ANADONTA				
		RAW	WORKED	RAW	WORKED	RAW	WORKED	RAW	WORKED	COM
SED. CLASS	CIVANO				1	1		1	1	2
COL.	SACATON	1		7	5	13	1	21	6	27
COL.	SANTA CRUZ					8	3	8	3	11
COL.	GILA BUTTE		5		1	12		12	6	18
PIONEER	SNAKETOWN	1	3			8		9	3	12
PIONEER	SWEETWATER	3				17		20	0	20
PIONEER	ESTRELLA	1				9		10	0	10
PIONEER	VAHKI		2			3		3	2	5
PIONEER	PIONEER		2			7		7	2	9
	UNPLACED	1	2			2	1	3	3	6
	TOTALS	7	14	7	7	80	5	94	26	120

Fig. 15.11. Occurrences of nacreous shell.

Figure 15.10 illustrates the distribution of shell by genus through time based on the data of the 1964–65 work. A test of this kind highlights the vagaries of digging, for it may be assumed that certain shells, as for example *Cerithidea, Spondylus, Haliotis, Trivia,* and *Dosinia* were present, though not found, in those phases bracketed by occurrences. The absence of *Laevicardium* in the Vahki Phase must be attributed to sampling because it was not only one of the commoner shells but was probably the first marine import into southern Arizona, as suggested by its presence in the pre-10,000 B.P. level of Ventana Cave (Haury 1950: 189-90). Some genera, as, for example, *Conus* and *Nassarius,* appear to have been late additions to the inventory, and there are always a few shells, as the limpet *Nomaeopelta,* which are represented by single occurrences and may be viewed as curiosities. A general increase in the number of species used from early to late is evident, a trend coupled with the proliferation of shell products.

Shells of the genus *Glycymeris,* notably *G. maculata* and *G. gigantea,* were most sought for by the Hohokam. Discounting whole shells, such as *Olivella,* easily modified into beads, *Glycymeris* outnumbered *Laevicardium elatum,* the next most abundant form, by a ratio of 10:1. No appreciable change is observed in this ratio throughout Snaketown's span of life.

The abundance of *Glycymeris,* more than 2,200 units, invites a closer examination of the source of supply. The distribution of *G. gigantea,* the commoner of the two species, is "... confined to the Gulf of California area, from Magdalena Bay, lower California, to Zorritos, Peru ..." (Keen 1958: 42-43). The northern limits of the distribution were within the Hohokam range. Although not deep water forms, live specimens must be dredged; they do not thrive in intertidal conditions. Single valves are noted to be common as beach drift. The rich coloration of the live specimen has been lost on these. In the entire collection, only a single bracelet fragment retains the attractive brown markings, good evidence that the Hohokam combed the beaches for their supply, and only now and again did nature provide the chance to pick up a fresh unbleached shell.

Nacreous shell must have held a special attraction for the Hohokam; yet extensive use of it was inhibited by the difficulty of obtaining adequate supplies of raw material. The following conclusions may be drawn, based on the frequencies given in Figure 15.11.

Of the three iridescent shells used, *Haliotis* not only was the most common but was known from the Vahki Phase on to at least the Classic Period. The spotty distribution is most likely attributable to sampling rather than as an indicator of true presence or absence. *Pteria sterna* Gould, the pearl oyster, noted for its delicately colored nacre, was formerly common in the Gulf of California in shallow water and was not difficult to collect. Because the shell is thin and brittle, it would not last long as beach casts. The freshness of the unworked pieces suggests that the species may have been collected directly, as live specimens during low-tide conditions. The temporal distribution is late, heaviest in the Sacaton Phase.

Before the building of Coolidge Dam, the freshwater *Anadonta dejecta* lived in the Gila River whence it was collected by the Hohokam. The shell is thin and brittle, but the inner surface is delicately nacreous, which made it a desirable material for ornaments. Of the 630 lots of shell derived from controlled digging, 80 produced *Anadonta,* usually highly fragmented, and only five pieces show some workmanship. The presence of *Anadonta* in about 13% of the shell samples representing all phases, but the low number of worked pieces once again raises the question as to whether or not the clam was a food source. An alternative explanation is that the shell fragments represent the wastage from shaping the valves into ornaments. In all probability the freshwater clam served both needs, food and raw material for jewelry. The ethnological literature makes no mention of Pima use of the clam as food.

Physa virgata is a small gastropod extant today, in the early 1970s, in permanent water pools. Too small and fragile for conversion into ornaments or for food, its presence is little more than a reflection of a former watery environment. Although single shells were widely scattered in the site, two concentrated occurrences are of special interest. One of these was in Pit 12:11G in the west end of the cut through Mound 39. This was a large pit (sectioned only), at least 3 m in diameter and penetrating the subsoil below the original desert surface to a depth of 2 m. The presence of *Physa* in some numbers in the bottom of the pit indicates that water stood for a time long enough to allow the snail to establish itself. It is doubtful if surface run-off would provide the necessary conditions; rather, because this pit is not far from the area where well penetrations were made to tap a shallow aquifer, it is likely that Pit 12 was another example of well-digging. The pool of permanent wells thus exposed would have provided the habitat favorable for the snail.

The second source was the sedimentary fill of the Pioneer Period irrigation canal. The specific sample of *Physa* at hand came from a Vahki Phase context, and shells were observed in later contexts of canal sediments as well. The inference to be drawn is that canal water was constant over long enough periods of time for colonies of *Physa* to become established, an important point when considering the constancy of canal use.

As for the other species in the inventory, all exist today. The most one can say is that environmental conditions then and now were similar enough for the species to tolerate them.

Technology

The general aspects of shell technology remain the same as described in 1937 (Gladwin and others 1937: 138). More can be said now, however, than was possible before, as to when certain specialized methods of working shell appeared. Simple drilling of holes conical or biconical for bead perforating or pendant suspension was practiced through all phases. So also was the use of a reamer for making larger holes, as in the case of rings. The method of making bracelets, already described, was unchanged from early to late, as was the cutting and grinding of shell fragments to make pendants, and the grinding off of shell spires to produce whole shell beads. The major differences noted with respect to previous data are the extension of cut shell as pendants from the Sweetwater into the Vahki Phase and carving shell as, for example, frogs on bracelets, from the Snaketown to the Vahki Phase. The time placement of acid-etching remains unchanged, Sacaton Phase.

Seen broadly, except for the specialized acid-etching technique, all basic methods of bringing shell to the desired form were known from the time of Snaketown's founding. With almost nothing in the way of shell use during the San Pedro Stage by the Cochise people to introduce a shell industry, we are left with the idea that the knowledge was brought in as a part of the techniculture when immigration took place.

Although the present sample generally duplicates the material recovered in the first excavation, the quantity of finished products is smaller because less work was done in the highly productive cremation areas. At the same time fragmentary specimens derived from controlled excavation units bulk infinitely larger. These assume particular significance when judgments are made regarding trait longevity, or the time of appearance and disappearance of elements or techniques, and form or style changes through time.

Unworked Shell

Most shells reached the Hohokam in an unworked state, and it is not surprising that some of these would turn up in the course of our digging. As previously noted, however, no large accumulations of raw shell were recovered.

Some species were useful as scoops and paint containers without modification. Large *Laevicardium elatum* shells were well suited as dippers or as liquid containers, and the record suggests that the species was used in this way as long ago as about 10,000 years (Haury 1950: 189-90). *L. elatum, Glycymeris maculata,* and *G. gigantea* also made handy paint containers, a use supported by the occasional survival of pigment stains on the concave surface. There doubtless were many other day-to-day uses of unmodified shell which left no evidence of the function for us to detect.

Worked Shell

The worked shell sample aggregates about 2,240 specimens, with good representations in all phases except those of the Classic Period because less work was done in sites of this age. In the tabulation of bead occurrences, whether disc or whole shell types, a frequency value of *one* was given, even though multiple units were present. Fewer than 200 specimens in the lot were either of unknown or mixed sample associations, leaving a useful balance of over 2,000 units. For these the cultural context is assumed to be the correct one, although it is recognized that some migration up or down in a temporal sense may have taken place. It is further assumed that the size of the sample and the repetition of the evidence will have erased the apparent significance of clashing disparities.

UTILITY

Shells intentionally modified for specialized work were not recognized in the present collection. They were never used in tempering pottery or as a scraping tool by potters in thinning the walls of vessels. Though noted earlier (Gladwin and others 1937: 139), shell needles were not recovered. On the basis of the evidence we may judge that the Hohokam valued shell primarily for its virtues in ornament production. Limited ritual use is suggested by shell trumpets and possibly some of the etched shell specimens. Among the Papago, a shell found in the sea during a salt pilgrimage was believed to have special power, and it was taken home (Underhill 1946: 234). If the Hohokam had a similar belief, there would be no way to segregate such a shell from those used secularly.

ORNAMENTS
Beads and Bead-pendants

Whole Shell. Small marine univalves were easily transported in bulk. By the simple operation of grinding off the spires or perforating the walls, they were quickly converted into beads. Little wonder, therefore, that they should be present in all phases. *Olivella* outnumbers all other species and is also the most consistent as to occurrence from the earliest times on (Fig. 15.12a). The smaller *Olivella* shells often were reduced by grinding away both ends (Fig. 15.12b), a treatment seen only in the Santa Cruz and Sacaton Phases. Among the other species *Trivia solandri* was most common (Fig. 15.12c and d), displaying two types of perforations, paired tiny holes in line on the dorsum or two large lateral holes. Although sporadically present, they begin in the Vahki Phase. A number of other shells were put to the same use (Fig. 15.12e-h). The general conclusion to be drawn is that many kinds of raw shells could be and were adapted as beads with a minimum of effort and that this practice prevailed throughout the life of Snaketown. Frequencies are too few to support meaningful conclusions about trends through time.

Disc. Disc beads, perhaps the most common form of ornament wherever shell was used, range through all phases at Snaketown (Fig. 15.13a). Their presence in the early part of the Pioneer Period

PHASE	a	b	c	d	e	f	g	h	TOTALS
CIVANO	3			1			1		5
SACATON	6	3			2				11
SANTA CRUZ	8						1	1	10
GILA BUTTE	4				1				5
SNAKETOWN	3								3
SWEETWATER	12								12
ESTRELLA	6				1	1			8
VAHKI	6		1						7
PIONEER P.	2		1						3
UNPLACED	3		1		1				5
TOTALS	53	3	3	1	5	1	2	1	69

Fig. 15.12. Whole shell beads: (a) *Olivella* sp., Ariz. U:13:21, Civano Phase; (b) *Olivella* sp., five shells welded by crematory fire, Sacaton Phase; (c) *Trivia solandri*, Pioneer Period; (d) *Trivia solandri*, Ariz. U:13:21, Civano Phase; (e) *Pyrene strombiformis*, Estrella Phase; (f) *Neritina luteofasciata*, Estrella Phase; (g) *Conus* sp., Santa Cruz Phase; (h) *Cerithidea albonodosa*, Santa Cruz Phase. Length of *c*, 1.8 cm.

PHASE	a	b	c	d	e	f	TOTALS
CIVANO	2						2
SACATON	15	2	1	4	1		23
SANTA CRUZ	5		1	1			7
GILA BUTTE	4			1		1	6
SNAKETOWN	8	1		1			10
SWEETWATER	10			2			12
ESTRELLA	4			1			5
VAHKI	5			1		1	7
PIONEER P.	7		1				8
UNPLACED	3						3
TOTALS	63	3	3	11	1	2	83

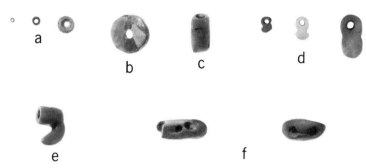

Fig. 15.13. Shell beads: (a) disc, diameter range 1.5 to 11.0 mm; (b) disc, probably *Haliotis;* (c) cylindrical, probably *Spondylus;* (d) bi-lobed, shell type unknown, length range 4.0 to 15.0 mm; (e) claw-shaped, probably *Spondylus;* (f) irregular lumps, side drilled, shell type unknown. Length of *f* (left), 16.5 mm.

was not certainly established before, but nine instances in the Vahki and Estrella Phases now leave no doubt that they were known to the Hohokam from the start. The most definitive evidence came from the floor of a large Vahki Phase house, House 1:9F (Fig. 15.13). Adjacent to the northernmost of two hearths, an area on the floor several meters square carried the impression of a mat. Pressed into the clay of the floor under the matting imprint were a half-dozen beads evidently lost by the wearer while the house was in use. These would easily have vanished through the interstices of the coarse matting elements. The other occurrences were all from reasonably pure trash contexts.

Associated with every phase were pink or deep purple beads, most likely derived from the massive-walled *Spondylus.* Crematory burning has destroyed the chance to make valid judgments as to the relative frequency of the tinted versus the normal white shell beads, though the impression remains that the latter were the most common. The method of producing shell beads was doubtless the same as that for stone bead manufacture, as well illustrated by a bead-maker's kit from the Mimbres valley (Cosgrove 1932: 62, Pl. 69).

A standard procedure in bead shaping was the flattening of the faces, eliminating the concave-convex contours of the natural shell. Only two exceptions were noted in Vahki Phase beads. This treatment is a minor detail, but it provides a contrast to the typically saucer-shaped bead of the early Anasazi beads and therefore may have some diagnostic value.

Drilling the string-hole was something of a technological achievement, especially in the smaller beads. Generally, the perforations are biconical, but many also show a bore of uniform diameter which could not readily have been made by a tapered drill. This characteristic, together with the smallness of the perforation, a minimum of 0.45 mm in a bead 1.50 mm in diameter, in all probability could not have been accomplished with a stone drill.

Tests have indicated that cactus spines and a fine abrasive may have been used (Haury 1931).

The evidence suggests that early Pioneer Period beads were relatively large, from 3.5 to 7.5 mm in diameter (average 5 mm) and from 1 to 2.5 mm thick. Later, the size range and average thickness were somewhat greater. The tiny bead, less than 2 mm in diameter, first appears in the Snaketown Phase, persisting into Classic Period times. Miniaturization and increasing thickness were two trends that appear to work against each other, but this may be associated with what may have been an increasing use of the disc bead from early to late.

Large thin discs, usually made of nacreous shell (Fig. 15.13b), were not common and appear to be late in the time scale, though one instance in the Snaketown Phase was noted.

Although the number of occurrences of disc beads is only about half as great as noted in the original work at Snaketown, the results are broadly comparable except that we now can demonstrate the presence of them in the Vahki Phase. The two occurrences in the Civano Phase are somewhat misleading, the product of the little work we did in Classic Period sites. From other evidence it is known that the disc bead was a common attribute of that Period.

Cylindrical. Chronological evidence for cylindrical beads (Fig. 15.13c) is not good because of the low frequency. One occurrence in mixed Pioneer Period trash may hint at a longer life than was previously noted.

Bilobed. This curious bead type occurs widely through the southern part of the Southwest, as well as in northwestern Mexico (Kelly 1945a: Fig. 72 l, m; Ekholm 1942: Fig. 21b). It matches the disc beads in terms of longevity. The earliest specimens are small, and the late forms are large, although the small form was not replaced. A necklace, combining disc and bilobed beads is shown in Figure 15.14. The small white bilobed units are old and much worn, while the large pink units are fresh-looking, with sharp edges, and they retain the abrading marks from shaping.

Claw-shaped. Although not common, a claw-shaped bead-pendant (Fig. 15.14e) (Gladwin and others 1937: Pl. CXV d, left) has so specific a configuration that it should be traceable in other areas and therefore be further indication of possible areas of contact. The type is assignable to the Santa Cruz and Sacaton Phases.

Side-drilled. Two units are different from all the rest (Fig. 15.13f) in that the perforation was on the side, not central as in the cylindrical form, made by slanted drill-holes meeting near the midpoint of the shell mass. One (left) was also end perforated.

The earliest phase association is the Vahki, a further indication that a rather special drilling procedure, leading to an unconventional stringing method, was already known to the shell craftsmen.

Bead-pendants. Previously listed as ground-shell pendants (Gladwin and others 1937: 141), this group of objects is of special interest because some show perforation styles that differ from all other shell products. These were fashioned of thick irregular pieces of shell smoothed by grinding but not enough to bring all to a uniform size or shape. The shell itself has not been certainly identified, though in unburned specimens the pink color, as well as the mass, suggests that *Spondylus* was the source. Judd (1954: Fig. 16) illustrates similar units from Pueblo Bonito which were identified as *Chama* shell.

Figure 15.15a illustrates units selected from a large sample with single perforations; *b,* double perforations having the same axis; and *c,* multiple perforations with variable axes. These variations in drilling are probably associated with a stringing mode that cannot now be reconstructed. It is worth noting that complicated necklace assemblies are more often seen in Mexico than in the Southwest.

The four occurrences of ornaments of this type were associated with cremations, two dating from the Sacaton Phase, one from the

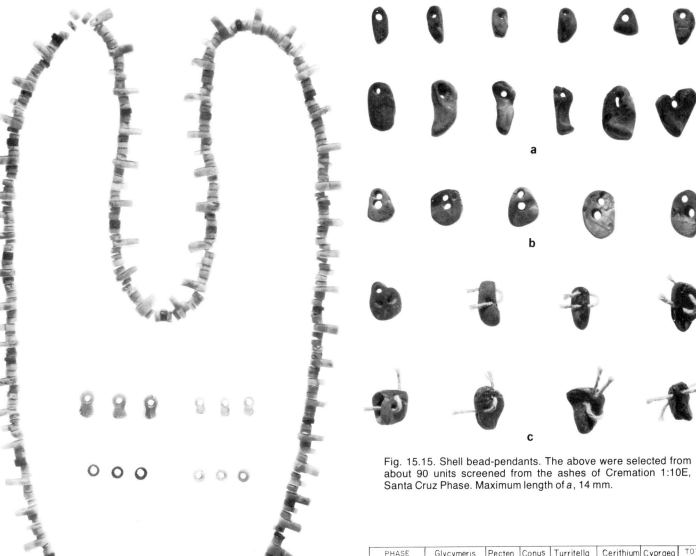

Fig. 15.15. Shell bead-pendants. The above were selected from about 90 units screened from the ashes of Cremation 1:10E, Santa Cruz Phase. Maximum length of *a*, 14 mm.

Fig. 15.14. Necklace of pink, purple, and white shell, including disc and bi-lobed types. Stringing conjectural. Probably Sacaton Phase. Length of strand, 80 cm.

PHASE	Glycymeris	Pecten	Conus	Turritella	Cerithium	Cypraea	TOTALS
CIVANO	1		1				2
SACATON	1	3		3	3	1	11
SANTA CRUZ	1	4		1	1		7
GILA BUTTE	2						2
SNAKETOWN	1	1					2
SWEETWATER		1			1		2
ESTRELLA		1					1
VAHKI							
PIONEER P.							
UNPLACED		2					2
TOTALS	6	12	1	4	5	1	29

Fig. 15.16. Frequency of whole shell pendants by genus and phase.

Santa Cruz Phase and one unplaced. During the original work at Snaketown the record showed the following associations: Sacaton Phase, 15; Santa Cruz Phase, 24; unplaced, 15 (Gladwin and others 1937: Pl. CXV). Lateness of the trait would appear to be well established.

Pendants

Whole shell. Simple perforation of shells, through the umbo if bivalves and through the lip if univalves, easily converted them to pendants. The accompanying chart (Fig. 15.16) gives the distribution by species through time. Taking the collections from both operations into account, the number of whole shell pendants is surprisingly small, a total of 57 occurrences (Gladwin and others 1937: Pl. CXIV). The greatest frequency is noted during the Sacaton and Santa Cruz Phases, although the custom of converting shells in this way must have been followed from the beginning of Hohokam history.

Cut shell. Cut shell pendants are distinguished from carved products by the fact that they were cut from relatively flat pieces of shell either with no elaborations except suspension holes, as in the case of geometric forms, or with the addition of anatomic details, usually by incising, as in the case of animal forms. In carved shell a distinct effort at three-dimensional portrayal was made.

The ratio of nacreous to ordinary shell is about 1:3. The former category includes *Haliotes*, *Pteria* and the freshwater *Anadonta*. *Laevicardium*, *Glycymeris*, and *Spondylus* were evidently the main suppliers of material for the rest.

Figure 15.17 illustrates the form range as well as frequencies. Geometric pendants are in the minority (*a, g*), assignable to the

PHASE	a	b-c	d	e	f	g	h	i-j,l	k,n	m	o	p	q	r	s	t	u	v	w	y	z	DD	bb-cc	x	TOTALS
CIVANO	l																								l
SACATON		2						2	l		l			l	2			l			2				12
SANTA CRUZ			l						l		l			l											4
GILA BUTTE					l								l		2	l									5
SNAKETOWN		l										l													2
SWEETWATER					4											l									5
ESTRELLA																									
VAHKI																				l					l
PIONEER P.								l											l						2
UNPLACED		l		l	l																				3
TOTALS	l	3	l	l	l	l	l	4	2	l	l	l	l	l	l	2	l	l	l	4	l		3		35

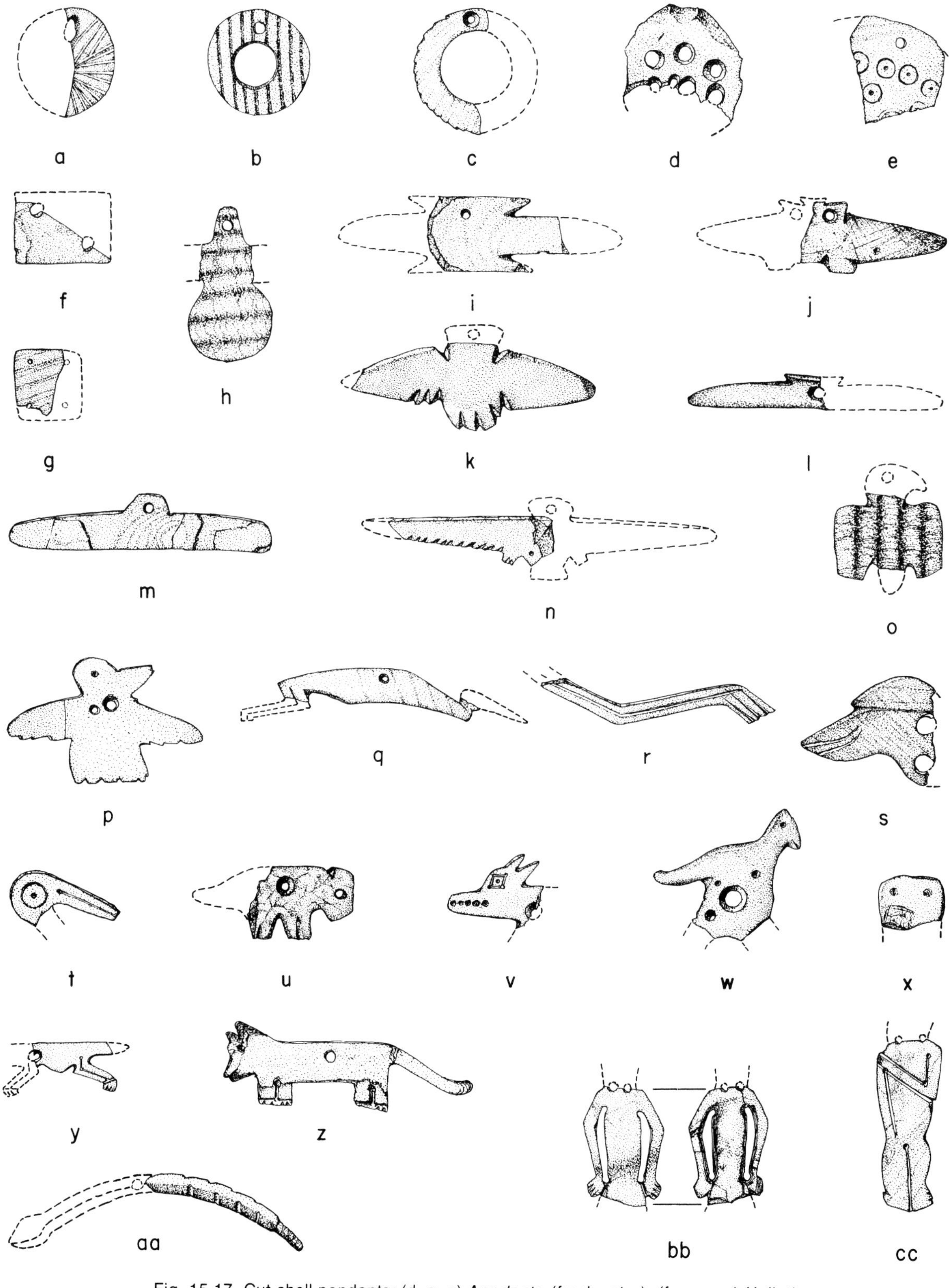

Fig. 15.17. Cut shell pendants: (d, g, p) *Anadonta* (freshwater); (f, m, x, z) *Haliotis*; (bb, cc) *Pteria*; all others *Laevicardium* or *Giycymeris*. Length of *m*, 5.3 cm.

later phases where placement is possible, while life forms (*h-cc*) not only dominate numerically but also were produced throughout the occupation of Snaketown. Attention is called to the following points, which have more than passing interest:

1. Specimen *e*, a fragment of delicate freshwater clam exhibits a series of precisely-made dotted circles, and the eye of *t* is similarly produced. The tool used to achieve this effect must have been a double-pointed stone engraver, the pivotal prong being slightly longer and blunter than the other one, which was slender and sharp. Rotation as with a compass would produce the results seen. This type of shell decoration appears to be lacking or at least rare, in the Southwest outside of the Hohokam territory; but instances are reported to the south at least to Jalisco (Ekholm 1942: Fig. 21r; Kelly 1949: Fig. 88p). A fragment reported in the 1937 Snaketown report (Pl. CXXI g) is closely matched in form and circle placement by one shown to me by Ekholm from Huatabampo. Relatively minor but distinctive characteristics of this kind strengthen the idea of ties between the Hohokam and the cultures to the south. The trait appears to be Santa Cruz Phase and later.

2. Bird-effigy pendants manifest several abstract forms (*h-m*), which appear as early as the Sweetwater Phase and continue to late times (Gladwin and others 1937: Pl. CXVI d), and more realistic representations (*n-t*) which are noted first in the Santa Cruz Phase. Some doubt may exist as to whether or not the early conventional types actually do represent birds, but a typological continuity through time is traceable. Whatever the true inspiration of the form, similar shell pendants were widely diffused through the Southwest, mostly after A.D. 1000, Pueblo Bonito (Judd 1954: Fig. 15,l-p) and the Mimbres Valley (Cosgrove 1932: Pl. 76c) being examples.

3. Specimen *q* is a fragment of a waterbird in flight (probably pelican) adapted from a bracelet fragment.

Animal pendants (Fig. 15.17u-w, y, and z) range upwards in time at least from the Sweetwater Phase onward, although the sample is too small to discern any typological changes through time. Specimen *aa,* again a bracelet fragment, was converted into a reptile.

Three fragments represent the human form (*x, bb, cc*), the latter two made of pearly oyster, *Pteria,* and the third probably *Haliotis.* Specimen *bb* was associated with Vahki Phase material which tenuously extends the trait to the earliest part of the Hohokam record. The other two instances were in certain Sacaton Phase contexts, as was also the one example found in the 1934–35 work (Gladwin and others 1937: Pl. CXVI h). The postures of the arms, over the chest (*cc*) or limply akimbo (*bb*), duplicate the style seen in the clay figurines. Remarkably comparable specimens are in the Norton Allen collection from the Citrus site near Gila Bend (Wasley and Johnson 1965: 102). These specimens, part of a large carved shell cache, are datable to the Sacaton Phase.

The human form carved in shell may be regarded as characteristically Hohokam as far as the Southwest is concerned. When it occurs outside of the Hohokam territory, the typological similarity draws attention to the source of the inspiration. The most dramatic example of this is seen in the Mimbres, where the likenesses to specimens from the Citrus site near Gila Bend are specific (Cosgrove 1932: Pl. 76; Wasley and Johnson 1965: Fig. 77). One concludes that the Hohokam of southern Arizona and the Mimbreños of southwestern New Mexico were in reasonably close contact. Further, the parallels tend to equate the Sacaton Phase with the nascent and classic Mimbres developments, a fact which is also well supported by the repeated occurrence of Mimbres Bold-face and Mimbres Black-on-white sherds in Sacaton Phase contexts at Snaketown.

In all probability, the Hohokam were not the originators of the human-form shell pendant. Almost identical specimens have been found in the vicinity of Guadalajara, Jalisco, Mexico. The parallelisms pertain not only to shape but also to the method of production. Open spaces, that is, leg and arm separations from the body, were started by drilling holes between which the shell was removed, as in Figure 15.17bb, presumably with a sharp stone graver. The drilled hole not only served as a convenient starting point for the cutting process but also reduced the chance of splitting the shell. This is a method frequently used today to stop cracks in flat materials like metal sheets. Pitting the surface with shallow drill-holes where features were to be shown by scoring (Fig. 15.17cc) may have served the same purpose in addition to establishing beginning and ending points of incised lines.

Bracelets

Plain. Three bracelet variants may be recognized, using band size, cross section shape, and umbonal treatment as criteria. Band size and shape are dependent on the extent to which the shell was ground down. In expressing dimensions, band width is measured on the axis of the shell's diameter, and thickness is taken at right angles thereto.

Type 1: (Fig. 15.18a) Thin band; width 2.5-4.0 mm, thickness 2.0-4.0 mm; section often quadrate ranging to triangular; umbo extensively reduced in size, predominantly square, sometimes rounded and worn thin; seldom perforated.

Type 2: (Fig. 15.18b) Medium band; width 4.0-6.0 mm, thickness 4.0-5.0 mm; section usually quadrant, sometimes a skewed parallelogram, rarely quadrate; umbo rounded, occasionally pointed, rarely squared, and perforated in about 50% of the examples.

Type 3: (Fig. 15.18c) Broad band; width 6.0-10.0 mm, thickness 5.0-17.0 mm; section irregularly oval to lenticular, occasionally quadrate; umbo little modified as a rule, band often widens over umbonal area, umbo occasionally perforated.

Values in the frequency chart accompanying Figure 15.18 are based on bracelet occurrences in controlled excavation units. Because many fragments are of band parts without umbo, typing was done on band size only, which tends to weaken the sharpness of the classification. It is also necessary to recognize that some mixing may be represented, that is, that the figures for Type 1 in the later phases may be higher than they should be. Nevertheless, trends are apparent. Type 1 bracelets, thin and delicate, were dominant in the early phases, but the type survived into later times. The Type 2 bracelet is essentially a late Pioneer, Colonial, and Sedentary Periods form, while Type 3 was dominant in the Sedentary Period and doubtless carried on into the Classic Period. In summary, the trend was from a thin-banded, delicate bracelet with extensively reduced umbo to a heavy-banded, bulky form with little or no modification of the umbo. The intermediate form, Type 2, is also intermediate in terms of time-frequency placement.

The production of Types 1 and 2 bracelets called for extensive reduction of the shell in which process the natural crenulations along the margin of the *Glycymeris* shells were eliminated. That these may have had some decorative value in the minds of bracelet makers is suggested by the fact that in a number of cases fine nicks were added to the margin of the band (Fig. 15.19). This feature is most commonly seen on Type 1 bracelets.

Although bracelets are often associated with cremations, the custom of cremating has erased opportunities to observe how and where the bracelets were worn. What are probably bracelet representations on figurines (Fig. 13.15h) suggest that they were worn about the wrist. This does not rule out upper-arm or leg use. Further, the range of size hints at use by individuals of all ages, and whether they were worn by both sexes is a matter for conjecture. Perforations in the umbo may mean that some bracelets were worn as pendants, or that small objects were attached to the bracelets. The large number of fragments in the collection, coming from all parts of the site and from rubbish of all phases, makes the bracelet the most common of all objects made of shell.

PHASE	TYPE 1	TYPE 2	TYPE 3	TOTALS
CIVANO				
SACATON	118	181	11	310
SANTA CRUZ	121	147		268
GILA BUTTE	251	151		402
SNAKETOWN	238	33		271
SWEETWATER	185	8		193
ESTRELLA	102	4		106
VAHKI	50	6		56
PIONEER P.	82	9		91
UNPLACED	95	32	2	129
TOTALS	1242	571	13	1826

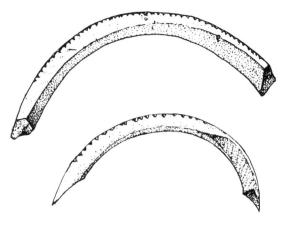

Fig. 15.19. Bracelet fragments showing marginal nicking. Actual size.

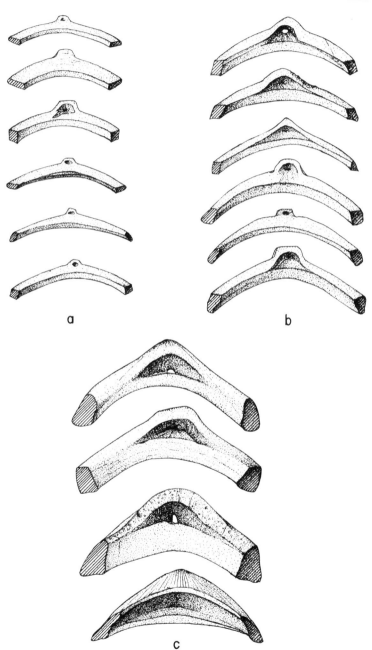

Fig. 15.18. Shell bracelet types: (a) Type 1; (b) Type 2; (c) Type 3.

Carved. A small fraction of bracelets, 10% by earlier calculations (Gladwin and others 1937: 142) and less than 3% on the basis of the present collection, were carved. This treatment includes geometric incising of the band, and the conversion of the umbo into frogs or bird-snake combinations. In the latter instance the bracelet band was easily adapted to the reptilian body.

Looking more particularly at the available evidence (Fig.

15.20), the following observations are in order: Geometric incising of bands (a-c) in chevron patterns appears to begin in the Colonial Period, extending through the Sedentary and into the Classic Periods. It may in fact represent an abstraction of the reptilian body. By Classic Period times, life-form carvings described below appear to have been replaced by geometric arrangements in which both paint and turquoise inlays were sometimes associated (Haury 1945a: 156-58; Di Peso 1956: 95-97).

A significant modification of earlier conclusions about the time of appearance of shell carving can now be stated. Attributed then to the late Pioneer Period (Gladwin and others 1937: 142), carving in simple form, as represented by Figure 15.20d-g, is now assignable to the beginning, the Vahki Phase. It is not absolutely certain that a snake was being portrayed by the undulating bracelet band, but specimen *e*, with incisions that appear to be rattles, suggests the possibility. In later phases when the snake becomes clear as the subject there was also a change in the technological manner of showing it. From modifying the edges of bands to produce a wavy configuration, the shift was toward carving the serpent in relief on the band (*h-o*).

The arrangement of reptiles varies from head-to-tail, head-to-head, and tail-to-tail. Specimens *n* and *o* are interesting because they appear to show a snake in the act of swallowing another one. In these the shell craftsman's mastery over a resistant medium is shown to good advantage. Attention is called particularly to specimen *i* in which the subject is delicate and stands out in high relief. This refinement in craftsmanship was well established by the Santa Cruz Phase, beginning possibly in Gila Butte times, and continued on through the Sacaton Phase, after which it deteriorated.

While on the subject of representing the serpent body, the Hohokam made use of an abstract art form when two reptiles were intertwined, which probably was not their invention (compare Fig. 15.28a and b).

Combining a bird and a serpent was a favorite motif (Fig. 15.20p-s). These range from naturalistic to stylized versions. When a single bird and a single snake were shown, the bird holds the serpent behind the head, and curiously the snakehead is always directed to the left of the bird (10 examples from Snaketown). When paired birds and snakes are shown, the birds are back-to-back and the snakeheads are grasped in the birds' beaks. A single example of the bird-serpent combination as used in bracelets is assignable to the Gila Butte Phase (Gladwin and others 1937: Fig. 55e), the rest are datable to the Santa Cruz and Sacaton Phases.

Finally, among the carved bracelets we come to the portrayal of the frog (Fig. 15.20t-y). The standard procedure was to develop the frog by carving the shell's umbo, sometimes with extraordinary realism and in high relief. The temporal spread was long, cer-

PHASE	a-c	d-g	h-o	p-s	t-y	z	TOTALS
CIVANO						I	I
SACATON			6	I	2		9
SANTA CRUZ	3	2	2	4	I		I2
GILA BUTTE	2	I			4		7
SNAKETOWN		2			2		4
SWEETWATER							
ESTRELLA		I					I
VAHKI		2			I		3
PIONEER P.							
UNPLACED		3			I		4
TOTALS	5	II	8	5	II	I	41

Fig. 15.20. Carved shell bracelets: (a-c) geometric; (d-g) probably reptilian motif; (h-o) reptilian; (p-s) bird-serpent; (t-z) frog. Diameter of *m*, 8.5 cm.

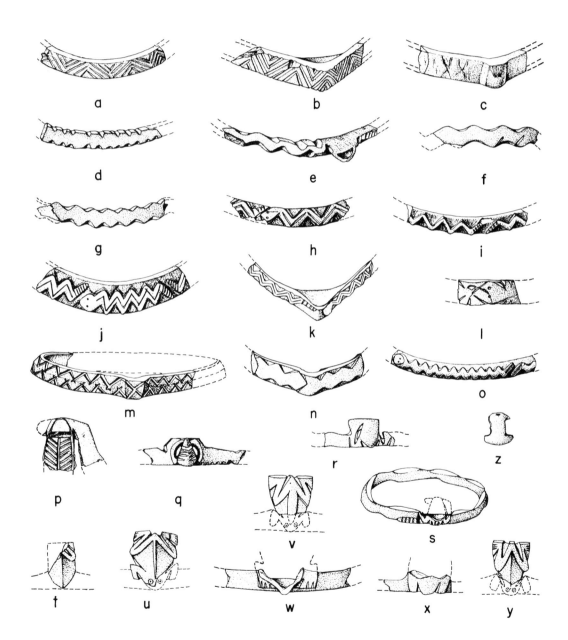

Miscellaneous Carvings

tainly from the Snaketown Phase and possibly as early as the Vahki Phase, for which one example exists. Stylistic changes in the frog on armlets are not observable on the basis of the specimens at hand, although the frog as a free form pendant (*z*), with or without mosaic turquoise overlay, was a fairly common feature during the Classic Period (Haury 1945a: 152).

Miscellaneous Carvings

Bracelet fragments occasionally presented a challenge to do something with them. In converting them to life forms, the artists had to capture the characteristic posture of the animal and fit it to the curvature of the band. In the case of a snake this was not difficult to do (Fig. 15.21a). If a bird was in the craftsman's mind, the pelican lent itself most readily to the material at hand. Figure 15.21b-e gives several examples. Why suspension holes were not provided (only started in *b*) is not known. The temporal distribution of these objects is spotty, mostly Sacaton Phase, although the presumed snake (*a*) was recovered from an early Pioneer Period trash context.

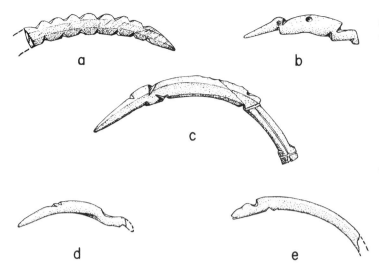

Fig. 15.21. Worked bracelet fragments: (a) snake, early Pioneer Period; (b, c) (?) pelican, unplaced; (d, e) (?) pelican, Sacaton Phase. Length of c, 5.85 cm.

cavity of the shell fits easily over the little-finger knuckle to produce a not unpleasing effect (Fig. 15.24). The fragile nature of the shell would lead to frequent breakage, and it should be noted that almost all examples are fragments. The left valve of *P. vogdesi* is slightly concave externally and therefore was not adaptable to this use, at least no examples of the left valve perforated in this way occur in the collection. The trait ranges from early to late in Snaketown, and its persistence into the Classic Period has not been clearly demonstrated.

From the Gila Butte Phase on, the central parts of large *Laevicardium* shells were removed to produce an object resembling a bracelet (Fig. 15.23d-f). The hole was always smoothly finished, inwardly beveled, and the natural crenulations of the shells' outer margins were also ground away to provide uniform edges. It is possible that these were a form of bracelet, even though fragile and cumbersome; but a suggestion of another, though unknown use, is seen in a lump of fine sand tempered stucco-like material adhering to the inner surface of one fragment. Unbroken specimens have not been found to my knowledge under circumstances that would clarify how they were used.

Rings

Two sizes of *Glycymeris* valves were used in the production of rings in pre-Civano phase times. For large shells the outer margin was chipped away, leaving the thick umbonal part which was reduced by grinding on an abrasive slab until a hole was produced, followed by chipping, reaming, and finally grinding the outer surface to bring the band to the desired thickness (Fig. 15.22a-c). This type of ring had a heavy band which lent itself to shaping the umbo into a bezel (*d*) and for carving (*e*) or grooving (*f, g*).

Small shells of suitable finger-ring size range from little modification of the circle (*h*) to those in which the umbo remains as a small bezel (*i*) or band decoration was expressed as a simple serration (*j*). Temporally, the evidence suggests that the small shell fashioned into a delicate ring was early, and although it continued as a tradition, the heavier banded ring with carving or with other embellishments was in style during the Colonial and Sedentary Periods. Generally speaking, the history of the ring matched that of the bracelet.

The final type of ring was one made of either a large *Oliva* or a *Conus*, producing a broad band (Fig. 15.22k). It appears to have been a Classic Period innovation and not infrequently carried an engraved and painted pattern (Haury 1945a: 156). Di Peso (1956: Pls. 14a and 17a) demonstrates that the broad-banded shell circle was used both as a ring and as a necklace.

The present evidence indicates that the *Glycymeris* shell ring appeared in the Vahki Phase and not in the Santa Cruz Phase, as was stated in the original study (Gladwin and others 1937: 144-45).

Perforated Shells

Bivalves with large perforations constitute a group of shell products, the specific purposes of which are not obvious, although ornamentation in a broad sense may be inferred. The first of these (Fig. 15.23a), represented by a single specimen from Ariz. U:13:22, is a much-worn *Glycymeris* with a central hole and an umbonal perforation. Probably a pendant, the type is not uncommon during the Classic Period, and no whole or fragmentary pieces were recovered at Snaketown. The second type (Fig. 15.23b and c) consistently made of the right valve of *Pecten*, mostly *P. vogdesi,* has a finger-sized hole near the umbo. The margins of these apertures as well as the edges of the shell are often heavily worn in a manner which would result from wearing the shell as a ring. Although somewhat cumbersome, the con-

PHASE	a-c	d	e	f-g	h	i	j	k	TOTALS
CIVANO		1			1			2	4
SACATON	21	4	2	3	8	2			40
SANTA CRUZ		3				4	1		8
GILA BUTTE	1								1
SNAKETOWN	1								1
SWEETWATER						1			1
ESTRELLA						1			1
VAHKI						3			3
PIONEER P.			1			4			5
UNPLACED	6			1	4	3			14
TOTALS	29	8	3	4	13	18	1	2	78

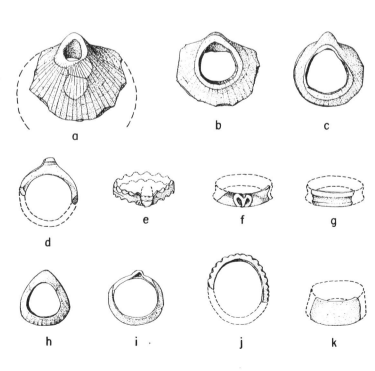

Fig. 15.22. Shell rings: (a-c) stages in ring production from large *Glycymeris* shells; (d-g) plain and carved heavy-banded rings; (h-j) rings made of small *Glycymeris* shells; (k) broad-band ring, probably of *Conus* (Ariz. U:13:21). Width of *a*, 3.9 cm.

PHASE	a	b-c	d-f	TOTALS
CIVANO	1			1
SACATON		6	8	14
SANTA CRUZ		5		5
GILA BUTTE		9	3	12
SNAKETOWN		8		8
SWEETWATER		8		8
ESTRELLA		5		5
VAHKI		1		1
PIONEER P.		5		5
UNPLACED		2	1	3
TOTALS	1	49	12	62

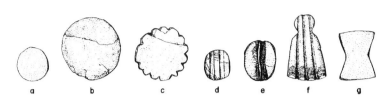

Fig. 15.25. Shell cut into geometric forms: (a) probably *Haliotis*, Sacaton Phase; (b) burned shell, Santa Cruz Phase; (c) *Pteria*, Civano Phase; (d) *Laevicardium*, Sacaton Phase; (e) *Spondylus*, unplaced; (f) *Pecten*, Santa Cruz Phase; (g) *Laevicardium*, unplaced. Diameter of *b*, 2.95 cm.

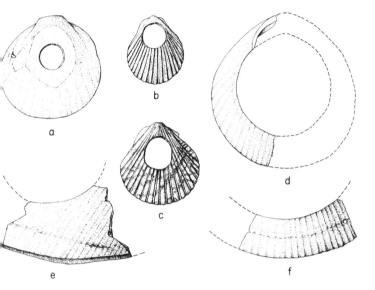

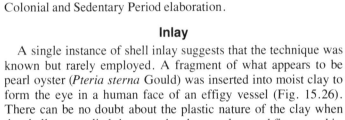

Fig. 15.23. Perforated shells: (a) *Glycymeris*; (b, c) *Pecten*, possibly used as finger rings; (d-f) *Laevicardium*. Diameter of *a*, 5.75 cm.

and Burgh 1954: Fig. 95) were evidently rare or absent among the Hohokam.

Although the evidence indicates that turquoise mosaics were produced from the Vahki Phase onward at Snaketown, the introduction of shell in mosaic assemblies appears to have been a Colonial and Sedentary Period elaboration.

Inlay

A single instance of shell inlay suggests that the technique was known but rarely employed. A fragment of what appears to be pearl oyster (*Pteria sterna* Gould) was inserted into moist clay to form the eye in a human face of an effigy vessel (Fig. 15.26). There can be no doubt about the plastic nature of the clay when the shell was applied, because the clay overlaps and fits around it. The remarkable aspect of the composition is that the shell withstood the firing process. The heavily eroded face indicates that the firing temperature was lower than usual, perhaps purposely restrained by the maker to prevent the shell from crumbling.

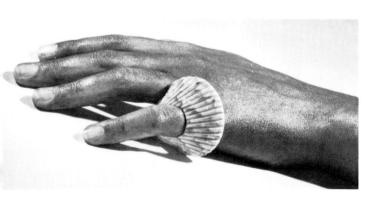

Fig. 15.24. Conjectural use of *Pecten* shells as rings.

Geometrics

Figure 15.25 illustrates almost the entire collection of shell cut into geometric forms, a small sample compared with the one of the 1934–35 excavations (Gladwin and others 1937: 146). Several of the pieces illustrated here have the beveled edges which indicate use in mosaic assemblies, but others do not. Two discs (*d, e*) retain the natural sculpturing of the exterior shell surfaces, *Laevicardium* and *Spondylus* respectively, in a way which suggests possible use of the objects as dice. Gaming pieces, either of bone or shell, of the kind so common among the Anasazi (Morris

Fig. 15.26. Fragmentary face of a clay effigy jar with traces of red paint and a shell inlaid eye. Height, 6.2 cm.

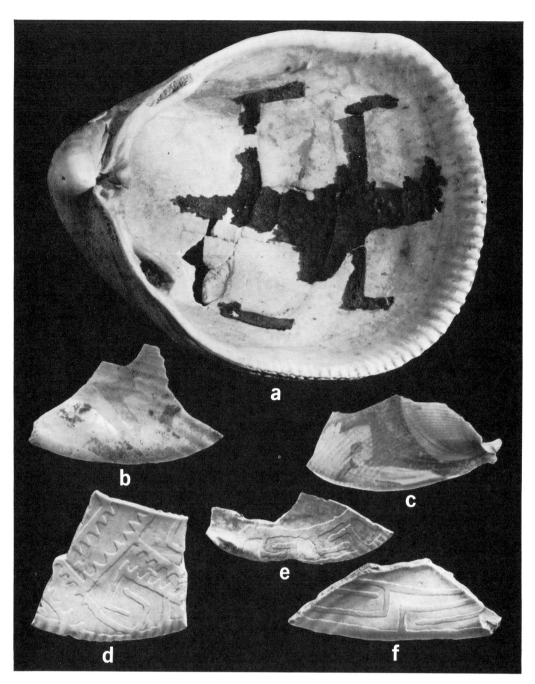

Fig. 15.27. Etched shell: (a, c) *Laevicardium* shells retaining organic resist applied before etching; (b) lightly etched; (d-f) fragments of finished examples, all on shell interiors. Sacaton Phase. Length of *a*, 17.4 cm.

Etched Shell

Acid etching of shell continues to stand out as a technological achievement unique to the Hohokam. The successful production of intaglio patterns by this method is dependent upon the following steps: (1) employment of a wax or pitch as a resistant material, applied on the shell surfaces in those areas to be protected against the corrosive effect of the acid and (2) use of an acid to chemically reduce the calcium carbonate of the shell where not protected by wax or pitch, thereby producing a pattern in relief. Experiments have demonstrated that the fermented juice of the giant cactus, saguaro, is an effective acid. We know from the presence of carbonized seeds that saguaro fruit was collected aboriginally, no doubt mainly for its food value. Soured juice, a weak acetic acid, would have been a natural by-product of making wine from cactus fruit juice, a deeply ingrained custom among the Pima and Papago and, inferentially, among the Hohokam as well.

In the original description of the process (Gladwin and others 1937: 148-51), the use of a resist was postulated for want of tangible evidence for it. Pomeroy (1959: 13) notes that two specimens, one from the Hodges ruin near Tucson and the other in the 1934–35 Snaketown collection which was not detected at the time, exhibited remnants of a pitch or tarry substance but only minimal effects of acid immersion. He concluded that these were evidences of the resist, though specific identification of the material was not made.

As the result of the recent Snaketown work we now have available a specimen which settles the point and removes any lingering doubts. From a mixed Santa Cruz-Sacaton Phase trash context and immediately below a late Sacaton Phase house floor (House 1:10F) came the large *Laevicardium* shell illustrated in Figure 15.27a. Its inner surface carries a figure of a horned lizard executed in a heavy, dark brown substance that appears to have been tacky when applied. A match test showed it to be highly volatile, giving off a pitchy odor. Tests of the lipid soluble fraction, amounting to 14.53% of the sample, produced the following results (supplied by W. F. McCaughey and E. T. Sheehan, Department of Agricultural Biochemistry, University of Arizona):

Carbon No.	Fatty Acid	% of Extract
C_{10}	Capric Acid	5.0%
C_{12}	Lauric Acid	5.6
C_{14}	Myriatic Acid	5.5
C_{15}	Pentadecanoic Acid	4.4
C_{16}	Palmitic Acid	38.4
$C_{16:1}$	Palmitoleic Acid	7.1
C_{17}	Heptadecanoic Acid	9.3
C_{18}	Stearic Acid	12.8
$C_{18:1}$	Oleic Acid	6.6
$C_{18:2}$	Linoleic Acid	5.3

The C_{16} suggests a biological source for the material, but the specific origin is not determinable.

For reasons unknown, the craftsman did not get around to finishing his product by following through with the acid treatment, a fortunate circumstance in this case, for had he done so we would have been deprived of the evidence for the missing step in the etching process. The apparent absence of shell etching in areas adjacent to the Hohokam domain and the presence of pieces that illustrate the steps in the process, as well as finished specimens, identify the technique as a Hohokam invention. To my knowledge, no examples have been reported from Mexico. Viewed globally, etching on bronze appeared in China at the end of the Chou Dynasty, before about 250 B.C., and in Europe, iron swords of the La Teñe period were etched just before the time of Christ, after which the process disappeared until about the fifteenth century (Smith 1972: 120-22). If shell was used as a substitute for metal elsewhere, I am not aware of it.

Discussion

Shellwork occupied a special niche in the total context of the Hohokam life-way. That an inland people, several hundred kilometers from the source of supply, should have been so heavily committed to using imported marine materials, is paradoxical. Among maritime folk who were heavily dependent upon the sea for food, the shaping of shell into a variety of implements and ornaments is a subordinate activity. For the Hohokam, however, food from shell fish was not a factor, and the raw supplies of shell had to be brought into an unlikely environment as a response to an intense cultural urge and demand. This situation raises a number of interesting questions, some of which can be partly answered by a review of the combined shell collections from Snaketown, and others still beg speculation.

In searching for the beginnings of a lively shell industry, one turns not only to the sources of the material but also to a comparative evaluation of the products and the art styles manifested by them. The coastal Indians of southern California in recent and pre-Columbian times elaborated shell extensively, but the products impress one as being of a different tradition and as having had little or no connection with the Hohokam. The sparse use of shell and the limited range of products rule out the eastern and northern neighbors as the sources of the inspiration.

The only open door is to the south, Mexico. However, a review of the available literature on the sites of northwestern and western Mexico leads us into a contradiction. The emphasis on shell manufacturing fluctuates as one goes south: it is strong in northern Sonora (Woodward 1936), in Guasave (Ekholm 1942: 109-11), and in Huatabampo, southern Sonora. It is scarce at Culiacan and absent at Chametla (Kelly 1945b: 144) in Sinaloa. From here southward, dependence on shell picks up again, as in the Autlán-Tuxcacuesco area of Jalisco (Kelly 1949: 129-32), in the Guadalajara region and apparently climaxing in the Rio Balsas of Guerrero (Personal information from Jose Luis Lorenzo). The time range of the listed sites is generally late, probably broadly equivalent with the Sedentary Period of the Hohokam and to a limited extent overlapping the Colonial Period. Stylistic similarities southward exist, but there are enough mutually excluded traits to weaken the value of assemblage comparisons. Nevertheless, it seems clear that a connection did exist. The answer probably lies buried in the sites of Jalisco and Guerrero.

Until this problem is cleared up we may infer that the Hohokam, having developed a liking for shell because of a probable closeness to the sea in their ancestral home and having firmly established themselves in the irrigable country of southern Arizona, continued the intensity of shell use as a function of their relative closeness to the extraordinarily rich collecting grounds on the mud and sandy flats of Adair Bay near the head of the Gulf of California. Refinements in our ideas of Hohokam-Mexican shell industry ties, particularly with respect to specific areas and time periods, must await detailed exploration in that part of the New World.

Even so, it is worth toying with a few art style comparisons that have more than passing interest. The subject matter of life forms, in Hohokam shell pieces, could have been predominantly locally derived. The frog, rattlesnake, birds, notably the pelican, and a variety of four-footed animals were creatures known to them; but the method of execution and stylistic details cast some doubt on the tenet that everything was locally inspired. The intertwining of two serpents, snake swallowing snake, the bird-snake partnership, the frog (Fig. 15.28a-i), and the manner of depicting the human body were not the monopoly of the Hohokam. Indeed, they occur in more developed ways and often in materials other than shell in the art of Mexico. As an aside, it should be noted that a serpent-bird combination both represented and served as a disguise for *Quetzalcoatl* (Caso 1947: 11).

Not uncommonly among the Hohokam shell pendants one sees a quadruped that matches no local life form. This is shown as a long-snouted, many-toothed animal, usually with a retroussé snout. Several examples in shell and a depiction of the same creature on a pottery vessel found near Tucson are illustrated in Figure 15.28n-q. What animal was in the minds of the artists is unclear, though the geographic spread from Tucson to Gila Bend suggests that the idea of the form was widely held. The coatimundi, native to northern Mexico and in recent years, an immigrant into southern Arizona, is a possible candidate as a model. However, bones of this mammal were not recovered in our excavations. In all probability the motif is a northern extension of the Mexican depiction of *cipactli*, the crocodile, often converted into a mythical monster (Fig. 15.28m). Meighan suggests (1969: 18-20) that the figure, whether depicted in Peru, Nayarit, or the Southwest, has a common ancestry. Since numerous and impressive analogies exist between the art products of the Hohokam and the people of Guerrero, the "borrowing" and subsequent modification of *cipactli* by the Hohokam does not seem unreasonable.

Beginning in the Sweetwater Phase, perhaps by A.D. 300, a geometric figure, which I have called a stylized bird, makes its appearance. It is seen first as cut shell pendants (Fig. 15.28k and l), and in the Snaketown Phase it shows up as a painted element on pottery as well (compare with Chupícuaro) (Fig. 12.98). It is tempting, as a speculation, to see a parallelism between this figure and the so-called Cross of Quetzalcoatl (Fig. 15.17i) of Mexican art (Kurath and Marti 1964: 206).

New data require modification of some of the conclusions drawn in 1937. The most noteworthy revision bears on the then expressed belief that from a simple beginning in the Vahki Phase shell work became progressively more advanced as time passed. In the main, the latter part of this statement is still true, but the evidence now supports the contention that even in the Vahki Phase there was already an intense shell manufacturing activity, employing numerous species which led to a remarkable array of finished products, including frog and probably snake carvings. The curve illustrating shell development (Gladwin and others 1937: Fig. 58, inset) is, therefore, not correct. A recasting of it would bring both the species and traits up at least to a value of 10. The obvious inference to be drawn from this is that, even as early as the Vahki Phase, the Hohokam were already some distance beyond the incipient stages of shell working and that antecedents to the tradition are still to be found.

On specific points, a comparison of the frequency charts associated with the illustrations in this section with Figure 58 in Gladwin and others (1937) will reveal the extension of a number of traits into earlier horizons, a fact which is consistent with the observed developed shell work of the Vahki Phase. Acid etching remains a Sedentary Period hallmark, one of the best horizon indicators. Tower (1945: 30) has raised the possibility of the functional misidentification of the *Conus* tinkler as beads in the original Snaketown work, but the fact is, that in both collections, this artifact is absent. It was a common associate of the Classic Period.

It is probable that the intensity of shell use increased with the passage of time, peaking in the Colonial and Sedentary Periods;

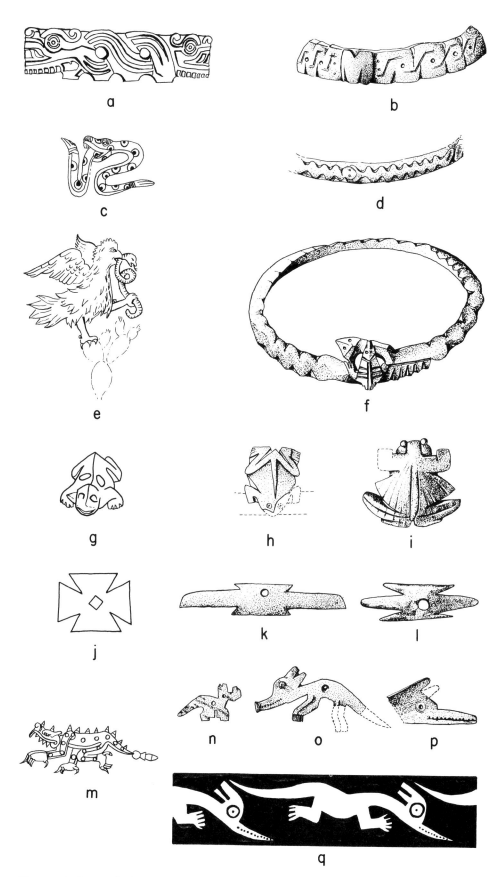

Fig. 15.28. Art motifs from various sources in Mexico (left column) and Hohokam portrayals, possibly of the same motifs (right column): (a) intertwined snakes, stone sculpture from Guerrero (one-half of unit shown) Rubin de la Borbolla 1964: illustration 199, p. 122; compare with rectilinear treatment of intertwined snakes (b) from Snaketown; (c) snake swallowing snake, Codex Borgia, Flor y Canto del Arte Prehispánico de México (anonymous) 1964: 363; compare with (d) shell bracelet carving from Snaketown; (e) bird with snake in beak and talons (Caso 1958: 91, taken from Durán Atlas); compare with (f) shell bracelet from Snaketown; (g) frog, probably stone (Rubin de la Borbolla 1964: illustration 206); compare with carved shell frog on bracelet from Snaketown (h), and (i), a pendant from Los Muertos (Haury 1945: Fig. 93g); (j) so-called cross of Quetzalcoatl (Kurath and Marti 1964: Figs. 133, 206); compare with shell pendants (k) from Snaketown and (l) from the Citrus site (Wasley and Johnson 1965: Fig. 76); (m) "monster" in Codex Nutall (Mendoza and Loto Loria 1959: 918); compare with (q), in negative painting (not resist painting) on Rillito Red-on-brown bowl from near Tucson and shell pendants (n) (from Citrus site, Wasley and Johnson, 1965: Fig. 76), (o), (from Los Muertos, Haury 1945: Fig. 94i) and (p), (from Las Canopas, Haury 1945: Fig. 121f). Not drawn to scale.

but an obviously increased population and relatively more excavations in these time zones than in the Pioneer Period may indicate that this impression is more apparent than real.

Sociological implications of shell-working are not easily assessed. Style uniformity could mean either strict observance of a cultural mode, if many people were engaged in shell fabricating, or, the existence of specialists who supplied the products to the community as a whole. In general, shell wastage, the by-products of manufacturing, was evenly scattered in the rubbish; yet, in several instances, concentrations of waste materials were observed in mounded trash and in pits filled with trash. Also several houses (House 1:8B and House 2:11J, both Sacaton Phase) produced exceptional concentrations of shell material. From this we may guess that there may have been individuals who made the fashioning of shell a specialty.

The practice of cremation has deprived us from making any meaningful observations as to possible differences in the age and sex of those who wore shell. Of the more than 500 cremations excavated in 1934–35, shell artifacts accompanied about 25% of them; in the current operation shell products were associated with 20% of the 90 cremations recovered. Although the earlier sample of burned bones is no longer available, an examination of the smaller lot indicates that shell artifacts occurred with persons of all ages; sex determinations generally cannot be certainly made, at least consistently enough to derive any conclusions therefrom. Until evidence to the contrary is forthcoming, we may suppose that the wearing of shell was perhaps largely a matter of personal option and that rank or class distinctions were not implied when it was worn.

Considering the importance of shell ceremonially in Mesoamerica, notably the *Pecten* at Teotihuacan, we may guess that this idea extended also to the Hohokam; but the evidence to support this is thin. Shell trumpets, only two of which were found at Snaketown (Gladwin and others 1937: 147, Pl. CXXII) are generally not common in Hohokam sites. The precise use of the handsome turquoise and shell assemblages found at Casa Grande and dating from the Classic Period (Pinkley 1931: 22), whether richly ornamental or ritual, is not known. Perhaps the best indicator of all was the large deposit of incinerated shell mosaic fragments in what was termed a cremation mound, evidently the site of mourning rite observances, discovered in 1934–35 (Gladwin and others 1937: 146). The subject matter, though seen only in the most fragmentary form—snakes, birds, and frogs— parallels the occurrence of these creatures on carved stone vessels whose use must have been more sacred than secular. One can only bemoan the practice of cremation, so wasteful from our point of view, in having deprived us of gaining a clearer picture of shell and its role in the realm of the supernatural.

Tower's helpful study of shell points to the Gila Basin not only as the area of greatest concentration of shell species but as a major cross-roads in the trade-route system (1945: 18, 44). To the

Hohokam this marine resource must have been a stock-in-trade, an important export item. I do not believe that people to the north and east of the Hohokam were wholly dependent on them for either raw materials or finished products; but the appearance of artifacts in the distinctive Hohokam style as far away as Pueblo Bonito, and especially in the Mimbres area of New Mexico, leads to the conclusion that the influence of the Hohokam was not inconsiderable. This general subject deserves a far more detailed study than can be given it in these pages.

On the basis of his careful work at San Cayetano del Tumacacori and other sites in southwestern Arizona, Di Peso has synthesized the prehistory of Pimeria Alta (1956: 559-68). A point which has particular relevance to the work at Snaketown is his recognition of a Hohokam intrusion or migration into the area occupied by an indigenous people called the Ootam, the period being dated from A.D. 900–1000 to 1250–1300. It is stated that the Hohokam "took over Snaketown (562)" and that they "... had great ability in the working of shell ..." and "... were able to produce items which the indigenes (Ootam-*mine*) had never known ... (564)."

The question at stake is whether or not Snaketown shellwork evidences the kind of technological shift which would lend support to these observations. Di Peso notes (1956: 113) that "The Hohokam featured the frog, serpent, bird, and human motifs as the central theme of their jewelry art while the Upper Pima were bound strictly to use of geometric designs created around the element of the flying triangle...." The Snaketown data indicate that the frog, snake and birds, although emphasized most heavily after the Snaketown Phase, did begin in the Pioneer Period, perhaps as much as 1,000 years before the so-called intrusion. Even the human form may have been known as early as the Vahki Phase. Life forms did not die out at the end of Di Peso's Hohokam Intrusion Period (1250–1300) but continued into the Classic Period (Di Peso's Ootam Reassertion Period, 1250–1300 to 1690). This is borne out by the evidence from sites like Casa Grande (Fewkes 1912: 145) and Los Muertos (Haury 1945a: 153). Di Peso is correct in asserting that geometric art, expressed as engraved and sometimes paint-filled patterns in rings and bracelets, was late, or a Classic Period achievement.

The question which emerges is: Were these minimal changes in form, the addition of new techniques and some changes in shell species associated with the arrival and subsequent withdrawal of a new group of people, or were they the normal products of the passage of time, the shifts in cultural "tastes" and the maturing of the shell industry? Looking at the total spectrum of Hohokam shellwork, the latter choice is the more acceptable one. Except for local innovations, as for example the invention of shell-etching, and art motif imports, as for example *cipactli* (monster), I see nothing in the rich evidence of Snaketown shellwork that supports the hypothesis of the arrival of a migrant society late in the village's history.

PART SIX

HOW OLD IS SNAKETOWN?

16. Chronology Building

In the preceding pages efforts have been made to arrange the cultural remnants uncovered in Snaketown into a meaningful progressive scheme, based on relative time assignments revealed by stratigraphic relationships. Changes in architecture, in canals, and in burial practices have been noted. It has been possible to develop a pottery "clock" by combining the simple principles of stratigraphy and typology. We are ready now to examine the problem of Snaketown's age in terms of the time-reckoning system we know and use, the Christian calendar.

No subject related to the Hohokam has provoked more debate than this one. Students of the past recognize the premise that a time-ordering of cultural phenomena provides the backbone around which the story of a people can be written. A sense of time is needed, not only to see what transpired at a given moment but also to measure the order and the rate of change, to search for causes thereof, to determine the appearance and disappearance of attributes, to evaluate the long- or short-term effects of migrations or other cultural dynamics, to pinpoint climaxes, and to weigh comparatively the achievements of one people against those of another. All of this is being said with the full realization that the historical approach is not the sole goal of archaeology. It is, however, the principal framework on which all other efforts to interpret society are dependent, and it is the key to our assessment of the Hohokam.

The task of chronology building for Snaketown is not an easy one. The problem derives more from conflicting perceptions as to the meaning of the evidence than to the nature of the evidence itself. The Hohokam left no inscriptions or texts to lead, or mislead, us. At best they probably had no more than a simple notation system comparable to the Pima calendar stick (Russell 1908: 36–66) to record events or to guide crop planting. Our recourse is to superimpose on the physical remains of the Hohokam year values derived from a variety of sources. History thus expressed, applied to a society as a whole but excluding the role of important personages and the impact of specific events, does no violence, in my opinion, to the attempt to measure the organic growth of a people. At the same time, the pinpointing of moments in a cultural continuum as, for example, phase beginnings and endings, introduces an arbitrariness which makes the system look artificial, when, in fact, a grading of changes in cultural phenomena along a time scale is implied.

The subjective nature of chronology building, when specific controls are wanting or inconclusive, is nowhere better shown than by what has happened through the years to the Snaketown sequence as originally published in 1937 (Gladwin and others). It has been most illuminating to see how a little time for thinking has changed our thinking about time. In spite of the fact that we are reaping the benefits of continually more refined techniques for measuring time, developed outside of archaeology, we still bow strongly to our individual ways of looking at and weighing the physical evidence we dig up. And our own concepts about how fast a culture unfolded in a given environment or in a given segment of prehistory shades our willingness to accept some dates and to reject others. At the same time, there are other defensible reasons for making such judgments too, as for example, internal consistency in a series of dates or measurements and compatibility with various ancillary lines of evidence that tend to build confidence in the system.

Before unfolding the dating problem for Snaketown, my advocacy of the long chronology as originally published in 1937 must be understood. My confidence in the reliability of the initial work was never seriously shaken. The central issue is the different weight each of us puts on the evidence and varying views of the rationale that motivate us in interpreting archaeological data.

Returning to the 1937 sequence, the anchor-points were the Sacaton and Santa Cruz Phases fixed approximately in time by a moderately extensive range of associated foreign pottery types which were dated by tree-rings. These two phases were given duration values of about 200 years each. The next step was assigning speculative time spans to the phases that preceded these two. Having few chronological landmarks to do this and believing that the antecedent phases would be no shorter than the "dated" horizons, a duration factor of 200 years was used, admittedly an arbitrary value. Most of the objections were directed against this formula and the attempts at making revisions followed.

Figure 16.1 brings together several of these efforts. Reassignments of phases to different cultural labels, as Vahki-Snaketown to Mogollon, deleting the Gila Butte Phase (Gladwin 1948), and relegating Vahki-Sweetwater Phases to the Ootam (Di Peso 1956) need not concern us now. Nor do we need at this time to spell out the detailed reasoning that prompted the positions taken. What is of concern is that chronology rebuilding could produce such disparate results. In essence, the "old" system was torn to shreds on arguments that seemed less valid to me than did those which were used in developing the chronology in the first place.

Compression of the time scale characterizes all efforts save one (Wheat 1955), and that approach was to vary the length of the phases. Shortening the sequence introduces irreconcilable conflicts with the information now available, and lifting the Snaketown-to-Sacaton phases to an A.D. 900–1300 period cannot be applied at all. Bullard (1962), in addition to shortening the sequence, makes much of the concept of overlapping. This factor is reviewed elsewhere (Chap. 12). The only phase about which there was reasonable agreement by nearly all authors was the Sacaton.

It is fair to note that there was support for the original sequence based on a fresh look at the data by Dixon (1956), Lehmer (1950), and Schroeder (1951). My own recent view, slightly more conservative than expressed in 1937, held that the Hohokam lived in Ventana Cave "possibly as early as the beginning of the Christian Era (1950: 526, 546)."

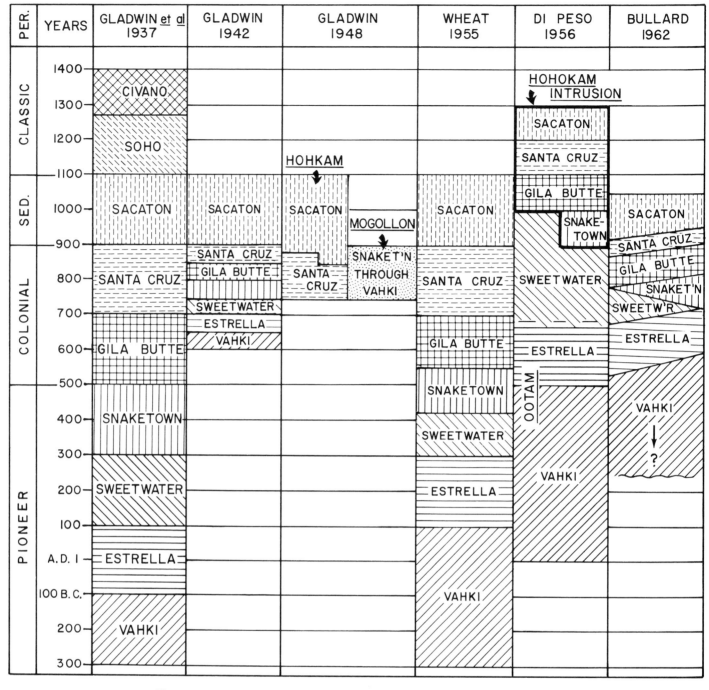

Fig. 16.1. A comparison of Hohokam chronologies illustrating the chaotic state that developed after the initial classification of 1937. Period names apply only to Gladwin and others 1937 and Wheat 1955.

As time passed it became abundantly clear that resolution of the conflicts could not be achieved by more revisions, which would only further confound the issue. Fresh data derived from new digging, and the application of dating techniques not available in 1934–35, offered the best hope. One of the prime motives for returning to Snaketown was to accomplish this end. Whether or not we were successful depends on the credence the reader places upon the following data and the interpretations thereof. It must be emphasized that the chronology which now emerges is meant to apply only to Snaketown, although, in all probability, it is also valid for most of the Hohokam domain.

Those methods of dating which provide calendrical values will be taken up in turn. The order of presentation, in a sense, expresses my feelings about the relative reliability and the degree of precision of the various methods. Thus, tree-ring dated intrusive pottery is considered to be more dependable than paleomagnetic dating, partly because there are more data of a repetitive nature and partly because of the greater degree of control that ring-counting provides.

TREE-RING DATING

The unusually dependable method of dating by tree-rings cannot be used directly because the desert failed to provide the types of wood that lend themselves to the successful application of the technique. However, a few logs of architectural wood of Ponderosa Pine and Douglas Fir, normally datable, were recovered. These came from some distance, though the means of transport and the sources are not known. Four specimens have been cross-dated by the Laboratory of Tree-Ring Research of the University of Arizona (letter from William J. Robinson, 22 Jan. 1968), listed as follows:

TR-1-64 from House 3: 10F (1964–65) Ponderosa Pine
TR-3-64 from House 3: 10F (1964–65) Douglas Fir
GP-1078 from House 8: 6G (1934–35) Ponderosa Pine
GP-1082 from House 1: 10F (1934–35) Douglas Fir

The composite chronology of these four specimens from three different architectural units is only 41 years long, too short to be dependable for dating, but the ring pattern bears some resemblance to the master chronology from A.D. 1140 to the early 1180s. The Laboratory of Tree-Ring Research is unwilling to assign dates to the specimens on the basis of this resemblance, and I hesitate to do so myself. If the dates are correct, they would tend to raise the abandonment of Snaketown, now stated at about 1100, by nearly a century. This does not seem likely.

It is of no small interest, however, that datable specimens, and in this case pieces that were cross-dated from different structures, were recovered. It holds out some promise for finding datable wood in future work. As a further observation, it was noted that the specimens have complete terminal rings, meaning that no erosion or wear of the logs had taken place prior to their use as building material. This condition tends to rule out the idea that the logs were salvaged as driftwood along the Gila River. If the logs were hand transported, it was over a distance of at least 125 km (75 mi) from the Pinal Mountains near Globe, the nearest source of Ponderosa Pine and Douglas Fir today, in the early 1970s. The supposition is that there has been no change in the distribution of these trees in the last 1,000 years.

The indirect application of tree-ring dating at Snaketown has high utility, which, in a way, makes up for the inability to apply the method directly. This is in reference to trade pottery which has been dated as will be seen in the following pages.

INTRUSIVE POTTERY

Pottery found in Snaketown but made elsewhere is useful in reflecting the contacts the Hohokam had with other people in the Southwest. Fortunately, most of it is easily distinguished from the indigenous red-on-buff, although exact type identification is often troublesome. It is a happy circumstance that much of the foreign pottery has been well dated by tree-rings. Because of this, trade pottery was heavily relied upon in 1937 (Gladwin and others: 212–220) to assign calendrical values to the Sacaton and Santa Cruz Phases and to equate the Hohokam and Anasazi cultural complexes. Furthermore, the "dated" horizons were then used as a yardstick for ascribing units of time to the undated horizons. These advantages still reside in the new collection of trade wares. Refinements in the application of tree-ring dating since 1937 have made the Anasazi pottery in Snaketown more useful than ever.

In the 1934–35 operation 408 fragments and six whole or restorable vessels not native to Snaketown were recognized. In the 1964–65 excavations, the totals for fragments are amazingly similar, 413, though no whole vessels were found. It must be noted that the units in the recent collection are generally better placed with respect to phase association than was the case in the earlier lot. The aggregate represents a large and significant sample from which useful inferences may be drawn. It is doubtful if many other Southwestern sites have produced as high a density of trade pottery as has Snaketown. A few examples are illustrated in Figure 16.2.

A measure of the frequency, though not necessarily the only one, is found in the occurrence of trade sherds in the controlled stratigraphic tests made in Mound 39. Each level by volume consisted of 2 m³ of refuse, an area 2 m² and 0.5 in depth. Foreign sherds ranged from none to seven per stratigraphic unit. The 44 m³ comprising the test yielded 40 fragments of pottery foreign to Snaketown, or a little less than one per screened unit. Mound 29, tested in 1934–35, produced 57 intrusives in a little over 100 m³ of trash, a somewhat lower density than Mound 39. Foreign sherds are not limited to refuse because house clearing and general digging produced them frequently. Although difficult to quantify the phenomenon, it is evident that lines of communication between the Hohokam and other people were open, fairly intimate and geographically extensive. We do not know much about the nature of the goods that were flowing out from the

Fig. 16.2. Examples of pottery foreign to Snaketown: (a) Kana-a Black-on-white; (b, c) Floyd Black-on-gray; (d, e) Black Mesa Black-on-white; (f, h) Deadmans Black-on-red; (g) Red Mesa Black-on-white; (i) Dragoon Red-on-brown; (j) Mogollon Red-on-brown; (k) Three Circle Red-on-white; (l) Trincheras Purple-on-red; (m) Mimbres Bold Face Black-on-white; (n) Mimbres Black-on-white; (o) vessel leg, Mexico, unidentified. Length of o, 12.9 cm.

Hohokam in exchange, or even if exchange was involved. Hohokam pottery in Anasazi and Mogollon sites is much less abundant than is the reverse situation, hinting that there was no particular premium on Hohokam pottery abroad.

The intrusive pottery recovered during both operations at Snaketown is tabulated in Figure 16.3. It is fair to assume that most, if not all, of the fragments came from pots that were brought to Snaketown as whole pieces. The introduction of potsherds into the village as curiosities picked up by itinerants appeals to me as the less likely explanation of their presence. Clearly, the meaning of foreign ceramics as an associate of Hohokam remains is dependent on the manner of introduction. If this pottery was brought in as whole vessels, a time equivalency between foreign and native goods, under normal circumstances of association, may be assumed; potsherds introduced as "collector's items" would be essentially valueless as a key to measuring age. The following discussion is based on the acceptance of the former alternative.

Using numbers of potsherds and types as the basis for assessing the intensity of regional contacts, Figure 16.3 makes it clear that contact with the Mogollon to the east was both close and over the longest period of time. Western Anasazi in the Flagstaff area were also prominent contributors but during a much shorter period of time. Connections with eastern Anasazi appear to have been weak and, reciprocally, it is there that few recognizable Hohokam elements occur. A mere half dozen or so sherds are clearly out of

The table below tabulates trade pottery by phase association. Notation used in cells: plain number = count; [n] = 1934–35 count (boxed in original); (n) = whole vessel (circled in original); I = age based on tree-rings; ⋮ = estimated extension; ★ = estimated (Haury 1936:9); ⊙ = based on new tree-ring data.

PERIOD	PHASE	LINO BL-ON-GRAY	LINO GRAY	KANA-A BL-ON-WH	KANA-A GRAY	FLOYD BL-ON-GRAY	WHITE MOUND BL/WH	KIATUTHLANNA BL/WH	RED MESA BL/WH	BLACK MESA BL/WH	DEADMANS BL/WH	RESERVE BL/WH	UNID. BL/WH	UNID. BL/RED	SAN LORENZO RED/BRN	MOGOLLON RED/BRN	THREE CIRCLE RED/WH	MIMBRES BOLD FACE B/W	MIMBRES BL/WH	SAN FRANCISCO RED	UNID. RED	FORESTDALE SMUDGED	RESERVE SMUDGED	ALMA PLAIN	ALMA NECK BANDED	THREE CIRCLE NECK COR	UNID. CORRUG	DRAGOON RED/BRN	RILLITO RED/BRN	RINCON RED/BRN	RINCON POLY	TANQUE VERDE RED/BR	WINGFIELD PLAIN	TRINCHERAS PURPLE/RED	TRINCHERAS POLY	NOGALES POLY	UNID. PLAIN	MISCL. UNID.	RED-ON-BROWN	REDWARE	BROWNWARE	BLACK SLIP
CLAS.	CIVANO												I																			7										
SED.	SOHO —1100																																									
SED.	SACATON —900		4 [7]	I			8 [7](1)	17 [11]		6	I				I	13 [9](1)	3			55 [21](1)	16		5	10 [3]	3 [3]		3	I	4 [8](1)	I	3	2							6	2	I	2 I I
COLONIAL	SANTA CRUZ —700		I	10 [2](1)	I		(1)		I	I	3 [2](1)				★	⊙ [2](1)	I	4		30 [10]	4		4 [4]	4 (1)	[1]	[2]	[1]	[2]	2	I				I		I				2	I
COLONIAL	GILA BUTTE	[I]			I												I 4	I		11 [2](1)	8 [4]													I							I	
PIONEER	SNAKETOWN												I			I				13 [3]	4											[I]							I	I		
PIONEER	SWEETWATER												I			I				10 [3]	2						I					2 [2]										
PIONEER	ESTRELLA																			3 [4]												[I]										
PIONEER	VAHKI																			3 [I]	2											I										
	UNPLACED	[4]	12 [46] (1)	I	I [1]		6	2 [35]	6 [29]	I	8				[2]	I [3]		8 [22]	[5]	37 [71]	6		[34]	2	I [1]		I		[9]	I					3 [6]	2		I	[16]		3	[2]
	TOTALS	[5]	I 26 [55] (1)	I (1)	4 [1]	7	11 [42] (2)	28 [42] (1)	I	15 (1)	I				2 [2]	6 [5]	3	25 [31] (1)	3 [5]	162 [115] (2)	42		16 [47]	2 [5]	[2] (1)	[4]	I		4 [19] (1)	4	4	2 [I]	7	I	9 [9]	2 [2]	I	8	5 [16]	2	3	4 I [4]

7 = 1964-65   [7] = 1934-35   (2) = WHOLE VESSELS   I = AGE BASED ON TREE-RINGS (BRETERNITZ :1966)   ⋮ = ESTIMATED EXTENSIONS
★ = ESTIMATED (HAURY 1936:9)   ⊙ = BASED ON NEW TREE-RING DATA (BANNISTER, HANNAH & ROBINSON 1970:64)

Fig. 16.3. Tabulation of trade pottery in Snaketown by phase associations. Tree-ring dated ages are supplied where applicable. High incidence of unplaced pieces is due mainly to surface finds.

west-central Mexico, but specific places and horizons are not assignable. The Trincheras Culture of northern Mexico is somewhat better represented. Nonetheless, it is something of a puzzle why ceramic bonds with the south were not stronger when so much else in Hohokam life ultimately came from there. The archaeological buffware of the Yumans to the west in the lower Colorado River valley has not been identified at Snaketown, a curious lack since the Yumans and Hohokam were immediate neighbors. They shared a similar environment as well as many cultural features, and the former were producing pottery early enough to make it available in Snaketown before it was abandoned. Some intermingling has been reported in the Gila Bend area (Wasley and Johnson 1965: 70–72), but on the whole, fraternization as expressed by pottery was next to absent.

Inferences drawn from intrusive pottery are dependent upon two important variables: (1) the proper identification of the type which refers a given specimen to a larger group about which the age, regional origin, cultural and physical characteristics, are well known, and (2) the validity of the association of the trade pieces in specific contexts at Snaketown.

As for the former problem, a number of experts, among them David Breternitz, J. Charles Kelley, and Gwinn Vivian, have been called upon to assist in the identification. No better way has yet been devised to recognize pottery; but even so, differences of opinion do occur. Specimens of doubtful identity, though figuring in the totals, have not been used where specific correlations are attempted.

The validity of the association, the most critical variable of the two, poses a different problem because we know that upward or downward intrusions of chronologically heterogeneous materials

did occur. The guidelines as stated in 1937 (Gladwin and others: 212) were: trade sherds in "pure" rubbish contexts and in house fill material were regarded as indicative of contemporaneity if the associations were repetitive and not merely single occurrences. Whole vessels in cremations were considered the most useful line of evidence in determining contemporaneity.

The intrusives from Snaketown reported in 1937 (Gladwin and others: 212–220) have been discussed in the literature with wide-ranging interpretations. My concern here now is only with Gladwin's meticulous re-analysis of the exotics from Mound 29 (1948: 82–94) because some of the conclusions drawn from his quantitative results are most misleading. Basic to the understanding of the meaning of foreign pottery in a site is the phenomenon of association. In his hands the co-occurrence of trade and in-digenous pottery types assumes spectral dimensions which lead one away from a rational and realistic consideration of the data. For example, Gladwin's Figure 25 (1948: 86) shows seven selected foreign types and their ocurrences with each of the local pottery types in sections of Trench 1 of Mound 29.

Choosing one of these as a test case, the number of times Kana-a Black-on-white was associated with Hohokam pottery types was as follows: Sacaton Red-on-buff 8, Santa Cruz Red-on-buff 3, Gila Butte Red-on-buff 10, Snaketown Red-on-buff 10, Sweetwater Red-on-gray 3, Estrella Red-on-gray 0. Gladwin states (87) "... *each one of these foreign types is found to have been associated in varying amounts with the same five types of local decorated pottery*" [italics his], from which he then concludes (88) "The uniformity of the association of the five local types with all six (?7) of the foreign types indicates that the overall span of the five local types was very much shorter than has heretofore been thought possible...." The assumption is that Kana-a Black-on-white is a valid indicator of the essential contemporaneity of the five Hohokam types, an interpretation I cannot accept. Gladwin ignores the stratigraphic evidence for an evolving ceramic tradition, and he pays no attention to quantitative differences which surely must have some meaning. This latter point needs further attention. Going back to the raw data (Gladwin 1948: 241–252), we can tabulate the presence of Kana-a Black-on-white in sections of Trench 1, Mound 29, and the numbers of sherds of local pottery types as shown in Figure 16.4.

What we learn from this is that Kana-a Black-on-white was associated predominantly with Sacaton Red-on-buff and Santa Cruz Red-on-buff and that all the other local types were present as tiny minorities, units of which found their way into the mound as a product of mixing, a phenomenon discussed at some length elsewhere (Chap. 12). Unfortunately, Gladwin rejects or ignores the fact that materials in an archaeological site can occur out of their normal temporal contexts. If this principle is not accepted, then one would expect to find Kana-a Black-on-white in deposits where Sweetwater Red-on-gray, Snaketown Red-on-buff and Gila Butte Red-on-buff were the dominant types. This did not happen.

It does not seem profitable now to engage in a long rebuttal of other points Gladwin made with respect to chronological problems that led to the evisceration of the original sequence. I am content to have my position supported by the new data. There are, however, some differences in quantification which will cause trouble for the reader unless explained. Mogollon Red-on-brown, for example, was listed (Gladwin and others 1937: 213) as having occured five times. Gladwin (1948: 86, Fig. 25) records the type in eight sections of Mound 29 alone, and there are other discrepancies as well. The sources of these figures are not clear to me. His tabulation and mine, therefore, as recorded in Figure 16.3, will not agree because the 1934–35 frequencies are based on my original count. Gladwin further states (1948: 34) "... I also wish to make it clear that I have not made, and have no intention of making, any changes in Haury's identifications...." However, Deadmans Black-on-red in the original list which dates from A.D. 775 to 1066 was changed to Tusayan Black-on-red with dates of 1050 to 1200 (Gladwin 1948: Fig. 9) for no apparent reason. I stand by the original identification.

All of the exotic pottery from Snaketown cannot be identified as established types, and all of those that can be typed have not been dated by tree-rings. However, those which have been typed and age-determined carry special value for us now. The task is to develop a time structure from the data they provide and to superimpose it upon the Hohokam remains.

For the best estimates of the time spans of dated types, Breternitz' useful study (1966) will be relied on. His longevity figures have been plotted as vertical bars on a time scale in the related pottery type column, dashed ends meaning that the beginning or the terminal dates are uncertain (Figure 16.3). The incidences of association with Hohokam materials of identified phase, appropriately coded for the year of recovery of the sample, are also shown. Whole vessels, usually in cremations, are particularly significant in this study.

Up to this point, the sources of error would be misidentification of a type, a grossly wrong temporal evaluation by Breternitz or erratic associations arising from disturbances. The numbers below a type time bar represent single or infrequent occurrences completely out of context compared with equivalent units appearing in multiple numbers within the time scale. An example is Deadmans Black-on-red, occurring in the Sweetwater and Snaketown Phases. As strays, they may be discounted as having any time value in dating the matrix in which they occurred.

Since we have become accustomed in our thinking to divide time into segments for taxonomic purposes, to provide chronological check points along a cultural continuum, the next task is to determine boundaries of sorts between phases. Because these interfaces are arbitrary and artificial, no two people are likely to establish them in the same way. To develop the borderlines for the Gila Butte, Santa Cruz, Sacaton, Soho, and Civano Phases, trade pottery coming into Snaketown is helpful.

It is significant that in the two operations at Snaketown only one certain Anasazi sherd was found in association with dominant Gila Butte Phase material, a statement worth reiterating in spite of Gladwin's different appraisal (1948: 85–86). This was a piece of Lino Black-on-gray with inclusive dates of A.D. 575 to 875 (Breternitz 1966: 82). Subsequently, Anasazi pottery occurs in substantial amounts, indicating that the trade channels were open. The inferences to be drawn from early scarcity are that (1) little contact existed between the two groups at this time, or (2) because the Anasazi were just coming into their own in the ceramic art, there was not only little pottery being made but little incentive to trade with the southern culture. Gila Butte Phase potters were already a long way down the ceramic road. Only one other type of equivalent age, representing the early efforts of the northern potters, Lino Gray, is represented by a single sherd in a Santa Cruz Phase context. Since production of several other northern types, namely, Kana-a Black-on-white, Floyd Black-on-gray, Deadmans Black-on-red, and others somewhat less certain, began in the 700s and were present in Santa Cruz Phase contexts, I favor using the A.D. 700 line as the border between the Gila Butte and Santa Cruz Phases.

Reciprocal evidence, the occurrence of Gila Butte Red-on-buff pottery away from home, is consistent with the foregoing conclusion. To be noted are six sherds of this type in the Forestdale Phase of the Bear Ruin, Forestdale Valley, (Haury 1940: 85–86) associated with ten tree-ring specimens giving a time span from about A.D. 575 to 700, although none of the specimens yielded true outside dates (Bannister, Gell, and Hannah 1966: Fig. 5, p. 11, 29–30). The main life span of the village appears to have been in the seventh century, although other evidence suggests that the occupation lasted into the first part of the eighth century. The circumstances permitting the arrival of Gila Butte Red-on-buff in

SOURCES	POTTERY TYPES				
TEST SECTION DESIGNATIONS	SACATON RED-ON-BUFF	SANTA CRUZ RED-ON-BUFF	GILA BUTTE RED-ON-BUFF	SNAKETOWN RED-ON-BUFF	SWEETWATER RED-ON-GRAY
F-5	I	771	I0	3	I
H-6		645	I0	2	
L-4	538		4	4	I
N-3	492		4	3	
O-6	839		24	6	
O-7	186		15	2	
P-5	577		20	I	
Q-4	255		22	2	
Q-6	562		21	3	I
U-9		297	2	5	
TOTAL	3450	1713	132	31	3

Fig. 16.4. Test sections in Trench 1, Mound 29, in which Kana-a Black-on-white occurred as an associate of Hohokam types, frequencies given.

the seventh century were present. The Crooked Ridge village at Point of Pines produced seven Gila Butte Red-on-buff sherds (Wheat 1954: 92–93) in the San Francisco Phase, but the site's position in time has not been clearly determined by tree-rings. Other elements indicate it to be coeval with the Forestdale Phase of the Bear Ruin. Another case of association is the Stove Canyon village at Point of Pines in a Stove Canyon Phase context with estimated dates of A.D. 600–800 and one tree-ring date of 677 (Neely 1974). Perhaps the most convincing of all associations is Lino Gray, White Mound Black-on-white (675–?900), and Gila Butte Red-on-buff in a site under investigation by Arizona State University on Walnut Creek, 15 km (9 mi) southeast of Young, Arizona (Dittert 1967: 1). Here also, the equivalency of Kana-a Black-on-white and Santa Cruz Red-on-buff has been demonstrated (Morris 1969a: 5; 1970: 54). While all of the foregoing instances are not as firm as might be desired, they nevertheless are better than none, and what we have supports an A.D. 700 break-point between the Gila Butte and Santa Cruz Phases.

Breternitz gives the dates for Mogollon Red-on-brown as 775 to about 950, with 875 to 925 as the time of greatest abundance (1966: 86–87). Recent restudy of the tree-ring material from the Mogollon and Harris villages suggests that these dates are too young (Bannister, Hannah, and Robinson 1970: 48–49, 63–64). An age range of about 625 to 850 (ibid.: 64) fits much better, considering also the post-850 dates now available for the Three Circle Phase which stratigraphically follows the San Francisco Phase for which Mogollon Red-on-brown is the main pottery component. The occurrences of this pottery in Snaketown were with Santa Cruz and Gila Butte Red-on-buff, diagnostics of the Santa Cruz and Gila Butte Phases respectively. The Mogollon Red-on-brown dates are thus helpful and significant in establishing the 550–900 interval for the two Hohokam phases concerned.

If further emphasis is needed to call attention to the earliness of the Hohokam pottery tradition, the presence of a red-on-buff sherd in the Bluff site, Forestdale valley, provides it (Haury and Sayles 1947: 57). While not specifically identifiable as to type, because it was badly weathered, the sherd was neither of the earliest or the latest types in the Hohokam series. Tree-ring dates for the site are early, with near outside dates ranging from A.D. 238–322 (Bannister, Gell, and Hannah 1966: 34).

The foregoing collateral information, taken with the direct evidence from Snaketown, tends to dispel the idea that there was any great lag between manufacture and the arrival of pottery in a foreign situation, that the associations reinforce each other by their consistency, and that we are indeed dealing with an advanced and early ceramic tradition. If, then, the Gila Butte-Santa Cruz Phase boundary is established as A.D. 700, the length of the Santa Cruz Phase can be put roughly in the order of 200 years. Gladwin's arguments (1937: 247–250) are still sound. But in examining Figure 16.3, one senses that had the Santa Cruz Phase extended much beyond 900, then such types as Red Mesa Black-on-white, Black Mesa Black-on-white, Reserve Black-on-white, and Mimbres Bold Face Black-on-white would have been associated as frequently with Santa Cruz Red-on-buff as with Sacaton Red-on-buff.

A beginning date for the Sacaton Phase of 900 appears to be justified by the relatively high association of Kana-a Black-on-white which passed out of style by about 950 and the frequencies of Black Mesa Black-on-white and Deadmans Black-on-red with life spans predominantly in the 900–1100 range. Mimbres Bold Face Black-on-white appears much stronger in Snaketown with Sacaton Phase materials than in earlier contexts, although the dates are about 775 to 927 (Breternitz 1966: 86). While this tends to pull Sacaton materials down a bit, it may also mean that Bold Face Black-on-white persisted longer than is now believed. The near absence of classic Mimbres Black-on-white is significant because it probably evolved mainly after Snaketown died as a village. On the basis of the total inventory of trade pottery, it does not appear that the terminal date for Snaketown can go much

beyond 1100. In support of this idea are the absences of pottery types that were in vogue in the twelfth century and were known to have been widely diffused, namely St. Johns Polychrome, Tularosa Black-on-white, and Tusayan Black-on-white, to mention but a few examples.

The intrusive redwares in Snaketown present one of the more difficult problems with respect to type identification and the pinning down of origins and ages. Polished and slipped redware potsherds were present in all phases, increasing in abundance from early to late, although the products did not improve technically as time passed. They show considerable variability as to color, finish, and paste characteristics, probably reflecting regional and age differences. Scarcity or absence of mica, a hard slip, and a high degree of polish distinguish them from the locally produced Vahki and Sacaton Reds, the Classic Period red and smudged types and the red pottery of the Pimas of historic times.

My conclusion, based on a number of specific identities, is that the principal donor was the Mogollon Culture in west central New Mexico and that what we have is San Francisco Red and variations thereof. The demonstrably long life of San Francisco Red (Haury 1936b: 28–31; Martin and others 1952: 492) is borne out by its omnipresence at Snaketown. A few specimens may have come from far south in Mexico, from southern Sonora (Guasave Red, Ekholm 1942: 74–77), or even from Papaguería (Valshni Red, Withers 1941). Except deep in Mexico, southern redwares appear to be late, after A.D. 1000. This fact, and Wasley's lack of success in identifying remains in northern and central Sonora with much time depth in his recent survey, further convinces me that the foreign red pottery in Snaketown came from the east.

In Figure 16.3, the associations of San Francisco Red by phases are given, closely following the pattern determined in the prior excavation (Gladwin and others 1937: 214). A few units, clearly something else than San Francisco Red, are shown as "Unidentified." The inference that emerges from the evidence is that Hohokam and Mogollon ceramics followed somewhat similar paths in type and time, both "fabrics" having been characterized by brown and red pottery from the start, the latter slipped and polished but without designs. It is probable that Vahki Red and San Francisco Red were derived from a common Mesoamerican base, and it now seems less likely that Vahki Red was a derivative of San Francisco Red as was claimed earlier (Gladwin and others 1937: 218). They may have entered the Southwest by different routes, San Francisco Red having moved north through the mountain corridor and Vahki Red having been introduced by the migratory Hohokam via a desertic route. The two types could be listed as "cousins," the oldest manifestations having been of comparable age. It is not surprising that there was interchange between these two pottery-making groups based on a shared inspiration for the craft.

A puzzling type of pottery which occurred in every phase, though in minuscule amounts, has been labeled Trincheras Purple-on-red (Sonora Red-on-brown, Gladwin and others 1937: 214). Trincheras Purple-on-red, indigenous to northern Sonora, is most commonly associated with Santa Cruz and Sacaton Red-on-buffs in Hohokam sites north of the Mexican border. The earlier Snaketown instances hint at a possible purple-on-red tradition, somewhere in northern Mexico, which had a long history but has gone unrecognized. Thomas Bowen, who has worked extensively in northwestern Mexico, tells me that his findings support this idea, that purple-on-red pottery is associated, though sparsely, with lithic assemblages reminiscent of the Cochise Culture. The alternative explanation is to regard the instances in the early phases as erratics. If that were so, one would have expected a much higher incidence of the pottery in late phases, less chronologically consistent associations in all early phases, and the same errant distribution of other traded types.

Pottery attributed to the Hohokam but made elsewhere than in the Gila Basin came mainly from the Tucson area. The types include Rillito, Rincon and Tanque Verde Red-on-brown (Fig. 12.10 j-1) and a rare Rincon Polychrome (Greenleaf 1975), and are useful chiefly in establishing phase equivalencies in the two areas.

The few fragments of pottery with sources in Mexico (Fig. 16.2 o) cannot be used in calendar-building because they are not specifically identifiable as to type and their ages are not known (Chap. 17).

In summary, the application of the tree-ring method of dating at Snaketown has been by indirect means, through using dated Anasazi, and in a few cases Mogollon, pottery types as the vehicle for determining the age of associated Hohokam materials. The repetitive nature of the data, as well as its internal consistency, convinces me that the method is valid. However, the system is effective only for the centuries following A.D. 500 which was near the beginning of Anasazi pottery production. To gain some notion of the time intervals for older Hohokam horizons, it is necessary to examine other methods of dating.

ARCHAEOMAGNETIC DATING

Throughout the work at Snaketown we were fortunate to have Robert L. DuBois, then of the University of Arizona, and his assistants work closely with us in gathering baked clay samples from the hearths of houses for archaeomagnetic analysis. The utility of this method is based on reestablishing the wanderings of the north magnetic pole by measuring clay samples whose ages have been established either by tree-rings, radiocarbon, or other means. It has a little of the chicken-or-the-egg syndrome about it, but fortunately, in the Southwest, enough dated materials have become available to permit the method to yield internally coherent and helpful results (Weaver 1967: 696–701).

DuBois' high precision-reading of ancient magnetic forces, noting both inclination and declination, makes possible the detection of which particular point the pole occupied in a vermicular path when two or three choices are possible because the magnetic alignment of a sample crosses all paths (Weaver 1967: 698–699). With the polar wandering established, DuBois states that his method achieves an accuracy within fifty years; in fact, the figures he has supplied show a plus or minus range averaging well below that.

The information DuBois has developed is tabulated and arranged chronologically in Figure 16.5 (all samples from Snaketown unless otherwise shown).

The question of the correctness of these data depends, of course, on the validity of the ages determined for the control samples from which the polar curve was built in the first place. Perhaps a measure of accuracy or closeness to reality is the degree of internal consistency in the results obtained from the Snaketown material and the concordance between the succession of archaeomagnetic dates and the stratigraphic sequence. On both counts there are no serious discrepancies.

LAB. NO.	SITE DESIGNATION	PHASE	ARCHAEO-MAGNETIC AGE A.D. YEARS	PRECISION AT 95% CONFIDENCE LEVEL/YEARS
49	ARIZ. U:13:22, ROOM 10	CIVANO	A.D. 1440	± 20
50	" ROOM 8	CIVANO	1410	± 27
53	" ROOM 7	CIVANO	1410	± 44
51	" ROOM 4	CIVANO	1350	± 17
41	HOUSE 1:5F	SACATON	1145	± 15
44	HOUSE 5:5F	SACATON	1120	± 23
42	HOUSE 4:11I	SACATON	1120	± 13
43	HOUSE 3:11I	SACATON	1105	± 29
48	HOUSE 9:5G	SACATON	1065	± 13
38	HOUSE 7:10G	SANTA CRUZ	965	± 30
52	HOUSE 19:10G	SNAKETOWN	770	± 24
56	HEARTH, BELOW CREM. FL.	GILA BUTTE OR LATER	765	± 15
57	HOUSE 2:9G	SANTA CRUZ	740	± 24
32	HOUSE 8:9F	GILA BUTTE	740	± 7
55	HOUSE 1:9I	GILA BUTTE	630	± 14
33	HOUSE 2:9E	SWEETWATER	330	± 37
31	HOUSE 1:7H	VAHKI[1]	1 B.C.	± 23
39	HOUSE 2:11F	VAHKI[2]	-200	± 41
34	HEARTH IN FLOOR FRAG. PIT 1:10F	VAHKI	-250	± 39
40	HOUSE 1:9F	VAHKI	-300	± 37

1. FIELD DETERMINATION WAS VAHKI PHASE BUT COULD BE ESTRELLA PHASE, CONSIDERING LOW INCIDENCE OF ESTRELLA RED-ON-GRAY POTTERY PRODUCED AT THIS TIME, THE MAIN DIAGNOSTIC.

2. REPRESENTS AN EARLY FLOOR REMNANT EXTENSIVELY DISTURBED BY LATER ACTIVITY; COULD NOT BE ASSIGNED TO PHASE BY ASSOCIATED CULTURAL REMAINS.

Fig. 16.5. List of archaeomagnetic dates.

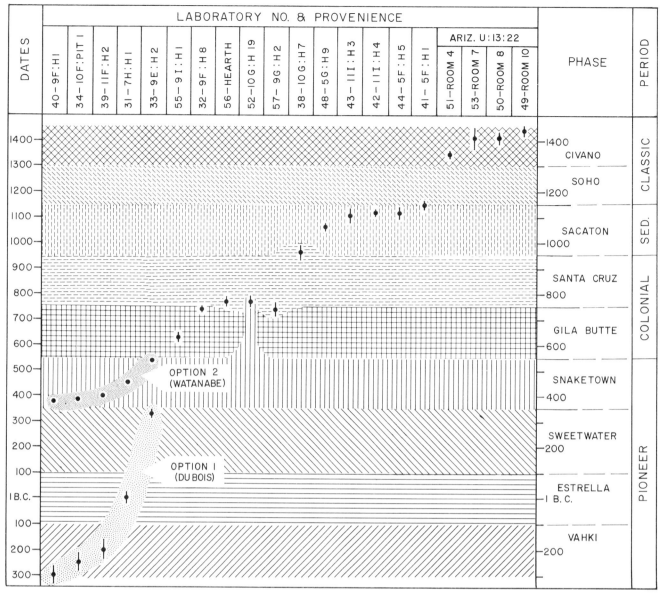

Fig. 16.6. Archaeomagnetic dates arranged in accordance with the cultural stratigraphy in Snaketown.

The data used for cross-correlation by DuBois are briefly summarized as follows: (1) for dates after A.D. 1100: Specimens from numerous sites including ruins in the Houck area, Pueblo Bonito, Cochiti, Tsia, Ft. Burgwin and Ft. Fillmore; (2) for dates in the A.D. 600–700 range: architectural remains in the Mesa Verde and Red Rock country, tree-ring dated; (3) for older horizons, including Vahki to Sweetwater Phases: two available options: (a) radiocarbon dated material from southern Arizona collected by Haynes and Agenbroad: Coyote Draw 1360±190, 2270 ± 150, 3210 ± 240, and Red Hill, 3300 (all dates B.P.); (b) radiocarbon date of Laboratory Specimen No. 31, dated by Naotune Watanabe in Japan, based on two assays averaged to A.D. 450±110 calculated from 1950. If this correlation is used it would place the ages of DuBois' samples as follows: Lab. No. 31, A.D. 450; Lab. No. 33, A.D. 535; Lab. No. 34, A.D. 385; Lab. No. 39, A.D. 400; Lab. No. 40, A.D. 375.

In Figure 16.6 the archaeomagnetic values have been plotted on a time scale, and both options available for pre-Sweetwater Phase associations are shown. Since both cannot be right, a choice of one must be made as being the more probable. My inclination is to favor the "long count," or Option 1, based on cross-correlated southern Arizona radiocarbon data, for the following reasons:

1. It provides a better fit for the rate of cultural change as seen in the post-A.D. 500 part of the sequence. Option 2 would require cultural development from Vahki through Estrella, Sweetwater to Snaketown Phases in the inordinately short time of a little less than 150 years.

2. Option 2 would bring the sequence within the time period when Anasazi trade pieces might have been expected, but these do not show up until the second phase after the Sweetwater, namely Gila Butte, and then only sparingly.

3. Option 1 can be reconciled with the older radiocarbon dates for the early phases, although some of the radiocarbon dates are consistent with Option 2 values. I favor the former alternative.

The glaring inconsistency of sample No. 52, dated at 770±24 from a presumed Snaketown Phase context, can best be explained as a possible misidentification of the house. Both fill and floor pottery samples contained Santa Cruz and Sacaton Red-on-buff mixed with a predominance of Snaketown Red-on-buff.

On the basis of the archaeomagnetic dates available and taking into account the above judgments, a trial calendar for the phases would look as follows, allowing for some rounding off of values:

Civano	1300–1450
Soho	1150–1300
Sacaton	950–1150
Santa Cruz	750–950
Gila Butte	550–750
Snaketown	350–550
Sweetwater	100–350
Estrella	100 B.C. to A.D. 100
	(Assuming that No. 31 is Estrella)
Vahki	300–100 B.C.

The reader must be cautioned that this is only a trial step in the development of a chronology for Snaketown. So far I see nothing basically inconsistent with the evidence of trade pottery and that of archaeomagnetic dating. The latter permits the extension of the sequence into earlier centuries.

Paleomagnetism has another potential use in archaeology which is only now under development. This involves measuring the changes in the intensity of the magnetic forces through time. Means have been devised to recover these values from fired clay, including bricks and pottery. In DuBois' kind of work, the precise orientation of a burned clay sample in the ground when collected is vital to successful analysis. For paleointensity studies the orientation is unimportant, which therefore opens a vast new area for investigation.

Although the objective in looking at west Mexican and Arizona pottery in the last 2,000 to 3,000 years was to demonstrate that the earth's magnetic intensity has changed through time in the Western hemisphere as had been shown to be the case for Eurasia (Bucha 1967: 12), the technique yields a fringe benefit that is of interest here. A comparison of 20 specimens, mostly pottery, from Western Mexico, arranged chronologically by stratigraphic, radiocarbon, and stylistic means, with 13 specimens from Arizona (10 measured from Snaketown), variously dated, produced strikingly similar average intensity ratio curves (Bucha, Taylor, Berger, and Haury 1969). This suggests a way of correlating ceramic chronologies from different areas. Once the basic curve has been established that registers the changes in geomagnetic intensity during the time pottery was produced in the Western Hemisphere, it might provide the mechanism for determining the age of a sample whose temporal position is not known. For the present, however, the parallelism between curves of the West Mexican and the Snaketown samples hints strongly that the sequences as established are probably correct even though there may be some hidden errors in the assigned time values.

RADIOCARBON DATING

The first radiocarbon date for Snaketown was determined in 1958 from carbonized cordage and textile contained in a crushed jar resting on the floor of House 8:6G (Crane and Griffin 1958: 1102, Sample No. M-324). The material was recovered in 1934–35, and at that time the house was assigned to the Sacaton Phase. Calculated from 1958, the expressed radiocarbon age of 700±250 B.P. states that the specimen could be as old as A.D. 1008 or as young as 1508. The older value is within the age bracket we have already been talking about for the Sacaton Phase as determined by other methods.

A total of 32 radiocarbon assays were made of carbonized organic and other materials gathered during 1964–65. Four laboratories participated: The University of Arizona Radiocarbon Dating Laboratory; Balcones Research Center, The University of Texas, Austin; Radiation Biology Laboratory, Smithsonian Institution; and Geochron Laboratories, Inc., Cambridge, Massachusetts. It would be an understatement to record that the results were in agreement with each other. The opposite is the case. The task of sorting out those dates that appear to be usable from those which are obviously incorrect and justify one's selections is not simple. It is unthinkable, however, that dates for Vahki Phase materials as far apart as 425±115 B.C. and A.D. 1010±120, or for the Sacaton Phase of A.D. 990±100 and 1820±110, can all be correct. These discrepancies force a choice. To do otherwise would land us in a chronological quagmire.

The reason or reasons for the disparities may be many, ranging from the selection, collection, and recording of samples in the field, to contamination, analytical errors in laboratory processing, and even to the assumptions on which isotope dating is based. It is not my intent to try to determine where the problem lies. However, I firmly believe that in making a qualitative judgment about the value of dates, an intimate knowledge of field problems and of

the nature of the cultural complex under study is fundamental to the decision. In addition, support from other and independent means of ordering cultural phenomena is available and may be used. Given these conditions, the qualitative test of a date reduces itself simply to its usefulness, to its "fit" within the total cultural frame and its value and harmony in relation to other data as an interpretive element. My dependence on certain radiocarbon dates and rejection of others will not be pleasing to everyone, but these judgments must be made. If the complications arising from the establishment of a chronology for Snaketown, involving only a few millennia, have taught us anything, it is that we are far from having reached a finite level of expertness in the art of dating as applied to archaeology.

Figure 16.7 itemizes the radiocarbon results obtained by several laboratories. The field catalog number determines the order of presentation. Cultural assignments were made in the field at the time of excavation if the association was clear, or, after laboratory work on related materials if the circumstances were unclear. Somewhat less than 50 percent of the samples were submitted for age determinations. It is evident that most of them were associated with the phases of the Pioneer Period. The thinking behind this was that efforts should be concentrated on the stratigraphically older materials because acceptable controls exist for the later horizons. Inasmuch as the University of Arizona's Radiocarbon Dating Laboratory produced most of the determinations under the guidance of Vance Haynes and Austin Long, I invited them to evaluate the results, with the warning, however, that I reserved the right to respond to their views.

RADIOCARBON DATING AT SNAKETOWN
by
C. Vance Haynes and Austin Long

Most of the samples analyzed were charcoal, three were burnt corn, and one was tufa (calcium carbonate). All charcoal and burnt corn samples were treated in the laboratory to remove extraneous organic and inorganic sources of carbon, and all dates are based on the Libby half-life 5,570 years and the NBS oxalic acid standard normalized to 1950 as the zero year. A "B.P." (before present) date thus refers to A.D. 1950 as "the present" and is converted to the A.D./B.C. scale by subtracting 1950 from it. If the result is positive, label it B.C., if negative, A.D.

Snaketown radiocarbon dates are shown in Figure 16.8 plotted in order from youngest to oldest within each cultural phase. The Texas dates are omitted. The solid horizontal lines represent the statistical precision of the C^{14} analysis only at the 67 percent confidence level (plus or minus one sigma).

Ferguson (1968, 1969) has cooperated with the Pennsylvania, La Jolla, and Arizona radiocarbon dating laboratories by providing dendrochronologically dated bristlecone pine wood specimens. Since the C^{14} content of a wood sample depends not only on the age but also on the C^{14} content of the atmosphere in which the wood grew, one can calculate the paleo-atmospheric C^{14} content from the C^{14} date on a sample of known age. Thus, a radiocarbon date younger than the tree ring date, which we assume to be equivalent to the calendar date, simply means that at that time the atmosphere had a relatively high C^{14} content. By analyzing enough wood of known calendar age, not only can we learn the nature and perhaps the cause of these interesting fluctuations, but, of more interest to archaeologists, we can develop a relationship enabling precise conversion of radiocarbon dates to calendar dates. These data are now available for the past seven and a half millennia. See Neustupny (1970) for a summary of the Nobel Symposium held on this topic, or for details see Olsson (1970).

The radiocarbon laboratories performing these analyses agree on the real but relatively minor deviations of radiocarbon ages from calendar (tree ring) ages. Figure 16.9 shows radiocarbon years plotted against tree ring years as well as the 45 degree line that would result if the two sets of values were equivalent. The curve has connected 50 year averages of all plotted data. This curve, including data of Suess (1965), Stuiver and Suess (1966), and Damon and others (1966 and personal communication), is essentially a calibration curve by which one may correct

FIELD NO.	LAB. NO.	PROVENIENCE	MATERIAL	YEARS B.P. UNCORRECTED ^{14}C DATE ON 5570 HALF-LIFE	UNCORRECTED CALENDAR ^{14}C DATE	TREE-RING CORR. DATE (AND RANGE OF POSSIBLE DATES)	CORRECTED CALENDAR DATE (WITH RANGE)	PHASE ASSIGNMENT
2	A-596[1]	STRAT. TEST 1:10D LEVEL 4	CHARCOAL FINE	950 1050±100 1150	900	1015 (930-1085)	935 (865-1020)	SWEETWATER-SNAKETOWN TRANSITION
4	A-598	CREMATORIUM 1:10D	CHARCOAL FINE	110 220±110 330	1730	290 (90-390)	1660 (1560-1760)	SACATON
5A	A-599	HOUSE 2:9E	BURNT CORN	800 920±120 1040	1030	1130 (1020-1290)	820 (660-930)	SWEETWATER
7	A-601	PIT 6:9E, FILL	CHARCOAL FINE	1240 1370±130 1500	580	1340 (1170-1490)	610 (460-780)	GILA BUTTE
9	A-603	HOUSE 1:10F	CHARCOAL	910 1010±100 1110	940	985 (875-1055)	965 (895-1075)	SACATON
10	A-604	HOUSE 1:10F	CHARCOAL	950 1050±100 1150	900	1015 (930-1085)	935 (865-1020)	SACATON
16	A-689	CREMATORIUM 1:8E	CHARCOAL	910 1030±120 1150	920	1100 (990-1195)	850 (755-960)	? VAHKI
17	A-1072	CREMATORIUM 1:8E	CHARCOAL	1540±70	410	1530 (1410-1600)	420 (350-540)	? EARLY PIONEER
25	A-731	MD. 40:11F, TIER 1, LEVEL 6	CHARCOAL FINE	1080 1240±160 1400	710	1210 (1040-1380)	740 (570-910)	SNAKETOWN
31A	A-734	HOUSE 1:15E	CHARCOAL	1240 1340±100 1440	610	1315 (1165-1395)	645 (555-785)	SNAKETOWN
41	A-735	MD. 40:11F, TIER 12, LEVEL 9	CHARCOAL FINE	1130 1240±110 1350	710	1195 (1065-1325)	755 (625-885)	EARLY PIONEER
46	A-741-1	PIT 33:11F, LEVEL 3	CHARCOAL FINE	1320 1430±110 1540	520	1390 (1310-1530)	560 (420-640)	GILA BUTTE-SNAKETOWN TRANSITION
52	A-873	ROASTING PIT 1:11 I	CHARCOAL	1670 1890±220 2110	60	1900 (1660-2110)	50 (160 B.C.-A.D. 290)	VAHKI
57	A-742	TEST 4:10G, LEVEL 6	CHARCOAL FINE	1420 1510±90 1600	440	1500 (1385-1590)	450 (360-565)	ESTRELLA
58	A-743	PIT 42:11F, TEST 1, LEVELS 3-4-5	CHARCOAL FINE	1390 1640±250 1890	310	1640 (1360-1890)	310 (60-590)	ESTRELLA
59	A-771	HOUSE 12:11F, SUB-FLOOR PIT	CHARCOAL FINE	1510 1810±300 2110	140	1800 (1500-2100)	150 (150 B.C.-A.D. 450)	VAHKI-ESTRELLA TRANSITION
61	A-786	HOUSE 1:5G, SUB-FLOOR TEST, LEVEL 3	CHARCOAL FINE	1270 1350±80 1430	600	1320 (1290-1390)	630 (560-660)	ESTRELLA
63	A-788	HOUSE 1:7H	BURNT CORN	780 900±120 1020	1050	1095 (1000-1290)	855 (660-950)	? VAHKI
65	A-814	PIT 42:11F, TEST 3, LEVELS 7-8	CHARCOAL FINE	1450 1540±90 1630	410	1530 (1400-1630)	420 (320-550)	ESTRELLA
66	A-815	HOUSE 2:6G, SUB-FLOOR TEST, LEVELS 3-4	CHARCOAL FINE	1030 1150±120 1270	800	1095 (1000-1290)	855 (660-950)	VAHKI
68	A-816	HOUSE 2:6G, SUB-FLOOR TEST, LEVELS 5-6	CHARCOAL FINE	1600 1710±110 1820	240	1680 (1590-1860)	270 (90-360)	VAHKI
69	A-817	HEARTH, UNDER CREMA-TORY FLOOR, MD. 38	CHARCOAL	1130 1310±180 1490	640	1305 (1065-1475)	645 (475-885)	GILA BUTTE
72	A-818	PIT 42:11F, TEST 2, LEVEL 8	CHARCOAL FINE	1280 1400±120 1520	550	1370 (1290-1510)	580 (440-660)	VAHKI
	TX-888[2]	GILA RIVER FLOOD PLAIN	CHARCOAL	530±80	1420			
	TX-891	CANAL LINING	MOSTLY CaCO$_3$	1580±60	370			CIVANO
3	SI-187[3]	STRAT. TEST 1:10D, LEVEL 6	CHARCOAL FINE	1060 1130±70 1200	820	1070 (1030-1150)	880 (800-920)	SWEETWATER-SNAKETOWN TRANSITION
5	SI-188	HOUSE 2:9E	BURNT CORN	920 990±70 1060	960	1220 (1130-1310)	730 (640-820)	SWEETWATER
6	SI-189	HOUSE 2:9E	CHARCOAL	1190 1260±70 1330	700	1280 (1120-1310)	670 (640-830)	SWEETWATER
8	SI-190	PIT 6:9E, FILL	CHARCOAL FINE	1130 1200±70 1270	750	1145 (1065-1285)	805 (665-885)	GILA BUTTE
35	GX-328[4]	PIT 14:11F, TIER 2 LEVEL 5	CHARCOAL FINE	1475 1580±105 1685	370			SWEETWATER
42	GX-329	TEST 1:10F, LEVELS 3-4-5 UNDER HOUSE 5	CHARCOAL FINE	2265 2375±110 2485	425 B.C.			VAHKI

(1) University of Arizona Radiocarbon Dating Laboratory.
(2) Balcones Research Center, The University of Texas at Austin. Courtesy of E. Mott Davis and Samuel Valastro. TX-888 collected by Vance Haynes; TX-891 by E.W. Haury.
(3) Smithsonian Institution, Radiation Biology Laboratory. Long and Mielke, 1967:375. Tree-ring corrected by Vance Haynes.
(4) Geochron Laboratories, Inc. Krueger and Weeks, 1966:150-151.
(5) All dates A.D. unless otherwise specified.

Fig. 16.7. Inventory of radiocarbon dates from Snaketown.

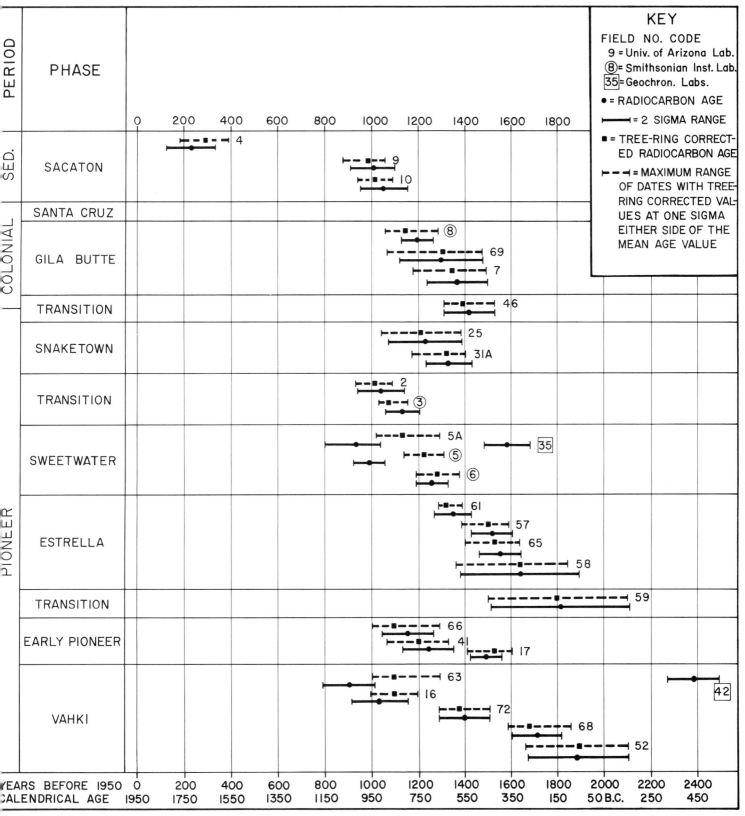

Fig. 16.8. Snaketown radiocarbon dates and their tree-ring corrected values.

radiocarbon dates to their tree ring (presumably calendar) year equivalent. We thus corrected the Snaketown dates. Original dates are published by Haynes et al (1971). From Figure 16.9 it is obvious that some radiocarbon values have more than one possible tree ring value. For each radiocarbon date, we graphically determined every possible tree ring corrected date and its maximum and minimum 67% confidence limits, then plotted them in dashed horizontal lines in Figure 16.8.

The result of the corrections from the C^{14} fluctuation is that all of the Snaketown dates average about 50 years younger, and the minimum possible ages (at the 67% confidence level) are extended by as much as 120 years.

Corn samples are a special case. Corn kernel analyses can be improved by assuming an average heavy isotopic enrichment with respect to charcoal equivalent to 250 years (Lowdon 1969). Thus, adding 250 years to all corn dates, they fall into line with charcoal (for example, Sweetwater Phase). The dashed horizontal lines on Figure 16.8 include this isotopic correction for samples numbered 5, 5A, and 63.

Adjusted as above, these radiocarbon dates represent the closest possible approximations to calendar ages. Repeated agreement between the Smithsonian and Arizona laboratories and the consistency within a given phase virtually eliminate the possibility of laboratory error and chemical contamination as explanations for unaccountable results. Three dates plotted in Figure 16.8 are clearly outside the main group of their respective phases (Field Nos. 4, 35, and 42), and we therefore choose to disregard them. Only one of these is an Arizona number. We ran

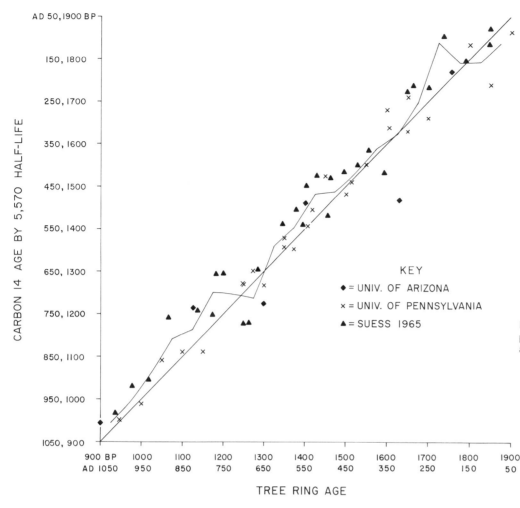

Fig. 16.9. Plot of Snaketown dated samples comparing radiocarbon and tree-ring ages.

KEY

♦ = UNIV. OF ARIZONA

× = UNIV. OF PENNSYLVANIA

▲ = SUESS 1965

all Arizona analyses over a period of three years, during which time we were also analyzing Ferguson's tree ring dated samples, and our results have been consistent with other precise radiocarbon laboratories' results. Thus, in Snaketown we have in effect a tight calibration with calendar dates.

The data coherence within each phase (exception: Vahki) and the agreement of charcoal dates with adjusted corn dates both suggest that most samples submitted indeed represent their associated cultural phases. Corn is especially significant because it cannot have a tree growth or driftwood age bias, and as it usually occupies a ceramic container, has clear association, and is not usually stratigraphically mobile.

Non-radiometric dating methods such as paleomagnetic intensity and obsidian hydration are calibrated either directly by radiocarbon dates or by tree ring dates analogously to our corrected C^{14} dates. Therefore all four dating methods discussed are interrelated in such a way that to question one is to question them all. A possible explanation of the discrepancies between the radiocarbon dating and archaeological dating is that some of the charcoal samples were not contemporary with the event they are assumed to represent; that is, either old wood was used or younger charcoal intruded older cultural levels.

The adjusted radiocarbon dates suggest that the time range of occupation of Snaketown extends about from the time of Christ to A.D. 1200. It also appears that certain cultural phases are less sequential and more contemporaneous than previously assumed. From Figure 16.8, two, possibly three, overlapping sequences are apparent. The least obvious sequence extends from Vahki through Early Pioneer, about A.D. 1 to 800. The most clearcut one is even more apparent after deleting the Geochron Labs' No. 329 and adjusting the corn dates (Nos. 5 and 5a) 250 years older; the sequence then clearly extends from the Early Pioneer-Estrella Transition Phase through the Sweetwater-Snaketown Transition Phase, about A.D. 150 to 900. The final sequence begins during the Snaketown-Gila Butte Transition and extends through the Sacaton Phase, about A.D. 700 to 850.

*   *   *

The Haynes-Long conclusions may now be summed up with a few comments:

1. The inclusive dates for the occupation of Snaketown are given as A.D. 1 to 1200. While the terminal date is acceptable, the founding date appears to be too conservative. It ignores the older archaeomagnetic readings and the correlative radiocarbon date of 425 B.C. (Geochron Lab. No. 329). In terms of ancillary cultural information endemic to the Snaketown sequence, namely, the need for time to accommodate the evolving stages of the Hohokam, a somewhat earlier date would provide a more logical fit.

2. The principal problem emerges from the statement ''... that certain cultural phases are less sequential and more contemporaneous than previously assumed.'' Implied is the phenomenon of overlapping, or, the simultaneous production of pottery types and other attributes which heretofore have been arranged in sequential order on the basis of stratigraphic controls. My disbelief in this phenomenon has been stated elsewhere (Chap. 12). To express the problem in another way: Accepting the radiocarbon dates for the phases at face value and giving them as mean averages, tree-ring corrected, we would have, Sacaton, 950; Santa Cruz, no dates available; Gila Butte, 685; Snaketown, 690; Sweetwater, 650; Estrella, 450; Vahki, 555. The A.D. 950 date for Sacaton agrees with other data, though it would mark the early part of the horizon. The problem lies in the Sweetwater-to-Gila Butte steps, encompassing 40 years with the Snaketown Phase out of sequence. Also, the Vahki and Estrella values are not only reversed but much too young. Added to the others the total sequence from Vahki to Gila Butte, inclusive, would be no more than 250 years, a totally unlikely figure denied by the physical evidence in the ground and by other lines of inference as well. However, Haynes and Long do see justification for a beginning date near the time of Christ.

If the radiocarbon dates from all laboratories are now arranged by chronological values in descending order within each phase (Fig. 16.10), the inconsistencies and overlap are further accentuated. This strengthens the case for having to make value judgments about the dates, the alternatives being to ignore them all or to accept them all and give up any idea that the archaeological record makes any temporal sense. Both alternatives must be rejected out of hand.

Since a high order of validity is placed on the phase succession as determined by stratigraphy, a sequence confirmed by initial alpha-recoil track measurements, on the reliability of the dates established for phases by tree-ring dated pottery and a reasonable confidence in the coherent archaeomagnetic ages, I will use these factors as the bases for judging the radiocarbon dates. Additionally, it must be repeated, I am influenced by the belief that Hohokam cultural evolvement was slow and steady. Evidence of differing rates of maturing, such as spurts and lapses, have not been demonstrated.

The tenth century values for the Sacaton Phase are fully acceptable, although the 1660 date is obviously in error. Happily, the Santa Cruz Phase, while not radiocarbon-dated, is well placed by associated intrusive pottery and by the appearance of Santa Cruz Red-on-buff as an intrusive in northern tree-ring dated sites, and a beginning date for the horizon of A.D. 700 seems reasonable. This then means that any radiocarbon dates after 700 derived from pre-Santa Cruz Phase cultural materials are in question. Only A-601 at 610 and the value of A-817 at 645 fit the projected age of the Gila Butte Phase. The Snaketown Phase dates are not acceptable, although the Snaketown-Gila Butte transitional date of 560 (A-741-1) is reasonable. The Sweetwater-Snaketown Phase transitional values are inconsistent with the stratigraphic record. For the Sweetwater Phase only sample GX-328, dating 370, would appear to fit the probable schedule. The determinations for the Estrella Phase, clustering earlier than any other group of dates, also appear to be too young. The Estrella-Vahki transitional value of 150 (A-771) is not out of "register." But for the Vahki Phase we once again find ourselves in trouble. The range is 425 B.C. to A.D. 855, and strangely enough three dates fall at mid-ninth century, an impossible place in the time scale because the Santa Cruz stage of development was then in full swing. Dates of 50, 270, 420, and 580 are equally difficult to reconcile as reflective of the founding time of Snaketown. One eyes, therefore, the 425 B.C. value (GX-329) as a possible legitimate contender for representing the true situation. It should be noted once again that the identification of cultural levels in the early Pioneer Period is difficult because of the low production of diagnostic pottery. This factor may account in part for the high variability in Vahki and Estrella Phase dates.

Support for the 425 ± 110 B.C. value for the Vahki Phase comes strongly from three archaeomagnetic assays of 300, 250, and 200 B.C. (Lab. Nos. 40, 34, and 39). A fourth date of 1 B.C. (No. 31) is also within the probable range. In sum, it is my opinion that there is justification for viewing the oldest occupational horizon at Snaketown as being before the time of Christ and that an initial age of 300 B.C., give or take 100 years, is supported by the best supplementary data that can now be offered. Other views would mean rejecting archaeomagnetic dating as having no value and seeing Hohokam evolution moving at a faster clip than was likely, particularly now that equally long and even longer periods of time are being determined for the pre-Classic stages in Mexico.

I see no clear way of pinning down the Estrella Phase other than by extrapolation, and a date somewhere within the range of the time of Christ is indicated. For the Sweetwater Phase, two fourth-century dates are in close agreement, GX-328 at 370 and archaeomagnetic sample No. 33 at 330.

If we now organize those dates from the various dating systems which are compatible sequentially, only a small residue of dates remains to use as a guide in developing the Hohokam time

PERIOD	PHASE	LABORATORY CODE & NO.	YEARS A.D., CORRECTED
SED.	SACATON	A-598	1660
		A-603	965
		A-604	935
COLONIAL	SANTA CRUZ		NO DATES AVAILABLE
	GILA BUTTE	SI-190	805
		A-817	645
		A-601	610
PIONEER	TRANSITIONAL	A-741-1	560
	SNAKETOWN	A-731	740
		A-734	645
	TRANSITIONAL	A-596	935
		SI-187	880
	SWEETWATER	A-599	820
		SI-188	730
		SI-189	670
		GX-328	370★
	ESTRELLA	A-786	630
		A-742	450
		A-814	420
		A-743	310
	TRANSITIONAL	A-771	150
	EARLY PIONEER	A-735	755
	VAHKI	A-689	850
		A-815	855
		A-818	580
		A-1072	420
		A-816	270
		A-873	50
		A-788	855
		GX-329	425 B.C.★

★ - NOT TREE-RING CORRECTED.

Fig. 16.10. Radiocarbon dates (sigma omitted) arranged according to phase on the basis of associated cultural materials.

structure. These are given in Figure 16.11. It seems reasonably certain that we are dealing with a substantial span of time. To assume that the older dates are in error and the younger dates are correct, that is, placing the Vahki Phase near or after the time of Christ, would mean discrediting archaeomagnetic dating, reducing phases to insupportably short intervals, require the dropping of the older radiocarbon values, raise questions about the usefulness of associated trade pottery, and disregard basic theory about cultural evolution. Either way the process of juggling will be open to attack. It should be clear that my stance toward dating is that all methods may have something to say; identification of the harmonious elements and the elimination of discordant values, however, are necessary and that has been attempted.

According to my reconstruction, from the presumed time of founding of Snaketown near 300 B.C., the Hohokam chronicle

| PERIOD | PHASE | TREE-RING DATES | | ARCHAEO-MAGNETISM | RADIO-CARBON |
		DIRECT	INDIRECT		
CLASSIC	CIVANO			1440 1410 (2) 1350	
	SOHO				
SED.	SACATON	? 1180's	900-1100	1145 1120 (2) 1105 1065	965 935 1250 ★
COLONIAL	SANTA CRUZ		700-900	965 740	
	GILA BUTTE			765 740 630	645 610 560
PIONEER	SNAKETOWN				
	SWEETWATER			330	370
	ESTRELLA			I B.C.	
	VAHKI			200 B.C. 250 " 300 "	425 B.C.

★ -MICHIGAN M-324

Fig. 16.11. Selected dates from various methods of dating which are compatible with a calculated timetable of Hohokam development.

continued unbroken through the centuries to the present moment, the Pima and the Papago Indians being the inheritors of an ancient tradition. The oft-stated terminal date of about A.D. 1450 is arbitrary and misleading. It is based on the fact that the archaeological record fades at this point with the abandonment of the large communities such as Casa Grande and Los Muertos. It does not mean that the people disappeared, though connecting their traces with modern survivors has not been easy. The question now arises as to how to subdivide the above noted 1,750 years in prehistory into manageable sub-units, how to determine phase lengths as a basis for measuring other aspects of the society as, for example, the speed of culture change.

Though it pleased no one, including its creators, the arbitrary 200-year span assigned to phases in 1937 (Gladwin and others) was the best judgment that could be made at that time. The truth of the matter is that even today we still do not have reliable methods for determining phase intervals, exemplified by the fact that as trial chronologies are made, they often differ significantly, depending on the mood and the depth of knowledge of the moment. So, keeping this problem in mind, and to satisfy those who feel the need of operating within precise dates, I submit the chronology given in Table 16.1.

While it seems pointless to further belabor the issue of the reliability of radiocarbon dates for Snaketown, I do wish to note that the disparities must be attributed to variables that are not identifiable at the present time. Until an explanation is found I am

TABLE 16.1

Suggested Chronology of Periods and Phases

Period	Phase	Approximate Time
Classic	Civano Soho	A.D. 1450–1300 1300–1100
Sedentary	Sacaton	1100–900
Colonial	Santa Cruz Gila Butte	900–700 700–550
Pioneer	Snaketown Sweetwater Estrella Vahki	550–350 350–200 200–A.D. 1 A.D. 1–300 B.C.

forced to place my faith in the stratigraphic and typological records and their compatibility with what we know about cultural development in the Southwest generally.

OBSIDIAN HYDRATION DATING

Obsidian was a rare mineral at Snaketown. For this reason the sample studied for hydration dating purposes by Clement W. Meighan and L. J. Foote of the Obsidian Hydration Laboratory, University of California, Los Angeles, numbered only 18 pieces, 10 of which were surface finds. Although the latter were measured, they have little value because of the uncertain association and are therefore not included in the tabulation.

Admittedly, obsidian hydration dating is still under development, but Meighan and colleagues (Meighan, Foote, and Aiello 1968) have evolved an age table for West Mexican obsidian which promises to yield useful results in the Southwest as well. The Snaketown specimens were investigated to test comparability of the hydration phenomenon in the two areas.

Meighan points out (letter, 17 October 1969) that two assumptions must be made before the West Mexican hydration rate can be applied to Snaketown: (1) Hohokam obsidian is chemically like Mexican obsidian. This has not been determined, but it was observed that one Snaketown specimen (No. 6-2) is green obsidian which appears not to occur naturally outside of Mexico and is known to have been widely traded. (2) The average annual temperature at Snaketown does not differ much from that in West Mexico, given as 20-25° centigrade. The mean annual air temperature for Phoenix is 20.8° centigrade, probably close to what it is at Snaketown 35 km (22 mi) to the southeast in a similar setting. The figures suggest that assumption 2 may be correct.

The West Mexican hydration rate applied to the Snaketown obsidian produced the results given in Figure 16.12. The derived

SPEC. NO.	PROVENIENCE	CULTURAL ASSOCIATION	HYDRATION (CORRECTED μ)	HYDRATION DATES	DATES DET. BY OTHER MEANS
1-1	MOUND 39 COL. 2, LEV. 1	MIXED SANTA CRUZ-SACATON ★	4.4	A.D. 740-897	A.D. 700-1100
1-2	"	"	4.3	767-897	"
1-3	"	"	4.4	740-897	"
2	MOUND 39 COL. 3, LEV. 3	"	4.3	767-897	"
3-1	MOUND 40 TEST I, LEV. 1	GILA BUTTE	5.7	382-554	550-700
3-2	"	"	NO VISIBLE HYDRATION		
4	PIT 14:11F TEST I, LEV. 2	SANTA CRUZ	4.8	630-774	700-900
5	HOUSE 7:5F FLOOR	SACATON	4.1	822-946	900-1100

★ - THESE DEPOSITS RESULTED FROM PHYSICAL TRANSFER OF REFUSE FROM THE TWO PHASES CONCERNED IN THE BUILDING OF A PLATFORM MOUND.

Fig. 16.12. Tabulation of obsidian hydration study results conducted by Meighan and Foote.

dates manifest consistency in relation to the stratigraphic record, and they follow a pattern, although tending to be early by about 100 years. Considering the smallness of the sample and the fact that the dating effort was exploratory, one cannot take the results too seriously (Meighan 1970). However, because the determinations are clearly within the range of dates established by other means, the technique holds bright prospects for the future.

ALPHA-RECOIL TRACK DATING

A technique enabling archaeologists to determine the firing date of pottery vessels is presently under development by Charles R. McGimsey III and Ervan Garrison of the Arkansas Archaeological Survey and the University of Arkansas, Fayetteville, and Otto H. Zinke of the Department of Physics of the University of Arkansas. Said to offer a 3,000-fold increase in sensitivity over the developed fission track dating method, the alpha-recoil track system is based on the following hypothesis, as stated by Garrison, who has carried out the basic research. "Nuclear-recoil tracks caused by alpha decay of uranium and thorium trace elements are observable on mica platelets often occurring as inclusions in prehistoric pottery. Heating mica to temperatures sufficient to fire pottery anneals out all previously caused alpha-recoil events. Thus, since alpha-recoil tracks appear at an essentially constant rate over archaeological time, the number of tracks observed on mica inclusions in pottery clay is directly proportional to the time which has elapsed since the vessel was fired."

A set of Hohokam sherds from Snaketown and an immediately adjacent site were submitted as suitable test material because the stratigraphic order was known and the elapsed time was believed to be long enough to permit the detection of differences in the densities of alpha-recoil tracks. They have graciously permitted my use of their present data as expressed in Figure 16.13 with the admonition, however, that these results are of the most tentative and preliminary nature. It is important to understand that the year-values supplied for the various types were my best estimates and that they were useful only in suggesting the probable amount of time involved and the chronological order of the potsherds examined.

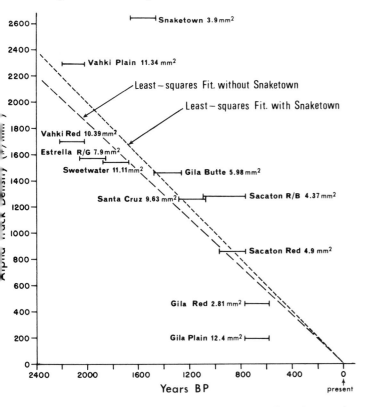

Fig. 16.13. Measured surface density of alpha-recoil tracks on mica inclusions in Snaketown potsherds.

The linear curves on Figure 16.13 are least-squares fits with and without the Snaketown point. Experience indicated that insufficient data were obtained for confidence in the Snaketown point. The curves extrapolate to 19 and 10 years B.P. respectively.

For the present, the results indicate an increase in track density through time of the expected magnitude and linearity and with only the Gila Plain representing a serious anomaly. It is interesting that the slope of the curve in terms of tracks per mm² and time measured before present is approximately 1 (one). For example, approximately 2,000 tracks per mm² would be expected on mica inclusions from pottery fired 2,000 years ago.

Full application of the alpha-recoil track technique awaits further research and testing to establish counting criteria. Meanwhile, McGimsey has prepared the following statement in which calendrical values for Snaketown are suggested (see also Garrison, McGimsey, and Zinke; in press). The tentative nature of these results must be borne in mind.

While absolute solving of the dating equation is possible, it is costly, requires equipment not normally available to archaeologists, and the results have a wide variance. On the other hand, an empirical test of the hypothesis is possible. One end of the dating curve is zero years ago and since the tracks will increase as essentially a straight line function over archaeological periods of time, determination of a single point on the line will enable the archaeologist to determine the slope of the dating line, thus permitting the dating of other samples.

This test was applied to the Snaketown sample using the Gila Butte date of A.D. 650 and the average counts of the Gila Butte sherds as the basis for establishing the rate or slope of the line. Calculation of dates for the other samples using the rate so derived yielded results which conform consistently with the results obtained by other dating methods. Vahki: 270 B.C. ± 270, and 130 B.C. ± 115; Estrella: 10 B.C. ± 65, and A.D. 150 ± 180; Sweetwater: A.D. 310 ± 180, and A.D. 810 ± 195 (this was a Gila Plain sherd whose provenience could be suspect); Snaketown: A.D. 400 ± 190, and A.D. 440 ± 170; Gila Butte: A.D. 610 ± 45, and A.D. 690 ± 105 (remember the counts on these sherds were used to establish the rate, so close conformance to A.D. 650 is to be expected); Santa Cruz: A.D. 800 ± 40, and A.D. 940 ± 105; Sacaton: A.D. 820 ± 185, A.D. 1080 ± 110, and A.D. 1170 ± 190; Civano: A.D. 1510 ± 6, A.D. 1550 ± 140, and A.D. 1643 ± 25.

The Civano and some of the Sacaton values appear too late, but this may simply reflect that on late samples with consequent lower counts the area counted must be higher for consistent accuracy. These highly interesting initial results are being further tested on samples from other archaeological areas.

Alpha-recoil track findings are significant on two counts: (1) they independently confirm the correctness of the stratigraphic sequence in Snaketown as determined by excavation, and (2) the derived year values, though tentative, are broadly consistent with those provided by several other dating methods.

OTHER DATING APPROACHES

Spectra of plant pollens are finding increased use in archaeology, primarily as a means of evaluating environmental conditions and changes in them. Implicit in environmental fluctuations is the passage of time, but the application of year values must come from other means. Bohrer worked diligently to collect pollen by sampling profile after profile in our excavations. Her efforts produced less than hoped for results because the physical conditions in Snaketown were detrimental to pollen preservation (Bohrer 1970: 426–428). Apart from the chronological aspect, the loss also extends to our inability to learn more of the details of the natural conditions under which the Hohokam lived. Changes favorable or less favorable to agricultural pursuits have been suggested (Bohrer 1971), and while these reflect the passage of time, they do not constitute a useful way of measuring time.

Aside from the subjective feeling I have, derived from working so intensely with Hohokam remains for so long, that the unfolding of their culture was a slow process, little different in fact from the tempo of development of the older societies of Mesoamerica, one is inclined to look for supporting evidence to which no year values are attached. The gross amount of refuse, the unbelievable amount of pottery, the wide-scale disturbances of the subsoil in the excavation of pits, wells, and other holes, the large array of houses, complete ones and especially those detectable only by remnants, and the complicated tangle of canals resulting from overbuilding and realigning the new over the old systems, hint at more rather than less time. Genetic changes in economic plants need not take much time, but Cutler's conclusion that the early corn was replaced by a more evolved type (Appendix 4) carries with it also the suggestion of some time depth.

A holistic view of the problem, the putting together of all lines of evidence—and many more are available now than we had in 1934–35—convinces me that the Hohokam tenure of the arid Southwestern valleys must be reckoned on the basis of a "long count," close to the calendrical values I have indicated by picking a tortuous and obstacle-ridden route through a maze of conflicting data.

PART SEVEN

THE HOHOKAM AND MESOAMERICA

17. Transmission of Culture

Efforts to link the pre-Columbian societies in the Southwest with those of Mesoamerica have been made for many decades and by many authors. One feature characterizes all of these attempts, namely, a belief that a connection did exist, but the documentation of the idea is wanting in the kind of details that encourages its full acceptance. Parallels in culture elements are demonstrable, but absolute identities are more difficult to establish. Exact sources, dispersal routes, and the mechanics and time of diffusion are usually the subjects of speculation. The excavations at Snaketown in 1934–35 and again those reported on herein have quickened the interest in this important interregional problem. Even though some new insights have been gained, the picture is far from clear. Thin knowledge of the vast territory between the Mesoamerican highlands and the Southwest remains a major hurdle. Although geography is a fixed dimension with describable qualities, we know too little of the fluid cultural events in the part of the continent concerned to permit a step-by-step reconstruction.

Helpful and significant studies are on record, however, to provide a few hints of what happened. They all point in the same direction, namely, that there was a wide dispersion of Mesoamerican elements (Haury 1945b) and living patterns and that these thinned out going northward as functions of distance and the reduction in the intensity of contacts. Lister's distributional study (1955) is the best source for references to 1951. Following that, a few key contributions may be identified: Jennings 1956, Johnson 1958, Di Peso 1968, Meighan and Foote 1968, and Mountjoy 1970. Kelley's review (1966) of Mesoamerican and Southwestern connections stands as the best and most perceptive analysis of the problem to date and much of what he says is fundamental to my remarks. It is encouraging that Mexican scholars are beginning to pay attention to the northern frontiers of the Mesoamerican high cultures (Braniff 1966).

Unfortunately, the archaeologist tends to think of his materials as cultural isolates, a state of mind which discourages relating people in geographically adjacent areas in a graded fashion. This unrealistic view has been overcome by ethnologists, notably Beals (1932) and Kirchhoff (1954) who, in their respective ways, see the living patterns of contiguous groups changing gradually as one passes from one tribe to another. The condition of today may well be the model that establishes how the events of prehistory should be viewed.

The inferences and conclusions drawn in connection with the Hohokam and their relationship with the cultures to the south are based on the following premises:

1. That Mesoamerican societies reached a high level of cultural achievement one to two millennia before the rise of the higher societies in the Southwest.
2. That radiations from the southern cultural reservoir passed northward over a long period of time, over several routes and by various means, shaping in differing degrees the Southwestern groups.
3. That those cultural attributes which are indicative of connections occur earlier in Mesoamerica than in the Southwest.
4. That the data now available do not permit the certain establishment of connections between any Southwestern culture and any specific culture center in Mesoamerica, or precisely when and by what route and mechanism cultural transmissions were made.

At this point in the discussion it is appropriate to introduce a chart which relates, in an over-simplified way, the Hohokam sequence to several southern chronologies (Fig. 17.1). The attempt will be far from satisfactory for those who have an intimate knowledge of the areas included, but it is intended to do no more than serve the single purpose of broadly equating the Hohokam and Mexico. In the Valley of Mexico and particularly at Teotihuacan, the record is long and complex and better known than are the sequences for other parts of Mexico. The Pre-Classic manifestations there make it clear that high cultural development existed long enough ago to qualify the region as a donor area. Chupícuaro stands by itself. It is included to show Jiménez Moreno's thinking as to where it fits in the Mesoamerican time scale. Kelley informs me (letter September 28, 1971) that some Mesoamericanists now suggest that Chupícuaro was contemporary with Cuanalan (Ticoman-Cuicuilco). In part, at least, Chupícuaro equates with Pioneer Hohokam. The feeling is strong that it may have been one of the reservoirs of culture from which stimuli emanated and that it holds the clues to many of the events in the north. The Durango-Zacatecas and west coast sequences are also included because they represent intermediate regions through which southern elements must have been transmitted. A puzzling situation arises from the Chihuahua (Casas Grandes) sequence because the late resplendent cultural development there had such a short antecedent history.

If the Pre-Classic, Classic, and Post-Classic designations for Mexican cultures are equated with the Hohokam, the Pre-Classic-Classic interface would come at the end of the Pioneer Period, and the Colonial Period equates with the Classic horizon of Mexico. This disagrees with the correlation proposed by Kelley (1960: 71), but it comes closer to fitting the spirit of the Mesoamerican taxonomy. The reader is cautioned, however, against confusing the Hohokam Classic with the Mexican Classic because the bases for each label are sharply different. Viewed broadly, the suggested correlation provides adequate time for Mexican people and influences to reach the Southwest and generate the Hohokam.

If the two kinds of Mesoamerican elements that reached the Hohokam are categorized, two classes may be recognized: (1) direct imports and (2) transmitted ideas that led to the local production of items as copies of southern prototypes, and the adoption of practices. In the former group copper bells, pyrite incrusted plaques, and macaws stand out; in the latter, the ball court, platform mounds, and the role of incense may be mentioned.

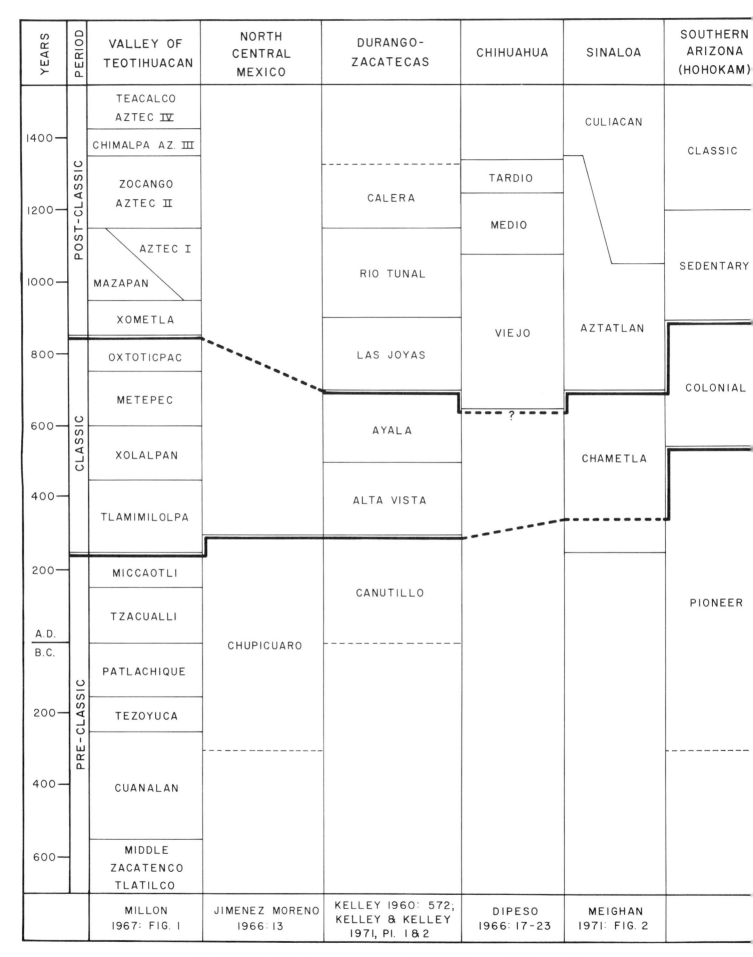

Fig. 17.1. The Hohokam sequence correlated with several Mesoamerican
chronologies. Greatly simplified.

Among the distant imports that have not been adequately discussed up to now are eleven potsherds which were separated from the vast Snaketown pottery sample on the basis of form, surface treatment, and color. These were seen in whole or in part by Meighan, Foote, Kelley, Lister, and Braniff. The following opinions, not attributed to the author, underscore the difficulty in working with material that has low diagnostic value. All agreed that the specimens came from Mexico but also that specific types and times were impossible to pin down. One judgment held that the pieces could easily be fitted into the Amapa, or west Mexican series.

A red-on-brown fragment (A-26,187), highly polished after painting, suggests a highland source, or derivation from the Cohumatlan (Michoacan) tradition or from the Totoate area of Jalisco. This specimen, together with another red-on-brown fragment (A-31,437), is also suggestive of Coyotlatelco. The difficulty of identification arises from the fact that red-on-brown pottery was produced almost everywhere in western Mexico (Lister 1955: 106). The first of these two specimens was associated with Santa Cruz Phase materials and the second from a mixed Santa Cruz-Sacaton Phase context. Only superficial resemblances between Snaketown units and the pottery of Zacatecas and Durango were noted. Perhaps the most diagnostic fragment is the leg of a tripod vessel (Fig. 16.2o) of redware, heavily fire-clouded (A-25,569), found on a Sacaton Phase house floor. This vessel form is said not to be common in western Mexico (Lister 1955: 22), but it fits well in the shape categories of Guanajuato (Braniff 1966). A highly polished red sherd, inside and out (A-27,572), is said to be of highland origin after A.D. 500. Its association was the Gila Butte Phase. The remaining fragments are mainly brownware, and except for the fact that they are Mexican in origin, not much else can be said about them.

The time range of this small collection of fragments spans the Colonial and Sedentary Periods, or about A.D.550–1100, not inconsistent with what is believed to be the time range of similar pottery types in Mexico.

Why so little southern pottery found its way into Arizona is most logically explained by the fact that it had little chance to survive up to 1,000 km of human back-packing. The absence of "show-case" pieces, excepting possibly the single leg of a tripod vessel, suggests that the specimens we do have were accessories, the containers, for the goods being traded. In this respect the Mexican collection differs markedly from the trade pottery that came in from the Anasazi.

The two points that deserve special emphasis in connection with the Mexican intrusive pottery are that its presence further reinforces the mounting evidence of southern contacts and that the points of origin appear to be far to the south, in Guanajuato, Michoacan, Jalisco and Nayarit. This leads to the question as to whether or not the Rio Grande de Santiago played a role in funneling trade from the Mexican highlands toward the coast where it turned north in the vicinity of Tepic, the Aztatlán of old (Sauer and Brand 1932). The fact that an alternate route of the Inter-American Highway (No. 15) follows a coastal path from Tepic to Guaymas whence it turns directly north to Tucson and Phoenix, the old Hohokam heartland, may represent a modern analogue of what happened in antiquity. Parallels in art styles between the pottery of the Chalchihuites Culture of Durango and Zacatecas and the Hohokam (Kelley and Kelley 1971; Johnson 1958) suggest the existence of an eastern route of contact as well; but as of now, the coastal path appears to have been more active and direct.

It is not my intention to review all of the possible ways in which the cultural resources of one area could be transmitted to another. Beyond the proposed initial migration which brought the Hohokam into the Southwest, various ways of maintaining contact could have been followed. Trade goods from Mexico serve notice that routes of contact were open. Some of these artifacts may have passed from hand to hand, or tribe to tribe,

Fig. 17.2. Burden carriers: (a) Gila Butte Red-on-buff, Snaketown; (b) Codex Mendocino and (c, e) Codex Fejérváry-Mayer (after Piña Chan 1959); (d) from a Sacaton Red-on-buff plate in the possession of L. G. Lewis, Tucson.

eventually landing among the Hohokam. But it seems far more likely that the contacts were direct, between a trader as a long distance traveler, and the receiving people. Support for this thought comes from the depiction of the burden carrier on pottery. He is consistently shown with a back-pack, a basket or a bag, supported by a tumpline to the head which is being steadied by one hand while the other hand clutches a helping stick with a crook on the upper end (Fig. 17.2a).

A similar subject, though rendered in greater detail, appears in some of the codices (Fig. 17.2b,c). At Snaketown, the earliest rendition of this figure is about A.D. 550–600. Piña Chan (1959: 921) observes that commercialism was born in Mesoamerica in the first millennium B.C. and that eventually routes extended to the Pacific and south to Guatemala and Honduras. We may assume that these lines of exchange extended north as well. It may be further assumed that lanes of contact operated considerably before the earliest drawings of the burden carrier.

A variation of the latter, taken from a Sacaton Red-on-buff plate, shows the shoulder yoke in use with the cargo suspended from each end (Fig. 17.2d). In what is probably the left hand the figure grasps a bow and arrows, the weapons an itinerant merchant would most likely have with him. The carrying yoke appears not to be known archaeologically in the Southwest other than in picture form. The Pimas did not use it and it evidently was not known among other Southwestern tribes. In Mexico the device is still frequently seen in mountain villages. The curious pincer-like projection in front of the featureless face makes one wonder whether this could have been inspired by the elaborate headdresses with which the traders are often shown in the codices (Fig. 17.2e).

We have heard much about the *pochtecas*, the highly organized merchantmen who were an important segment of

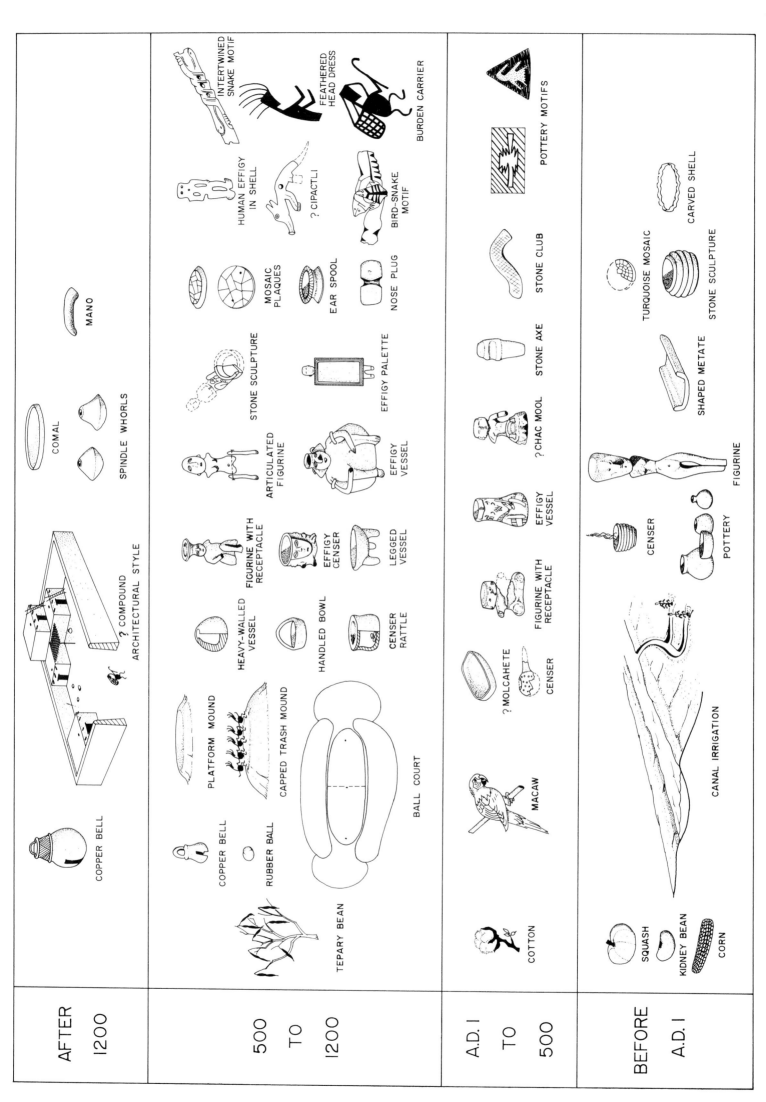

Fig. 17.3. The Mesoamerican impact on the Hohokam seen through the arrival of cultural elements during four time periods.

Aztec society (Romerovargas Iturbide 1959: 745–748) and how their Toltec-Chichimecan forerunners exploited the northern borderlands (Di Peso 1968). Ferdon has suggested (1955) the *pochtecas* may have had far-reaching effects cross-culturally in the Southwest. A broad view of the problem of Mesoamerican influences suggests that contacts were maintained throughout the life of Snaketown, but that the intensity of contacts was low at all times, though perhaps variable. The small number of actual identified imports, not only at Snaketown but from everywhere in the Southwest, suggests this. If all the Mexican goods recovered from precontact sites are brought together, aggregating several hundred bells of copper, a handful of mirror backs, and some miscellaneous materials, the combined weight would not exceed a few kilograms, barely enough to make it worth a trader's time and effort to pack it northward over an arduous trail. It is probably true that much of what was imported was bulky and light in weight, notably feathers and textiles, and such materials would not have survived; but there is no proof of this. The evidence we do have does not support the idea of large-scale importations by the *pochtecas*. I fail to see that the formalized trading system which was so effective in Mesoamerica reached the Southwest with any appreciable force. As far as the Hohokam were concerned, we appear to be dealing with a casual and informal exchange arrangement. The *pochteca* institution, in its most active form, was a derivative of Aztec imperialistic expansion, too late to be felt in Snaketown, and the impact on Classic Period Hohokam was only nominal.

Instead of making a highly detailed comparative analysis of elements in the Hohokam world which I regard as Mesoamerican in origin, the theme is simplified and developed visually (Fig. 17.3). The problem is viewed from the standpoint of four time periods which is about as close as it is possible to come now in assigning dates. The attributes are drawn from the record as preserved in Snaketown and after A.D. 1200, from sites of the Classic Period.

Before A.D. 1. At this time a constellation of traits was introduced by the migrant Hohokam into the Southwest where the complex as a whole, or even the integral parts of it, were without local prototypes. A new cultural orientation and a new way of life were represented. The elements can only be attributed to a southern source where they were not only earlier but also more developed. It is impossible to show visually the inferred mental attitudes that were a part of the new outlook related to ceremonialism and sociopolitical aspects of the society, such as sacrifice, the power of incense, incantations, and political and social arrangements related to an agricultural economy. The contrast between what was native and what was introduced is emphasized by the arrival of new crops, new ways to grow and process them, and new arts and crafts.

The impact of the southerners' arrival was undoubtedly felt soon by the indigenous people of the Cochise, or Desert, Culture, for in a relatively short time they began to change their ways to match those of their new neighbors. More important to our considerations now, however, was the fact that the contacts with the south did not cease. A flow of ideas and traits continued through the centuries.

A.D. 1 to 500. During this segment of time, the Hohokam were slowly shaping a way of life that became peculiarly their own. They were helped incrementally by a steady flow of new ideas and materials. A stone copy of a probable throwing club, a Chac Mool-like figure, the handled incense burner, and the macaw would make it appear that ceremonial gear and doubtless ceremonialism were on the increase. At the same time art styles in pottery began to appear, including the basic step of pottery painting. Kelley suggests that this important advance was inspired by the Chupícuaro complex or a northern outpost thereof in Jalisco or Zacatecas (1966: 102). Guanajuato should also be added as a likely source (Braniff 1966). The human and bird effigy jars were established, and, indeed, they may have

been included in the first wave of elements since they were being produced in a variety of forms in the Valley of Mexico before the time of Christ (Porter 1953, Pls. 8, 9; Piña Chan 1958). The important economic fiber, cotton, is first detected at this time, but it, too, may have been an element in the original constellation of cultural items.

A.D. 500 to 1200. This appears to have been the time when the Hohokam received the most massive infusions out of the south. Cutler and Blake (Appendix 4) recognize A.D. 700 as about the moment when the kinds of corn grown by the Hohokam increased markedly. The adoption of the platform mound and the ball court stand preeminently. In both cases the architectural vestiges are only the tangible evidence for a complex of ideas, activities, and behavior patterns associated with them. Furthermore, these may have been the main "vehicles" on which lesser and perhaps unrelated ideas and things rode in. Other than macaws, the first trade goods appear: copper bells, mosaic mirrors, and a few pieces of pottery. Personal ornaments as, for example, earplugs, pottery shapes, and art themes become increasingly more reflective of the Mesoamerican idiom. Additionally, the burden carrier, the plumed headdress, *cipactli* the mythical monster, snake symbolism, and certainly textile techniques reinforce the idea that the Hohokam were indeed an abridged Mesoamerican society.

The flood of southern traits is at the heart of the concept that the Hohokam migration took place at this time, as enunciated by Gladwin and Di Peso. My preference, however, is to view the period as one of great activity in the south and high receptivity of influences in the north, a state of affairs conditioned by some 800 years of exposure beforehand. The "national" character of the Hohokam had already long been in the molding process before this Mesoamerican flare took place.

Jiménez Moreno (1966: 52) places the end of Teotihuacan at about A.D. 650, and he believes that a wide dispersion of Mesoamerican elements followed. The time is not inconsistent with what we observe as a new thrust from the south among the Hohokam, and it may be that they were the inheritors of this major event. The alleged control of the northern frontier at this time through strongholds and garrisons established by southern politically potent states (Palerm and Wolf 1957: 2–6) may also have been a significant factor in the spread of culture.

Before leaving this segment of time, the importance of the pyrite-encrusted mirror needs to be reviewed. As a dating vehicle it probably is the most meaningful of all intrusive items from Mexico. The typological order of appearance of the plaques in Snaketown matches that established at Kaminaljuyu (Kidder, Jennings, and Shook 1946: 126–133) in Guatemala and also in western Mexico (Furst, personal communication). The chronological age probably is close to being the same in all areas, though a slight time lag for the mirrors in the peripheries is probable. Furst informs me that he considers the mirrors to be shamanistic devices because many were found together in a shaft grave in a manner suggesting they had been attached to the clothing of one person. In Snaketown they occurred most often with cremations and caches, and a number of fragments were recovered in the crematory mound in Block 6G. They almost always appeared in multiples and generally with other classes of objects of a probable esoteric nature. Furst's shamanic hypothesis seems to have some support in these circumstances. The Huichol shamans of west Mexico make extensive use of modern mirrors to put themselves in a trance so they can "see the world."

After A.D. 1200. The strength of Mesoamerican influences faded after 1200, possibly correlated with the crumbling of the Toltecs, the increasing pressure exerted by the Chichimecs, and in spite of the rising supremacy of the Aztecs characterized by their empire-building successes. The strongly organized trading system of the Aztecs had little or no impact on the Hohokam because their culture had already climaxed and was in the process of losing its vitality. But from a northern *pochteca* outpost, Casas Grandes in Chihuahua (Di Peso 1968), contacts with the late Anasazi were maintained. A weak lane of contact along the west coast did exist and through it the Hohokam picked up the *comal,* or baking griddle of clay and, inferentially, a new way of preparing maize, the *tortilla;* the specially made pottery spindle whorl; possibly the compound as an architectural form although this is debatable; the *mano* with drooping ends and some other elements of minor importance. By the time of the Spanish Conquest the cultural conditions in both the donor and receiver areas had totally changed and a fascinating era of acculturation had drawn to a close.

As a footnote to this moment in Mesoamerican-Southwestern connections, a speculation about the *trincheras* of northwestern Mexico and southern Arizona is in order. The classic example of terracing a hillside exists in northern Sonora near the small town of Las Trincheras (Sauer and Brand 1931: 91–92). The same manner of modifying hills is seen repeatedly elsewhere in Sonora and in Papaguería (Hoover 1941). Without attempting to argue for or against the many ideas that have been expressed explaining the existence of *trincheras,* whether for agriculture, domestic home sites, defensive measures, and others, it seems worth considering the possibility that they represent a northern modification of the terraced pyramid, using a natural hill as a substitute for a totally artificial structure. The Schroeder site in Durango (Kelley 1971: 788) exemplifies the terracing of a natural hill for sacred uses. The Sonora and Arizona instances, generally datable to after A.D. 1200, appear to have primarily served secular functions.

With so much Mesoamerican cultural substance evident in surviving Hohokam vestiges, it is perplexing that some of the more explicit details did not show up. One might have expected exact parallels in the fine arts, in painting, ceramics, sculpture, musical instruments, in representations of the dance and religious or god-connected symbolism; but they do not exist or have not been recognized. No doubt this is due in part to a fundamental difference in the approach to art as related to societal complexity in the two areas: an enormous array of subject matter, shown in great detail, springing from intricate religious and political systems and an advanced technology in Mesoamerica, and a limited art repertoire, broadly topical subjects, portrayed with little or no detail befitting a simple social organization and technology in the arid southwest. From Culiacan in Sinaloa southward, Mexican cultures had so much more than the Hohokam ever knew. What was it that let some attributes go northward and prevented others from doing so? The filtering system must have been a combination of lessening of cultural values and meanings as a function of distance and a decreasing ability, or even inclination, to maintain complex art and mental forms by societies that were increasingly more peasant-like the farther they were removed from the Mesoamerican hearth. I do not believe that environment was a significant factor in generating the difference.

Specifically, such symbols as speech scrolls, name glyphs, calendrical values, ornamental staffs, personalized headdresses, and a penchant for story-telling in art did not survive the passage. Instead, we think we see only faint echoes of some of these as, for example, the possible survival of the glyph and calendrical values of Mexico in the emphasis on the use of myriad small repeated design elements among the Hohokam. Granted that Mesoamerica was the donor of cultural fundamentals and that the lifeline continued to feed vitality northward, it must also be recognized that the Hohokam reshaped the elements inherited from a polished and hierarchic social system to make them compatible with their own, which, at best, was weakly class-structured and feebly hierarchical.

PART EIGHT

CONCLUDING THOUGHTS

18. General Issues

Throughout these pages attention has been given to drawing inferences and interpretations from topical data and to separate phenomena that are coincidental from those that appear to be consequential. The need to summarize the findings in detail is thereby eliminated, permitting this final section to be devoted to the more general issues related to the Hohokam. The goals of the project outlined in the proposal to the National Science Foundation, stated succinctly, were as follows: (1) to re-examine the basis for the Hohokam chronology and by employing new dating tools to develop a more accurate correlation with the Christian calendar than was possible in the 1930s; (2) to focus on Hohokam origins and attempt to link the Hohokam with the Cochise Culture, correlates of this problem being the emergence of settled village living, the development of agriculture, and the effects on the Hohokam of arid-land environmental factors; (3) on the basis of expected new data, to reassess the Mesoamerican influences on the Hohokam.

How well these stated goals were achieved will be up to the reader to decide. Because archaeological data can almost never be used to reach a finite conclusion, and because a given set of information can be interpreted in two ways by two investigators, I am the first to admit that the results stated herein are subject to refinements as fresh information is gathered. For the moment I must express what I think we have learned.

Two points about the Snaketown chronology need reiteration. First, the order of phases as determined in 1934–35 was upheld. I am not concerned here with differences of opinion as to our use of the phase concept or as to where the division between two phases has been drawn. What does matter is the nature of the evolutionary thread that was identified. This is known reasonably well even though all the related factors which determined Hohokam destiny are not well understood. The orderly nature, magnitude, and direction of the development can be described, and the basis for the succession of events is what appears to be an unimpeachable stratigraphic record.

Second, the importance of year-values in making all manner of archaeological assessments needs no justification. For Snaketown, to know when Hohokam evolution took place in relation to the Christian calendar is essential if measurements are to be made of cultural longevity, vitality, and its place in a regional and indeed, continental, context. By using the stratigraphic record, and somewhat subjective estimates of the speed of cultural unfolding drawn from well-dated segments of their history, and by merging the best data available derived from tree-ring dated intrusive pottery, from radiocarbon analyses, from archaeomagnetic and alpha-recoil track studies, an initial value of 300 B.C. has been derived. I will not be overly disturbed by opposition to this value, provided that it departs only nominally from that figure and that the objections voiced adequately explain possible errors in the data at hand, nor will I be too worried over juggling of phase durations. What does count is the proposition that Hohokam prehistory had a respectable longevity and that a 300 B.C. beginning date, and A.D. 1450 date of the phasing-out from a stage of cultural supremacy but not a terminal date for the culture, are acceptable. These anchor points in the Christian calendar are justifiable on the basis of the data at hand, and I subscribe to them.

The second expressed goal dealt with Hohokam origins, and this demanded a sharper delineation of the Vahki Phase than was available before the studies were begun. Progress in this direction was responsible for a 180-degree switch from my former position. Instead of thinking of the San Pedro Stage of the Cochise Culture as the seed-bed for Mesoamerican ideas out of which the Hohokam grew, I now see them as immigrants out of the south, as an abridged Mesoamerican society in search of a new home. But more of that later.

As for the third goal, the answer already has been anticipated by the statement above. The Hohokam were, indeed, a frontier, spatially displaced Mesoamerican society. As such, they were unique in the Southwest, not only in terms of their culture history but also in the complexion of their way of life.

Disregarding the order set by the enumeration of goals above, several topics demand fuller articulation than they have received up to this point.

HOHOKAM ORIGINS

From the moment the first Hohokam are recognized, the cluster of elements that constitute the Vahki Phase, one sees a cultural phenomenon without precedent in the Southwest's long record of human occupancy: the presence of a constellation of attributes for which there are no local antecedents. What appears to be a sudden burst of cultural vitality, of traces of a totally different way of life, is most logically explained as the result of a newly arrived people. While other explanations may be adduced, as, for example, cultural mutation, or diffusion, I elect the migration concept as the soundest at this time. Let us examine in review what the Hohokam had.

The most significant characteristics were a developed water-managing capability, coupled with a tillage technology, and a roster of domesticated plants probably including one or more races of maize new to the Southwest, cotton and the old stand-bys, beans and squash. Well-digging was known. Domestic houses were exceptionally large, squarish, with sunken floors, an architectural form not yet identified in Mexico. Extended family living is suggested by the house size, but more importantly the building type implies established village living, itself probably an imported idea. Disposal of the dead was by cremation. Among the crafts, pottery-making was well established. Although none of it was painted, the gray-brown and red-slipped types echo the early Mexican ceramic fabric. Technically, the art was a long way beyond the inventive stages of pottery production. Other traits included a human clay figurine complex, the intensive use of marine shells for jewelry, including the carving of the same, sculpturing of stone, the full-troughed exteriorly shaped metate as a sophisticated replacement of the indigenous and long-lived basin grinding stone, incised bone tubes, and turquoise mosaics. Skills in the textile arts may be inferred, though we know they had twilled mats. Social and political leadership had to be adequate to guide the development of waterworks, but at best, it probably was no more complex than that of a simple peasant society.

These elements constitute a block of traits large enough and complex enough to identify the bearers as a cultural unit. Synchroneity of appearance and absence of local prototypes argue that the elements moved as a cluster and were not the result of normal stimulus diffusion. Even though we cannot at this time meet all the conditions for a migration as spelled out by Rouse (1958), this mechanism best explains the presence in southern Arizona of a totally new people and a new pattern of living, and it requires fewer assumptions than does any other explanation.

The idea that the Hohokam were a migratory people, coming out of Mexico into what is now Arizona, is not new. Gladwin proposed this in 1948 (232) and categorically supported the view again in 1957 (81–94). Sauer implied as much (1954), and further endorsement came from Ferdon (1955: 29), Jennings (1956: 92–93), Di Peso (1956: 259–64, 562–64), and Schroeder (1960; 1965: 302). This is a formidably held position, and I seem to have been the only one who believed otherwise. My early opinion was that the late Cochise Gatherers, people of the San Pedro Stage, having been inoculated with a host of new cultural factors flowing from Mesoamerica, became the Hohokam with the adoption of the same, leading to the eventual efficient exploitation of their arid environment. This view I now reject in favor of the migration hypothesis, putting me in the Gladwin-Di Peso camp. However, there is a fundamental and important difference in our positions which I do not wish to have misunderstood.

In Di Peso's reconstruction, the Hohokam arrived after A.D. 900, in Gladwin's about A.D. 700, after which the irrigation system was put into use. Gladwin recognizes nothing as introductory to Colonial Hohokam, which leads to the query as to what is to be done with all the pre-Colonial remains known to have existed at Snaketown. They cannot be ignored. Di Peso, on the other hand, does recognize cultural time depth, but the pre-Colonial remains are put into a different category, the Ootam. In simple terms, I see the pre-Colonial evidences as directly and lineally antecedent to the Colonial Period and therefore prefer to call the whole continuum Hohokam. My reconstruction proposes that a group of people came from Mexico probably as early as 300 B.C. and that after having "settled-in" the society enjoyed a long local development, though nudged to greater cultural heights from time to time by infusions from Mesoamerica.

It is impossible at this time to pin down a spot in Mexico which might have been the Hohokam base before they drifted northward. The fact is we may be expecting too much to think that "the place" can ever be found. Yet, a few speculations should be stated.

Because initial cultural elements were already considerably diluted in form and quantity over truly southern complexes, the idea that the ancient Hohokam lived somewhere in the Mesoamerican frontier, perhaps in an arid part of it, is not unreasonable. Here they could have matured their skills in

controlling water. The time would have been in the Pre-Classic horizon of Mesoamerica and, in terms of my dating scheme, well before 300 B.C. Northern Michoacan, Guanajuato, Aguascalientes, and southern Zacatecas might be likely places of origin. Another possible staging area was coastal, in the valleys of rivers emptying into the Pacific or the Gulf of California from Sinaloa north. The modern farming developments here under irrigation amply demonstrate the productive capability of the land, but the present reclamation may have gone a long way toward eliminating the old record of the area's use.

It would be most helpful to find tracks of the Hohokam in far northwestern Mexico. To identify such evanescent spoors is probably too much to hope for. Before his untimely death, Wasley spent nearly a year in Sonora searching for possible Hohokam antecedents or traces of them; but his work, along with that of all others in northwestern Mexico, failed to produce any clues. The time depth for the remains found is too shallow, and the cultural vestiges do not match. In Sinaloa, the San Blas complex (Mountjoy 1970) provides vague similarities with Pioneer Hohokam, and these intensify on going south into Michoacan. The cultural horizons old enough to qualify as donor sources must lie well to the south in western Mexico.

A logical question rising from the migration concept concerns the route by which the Hohokam went north. Here, the trade routes which have already been touched on, may show the way. The coastal path appears to be the most likely one. Support for this approach comes from such collateral lines of evidence as, for example, maize, for the early Hohokam variety most likely came out of western Mexico, and the shell industry, already well established in the oldest Hohokam horizon, suggests maritime connections.

As for the mode of transit, foot travel over a land route seems the only acceptable way in the light of present knowledge. A waterborne diffusion has been postulated (Gritzner 1966: 134), but the arguments for this view, including the alleged possession by the Hohokam of reed boats, are not upheld by the data.

While food gathering was still important to the immigrants, their main thrust was food production. They already had traveled far down the path toward developing a stable and efficient agricultural economy. But the territory into which they moved was itself the domain of the San Pedro people of the Cochise complex who were dependent mainly, if not wholly, on the plant and animal resources supplied by nature. The mode of life that characterized the newly arrived Hohokam was foreign to the indigenes.

The intrusion of a strange people into a territory already occupied holds the ingredients for conflict. But no evidence of a confrontation exists. The probable explanation for the apparent smooth integration resides in the fact that two different parts of the arid environment were being exploited, as determined by the two vastly different economies and related technologies used by the food collectors on the one hand and by the producers on the other. The hilly submountain environment suited the former, the low-lying, broad, fertile valleys with living streams attracted the latter. The conflict for territory was thus reduced to a minimum, and for several centuries the two economies coexisted. The contact, however, was not without its effects, for the advantages of the introduced lifeway were not lost on the resident foragers. Within a few centuries, the San Pedro Cochise themselves became sedents by adopting the customs and crafts of their new neighbors. This transition is recognized in the oldest villages within the era of pottery-making lying to the southeast of the Hohokam heartland.

Since the Hohokam are characterized from the start as a

water-managing people, the assumption follows that this capability was long established and widely practiced in Mexico. Until recently we had no knowledge that this was the case. The old view that the Hohokam may have originated canal irrigation, now clearly in error, was based on this void in the data.

Studies in the Tehuacan Valley by MacNeish (1964) and in the Oaxaca Valley (Neely 1967; Flannery, Kirkby, Kirkby, and Williams 1967) have demonstrated that water control practices were well known in the first millennium B.C. in those parts of Mexico. On the basis of this information, it may be assumed that the art of irrigating crops was also practiced in other parts of Mexico wherever irrigation was possible and necessary for survival. The wide and early dispersal of this economic pattern over central Mexico may have extended it as well into the northern frontier of Mesoamerica, if not even into the southern part of the Greater Southwest. In short, hydraulic engineering was already a part of the way of life in Mexico before the river valleys of the arid Southwest were settled by farmers. In the outward expansion from the nuclear area, the factors of time, distance, and reduced intimacy of contact with the higher culture centers worked together to dilute the Mesoamerican complexion of the immigrant populations; as a consequence, specific comparisons with southern groups cannot be made. But what happened from this time on, in bare outline, has been noted in the previous section of this report.

As already indicated, the place of origin of the Hohokam in Mexico cannot be pinpointed. Inferentially, the movement into the Southwest may have been linked with an apparent expansion of Mesoamerican groups in upper Pre-Classic times, roughly between 600 and 100 B.C. (Braniff 1966). This was a time of considerable activity, of what might be called the "urban revolution." The Chupícuaro culture was exerting its influence widely (Jiménez Moreno 1966: 25) and it may be that its effects were felt as far away as the Southwest.

Although several options have been suggested with respect to routes of passage, the corridor between the western face of the Sierra Madre Occidental and the coast seems the most likely. Hayden has proposed one interesting hypothesis (1970) which recognizes a number of factors, including linguistic distributions, that focus attention on the western route.

Once in arid Arizona, settling-in took place along the Gila and Salt Rivers after these streams debouched from the mountains on the open desert plains. Snaketown was not the only place where the Hohokam settled, for there are hints of their early presence in other communities as well. But Snaketown stands as the only place now known where the evidence has enough substance and volume to reflect the existence of a sizable community and to show that it was there continuously for a long time.

As a part of the process of growing roots, the transplanted people began the inevitable development of a life style that befitted the setting. This required a merging, mostly undirected, of their responses to the environment, of the ways in which they saw themselves meeting the needs of survival, and of their own "Weltanshauung." Out of these thrusts the Hohokam character was shaped. To identify the distinguishing qualities is not an easy task. In spite of the risks in drawing on a modern ethnological model to explain the old, I nevertheless believe that Piman culture at the time of white contact was a watered-down version of the Hohokam system. In general terms they had an elected head chief, elected village leaders, community councils, patrilocality, a number of social groups which exerted no strong restraints on marriage or other social customs. Religion was mainly person-oriented, and there were few community rituals. Public opinion was a strong force in determining personal relationships, and life and property were secure. Sensitivity toward group welfare, and a feeling of in-

dividual responsibility, particularly in agricultural pursuits, were probably more important than was strongly developed political leadership.

While one cannot be certain that the Hohokam operated along these lines, it does seem likely that they were a benign primitive democracy rather than a theocracy or a strong politically oriented society. We may assume that the Hohokam were more ritually directed and their technology was more developed than was the case among the Pima. Social and economic factors probably superseded all others in determining how the Hohokam reacted toward each other. The absence of formality in the village layout and, most of all, the apparent disregard for house and trash mound placement with respect to ball court and platform mound, emphasize the secularity of the Hohokam way of life. Rules of residence and lines of descent were weak.

On the whole, the Hohokam impress one as having been a conservative people, not given to extravagancies, held in check, as it were, by unseen forces. Possessed of technological mastery over the desert environment, they had to fear only the momentary disruption of their life style by nature's imbalances, of too much water or too little, or by occasional upsets caused by people or pests. They preferred to live at arm's length from their tribal neighbors and from each other. In some ways the Hohokam were people with sharp contradictions. On the one hand they engineered large and efficient irrigation canals, but their homes were drab huts, the floors depressed into the desert, and roofs dirt covered. Although their agricultural products were plentiful most of the time, they were hungry for protein and ate anything that would supply it.

They were especially gifted in the carving of stone and shell, but the quality of their pottery and the wielding of the paintbrush showed that the potter's skill lagged. While they observed rituals at death and probably at harvest time, they seem not to have symbolized the elements of their pantheon by art forms or honored them with monumental shrines and buildings as material measures of the depth of their religious emotions. Yet we know that drama in ritual was recognized by group participation, by the dance step, by the use of feathered headdresses, flutes, and rattles, hand-held and attached to the body, and the burning of incense.

In our terms, a touch of the flamboyant shines through. They had a certain flare for luxury goods, notably in shell jewelry. The range of types and the quantity were clearly linked with closeness to the source of raw materials and their manufacturing skills, culminating in the etching of shell. But nothing that has survived for us to examine hints at humor; there are no smiles on figurines, no postures that portray the lighter activities. While the painting of life forms on pottery appears deadly serious, decorative more than declarative, only now and again the stance of an animal or a human figure conveys a whimsical note.

What were the restraints? What kept them throttled? Or, if we are misreading the signs, how else did they convey the idea that they were a happy people? We do not know. It may be that a basically gaunt land had an impact upon them, and it may also be that, being far removed from the sources of cultural energy, Mexico, they did little more than was consistent with the conditions imposed or permitted by their environment.

I cannot conclude this review of Hohokam origins without reference to an interesting and scholarly study of 13 Pima and Papago myths for historical evidence of Hohokam identity (Bahr 1971). Bahr holds that myths involving the Hohokam talk about a death and rebirth ideology which may be attributed to several influences, the most likely of which was Central Mexico. Above all, he demonstrates that drawing history out of myths is complex and uncertain.

SNAKETOWN'S LONGEVITY

Living on the same spot for a long time has been a characteristic of man the world over. In Mesopotamia, a city mound may show a succession of occupancies: Sumerian, Babylonian, Persian, Greek, and contemporary tribesmen who have no knowledge of what lies underfoot. People changed but the place of residence did not. Water, land, commercial crossroads, and other resources provided the anchorage. For a calculated 1,400 years, Snaketown was a viable village, but unlike so many tells in the Near East, the people remained the same while their culture changed. The smoothly graded typological sequences for most attributes suggest to me that the ethnic identity of the inhabitants was not interrupted, that they were one and the same people experiencing normal internal evolutionary cultural modifications with occasional boosts of features and ideas newly arrived from the outside.

The natural advantages of closeness to a thousand tillable acres on the lower terrace, uncounted more acres on the upper terrace, a topography favorable to canal building and a location convenient logistically for maintenance thereof, an underground domestic water supply tappable by shallow wells, closeness to the Gila River, and a riverine environment rich in natural foods, contributed basically to Snaketown's long existence. Social and political tranquility within the people and regional calmness had also to exist. Greed for territory and goods appears to have been lacking, so that conflict, the destroyer of residence, was held to a minimum.

To restate the problem, two conditions stand out as the primary ingredients accountable for Hohokam stability. First, the natural surroundings determined what the people *could* do. Second, man's responses to the opportunities provided by the physical resources of the earth became functions of culture through the application of the technology available to them. To a point, the natural surroundings determined Hohokam behavior, but it was their attitude, will, and skills that decided the effective use of the habitat. Their technological mastery of water they brought with them. While through the centuries there were refinements in water management, increases in canal mileage, and expansion of acreage brought under cultivation, I see no great breakthroughs that would have led to major shifts in cultural orientation. The key barrier to progress, a parched land, they solved from the start by taking the water from the river and putting it where it was needed. The only reconstruction of the geography they resorted to was canal building and field clearing, and these rested lightly upon the land, leaving traces that are not easily found in the early 1970s.

My view of Hohokam successes, epitomized by their long history, is that they effectively blended their technical know-how with the resources of nature available to them. It was a case of environmental and cultural determinism working harmoniously together to achieve a state of long-lasting equilibrium. The natural resources were used and not abused.

We hear much these days about how our technology is freeing us from environmental restraints, our successes in ruling nature rather than being ruled by it. In one important sense the Hohokam broke the fetters that dictated where they should live. Closeness to an unfailing water supply has always ruled man's residence; but an improved technology: digging wells, and the installation of pumps and pipes, have widened the choices for us. They, with their canals, founded villages many miles from naturally occurring water, a development shared by no other people north of Mexico in pre-Columbian times, and a kind of emancipation unique in aboriginal America. Maintaining the flow of water in the canals became absolutely imperative for village survival. If more than one village drew upon the waters of the same ditch, agreements with respect to management responsibilities and water allocation had to be reached. That discipline was achieved on an inter-village basis is supported by the archaeological record which shows the system survived for a century or more during the Classic Period (Haury 1956: 9).

The benefits to the archaeologist of long residence in one place have become apparent in the analyses of material goods presented in earlier pages of this report. Rubbish depth and house overbuilding have been essential to chronology development. But this stage in the examination would not have been possible without typological change in the artifactual remains. The stratigraphic context determined the order of progression of artifacts; artifact details subject to modification became the hallmarks of assigning objects to a place in the sequence.

The fact that there was change in the hardware and in the institutions of culture sets up other kinds of investigations that can be pursued. Measurements of change with respect to rate, direction, scope, and reasons are not always easy to devise, but progress is being made in the development of ways to assess the problems. At Snaketown we employed no techniques directed specifically toward these ends, but a few observations are in order, subjective though they may be.

Our notion as to what did happen in the area of culture change at Snaketown is based primarily on the objects and features that were exhumed. Sociopolitical and religious changes must be inferred. An immediate generalization is that change was smooth, orderly, and without the kind of leaps that hint at cultural replacement, enforced or otherwise. The initial agricultural efficiency the Hohokam had was little improved on as time passed. There were refinements in canal technology, increases in tilled acreage, and doubtless also in crop yield. The gross effect of this was a gradual population increase which, in Snaketown, reached climax just before the village died, about A.D. 1100. This judgment is based on the territory encompassed and the amount of trash accumulated by the people during the Sacaton Phase. The more subtle effects may have been a cultural enrichment based on numerically more material attributes than were in evidence before and possibly a more formalized ritual system testified to by the construction of totally artificial platform mounds believed to have filled sacred needs. Death was followed by cremation until the Classic Period when there was some increase in inhumation, linked with the introduction of other, non-Hohokam, elements. But only nominal changes took place in the manner of disposing incinerated bones, from trench to pit deposits and finally to entombment in a jar, a trend rather than a clear sequential order. There was a noticeable average increase in grave goods, a probable reflection of a richer material culture.

The architectural record is complicated, starting with a suggestion of extended family occupancy of large houses, quickly changing to small houses serving presumed single families. Form changes were minimal during many centuries and evidently prompted by mood rather than mode or environmental and cultural factors. The pronounced shift came in the Classic Period when above ground, adobe-walled, contiguous dwellings were put up, an introduction from the outside which did not last beyond the middle of the fifteenth century.

Practically all of the crafts manifest what I regard to be a smooth unfolding and maturing of skills. This includes pottery making; shell, bone, and stone carving; other kinds of lithic treatment; figurine production; and probably also arts of perishable nature. With some fluctuation, this situation held true to the end of the Sedentary Period when a pronounced shift took place to which we will return later.

It is my opinion that pottery painting, stone sculpturing of receptacles and palettes reached a state of highest elegance towards the end of the Colonial Period, from A.D. 700–900. Thereafter there was a decline in excellence, most noticeable in pottery decoration, which one is tempted to link with a trend toward the mass production of goods. The Colonial Period efflorescence created the impression that a new core of cultural elements arrived from Mexico, brought in by immigrants identified as the Hohokam by some scholars. The large village concept, ball courts, new death practices, different pottery in form and decoration, new skills in shell and stone manufacturing, the irrigation system, and changes in social and religious functions are cited as evidence of the advent of a new people. Careful examination of the data, however, does not support this view. Most of the elements in question had local prototypes and were no more than the peaking of the evolutionary process to which culture is subject. Change, in this instance, has been misjudged as to cause. There was some intensification of Mesoamerican contacts in the Colonial Period, evidenced by the importation of mosaic mirrors of pyrites as an example, but, in aggregate, the net result did not greatly deflect the direction or rate of Hohokam development.

The significant change in the Hohokam regime came after Snaketown as a coherent village was abandoned. Satellite communities did spring up in the east and west margins of the 250-acre village; but the settlement pattern had changed from open *rancheria* to compact, contiguous-roomed residence units, a shift associated with other introductions, namely, polychrome pottery, inhumation, and doubtless a different social order. This was the so-called Salado intrusion, best exemplified by such places as Casa Grande and Los Muertos (Haury 1945a: 204– 210). A pronounced change in Hohokam painted ceramics took place as a related phenomenon. In terms of this discussion the change was due to the arrival of a new cultural element, not to internal or direct environmental forces. The withdrawal of the Puebloid people close to A.D. 1450 brought the pattern of the big village, of the centers with high population density, to a close. The people left behind, the residual Hohokam, continued dispersed *rancheria* living in a manner that lasted into the 19th century.

THE DECLINE

The reasons for decentralization and community break-up in the fifteenth century have been much debated. Our work at Snaketown produced no new insights to the problem. The most frequently-heard reasons given for the collapse were water logging and salt concentration in the fields due to over irrigation, thereby making the soil unfit for cultivation. While these conditions may have been factors, I cannot accept them as the sole ones. Communities not dependent on canal irrigation, as those in Papagería, fell victim to the same fate. Of more importance is the fact that the collapse was taking place over much of the Southwest, affecting settlements in the mountains and on the plateau where different living patterns were followed. Without attempting to identify causes, whatever the forces were, these had to be broad in nature, cutting across cultural and environmental boundaries.

In summary, the Hohokam record illustrates a not uncommon growth and decline pattern: a thousand years of slow ascendency, peaking from A.D. 700–900; followed by a population rise but with an associated decline in aesthetic values; the infusion of a new cultural system, the Salado, which materially altered settlements; and with their withdrawal, a weakened Hohokam left behind. It was they who survived to modern times by dint of will and an illustrious inheritance to become the Pima. As far as we know now, greater Snaketown can lay claim to having been the longest continuously inhabited open site in the desert, if not in the Southwest: from about 300 B.C. to A.D. 1450, followed by a hiatus and a reoccupation by the Pima Indians in the nineteenth century. Apart from the interest factor, this underlines a kind of stable living that I believe to be directly correlated with the successful merging of technology and environment. Unhappily, we do not yet have adequate data about climatic fluctuations, about variations in plant and animal communities, to talk about how these may have influenced the life of the Hohokam.

AGE PRIORITY

The dating priority the Hohokam had in the skills associated with sedentism—for example, irrigated agriculture, pottery making, stone sculpturing, shell working—over most other Southwestern groups, places them in the position of a donor culture. The immediate impact may well have been on the scattered communities of gatherers of the late Cochise Culture, but the fruits of Mexican-derived cultural achievements were also diffused farther afield at an early time as significant forces in shaping Southwestern people in general.

It is a temptation to view Snaketown as a trading center, as the home base for organized groups trafficking with neighbors in ideas and commodities. Our failure to find large stocks of raw materials as, for example, marine shells, does not support this idea. Furthermore, looking at the complexion of Hohokam society, at least as we see it from highly sketchy information, this kind of commercial endeavor would not appear to have fitted their pattern. Normal, or unorganized, trade, engaged in by individuals rather than groups, can be visualized as the mechanism whereby the Hohokam reached other people. That influences did extend out is demonstrable, and the consequence could be made the subject of a detailed study. A fascinating aspect of cultural diffusion from the Hohokam to the Anasazi, for example, is the lag time between possession and acquisition. Why should it have taken perhaps as long as 700 years for the knowledge of pottery making to have spread from southern to northern Arizona? Or a lesser, but still a long time, for the transmission of cotton? These delays in acquision of highly useful cultural attributes by the Anasazi and to a somewhat lesser extent by the Mogollon, emphasize the ineffective unorganized status of Hohokam commercialism. In actuality, the major impact of the Hohokam seems not to have been felt by neighbors until after A.D. 700 when optimum development had been reached by them. It was then that highly specific elements were borrowed, cribbed, or traded, making the identification of cross-cultural contacts less speculative.

Closely linked with the foregoing problem of analyzing Hohokam culture is the question of Hohokam colonization. Pioneer Period remains are mainly confined to the Phoenix, Sacaton, and Tucson areas of the Salt, Gila, and Santa Cruz Rivers respectively. Radiations northward up the Agua Fria, New, and Verde rivers, going as far as Flagstaff, and eastward into the Tonto Basin and beyond, up the Gila River to Safford, and southward into the valleys of the San Pedro and Santa Cruz rivers, and even into Papaguería, are identified as having taken place in the Colonial Period, an aptly named segment of Hohokam history. It is probably no accident that territorial expansion coincided with the climaxing of Hohokam culture. The nature of the mixing that took place with other people in the fringes of this large part of the arid Southwest does not impress one as having been a matter of conquest, but rather the peaceful expansion into new valleys by extending their irrigation technology. It seems to have been a case of a gentle but stubborn breed of people soft-selling their way of life and in the process achieving some degree of cultural blending. In a few instances, as at Winona Ridge Ruin east of Flagstaff and Walnut Creek near Young, factors other than irrigation practices ruled. Application of water-control knowledge was no longer important in those environments. All evidence points to the fact that the Hohokam were more versatile and adaptable to changing habitats than has seemed apparent until now.

DEMOGRAPHY

Because the factors bearing on population are vague and inconclusive, I do not intend to make much of this subject. A few speculations have been offered, and little more that is meaningful can be added. A detailed analysis of all survey resources would probably be fruitful although the data cannot be verified because so much of the archaeological record has been sacrificed to land subjugation. What remains today does not accurately reflect the past use of the land.

The internal record at Snaketown, namely, the amount of trash and numbers of houses by phase, the area inhabited, suggests in a gross way that population was expanding and that the peak was reached at the time of village disintegration. The population climax was judged to be near 2,000 people, a figure that may be as much as 50% wide of the mark. However, considering the fact that a mid-nineteenth century Pima Village numbered a few less than 1,000 souls (Russell 1908: 21), this estimate seems within reason. Whatever the total, Snaketown was a large settlement matching, if not exceeding, any other *rancheria* type village in the desert before A.D. 1100.

Regionally, the population climaxed between 1200 and 1400 to 1450, when there were many large settlements sheltering both Hohokam and the expansionist-minded puebloid people. This was the time the canal systems reached their maximum extent and the greatest acreage was tilled. With the collapse of the big settlements about A.D. 1450, the number of people in the desert valleys dropped drastically. Granted that the first Europeans to see the Pimas would not have visited all of their villages, their references, however, suggest that they were both sparse in number and, with a few exceptions, small as to the number of inhabitants. This situation persisted into the present century. Russell (1908: 23) lists only 18 villages along the Gila River in what is now Pima and Maricopa country, but he provides no estimate of the number of people. An 1858 census accounts for 4,117 Pimas in nine villages, and only 518 Maricopas in two villages (Russell 1908: 20–21). For a variety of reasons, including such factors as seasonal mobility, firm contemporary census figures are difficult to establish for the Gila River Indian Reservation. Somewhat diverse values have been given by the following agencies: the Indian Development District of Arizona, 6,140 in 1969; Bureau of Indian Affairs, 5,241 in 1970; and the Indian Health Service, 6,450 in 1970 (information supplied by Thomas Weaver, Director, Bureau of Ethnic Research, University of Arizona). From these we derive an average of about 6,000 Pimas and Maricopas, a slight gain during the twentieth century, taking the two base figures at face value.

Considering the difficulty of making an accurate count in the early 1970s, projecting population values into prehistory becomes hazardous indeed. A guess as to the number of inhabitants in the Gila-Salt region during the Classic Period can be made to show the nature of the contrast, inaccurate as it probably is. Various archaeological surveys have shown that there were numerous small communities of this period, some of which have been excavated (Johnson 1964; Ambler 1961). In addition, there were the many major settlements, Casa Grande, Pueblo Grande, Los Muertos, and some others. To repopulate all of these places would appear to require an increase by a factor of at least 8 to 10 over the contemporary value given for Pima and Maricopa Indians. This would have put roughly from 50,000 to 60,000 people in the area during the fourteenth century. A reduction of those figures by half may be close to the mark for the number of Colonial and Sedentary Period inhabitants. I recognize that no quantitative basis for these figures is being expressed, but identification of the demographic trend does seem worth noting, even though subjective. If these figures are sufficiently annoying to someone to goad him into a detailed demographic study of the Hohokam country, my purpose will have been served.

A NOTE ON HOHOKAM ART

The use made of Hohokam art forms in the preceding analyses has been of practical nature: changes have been relied upon as hallmarks of the position of an object in the time scale, and art elements have served as a basis for tracing relationships of the Hohokam and the people of Mesoamerica. No one has yet attempted a full-scale study of Hohokam art with the idea of using esthetics as an index of innate capacities, as measures of profoundly held religious concepts, group psychology, or other aspects of their society. Rippeteau's results in this direction (1972) have been somewhat less than hoped for. The complexity of materials on which art was lavished and the range of technological processes suggest that to explain it all as remarkable embellishments, as a cultural flamboyance without meaning, is not enough. Shifts in style, form, motif, the evolutionary trends, technological processes, the origins and derivations, and reasons for being deserve attention for they still have much to tell us.

The durable products of the Hohokam craftsmen on which time was spent to lift them above the level of pure functional efficiency, have been reviewed in some detail. In sum, we have seen the application of paint on an object more widely employed than any other form of modification. Pottery vessels, incense burners, and figurines among clay products; palettes (Gladwin and others 1937: Pl. CIVc), sculptures, pipes (Haury 1950: 329–332) in stone; shell (Gladwin and others 1937: Pl. CXXIII) and bone (*ibid.*, Pl. CXXX) were decorated in this manner. Painting articles of wood, woven materials such as baskets and cloth, and the human body may be inferred. Another use of paint was the filling of incised patterns. Not only were pigments abundant, but the Hohokam saw painting as a means of adding interest to an object. Furthermore, applying paint required no specialized skills and could be done by anyone. In stone, bone, and shell sculpturing, incising, and carving; in the special etching process of shell; and in the modelling of clay, the true genre of Hohokam creativity and skill appears. A similar quality in the woven products must have existed. Figurines with movable parts and flowing headdresses, probably representing feathers, and the inferred use of feathers in some clay figurines add a note of dynamism. The inlaying of shell in clay, turquoise in shell (Haury 1945a: 156–158), and mosaics of shell and turquoise add further luster in the realm of craft achievements. It will be recalled that copper bells and false cloisonné on mirror bases were imports from the South.

The role of music and the dance in Hohokam life must be assessed largely on the basis of indirect evidence. A few sound-making instruments exist, namely, shell tinklers and trumpets, pottery censer rattles, and copper bells; hand-held and leg rattles, and flutes are depicted on pottery. The possession of drums and rasps may be inferred as may also the use of the human voice in song and word. If the musical bow, basket drum, bone whistle, and percussion stones were known, traces of them have not been recognized. In general, the evidence for music among the Hohokam comes in the Colonial Period and later. Brown (1967: 84) observes that the spread of musical instruments is associated with stimuli from Mexico and that this was most active after about A.D. 1000.

The existence of platform mounds, hard-surfaced trash dumps, and the crematory floor presuppose the dance to have been an important art form. This idea finds support in the depictions on pottery and stone of dancers, singly, in pairs, but most commonly in hand-holding lines, perhaps indicative of the circle dance. Costuming, elaborate headdresses, wands, and other material symbols, the burning of incense, instrumental music and song, along with the dance, add up to a dynamic and complex expression of what must have been religiously motivated actions.

What fraction of their artistic efforts were prompted by the sheer joy of doing them or for other reasons cannot be surely judged. Much decorated pottery and personal jewelry perhaps carried no other meanings than satisfying the esthetic urge. But the animal additions to palettes and indeed the effigy palettes, the snakes, lizards, birds, and other animals drawn from the desert environment which so richly decorate stone receptacles, seem to qualify as esoterica rather than commonly possessed items. Beliefs in the power of animals as the cause of illnesses and that effigies of them can effect cures are not unknown among existing desert tribes. That art played a dual role among the Hohokam, to please and to protect, to erase drabness, and to be iconographic, seems certain. There is, however, no apparent line that may be drawn to separate the two polar extremes, and it may be that the real strength of Hohokam art lies in the clever blending of the two.

I am convinced that the quality of Hohokam esthetic expressions is a better measure of their intellectual capacities than is the technical excellence revealed by any other cultural vestiges remaining for us to examine. Such a comparison must include their capabilities in the area of irrigation and agriculture even though these were fundamental to survival.

THE RIVER PEOPLE

During our excavations in 1964–65 we sensed an increasing awakening of interest on the part of our Pima workers in the remains they were exposing. Questions were being asked, and there were more and more attempts to explain to us the meanings of findings in terms of their culture, "how it once was." On March 10, 1965, the members of the Gila River Indian Community Council toured Snaketown, at the end of which several of them became engaged in a serious discussion. Questions were shortly put to me: "Who were the Hohokam? Were they our ancestors?" After outlining reasons why I believed the Pimas to be latter-day Hohokam, and hearing a chorus of assents, the then Governor of the Gila River Indian Community and Chairman of the Council, Lloyde Allison, said with a wry smile: "I'll ask the Council to pass a resolution declaring that the Pimas *are* the descendents of the Hohokam." Obviously, this is not a problem to be solved by fiat; but the acceptance of a relationship on the part of a forward-looking Indian community is not without interest.

In spite of this growing feeling of kinship, not once did we encounter expressions of unhappiness or antagonisms against us because we were "disturbing" the homes and other traces of their possible forerunners. Indeed, the opposite attitude prevailed, for repeatedly we were told: "We had no idea these things were here under the ground," and "We want to know more about the Hohokam." The final test of their sensibility toward the problem was the council-endorsed request to the federal government to establish Snaketown as an element in the National Park system, thereby memorializing the achievements of the early desert dwellers.

Reasons for believing in the probability of a Hohokam-Pima continuity (including the Papago) have been outlined a number of times (Bandelier 1892: 463–464; Haury 1945a: 211–212; 1950: 542–543) and repeatedly alluded to herein. Ezell's treatment of the problem (1963) is perhaps the completest statement and raises some of the main doubts that relate to the hypothesis. Long involvement with both the Hohokam remains and the Pima leads one into the gray area of subjectivity in thinking about their kinship. Such behavior among the Pima as holding victory dances on natural mounds becomes a signal of connections with observances held on artifical mounds of old; apparent similarities in the dance form, the circle dance, the enclosing of ritual areas with palisades, Mound 16, and the contemporary Children's Shrine, assume increasing importance as elements in the puzzle. Not the least of these factors is an inferred similarity in tribal outlook toward others. Snaketown was not a defensive site. It enjoyed an exceptionally long life and its occupants had no over-developed weaponry. It appears that the Pima reputation as a peaceful, nonaggressive people so well demonstrated in their helpfulness to whites during their westward expansion in the nineteenth century has been honestly won as an inheritance from antiquity. At the more basic level of economic dependence, similar irrigation practices, the same varieties of corn, heavy use of the tepary bean, and fish-eating have something to say about the continuity of product and habit.

But looking beyond these points, to assert that there was no connection between the Piman people and the Hohokam requires the removal of the latter from the area by about A.D. 1450 and the introduction of the Pimans with an impressively similar lifeway almost immediately. Contacts in the sixteenth and seventeenth centuries by Europeans indicate that the Pimas were comfortably adjusted to their desert habitat, a "fit" that bespeaks a long residence rather than exceptional cultural adaptability.

The Hohokam were not one of the world's great societies, but they revealed a strain of greatness characterized by a cultural form or style that insured unusual stability. By placing primacy on the earth and by being protective of their environment, they forged a social and economic system that enjoyed 1,500 years of ascendency, and endured, on a reduced scale, for nearly 800 years more to the present day. Few people can match that record.

APPENDIX SECTION

APPENDIX 1

The Cartography of Snaketown

Jonathan Gell

The original plan adopted in 1934–35 to maintain horizontal control of Snaketown was the establishment of a system of coordinates that divided the site into blocks each 60 m square. Grid intersections thus provided benchmarks for triangulation purposes relatively close to any feature excavated within the block. Wooden posts were used to mark block intersections, designated by a letter of the alphabet west to east and by numerals north to south. The 1A post was the northwesternmost point in the grid system, and the benchmark forming the northwest corner of each block then became designator for that block.

The initial cartographic task was to reestablish the network of grid points used by Gila Pueblo in 1934–35 so that the excavations of the second campaign might be fully coordinated with the earlier findings. Second, though in fact of subsidiary importance for the archaeological control, it was advisable to relate the vertical datum of 1964–65 with that of the earlier project. Third, permanent markers to preserve the 1964–65 grid system were to be erected for the guidance of future excavations or plane surveys at Snaketown.

1. RECOVERY OF THE 1934 GRID SYSTEM

No immediately recognizable permanent markers or monuments from the 1934 survey had survived; eventually we did discover three grid corner stakes *in situ*. Our strategy was based on the attempt to rediscover undisturbed surviving markers of grid block corners by measuring "backward" from preserved 1934 houses, using scaled plans and logged chain distances. Reversing the process by which the large ball court had been mapped, a good approximation to the 1934 position of stake 8D was made; from House 2 in Block 7I grid corner 8J similarly was located. From this beginning, the search for 8H in a small area led to the discovery of the remains of the 8H wooden stake. The provisional grid network of 1964 was based upon these three points. Later in the season the hub at 11N was found.

2. VERTICAL CONTROL

For the recording of "elevations," or depths, in the 1964–65 season, a datum plane was assumed which lay 4.20 m above Corps of Engineers Benchmark TTU-22, close by the meeting of

Sections 2, 3, 10, and 11, about 0.5 km northwest of field headquarters. The datum plane was set arbitrarily at an elevation higher than ground surface within about 3 km radius of field headquarters, making possible the recording of vertical measurements altogether *below* the datum, that is, depth readings from the 0.00 m level, and nowhere, except perhaps in the flood plain, exceeding 10.00 m. As far as can be determined from a minimum of leveling (cf. Cartographer's Book 2:46–7), the 1934 assumed datum of 100.00 m is equivalent to 3.86 m in the 1964 system. Conversely, the assumed datum of 1964–65 is approximately equivalent to 103.86 m in terms of the 1934 datum.

3. PERMANENT MARKING OF THE GRID SYSTEM

Stamped brass plates set in concrete cylinders mark 8H and 11N. They have been positioned in the place of the hub remnants from the Gila Pueblo survey. Careful triangulation and chaining established as good an approximation as possible to the position of 11H, at the foot of the perpendicular in the right triangle 8H-11H-11N. The position of 8D was then determined by triangulation and chaining from this first right triangle. Next, 8J was determined, on the same base. While the hole was being dug to emplace the concrete cylinder there, the post-hole digger of 15 cm diameter brought up the pointed base of the 1934 8J hub. This finding was a noteworthy and satisfying confirmation of the accuracy of the recovery survey.

Furthermore, brass markers were set at 5H, 15D, and 15J. The eight brass plates comprise the framework, the "First Order" coordinate points, for the permanent marking of the Snaketown archaeological survey grid. They are supplemented by 23 iron pipes, some set in concrete, some driven into the ground, for the quick convenience of those who need to orient themselves in the grid or to carry out rough surveys without working from the "First Order" grid points. Attention is drawn to 10 permanent markers lying along the Snaketown Canal opposite the main area of settlement.

It must be made clear that the permanently marked coordinate points represent an attempt to re-establish and preserve the 1934 grid, *not* to construct a network of a high order of precision in azimuthal orientation and in coordinate dimensions.

APPENDIX 2

Inventory of Snaketown Houses

The following tabulation (Fig. A2.1) attempts to bring house data together more explicitly than has been possible in the text and to supplement the information given in Figure 3.2. Those houses identified by Sayles in the 1934–35 operation (Gladwin and others 1937: Fig. 19) have been included and are shown as *italic* entries. All other listings represent the 1964–65 work. Some discrepancies between this tabulation and the site map, Figure 1.6, may be detected. Several houses were plotted by cartographer Gell, exposed in 1934–35, but were not identifiable to phase and therefore not listed by Sayles. Yet they add to the general pattern of house distribution. Other symbols used are:

$\dagger\dagger$ = The same house given two numbers.
* = Too fragmentary to type.
** = Not typed; resemble P-7.
*** = Not typed; see Figure 3.20d.

Column group 1

PER PHASE	BLOCK OR SITE	HOUSE NO.	TYPE	TYPE FREQ/PHASE	TOTAL ALL TYPES BY PERIOD
CLASSIC / CIVANO	AZ. U 13:21	1	CL-1	CL-1: 4	16
		2	CL-1	CL-2:12	
		3	CL-1		
		4	CL-1		
		5	CL-2		
		6	CL-2		
	AZ. U 13:22	1-10	CL-2		
CLASSIC / SOHO	←———— NO DATA ————→				
SEDENTARY / SACATON	3C	*1*	S-1	S-1:66	102-2=100
		2	S-1	S-2: 8	(DISCOUNTING
	4H	*1*	S-1	S-3: 3	TWO HOUSES
		2	S-1	S-4: 2	NUMBERED
	5F	1	S-1	S-5: 2	TWICE)
		3	*	* :21	
		4	S-1		
		5	S-1		
		7	S-1		
	5G	1	S-2		
		2	S-1		
		4	S-1		
		6	S-1		
		8	S-5		
		9	S-4		
		10	*		
		11	*		
		12	S-1		
		13	*		
		14	S-1		
	6E	*1*	S-1		
		2	**		
	6F	*1*	**		
	6G	*8*	S-1		
		1	S-2		
		3	S-1		
	7J	*3*	S-1		
	8B	1	S-1		
	8E	3	S-1		
		12	S-5		
	8F	4	S-1		
		5	S-1		
	8I	2	S-1		
		3	S-1		
	9F	4	S-1		
		6	*		
		10	S-1		
	9G	3	S-3		
	10D	1	S-2		
		3	S-2		
	10F	*9*	S-1		
		1	S-2		
		2	*		
		3	S-2		
		4	S-1		
		6	S-1		
		7	*		
		8	S-1		
		9	S-1		
		10	S-1		
		11	S-2		
		12	*		
		13	*		
		14	S-1		

CONTINUED NEXT COLUMN

Column group 2

PER PHASE	BLOCK OR SITE	HOUSE NO.	TYPE	TYPE FREQ/PHASE	TOTAL ALL TYPES BY PERIOD
(SEDENTARY) / (SACATON)		15	S-1		
		16	S-1		
		17	S-1		
		18	*		
		19	S-1		
		21	S-1		
		22	*		
		23	S-1		
		24	S-1		
		25	*		
		26	S-1		
	10G	5+	S-1		
		6++	S-1		
		2	S-1		
		3	S-1		
		4	S-2		
		6	S-1		
		8	S-1		
		9	S-3		
		10	S-1		
		13+	S-1		
		16++	S-1		
		18	S-3		
	10H 10I	1	S-1		
	10I	1	S-1		
		2	*		
		3	S-1		
		5	S-1		
	10J	1	S-1		
		2	S-4		
		3	S-1		
		4	S-1		
		6	*		
		7	S-1		
		9	*		
	11F	1	*		
		3	*		
		5	S-1		
		8	S-1		
		9	S-1		
		10	S-1		
		14	*		
		15	S-1		
	11I	2	S-1		
		3	S-1		
		4	S-1		
	11J	1	***		
		2	S-1		
COLONIAL / SANTA CRUZ	5G	7	C-2	C-1: 4	C-1: 6
	6F	*7*	C-2	C-2: 11	C-2:20
	6G	*1*	C-2	C-3: 3	C-3: 6
		13	C-2	* : 5	* :11
		2	*	23	43
	8E	2	C-2		
		6	C-3		
	8F	1	C-2		
		2	*		
	8I	*1*	C-1		
	9E	*3*	C-2		
		7	*		
	9F	2	C-2		
	9G	6	C-2		
		2	C-3		
	9H	5	C-2		
	10D	4	C-1		
	10F	5	C-1		
	10G	7	C-2		
		11	C-3		
		14	*		

CONTINUED NEXT COLUMN

Column group 3

PER PHASE	BLOCK OR SITE	HOUSE NO.	TYPE	TYPE FREQ/PHASE	TOTAL ALL TYPES BY PERIOD
GILA BUTTE (Colonial)	11H	15	*		
		1	C-1		
	5F	6	C-2	C-1: 1	
		8	*	C-2: 7	
	5G	5	C-2	C-3: 2	
	6G	4	*	* : 4	
	8E	7	C-2	14	
	8F	3	*		
	9E	1	C-3		
		3	C-2		
	9F	8	C-3		
	9I	1	C-2		
		2	C-2		
	10I	4	C-1		
	11F	7	*		
		13	C-2		
	8E	8	C-2	C-1: 1	
		11	C-2	C-2: 2	
	9E	9	*	C-3: 1	
	9F	3	C-1	* : 2	
		9	C-3	6	
	10G	17	*		
PIONEER / SNAKETOWN	6G	*12*	P-1	P-1: 4	P-1: 5
	6H	*1*	P-1	P-2: 1	P-2: 7
	6I	*1*	P-1	P-3: 7	P-3: 9
	7F	*9*	P-2	* : 2	P-4: 6
	7I	*2*	P-3	14	P-5: 1
	8F	*2*	P-1		P-6: 1
	9E	*1*	P-3		P-7: 1
		8	*		* :12
	9G	1	P-3		42
		6	P-3		
	10F	20	P-3		
	10G	19	P-3		
	11F	6	*		
	15E	1	P-3		
PIONEER / SWEETWATER	6H	*2*	P-3	P-1: 1	
	9E	*4*	P-3	P-2: 1	
		2	P-1	P-3: 2	
		4	P-2	P-6: 1	
		6	*	* : 3	
	10G	1	*	8	
	10J	5	*		
	11I	1	P-6		
PIONEER / EST. VAHKI	6G	*11*	P-4	P-2: 1	
	9E	5	P-4	P-4: 2	
	9G	5	P-2	3	
	7F	*8*	P-4	P-4: 4	
	7H	*1*	P-4	4	
		1	P-4		
	9F	1	P-4		
PIONEER / (Pioneer)	5F	2	P-2	P-2: 4	
	8E	1	P-2	P-5: 1	
		4	*	P-7: 1	
		5	P-5	* : 7	
		10	P-2	13	
		13	P-7		
	9E	11	*		
	9F	7	P-2		
	9G	4	*		
	10G	20	*		
		21	*		
	11F	11	*		
		12	*		
	TOTAL				201
	UNPLACED HOUSES				20
	GRAND TOTAL				221

Fig. A2.1. Complete tabulation of houses excavated in Snaketown and neighboring Classic Period sites.

APPENDIX 3
Instrument Surveys at Snaketown
Hugh Bergh

Three instruments, proton magnetometer,[1] geohm,[2] and seismiktron[3] were tried out at Snaketown in the Arizona desert during the week January 15-20, 1965. The site, in occupation from about 300 B.C. to A.D. 1100, is characterized on the surface by numerous large trash mounds, a well-marked ball court, and a clearly defined ridge formed by the filling of a former irrigation canal and at least one subsidiary canal. The excavations were well advanced and a large number of hard packed floors had been exposed. These house floors usually have a small clay firepit just inside the entrance and are, on the average, about 0.5 to 1.0 m below the present surface. A large gash had been cut through the center of one of the trash mounds, giving a clear picture of about 1,000 years of layering. Several deep trenches cut across the main canal exposed profile details at a number of points along its length. A few extremely large firepits were found on the site. In looking at them a hungry gleam comes into the eye of anyone intending a magnetometer survey of the site.

Preliminary experiments on the excavated house floors were not encouraging. The small firepits gave magnetic anomalies of 5 γ or less and the compact floors showed little contrast in resistivity from the surroundings.

Magnetometer readings were then taken along two parallel lines about 500 m long and 20 m apart, extending roughly eastward from the intensively excavated portions of the site in Blocks 10F and 10G. Readings were taken approximately every 1 m and eleven interesting spots were marked with stakes and afterward carefully surveyed. The results were extremely rewarding. Contours obtained by surveying two of the "hotspots" are shown in Figures A3.1 and A3.2. These were excavated immediately after surveying and firepits were found. Nearly all the other "hotspots" gave anomalies just as well defined, though the one shown in Figure A3.1 was the most intensely magnetic. One interesting point worth mentioning here is the well-defined direction from the center of the anomaly to the center of the reverse anomaly (marked by arrow). This direction should be roughly the same as that of the geomagnetic field at the time of last firing of the clay lining. This statement should not be taken too literally, as there are several complicating factors, although it should hold in certain cases. Assuming this and having some knowledge of the variation in declination of the geomagnetic field with time for the region considered, a rough relative chronology could be built and applied to these firepit anomalies *before* excavating. This provides a further incentive for doing a thorough magnetometer survey of the unexcavated areas of the site and then picking out anomalies lying

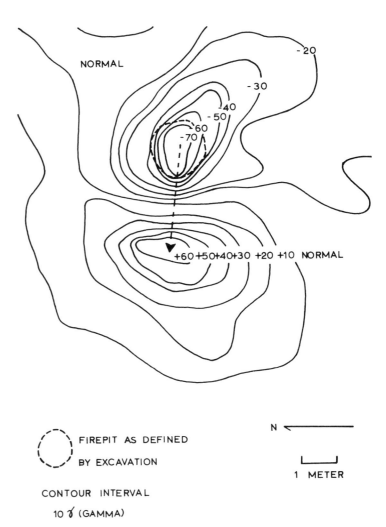

FIREPIT AS DEFINED BY EXCAVATION

CONTOUR INTERVAL

10 γ (GAMMA)

N

1 METER

Fig. A3.1. Positive and negative magnetometer contours created by Roasting Pit 1:11I (see also Fig. 9.9c).

[1] The Elsec proton magnetometer is manufactured by the Littlemore Scientific Engineering Co., Oxford, England.
[2] The Geohm is maufactured by the Gossen Company, Erlanden, Germany.
[3] The Seismiktron is manufactured by Advanced Systems Laboratories, Inc., 9 Fayette Street, Rockville, Maryland. (We are grateful to Manuel Cebollero, President of Advanced Systems Laboratories, for the loan of this instrument for these tests.)

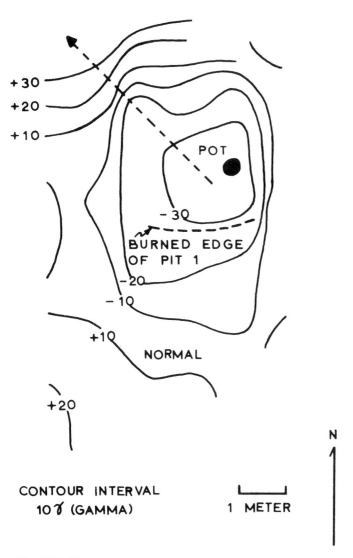

+30

+20

+10

POT

−30

BURNED EDGE
OF PIT 1

−20

−10

+10

NORMAL

+20

CONTOUR INTERVAL
10 γ (GAMMA)

1 METER

N

Fig. A3.2. Magnetometer readings which led to discovery of Pit
1:10I and large pottery cauldron shown in Fig. 12.19d.

in an age-range of most interest. A rough curve of declination versus time derived from DuBois' archaeometric work would be useful; in return, the magnetometer survey might help him in the selection of more suitable material.

Figure A3.2 gives the contours associated with a partially burned pit in which rested a large pottery vessel.

Two magnetometer and resistivity surveys were also run across the canal system (Fig. A3.3). Both showed sharp anomalies over a gray silt layer north of the main canal but were not specific in showing the actual canal positions. The gray silt is probably a combination of spoil dirt and material from canal cleanings.

Resistivity measurements across the ball court clearly picked up the well compacted central floor area. Of interest here also is the fact that readings were unchanged on traversing across the mounds on either side of the central floor. This is somewhat surprising since tests have revealed hard sloping surfaces in the embankments.

Mound 40, investigated with the geohm, showed little variation. This was disappointing as several hard capping layers were evident in the cut made through the mound. However, they were not thick and heavily compacted, and this most probably accounts for the geohm's failure to detect them.

The seismiktron worked nicely and consistently. Unfortunately refraction seismology appears to have little application to archaeological sites of this nature. The instrument is designed to pick up features of relatively large horizontal extent, and this it does well. However, such features usually have more geological than archaeological significance.

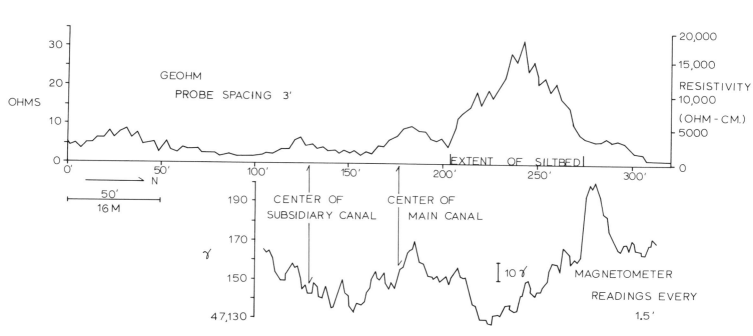

OHMS

GEOHM
PROBE SPACING 3'

30
20
10
0

20,000
15,000
RESISTIVITY
10,000
(OHM - CM.)
5000
0

0'   50'   100'   150'   200'   250'   300'

EXTENT OF SILTBED

50'
16 M

N

190

170

150

47,130

γ

CENTER OF
SUBSIDIARY CANAL

CENTER OF
MAIN CANAL

10 γ

MAGNETOMETER

READINGS EVERY

1.5'

Fig. A3.3. Comparison of geohm and magnetometer surveys across diversion and
main canals at the Four Canal Station.

APPENDIX 4
Corn From Snaketown
Hugh C. Cutler and Leonard W. Blake

Living things continually change. Plants growing any place today are always different to some extent from those present some years past. Actions of man greatly accelerate such change, especially in his cultivated plants and weeds. In any series of collections of plants which have been associated with man, a period of great change usually coincides with intensified cultural changes. Plants, thus, may be records of man's history.

From Snaketown we have a series of carbonized corn grains and ear fragments covering roughly 1,400 years. The sample is small, but it has the value of being from a single site. Collections we have seen from other dated sites in southern Arizona confirm information derived from the Snaketown material.

Corn from Snaketown falls into a series of types, usually termed races, with intermediates which make it difficult to define limits. The series begins with small-grained and small-cobbed, popcorn and progresses gradually to large-grained, larger-cobbed, flour corn. Dent corn is not present. It may be late, possibly post-Spanish, in southern Arizona. The series from oldest, hardest, and smallest-grained, to most recent, softest, and largest-grained now follows:

Chapalote: a small popcorn, usually 12- or 14-rowed, but some early forms may have as few as 8 or as many as 18 rows.

Reventador: similar to the above but with slightly flatter and larger grains, a pop or hard flint, sometimes with shriveled grains.

Onaveño: a hard flint, continuing the progression towards larger grains and ears.

Mais Blando de Sonora: usually soft flour corn, with larger grains and ears.

8-Rowed, or Harinoso de Ocho: usually a flour corn with 8 rows, but in some areas until recently, flint forms of this were common. Large forms of this probably were rare until A.D. 700 in the Southwest. These last three races are closely related and are sometimes combined to form the Pima-Papago race.

Sweet corn: usually 12 or 14 rows of grains, ears with rounded tips and butts and relatively small cob. None could be identified in Snaketown but it probably was grown.

The above kinds of corn were grown until a few years ago by Indians of southern Arizona.

All of the corn from the Vahki Phase (300–100 B.C.) would be classified as Chapalote, Reventador, and small Onaveño (Wellhausen and others 1952). Only grains were found. These were mostly about 4 mm thick, 6 mm wide, and 6 mm long, and came from 12- to 14-rowed ears. A few grains could have come from 8- and 10-rowed ears. A mass of about a cupful was bordered on two sides by small parallel sticks (House 1:7H). A similar mass from the floor of the same house was rounded on one side in a shape suggesting it was burned in a container of about 16 to 20 cm diameter. The average grains were slightly smaller in size than those of the first lot. Most of two cupfuls of corn grains

from the Sweetwater Phase (House 2:9E, A.D. 200–350) were similar in size to those of the Vahki Phase, but there were a few larger grains and several slender and longer grains (4.5 mm thick x 5.5 mm wide x 7.5 mm long) from 12- or 14-rowed ears, probably variants of Onaveño. We have ears with similar grains in some 1914 Papago Indian corn in our collection. The grains are not those of dent corn. There were far more grains from 8- and 10-rowed ears than in the Vahki Phase, but none of the grains approached the size of grains usually found in large Onaveño or in Harinoso de Ocho, the 8-rowed race.

The few corn grains found in Snaketown Phase (A.D. 350–550, House 1:15E; House 13:8E, Strat. Test level 3) include all the kinds found in previous levels but the proportion of medium-sized grains is greater. Three of the 8 cob fragments (from House 1:10D; Pit 34:11F, level 6; Mound 40, Strat. Test 1, Tier 1, level 5) are 14- and 16-rowed and small, similar to ancient but persisting kinds of popcorn. In general the corn is similar to that from the Sweetwater Phase, but the sample is small.

From the Gila Butte Phase (A.D. 550–700) we have only half a cupful (cupule width 4.8 mm) of carbonized corn kernels, all small (Mound 40, Strat. Test 1, Tier 2, level 1), and a single small 12-rowed cob fragment (Mound 40, Strat. Test 1, Tier 4, level 3). These would be classified as Chapalote or Reventador, small popcorns or flints. A single and slightly smaller 16-rowed cob was found in Arizona T:13:9, a Gila Butte Phase site (Cutler, in Wasley and Johnson 1965: 108). The Gila Butte Phase coincides with the Georgetown Phase of the Mogollon culture, Tularosa Cave (Martin and others 1952), a period of great change during which the preparation of gathered plant foods increased greatly, suggesting a time of stress. Our collections from southern Arizona are still too small to be sure that corn agriculture was reduced during the Gila Butte Phase, but it is likely that much of the change in agriculture followed this period. The dates for the first moschata squash *(Cucurbita moschata),* cushaw *(Cucurbita mixta),* and perhaps the tepary bean probably are near A.D. 700.

In the Santa Cruz Phase (A.D. 700–900) there was a rapid increase in the kinds of corn. In about a cup of loose kernels and a few cob fragments with grains, were found all the kinds of corn grown by recent Papago Indians, except for the largest of the 8-rowed flour corn and the dent types.

By Sacaton Phase time (A.D. 900–1100) the inhabitants of Snaketown probably were growing all the kinds, including the large-grained 8-rowed flour corn of recent Papagos, except for dent corn. The only cobs recovered from Sacaton Phase contexts during the recent excavations are two small ones, 12- and 16-rowed, which belong to the hard flint Reventador race. In a lot of eighteen cobs from the Sacaton Phase of the Gatlin Site (Arizona Z:2:1) (Cutler, in Wasley and Johnson 1965), two are large 8-rowed, three are Mais Blando or large forms of Onaveño, six are typical Onaveño and seven are Reventador and mixtures of it with Onaveño. Jones, who studied earlier recoveries of corn from

SITE, PHASE, DATE	COBS IN SAMPLE	PERCENT OF COBS WITH:				
		8 ROWS	10 ROWS	12 ROWS	14 ROWS	16 ROWS
ARIZONA T:13:8, ? , 1200-1300	42	15	50	23	12	
O-BLOCK, RESERVE P., 1000-1100	59	46	27	17	8	2
O-BLOCK, THREE CIRCLE P., 900-1100	136	52	29	12	6	1
ARIZONA Z:2:1, SACATON P., 900-1100	18	11	17	55	11	6
SNAKETOWN, PRE-SACATON P., BEFORE 900	EST.	10	18	50	15	7
TULAROSA CAVE, SAN FRANCISCO P., 700-900	239	73	21	4	1	1
TULAROSA CAVE, SAN FRANCISCO P., 700-900	401	65	25	4	3	3
TULAROSA CAVE, GEORGETOWN P., 500-700	224	34	19	29	13	5
TULAROSA CAVE, GEORGETOWN P., 500-700	357	23	25	35	10	7
SNAKETOWN, SNAKETOWN P., 350-550	11	9	18	46	18	9
TULAROSA CAVE, PINELAWN P., 150 B.C.-A.D. 500	457	7	22	45	18	8
TULAROSA CAVE, PREPOTTERY P., BEFORE 150 B.C.	618	4	15	45	25	11

Fig. A4.1. Comparison of numbers of rows of kernels on corn ears from Snaketown and selected southwestern sites.

Snaketown (in Castetter and Bell 1942: 31) mentions several kinds of grains, including large and crescent shaped ones which apparently came from the large 8-rowed race.

The progression from mainly small-grained corn in the lower levels of Snaketown to greater diversity in upper levels agrees with the reports of Jones.

We do not have enough corn material from nearby sites to make thorough comparison and analysis of the Snaketown collections. Comparisons with distant sites, or even nearby sites which may have slightly different growing conditions must consider many variables. Under more severe growing conditions, smaller plants will result. Most obvious effect is a decrease in the number of rows of grains on the ear (Emerson and Smith 1950), although many other effects can be noted in plant and ear characters. Eight-rowed and slightly harder ears are more common as one goes to higher elevations and farther north where days are shorter. Thus, more 8-rowed ears are found in farther north Mogollon area sites like Tularosa and O-Block Caves (Fig. A4.1), but the corn is closely related to the kinds of corn grown at Snaketown.

Faunal Study of Unworked Mammalian Bones

Jerry L. Greene and Thomas W. Mathews

Approximately 33% of the Snaketown collection of mammal bones was examined in this study, leading to the identification of 1,688 specimens. Four orders are represented: Lagamorpha, Rodentia, Carnivora, and Artiodactyla. In terms of minimal faunal count, the bones represent 656 individuals. The percentage composition of the total number of specimens is given in Figure A5.1a; the minimal faunal count (MFC), reduced to percentage values, is shown in Figure A5.1b. The list of species, together with other pertinent data, will be found in Figures A5.2-A5.9.

LAGAMORPHA

The minimal faunal count (MFC) of Lagamorpha is 63.49% of the collection. *Sylvilagus* and *Lepus alleni* are about equal in number, 11%. *Lepus californicus* is 41% and represents the largest number of individuals per species in the faunal list (Fig. A5.2).

Rabbits and hares are still important food items for the peoples of the low desert region surrounding Snaketown. The three forms occurring in that area today, *L. alleni*, *L.c. eremicus* and *L.c. deserticola*, are hunted. In addition to the communal drive just before the Papago drinking ceremony, these animals were regularly hunted by boys who were expected to keep the family supplied. In times of inadequate water supply and crop failure the people relied heavily upon "jackrabbits, and less numerous deer and mountain sheep" (Castetter and Bell 1942:57). One early reference describes the Papago as living on seeds, grass, rabbits, nuts, and wild fruits (Documentos 3rd ser., IV: 554).

Sylvilagus auduboni. The cottontails rank fourth in total MFC. Skeletal material representing this species has a size range smaller than *S.a. cedrophilus*, the rabbit of the pinyon-juniper belt, many of the skeletons of mature individuals being very small. Since there is no overlap in these specimens and *S.a. cedrophilus*, they could be referred to *S.a. arizonae* (Anthony 1928: 501–2, Fig. 108). Today this subspecies, one of three in the state of Arizona, is found in the southwest section, including the vicinity of Snaketown (Cockrum 1960: 73–75, Fig. 34).

Lepus californicus. The Blacktail jackrabbit is the most common mammal encountered in the Snaketown collection. Again, this animal is small compared to those in our collection. In considering sex dimorphism one of two problems exists concerning specimens of this species. Either disproportionate numbers of males were taken in hunting or the specimens examined are of a different subspecies than those used for comparison. Even elements representing the largest individuals are more male-like in structure, (females are larger than males in Lagamorpha). Study of this material indicates a separation of elements into two groups —small females and smaller males—is possible. Further analysis may determine if other subspecific varieties than *Lepus californicus eremicus* and *L.c. texianus* used in this study are present. Hall and Kelson (1959) show *L.c. deserticola* inhabits the Snaketown area today. This subspecies is smaller than the other two forms (Anthony 1928: 490).

Lepus alleni. The Antelope jackrabbit ranks third in the collection. There is no overlap of these specimens with *Lepus*

californicus except in the fore and hind paw elements. Some of the long bones, however, are large, representing individuals well within the upper limits of their size range. Most of the bone material of this species is of fully adult age with only one immature specimen in ten. This is a larger proportion than for

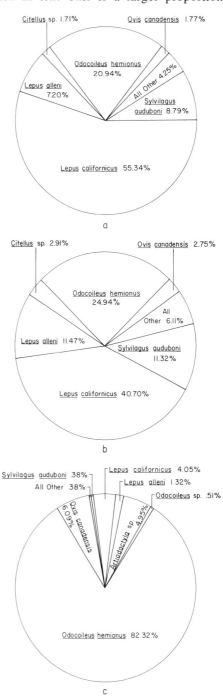

Fig. A5.1. The Snaketown mammalian bone collection: (a) percentage composition of total specimens; (b) percentages of minimal faunal count of identified bones; (c) percentage of usable meat.

SPECIES	PIONEER PERIOD	VAHKI-SWEETWATER	VAHKI-ESTRELLA	VAHKI	ESTRELLA	SWEETWATER-SNAKETOWN	SWEETWATER	SNAKETOWN-GILA BUTTE	SNAKETOWN	GILA BUTTE	SANTA CRUZ-SACATON	SANTA CRUZ	SACATON	NO ASSOCIATION	NO INFORMATION	TOTAL	TOTAL PERCENT
Sylvilagus auduboni	6 *6* 13.98	2 *2* 20.00		17 *8* 12.32			8 *6* 10.56	46 *19* 8.93	3 *3* 11.10	17 *12* 24.48	5 *2* 8.70	16 *3* 13.05		9 *4* 12.92	20 *9* 11.43	149 *74*	8.79 11.32
Lepus californicus	55 *16* 34.95	14 *6* 60.00	18 *4* 40.00	91 *27* 41.58	15 *6* 40.02	18 *4* 57.16	70 *24* 42.96	297 *81* 38.07	45 *17* 62.90	47 *22* 44.88	44 *6* 26.10	45 *6* 26.10	3 *1* 25.00	43 *14* 45.22	133 *33* 41.91	938 *267*	55.34 40.70
Lepus alleni	7 *6* 13.98		2 *1* 10.00	22 *10* 15.38		3 *2* 28.58	13 *9* 16.11	27 *19* 8.93	7 *3* 11.10	1 *1* 2.04	7 *4* 17.40	2 *2* 8.70		12 *8* 25.84	19 *10* 12.66	122 *75*	7.20 11.47
Citellus sp.	1		6 *2* 20.00	6 *4* 6.16	1 *1* 6.67		2 *2* 3.58	5 *3* 1.41	1 *1* 3.70	1 *1* 2.04	1 *1* 4.35	*1* 4.35			5 *3* 3.81	29 *19*	1.71 2.91
Thomomys bottae		2 *1* 10.00		1 *1* 1.54	3 *1* 6.67			4 *4* 1.88			2 *2* 8.70				1 *1* 1.27	13 *10*	.77 1.53
Dipodomys sp.	1 *1* 2.33	1 *1* 10.00						1 *1* .47								3 *3*	.18 .46
Dipodomys deserti								5 *1* .47								5 *1*	.30 .15
Onychomys sp. cf. torridus														1	*1* 1.27	1 *1*	.06 .15
Neotoma sp.								1 *1* .47								1 *1*	.06 .15
Canis sp.				1 *1* 1.54				5 *1* .47								6 *2*	.35 .31
Canis familiaris				3 *1* 1.54	12 *1* 6.67											15 *2*	.89 .31
Vulpes macrotis	1 *1* 2.33							1 *1* .47								2 *2*	.12 .31
Taxidea taxus				1 *1* 1.54												1 *1*	.06 .15
Artiodactyla sp.	1 *1* 2.33		1 *1* 10.00	2 *2* 3.08				6 *6* 2.82		1 *1* 2.04	1 *1* 4.35	1 *1* 4.35			1 *1* 1.27	14 *14*	.83 2.14
Odocoileus sp.								1 *1* .47								1 *1*	.06 .15
Odocoileus hemionus	19 *12* 27.96		3 *2* 20.00	26 *10* 15.38	12 *6* 40.02	1 *1* 14.29	19 *14* 25.06	156 *65* 30.55	3 *3* 11.10	17 *12* 24.48	6 *4* 17.40	36 *9* 39.15	6 *2* 50.00	10 *5* 16.15	41 *18* 22.86	355 *163*	20.94 24.94
Antilocapra americana								1 *1* .47								1 *1*	.06 .15
Bos taurus															2 *1* 1.27	2 *1*	.12 .15
Ovis canadensis	1 *1* 2.33						8 *1* 1.79	11 *9* 4.23			3 *3* 13.05	1 *1* 4.35	1 *1* 25.00		5 *2* 2.54	30 *18*	1.77 2.75
TOTAL	92 *44* 100.19	19 *10* 100.00	30 *10* 100.00	170 *65* 100.06	43 *15* 100.05	22 *7* 100.03	120 *56* 100.06	567 *213* 100.11	59 *27* 100.90	84 *49* 99.96	69 *23* 100.05	101 *23* 100.05	10 *4* 100.00	75 *31* 100.13	227 *79* 100.29	1688 *656*	99.61 100.20

Fig. A5.2. Tabulation of number of specimens of each identified species, minimal faunal count, and percent in relation to provenience.

Blacktails, which had an immature individual in every four specimens identified.

"White-sided jackrabbits range for the most part in semiarid zones supporting a fairly dense ground vegetation—particularly mesquite—grassland and thorn forest. Only in western Sonora does *L. callotis* [= *L. alleni*] occur in true desert, and even there it frequents brushy watercourses rather than the bare desert plains" (Leopold 1959).

In the above quote Leopold refers to *Lepus callotis* as a group name for the four "species" of white-sided jackrabbits occurring in Mexico, in which *L. alleni* is included. *L. alleni* is that hare inhabiting the country west of the continental divide and south into Nayarit (Leopold 1959: 347). *Lepus callotis* is the earliest name used for the white-sided jackrabbit group by Wagler in 1830 (Miller and Kellogg 1955: 153), and was adopted by Nelson in 1909 in his monograph on American Leporidae (Leopold 1959: 345).

RODENTIA

Only four rodents have been identified in the Snaketown collection at the present time. This is undoubtedly due to sample selection, for much of the smaller material was gleaned from flotation, stored separately, and has not been studied. In scanning this small and broken material, we find rodent and leporid mixed with fish, reptile, and other vertebrates. The bulk of this, again, is probably rabbit bones broken into tiny fragments.

Castetter and Bell note (1942: 68–69) that "various rats were eaten, particularly by the Papago, the packrat (*Neotoma* sp.), most common food in the group, being rather extensively utilized."

Citellus sp. The ground squirrel ranks as the fifth most numerous species in the MFC list. The specimens that were examined have been compared to Harris' antelope squirrel, *Ammospermophilus harrisii*, in the Southwest Archeological Center specimen and those recorded by Howell (1938: 187–88). Furthermore, Howell's record shows *Citellus spilosoma canascens*, the Round-tailed ground squirrel, occurring in the Snaketown area. He notes it is smaller than *A. harrisii* in tooth row measurement too. The specimens in question all measure more than 7.5 mm in this area, matching the size range of *C. tereticaudus*, the suggested species.

	*C.s.c.** (mm)	*A.h.h.** (mm)	*C.t.n.** (mm)
Total length	210–247	225–250	204–247
Tail	67–86	74–94	60–84
Hind foot	30–34	38–42	32–37
Skull	37.5–38.7	38.8–41.2	35.3–39.3
Maximum tooth rows	6.5–7.4	6.8–7.5	7.3–8.0

**Citellus spilosoma canascens; Ammospermophilus harrisii harrisii; Citellus tereticaudus neglectus*

Thomomys bottae. The Valley pocket gopher represents 1.53% of the MFC, totaling ten individuals. Because pocket gophers are often found in localized isolated populations, there tends to be great morphologic variation, each individual population possessing some degree of uniqueness. Nomenclatural recognition of these populations is still a taxonomic problem. At present more than 300 kinds of pocket gophers have been named (Hall and Kelson 1959).

Several specimens of *T. bottae cervinus*, collected in the Phoenix area, were used to compare with the Snaketown gophers. They are similar in size and morphology.

Dipodomys sp. The five large individuals of this genus are similar to *D. deserti* and *D. spectabilis*. The cranial material, an auditory bulla and premaxilla, are from a large male *D. deserti*. Studies made by Vorhies and Taylor (1922: 7–9) show that there are distinct habitat preferences in these species. *D. deserti* inhabits sandier (less firm) soil than *D. spectabilis*.

Environmental factors favoring *Dipodomys* are (1) arid or semi-arid climate, (2) proper drainage, (3) any combination of soil and climatic factors to provide an abundance of seed plants with light ground cover, (4) some provision for shelter, and (5) the availability of dusting places for at least a part of the year (Dale 1939: 730).

Onychomys sp. cf. *torridus*. One specimen of the Grasshopper mouse has been identified. Though it resembles *O. leucogaster* morphologically (Olsen 1964: Fig. 95), it is smaller, indicating the suggested species. Today the Southern grasshopper mouse occurs in the Lower Sonoran Life Zone, whereas *O. leucogaster* is suited to the mesic biotic areas, that is, grassland at higher elevations (Hall and Kelson 1959: 662).

Neotoma sp. It seems indeed unusual to find only one pack rat bone among the 1688 specimens recorded. A long bone of an immature individual, it is similar to the *N. albigula* used in the comparative collection. Since differences are small in the three species found in southwestern Arizona today, reference to species would need more adequate comparative material.

CARNIVORA

In contrast to other southwestern sites, Snaketown is deficient in carnivore remains. Three species were identified in this collection: dog, fox, and badger. In MFC all carnivores make up only 1.08% of the collection sample.

Canis sp. Six specimens of neonate pups are listed in this category. Five are long bones of one individual and the sixth, a dentary fragment of another.

Canis familiaris. Cranial material from two dogs is considered. They were both excavated from early stratigraphy, one from material of the Vahki Phase, the other from the Estrella. The carnassial of the latter, the only measurable part of a fragmented dentary, is 19.3 mm long. This is about the mean for the range recorded by Haag (1948: 154) of seventeen southwestern aboriginal dogs. The other dog has a lower incisor equal in size to Chaco Canyon and Gran Quivira dogs. This tooth is larger at the base and less curved anteroposteriorly than that of the coyote. Measurements indicate these specimens could be grouped within the range of the Small Indian Dog described by Allen (1920).

Vulpes macrotis. Two specimens were identified belonging to this species. One had been scorched. Although kit foxes are rare inhabitants in the Snaketown area today, we have been told that a pair had a den in the large ball court when excavations were begun in 1964. According to Cahalane (1947: 236), "The kangaroo rat is the most frequent victim. The kit fox is rarely or never found outside the range of this grotesque, long-legged creature."

Taxidea taxus. This species is represented by a single, thoroughly calcined, long-bone. The badger is a regular consumer of rodents, lizards, and snakes and is likely to be seen anywhere a diet of this sort can be obtained.

ARTIODACTYLA

This order constitutes 30% of the total MFC. When the amount of usable meat is considered, the Artiodactyls are found to outrank all the other game food forms (Figs. A5.7, A5.8). They account for 94% of the total (Fig. A5.1c).

Odocoileus sp. One specimen has been placed in this category. The element, a metatarsal, is plainly deer, but it lacks an articular surface and cannot be distinguished as to species. Although Whitetail deer occur in the surrounding mountains today, they have not been noted in the bone refuse of Snaketown examined thus far.

Odocoileus hemionus. In numbers the mule deer ranks second to blacktail jackrabbit with an MFC of 163 individuals made up of 355 specimens. Though there are more than twice as many hares and rabbits in the Snaketown collection, their priority is lost when weight per individual is considered. Comparing figures from a list

PERIOD / SPECIES	TOTAL SPECIMENS			PERCENT SPECIMENS			TOTAL MFC			PERCENT MFC		
	PIONEER	COLONIAL	SEDENTARY	PIONEER	COLONIAL	SEDENTARY	PIONEER	COLONIAL	SEDENTARY	PIONEER	COLONIAL	SEDENTARY
Sylvilagus auduboni	36	23		6.48	13.16		25	15		10.73	20.85	
Lepus californicus	326	92	3	58.68	52.62	30.00	103	28	1	44.19	38.92	25.00
Lepus alleni	54	3		9.72	1.71		31	3		13.30	4.17	
Citellus sp.	17	1		3.06	.57		10	2		4.29	2.78	
Thomomys bottae	6			1.08			3			1.29		
Dipodomys sp.	2			.36			2			.86		
Canis sp.	1			.18			1			.43		
Canis familiaris	15			2.70			2			.86		
Vulpes macrotis	1			.18			1			.43		
Taxidea taxus	1			.18			1			.43		
Artiodactyla sp.	4	2		.72	1.14		4	2		1.72	2.78	
Odocoileus hemionus	83	53	6	14.94	30.32	60.00	48	21	2	20.59	29.19	50.00
Ovis canadensis	9	1	1	1.62	.57	10.00	2	1	1	.86	1.39	25.00
TOTALS	555	175	10	99.90	100.09	100.00	233	72	4	99.98	100.08	100.00

Fig. A5.3. Frequency and percentage comparisons of total number of specimens of a given species and the minimal faunal count, by period.

BODY PARTS / SPECIES	CRANIA	VERTEBRAE	CAUDAL VERTEBRAE	RIBS	SCAPULAE	FORELEGS	INNOMINATES	HINDLEGS	MANI & PES	SACRA	TOTAL	RATIO OF CRANIA/TOTAL
Sylvilagus auduboni	*14*	*7*		*10*	*16*	*14*		*35*	*4*	*18*	*100*	
	18	9		13	21	18		45	5	1	130	1:7
Lepus californicus	*6*	*10*		*4*	*9*	*24*	*10*	*28*	*8*	*1*	*100*	
	53	87		34	73	204	89	243	68	9	860	1:16
Lepus alleni	*7*	*5*		*11*	*12*	*27*	*9*	*21*	*11*	*1*	*100*	
	7	5		11	12	27	9	21	11	1	104	1:15
Citellus sp.	7					3	2	11			23	1:3
Thomomys bottae	5					3	1	3			12	1:2
Dipodomys sp.								3			3	
Dipodomys deserti	1										1	1:1
Onychomys sp. cf. torridus								1			1	
Neotoma sp.								1			1	
Canis sp.	1			1		3		1			6	1:6
Canis familiaris	3										3	
Vulpes macrotis						2					2	
Taxidea taxus						1					1	
Artiodactyla sp.	*7*	*7*	*7*	*7*	*36*	*14*		*21*			*100*	
	1	1	1	1	5	2		3			14	1:14
Odocoileus sp.									1		1	
Odocoileus hemionus	*3*	*23*	*3*	*8*	*16*	*12*	*19*	*7*	*2*		*100*	
	10	67	1	24	45	35	56	20	5		290	1:29
Antilocapra americana						1					1	
Bos taurus									2		2	
Ovis canadensis	*5*	*9*	*5*	*5*		*23*	*36*	*18*			*100*	
	1	2	1	1		5	8	4			22	1:22
TOTAL											1475	

Fig. A5.4. Comparison of body parts by numbers of specimens and by percent for the most abundant species.

AGE GROUPS BY MINIMUM FAUNAL COUNT / SPECIES	ADULT MALE	ADULT FEMALE	YOUNG ADULT MALE	YOUNG ADULT FEMALE	IMMATURE MALE	IMMATURE FEMALE	ADULT, SEX ?	IMMATURE, SEX ?	TOTALS	SUBADULT	ADULT	RATIO OF IMMATURE / ADULT
Sylvilagus auduboni	42	19	2	1		2	1	7	74	12	62	1:5
Lepus californicus	114	92	6	6	4	9	5	31	267	56	211	1:4
Lepus alleni	22	30	1	0	3	2	16	1	75	7	68	1:10
Citellus sp.							12	7	19	7	12	1:2
Thomomys bottae	6	1					1	2	10	2	8	1:4
Dipodomys sp.					1		2		3	1	2	1:2
Dipodomys deserti	1								1		1	
Onychomys sp. cf. torridus								1	1	1		
Neotoma sp.					1				1	1		
Canis sp.								2	2	2		
Canis familiaris							2		2		2	
Vulpes macrotis	1	1							2		2	
Taxidea taxus		1							1		1	
Artiodactyla sp.	1	2					3	8	14	8	6	1:1
Odocoileus sp.							1		1		1	
Odocoileus hemionus	45	56	4	7	10	3	12	26	163	50	113	1:2
Antilocapra americana		1							1		1	
Bos taurus		1							1		1	
Ovis canadensis	6	6					6		18		18	
TOTALS	238	210	13	14	19	16	61	85	656			

Fig. A5.5. Tabulation of age groups by minimal faunal count and ratio of subadult individuals.

compiled by Theodore White (1953: 396), for calculating the dietary percentage of various food animals, we find that for every mule deer it takes 33 jackrabbits to furnish an equal amount of usable meat. In light of this the mule deer is shown to be the most utilized mammal food source of the Hohokam, contributing 82% of the total (Fig. A5.1c).

In the Snaketown collection deer specimens are larger than comparative material at Southwest Archeological Center. The comparative specimen most often used was a deer taken in the Upper Sonoran Life Zone of north-central Arizona, and probably belongs to the subspecies *O.h. crooki*. Other specimens are from the Transition Zone of the Elevated Central Tract. The population that occurs in the lower desert environment below 1,500 feet is *O.h. eremicus*, where the chief vegetation is mesquite, willow, screwbean, arrowweed, ironwood, and paloverde. This subspecies is larger than the Desert Mule deer (Taylor 1956: 353).

According to Mearns (1907: 210) these deer were hunted by the Papagos.

Today the geographical range of this subspecies is on "both sides of the Colorado River and around the head of the Gulf of California." Specimens are not recorded as occurring nearer than the Ajo Mountains (Mearns 1907: 210). In former times, however, it seems possible that the burro deer could have occupied the bottom land of the Gila extending to the vicinity of Snaketown. With improved collections and greater refinement in the criteria used in identifications, leads such as this will certainly contribute to the environmental detail of a given time period.

The Hohokam seemed to draw from much the same faunal

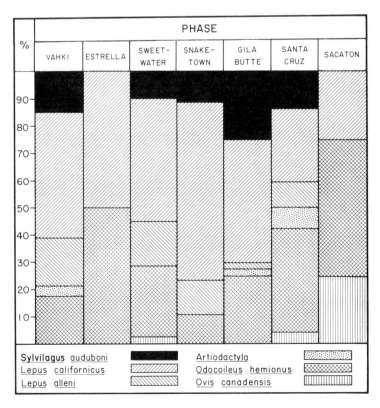

Fig. A5.6. Bone occurrences of the principal meat-producing animals by phase, calculated as percentages of the minimal faunal count.

SPECIES	MINIMUM FAUNAL COUNT	POUNDS USABLE MEAT PER INDIVIDUAL	TOTAL USABLE MEAT IN POUNDS	PERCENT TOTAL USABLE MEAT
Sylvilagus auduboni	74	1.0	74.0	.38
Lepus californicus	267	3.0	801.0	4.05
Lepus alleni	75	3.5	262.5	1.32
Citellus sp.	19	.17	3.2	.02
Thomomys bottae	10	.13	1.3	.01
Dipodomys sp.	3	.35	1.0	
Neotoma sp.	1	.7	.7	
Canis familiaris	2	12.5	25.0	.13
Vulpes macrotis	2	3.0	6.0	.03
Taxidea taxus	1	12.5	12.5	.06
Artiodactyla sp.	14	70	980.0	4.95
Odocoileus sp.	1	100	100.0	.51
Odocoileus hemionus	163	100	16,300.0	82.32
Antilocapra americana	1	44.0	44.0	.22
Ovis canadensis	18	67	1206.0	6.09
TOTAL	656		19,817.0	100.09

Fig. A5.7. Analysis of the relative amounts of usable meat produced by various animals.

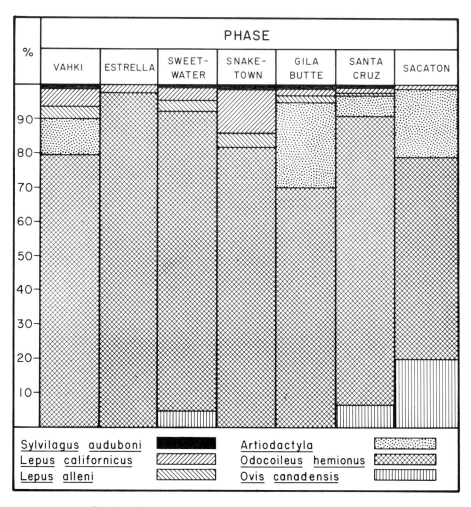

Fig. A5.8. Percentage composition of usable meat per phase.

PHASE \ SPECIES	PIONEER	VAHKI-SWEETWATER	VAHKI-ESTRELLA	VAHKI	ESTRELLA	SWEETWATER-SNAKETOWN	SWEETWATER	SNAKETOWN-GILA BUTTE	SNAKETOWN	GILA BUTTE	SANTA CRUZ-SACATON	SANTA CRUZ	SACATON	NO ASSOCIATION	NO INFORMATION	TOTAL SPECIMENS
Sylvilagus auduboni				8 / 47.0				3 / 6.5	1 / 33.3	7 / 41.2				2 / 22.2	6 / 30.0	27 / 18.1
Lepus californicus	13 / 23.6	6 / 42.8	3 / 16.7	28 / 30.8	3 / 20.0	2 / 11.2	6 / 8.6	55 / 18.5	8 / 17.8	19 / 40.5	7 / 15.9	7 / 15.6		3 / 7.0	11 / 8.3	171 / 18.2
Lepus alleni	2 / 28.6		1 / 50.0	4 / 18.2			3 / 23.1	6 / 22.2		1 / 100.0		2 / 100.0		4 / 33.4	1 / 5.3	24 / 19.7
Odocoileus hemionus	9 / 47.5		2 / 66.6	6 / 23.1	5 / 41.6	1 / 100.0	12 / 63.2	70 / 44.9	1 / 33.3	7 / 41.2	2 / 33.3	15 / 41.7	1 / 16.7	5 / 50.0	14 / 29.3	150 / 42.3
Ovis canadensis	1 / 100.0						2 / 25.0	6 / 54.5			1 / 33.3		1 / 100.0		3 / 60.0	14 / 46.7
TOTAL SPECIMENS	25	6	6	46	8	3	23	140	10	34	10	24	2	14	36	386

Fig. A5.9. Burned bones of principal meat-producing animals plotted by frequency and phase. Percentage values represent the fraction of burned to unburned bone.

resources as the Pima and Papago of a later time. Pima informants maintained that deer as a food source was second only to blacktail jackrabbits (Castetter and Bell 1942: 64). Concerning the Papago they write, "Among animals their reliance was upon deer, and in diminishing order, rabbits, antelope, mountain sheep, rats, and larvae. A family group formerly had no more than one or two hunters, each killing about twelve to fifteen deer per year. Many families had no hunter, so the kill was distributed among the entire economic unit with which they were affiliated, ranging usually from two to ten families" (1942: 58).

Castetter and Bell also quote Grossman in 1871 as stating, "The younger men built or repaired ditches and houses, and in winter, fought enemies or hunted, especially deer. In some cases, one man of a family was the hunter, the others caring for the land, as deer hunting involved the development of a specialized technique entailing a long apprenticeship begun in boyhood" (1942: 133).

Antilocapra americana. A single specimen has been identified in the collection. It seems unusual that more pronghorn were not found. The pronghorn is an animal adapted to open country and had a diet consisting mainly of weeds and forbs, with grass and browse being of lesser importance (Leopold 1959: 522). But perhaps the only community that supports this kind of plant life for any length of time in the Sonoran Zone would be along the few streams and river courses. These areas are covered however, by larger forms of vegetation thus making the pronghorn, on entering this cover extremely vulnerable to attackers. At best the Sonoran desert could support small bands of this species, probably rarely ever reaching a sizable population. Since the northern Sonoran desert was heavily peopled during the Snaketown occupation, it would have taken little time at all to have depleted bands of pronghorn thus keeping them below a balance of productivity.

The herds that ranged the desert regions of southwestern Arizona were probably the subspecies *A.a. sonoriensis.* Goldman described a specimen in 1945 from Crittenden, Santa Cruz County, Arizona.

Bos taurus. Three specimens of domestic cattle were identified in this sample. Two of these elements are foot bones of a small adult, significantly below the size range of bison. The third specimen is a portion of long bone, definitely modern, which had been cut transversely with a metal saw, resulting in a ring and indicating butchering.

Ovis canadensis. The collection consists of an MFC of 2.75%, or 31 specimens, in the material identified as Bighorn (Fig. A5.1b). Their numbers are few compared to deer, and were probably not of local origin. They occur today in mountainous areas or, during drought conditions, at waterholes where they may remain until the rains let them disperse. Within their restricted environmental niche, however, these animals seemingly occurred in good numbers. But being adapted to climbing, they are "loath to leave the mountains since they are poor runners on flat terrain" (Leopold 1959: 526).

Mearns' description of the characteristics of this animal indicates that it was an easy take for any greenhorn who had the capacity to climb. "When first seen all three leaped upon a boulder and gazed down at the hunter. One was shot, and the others in rapid succession when they stopped, out of curiosity, to look at the hunter. To judge by our own experiences, this tameness or stupidity is characteristic, and only the inaccessible nature of its retreats has enabled the remnant of the species to exist up to the present time" (1907: 238).

According to early reports, Bighorns were used extensively by the Pima and Papago. At certain places there were skulls with horns piled high by the hunters. One seventeenth century observer, Mange, encountered at the Pima village of Tusonimo in the vicinity of present-day Blackwater on the Gila, a large mound or hill of mountain-sheep horns which he estimated contained more than 100,000, and this abundance led him to conclude that sheep must have been their common source of food (Castetter and Bell 1942: 67). Mearns saw other heaps of horns of *O.c. gaillardi* [= *O.c. mexicana*] in the Tule and Granite Mountains (1907: 244).

APPENDIX 6

Avifauna

Charmion Randolph McKusick

The identification study of the Snaketown avifauna could not have been undertaken without the generous cooperation of Chester A. Thomas, Chief, Southwest Archaeological Center, and Thomas W. Mathews, Chief, Preservation Laboratory. In addition to the National Park Service avian comparative collection, specimens were loaned by Stephen Russell and Amadeo M. Rea of the University of Arizona and Lyndon L. Hargrave of Prescott College. Special thanks are due Bixby Demaree and Eleanor Radke who salvaged carcasses of a great many birds from the Phoenix area for preparation of modern comparative specimens used in this study.

NATURE OF THE SPECIMENS

The avian remains considered here consist of about a cupful of specimens sorted from eight large boxes of bone, mostly composed of rodent, rabbit, hare, and large mammal bone, but including an unusually large proportion of fish, amphibian, reptile, and arthropod remains. An impression that the Hohokam utilized almost anything that moved has been borne out by the identifiable portion of the avian collection. Approximately a third of the specimens were derived from what is believed to be fecal remains. These specimens are extremely fragmentary. Most of those which remain unidentified appear to be bones of sparrow-sized Fringillidae. Many more specimens are burned than is usual at later sites in other areas of the Southwest. This is not a scorching of exposed ends such as occurs in roasting, or isolated charred spots produced by contact with live coals, but is much more extensive, suggesting that the trash dump itself may have been burned from time to time. There was little gnawing of bones by either carnivores or rodents.

NOTES ON THE COLLECTION

A minimum faunal count of 68 specimens, representing 26 species, 2 subspecies, and 4 genera, has been secured from the identification study (Fig. A6.1). The low usage of a variety of species is reflected by a minimum faunal count of eight, or 11.76% of the collection, for the most numerous species. Low usage of birds may be illustrated by an average of fewer than three individuals per species at Snaketown, as contrasted to an average of as many as 40 individuals per species where birds are used in large numbers (McKusick 1970: Ms., avian remains, Gran Quivira, N.M., Mound 7).

The avian identifications are discussed by family groupings in accepted taxonomic order. Minimal faunal counts and other pertinent information are given in Figure A6.1.

Herons

The Great Blue Heron is the most conspicuous large water bird in Arizona. It formerly nested in colonies in the Salt River Valley (Phillips, Marshall and Monson 1964: 5), and still does locally (Amadeo Rea, personal correspondence, 1970).

Ardea herodias. A single specimen, part of the left radius, has been gnawed by small rodents and burned.

Geese and Ducks

Of 15 specimens in this family, 13 are assignable to time periods. These extend from about 300 B.C. to A.D. 700. Fourteen specimens are bones of the wing or pectoral girdle, suggesting that feathers may have been valued more than or instead of the meat of the fowl. All of the ducks and geese would have been available as wintering or transient birds; the Ruddy Duck might also have been obtained during the summer. White-fronted Geese, which are now rare, occur in equal numbers to Snow Geese.

Although dabbling ducks, which do well in shallow water, are most numerous, a diving duck and a stiff-tailed duck imply the presence of some fairly deep still water.

Geese

Branta canadensis. The Canada Goose is represented by a burned left humerus.

Anser albifrons. White-fronted Goose specimens include a humerus, an ulna, two radii, and a carpometacarpus; two bones are burned.

Chen hyperborea. Snow Goose specimens consist of three carpometacarpi, two of which are burned, and a humerus.

Dabbling Ducks

Anas platyrhynchos. Mallard specimens include a humerus, ulna, and carpometacarpus.

Anas acuta. The Pintail is represented by a burned left ulna.

Anas carolinensis. Green-winged Teal is represented by a right coracoid.

Diving Ducks

Aythya affinis. A left carpometacarpus was identified as Lesser Scaup.

Stiff-tailed Ducks

Oxyura jamaicensis. The Ruddy Duck, the only stiff-tailed duck found in Arizona, is represented by a scorched tarsometatarsus.

FAMILY	SPECIES	VAHKI	ESTRELLA	VAHKI-SWEETWATER	ESTRELLA-SWEETWATER	SWEETWATER	SWEETWATER-SNAKETOWN	SNAKETOWN	PIONEER GENERAL	SNAKETOWN-GILA BUTTE	GILA BUTTE	SANTA CRUZ	SANTA CRUZ-SACATON	GENERAL	MINIMUM FAUNAL COUNT	PERCENTAGE OF COLLECTION	PERCENTAGE OF MINIMUM FAUNAL COUNT
ARDEIDAE	Ardea herodias									I					1	1.47	1.47
ANATIDAE	Branta canadensis								I						1	1.47	22.05
	Anser albifrons				I			I		2					4	5.88	
	Chen hyperborea	I		I				I	I						4	5.88	
	Anas platyrhynchos		I			I									2	2.94	
	Anas acuta													I	1	1.47	
	Anas carolinensis					I									1	1.47	
	Aythya affinis	I													1	1.47	
	Oxyura jamaicensis													I	1	1.47	
ACCIPITRIDAE	Accipiter cooperii												I		1	1.47	8.82
	Buteo swainsoni													I	1	1.47	
	Circus cyaneus					I					I			2	4	5.88	
FALCONIDAE	Falco sparvarius	I			I		I								3	4.41	4.41
PHASIANIDAE	Lophortyx gambelii	I				I			I		2	I		2	8	11.76	11.76
GRUIDAE	Grus canadensis					I								I	2	2.94	2.94
RECURVIROSTRIADE	Recurvirostre americana						I								1	1.47	1.47
COLUMBIDAE	Zenaidura macroura	I		I					I						3	4.41	4.41
PSITTACIDAE	Ara sp.					I			I						2	2.94	7.35
	Ara macao					I									1	1.47	
	Rhynchopsitta pachyrhyncha					I						I			2	2.94	
CUCULIDAE	Geococcyx californianus					I									1	1.47	1.47
PICIDAE	Colaptes auratus mearnsi					I									1	1.47	1.47
CORVIDAE	Aphelocoma coerulescens										I				1	1.47	2.94
	Corvus corax							I							1	1.47	
MIMIDAE	Mimus polyglottos						I							I	2	2.94	2.94
ICTERIDAE	Sturnella sp.		I											I	2	2.94	22.05
	Xanthocephalus xanthocephalus	I													1	1.47	
	Agelaius phoenecius			I		I					I			I	4	5.88	
	Icterus cucullatus						I							7	8	11.76	
FRINGILLIDAE	Aimophila sp.													I	1	1.47	4.41
	Junco sp.													2	2	2.94	
	TOTALS	5	2	3	2	11	2	4	4	3	8	2	1	21	68		

Fig. A6.1. Minimal faunal counts of bird species and genera by phases.

Hawks and Falcons

Occurrences of the Sparrow Hawk fell between 300 B.C. and A.D. 550, the Marsh Hawk between A.D. 200 and 700, and the Cooper's Hawk between A.D. 700 and 1100. The single Swainson's Hawk is undated. There appears to be a tendency to utilize Sparrow Hawks at an early period in the Southwest with an emphasis on large hawks and eagles developing rather late. All hawk and falcon bones are from the wings or pectoral girdle. None are burned.

Accipiter cooperii. The Cooper's Hawk is represented by a right ulna.

Buteo swainsoni. Swainson's Hawk is identified from a left humerus.

Circus cyaneus. Marsh Hawk specimens consist of two right

ulnae, a right corcacoid, and a right carpometacarpus. All are from large individuals of female size range.

Falco sparvarius. Sparrow Hawks are represented by right and left ulnae and a right carpometacarpus, all of large, presumably female, size.

Quail

Quail samples occur in the period between 300 B.C. and A.D. 900. All quail from the second Snaketown excavation compare well with modern skeletons of Gambel's Quail from the area. George O. Hand described this species as being present in this vicinity by the "millions" as late as 1862 (Phillips, Marshall and Monson 1964: 29).

Lophortyx gambelii. Gamble's Quail are represented by random bones from the wings, legs, and axial skeleton. None are burned.

Marsh Birds

Of two Sandhill Crane specimens, only one is referable to subspecies or phase; it is a Lesser Sandhill Crane dating between A.D. 200 and 350. The American Avocet has been considered to be occasional but not breeding in central Arizona. On June 20, 1968, Bixby Demaree salvaged the carcass of an avocet in breeding plumage. Upon preparation at the Southwest Archeological Center, it was found to be a female with three enlarged ova, one of which was ready to enter the oviduct. Encouraged by this indication of breeding in the Phoenix area, she found in 1969 an avocet nest with three eggs between those of two pairs of Black-necked Stilts at the West Phoenix Sewerage Ponds. Unfortunately these nests were drowned out by an increase in water level, but the probability of avocets being more common in the area before the construction of the present dam complex is certainly reinforced. The avocet from Snaketown dated A.D. 200–350 or later.

Grus canadensis. The Sandhill Crane is represented by two right ulnae.

Recurvirostre americana. The American Avocet specimen is a fragmentary right humerus.

Ground Cuckoos

Geococcyx californianus. The only Roadrunner bone recovered is a left tarsometatarsus.

Woodpeckers

One woodpecker, a flicker, dates between A.D. 200 and 350. All flickers have now been included in the species *Colaptes auratus.* This specimen falls within the size range of the small, yellow, desert subspecies, *mearnsi.*

Colaptes auratus mearnsi. The Gilded Flicker is represented by a left tarsometatarsus.

Corvids

Phillips, Marshall, and Monson (1964: 104) list the Scrub Jay as the only one which regularly descends into the desert. No large concentrations of Common Ravens are known from southern Arizona, but they are rare summer residents in the Phoenix area (Phillips, Marshall and Monson 1964: 106). The raven is from a Pioneer Period time level.

Aphelocoma coerulescens. The Scrub Jay specimen is an intact left ulna.

Corvus corax. A left carpometacarpus is the only raven bone recovered.

Doves

Occurrences of Mourning Doves, *Zenaidura macroura,* date between 300 B.C. and A.D. 700.

Macaws and Parrots

Snaketown is by far the earliest known site at which either macaws or parrots have been found in the Southwest. Macaws are dated between A.D. 200 and 900. No macaw or parrot burials were recovered as is often the case in later sites. Only random bones were found.

Ara sp. Macaws are represented by a right ulna and a fragmentary pelvis.

Ara macao. The Scarlet Macaw specimens include the manubrium and four fragmentary vertebrae.

Rhynchopsitta pachyrhyncha. Thick-billed Parrot specimens are a left carpometacarpus and a right femur.

Mockingbirds

Mockingbirds, *Mimus polyglottos,* would have been available in the area as transients or winter residents, and undoubtedly bred in moist agricultural areas (Amadeo Rea, personal correspondence 1970).

Icterids

The Icterids, meadowlarks, orioles, and blackbirds, equal the waterfowl in number of individuals. All four species represented are still abundant in the area where there are irrigated fields. Datable Icterids occupy time ranges of from 300 B.C. to A.D. 200 for meadowlarks and Yellow-headed Blackbirds, 300 B.C. to A.D. 700 for Red-winged Blackbirds, and A.D. 350 to 550 for Hooded Orioles.

Sturnella sp. Both meadowlark specimens are mandibles.

Xanthocephalus xanthocephalus. The Yellow-headed Blackbird is represented by a mandible.

Agelaius phoenecius. Red-winged Blackbird specimens include two right humeri, a left ulna, and a burned left tibiotarsus.

Icterus cucullatus. Hooded Oriole specimens comprise seven tibiotarsi, two of which are burned, a manual phalanx, and a cranium.

Sparrows and Finches

Most of the unidentified specimens are undoubtedly Fringillidae.

Aimophila sp. The Aimophila sparrow is represented by a fragmentary mandible.

Junco sp. The Junco specimen is a fragmentary right tarsometatarsus.

SUMMARY

Attempting to sketch the usage of avifauna over 1,400 years from only 68 identified individuals is impractical. For this reason the few specimens available have been noted in some detail in the hope that they may be combined with future data to form a better picture of Hohokam bird usage. One outstanding characteristic of Hohokam faunal collections, at least through Sedentary times, is the paucity of bird bone in what little refuse bone is present. Apparently agriculture was dominant, and the inhabitants of Snaketown were more dependent on fish than they were on small birds. Fecal remains include the bones of many fish and small rodents, but relatively few remains of mockingbirds, orioles, blackbirds, and sparrows, the only avian species identifiable from this source.

Some trends are suggested by the material now available which will probably be confirmed by additional specimens. The Snaketown bird bone identifications fall naturally into three groups. The first, including only Vahki Phase material, is a rather basic assortment of species found in the early phases of other sites in southern Arizona and southwestern New Mexico. Typically this includes waterfowl, quail, doves, and Sparrow Hawks.

The second division extends from Estrella through Gila Butte. It appears to be a developmental period characterized by a wider usage of species including the Common Raven and Marsh Hawk, but is more conspicuous for the utilization at an extremely early time of macaws and parrots. The macaws suggest Mexican influence of a different sort and perhaps source than that responsible for the introduction of pyrite mirrors and accompanying traits at a later period (Di Peso 1968: 7).

The third grouping, from Santa Cruz and Sacaton phases, is completely lacking in waterfowl, Sparrow Hawks, and macaws. With this shift comes an increasing emphasis on hawks, reminiscent of late Mogollon or Western Pueblo species distributions.

There are no owls, turkeys, or eagles. Apparently usage of turkeys, and perhaps eagles in this area is contemporaneous with the introduction of the Gila Polychrome Series (Fewkes 1912: 91, 93; Haury 1945a: 207). The only turkey bone from a Hohokam site which was available for examination was one specimen of Indian domestic turkey from the University Indian Ruin which dates in the 1300s (Hayden 1957: 126), so turkey bone would not be expected from a Hohokam site occupied at this time period. Owls were certainly available to the Hohokam if they had wished to use them. It may be that utilization of owls is referable to a later time period or another cultural complex.

The pattern of development of avifaunal usage at Snaketown is not in itself unusual; what is unusual is its placement in time earlier than parallel developments in neighboring areas.

The use for which the birds were intended may have been multiple. Hooded Oriole and Red-winged Blackbird remains, which come from samples of fecal material, are all in the size range of the more colorful males. The birds could have been stripped of desirable feathers, and then eaten, apparently whole. Yellow birds are conspicuous and include a Yellow-headed Blackbird, a meadowlark, and a Gilded Flicker, as well as the eight Hooded Orioles.

Hawks and Marsh Hawks are in the female size range, suggesting a preference for the banded feathers of the females of these species over the more uniformly colored feathers of the males.

Quail were in all probability eaten, as may have been doves. Both are eaten by the Papagos and Pimas. The latter group also keeps doves for their feathers (Castetter and Bell 1942: 69–71; Underhill 1951).

Except for the imported parrots and macaws, the species list is what one would have found in an area characterized by natural riparian vegetarian bordered by irrigated fields, with desert beyond.

APPENDIX 7
Micro-Vertebrates
Stanley J. Olsen

The smaller vertebrates, discussed here, are of unusual interest because they represent animals the bones of which are generally missed by archaeologists. Recovery methods at Snaketown included the use of fine screens which caught tiny bones, fragmented and whole (Fig. 8.1), that passed through the coarser screens. Ideas of Hohokam food habits not previously stated have been stimulated by this evidence.

The fauna is representative of "bite-sized" animals easily collected by children or old adults in the immediate vicinity of their dwellings. There is little doubt that these animals constituted an accepted diet, particularly if the usual deer and rabbit, common to most southwestern sites, were in short supply.

CLASSIFICATION

Most of the specific taxonomic classifications of vertebrates are based on living animals, the emphasis being placed on their soft anatomy and color patterns. Excessive fragmentation of the Snaketown material has made positive specific assignment difficult for some of it and in many cases impossible. This problem is recognized in the listings as, for example, *Sceloperus* cf. *graciosus*. Since this species is the more common of those present in the area of the same genus, it is indicated. I believe that this specific choice will not markedly change the overall evaluation as to the importance of these animals to the Snaketown inhabitants. Most of the *Sceloperus* species represent animals with the same ecological requirements. Some ecologists believe that an "ecological species" is important and a taxonomic species is not. If bluegill, bream, or sunfish—fish of similar size—inhabit the same environmental niche, equally fill the food requirements, and offer the same problems of capture to the fisherman, it matters little which taxonomic species they are.

Fish

Family Cyprinidae: Minnows
Ptychocheilus lucius, Colorado River Squawfish
Gila cf. *cypha*, Humpback chub

The Colorado River Squawfish *(Ptychocheilus lucius)* was apparently a common and preferred food fish in pre-Columbian Arizona reaching a length of some 2 m and weighing over 45 kg (100 lb) (Lowe 1967). Numerous vertebrae recovered from the fine screening and by flotation indicate that small (200 mm) fry were also collected. Several pharangeal arches with teeth of the chub *(Gila* cf. *cypha)* were also identified. These compared well with recent fish that were 62 mm in length.

Glover M. Allen, Curator of Mammals at the Museum of Comparative Zoology at Harvard University, identified fish bones as representing the sturgeon, *Acipenser* (Gladwin and others 1937: 157). Robert Miller (1955) reported that the sturgeon would have been considerably out of its known range to have occurred in the Snaketown area and also that bones of this genus are rarely preserved in archaeological sites due to their cartilagenous nature. Miller stated that these remains probably represented the Squawfish *(Ptychocheilus)*. With this I wholeheartedly concur. The bones were subsequently lost, so that this problem cannot now be resolved to everyone's satisfaction.

Lizards

Family Iguanidae: Iguanas
Sceloporus cf. *graciosus*, Sagebrush Lizard
Sceloporus cf. *magister*, Desert Spiny Lizard
Family Teidae: Teids
Cnemidophorus cf. *tigris*, Western Whiptailed Lizard

These small lizards are commonly found around dwellings and walls in arid and semiarid environments. Although swift-moving, they can be easily caught by anticipating their movements. Vertebrae as well as mandibles with dentitions were collected from the excavations.

Snakes

Family Colubridae: Garter Snakes, Rat Snakes, Gopher Snakes, etc.
Colubrid, gen. et. sp. indet.

Vertebrae of small harmless snakes of this family turned up in several areas of the site. One sample from Pit 9:10E was burned, perhaps from meal preparation.

It is impractical from such scanty material to assign generic or specific names to the remains.

Mammals

Family Sciuridae: Squirrels
Citellus cf. *harrisii*, Yuma Antelope Squirrel, or *Citellus tereticaudus*, Round-tailed Ground Squirrel
Family Cricetidae: Native Rats and Mice
Peromyscus boylii, Brush Mouse

Two small mammals, the Antelope Squirrel *(Citellus* cf. *harrisii)* and mouse *(Peromyscus boylii)* constitute the bulk of the recovered small mammal bones. Nearly all elements of the skeletons were represented, most were incomplete or broken. Young as well as old individuals were identified. All of the sample from Pit 9:10E was burned.

The entire vertebrate bone sample seems to indicate that most of the common or abundant small animals were taken by the Snaketown inhabitants.

ACKNOWLEDGMENTS

I wish to thank Robert Miller for the generous loan of comparative fish skeletons from his excellent collections and my son John, and James Kelley (a student at Florida State University) for their generous aid in making faunal comparisons and collecting the needed fresh animal skeletons.

APPENDIX 8
Fishes
W. L. Minckley

A total of 277 bones, whole and fragmentary, were received for study. Considering the fragmentation, nature of the material (which appeared largely to be dry-screened), and the scattering of the material throughout vertical and horizontal space, no interpretations may be made as to changes in species utilization through time. One hundred thirty-two bones were identifiable as fishes known to have occurred in the fresh waters of the region (with exceptions noted below). About 30% of the fish bone sample could be identified as to species. The bone fragments not identifiable as fish were reptilian—snakes, lizards, and one shell fragment of the native turtle, genus *Kinosternon*.

Few fragments were charred, indicating to me fishes were used by boiling or were simply eaten raw. There is good evidence from localities on the Verde River that fish were dried for preservation (unpublished data). All material I examined represents individuals 25 cm (10 in) in length or larger. The most common form was a sucker, Family Catostomidae—*Catostomus insignis* Baird and Girard (Gila coarse-scaled sucker); the second-most was the Gila mountain sucker, *Pantosteus clarki* (Baird and Girard). These were followed in decreasing order by Colorado chub, *Gila robusta* Baird and Girard, razorback sucker, *Xyrauchen texanus* (Abbott), and one large vertebra, badly damaged, that I refer to the Colorado River Squawfish, *Ptychocheilus lucius* Girard. This last form was thought to be the "sturgeon" reported in 1937 (Gladwin and others: 157) and questioned by Miller (1955). One caudal vertebra is reminiscent of *Gila elegans* Girard, the bonytail chub, but must be considered *incerti sedis* because of fragmentation.

Two fragments not included above appear to represent earbones (or otoliths) of marine Sciaenidae, drums or croakers. They are hard white bones and likely intended for ornamental use or as trade items. One is almost certainly corvina, genus *Cynoscion*, as may both well be. These fish would have been available only from the Sea of Cortez, or from off the California coast.

All species found in the Snaketown collection have been historically present in the Phoenix canal system, at least seasonally. Of the five listed the *Catostomus, Pantosteus,* and *Gila* persist there, at least locally, in large numbers today. Diversion of water and drying of a canal segment make them simple prey to man and other animals.

APPENDIX 9

Cremated Human Remains

Walter H. Birkby

Surely Thomas Paine must have been thinking of cremation analyses when he wrote, "These are the times that try men's souls," for to no other osteological study can so much time and effort be devoted for such a small amount of recoverable data.

This is not to say that cremated remains have no redeeming value, or that they should be ignored after an excavator once passes them through a screen to recover associated artifacts. Indeed, cremated human remains offer a distinct challenge to the osteologist because they are difficult to analyze.

While some techniques ordinarily employed in human identification cases can be used in the examination of well-cremated remains, such techniques are limited by the nature of the material almost solely to morphological analyses. Generally, there can be no recourse to the calipers—except in limited situations (Gejvall 1963). Even the dentition, as a rule, is reduced to fragments of crowns without their enamel and to remnants of tooth roots.

Nevertheless, with all of these inherent problems, some biological data are recoverable from fired osseous debris. A few, though certainly not all, cremations will yield information on the least possible number of individuals represented, their probable sex, age, dental and osseous pathologies, and nonmetric or discontinuous traits. From most of the remains, conjectures can be made as to whether the bones were dry or "green" at the time of incineration.

Little biological data have been reported on the burned human bones from the Southwest, although many excavated sites have yielded cremations. Most notable of the few published analyses are that of Haury (1945a) on the Los Muertos material and more recently that of Merbs (1967) on the cremations from two Point of Pines sites. The biological data suggested as useful in these reports, as well as those of Baby (1954), Gejvall (1963), and Binford (1972a; 1972b), have been utilized to some extent in the analysis of the burned human bones recovered from Snaketown.

THE SNAKETOWN REMAINS

The fired Snaketown remains consisted of reputedly 110 individuals retrieved from two immediately adjacent but temporally separated sites. Ninety-five of the cremations were excavated from Snaketown while 15 others were taken from the later Classic Period site, Arizona U: 13:24.

Every identifiable fragment of each cremation was carefully sorted into its anatomic component after initial separation into a cranial or postcranial category. Occasionally, and whenever the situation warranted, temporary reconstructions were made if several of the fragments of an element could be pieced together. Such reconstructions were always attempted when nonhuman bone artifacts were encountered.

After each cremation had been sorted fully, and any artifacts or other extraneous material removed, the following observations were recorded: the degree of calcination of the total cremation, the bones represented, the duplication of osseous elements, the probable sex and age of the individual, the state of the dentition,

bone and tooth pathologies, and nonmetric traits. The final recorded observation was the total weight of all human remains from the cremation, regardless of whether the debris could be anatomically identified.

Numbers, Age, and Sex of Individuals

Multiple individuals isolated from supposedly single cremations were found in only three instances, all from Snaketown. Cremation 4:11I contained the remains of a child aged 6-9 years and an adult female of indeterminate age. Crematorium 1:8E consisted of an adult female, an adult of indeterminate sex (isolated by a duplication of mandibular fragments and teeth), and an adolescent less than 14 years old. Crematorium 7:11H could be separated into remnants of an adult of unknown sex and age, and a young child.

One bag of cremated bone from Block 12G was listed in the field as being double and thus labeled as "Cremations 1 and 2." Examination in the laboratory, however, revealed neither a duplication of skeletal elements nor indications of dissimilarities in cranial vault or cortex thicknesses, nor a differential firing of skeletal parts. Therefore, for purposes of this study, the "double" cremation was classified as a single.

The age assessment of the three adult cremations from Snaketown (Fig. A9.1) was based on endocranial and ectocranial suture closure, and on the incomplete closure of the basilar synchondrosis in the case of the youngest individual. All other adults from both sites to whom specific age categories could not be assigned were aged primarily on their overall robusticity and on the cortical thicknesses of the long bone fragments. The next most frequent adult aging mechanism was the remnants of dentition or the molar sockets when the teeth were missing postmortem. Occasionally, however, the fusion and obliteration of epiphyseal lines from the ends of the long bones were suggestive that the remains were probably those of an adult. Eighty-six percent (81/94) of the adult material could not be assigned to a specific age category. This differs markedly from the 31% reported for Point of Pines cremations (Merbs 1967: 502) but comes closer to the recorded frequency at Los Muertos where as many as 51% (60/117) of the adults could not be age assigned (Haury 1945a: 46). Indeed, the Los Muertos figure might have been even larger if more than 137 of the 300 to 400 cremations recovered had been available for analysis. Nevertheless, these findings suggest that incineration as practiced by the Hohokam resulted in more complete degradation of the bone than was true at Point of Pines.

The ten nonadults, all from Snaketown, were aged predominately by dental maturation and epiphyseal union. There were no specimens observed which could be considered younger than one year of age. I strongly doubt, judging from the state of destruction to the remains of the few infants and children, that material any younger could have withstood incineration and still have been identifiable.

Sex determinations were derived primarily from both cranial

CREMATIONS	ADULTS						NON-ADULTS		SEX ? AGE ?		TOTAL		
	MALE*		FEMALE*		SEX ?								
	(:1)	(:24)	(:1)	(:24)	(:1)	(:24)	(:1)	(:24)	(:1)	(:24)	ADULTS	NON-ADULT	?
INFANTS: BIRTH-2 YRS.							3					3	
CHILDREN: 3-11 YRS.							5					5	
ADOLESCENTS: 12-17 YRS.							2					2	
ADULTS: 18-30 YRS.	1										1		
30-40 YRS.	1										1		
OVER 40 YRS.			1								1		
AGE UNKNOWN	10	7	8		62	4			2	4	91		6
SITE TOTAL	12	7	9		62	4	10		2	4	94	10	6
TOTAL CREMATIONS	19		9		66		10		6		110		

* = Includes those individuals classified as Male (?) and Female (?).

Fig. A9.1. Sex and age distribution of cremations from Snaketown and Arizona U:13:24.

and postcranial morphology, using criteria developed from the more typical skeletal analysis (Krogman 1962). The most frequent cranial features used for sexing were the appearance of the supraorbital borders, the mandibular ramus and chin, and the nuchal area of the occipital. In three instances, frontal sinus development played a major supporting role in sex identification. Postcranially, robusticity figured most prominently in ascribing the sex of the remains. The os pubis was identifiable in only two cremations (both males); the presence of a preauricular sulcus was observed in one female and its absence noted in the sexual determination of one male.

In only 6 of the 110 specimens was it impossible to at least suggest a probable sex or general age of the remains. These nonidentifiable specimens were grossly incomplete, ranging in weight from 2 to 27 grams. Despite a most careful effort to sex the adult remains from Snaketown, limiting the investigation to morphology rather than using metric standards developed on European material (Gejvall 1963: 385), only 30% of the adults could be so classified. Such results again differ markedly from the 69% obtained by Merbs (1967: 501) on late Mogollon material at Point of Pines.

The Los Muertos adults were sexed in 57% (67/117) of the cases (Haury 1945a: 47), but the field selection at that site was so great (only 137 remain of the 300-400 recovered) that these results can only be considered questionably high. Haury himself suggests that "... the members of the Expedition [may have] selected only those lots with larger amounts and better preserved fragments" (1945a: 46).

Types of Incineration

The predominant type of firing noted on the submitted material from both sites was most similar to the "completely incinerated" classification established by Baby (1954: 2). At least 66% of the cremations examined (Fig. A9.2) fell into this category by their color range, the presence of deep "checking," and "diagonal transverse fractures and warping." The smallest number (10.3% of cremations) matched Baby's classification of "incompletely incinerated, or smoked." There were no cases of "nonincinerated or normal bone." These findings are generally similar to what Merbs (1967) reported for the Mogollon sites.

However, unlike the material reported by Merbs and Baby, the Hohokam cremations have a 23.4% incidence of a type of burning which goes beyond the "completely incinerated" classification. An examination of these cremations indicated that they were so well calcined that the bones could be used to write on a chalkboard or could be powdered between the fingers. This suggests either the use of a hotter crematory fire or an increase in the length of actual incineration time, or both. It will be noted in

CATEGORY	CHALKY	COMPLETELY INCINERATED(1)	INCOMPLETELY INCINERATED; SMOKED (1)	NON-INCINERATED OR NORMAL (1)	TOTAL
ALL CREMATIONS.......	25 gr.	71	11	NONE	107(2)
%....................	23.4	66.3	10.3		100%
ADULT CREMATIONS.......	22	60	10		92(3)
ADULT TOTAL WEIGHTS...........	3,110 gr.	16,433	6,472		26,015 gr.
ADULT WEIGHT RANGE.............	9-400 gr.	9-1675	28-2353		9-2353 gr.
AVERAGE ADULT CREMATION WEIGHT.............	141.4 gr.	273.8	647.2		282.8 gr.

(1) Classifications established by Baby (1954: 2).
(2) Three individuals (2 adults, 1 adolescent) from multiple cremation (Crematorium 1:8E) could not be counted due to differential firing of the mixed remains.
(3) Two adults not included from Crematorium 1:8E. See (2) above.

Fig. A9.2. Classification and weights (in grams) of the incinerated bones from Snaketown and Arizona U:13:24, combined.

Figure A9.2 that the "chalky" type bone residues, when examined by weight, do indeed fit nicely at the proposed "hottest" end of the incineration gradient. The cremations in this category not only had a smaller adult average weight but the weight range also was the shortest.

Another slightly different form of burned bone was observed among the submitted remains. This I classified as "porcelainized bone" because of its somewhat shell-like appearance and brittle condition. When tapped with another fragment, this material produced a "brittle" sound not unlike highly fired ceramic materials when struck. Eight cremations from Snaketown and one from Arizona U:13:24 exhibited this condition, but inasmuch as they otherwise had the characteristics of the "completely incinerated" classification, they were tabulated under that heading.

Since Merbs (1967) did not classify his sample into either the "chalky" or "porcelainized" conditions, a check was made of Point of Pines material for evidence of these occurrences. Forty cremations from this collection were examined (29 from Arizona W:10:50 and 11 from Arizona W:10:78). Not a single instance of a "chalky" type incineration was observed, although four cremations (two from each site) were encountered which could be classified as "porcelainized bone." Three of the remaining 36 randomly sampled Mogollon cremations were of the "incompletely incinerated" type, with the rest falling into the "completely incinerated" class.

"In-the-Flesh" Cremation

The general condition of the burned human remains from Snaketown indicates that cremation was performed on flesh-covered or "green" bones rather than on dried osseous material. Previoius test burnings by Baby (1954: 4) on a whole fleshed cadaver, on "green bones" from dissections, and on dry bones were reported as showing certain fundamental differences in surface "checking," deep longitudinal fracturing, and warpage. Binford (1972a: 375–76) attempted to duplicate these tests using in some instances a partially dissected monkey cadaver. The results of his tests were comparable to those of Baby, for example, cremated dry bones exhibited little or no warpage, no deep longitudinal fracturing, but had straight transverse fracture lines.

The "completely incinerated" Snaketown cremations predominately contained cranial and postcranial material which was badly warped and deeply "checked" and had curving transverse fractures of the long bones—all of which are most characteristic of cremated "green" or flesh-covered skeletons. The condition of the worked nonhuman bone artifacts recovered from the osseous debris of nineteen cremations supports this contention for burning "in-the-flesh." These artifacts, most often constructed from Artiodactyla metapodials, presumably would have been dry (or nearly dry) tools prior to incineration. Invariably, when found with a human cremation, each exhibited characteristics which have been demonstrated for fired dry bones, and the human remains all bore features of "in-the-flesh" or "green bone" incineration.

Identifiable Surviving Bones

The identifiable cranial bones from both sites which best survived the flames are (with their percent occurrence) as follows: temporal (45%), mandible (44%), parietals (33%), frontal (31%), occipital squamous (27%), and the maxillae (16%). The most frequently identified postcranial elements were: ribs (44%), vertebrae (31%), femoral shafts and phalanges (28%), and the tarsals and the distal humerus (16%).

By contrast the most frequently appearing (43%) cranial element at Los Muertos, unlike at Snaketown, was the nuchal area of the occipital (Haury 1945a: 45); presumably the same was true also for the Point of Pines sites, although Merbs does not specifically state a frequency. Haury found ribs and vertebrae among the Los Muertos cremations but does not mention in what numbers. Merbs mentions neither of these bones as surviving

incineration at Point of Pines. It is interesting to note that ribs and the temporal bone are the most readily identifiable element in cremations. Generally, however, the bone survival lists given by Haury and Merbs match fairly well the one for the Snaketown material.

Ten Snaketown cremations (5 from Block 5F, 2 from Block 8E, and 3 from the Classic Period site) totally lacked cranial fragments. Eight of the 10 were definitely adults (two from Arizona U:13:24 were of unknown age) and, except for two "chalky" cremations, were classified as "completely incinerated." The burned bone weights were all low and ranged from 3 to 49 gr. Cremation 13 from the Classic Period site lacked not only cranial fragments but also long-bone fragments. It was noted in all cremations that remnants of the lower arms, the lower legs, and the innominates were poorly represented. No explanation can be offered for this condition.

Dental Observations

Only 29.8% of the 94 adult cremations from Snaketown had maxillary and mandibular fragments which exhibited either sockets or an alveolar process undergoing or completing bony resorption. This percentage is considerably lower than the 53% reported by Merbs (1967: 502) for the Late Mogollon.

No attempt was made to analyze separately the dental conditions of the major Snaketown site and the adjacent Classic Period site since only a single adult (male) from the latter had mandibular fragments on which such observations could be made. Therefore, data from both Hohokam sites were tabulated together as if from one site. Non-adult observations could also be made in only one instance and for this reason were excluded from the analysis.

There was a slight (59%) tendency for the left maxillary and mandibular sockets and alveoli to survive destruction by fire. Out of a total of 53 observable maxillary tooth positions, 38 (72%) were from the left side, while 98 of 176 (56%) mandibular tooth positions were from that side. A corrected chi-square (Simpson and others 1960: 190) was computed to test the significance of these observed differences, but the results ($X^2_c = 5.07_{df = 1}$) were not wholly satisfactory, that is, $0.05 < P < .02$. The initial assumption was that these observed differences might be indicative of a differential burning of the body, for whatever reason. This was rejected after an additional check of the surviving bones *by side* produced negative or inconclusive results.

A checklist of the preserved maxillary sockets and alveoli (n = 53) indicated that the two left incisors (n = 7 and 8 respectively) and the canine (7) survived with the highest frequencies (13-15%) in either upper jaw. However, the most frequently surviving mandibular sockets and alveolar spaces, out of the 176 observed, ranged from only 7-8% (12-13 sockets) and covered a broader area of the dental arcade. These mandibular survivors were the right second incisor and the canine sockets, all of the left anterior tooth positions, plus those of the two premolars and the last two molars. A total of 188 fragmentary and nonidentifiable roots were recovered from the adult cremations, with an additional 22 isolated from nonadult material.

Dental pathologies were limited to 53 (23%) of the 229 observable sockets and alveolar spaces. Antemortem missing teeth, as evidenced by slight to complete alveolar resorption, accounted for 45 of the 53 (85%) pathologies. Thirty-three of these 45 were from the mandibular fragments alone. Only 7 sockets (2 maxillary, 5 mandibular) bore traces of abscessing, and all had indications that the tooth had been extant at the time of death. There was only one observable case in which an abscessed tooth had been lost sometime prior to death. Two instances were recorded for peridontal disease, one each in upper and lower jaw fragments.

A single case was noted for suspected congenitally missing third molars. Both maxillary and the mandibular right alveoli did not have the appearance of being resorbed and for this reason were suspected of third molar agenesis. Radiographs were not taken of these areas, and a more definitive statement cannot be made at present.

It is unfortunate that at the time these observations were being recorded, no data were collected on the presence and absence of bifurcated premolar roots or three-rooted mandibular first molars. Both of these supposedly genetic conditions would have been visible on the extant sockets had they occurred. All materials were too fragmentary and incomplete to make observations for shovel-shaped incisors.

Osseous Pathologies

The adult cremations provided evidence for at least five cases of vertebral osteophytosis, one case of hypertrophic changes in the phalanges of a foot, and one case of hypertrophy of the temporomandibular joint. All of these bony changes were suggestive of "osteoarthritis" with the possible exception of the latter. The breakdown in that fossa could also have come about through alterations in the normal bite possibly due to extensive antemortem tooth loss. Only one individual from Arizona U:13:24 had an osteophytic condition of the vertebral centra. An osteitis or possibly an osteomyelitis of an unidentified long-bone fragment occurred with adult Cremation 4:9E from Snaketown.

One 6-9-year old child (Cremation 4A:11I) had the only recorded nonadult bony anomaly—a premature closure of the sagittal suture. Whether this was part of a truly pathological condition, which would have led to microcephaly if the other vault sutures were also involved, could not be determined from the available fragments. Premature craniosynostosis has been reported (Bennett 1967) for a few other sites in the prehistoric Southwest, but I believe this to be the first recorded evidence for the condition among the pre-Classic Hohokam.

Nonmetric Traits

Merbs (1967) was apparently the first to attempt a nonmetric trait analysis on cremated human remains using criteria derived from the noncremated skeletal studies by various investigators. The present examination of the nonmetric traits of the Snaketown Hohokam follows the lead established by his investigations.

Each of the 94 adult cremations was carefully examined for the presence or absence of nonmetric or discontinuous traits. Inasmuch as the identifiable postcranial skeleton was so poorly represented numerically, the nonmetric observations were limited in this study to the cranial fragments. Again, the material from both villages was pooled since only two adults from the Classic Period site had traits observable on their cranial fragments.

An attempt was made to collect data for the 54 cranial traits which are listed on the Arizona State Museum Human Identification Laboratory's standard skeletal data sheets. However, observations could be obtained on only 37 of those attempted. There was an additional but arbitrary deletion of 13 other traits which were deemed too infrequent (less than 3) by their occurrence to be included with the others. The 24 traits which remained after this paring are given in Figure A9.3; unless otherwise stated, these have all been scored as "trait present."

All of the listed traits have been discussed elsewhere in the osteological literature or can be found in standard anatomy textbooks. Three, however, may need clarification either because they are terms coined by this author (e.g., zygo-root foramen and posterior malar foramen) or are not easily found in the suggested texts (e.g., frontal foramen).

The frontal foramen is a well-defined vascular perforation which, when present, is usually located lateral to the supraorbital foramen. The posterior orifice does not open into the orbital cavity, as does the former, but directly into the diploic space. It possibly houses a lateral branch of the supraorbital artery.

The zygo-root foramen is an occasionally appearing vascular orifice located on the superior medial surface of the junction of the temporal squamous and the zygomatic process. It possibly transmits a minor branch of the middle temporal artery.

The posterior malar foramen appears inconsistently on the

TRAIT	FREQUENCY						OBSERVATION RATE			
	SNAKETOWN		POINT OF PINES[1]				SNAKETOWN		POINT OF PINES[1]	
			AZ. W:10:50		AZ. W:10:78					
Mandibular torus	1/6	.17					6/56	.11		
Bregmatic ossicle	0/4	.00					4/28	.14		
Os Inca	0/7	.00					7/28	.25		
Os japonicum	0/3	.00					3/56	.05		
Lacrimal foramen	3/3	1.00					3/56	.05		
Zygo-facial foramen absent	0/7	.00	1/9	.11	1/5	.20	7/56	.12	14/144	.10
Access. Zygo-facial foramen	6/7	.86	1/9	.11	1/5	.20	7/56	.12	14/144	.10
Supraorbital foramen	12/13	.92	8/16	.50	2/8	.25	13/56	.23	14/144	.17
Supraorbital notch	3/6	.50					6/56	.11		
Frontal foramen	1/5	.20					5/56	.09		
Parietal foramen	11/12	.92					12/56	.21		
Mastoid foramen	5/5	1.00					5/56	.09		
Mastoid foramen, extra-sutural	3/5	.60					5/56	.09		
Zygo-root foramen	3/7	.43					7/56	.12		
Posterior condylar canal absent	1/6	.17	0/8	.00	0/7	.00	6/56	.11	15/144	.10
Hypoglossal canal double	1/8	.12	0/7	.00	2/10	.20	8/56	.14	17/144	.12
Foramen spinosum open	0/6	.00					6/56	.11		
Canaliculus innominatus	1/6	.17					6/56	.11		
Foramen ovale incomplete	0/5	.00					5/56	.09		
Posterior malar foramen	4/5	.80					5/56	.09		
Double mental foramen	0/4	.00					4/56	.07		
Access. mandibular foramen	2/3	.67					3/56	.05		
Metopic suture	0/7	.00					7/28	.25		
External frontal sulcus	1/3	.33					3/56	.05		

From Data Table 2, Merbs (1967: 504)

Fig. A9.3. Selected cranial nonmetric traits of adult cremations from Snaketown.

temporal (posterior) surface of the malar, usually at the junction of the large ascending frontal process and the main body of the bone. The orifice is most often as large as that of the foramen spinosum, and generally courses in a medial direction. The feature should not be mistaken for the more consistent but smaller and more superiorly positioned zygomaticotemporal, foramen. This foramen may house an inconsistent branch of the anterior deep temporal artery.

Comparisons could be made with only five of the seven cranial traits listed for the cremations at the Point of Pines sites (Fig. A9.3). The observations for the absence of the zygo-facial foramen at those sites (1 of 9 and 1 of 5, respectively) differed but little from those recorded for Snaketown (0/7). The same may be said when the observed differences in the absence of the posterior condylar canal and the divided hypoglossal canal at the two Mogollon sites were compared with the Hohokam frequencies.

However, two traits (the accessory zygo-facial and the supraorbital foramina) showed marked observational differences between the plateau and the desert cremations. Whether these two traits could be considered as possible population "markers" for the two culturally different groups is not presently known, although it could be indicative and certainly suggests an avenue of future research.

Artifacts

While sorting each individual fragment from a cremation, it was possible to isolate and salvage artifactual materials which might have otherwise gone unnoticed. No attempt was made by the author to analyze this debris, but their presence with a cremation was recorded prior to submitting them to the archaeologist for his observations and interpretation. Their presence illustrates the necessity for careful and detailed examination of cremated human remains, time consuming and tedious as it is.

Haury (1945a:45) was able to record only a 15% incidence of artifact recovery in the 137 Los Muertos cremations available for study. This was considerably lower than the 65% recovery rate among the Snaketown remains, and is probably an accurate reflection of the severe field selection—and probably the removal of easily identifiable artifacts—which was practiced by excavators at the Los Muertos site. It is still a not uncommon practice for archaeologists to screen cremated remains in order to retrieve associated funerary offerings.

CONCLUSIONS

When dealing with any cremated prehistoric population there is always the problem of defining the size of that population. Although it can sometimes be established, through a duplication of skeletal elements, that there are multiple individuals represented in the debris called "a cremation," there is no equally simple way of demonstrating that several discrete piles of burned bones are possibly the remains of a single individual. The *a priori* assumption by archaeologists and osteologists in the past has been that each individual lot of incinerated debris was much like a primary interment, that is, representative of one deceased person. This assumption has led investigators, perhaps erroneously, to treat numbered cremations as one would the numbered skeletal remains and thus arrive at a possible inflated *post-obitum* "burned body count." The question naturally arises, do the Snaketown cremations represent 110 incinerated *individuals,* or is the recorded number also the result of an *a priori* assumption?

The low bone weights observed (Fig. A9.2) for any one lot of adult bones indicate that much less than one complete individual constitutes a Snaketown "cremation." Binford (1972b: 385) has stated that it takes approximately 1,750 grams of calcined and leached bone debris to equal one adult male skeleton. In only three instances do the Snaketown residues approach or surpass that critical weight.

At least two crematory practices could account for the low weights obtained. The first, postcrematory "gleaning," would yield low bone residue if the people were negligent in recovering osseous fragments from the ashes. If this were the case, the crematory pits must not have been used more than once, since, aside from the one noted exception (Cremation 4:11 I), there were no cases for multiple cremations in the recovered individual lots of bone. Similarly, it would seem that if incomplete gleaning was practiced, the crematoria would have produced more multiple cremations than only the two observed cases (Crematoria 1 and 7: 11 H).

The second practice, for which there may be some ethnographic evidence from Southwestern American Indian groups, is the partition of each incinerated body into several or more lots with each lot being interred in a separate location. If the incinerated bodies at Snaketown were indeed being partitioned into random lots prior to interment, one would also expect the bone artifacts to be inadvertently involved in the division. To check this possibility, an attempt was made to match or fit together the fragments of worked bone recovered from one "cremation" with those from any other lot of bones. While the concept itself was sound, the attempt was a failure! The materials were far too fragmentary and incomplete, and the necessary proof for partitioning at Snaketown must remain inconclusive for the present.

Nevertheless, the fact remains that in 97% of the 92 alleged "single adult" bone lots, the observed weights were excessively low. Unless the prehistoric crematory fires were reducing the bones more than would be suspected for usual wood-fed fires, the suggestions for (1) multiple burial of a single cremated individual, or (2) poor postcrematory gleaning, seem the most plausible.

Both of these practices could have been in operation at the same time, and either or both explanations could account for 10 adult "cremations" which totally lacked any evidence for the presence of cranial material. Lest these ten cases conjure up, in the minds of some, images of the taking of trophy heads, body mutilation, or precremation dismemberment, I hasten to add that after close examination of the fragments, there was no evidence of cut-marks on any of the bones from Snaketown.

The Snaketown cremations (and possibly the Los Muertos material as well) differ in several respects from the Late Mogollon incinerations recovered from Point of Pines. The difficulty of making age and sex determinations on the more fragmentary adult remains plus the 23% incidence of a "chalky" type of fired bone observed only among the Hohokam material suggests that the possibly hotter mesquite fuels used by the desert peoples may have reduced the bodies to a greater extent than did the pine and fir which were available to the Mogollon.

A crematory practice of stirring the bones in the glowing embers for some time after the body was consumed could also account for a greater reduction of the osseous remains. So too could other cultural practices (for example, types of pyres selected) pursuant to the preparation of the corpse for destruction, although all would be hard to demonstrate archaeologically or osteologically.

There was only a 9% (10 of 110) recovery of nonadult material from Snaketown, as compared to the 25% reported for Point of Pines. A large series skeletal analysis usually shows that somewhere between 40% and 60% of the nonadults die prior to their reproductive years. If a similar mortality obtained for the Hohokam, and if the 9% recovery were a good and true sample, it would indicate either that the nonadults were not being cremated as frequently or that they were not being interred in the same localities as were the adults. However, this low frequency may be due to nothing more than sampling differences, since there was no concentrated effort to recover interments during the second Snaketown expedition (Haury, personal communication).

The data presented here on the Hohokam cremations and those given for the Late Mogollon (Merbs 1967) indicate that both cultural groups were practicing "in-the-flesh" or at least "green bone" incineration of the dead. The characteristic appearance of burned artifacts of old bone from Snaketown supports these data, at least with regard to the former group.

APPENDIX 10

Human Skeletal Remains

Kenneth A. Bennett

Four individuals from Arizona U:13:1 and three from Arizona U:13:22 constitute the total skeletal sample which was recovered from burials. In general, the material is fragmentary and friable, limiting the amount of useful information which can be derived from it. Since there is some doubt as to the archaeological affinity, these individuals are not treated as members of a population, but instead as single burials. Their physical characteristics are described below.

ARIZONA U:13:1, BURIAL No. 1

At least two individuals are present in this burial. The first, arbitrarily designated as "a," was in all likelihood a male, as determined by the large mastoid processes and a relatively robust mandible. The age at death, although difficult to assess, appears to have been between 12 and 15. This is evident from the facts that the mandibular third molars had not erupted, the second molars were not fully erupted, and dental attrition was slight, corresponding to Brothwell's (1963: 69) second category. Unfortunately, both pubic symphyses and innominates were missing.

Fragmentary portions of both parietals and part of the occipital show that the skull had been deformed occipitally. A few small Wormian bones are present on the right half of the lambdoid suture, but the same observation cannot be made on the left half. There was no metopic suture, no mylohyoid bridge on either side of the mandible, no torus mandibularis, and a parietal foramen was observed only on the right side. Other discontinuous variations which are commonly observed in cranial material, such as torus palatinus, ear exostoses, dehiscences of the tympanic element, and so forth, could not be checked for absence or presence due to the fragmentary nature of the material.

The dentition was present, although the maxillary teeth were loose. Occlusal caries occurred in the mandibular right M1 and left M1, left M2, and in the maxillary left M2. Enamel hypoplasia was observed, although slight, in the maxillary canines and all four incisors. In addition, the lateral and central upper incisors were double shovel-shaped, that is, the characteristic shoveling found in most American Indian populations was found both on the lingual and labial sides of the teeth. No periodontal disease was evident.

Skeletal changes of a pathological nature were limited to the skull. Slight osteoporotic pitting was observed in both parietals, concentrated in the area along the right and left halves of the lambdoid suture. The right half of the occiput was equally affected, but an attempt to diagnose the condition was not made due to the small amount of material present.

Measurements:

Width of ascending ramus	32 mm

Right femur:

Mid. shaft dia., ant.-post.	23
Mid. shaft dia., lateral	20
Circumference of shaft	67
Subtrochanteric dia., ant.-post.	21
Subtrochanteric dia., lateral	25
Pilastric index	115.0
Index of platymeria	84.0
Middle index	86.9

Left femur:

Mid. shaft dia., ant.-post.	24
Mid. shaft dia., lateral	21
Circumference of shaft	69
Pilastric index	114.3
Middle index	87.5

The second individual in Burial No. 1, designated as "b," was represented only by the shafts of 4 long bones, 5 small cranial fragments, 3 fragments of the sternum, 15 vertebral centra, and 8 unidentifiable fragments. While sex determination in children is not possible with any degree of accuracy, age, based on neural arch fusion in the thoracic and lumbar vertebrae, was between 5 and 8.

ARIZONA U:13:1, BURIAL No. 2

The wide angle of the greater sciatic notch and the presence of a pronounced preauricular sulcus indicate that this individual was a female between 25 and 35 years old. The age estimate was derived from epiphyseal maturation of the sacrum and clavicle. In addition, dental attrition in the mandible and maxilla was quite severe, corresponding to Brothwell's fifth category.

The fragmentary condition of the skull allowed only a few observations, but it is evident that there was no artifical deformation, no metopic suture, no mandibular or palatine tori, and several small Wormian bones on the right and left sides of the lambdoid suture.

Pathology in the skull was restricted to the maxilla and mandible, specifically in the form of periodontal disease, caries and abscesses, enamel hypoplasia, and cementum hyperplasia. Enamel hypoplasia was observed in the mandibular right C, right CI, left LI, and left C. Cementum hyperplasia was seen only at the apex of the maxillary right CI and on the roots of the upper left M1. Alveolar abscesses were found around the upper left LI and upper left M1. In the maxilla, occlusal caries occurred in the left

LI, mesial cervical caries in the right M2, left C, left PM1, and left M1. Distal cervical caries occurred in the left LI and left M1, and buccal cervical caries were found in the left PM1. In the mandible, mesial cervical caries were noted in the right PM2 and left PM1, with a single distal cervical caries in the right PM2. The crown of the right mandibular M3 was completely decayed. In conjunction with caries, dental attrition, abscesses, and perhaps general periodontal disease, several teeth were lost prior to death. These include the maxillary right M1 and M3, the left M2, and the mandibular right M1 and M2, left CI, PM2, and all three molars.

Osteoarthritic lipping, and in some cases, rarefaction, is present in all sections of the vertebral column, with no evidence of eburnation being present on any of the articular facets which are present. The inferior articular facets are essentially normal throughout the entire column, with the one exception being some slight lipping on the first cervical. In addition, the costal facets of the first and twelfth thoracic vertebrae exhibit porotic appearances along with some arthritic lipping. Otherwise, such lipping is restricted to the centra of all vertebrae, in general increasing in severity from the cervicals to the lumbars.

Arthritic lipping is also observed on the first sacral vertebra and on the right auricular surface, and on both acetabulae as well. Spurs, probably arthritic in origin, are present on the planar surface of the right calcaneous, right first metatarsal, left first and fifth metatarsals, and on one phalanx of the foot (probably a second or third). Such changes also are noted on the lateral condyles of both femora and on the glenoid fossae of both scapulae.

Measurements:
Mandible:
Symphyseal height .... 33 mm
Bigonial diameter 91
Bicondylar width.. 119
Height of ascending ramus 57
Width of ascending ramus 31
Corpal length 82
Right clavicle, maximum length.......................... 150
Left clavicle, maximum length 155
Right femur, max. dia. of head 42
Left femur, max. dia. of head 43
Right radius:
Maximum length... 247
Physiological length..................................... 238
Right scapula, maximum breadth 111
Left scapula, maximum height.......................... 146
Left scapula, maximum breadth 110

ARIZONA U:13:1, BURIAL No. 3

The remains are those of a male, 17 to 20 years old (based on epiphyseal maturation of the ischial tuberosity and pubic symphysis). Only the petrous portion of the left temporal and a few fragmentary parts of the postcranial skeleton were recovered. Stature of this individual, based on the formula for tibial length suggested by Trotter and Gleser (1958) for Mongoloid males, was 177.8 cm. No pathology was evident.

Measurements:
Left clavicle, maximum length........................... 156 mm
Left tibia:
Nutri. foramen, ant.-post. dia......................... 40
Nutri. foramen, lateral dia............................. 24
Index of platycnemia 60.0
Left fibula, maximum length............................. 401

ARIZONA U:13:22, BURIAL No. 1

Sex: Unknown
Age: Late fetal to newborn, based on the measurements of the long bones (Johnston 1962: 249–253).

Measurements:
Right humerus, maximum length........................ 62
Right radius, maximum length........................... 51
Left radius, maximum length 52
Right ulna, maximum length............................. 60
Left ulna, maximum length 59

Observations: Maxillary central and lateral incisors are shovel-shaped, although not erupted.

ARIZONA U:13:22, BURIAL No. 2

Sex: Unknown
Age: Pre-natal, probably spontaneous abortion.

ARIZONA U:13:22, BURIAL No. 3

Sex: Unknown
Age: Late fetal to newborn (based on the measurements of the long bones).

Measurements:
Right humerus, maximum length........................ 63
Right clavicle, maximum length......................... 44
Right femur, maximum length........................... 75
Left tibia, maximum length 65
Right radius, maximum length........................... 54
Right ulna, maximum length............................. 61
Left ulna, maximum length 61

APPENDIX 11

Catalogue Numbers of Specimens Illustrated

A = Arizona State Museum; GP = Gila Pueblo

Figure	Catalogue Number
2.1	A-26,405.
11.2	a, A-26,199; b, A-26,198; c, A-26,213; d, A-26,200.
11.3	a, A-26,201; b, A-26,204; c, A-26,202; d, A-26,210; e, A-26,216; f, A-26,209; g, A-26,217; h, A-26,206; i, A-26,207; j, A-26,203; k, A-26,212; l, A-26,208; m, A-26,214.
11.6	A-26,547-x-1-19.
11.7	a, A-26,495; b, A-26,494; c, A-26,530; d, A-26,493; e, A-26,506; f, A-26,507; h, A-26,498; i, A-26,508; j, A-26,505; k, A-26,503; l, A-26,504; m, A-26,489; n, A-26,491; o, A-26,488; p, A-26,492; q, A-26,542; r, A-26,501; s, A-26,502.
11.8	a, A-26,496; b, A-26,520; c, A-26,519; d, A-26,522; e, A-26,528; f, A-26,521; g, A-26,509; h, A-26,527; i, A-26,515; j, A-26,525; k, A-26,510; l, A-26,531; m, A-26,518; n, A-26,512; o, A-26,523; p, A-26,524.
11.9	a, A-26,546; b, A-26,545; c, A-25,536; d, A-26,541; e, A-26,539; f, A-26,514.
11.10	a, A-26,499; b, A-26,500; c, A-25,535.
11.11	a, A-26,516; b, A-26,517.
11.12	Shell, A-26,526; bracelets, A-26,544-x.
11.13	A-26,548.
11.16	a, A-26,908; b, A-26,901; c, A-26,910; d, A-26,777; e, A-26,909; f, A-26,902; g, A-26,914; h, A-26,780.
11.17	a, A-26,918; b, A-26,290; c, A-26,915.
11.18	upper, A-26,907; lower, A-26,778.
11.19	a, A-26,770; b, A-26,767; c, A-26,759; d, A-26,746; e, A-26,765; f, A-26,783; g, A-26,766; h, A-26,751; i, A-26,905; j, A-26,754.
11.20	a, A-26,764; b, A-26,906; c, A-26,758; d, A-26,900.
11.21	a, A-26,744; b, A-26,749; c, A-26,753; d, A-26,896; e, A-26,755.
11.22	a, A-26,763; b, A-26,741; c, A-26,740; d, A-26,927.
11.23	a, A-26,884; b, A-26,748; c, A-26,779; d, A-26,743; e, A-26,782.
11.24	a, A-26,757; b, A-26,781.
11.25	a, A-26,778; b, A-26,750.
11.26	a, A-26,747; b, A-26,761; c, A-26,760.
11.27	A-26,742.
11.28	a, A-26,935; b, A-26,937; c, A-26,926.
11.29	a, A-26,903; b, A-26,893.
11.30	a, A-26,886; b, A-26,897; c, A-26,424; d, A-26,887; e, A-26,895; f, A-26,917; g, A-27,807; h, A-26,883; i, A-26,916.
12.10	a-l, 39,774-x; m, A-27,270; n-q, A-39,774-x; r, A-27,313; s, t, A-39,774-x.
12.12	a, A-27,107; b, A-27,003; c, A-27,276; d, A-27,277; e, A-27,226; f, A-27,356; g, A-27,225.
12.13	A-27,314.
12.14	a, A-27,812; b, A-27,834.
12.16	a-g, A-39,775-x.
12.17	a, A-26,583; b, A-26,882; c, A-27,772.
12.18	a, A-27,450; b, A-27,008; c, A-26,625; d, A-25,087; e, A-27,762.
12.19	a, A-26,602; b, A-27,802; c, A-26,448; d, A-26,405.
12.20	a, A-26,957; b, A-25,379; c, A-26,988; d, A-27,006; e, A-26,550; f, A-27,760; g, A-26,117.
12.21	a, A-27,009; b, A-27,343.
12.22	A-41,137-x.
12.23	A-41,141-x.
12.24	A-41,140-x.
12.25	a, A-26,320; b, A-27,020.
12.27	a, A-27,350; b, A-26,732; c, A-25,417; d, A-26,991; e, A-26,598; f, A-27,451; g, A-27,348; h, A-25,293.
12.28	a, A-25,533; b, A-25,530; c, A-26,605; d, A-25,534; e, A-26,556.
12.29	a, A-27,347; b, A-25,025; c, A-25,689; d, A-27,281; e, A-27,349; f, A-26,376; g, A-26,989; h, A-27,765; i, A-27,385; j, A-27,766.
12.30	a, A-27,804; b, A-27,803.
12.31	A-42,841-x.
12.32	A-42,850-x.
12.33	a, A-42,842-x; b, A-42,843-x.
12.35	a, A-27,039; b, A-25,594; c, A-26,880.
12.36	a, A-27,371; b, A-25,955; c, A-27,386.
12.37	A-42,845-x.
12.38	a, A-42,853-x; b, A-42,854-x.
12.39	A-42,844-x.
12.40	a, A-25,652; b, A-25,636; c, A-25,641; d, A-27,317; e, A-27,318; f, A-25,222; g, A-25,639.
12.41	A-25,666.
12.43	a, A-27,316; b, A-25,654.
12.44	a, A-42,848-x; b, A-42,849-x.
12.45	A-42,851-x.
12.46	a, A-42,846-x; b, A-42,847-x.
12.47	A-27,769.
12.49	A-42,852-x.
12.50	a, A-25,061; b, A-25,062; c, A-25,065; d, A-25,063; e, A-25,064; f, A-25,366.
12.51	a, A-25,060; b, A-25,059.
12.52	A-41,143-x.
12.53	A-41,142-x.
12.57	A-41,146-x.
12.59	a, A-26,232; b, A-26,807; c, A-27,454; d, A-27,758; e, A-25,058.
12.60	a, A-27,768; b, A-27,767; c, A-27,774; d, A-27,805; e, A-27,806; f, A-26,061.
12.62	A-41,151-x.

Figure	Catalogue Number
12.64	Left, A-26,001; right, A-27,801.
12.65	a, A-26,695; b, A-25,121; c, A-25,122; d, A-25,410; e, A-27,452; f, A-26,845.
12.66	a, A-31,414; b, A-27,136; c, A-25,265; d, A-25,266; e, A-27,170; f, A-31,448.
12.67	A-25,040.
12.68	A-41,149-x.
12.69	A-41,150-x.
12.70	A-41,199-x.
12.71	A-41,147-x.
12.72	t, A-25,594; all others, A-41,148-x.
12.74	A-30,716.
12.75	A-41,153-x.
12.76	A-26,664.
12.77	A-41,152-x.
12.78	A-41,145-x.
12.79	a, A-26,880; b, A-27,402.
12.81	c, A-27,345; all others, A-39,776-x.
12.82	r, A-26,125; all others, A-41,139-x.
12.83	A-44,138-x.
12.84	A-30,715.
12.85	A-42,865-x.
12.88	A-42,864-x.
12.89	A-42,861-x.
12.90	A-42,868-x.
12.91	A-42,866-x.
12.92	v, 26,664; all others, A-42,867-x.
12.95	A-42,862-x.
12.96	A-42,869-x.
12.100	A-42,870-x.
12.101	A-42,863-x.
12.102	A-42,873-x.
12.103	A-42,872-x.
12.104	A-42,871-x.
12.105	A-42,860-x.
12.107	a, A-25,035; b, A-26,247; c, A-25,000; d, A-27,485; e, A-26,738; f, A-25,954; g, A-25,223; h, A-26,433; i, A-26,235.
12.108	A-26,676.
12.109	a, A-25,978; b, A-27,542; c, A-27,975; d, A-31,310; e, A-27,962; f, A-26,140; g, A-31,449; h, A-27,884; i, A-31,450; j, A-27,502; k, A-31,317; l, A-27,844; m, A-25,306; n, A-25,395; o, A-27,814; p, A-27,537; q, A-25,563; r, A-25,344; s, A-25,531; t, A-31,320; u, A-27,927; v, A-25,264.
12.111	A-25,075.
12.112	a, A-27,382; b, A-27,759; c, A-27,359; d, A-27,361; e, A-27,358; f, A-27,357; g, A-27,796; h, A-26,233.
12.113	a, A-27,779; b, A-27,786; c, A-27,778; d, A-27,784; e, A-27,783.
13.3	a, A-27,534; b, A-25,973; c, A-27,677-x-1; d, A-26,257; e, A-26,258; f, A-26,259; g, A-25,772; h, A-27,700; i, A-26,251; j, A-26,274; k, A-27,305; l, A-25,511; m, A-26,278; n, A-25,996; o, A-26,275; p, A-25,994.
13.4	a, A-27,532; b, A-26,249; c, A-26,250; d, A-27,699; e, A-25,984; f, A-25,995; g, A-26,277; h, A-26,260; i, A-27,626-x-2; j, A-25,985; k, A-25,514; l, A-27,691-x-2; m, A-27,669; n, A-27,695.
13.5	a, A-26,811; b, A-26,810; c, A-26,852; d, A-26,580; e, A-25,485; f, A-25,534; g, A-25,986; h, A-27,510; i, A-26,476; j, A-26,585; k, A-26,628; l, A-27,652; m, A-25,749; n, A-26,833; o, A-26,573; p, A-26,835; q, A-26,832.
13.6	a, A-26,662; b, A-25,747; c, A-25,748; d, A-26,813; e, A-26,633; f, A-27,471; g, A-27,191; h, A-26,632; i, A-26,683; j, A-26,851; k, A-26,812; l, A-26,639; m, A-27,692; n, A-27,650-x-3; o, A-27,686-x-2;

Figure	Catalogue Number
13.6 (*continued*)	p, A-27,660-x-3; q, A-27,650-x-4; r, A-27,686-x-1; s, A-27,642-x-1; t, A-27,694; u, A-27,642-x-3; v, A-27,682-x-4; w, A-27,660-x-1.
13.7	a, A-25,933; b, A-25,940; c, A-25,929; d, A-25,921; e, A-26,928; f, A-25,166; g, A-25,942; h, A-25,935; i, A-27,586; j, A-25,552; k, A-25,550; l, A-26,463; m, A-25,190; n, A-25,739; o, A-25,852; p, A-27,646-x-2; q, A-25,922; r, A-25,926; s, A-25,918; t, A-25,944; u, A-27,639.
13.8	a, A-25,702; b, A-25,919; c, A-25,795; d, A-25,648; e, A-25,721; f, A-25,923; g, A-26,472; h, A-27,680; i, A-25,687; j, A-25,183; k, A-25,257; l, A-25,941; m, A-25,924; n, A-25,925; o, A-25,920; p, A-25,938.
13.9	a, A-25,554; b, A-27,681; c, A-27,640; d, A-27,641-x-4; e, A-27,659; f, A-27,674-x-5; g, A-25,556; h, A-27,643-x-6; i, A-27,705; j, A-25,159; k, A-25,936; l, A-27,673; m, A-25,692; n, A-25,782; o, A-25,781; p, A-25,691; q, A-25,696; r, A-25,783; s, A-25,758; t, A-25,694; u, A-27,184; v, A-25,693.
13.10	a, A-27,688; b, A-26,255; c, A-26,616; d, A-25,270; e, A-25,292; f, A-26,615; g, A-25,078; h, A-26,460; i, A-26,185; j, A-26,182; k, A-25,983; l, A-25,302; m, A-25,435; n, A-27,631.
13.11	a, A-26,952; b, A-27,211; c, A-25,080; d, A-25,588; e, A-26,930; f, A-26,572; g, A-25,675; h, A-26,943; i, A-27,082; j, A-26,553; k, A-25,189; l, A-25,106; m, A-25,676; n, A-25,079; o, A-26,553; p, A-25,862; q, A-25,863; r, A-26,925; s, A-27,655-x-2.
13.12	a, A-27,288; b, A-26,094; c, A-26,856; d, A-27,658; e, A-25,492; f, A-25,343; g, A-25,493; h, A-25,573; i, A-25,431; j, A-27,406; k, A-25,562; l, A-27,162; m, A-27,407; n, A-27,001; o, A-26,666; p, A-27,436; q, A-27,684.
13.13	a, A-27,399; b, A-26,135; c, A-27,629; d, A-25,987; e, A-27,300; f, A-27,174; g, A-25,529; h, A-26,265.
13.14	a, A-27,191; b, A-26,250; c, A-25,749; d, A-26,925; e, A-25,721; f, A-25,983; g, A-26,182; h, A-27,642-x-8; i, A-27,682-x-4; j, A-25,994; k, A-26,615; l, GP-45,613; m, GP-45,022.
13.15	a, top to bottom, A-26,568, GP-47,484, A-26,931, A-26,585, A-26,832, A-26,476; b, GP-47,472; c, A-27,655-x-2; d, GP-47,484; e, GP-45,021; f, A-26,472; g, A-27,680; h, A-26,632; i, GP-45,021; j, left to right, A-25,696, A-25,852, A-26,251-x-1, A-26,476, A-26,585, A-27,510, GP-45,021.
13.17	GP-46,159.
13.19	A-38,875.
13.20	a, A-26,246; b, A-26,240; c, A-26,938; d, A-25,085; e, A-26,151.
13.21	a, A-26,326; b, A-26,045, c, A-26,877; d, A-26,547-x-5; e, A-26,547-x-7; f, A-26,547-x-4.
13.22	A-31,451.
13.23	a, A-27,643-x-4; b, A-27,395; c, A-27,649-x-2; d, A-27,642-x-2; e, A-27,666; f, A-26,635; g, A-27,504; h, A-25,993; i, A-27,648; j, A-27,633; k, A-26,661; l, A-27,672.
13.24	a, A-27,643-x-2; b, A-27,376; c, A-26,248; d, A-25,209; e, A-26,249; f, A-27,775; g, A-26,850; h, A-25,951; i, A-26,846; j, A-25,932; k, A-26,245.
13.25	a, A-26,280; b, A-27,689; c, A-27,405; d, A-27,647; e, A-27,776; f, A-27,700; g, A-27,088-x-1; h, A-27,088-x-3; i, A-27,696; j, A-27,654.
13.26	a, A-25,991; b, A-26,421; c, A-26,434; d, A-26,696; e, A-25,188; f, A-27,644; g, A-25,071; h, A-26,300; i, A-25,014; j, A-25,856; k, A-25,094.
13.28	a, A-25,365-x-2; b, A-25,365.

Figure	Catalogue Number
13.30	A-25,124.
14.3	a, A-26,840; b, A-26,841; c, A-26,839; d, A-26,604.
14.4	A-27,581.
14.6	a, A-27,481; b, A-27,482.
14.7	a, GP-45,332; b, GP-45,328; c, GP-43,259; d, GP-47,782; e, A-26,380.
14.8	a, A-25,560; b, A-26,701; c, A-25,204; d, A-26,470; e, A-25,091; f, A-27,034; g, A-25,010; h, A-26,703; i, A-27,459; j, A-26,079.
14.9	a, A-26,855; b, A-26,091; c, A-26,998; d, A-26,128; e, A-26,571.
14.10	a, A-26,645; b, A-27,298; c, A-27,099; d, A-25,813; e, A-26,959.
14.11	A-26,092.
14.12	a, A-25,592; b, A-26,059; c, A-26,060; d, A-27,076; e, A-27,365.
14.13	a, A-26,010; b, A-25,829; c, A-25,006; d, A-25,389; e, A-25,622; f, A-26,802.
14.14	a, A-26,960; b, A-26,009; c, A-26,704; d, A-25,868; e, A-25,181; f, A-25,118; g, A-25,506; h, A-25,421; i, A-26,152; j, A-26,419; k, A-26,003; l, A-25,522.
14.16	a, A-27,149; b, A-26,435.
14.17	a, A-25,148; b, A-27,328.
14.18	A-27,122.
14.19	a, A-25,338; b, A-25,673; c, A-26,387.
14.20	a, A-25,054; b, A-26,441; c, A-27,315; d, A-25,382; e, A-27,351; f, A-26,062; g, A-27,352; h, A-26,043; i, A-27,421; j, A-26,440.
14.21	A-26,440.
14.22	Left, A-26,199; right, A-26,198; palette, A-26,214.
14.24	b, GP-43,484.
14.25	a, A-25,428; b, A-25,449; c, A-27,369; d, A-25,143; e, A-27,204; f, A-27,598; g, A-25,685.
14.26	A-27,598.
14.27	a, A-26,364; b, A-26,673; c, A-25,443.
14.28	A-25,443.
14.30	A-25,034.
14.31	A-26,027.
14.32	a, A-25,831; b, A-25,871; c, A-26,999; d, A-25,142; e, A-26,986; f, A-26,332; g, A-27,628; h, A-26,597.
14.33	a, A-25,427; b, A-25,882; c, A-26,288; d, A-25,456; e, A-25,404.
14.34	a, A-25,141-x-6; b, A-25,047; c, A-25,044.
14.35	a, A-26,581; b, A-26,617; c, A-27,557; d, A-26,654; e, A-25,206; f, A-26,410; g, A-26,391; h, A-26,159.
14.36	a, A-25,049; b, A-26,006; c, A-26,329; d, A-26,821; e, A-25,303; f, A-25,776; g, A-25,760; h, A-25,735; i, A-26,563.
14.37	A-25,215.
14.38	a, A-27,405; b, A-26,849; c, A-25,481; d, A-25,110; e, A-25,680; f, A-26,474; g, A-25,093; h, A-25,476; i, A-25,318; j, A-25,316; k, A-27,487; l, A-25,808; m, A-25,501; n, A-27,133.
14.39	a, A-26,130; b, A-26,446, c, A-25,475; d, A-26,446-x; e, A-25,663; f, A-25,253; g, A-27,400; h, A-25,077; i, A-27,178; j, A-25,912; k, A-26,566; l, A-26,872; m, A-25,899; n, A-25,429; o, A-25,301.
14.40	A-26,446-x.
14.41	a, A-27,177; b, A-27,573; c, A-27,026; d, A-26,963; e, A-25,076.

Figure	Catalogue Number
14.42	a, A-26,692; b, A-26,967; c, A-25,444; d, A-25,840; e, A-26,478; f, A-25,441; g, A-26,362; h, A-26,831; i, A-25,119; j, various.
14.43	A-25,320.
14.44	a, A-25,445; b, A-25,815.
15.1	A-27,172.
15.2	a, A-27,373; b, A-25,582.
15.3	a, A-27,189; b, A-26,377; c, A-27,397; d, A-25,915; e, A-25,910; f, A-27,375; g, A-26,425; h, A-27,551; i, A-25,170; j, A-27,202.
15.4	A-26,954.
15.5	A-42,855.
15.6	a, A-25,415; b, A-25,718; c, A-25,724; d, A-25,770; e, A-25,725; f, A-26,795; g, A-26,455; h, A-26,549; i, A-26,805.
15.7	a, A-42,856; b, A-42,857; c, A-42,858-x; d, A-42,859.
15.9	A-40,778-x.
15.12	a, A-25,947; b, A-25,388; c, A-27,086; d, A-26,945; e, A-25,450; f, A-26,822; g, A-27,727; h, A-26,341.
15.13	a (l to r), A-27,322, A-27,321, A-27,615; b, A-25,889; c, A-27,410; d, A-25,283, A-26,869, A-25,149; e, A-25,370; f, A-27,625, A-27,736.
15.14	A-27,456.
15.15	A-25,798-x.
15.17	a, A-26,944; b, A-27,294; c, A-25,335; d, A-25,299; e, A-26,132; f, A-25,333; g, A-27,495; h, A-26,875; i, A-25,789; j, A-26,934; k, A-27,186; l, A-26,067; m, A-26,662; n, A-27,723; o, A-26,953; p, A-27,434; q, A-26,971; r, A-26,243; s, A-26,017; t, A-27,712; u, A-27,173; v, A-26,134; w, A-25,432; x, A-25,513; y, A-27,414; z, A-26,039; aa, A-26,718; bb, A-26,339; cc, A-25,859.
15.19	A-40,772-x.
15.20	a, A-27,543; b, A-26,360; c, A-27,726; d, A-25,907; e, A-25,569; f, A-27,626; g, A-25,428; h, A-26,837; i, A-26,052; j, A-25,763; k, A-25,437; l, A-26,111; m, A-25,860; n, A-26,123; o, A-25,294; p, A-25,839; q, A-26,301; r, A-25,322; s, A-26,806; t, A-27,306; u, A-25,300; v, A-25,347; w, A-27,732; x, A-27,217; y, A-25,095; z, A-26,946.
15.21	a, A-25,900; b, A-25,179; c, A-27,738; d, A-25,424; e, A-25,227.
15.22	a, A-27,200-x-1; b, A-26,978; c, A-26,977; d, A-27,739; e, A-25,184; f, A-26,118; g, A-26,973; h, A-26,096; i, A-26,195; j, A-26,069; k, A-27,068.
15.23	a, A-27,257; b, A-25,167; c, A-25,093; d, A-27,731-x-2; e, A-27,731-x-1; f, A-26,013.
15.25	a, A-26,177; b, A-27,717; c, A-27,096; d, A-26,023; e, A-26,024; f, A-26,133; g, A-25,019.
15.26	A-31,340.
15.27	a, A-25,570; b, A-26,871; c, A-26,046; d, A-26,469; e, A-25,564; f, A-27,499.
15.28	b, GP-45,589; d, A-25,294; f, GP-45,456; h, A-25,300; k, A-26,934; q, A-30,715.
16.2	a, A-26,281; b, A-27,205; c, A-31,418; d, A-25,837; e, A-26,950; f, A-25,185; g, A-26,606; h, A-25,664; i, A-26,165; j, A-27,208; k, A-27,835; l, A-25,651; m, A-27,293; n, A-27,216; o, A-25,569.

Bibliography

ALLEN, GLOVER M.
1920   Dogs of the American Aborigines. *Bulletin of the Museum of Comparative Zoology*, Vol. 43, No. 9, Cambridge.

AMBLER, JOHN R.
1961   Archaeological Survey and Excavations at Casa Grande National Monument, Arizona, MA Thesis, The University of Arizona, Tucson.

AMSDEN, C. A.
1936   An Analysis of Hohokam Pottery Designs. *Medallion Papers*, No. 22. Gila Pueblo, Globe, Arizona.

ANONYMOUS
1853–   *Documentos para la Historia de México*. 20 volumes in 4
1857   series. Series 3 in four parts referred to as volumes. México.

ANONYMOUS
1964   *Flor y Canto del Arte Prehispánico de México*. Fondo Editorial de la Plástica Mexicana, México, D.F.

ANTHONY, H. E.
1928   *Field Book of North American Mammals*. G. P. Putnam's Sons, New York.

BABY, RAYMOND S.
1954   *Hopewell Cremation Practices*. The Ohio Historical Society, Papers in Archaeology, No. 1, pp. 1–7. Columbus.

BAHR, DONALD M.
1971   Who Were the Hohokam? The Evidence from Pima-Papago Myths. *Ethnohistory*, Vol. 18, No. 3, pp. 245–266. Tucson.

BANCROFT, H. H.
1889   *History of Arizona and New Mexico, 1530–1888*, Vol. 17, The History Company, San Francisco.

BANDELIER, A. F.
1892   Final Report of Investigations Among the Indians of the Southwestern United States, Part II. *Papers of the Archaeological Institute of America*. American Series, Vol. 4. Cambridge.

BANDELIER, FANNY R.
1932   Translator of Sahagún's *A History of Ancient Mexico*, Vol. 1, Fisk Univ. Press. Nashville.

BANNISTER, BRYANT, ELIZABETH A. M. GELL,
    AND JOHN W. HANNAH
1966   *Tree-Ring Dates from Arizona N-Q, Verde-Showlow-St. Johns Area*. Laboratory of Tree-Ring Research, The University of Arizona, Tucson.

BANNISTER, BRYANT, JOHN W. HANNAH AND WILLIAM J. ROBINSON
1970   *Tree-Ring Dates from New Mexico M-N, S, Z, Southwestern New Mexico Area*. Laboratory of Tree-Ring Research, The University of Arizona, Tucson.

BARTLETT, JOHN RUSSELL
1854   *Personal Narrative of Exploration and Incidents in Texas, New Mexico, California, Sonora and Chihuahua*. United States and Mexican Boundary Commission, 1850–53, 2 Vols. D. Appleton & Company, New York.

BEALS, RALPH
1932   The Comparative Ethnology of Northern Mexico before 1750. *Ibero-Americana*, No. 2, pp. 93–225. Berkeley.

BENNETT, KENNETH A.
1967   Craniostenosis: A Review of the Etiology and a Report of New Cases. *Am. J. Phys. Anthrop.*, No. 27, Vol. 1, pp. 1–10. Wistar Press, Philadelphia.

BERRY, S. S.
1956   A Tidal Flat on the Vermilion Sea. *Journal of Conchology*, Vol. 24, No. 3, pp. 81–84. London.

BINFORD, LEWIS R.
1972a   An Analysis of Cremations from Three Michigan Sites. In *An Archaeological Perspective*. Seminar Press, New York. pp. 373–382.

1972b   Analysis of a Cremated Burial from the Riverside Cemetery, Menominee County, Michigan. In *An Archaeological Perspective*. Seminar Press, New York. pp. 383–89.

BOHRER, VORSILA L.
1970   Ethnobotanical Aspects of Snaketown, A Hohokam Village in Southern Arizona. *American Antiquity*, Vol. 35, No. 4, pp. 413–430. Salt Lake City.

1971   Paleoecology of Snaketown. *The Kiva*, Vol. 36, No. 3, pp. 11–19. Tucson.

BOHRER, VORSILA L., HUGH C. CUTLER AND JONATHAN D. SAUER
1969   Carbonized Plant Remains from Two Hohokam Sites, Arizona BB:13:41 and Arizona BB:13:50. *The Kiva*, Vol. 35, No. 1, pp. 1–10. Tucson.

BORBOLLA, F. RUBÍN DE LA
1964   *Escultura Precolombiana de Guerrero*. Universidad Nacional Autónoma de México, Museo de Ciencias Y Arte, México, D.F.

BORHEGYI, STEPHAN F.
1964   Frozen in Clay. *Lore*, Vol. 14, No. 3, pp. 80–87. Milwaukee.

1966   America's Oldest Dolls. *Lore*, pp. 87–91, Summer, 1966. Milwaukee.

BRAND, DONALD D.
1935   Prehistoric Trade in the Southwest. *New Mexico Business Review*, Vol. 4, No. 4, pp. 202–209. Albuquerque.

1937   Southwestern Trade in Shell Products. *American Antiquity*, Vol. 2, No. 4, pp. 300–302. Menasha.

1938   Aboriginal Trade Routes for Sea Shells in the Southwest. *Yearbook of the Association of Pacific Coast Geographers*, Vol. 4. Cheney, Washington.

BRANIFF, BEATRIZ
1965   Investigaciones Arqueológicas en Guanajuato, México, 1965. Consideraciones Preliminares. Unpublished MS.

1970   Greca Escalonada en el Norte de Mesoamérica. *Instituto Nacional de Antropología e Historia*, Boletín 42, pp. 38–41. México, D.F.

1972   Secuencias Arqueológicas en Guanajuato y la Cuenca de México: Intento de Correlación. In Teotihuacán XI, Mesa Redonda, Sociedad Méxicana de Antropología, pp. 273–323. México, D.F.

BRETERNITZ, DAVID A.
1960   Excavations at Three Sites in the Verde Valley, Arizona. *Museum of Northern Arizona Bulletin* 34, Flagstaff.

BRETERNITZ, DAVID A. (*continued*)
1966   An Appraisal of Tree-ring Dated Pottery in the Southwest. *Anthropological Papers of the University of Arizona*, No. 10. Tucson.

BREW, DOUGLAS C.
1970   The Naco Formation (Pennsylvanian) in Central Arizona. *Plateau*, Vol. 42, No. 4, pp. 126–138. Flagstaff.

BROMS, R. S. D. AND JAMES R. MORIARTY
1967   The Antiquity and Inferred Use of Stone Spheroids in Southwestern Archaeology. *The Masterkey*, Vol. 41, No. 3, pp. 98–112. Los Angeles.

BROTHWELL, D. R.
1963   Digging Up Bones. *British Museum of Natural History*, pp. 67–70. London.

BROWN, DONALD N.
1967   The Distribution of Sound Instruments in the Prehistoric Southwestern United States. *Ethnomusicology*, Vol. 11, No. 1, pp. 71–90. Middletown, Conn.

BRYAN, BRUCE
1963   A Hohokam "Venus." *The Masterkey*, Vol. 37, No. 3, p. 85. Los Angeles.

BRYAN, KIRK
1923a Erosion and Sedimentation in the Papago Country, Arizona. *Contributions to the Geography of the United States*, 1922, pp. 19–90. Washington.

1923b Types of Surface Water Supplies in the Lower Gila Region, Arizona by Clyde P. Ross, pp. 35–95. *United States Geological Survey Water-Supply Paper 498*. Washington.

1925   The Papago Country, Arizona. *United States Geological Survey Water-Supply Paper 499*. Washington.

BUCHA, V.
1967   Intensity of the Earth's Magnetic Field During Archaeological Times in Czecho-Slovakia. *Archaeometry*, Vol. 10, pp. 12–22. Oxford.

BUCHA, V., R. E. TAYLOR, RAINER BERGER AND E. W. HAURY
1970   Geomagnetic Intensity: Changes During the Past 3000 Years in the Western Hemisphere. *Science*, Vol. 168, No. 3927, pp. 111–14. Washington, D.C.

BULLARD, WILLIAM ROTCH, JR.
1962   The Cerro Colorado Site and Pithouse Architecture in the Southwestern United States Prior to A.D. 900. *Papers of the Peabody Museum of American Archaeology and Ethnology*, Vol. 44, No. 2. Cambridge.

CAHALANE, VICTOR H.
1947   *Mammals of North America*. The Macmillan Co., New York.

CALLEN, E. O.
1963   Diet as Revealed by Coprolites. In *Science In Archaeology*, pp. 186–94. Basic Books, Inc., New York.

CALLEN, E. O. AND T. W. M. CAMERON
1960   A Prehistoric Diet Revealed in Coprolites. *The New Scientist*, 8 (190), pp. 35–40. London.

CARLSON, R. L.
1963   Basketmaker III Sites near Durango, Colorado. The Earl Morris Papers, No. 1. University of Colorado Studies, *Series in Anthropology*, No. 8, pp. 1–82. Boulder.

CASO, ALFONSO
1932   Reading the Riddle of Ancient Jewels. *Natural History*, Vol. 32, No. 5, pp. 464–80. New York.

1947   The Eagle and the Nopal. *The Social Sciences in Mexico and News about the Social Sciences in South and Central America*, Vol. 1, No. 1, pp. 5–15, México, D.F.

1958   *The Aztec People of the Sun*. University of Oklahoma Press, Norman.

CASO, ALFONSO, IGNACIO BERNAL AND JORGE R. ACOSTA
1967   La Cerámica de Monte Albán. *Memorias del Instituto Nacional de Antropología e Historia*, 13. México, D.F.

CASTETTER, E. F. AND W. H. BELL
1942   Pima and Papago Indian Agriculture. *Inter-Americana Studies* 1, Albuquerque.

CHAPMAN, KENNETH M.
1916   The Evolution of the Bird in Decorative Art. *Art and Archaeology*, Vol. 4, No. 6, p. 307–16. Washington, D.C.

CHESKY, JANE
1942   The Wikita. *The Kiva*, Vol. 8, No. 1, pp. 3–5. Tucson.

CLARKE, FRANK WIGGLESWORTH
1924   The Data of Geochemistry. *United States Geological Survey, Bulletin* 770. Fifth Edition, Washington, D.C.

COCKRUM, LENDELL E.
1960   *The Recent Mammals of Arizona*. The University of Arizona Press, Tucson.

COFFIN, EDWIN F.
1932   Archaeological Exploration of a Rock Shelter in Brewster County, Texas. Museum of the American Indian, Heye Foundation, *Indian Notes and Monographs*, No. 48. New York.

COLBERG-SIGLEO, A. M.
1970   *Trace-element Geochemistry of Southwestern Turquoise*. M.A. Thesis, University of New Mexico. Unpublished.

COLBERG-SIGLEO, ANNE
1975   Turquoise Mine and Artifact Correlation for Snaketown Site, Arizona. *Science*, Vol. 189, No. 4201, pp. 459–60. Washington, D.C.

COLTON, HAROLD S.
1941   Prehistoric Trade in the Southwest. *The Scientific Monthly*, Vol. 52, pp. 308–19. Washington.

COSGROVE, H. S. AND C. B.
1932   The Swarts Ruin: A Typical Mimbres Site in Southwestern New Mexico. *Papers of the Peabody Museum of American Archaeology and Ethnology*, Vol. 15, No. 1. Cambridge.

COVARRUBIAS, MIGUEL
1957   *Indian Art of Mexico and Central America*. Alfred A. Knopf. New York.

CRABTREE, DON E.
1973   Experiments in Replicating Hohokam Points. *Tebiwa*, Vol. 16, No. 1, pp. 10–45. Pocatello.

CRABTREE, DON E. AND B. ROBERT BUTLER
1964   Notes on Experiment in Flint Knapping: I. Heat Treatment of Silica Minerals, *Tebiwa*, Vol. 7, No. 1, pp. 1–6. Pocatello.

CRABTREE, DON E. AND EARL H. SWANSON, JR.
1968   Edge-ground Cobbles and Blade-making in the Northwest. *Tebiwa*, Vol. 11, No. 2, pp. 50–58. Pocatello.

CRANE, H. R., AND JAMES B. GRIFFIN
1958   University of Michigan Radiocarbon Dates II., *Science*, Vol. 127, No. 3306, pp. 1098–1105. Washington.

CULIN, S.
1907   Games of the North American Indians. *Twenty-fourth Annual Report of the Bureau of American Ethnology*. Washington.

CUMMINGS, BYRON
1933   Cuicuilco and the Archaic Culture of Mexico. *Social Science Bulletin* No. 4; University of Arizona Bulletin, Vol. 4, No. 8, Tucson.

CUSHING, FRANK HAMILTON
1890   Preliminary Notes on the Origin, Working Hypothesis, and Primary Researches of the Hemenway Southwestern Archaeological Expedition. *Congrès International des Américanistes, Compte-rendu de la septième session*, pp. 151–94. Berlin.

DALE, F. H.
1939   Variability and Environmental Responses of the Kangaroo Rat, *Dipodomys heermani saxatilis*. *American Midland Naturalist*, Vol. 22, pp. 703–31, November. Notre Dame.

DAMON, P. E., AUSTIN LONG AND D. C. GREY
1966   Fluctuation of Atmospheric C^{14} During the Last Six Millennia. *Journal of Geophysical Research*, Vol. 71, pp. 1055–63. Washington.

DANSON, E. B.
1957   Pottery Type Descriptions (in Excavations, 1940, at University Indian Ruin by Julian D. Hayden). *Southwestern Monuments Association Technical Series*, Vol. 5, pp. 219–31. Globe.

DI PESO, CHARLES C.
1951   The Babocomari Village Site on Babocomari River. *The Amerind Foundation*, No. 5, pp. 195–209. Dragoon, Arizona.

1956   The Upper Pima of San Cayetano del Tumacacori: An Archaeo-historical Reconstruction of the Ootam of Pimería Alta. *The Amerind Foundation*, No. 7. Dragoon, Arizona.

DI PESO, CHARLES C. (*continued*)
1958 The Reeve Ruin of Southeastern Arizona. *The Amerind Foundation,* No. 8. Dragoon, Arizona.

1966 Archaeology and Ethnohistory of the Northern Sierra. *Handbook of Middle American Indians,* Robert Wauchope, ed., Vol. 4, pp. 3–25. University of Texas Press, Austin.

1968 Casas Grandes, a Fallen Trading Center of the Gran Chichimeca. *The Masterkey,* Vol. 42, No. 1, pp. 20–37. Los Angeles.

DITTERT, A. E.
1967 Archaeological Field Camp, Arizona State University. *Anthropology in Northern Arizona: A Research Letter, No. 5,* November. Flagstaff.

DIXON, KEITH A.
1956 Archaeological Objectives and Artifact Sorting Techniques: A Re-examination of the Snaketown Sequence. *Western Anthropology,* Vol. 1, No. 3. Missoula.

DOYEL, D. E.
1974 Excavations in the Escalante Ruin Group, Southern Arizona. Arizona State Museum, University of Arizona. Tucson.

DOZIER, EDWARD P.
1965 Southwestern Social Units and Archaeology. *American Antiquity,* Vol. 31, No. 1, pp. 38–47. Salt Lake City.

EKHOLM, GORDON F.
1939 Results of an Archaeological Survey of Sonora and Northern Sinaloa. *Revista Mexicana de Estudios Antropológicos,* Vol. 3, No. 1, pp. 7–10. México, D.F.

1942 Excavations at Guasave, Sinaloa, Mexico. *Anthropological Papers of the American Museum of Natural History,* Vol. 38, Pt. 2. New York.

EL-ZUR, ARIEH
1965 Soil, Water, and Man in the Desert Habitat of the Hohokam Culture. Ph.D. Dissertation, University of Arizona, Tucson.

EMERSON, R. A., AND H. H. SMITH
1950 Inheritance of Number of Kernel Rows in Maize. *Cornell University Agricultural Experiment Station Memoirs,* 296. Ithaca.

EZELL, PAUL H.
1963 Is There A Hohokam-Pima Culture Continuum? *American Antiquity,* Vol. 29, No. 1, pp. 61–66. Salt Lake City.

FERDON, EDWIN N., JR.
1955 A Trial Survey of Mexican-Southwestern Architectural Parallels. *School of American Research, Museum of New Mexico, Monographs,* 21. Santa Fe.

1967 The Hohokam "Ball Court": An Alternative View of its Function. *The Kiva,* Vol. 33, No. 1, pp. 1–14. Tucson.

FERGUSON, C. W.
1968 Bristlecone Pine: Science and Ethics. *Science,* Vol. 159, pp. 839–46. Washington.

1969 A 7104-year Annual Tree-ring Chronology for Bristlecone Pine, *Pinus aristata,* from the White Mountains, California. *Tree-Ring Bulletin,* Vol. 29, pp. 3–4. Tucson.

FERRY, J. F., AND H. S. WARD
1959 *Fundamentals of Plant Physiology.* The Macmillan Company, New York.

FEWKES, J. W.
1912 Casa Grande, Arizona. *Twenty-eighth Report of the Bureau of American Ethnology,* pp. 25–180. Washington.

FLANNERY, KENT W., ANNE V. T. KIRKBY, MICHAEL J. KIRKBY AND AUBREY W. WILLIAMS, JR.
1967 Farming Systems and Political Growth in Ancient Oaxaca. *Science,* Vol. 158, No. 3800, pp. 445–54. Washington.

FONTANA, BERNARD L., WILLIAM J. ROBINSON, CHARLES W. CORMACK AND ERNEST E. LEAVITT, JR.
1962 *Papago Indian Pottery.* Univ. of Washington Press, Seattle.

FOWLER, MELVIN L.
1968 Un Sistema Preclásico de Distribución de Agua en la Zona Arqueológica de Amalucan, Puebla. No. 2, *Instituto Poblano de Antropología e Historia.* Puebla.

FREEMAN, G. F.
1918 Southwestern Beans and Teparies. *Bulletin* No. 68, *Agricultural Experiment Station, University of Arizona,* rev. ed. Tucson.

FULTON, WILLIAM SHIRLEY
1941 A Ceremonial Cave in the Winchester Mountains, Arizona. *The Amerind Foundation,* No. 2, Dragoon, Arizona.

GABEL, NORMAN E.
1950 The Skeletal Remains of Ventana Cave. In *The Stratigraphy and Archaeology of Ventana Cave, Arizona,* by E. W. Haury, pp. 473–520. The Univ. of Arizona Press, Tucson, and the Univ. of New Mexico Press, Albuquerque.

GARRISON, ERVAN G., CHARLES R. MCGIMSEY III, AND OTTO H. ZINKE
In
Press Alpha-Recoil Tracks in Archaeological Dating. *Science.*

GEJVALL, NILS-GUSTAF
1963 Cremations. In *Science In Archaeology,* pp. 379–90. Basic Books, New York.

GIFFORD, E. W.
1946 Archaeology in the Punta Peñasco Region, Sonora. *American Antiquity,* Vol. 11, No. 4, pp. 215–21. Menasha.

GLADWIN, HAROLD S.
1942 Excavations at Snaketown III: Revisions. *Medallion Papers,* No. 30. Gila Pueblo, Globe, Arizona.

1948 Excavations at Snaketown IV. Review and Conclusions. *Medallion Papers,* No. 38. Gila Pueblo, Globe, Arizona.

1957 *A History of the Ancient Southwest.* The Bond Wheelwright Company, Portland, Maine.

GLADWIN, WINIFRED AND HAROLD S. GLADWIN
1929a The Red-on-Buff Culture of the Gila Basin. *Medallion Papers,* No. 3. Gila Pueblo, Globe, Arizona.

1929b The Red-on-Buff Culture of the Papaguería. *Medallion Papers,* No. 4. Gila Pueblo, Globe, Arizona.

1930a The Western Range of the Red-on-Buff Culture. *Medallion Papers,* No. 5. Gila Pueblo, Globe, Arizona.

1930b An Archaeological Survey of the Verde Valley. *Medallion Papers,* No. 6. Gila Pueblo, Globe, Arizona.

1930c Some Southwestern Pottery Types, Series I. *Medallion Papers,* No. 8. Gila Pueblo, Globe, Arizona.

1933 Some Southwestern Pottery Types, Series III. *Medallion Papers,* No. 13. Gila Pueblo, Globe, Arizona.

1935 The Eastern Range of the Red-on-Buff Culture. *Medallion Papers,* No. 16. Gila Pueblo, Globe, Arizona.

GLADWIN, H. S., EMIL W. HAURY, EDWIN B. SAYLES AND NORA GLADWIN
1937 Excavations at Snaketown, Material Culture. *Medallion Papers,* No. 25. Gila Pueblo, Globe, Arizona.

GORDON, G. E., K. RANDLE, G. C. GOLES, J. B. CORLISS, M. H. BEESON AND S. S. OXLEY
1968 Instrumental Activation Analysis of Standard Rocks with High Resolutions, γ-ray Detectors. *Geochim. et Cosmochim, Acta,* Vol. 32, pp. 369–96. Oxford.

GREENLEAF, J. CAMERON
1975 Excavations at Punta de Agua in the Santa Cruz Basin, Southeastern Arizona. *Anthropological Papers of the University of Arizona,* No. 26. Tucson.

GRITZNER, CHARLES F.
1966 Hohokam Culture Origin: A Geographical Interpretation (Abstract). *Journal of the Arizona Academy of Science,* Vol. 4, No. 2, p. 134. Tucson.

HAAG, W.
1948 An Osteometric Analysis of Some Aboriginal Dogs. *Univ. of Kentucky Reports in Anthropology,* Vol. 7, No. 3, pp. 107–264. Lexington.

HACK, JOHN T.
1942 The Changing Physical Environment of the Hopi Indians of Arizona. *Papers of the Peabody Museum of American Archaeology and Ethnology,* Vol. 35, No. 1. Cambridge.

HACKENBERG, ROBERT A.
1961 Aboriginal Land Use and Occupancy of the Pima-Maricopa Community. *Report to the U.S. Department of Justice.* September 1961, Vols. 1 and 2. Arizona State Museum Library Archives, Tucson.

HACKENBERG, ROBERT A. (*continued*)

1962   Economic Alternatives in Arid Lands: A Case Study of the Pima and Papago Indians. *Ethnology,* Vol. 1, No. 2, pp. 186–96. Pittsburgh.

1964   Changing Patterns of Pima Indian Land Use. In *Indian and Spanish Adjustments to Arid and Semi-arid Environments,* ed. Clark S. Knowlton, pp. 6–15. Contribution No. 7 of the Committee on Desert and Arid Zone Research, Texas Technological College, Lubbock.

HALL, E. RAYMOND, AND KEITH R. KELSON

1959   *The Mammals of North America.* Vols. 1 and 2. The Ronald Press Company, New York.

HALSETH, ODD S.

1947   Arizona's 1500 Years of Irrigation History. *The Reclamation Era.* Vol. 33, No. 12, pp. 251–54. Washington.

HAMMACK, LAURENS C.

1969   A Preliminary Report of the Excavations at Las Colinas. *The Kiva,* Vol. 35, No. 1, pp. 11–28. Tucson.

HAMMACK, LAURENS C., CAROL S. WEED, AND BRUCE B. HUCKELL

Las Colinas. In preparation.

HARGRAVE, LYNDON L.

1970   Mexican Macaws. Comparative Osteology and Survey of Remains from the Southwest. *Anthropological Papers of the University of Arizona.* No. 20. Tucson.

HASTINGS, RUSSELL

1934   Second Preliminary Report on Excavations at Casa Grande, 1934. *Southwestern Monuments Monthly Reports,* January, pp. 46–48. Casa Grande National Monument (Mimeographed).

HAURY, EMIL W.

1931   Minute Beads from Prehistoric Pueblos. *American Anthropologist,* Vol. 33, No. 1, pp. 80–87. Menasha.

1932   Roosevelt 9:6, A Hohokam Site of the Colonial Period. *Medallion Papers,* No. 11. Gila Pueblo, Globe, Arizona.

1936a   The Snaketown Canal. *The University of New Mexico Bulletin* No. 296, Anthropological Series, Vol. 1, No. 5, pp. 48–50. Albuquerque.

1936b   Some Southwestern Pottery Types, Series IV. *Medallion Papers,* No. 19. Gila Pueblo, Globe, Arizona.

1936c   The Mogollon Culture of Southwestern New Mexico. *Medallion Papers,* No. 20. Gila Pueblo, Globe, Arizona.

1937   A Pre-Spanish Rubber Ball from Arizona. *American Antiquity,* Vol. 2, No. 4, pp. 282–88. Menasha.

1940   Excavations in the Forestdale Valley, East Central Arizona. *University of Arizona Bulletin,* Vol. 11, No. 4, Social Science Bulletin No. 12. Tucson.

1945a   The Excavation of Los Muertos and Neighboring Ruins in the Salt River Valley, Southern Arizona. *Papers of the Peabody Museum of American Archaeology and Ethnology,* Vol. 24, No. 1. Cambridge.

1945b   The Problem of Contacts Between the Southwestern United States and Mexico. *Southwestern Journal of Anthropology,* Vol. 1, pp. 55–74. Albuquerque, Univ. of New Mexico Press.

1956   Speculations on Prehistoric Settlement Patterns in the Southwest. In *Prehistoric Settlement Patterns in the New World,* ed. G. R. Willey, Wenner-Gren Foundation for Anthropological Research, New York.

1957   An Alluvial Site on the San Carlos Indian Reservation, Arizona. *American Antiquity,* Vol. 23, No. 1, pp. 2–27. Salt Lake City.

HAURY, EMIL W., AND E. B. SAYLES

1947   An Early Pit House Village of the Mogollon Culture, Forestdale Valley, Arizona. *University of Arizona Bulletin,* Vol. 18, No. 4. Social Science Bulletin No. 16. Tucson.

HAURY, EMIL W., KIRK BRYAN, EDWIN H. COLBERT, NORMAN E. GABEL, CLARA LEE TANNER, AND T. F. BUEHRER

1950   *The Stratigraphy and Archaeology of Ventana Cave, Arizona.* Univ. of Arizona Press, Tucson, and Univ. of New Mexico Press, Albuquerque.

HAWLEY, F. G.

1937   Chemical Investigation of the Incrustation on Pottery Vessels from Snaketown, Appendix 4, pp. 282–89. In Excavations at Snaketown, by H. S. Gladwin, E. W. Haury, E. B. Sayles and N. Gladwin, *Medallion Papers,* No. 25, Gila Pueblo, Globe, Arizona.

HAWLEY, FLORENCE

1937   Kokopelli, of the Prehistoric Southwestern Pantheon. *American Anthropologist,* New Series, Vol. 39, No. 4 (Part 1), pp. 644–46. Menasha.

HAYDEN, JULIAN D.

1936–   Notes on the Excavation of Pueblo Grande, Phoenix, Ari-
1940   zona. Pueblo Grande Laboratory Archives, unpublished.

1957   Excavations, 1940, at University Indian Ruin. *Southwestern Monuments Association,* Technical Series, Vol. 5. Globe, Arizona.

1959   Notes on Pima Pottery Making. *The Kiva,* Vol. 24, No. 3, pp. 10–16. Tucson.

1969   Gyratory Crushers of the Sierra Pinacate, Sonora. *American Antiquity,* Vol. 34, No. 2, pp. 154–61. Salt Lake City.

1970   Of Hohokam Origins and Other Matters. *American Antiquity,* Vol. 35, No. 1, pp. 87–91. Salt Lake City.

1972   Hohokam Petroglyphs of the Sierra Pinacate, Sonora and the Hohokam Shell Expeditions. *The Kiva,* Vol. 37, No. 2, pp. 74–83. Tucson.

HAYNES, C. V., D. C. GREY AND A. LONG

1971   Arizona Radiocarbon Dates VIII. *Radiocarbon,* Vol. 13, pp. 1–18. New Haven.

HIBBEN, FRANK C.

1966   A Possible Pyramidal Structure and Other Mexican Influences at Pottery Mound, New Mexico. *American Antiquity,* Vol. 31, No. 4, pp. 522–29. Salt Lake City.

HILL, W. W.

1936   Notes on Pima Land Law and Tenure. *American Anthropologist,* Vol. 38, No. 4, pp. 586–89. Menasha.

HINE, ROBERT V.

1968   *Bartlett's West: Drawing the Mexican Boundary.* Yale Univ. Press, New Haven and London.

HODGE, F. W.

1893   Prehistoric Irrigation In Arizona. *American Anthropologist,* o.s., Vol. 6, pp. 323–30. Washington.

HOOVER, J. W.

1929   The Indian Country of Southern Arizona. *The Geographical Review,* Vol. 19, No. 3, pp. 38–60. New York.

1941   Cerros de Trincheras of the Arizona Papaguería. *The Geographical Review,* Vol. 31, No. 2, pp. 228–39. New York.

HOWELL, A. H.

1938   Revision of the North American Ground Squirrels. *North American Fauna,* No. 56. Washington.

IVES, RONALD L.

1965   Manje's Mercury Mines. *The Journal of Arizona History,* Vol. 4, No. 4, pp. 165–76. Tucson.

JENNINGS, JESSE D. (ED.)

1956   The American Southwest: A Problem in Cultural Isolation. In Seminars in American Archaeology: 1955. *American Antiquity,* Vol. 22, No. 2, Part 2, Memoirs of the Society for American Archaeology, No. 11. Salt Lake City.

JIMÉNEZ MORENO, WIGBERTO

1959   Síntesis de la Historia Pretolteca de Mesoamérica. In *Esplendor del México Antiguo,* pp. 1019–1108. Centro de Investigaciones Antropológicas de México, México, D.F.

1966   Mesoamerica Before the Toltecs. *Ancient Oaxaca,* ed. John Paddock, pp. 1–82. Stanford Univ. Press, Stanford.

JOHNSON, ALFRED E.

1960   The Place of the Trincheras Culture of Northern Sonora in Southwestern Archaeology. Master's Thesis, University of Arizona, Tucson.

JOHNSON, ALFRED E. (*continued*)
1964 Archaeological Excavations in Hohokam Sites of Southern Arizona. *American Antiquity,* Vol. 30, No. 2, Part 1, pp. 145–61. Salt Lake City.

1966 Archaeology of Sonora, Mexico. *Handbook of Middle American Indians,* Vol. 4, Archaeological Frontiers and External Connections, pp. 26–37. Univ. of Texas Press, Austin.

JOHNSON, ANN STOFER
1958 Similarities in Hohokam and Chalchihuites Artifacts. *American Antiquity,* Vol. 24, No. 2, pp. 126–30. Salt Lake City.

JUDD, N. M.
1931 Arizona's Prehistoric Canals from the Air. *Explorations and Field-Work of the Smithsonian Institution in 1930,* pp. 157–66. Washington, D.C.

1954 The Material Culture of Pueblo Bonito. *Smithsonian Miscellaneous Collections,* Vol. 124. Washington, D.C.

KAEMLEIN, WILMA
1955 Yuma Dolls and Yuma Flutes in the Arizona State Museum. *The Kiva,* Vol. 20, Nos. 2 and 3, pp. 1–10. Tucson.

1971 Large Hunting Nets in the Collections of the Arizona State Museum. *The Kiva,* Vol. 36, No. 3, pp. 20–52. Tucson.

KAPLAN, L.
1967 Archaeological Phaseolus from Tehuacan. In *The Prehistory of the Tehuacan Valley,* Vol. 1, Environment and Subsistence, ed. Douglas S. Byers. Robert S. Peabody Foundation, Phillips Academy, Andover, Mass., Univ. of Texas Press, Austin.

KEARNEY, THOMAS H., AND ROBERT H. PEEBLES
1960 *Arizona Flora.* Univ. of California Press, Berkeley and Los Angeles.

KEEN, A. MYRA
1958 *Sea Shells of Tropical West America: Marine Mollusks from Lower California to Colombia.* Stanford Univ. Press, Stanford.

KELLEY, J. CHARLES
1960 North Mexico and the Correlation of Mesoamerican and Southwestern Cultural Sequences. In *Selected Papers of the Fifth International Congress of Anthropological and Ethnological Sciences,* ed. Anthony F. C. Wallace, pp. 566–73. Univ. of Pennsylvania Press, Philadelphia.

1966 Mesoamerica and the Southwestern United States. *Handbook of Middle American Indians,* Vol. 4, Archaeological Frontiers and External Connections, pp. 95–110. Univ. of Texas Press, Austin.

1971 Archaeology of the Northern Frontier: Zacatecas and Durango. *Handbook of Middle American Indians,* ed. Robert Wauchope, Vol. 11, Part 2, pp. 768–801. Univ. of Texas Press, Austin.

KELLEY, J. CHARLES AND ELLEN ABBOTT
1966 The Cultural Sequence on the North Central Frontier of Mesoamerica. *XXXVI Congreso Internacional de Americanistas,* Vol. 1, pp. 325–44. Sevilla.

1971 An Introduction to the Ceramics of the Chalchihuites Culture of Zacatecas and Durango, Mexico. Part 1: The Decorated Wares. *Mesoamerican Studies,* No. 5. Carbondale.

KELLY, ISABEL T.
1938a The Hodges Site. Unpublished manuscript. Archives of the Arizona State Museum, University of Arizona, Tucson.

1938b Excavations at Chametla, Sinaloa. *Ibero-Americana:* 14. Berkeley.

1945a Excavations at Culiacán, Sinaloa, *Ibero-Americana:* 25. Berkeley.

1945b The Archaeology of the Autlán-Tuxcacuesco Area of Jalisco. I; The Autlan Zone. *Ibero-Americana:* 26. Berkeley.

1947 Excavations at Apatzingán, Michoacán. *Viking Fund Publications in Anthropology,* No. 7. New York.

1949 The Archaeology of the Autlán-Tuxcacuesco Area of Jalisco. II: The Tuxcacuesco-Zapotitlán Zone. *Ibero-Americana:* 27. Berkeley.

KELLY, ROGER E.
1963 The Socio-Religious Roles of Ball Courts and Great Kivas in the Prehistoric Southwest. Master's Thesis, University of Arizona, Tucson.

KENT, KATE PECK
1957 The Cultivation and Weaving of Cotton in the Prehistoric Southwestern United States. *Transactions of the American Philosophical Society,* n.s., Vol. 47, Pt. 3. Philadelphia.

KIDDER, A. V.
1932 The Artifacts of Pecos. *Papers of the Phillips Academy, Southwestern Expedition,* No. 6. New Haven.

KIDDER, A. V., JESSE D. JENNINGS, AND EDWIN M. SHOOK
1946 Excavations at Kaminaljuyú. *Carnegie Institution of Washington,* Publication 561. Washington.

KING, DALE S.
1949 Nalakihu: Excavations at a Pueblo III Site on Wupatki National Monument, Arizona. *Museum of Northern Arizona Bulletin* 23. Flagstaff.

KING, MARY ELIZABETH
1965 Prehistoric Textiles from the Gila Bend Area, Appendix C, pp. 110–14. In "Salvage Archaeology in Painted Rocks Reservoir, Western Arizona," by William W.Wasley and Alfred E. Johnson. *Anthropological Papers of the University of Arizona,* No. 9. Tucson.

KIRCHHOFF, PAUL
1954 Gatherers and Farmers in the Greater Southwest: A Problem in Classification. *American Anthropologist,* Vol. 56, No. 4, Part 1, pp. 529–50. Menasha.

KRIEGER, M. H.
1965 Geology of the Prescott and Paulden Quadrangles, Arizona. *U.S. Geological Survey Professional Paper,* No. 467, pp. 1–127. Washington.

KROGMAN, WILTON M.
1962 *The Human Skeleton in Forensic Medicine.* Charles C. Thomas, Springfield.

KRUEGER, HAROLD W., AND C. FRANCIS WEEKS
1966 Geochron Laboratories, Inc. Radiocarbon Measurements II. *Radiocarbon,* Vol. 8, pp. 142–60. New Haven.

KURATH, GERTRUDE P., AND SAMUEL MARTÍ
1964 Dances of the Anáhuac, the Choreography and Music of Precortesian Dances. *Viking Fund Publications in Anthropology,* No. 38. New York.

LAMBERT, MARJORIE F.
1966 A Unique Kokopelli Jar. *El Palacio,* Vol. 73, No. 2, pp. 21–25. Santa Fe.

LEAVITT, ERNEST E.
1962 Technical Differences in the Painted Decoration of Anasazi and Hohokam Pottery. M.A. Thesis, University of Arizona, Tucson.

LEHMER, DONALD J.
1950 Excavations at Snaketown IV. Reviews and Conclusions (Review of Gladwin, 1948). *American Anthropologist* n.s., Vol. 52, No. 3, pp. 415–18. Menasha.

LEOPOLD, A. STARKER
1959 *Wildlife of Mexico.* Univ. of California Press, Berkeley and Los Angeles.

LISTER, ROBERT H.
1955 The Present Status of the Archaeology of Western Mexico: A Distributional Study. *University of Colorado Studies,* Series in Anthropology, No. 5. Boulder.

LONG, AUSTIN AND JAMES E. MIELKE
1967 Smithsonian Institution Radiocarbon Measurements IV. *Radiocarbon,* Vol. 9, pp. 368–81. New Haven.

LOWDON, J. A.
1969 Isotopic Fractionation in Corn. *Radiocarbon,* Vol. 11, pp. 391–93. New Haven.

LOWE, CHARLES H.
1967 *The Vertebrates of Arizona.* Univ. of Arizona Press, Tucson.

McGregor, John C.
1941 Winona and Ridge Ruin, Part I. Architecture and Material Culture, *Museum of Northern Arizona*, Bulletin 18. Flagstaff.

McKusick, Charmion R.
1970 Faunal Remains of Mound 7, Gran Quivira National Monument, New Mexico. MS on file in the Arizona Archaeological Center, National Park Service, Tucson.

MacNeish, Richard S.
1964 Ancient Mesoamerican Civilization. *Science*, Vol. 143, No. 3606, pp. 531–37. Washington.

Manson, James
1961 Seri Indian Figurines. *The Kiva*, Vol. 26, No. 4, pp. 30–33. Tucson.

Martí, Samuel
1955 *Instrumentos Musicales Precortesianos*. Instituto Nacional de Antropología, México, D. F.

Martin, Paul S.
1959 Digging Into History: A Brief Account of Fifteen Years of Archaeological Work in New Mexico. *Chicago Natural History Museum, Popular Series*, Anthropology, No. 38. Chicago.

Martin, Paul S., John B. Rinaldo, Elaine Bluhm,
Hugh C. Cutler and Roger Grange, Jr.
1952 Mogollon Cultural Continuity and Change: The Stratigraphic Analysis of Tularosa and Cordova Caves. *Fieldiana: Anthropology*, Vol. 40. Chicago.

Mason, J. Alden
1929 Turquoise Mosaics from Northern Mexico. *The Museum Journal*, June, pp. 157–75. Philadelphia.

Mason, Ronald J., and Carol Irwin
1960 An Eden-Scottsbluff Burial in Northeastern Wisconsin. *American Antiquity*, Vol. 26, No. 1, pp. 43–57. Salt Lake City.

Mearns, E. A.
1907 Mammals of the Mexican Boundary of the United States. *United States National Museum Bulletin* 56. Washington.

Meighan, Clement W.
1969 Cultural Similarities Between Western Mexico and Andean Regions. In *Mesoamerican Studies*, No. 4. Pre-Columbian Contact Within Nuclear America, pp. 11–25. Carbondale.

1970 Obsidian Hydration Rates. *Science*, Vol. 170, No. 3953, pp. 99–100. Washington, D.C.

1971 Archaeology of Sinaloa. *Handbook of Middle American Indians*, ed. Robert Wauchope, Vol. 11, Part 2, pp. 754–67. Austin.

Meighan, Clement W., and Leonard J. Foote
1968 Excavations at Tizapan El Alto, Jalisco. *Latin American Studies*, Vol. 11. Los Angeles.

Meighan, Clement W., Leonard J. Foote and Paul V. Aiello
1968 Obsidian Dating in West Mexican Archaeology. *Science*, Vol. 160, No. 3832, pp. 1069–75. Washington.

Mendoza, Abel and Alfonso Lota Loria
1959 Caza y Pesca. *El Esplendor del México Antiguo*, pp. 905–20. Centro de Investigaciones Antropológicas de México, México, D.F.

Merbs, Charles F.
1967 Cremated Human Remains from Point of Pines, Arizona: A New Approach. *Am. Antiquity*, No. 32, Vol. 4, pp. 498–506. Salt Lake City.

Miles, Charles
1963 *Indian and Eskimo Artifacts of North America*. Henry Regenery Co. Chicago.

Miller, Gerritt S. and Remington Kellogg
1955 List of North American Recent Mammals. *United States National Museum Bulletins*, 205. Washington.

Miller, Robert R.
1955 Fish Remains from Archaeological Sites in the Lower Colorado River Basin, Arizona. Paper in *Mich. Acad. Sci., Arts, Lett.*, Vol. 46, pp. 125–136.

Millón, René
1959 La Agricultura Como Inicio de la Civilización. In *El Esplendor del México Antiguo*, pp. 907–1018. Centro de Investigaciones Antropológicas de México. México, D.F.

1967a Cronología y Periodificación: Datos estratigráficos sobre períodos cerámicos y sus relaciones con la pintura mural. *Sociedad Méxicana de Antropología*. 11th Mesa Redonda, 1966. México, D.F.

1967b Teotihuacán. *Scientific American*, Vol. 216, No. 6, pp. 38–48. Washington.

Morris, Donald H.
1969a A 9th Century Salado (?) Kiva at Walnut Creek, Arizona. *Plateau*, Vol. 42, No. 1, pp. 1–10. Flagstaff.

1969b Red Mountain: An Early Pioneer Period Hohokam Site in the Salt River Valley of Central Arizona. *American Antiquity*, Vol. 34, No. 1, pp. 40–53. Salt Lake City.

1970 Walnut Creek Village:A Ninth Century Hohokam-Anasazi Settlement in the Mountains of Central Arizona. *American Antiquity*, Vol. 35, No. 1, pp. 49–61. Salt Lake City.

Morris, Donald H., and Mahmoud El-Najjar
1971 An Unusual Classic Period Burial from Las Colinas, Salt River Valley, Central Arizona. *The Kiva*, Vol. 31, No. 4, pp. 31–35. Tucson.

Morris, Earl H., and Robert F. Burgh
1954 Basket Maker II Sites Near Durango, Colorado. *Carnegie Institution of Washington Publication* 604. Washington, D.C.

Morris, Elizabeth A.
1959 Basketmaker Flutes from the Prayer Rock District, Arizona. *American Antiquity*, Vol. 24, No. 4, Part 1, pp. 406–11. Salt Lake City.

Morris, Elizabeth Ann, and Volney H. Jones
1960 Seventh Century Evidence for the Use of Tobacco in Northern Arizona. Akten des 34. *Internationalen Amerikanistenkongresses*, pp. 306–09. Vienna.

Morss, Noel
1954 Clay Figurines of the American Southwest. *Peabody Museum Papers*, Vol. 49, No. 1. Cambridge.

Moser, Edward, and Richard S. White, Jr.
1968 Seri Clay Figurines. *The Kiva*, Vol. 33, No. 3, pp. 133–54. Tucson.

Mountjoy, Joseph B.
1970 San Blas Complex Ecology. Paper presented during 35th Annual Meeting of the Society for American Archaeology, May 2, 1970, Mexico City.

Murdoch, J., and R. W. Webb
1966 Minerals of California. *California Division of Mines*, Bulletin 189. San Francisco.

Neely, James A.
1967 Organización hidráulica y sistemas de irrigación prehistóricos en el Valle de Oaxaca. *Instituto Nacional de Antropología e Historia*, Boletín 27, pp. 15–17. México, D.F.

1974 The Prehistoric Lunt and Stove Canyon Sites, Point of Pines, Arizona. Ph.D. dissertation, The University of Arizona, Tucson.

Neustupný, Evžen
1970 A New Epoch in Radiocarbon Dating. *Antiquity*, Vol. 44, No. 173, pp. 38–45. Cambridge, England.

Olsen, Stanley J.
1964 Mammal Remains from Archaeological Sites. *Papers of the Peabody Museum of American Archaeology and Ethnology*, Vol. 56, No. 1. Cambridge.

Olsson, I. U.
1970 Radiocarbon Variation and Absolute Chronology. *Proceedings of the 12th Nobel Symposium*. Wiley Interscience, New York.

Owen, Roger C.
1956 Some Clay Figurines and Seri Dolls from Coastal Sonora, Mexico. *The Kiva*, Vol. 21, Nos. 3 and 4, pp. 1–11. Tucson.

Palerm, Angel and Eric H. Wolf
1957 Ecological Potential and Cultural Development in Mesoamerica. *Studies in Human Ecology*, Social Science Monographs, III, p. 37. Washington, D.C.

Parsons, Elsie C.
1919 Increase by Magic: A Zuni Pattern. *American Anthropologist*, n.s., Vol. 21, pp. 279–86. Lancaster.

1938 The Humpbacked Flute Player of the Southwest. *American Anthropologist*, n.s., Vol. 4, No. 2, pp. 337–38. Menasha.

PARSONS, ELSIE C. (*continued*)

1939 *Pueblo Indian Religion*. 2 Vols., Chicago Univ. Press. Chicago.

PENDERGAST, DAVID M.

1962 Metal Artifacts in Prehispanic Mesoamerica. *American Antiquity*, Vol. 27, No. 4, pp. 520–45. Salt Lake City.

PEPPER, GEORGE H.

1920 Pueblo Bonito. *Anthropological Papers of the American Museum of Natural History*, Vol. 27. New York.

PHILLIPS, ALLAN, JOE MARSHALL AND GALE MONSON

1964 *The Birds of Arizona*. Univ. of Arizona Press, Tucson.

PIÑA CHAN, ROMAN

1958 *Tlatilco*, Instituto Nacional de Antropología e Historia, México, D.F.

1959 Tianquiztli. *Esplendor del México Antiguo*, pp. 921–32. Centro de Investigaciones Antropológicas de México, México, D.F.

1960 *Mesoamérica: Ensayo Histórico Cultural*. Memorias, VI, Instituto Nacional de Antropología e Historia, México, D.F.

PINKLEY, F., AND E. T.

1931 *The Casa Grande National Monument in Arizona*. Privately printed.

POMEROY, J. ANTHONY

1959 Hohokam Etched Shell. *The Kiva*, Vol. 24, No. 4, pp. 12–21. Tucson.

PORTER, MURIEL N.

1953 Tlatilco and the Pre-Classic Cultures of the New World. *Viking Fund Publications in Anthropology*, No. 19. New York.

1956 Excavations at Chupícuaro, Guanajuato, México. *Transactions of the American Philosophical Society*, Vol. 46, Part 5. Philadelphia.

RIPPETEAU, BRUCE E.

1972 The Need-Achievement Test Applied to the Hohokam. *American Antiquity*, Vol. 37, No. 4, pp. 504–13. Washington, D.C.

ROMEROVARGAS YTURBIDE, IGNACIO

1959 Las Instituciones. *Esplendor del México Antiguo*, pp. 729–76. Centro de Investigaciones Antropológicas de México, México, D.F.

ROSS, CLYDE P.

1923 The Lower Gila Region, Arizona. *United States Geological Survey Water Supply Paper* 498. Washington.

ROUSE, IRVING

1958 The Inference of Migrations from Anthropological Evidence. In "Migrations in New World Culture History," ed. Raymond H. Thompson, *University of Arizona Social Science Bulletin* No. 27, Vol. 29, No. 2, pp. 63–68. Tucson.

RUSSELL, F.

1908 *The Pima Indians*. Twenty-sixth Annual Report of the Bureau of American Ethnology, Washington.

SAHAGÚN, BERNARDINO DE

1932 *A History of Ancient México*, Vol. 1. trans. Fanny R. Bandelier. Fisk. Univ. Press, Nashville.

SALDIVAR, GABRIEL

1934 *Historia de la Música en México, Epocas Precortesiana y Colonial*. Secretaría de Educación Pública, Publicaciones del Departamento de Bellas Artes, México, D.F.

SAUER, CARL O.

1954 Comments on Kirchhoff's Gatherers and Farmers in the Greater Southwest. *American Anthropologist*, Vol. 56, No. 4, Part 1, pp. 553–56. Menasha.

SAUER, CARL AND DONALD BRAND

1931 Prehistoric Settlements of Sonora with Special Reference to Cerro de Trincheras. *University of California Publications in Geography*, Vol. 5, No. 3, pp. 67–148. Berkeley.

1932 Aztatlán, Prehistoric Frontier on the Pacific Coast. *Ibero-Americana:* 1. Univ. of California Press, Berkeley.

SAYLES, E. B.

1945 The San Simon Branch Excavations at Cave Creek and in the San Simon Valley, I, Material Culture. *Medallion Papers*, No. 34. Gila Pueblo, Globe, Arizona.

SAYLES, E. B., AND ERNST ANTEVS

1941 The Cochise Culture. *Medallion Papers*, No. 29. Gila Pueblo, Globe, Arizona.

SCANTLING, F. H.

1940 Excavations at the Jackrabbit Ruin, Papago Indian Reservation, Arizona. Master's Thesis, University of Arizona. Tucson.

SCHROEDER, ALBERT HENRY

1940 A Stratigraphy Survey of Pre-Spanish Trash Mounds of the Salt River Valley, Arizona. Master's Thesis, University of Arizona. Tucson.

1951 Snaketown IV vs. the Facts. *American Antiquity*, Vol. 16, No. 3, pp. 263–65. Salt Lake City.

1953 The Bearing of Architecture on Developments in the Hohokam Classic Period. *Southwestern Journal of Anthropology*, Vol. 9, No. 2, pp. 174–94. Univ. of New Mexico Press, Albuquerque.

1958 Lower Colorado Buff Ware. In "Pottery Types of the Southwest," ed. Harold S. Colton, *Museum of Northern Arizona Ceramic Series*, No. 3D. Flagstaff.

1960 The Hohokam, Sinagua, and Hakataya. *Archives of Archaeology*, No. 5. Madison.

1965 Unregulated Diffusion from Mexico into the Southwest Prior to A.D. 700. *American Antiquity*, Vol. 30, No. 3, pp. 297–309. Salt Lake City.

SCOTT, STUART D.

1960 Pottery Figurines from Central Arizona. *The Kiva*, Vol. 26, No. 2, pp. 11–26. Tucson.

SEDAT, DAVID W.

1972 The Parker Collection of Hohokam Artifacts. M.A. Thesis. Claremont Colleges, Claremont.

SÉ JOURNÉ, LAURETTE

1966 *Arqueología de Teotihuacán: La Cerámica*. Fondo Cultura Económica, México.

SIMPSON, GEORGE, G. A. ROE AND R. C. LEWONTIN

1960 *Quantitative Zoology*. Harcourt, Brace and Co., New York.

SMILEY, TERAH L.

1949 Pithouse Number 1, Mesa Verde National Park. *American Antiquity*, Vol. 14, No. 3, pp. 167–71. Menasha.

SMITH, A. LEDYARD AND ALFRED V. KIDDER

1951 Excavations at Nebaj, Guatemala. *Carnegie Institution of Washington Publication* 594. Washington, D.C.

SMITH, CYRIL STANLEY

1972 Metallurgical Footnotes to the History of Art. *Proceedings of the American Philosophical Society*, Vol. 116, No. 2, pp. 97–135. Philadelphia.

SOLHEIM, WILHELM G., II

1960 The Use of Sherd Weights and Counts in the Handling of Archaeological Data. *Current Anthropology*, Vol. 1, No. 4, pp. 325–29. Chicago.

SOUTHWORTH, CLAY H.

1919 History of Irrigation on the Gila River. *Hearings before the Committee on Indian Affairs*, House of Representatives, 66th Congress, 1st Session, Vol. 2, pp. 103–223. Government Printing Office, Washington.

SPIER, LESLIE

1933 *Yuman Tribes of the Gila River*. The Univ. of Chicago Press, Chicago.

1936 Cultural Relations of the Gila River and Lower Colorado Tribes. *Yale University Publications in Anthropology*, No. 3. New Haven.

SPRAGUE, RODERICK AND ALDO SIGNORI

1963 Inventory of Prehistoric Southwestern Copper Bells. *The Kiva*, Vol. 28, No. 4, pp. 1–20. Tucson.

STANISLAWSKI, MICHAEL B.

1961 Two Prehistoric Shell Caches from Southern Arizona. *The Kiva*, Vol. 27, No. 2, pp. 22–27. Tucson.

STEWARD, J. H., R. M. ADAMS, D. COLLIER, A. PALERM, K. A. WITTFOGEL AND R. L. BEALS

1955 Irrigation Civilizations: A Comparative Study. *Social Science Monographs* I. Washington.

STRONG, WILLIAM DUNCAN
1927 An Analysis of Southwestern Society. *American Anthropologist*, Vol. 29, No. 1, pp. 1–61. Menasha.
STUIVER, M., AND H. E. SUESS
1966 On the Relationship Between Radiocarbon Dates and True Sample Age. *Radiocarbon*, Vol. 8, pp. 534–40. New Haven.
SUESS, H. E.
1965 Secular Variations of Cosmic Ray-produced Carbon-14 in the Atmosphere. *Journal of Geophysical Research*, Vol. 70, p. 5937. London.

TANNER, CLARA LEE
1950 Ventana Cave Textiles in *The Stratigraphy and Archaeology of Ventana Cave, Arizona*, Haury, pp. 443–459. The Univ. of Arizona Press, Tucson, and the Univ. of New Mexico Press, Albuquerque.
TAYLOR, WALTER P.
1956 *The Deer of North America*. The Wildlife Management Institute, Washington.
TITIEV, MISCHA
1939 The Story of Kokopele. *American Anthropologist*, n.s., Vol. 41, No. 1, pp. 91–98. Menasha.
TOWER, DONALD B.
1945 The Use of Marine Molusca and their Value in Reconstructing Trade Routes in the American Southwest. *Papers of the Excavators' Club*, Vol. 2, No. 3. Cambridge.
TREUTLEIN, THEODORA E. (TRANSLATOR AND ANNOTATOR)
1965 Missionary in Sonora: The Travel Reports of Joseph Och, S.J., 1755-1767. *California Historical Society Special Publication*, No. 4. San Francisco.
TRIK, AUBREY S.
1963 The Splendid Tomb of Temple I at Tikal, Guatemala. *Expedition, Bulletin of the Museum of the University of Pennsylvania*, Vol. 6, No. 1, pp. 2–18. Philadelphia.
TRISCHKA, C.
1933 Hohokam: A Chapter in the History of Red-on-Buff Culture of Arizona. *Scientific Monthly*, Vol. 37, pp. 417–33. Lancaster.
TROTTER, M., AND G. GLESER
1958 A Re-Evaluation of Estimation of Stature Based on Measurements of Stature Taken During Life and of Long Bones after Death. *American Journal of Physical Anthropology*, Vol. 16, No. 1, pp. 79–123. Philadelphia.
TUTHILL, CARR
1947 The Tres Alamos Site on the San Pedro River, Southeastern Arizona. *The Amerind Foundation*, No. 4. Dragoon, Arizona.

UNDERHILL, RUTH M.
1939 Social Organization of the Papago Indians. *Columbia University Contributions to Anthropology*, Vol. 30. New York.
1946 *Papago Indian Religion*. Columbia Univ. Press, New York.
1951 People of the Crimson Evening. Bureau of Indian Affairs, Education Branch. Lawrence, Kansas.

VAILLANT, GEORGE C.
1935 Excavations at El Arbolillo. *Anthropological Papers of the American Museum of Natural History*, Vol. 35, Part II. New York.
1938 A Correlation of Archaeological and Historical Sequences in the Valley of Mexico. *American Anthropologist*, n.s., Vol. 40, No. 4, pp. 535–73. Menasha.
VIVIAN, GWINN R.
1965 An Archaeological Survey of the Lower Gila River, Arizona. *The Kiva*, Vol. 30, No. 4. Tucson.
1974 Conservation and Diversion: Water-Control Systems in the Anasazi Southwest. In Irrigation's Impact on Society, eds. Theodore E. Downing and McGuire Gibson. *Anthropological Papers of the University of Arizona*, No. 25, pp. 95–112, The University of Arizona Press. Tucson.
VORHIES, CHARLES T., AND WALTER P. TAYLOR
1933 The Life Histories and Ecology of Jack Rabbits, *Lepus alleni* and *Lepus californicus* ssp. in Relation to Grazing in Arizona. *University of Arizona Agricultural Experiment Station Technical Bulletin* 49. Tucson.

WASLEY, W. W.
1960 A Hohokam Platform Mound at the Gatlin Site, Gila Bend, Arizona. *American Antiquity*, Vol. 26, No. 2, pp. 244–62. Salt Lake City.
WASLEY, W. W., AND BLAKE BENHAM
1968 Salvage Excavation in the Buttes Dam Site, Southern Arizona. *The Kiva*, Vol. 33, No. 4, pp. 244–79. Tucson.
WASLEY, W. W., AND ALFRED E. JOHNSON
1965 Salvage Archaeology in Painted Rocks Reservoir, Western Arizona. *Anthropological Papers of the University of Arizona*, No. 9. Tucson.
WEAVER, KENNETH F.
1967 Magnetic Clues Help Date the Past. *National Geographic*, May 1967, pp. 696–701. Washington.
WEED, CAROL S., AND ALBERT E. WARD
1970 The Henderson Site: Colonial Hohokam in North Central Arizona: A Preliminary Report. *The Kiva*, Vol. 36, No. 2, pp. 1–12. Tucson.
WELLHAUSEN, E. J., L. M. ROBERTS, E. HERNANDEZ X., AND P. C. MANGELSDORF
1952 *Races of Maize in Mexico*. Bussey Institute, Harvard Univ., Cambridge.
WHEAT, J. B.
1952 Prehistoric Water Sources of the Point of Pines Area. *American Antiquity*, Vol. 17, No. 3, pp. 185–96. Salt Lake City.
1954 Crooked Ridge Village. *University of Arizona Bulletin*, Vol. 25, No. 3, Social Science Bulletin No. 24. Tucson.
1955 Mogollon Culture Prior to A.D. 1000. *Memoirs of the Society for American Archaeology*, No. 10. Salt Lake City.
WHITE, THEODORE E.
1953 A Method of Calculating the Dietary Percentage of Various Food Animals Utilized by Aboriginal Peoples. *American Antiquity*, Vol. 18, No. 4, pp. 396–98. Salt Lake City.
WHITTEMORE, ISAAC T., AND CHARLES H. COOK
1893 *Among the Pimas, or the Mission to the Pima and Maricopa Indians*. Ladies' Union Mission School Association, Albany, New York.
WICKE, CHARLES R.
1965 Pyramids and Temple Mounds: Mesoamerican Ceremonial Architecture in Eastern North America. *American Antiquity*, Vol. 30, No. 4, pp. 409–20. Salt Lake City.
WINGERT, PAUL T.
1952 *Prehistoric Stone Sculpture of the Pacific Northwest*. Portland Art Museum, Portland.
WITHERS, ARNOLD M.
1973 Excavations at Valshni Village, Arizona. *The Arizona Archaeologist*, No. 7, ed. W. T. Duering, Arizona Archaeological Society Inc. Phoenix.
WOODBURY, RICHARD B.
1954 Prehistoric Stone Implements of Northeastern Arizona. *Papers of the Peabody Museum of American Archaeology and Ethnology*, Vol. 34, Reports of the Awatovi Expedition, No. 6. Cambridge.
1960a The ohokam Canals at Pueblo Grande, Arizona. *American Antiquity*, Vol. 26, No. 2, pp. 267–70. Salt Lake City.
1960b Social Implications of Prehistoric Arizona Irrigation. *Acts of the 6th International Congress of Anthropological and Ethnological Sciences*, Tome II (1st Volume), pp. 491–93. Paris.
1961 A Reappraisal of Hohokam Irrigation. *American Anthropologist*, Vol. 63, No. 3, pp. 550–60. Menasha.
WOODWARD, ARTHUR
1931 The Grewe Site. *Occasional Papers of the Los Angeles Museum of History, Science, and Art*, No. 1. Los Angeles.
1933 Ancient Houses of Modern Mexico. *Bulletin of the Southern California Academy of Sciences*, Vol. 32, Part 3, pp. 79–98. Los Angeles.
1936 A Shell Bracelet Manufactory. *American Antiquity*, Vol. 2, No. 2, pp. 117–25. Menasha.
1941 Hohokam Mosaic Mirrors. *Los Angeles County Museum Quarterly*, Vol. 1, No. 4, pp. 6–11. Los Angeles.

Index

tall   **Haury, Emil Walter,** 1904-
E   The Hohokam, desert farmers & craftsmen : excavations at
78   Snaketown, 1964-1965 / Emil W. Haury. — Tucson : University
A7   of Arizona Press, c1976.
H37

       xii, 412 p. : ill. (some col.) : 32 cm.

       Bibliography: p. 391-398.
       Includes index.
       ISBN 0-8165-0445-8 : $19.50

      1. Snaketown, Ariz.   2. Hohokam culture.   I. Title.
      3. Arizona-History.

317452 E78.A7H27   970'.004'97   74-31610
                                                            MARC

Library of Congress   76